Delinquency in Society

Delinquency in Society

Fifth Edition

Robert M. Regoli
University of Colorado

John D. Hewitt
Grand Valley State University

Boston   Burr Ridge, IL   Dubuque, IA   Madison, WI   New York
San Francisco   St. Louis   Bangkok   Bogotá   Caracas   Kuala Lumpur
Lisbon   London   Madrid   Mexico City   Milan   Montreal   New Delhi
Santiago   Seoul   Singapore   Sydney   Taipei   Toronto

McGraw-Hill Higher Education ⚡

A Division of The **McGraw-Hill** *Companies*

DELINQUENCY IN SOCIETY

Published by McGraw-Hill, a business unit of the McGraw-Hill Companies, Inc., 1221 Avenue of the Americas, New York, NY, 10020. Copyright 2003, 2000, 1997, 1994, 1991 by The McGraw-Hill Companies, Inc. All rights reserved. No part of this publication may be reproduced or distributed in any form or by any means, or stored in a database or retrieval system, without the prior written consent of The McGraw-Hill Companies, Inc., including, but not limited to, in any network or other electronic storage or transmission, or broadcast for distance learning. Some ancillaries, including electronic and print components, may not be available to customers outside the United States.

This book is printed on acid-free paper.

1 2 3 4 5 6 7 8 9 0 DOC/DOC 0 9 8 7 6 5 4 3 2

ISBN 0-07-248596-5

Editorial director: *Phillip A. Butcher*
Senior sponsoring editor: *Carolyn Henderson Meier*
Senior marketing manager: *Daniel M. Loch*
Media producer: *Shannon Rider*
Project manager: *Diane M. Folliard*
Lead production supervisor: *Lori Koetters*
Senior designer: *Jenny El-Shamy*
Photo research coordinator: *Judy Kausal*
Photo research: *Inge King*
Supplement producer: *Nate Perry*
Cover design: *Donna Cambra*
Typeface: *10/12 Berhold Baskerville*
Compositor: *GAC Indianapolis*
Printer: *R. R. Donnelley*

Library of Congress Cataloging-in-Publication Data

Regoli, Robert M.
    Delinquency in society / Robert M. Regoli, John D. Hewitt.–5th ed.
        p. cm.
    Includes indexes.
    ISBN 0-07-248596-5 (alk.paper)
    1. Juvenile delinquency–United States. 2. Juvenile justice, Administration of –United States. I. Hewitt, John D., 1945- II. Title.
HV9104 .R43 2003
364.36'0973–dc21

                                                        2002024626

http://www.mhhe.com

To the men and women who preserve freedom,
making it possible for us to follow more trivial pursuits.

RMR

JDH

About the Authors

Robert M. Regoli is professor of sociology at the University of Colorado in Boulder. In 1975, he received his Ph.D. in sociology from Washington State University, where he was elected to Phi Beta Kappa. Professor Regoli is the author of more than 100 journal publications and books and is past-president and fellow of the Academy of Criminal Justice Sciences and is a Fulbright scholar.

John D. Hewitt is professor of criminal justice at Grand Valley State University in Grand Rapids, Michigan. He received his Ph.D. in sociology from Washington State University in 1975. Professor Hewitt is the author or co-author of four books and more than 30 articles. His writings have been published in journals such as *Justice Quarterly, Crime and Delinquency, Law and Human Behavior, Social Forces, Journal of Social Research*, and *Law and Policy Quarterly*.

Brief Table of Contents

Table of Contents

Preface

If it is true that in teaching we learn, we have had the good fortune to do quite a bit of both since the first edition of *Delinquency in Society* was published in 1991. Its continued success is a reflection of what we learn from the comments and suggestions of our students, our professional colleagues, and their students around the country who read the book. We do enjoy hearing compliments, but we pay very careful attention to the suggestions for improvements. Such suggestions have resulted in a number of changes to the fifth edition, which we have detailed below. One change is actually a return to our commitment to a "child-centered approach" emphasized in earlier editions of the book, but somehow lost in later editions. Our child-centered approach suggests that juvenile delinquency represents the culmination of a process that begins at conception and evolves through adolescence. We believe that the vulnerable and unequal status of children in society, one which leads to their oppression, determines the nature of their relations with others, and hence, behaviors that come to be viewed as delinquency. It is the relationships in which children find themselves that serve as the breeding ground for juvenile delinquency. While this approach does not excuse the criminal behavior of children, we believe it helps to contextualize its origins and thus may provide better understanding for the eventual reduction of delinquent behavior.

The Fifth Edition

While this edition continues to provide a comprehensive theoretical framework for understanding the evolving phenomenon of delinquency and society's response to the problem, it has been thoroughly updated to reflect the most current trends and developments in delinquency, including discussions of the history, institutional context, and societal reactions to delinquent behavior. Among the more significant changes found in this edition are the following:

- The chapters on drugs and delinquency and on youth violence have been moved from the third section of the book on the social context of delinquency up to the first section of the book on the nature and extent of delinquency. This change places the discussion of serious delinquency immediately following the more general discussion of measuring delinquency.

- The chapter on female delinquency has been substantially revised and moved. The previous discussion on the nature and extent of female delinquency has been placed in the section on sex and delinquency in Chapter 2. The chapter now focuses largely on theories of female delinquency and is appropriately located in the section of the book dealing with theories of delinquency.

- There is expanded discussion of the relationship of race and delinquency throughout the book. For example, racial profiling is more extensively discussed in Chapter 13, "Police and Delinquency," and racial disparities in court appearance, detention, adjudication, disposition, and waiver are given extensive coverage in Chapter 14, "The Juvenile Court."

- There is expanded discussion of chronic offenders in Chapter 2, "Measuring Delinquency."

- With national concern over recent school shootings, Chapter 3, "Youth Violence," now has a greatly expanded discussion of the nature and extent of school violence and approaches to prevention of school violence.

- The discussion of Agnew's General Strain Theory and Gottfredson and Hirschi's General Theory of Crime has been expanded in Chapter 7.

- Chapter 8, "Labeling, Critical, and Conflict Theories," now contains a discussion of Left Realism.

- Chapter 10, "Family and Delinquency," contains new discussions of teen fathers, nonresident parents and failure to pay support, and consequences of court-ordered visitations on children.

- New material on bullying has been added to Chapter 11, "Schools and Delinquency," as a result of growing sensitivity to the consequences of bullying and its potential relationship to more serious forms of school violence.

- Chapter 13, "Police and Delinquency," contains new material on racial profiling and expanded discussion of police discretion. These initial discretionary contacts between police and juveniles create significant opportunities for determining whether a particular juvenile becomes identified as a delinquent.

- Chapter 14, "The Juvenile Court," has been revised to provide more extensive coverage of all the major court hearings juveniles face. Although most states continue to hold juvenile court hearings out of the public eye, it is critical that students understand this important process. Each stage in the juvenile court process, from intake, detention, and waiver hearings to adjudication and disposition hearings, produces opportunities for diversion out of the system as well as for disparities in treatment based on sex, race, age, and socioeconomic status.

- New coverage of the process of deciding appropriate dispositions and restorative justice has been added to Chapter 15, "Juvenile Corrections."

Overview of Contents

Section One, "Nature and Extent of Juvenile Delinquency," introduces students to historical and contemporary perceptions of children and how their misbehaviors have been defined as delinquent. It examines the major sources of data on delinquency and problems with measuring the extent of delinquency. Students are also given in-depth coverage of two of the most critical areas of contemporary delinquency in the chapters on youth violence and illegal drug use.

Section Two, "Causes of Delinquency," provides students with an easy-to-understand discussion of all the major theoretical approaches to explaining juvenile delinquency. Students will be able to examine early supernatural, Classical, and Neoclassical theories; the substantial contributions of biological and psychological theories; and the dominant sociological theories ranging from social disorganization, strain, and social control to labeling, conflict, and radical theories, as well as specialized explanations of female delinquency.

Section Three, "The Social Context of Delinquency," contextualizes delinquency within three major social settings: the family, the school, and the gang. Students will be introduced to provocative discussions dealing with the relationship of family structure and process on delinquency, the nature of delinquency within schools and how schools may contribute to the problem of delinquency, and the extensive problems related to juvenile gangs.

Section Four, "The Juvenile Justice System," examines the formal societal response to delinquency within the context of the police, the courts, and corrections. Each chapter provides extensive, cutting-edge coverage of procedures and issues critical in the juvenile justice system's attempt to prevent and control delinquency.

Learning Aids

The fifth edition of *Delinquency in Society* contains many of the same outstanding pedagogical features we introduced in previous editions, as well as a number of significant new learning aids.

- **Getting Connected.** At the end of each chapter, Internet sites are identified that will provide students with the most current information available on various chapter topics. Each of these sites is now accompanied by exercises students can use to guide their exploration of the topic.
- **Chapter Outlines.** Each chapter begins with an easy-to-follow outline of the major topics that will be discussed. These outlines immediately alert students to the central issues of the chapter as well as to the order in which they are presented.

- **Provocative Discussion Questions**. Each chapter contains a wealth of provocative discussion questions about important issues. The questions are located in the margins next to the topics they explore further and are designed to stimulate discussion in class and sharpen student critical thinking.
- **Critical-Thinking Questions for Photographs**. The wealth of new photographs in the book are accompanied by intriguing questions or extended narratives designed to encourage critical thinking.
- **Theory In a Nutshell Asides**. Many students have difficulty grasping the differences among the various theories of behavior. To make theories more manageable and understandable, each of the more important theories discussed in Section 2 is presented in brief encapsulated form in the chapter margins.
- **Unique and Exciting Boxes**. To make the text more relevant and interesting for students, we have created three different thematic boxes and inserted them where appropriate within the text:
  - **The Face of Delinquency** A series of boxes discussing various facets of delinquency personalize the story of delinquency and bring into focus the different life situations of victims and offenders.
  - **Cross-Cultural Perspectives on Delinquency** Thematic boxes providing students with brief glimpses into the nature of delinquency in other countries allow students to consider the similarities and differences among nations.
  - **Delinquency Prevention** A thematic box focusing on issues related to the prevention, reduction, or control of delinquency. Some of the programs discussed are well established and appear to most criminologists to be effective in achieving their goals. Other programs discussed hold great promise but are relatively new and untested.
- **Key Terms and Glossary**. Students are provided with succinct definitions of commonly used terms and descriptions of important concepts found in bold type throughout the text. For easy reference when students are preparing for exams, each chapter's key terms are defined at the end of the chapter in addition to being included in the Glossary.
- **Legal Case Index**. Each court case discussed in the chapters is alphabetically listed with its most current citations and is accompanied by a brief annotation of the case in the Legal Case Index, located at the back of the book.
- **Name and Subject Indexes**. Separate name and subject indexes are provided at the end of the book to help students in their search for particular issues or concerns.

Supplements

For the Student

- *Making the Grade Student CD-ROM* (prepared by Thomas McAninch of Scott Community College)–a free electronic study guide packaged with each new book that includes chapter self-tests with feedback indicating why the student's response is correct or incorrect, an Internet guide, and much more.

For the Instructor

- *Instructor's Manual/Testbank* (prepared by Beverly Quist of Mohawk Valley Community College)–chapter outlines, key terms, overviews, lecture notes, discussion questions, a complete testbank, and more.
- *Computerized Testbank*–easy-to-use computerized testing program for both Windows and Macintosh computers.
- *PowerPoint Slides*–complete chapter-by-chapter slide shows featuring text, tables, and illustrations.

Acknowledgments

We would like to thank our team at McGraw-Hill for their continued support of *Delinquency in Society*. Carolyn Henderson Meier, acquisitions editor and guiding light for this project, has brought the fifth edition of this book to a new level. Her insights and creative touches have amazed us, and we greatly appreciate her direction of the project. There are a number of other wonderful folks at McGraw-Hill who have contributed to this edition, including Julie Abodeely, editorial coordinator, Dan Loch, marketing manager, Shannon Rider, media producer, Diane Folliard, project manager, and Phil Butcher, publisher. In addition, we want to thank Inge King, our photo editor, who directed the fifth edition's wonderful photo program and Beverly Quist, who continues to produce the exceptional Instructor's Manual that accompanies this book.

A special thanks must go to Matt DeLisi of Iowa State University who developed the many provocative critical-thinking questions found in the chapter margins and photo captions.

We also would like to thank our many colleagues and students for their solicited and unsolicited insights, guidance, criticism, and assistance, with special thanks to Gregg Barak, Joanne Belknap, Ingrid Bennett, Bob Bohm, Sue Caulfield, Todd Clear, Frank Cullen, John Fuller, Mark Hamm, Lou Holscher, Charles Hou, Peter Iadicola, Richard Lawrence, Bill Miller, Hal Pepinsky, Tom Reed, George Rivera, Rick Rogers, Andrew Schmurr, Vic Streib, Jay Watterworth, Jules Wanderer, and Tom Winfree.

Other colleagues who were selected by McGraw-Hill to review the text helped improve this fifth edition in innumerable ways. We extend our sincere gratitude to:

Roy L. Austin, *Pennsylvania State University*

James J. Chriss, *Cleveland State University*

Matt DeLisi, *Iowa State University*

Mary Jackson, *East Carolina University*

David F. Machell, *Western Connecticut State University*

David Mackey, *Framingham State College*

John Quicker, *California State University, Dominguez Hills*

Stanley L. Swart, *University of North Florida*

Kevin Thompson, *North Dakota State University*

Major writing projects always take their toll on those people closest to the authors; for us, those people are our families. We would like to give very special thanks to our wives, Debbie and Avis, who stood beside us as we worked on this project, providing encouragement, love, and both solicited and unsolicited insights that strengthened the final product. We also must recognize Adam, Andrea, Eben, Sara, and new grandson, Henry, for their love and support.

Bob Regoli
regoli@spot.colorado.edu

John D. Hewitt
hewittj@gvsu.edu

A Guided Tour of *Delinquency in Society*

As noted in the Preface, this text reflects the authors' commitment to a "child-centered" approach to juvenile delinquency. This approach is based on the idea that juvenile delinquency is the culmination of a process that begins at conception and evolves through adolescence. In the authors' view, the vulnerable and unequal status of children in society—one which leads to their oppression—determines the nature of their relations with others, and hence, behaviors that come to be viewed as delinquency. It is the relationships in which children find themselves that serve as the breeding ground for juvenile delinquency. While this approach does not excuse the criminal behavior of children, it may help to contextualize the behavior's origins and thus may provide better understanding for the eventual reduction of delinquent behavior.

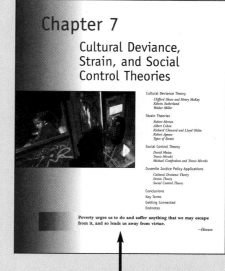

Absolutely critical to any course in juvenile delinquency is early, clear, comprehensive coverage of the major theoretical approaches to explaining juvenile delinquency.

This critical coverage is neatly encapsulated in **Theory in a Nutshell** boxes throughout section 2 of the text, making it easier for students to grasp the differences between important theories and study for exams.

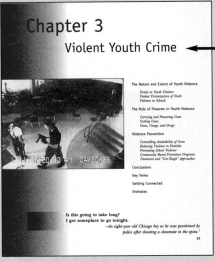

With national concern over recent school shootings, Chapter 3, "Youth Violence," now has a greatly expanded discussion of the nature and extent of school violence and approaches to prevention of school violence.

Thorough updates throughout reflect the most current trends and developments in delinquency.

Chapter 13, "Police and Delinquency," contains new material on racial profiling and expanded discussion of police discretion. These initial discretionary contacts between the police and juveniles create significant opportunities for determining whether a particular juvenile becomes identified as a delinquent.

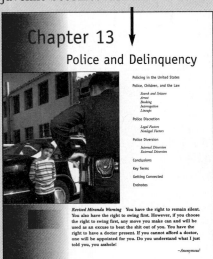

Chapter 10, "Family and Delinquency," contains new discussions of teen fathers, non-resident parents and failure to pay support, and the consequences of court-ordered visitations on children.

Easy-to-follow chapter-opening outlines of the major topics that will be discussed immediately alert students to the central issues of the chapter as well as the order in which they are presented.

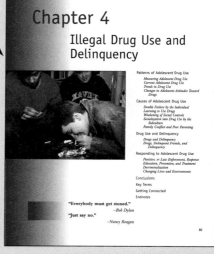

The wealth of new photographs in the book are accompanied by intriguing questions or extended narratives designed to stimulate class discussion and critical thinking.

Each chapter also contains a wealth of provocative discussion questions about important issues. The questions are located in the margins next to the topics they explore further and are designed to stimulate discussion in class and to sharpen students' critical-thinking skills.

Female behavior, including delinquent behavior, has historically been defined by stereotypical conceptions of femininity. Does this photo invoke any delinquent imagery? If so, why?

in the consumption and production spheres. Both parents work and have control positions outside the home, and both share child rearing responsibilities within the home. Parental control is redistributed so that the control over daughters is more like that over sons, and daughters, like sons, are prepared to enter the production sphere and given greater opportunities for risk taking. This differential treatment leads boys in such families, more so than girls, to engage in greater risk taking, and, consequently, delinquency.

However, Meda Chesney-Lind and Randall Shelden suggest that this is "essentially a not-too-subtle variation of the **liberation hypothesis**, that women's liberation directly led to increases in female criminality. Now, mother's liberation or employment causes daughter's crime."[60] They argue there is no evidence to support Hagan's claim that as women's participation in the labor force increases, so too will female delinquency. It should be noted, however, that Roy Austin's analysis of labor force participation, divorce rates, and female arrests for minor, major, and occupational offenses does lend support to the claim that female liberation is associated with an increase in female criminality.[61]

Numerous tests of power-control theory have been conducted over the past two decades, with rather inconsistent findings. For example, Simon Singer and Murray Levine analyzed data from 705 high school youth and 560 parents and found that, consistent with power-control theory, parents

---

relative inattention given to female delinquency was also due in part to the fact that most criminological theory has been policy driven; that is, because males made up most of the delinquent population in the courts and correctional institutions, policies designed to respond to delinquency sought out theories that dealt primarily with boys.

As more women entered the field of criminology during the past two decades, they brought with them a greater interest in female delinquency, its nature and causes, and how its origins may differ from those of male delinquency. In this section we will examine biological and psychological theories of female delinquency, consider how sociological theories may apply to girls, and look at the more recent feminist and critical theories.

Biological and Psychological Theories

Although the earliest explanations of delinquency located its causes in demons and, later, in free will, they did not make causal distinctions on the basis of the sex of the delinquent. It was not until the rise of positivistic criminology, with its early emphasis on biological and psychological causes of behavior, that female law violators were seen as uniquely "different" from male criminals (see Chapter 5).

Lombroso and Ferrero's "Atavistic Girl"   In *The Female Offender*,[26] published in 1895, Cesare Lombroso and William Ferrero applied to females the principles of Lombroso's earlier work on the male criminal. Inasmuch as criminals were viewed as "throwbacks," or atavistic by their nature, the female criminal was also seen as biologically distinct and inferior to noncriminal women. Lombroso and Ferrero believed that women were lower on the evolutionary scale than men and therefore closer to their "primitive" origins. Consequently, female criminals were not as visible as their male counterparts and showed fewer signs of degeneracy than males.

According to Lombroso and Ferrero, women are naturally more childlike, less intelligent, lacking in passion, more maternal, and weak-characteristics that make them less inclined to commit crimes. Women also share other traits with children: their moral sense is deficient and they are "revengeful, jealous, [and] inclined to vengeances of a refined cruelty."[27] However, because "women are big children; their evil tendencies are . . . more varied than men's, but generally . . . latent. When . . . awakened and excited they produce results proportionately greater."[28] Therefore, when a woman does turn to crime she is "a monster," as "her wickedness must have been enormous before it could triumph over so many obstacles."[29]

For Lombroso and Ferrero, women's criminality is a product of their biology, but this biology also keeps most women from crime. To the extent that woman's nature is antithetical to crime, and with criminality seen as a characteristic more common to men, the female criminal not only is an abnormal woman, but is biologically more like a man, only "often more ferocious."[30] It should be noted that Lombroso and Ferrero believed that most female delinquents were only "occasional criminals," as were most male delinquents. The

Will female involvement in delinquency ever match or exceed male involvement? Which social factors might facilitate or prevent this from occurring?

The Face of Delinquency. A series of boxes discussing various facets of delinquency or factors related to delinquency personalize the story of delinquency and bring to focus the different life situations of victims and offenders.

Unique, exciting box program makes material more relevant for students.

Cultural Perspectives on Delinquency. Thematic boxes providing students with brief glimpses into the nature of delinquency in other countries and how the problem is dealt with in other cultures allow students to consider the similarities and differences among nations.

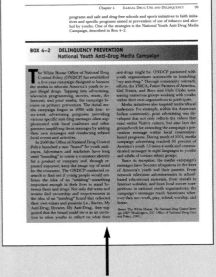

Delinquency Prevention. A thematic box focusing on issues related to the prevention, reduction, or control of delinquency. Some of the programs discussed are well established and appear to most criminologists to be effective in achieving their goals. Other programs discussed hold great promise but are relatively new and untested.

Brief end-of-chapter Conclusions sections summarize chapter material for students and help them prepare for exams.

Students are provided with succinct definitions of commonly used terms and descriptions of important concepts found in bold type throughout the text. For easy reference when students are preparing for exams, each chapter's key terms are defined at the end of the chapter in addition to being included in the glossary.

At the end of each chapter, Internet sites are also identified that will provide students with the most current information available on various chapter topics. Each of these sites is now accompanied by exercises students can use to guide their exploration of the topic.

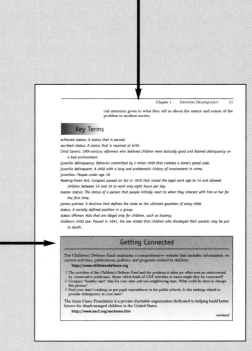

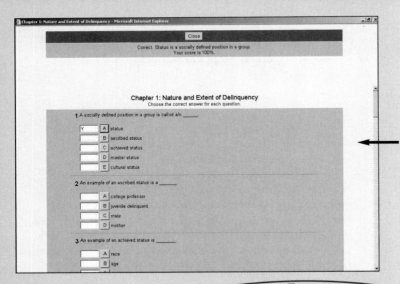

Multiple-choice quizzes with feedback indicating why the student's response is correct or incorrect enable students to master chapter material as they prepare for exams.

Free electronic study guide packaged with the text to help students improve their grades on exams.

In addition to 15–20 question quizzes, the **Making the Grade** electronic study guide includes such important student resources as an Internet guide, a study skills primer, and more.

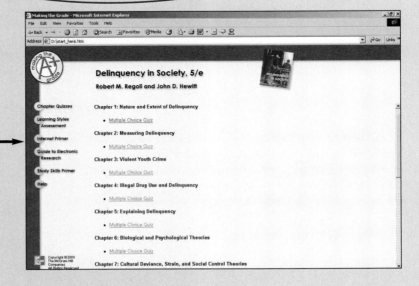

Delinquency in Society

Nature and Extent of Delinquency

I n Section 1 you are introduced to the problem of defining and measuring delinquency. Delinquency is not a simple problem that is easy to describe or measure. Just what delinquency is and how to measure it has been problematic for hundreds of years. This opening section will also introduce two specific problem areas of delinquency: youth violence and illegal drug use.

Chapter 1 reports on the status of children. Past and present definitions of delinquency also are reviewed. Legal definitions of delinquency that regulated the behavior of children in the American colonies, legal reforms of the child-saving movement at the end of the 19th century, and recent changes in state and federal laws are also discussed.

The focus of Chapter 2 is on the prevalence and incidence of delinquency. A student recently asked, "What difference does it make whether I know how much delinquency there is?" Knowing how much and what kind of delinquency is committed by juveniles with what characteristics, living in which neighborhoods, having what kinds of social networks, and leading what kinds of lives is vital to understanding where the problem of juvenile crime exists in U.S. society. Such knowledge helps us to understand the problem more completely. Is delinquency only a problem of lower-class males who live in the inner city? Does it also include females, middle-class children who attend quality schools, troubled children from good families, and "nice" children experimenting with drugs, alcohol, and sex? Chapter 2 reports on how delinquency is measured and what those measures tell us about the extent and nature of the problem.

Chapter 3 examines the current crisis of youth violence. The nature and extent of violent crimes committed by adolescents, the rise in violence, the role of firearms, and approaches to preventing juvenile violence are all discussed.

The last chapter in this section (Chapter 4) probes into illegal drug use by juveniles. Several factors are identified that help to explain why many people believe there is a drug crisis in the United States. Drawing on arrest data from the *Uniform Crime Reports* and self-report surveys of youth, however, we find adolescent drug use actually decreased during the late 1980s and only started to increase again in the mid-1990s. After a discussion of sociological theories of adolescent drug use, the relationship between drugs and delinquency is examined.

Chapter 1
Defining Delinquency

In a New York minute, everything can change.

—Don Henley, "New York Minute"

No song may be more prophetic. Monday, September 10, 2001, was just like any other day. I noticed a dent on my car door just as I was rushing off to work and thought life was unfair. I asked students how they were doing without caring much about their answers. Newspapers were filled with stories about the first week of the NFL season, with detailed team-by-team injury reports. I passed strangers on campus without noticing them. On Tuesday, September 11, all that changed. Different things seemed important. Somebody had tried to tear America apart. In a split second, several thousand people had been killed. Some had their limbs torn from their bodies; hundreds of others perished inside an inferno. Strangers died helping others.

Crime often occurs this way—suddenly and without warning. When it does, life is never the same. What happened to America on September 11 takes place on a much smaller scale every day. It is a tragedy whenever innocent people are killed. Sometimes children are the killers. In 2000, approximately 700 juveniles were arrested for murder (see Chapter 3).[1] One incident involved 6-year-old Tiffany Eunick, who was beaten to death by 12-year-old Lionel Tate. Tate kicked and slugged her, smashed her skull, lacerated her liver, and broke her ribs. Lionel was convicted of first-degree murder and sentenced to life in prison without parole. He did not receive the death penalty because of his age at the time of the crime (see Chapter 15). What is unusual about Tiffany's murder is why Lionel killed her. Lionel explained that he had been imitating pro wrestling moves. He didn't think he would hurt Tiffany if he punched her and threw her against the wall because he had seen wrestlers do this to each other without causing injuries.[2]

Tiffany Eunick's murder captured international attention. But every year tens of thousands of **juveniles** (people under age 18) are arrested for serious crimes (see Chapter 2). When they are, people ask a lot of questions such as: "Why do they do it?" and "What can be done to prevent it?" These questions invite others: What is the child's family like? Does the mother work outside the home? Where was the father? Who are the child's friends? Did the child watch too much television? How should society react to serious juvenile crime? Try to rehabilitate offenders? Punish them severely? Exactly how should we punish or treat juvenile offenders?

Should a child ever be sentenced to life in prison without parole? Are there crimes for which juveniles should be executed?

The first step in answering these questions is to review what it means to be a child in American society. As you read the next section, think about who children are in relation to you. What do you think about them? Are they equal to you? Are they inferior in some way? How does your perception of who children are affect your relations with them?

The Status of Children

Status refers to a socially defined position in a group. It affects how people interact with others and how others interact with them. Status may be

A jetliner is lined up on one of the World Trade Center towers in New York Tuesday, Sept. 11, 2001. In the most devastating terrorist onslaught ever waged against the United States, knife-wielding hijackers crashed two airliners into the World Trade Center, toppling its twin 110-story towers.

Lionel Tate, 13, left, looks at his mother, Kathleen Grossett-Tate, prior to opening statements in his murder trial in Fort Lauderdale, Florida. Lionel is being tried as an adult and faces a mandatory life sentence with no possibility of parole for 25 years if convicted of first-degree murder in the death of 6-year-old Tiffany Eunick. Tate says he accidentally killed Eunick while imitating pro wrestlers.

ascribed or achieved. An **ascribed status** is received at birth. It *cannot* be altered. Being born a Caucasian is an ascribed status. An **achieved status** is earned. Becoming a delinquent is an achieved status. In reality, statuses involve a mixture of ascription and achievement. Ascribed statuses influence achieved statuses. It is no more a coincidence that children from wealthy families usually score higher on standardized tests than children living in poverty than it is that black children are more likely than whites to be arrested (see Chapter 2). This is because ascription partly determines what opportunities are available and what people can achieve.

At any one time people occupy different statuses. Fourteen-year-old Felicia is a student council member, daughter, honor roll student, and a soccer player. These statuses vary in the degree they affect who Felicia is in relation to others. The most important of these statuses is that Felicia is a child. This is her **master status,** the one people react to first when they meet her.

The status of child is the least privileged of all statuses. Children sit at the bottom of the status hierarchy; thus, they have been forced to experience extraordinary physical, emotional, and sexual pain and suffering.

In the Greek, Roman, and Chinese empires, children were killed for offenses committed by their parents. In 19th century Europe, children were treated indifferently. Noisy children were given opium-filled pacifiers to suck on. In one year, 33,000 French children were deserted. In England, 4-year-old children worked cleaning chimneys because they were small enough to fit inside. Thousands died from lung disease at young ages. At age 7, children in England's poor class were indentured to textile mills where they worked until age 21. Five-year-olds worked 16 hours a day in coal mines.[3]

The victim in the first child abuse case in the United States was eight-year-old Mary Ellen Wilson. Laws preventing cruelty to animals had to be invoked to remove her from the home of her abusive foster parents.

Children in the United States did not fare any better. In 1874 in New York, laws preventing cruelty to animals had to be used to remove an abused child from the home of her foster parents. Eight-year-old Mary Ellen Wilson was living in the home of her foster parents, Francis and Mary Connolly. Mrs. Connolly abused and neglected Mary Ellen, beating her and not clothing her properly. Once Mary Ellen's living condition was discovered by a charity worker, Etta Wheller, it was referred to the New York City Department of Charities. But the case was turned away because the agency did not have custody of the girl. When Henry Berge, founder of the American Society for the Prevention of Cruelty to Animals, became aware of Mary Ellen's living arrangement, he brought the matter to the attention of his colleague, Elbridge Gerry, who petitioned the court to hear the case on the grounds that since Mary Ellen was a member of the animal kingdom, she was entitled to the same protection as abused animals—and the child needed protection. The court heard the case; the foster mother was tried, convicted of assault,

BOX 1–1   A WINDOW ON DELINQUENCY
Beating Children

Every year child protective service agencies receive reports on more than 3 million maltreated children. One recent child abuse incident captured attention worldwide. As you read about it, ask yourself: When should children be physically punished? Is it okay for parents to whip children under some circumstances? Should the law be allowed to interfere with the religious beliefs of parents?

In March of 2001, Atlanta police arrested a pastor and five members of his 130-member church who whipped children as a form of discipline. House of Prayer leader 68-year-old Arthur Allen and the church members were charged with cruelty to children. Yet, even though they have been arrested, church members said they will continue to whip unruly children. They believe parents have an absolute right to discipline their children however they see fit. What parents do to *their* children is no business of the state. The beatings were done at the church, executed by par-

ents and other adults with belts and switches under the supervision of Pastor Allen, who advised them on how severe the beatings should be. Allen based the decision on the seriousness of the infraction, a child's age, and whether the child had expressed remorse. For instance, teenage girls who had sex were whipped during church services, after having their skirts or dresses removed. Children who misbehaved at public school were then beaten at church. One 7-year-old boy was held in the air by three adults while his uncle whipped him with a switch as Allen stood by, giving instructions. A 16-year-old girl was beaten with belts for 30 minutes. Police photographs showed 3-inch-long welts on children, and a 10-year-old boy had open wounds on his stomach and side.

Sources: David Firestone, "Minister Defends Beating of Children," *Rocky Mountain News*, March 30:2A, 57A (2001); "Juvenile Judge Removes Children from Church," *Daily Camera*, March 29:11A (2001); "Pastor, 5 Others Held in Whippings," *Rocky Mountain News*, March 21:46A (2001).

Throughout history children have been abused and dominated by adults. Has this historical maltreatment of children created guilt in our national adult conscience? If so, does this guilt contribute to the inability to reduce serious delinquency?

and sentenced to one year in prison. Mary Ellen was removed from the foster home and placed with Etta Wheller's mother.[4]

Children are still second-class citizens. They are the only people without constitutional rights. Because children and adults are not equals in the eyes of the law, some adults think they can do things to children they would hesitate to do to another adult (see Box 1–1). For example, in a recent heinous incident, a father and mother whipped their 12-year-old daughter to death with a 5-foot stretch of electrical cable after she was tied down. Larry and Constance Slack delivered 160 blows to their daughter Laree, stuffing a towel in her mouth to silence her screams.[5] Children also are the only persons whose behavior is legally restrained because of their age. They cannot vote, possess firearms, decide their own medical treatment, wear the clothing of their choice to school, or read whatever material they choose.[6]

BOX 1–2   A CROSS-CULTURAL PERSPECTIVE ON DELINQUENCY
Slave Ships

In the United States in the 19th century, hundreds of thousands of poor and immigrant children were put on trains and transported to obscure locations in the West. These "orphan trains" operated for more than 70 years, from 1854–1929. Today, something similar is going on in a different part of the world. Slave ships are moving children from one country to another. Hundreds of West African children are being transported by ships to oil-rich Gabon, where they are sold into slavery. Some of the children are only 10 years old.

Selling children is common. In countries such as Benin, Togo, Mauritania, and Mali, parents sell children for only US$14 to slave rings that resell them in wealthier African nations for about US$340. The children are then forced to work on fishing vessels and cocoa plantations, in prostitution, and in sweatshops.

Child trafficking is widespread throughout Central and West Africa, where every year about 200,000 children are trafficked and sold into indentured servitude. The problem of child trafficking, however, extends beyond Central and West Africa. Millions of children worldwide are trafficking victims. For example, countless children are sold into bondage in Southeast Asia. They include Thai children enslaved to prostitution, Bangladesh children who were slipped into the United Arab Emirates, and Chinese children smuggled into Los Angeles. While many profit from exploiting children, the children suffer grievously every day of their lives.

Sources: Clarence Page, "Mystery Shines Light on Slavery," *Rocky Mountain News,* April 26:40A (2001); Glenn McKenzie, "Return of Ferry Leads to Search for Child Slaves," *Rocky Mountain News,* April 18:2A, 38A (2001); Holger Jensen, "Slavery Still Raising Its Ugly Head in Africa," *Rocky Mountain News,* April 17:20A (2001).

American Delinquency

The treatment of children in early America was similar to the care they received in England. The English who settled the colonies saw children as a source of labor. Until about 1880, child labor was widespread and the apprenticeship system was broadly practiced. Poor parents turned their children over to farmers or craftsmen who promised to teach them a trade. The practice of selling children into apprenticeship is one that takes place elsewhere today (see Box 1–2).[7]

The American Colonies

In the colonies, *all* children, rich and poor, faced strict control of their behavior. In 1641, the General Court of Massachusetts Bay Colony passed the **stubborn child law,** which stated that children who disobeyed their parents could be put to death.[8] The stubborn child law was based on the Puritans'

In colonial America, "frontier" justice was harsh by today's standards. Vigilantism and infanticide were hasty means of controlling problem and delinquent children. While these policies were certainly cruel, were they effective in controlling delinquency? Was delinquency more or less prevalent in the colonial era than today? Does the harsh frontier justice that was handed out explain why?

belief that unacknowledged social evils would bring the wrath of God down upon the entire colony. The Puritans believed they had no choice but to respond to juvenile misbehavior in a strict and calculated way. But not all of the colonies adopted the stubborn child law. Outside of Massachusetts, children guilty of serious crimes were typically whipped with a leather strap.[9]

It was more than the activity of children that bothered the colonists; their inactivity also upset them. In 1646 the Virginia General Assembly passed a law to prevent "sloth and idleness,"[10] and in 1672, the General Court of Massachusetts Bay Colony prohibited an adult from luring a child from his or her work. Rude, stubborn, and unruly children were taken from their parents and given to a master to "correct" the misbehavior of boys until they were 21 and girls until age 18.[11]

Puritans held mixed feelings about children. On the one hand, they believed children were born in sin and should submit to adult authority and hard labor. On the other hand, they also thought children required separate legal provisions. For instance, the Massachusetts Bay Colony laws of 1660 provided that

> for sodomy . . . children under fourteen were to be "severely punished" but not executed; for cursing and smiting parents, . . . only those "above sixteen years old, and of sufficient understanding" could be put to death; for being stubborn or rebellious sons . . . only those "of sufficient years and under-

The two young boys in this photo had been accused of stealing pigeons. The boys were beaten severely and sent to a reformatory.

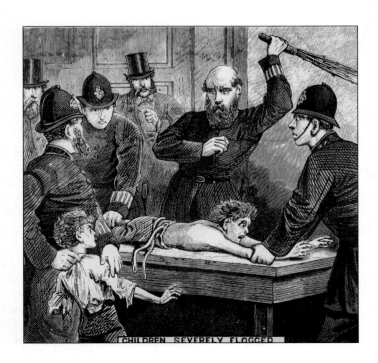

CHILDREN SEVERELY FLOGGED

To this day, underage American children toil in fields and factories. Six-year-old Graciela Perez carries a bucket of red chilies across a field during the morning harvest in Berino, New Mexico. The peppers ended up in Newman's Own salsa.

standing [sixteen years of age]" were liable; for arson, . . . the law also applied only to those "of the age of sixteen years and upward"; for "denying the Scriptures to be the infallible word of God," again the minimum age was sixteen for those who were liable to the death penalty.[12]

The Puritans made no distinction between delinquency and sin. The laws of the colony reflected the laws of God. Children who misbehaved violated God and God's law.

The Puritans were not the only ones concerned about children. By the 18th century, childhood was considered a special period of life during which children needed thoughtful guidance and discipline. Children were seen as "fragile, innocent, and sacred, on one hand, but corruptible, trying, and arrogant on the other hand."[13] This perspective of children was held by the upper class, who demanded the close observance of children, the need for discipline rather than coddling, the importance of modesty, and strict obedience to authority. Children had now been transformed from being miniature adults to being something "special."

Postcolonial Patterns of Delinquency

Once children had become special, new "children only" laws were passed. There was an increasing demand on the state to take responsibility for improving the lives of children, and eventually new regulations, such as child labor laws, were enacted.[14] In 1916, for instance, Congress passed the **Keating-Owen Act,** the first piece of child labor legislation in America. Even

> In contemporary America, disparaging people because of their race, ethnicity, sex, social class, or sexual orientation is taboo and sometimes illegal. However, there is no similar outcry for the subordination of children. Why? Will other "protected groups" mobilize for the equality of children? Will there be a new child-saving movement?

though the Act was overturned two years later in *Hammer v. Dagenhart*,[15] it did lay the groundwork for passage in 1938 of the *Fair Labor Standards Act*. Moreover, today, every state has established its own child labor laws.[16]

While early interest in children was motivated by humanitarian concern, the actual purpose of the reforms was to control the children of the immigrant poor. Their swarming, ragged presence on city streets made them highly visible to a worried and fearful public. For the first time, Americans were forced to confront large numbers of homeless children. The new concern for children was paradoxically tied to the fear that these children were a threat to society.[17] Fear of children was based on many different experiences. In the early 19th century, America was in the midst of a massive economic depression. Crime soared and lawlessness was rampant. Particularly distressful was the harassing and assaultive behavior of juvenile gangs (see Chapter 12).[18]

By the early 1800s, juvenile gangs had become an unwanted fixture in big cities. Their habits of hanging out on street corners, verbally abusing pedestrians, and pelting citizens with rocks and snowballs were among the least-threatening behaviors. More serious were the violent gangs of juvenile robbers that preyed on innocent citizens.[19]

The Child Savers

In the first quarter of the 19th century, America underwent rapid social change during the Industrial Revolution. Of the many changes that resulted from the Industrial Revolution, three are particularly relevant for understanding the emergence of delinquency in the United States. Most important may be that wealthy people had more leisure time. Yet, at the same time, there was a rise in public education, and communal life in the cities was beginning to break down. Affluent people needed something to do. Some satisfied their need by turning their attention to saving *other* people's children. These concerned citizens eventually formed a social activist group called the **Child Savers,** who believed children were born good and became bad. Juvenile crime was blamed on bad environments. The best way to save children was to get them out of "bad" homes and placed in "good" ones.[20]

The Early History of Institutional Control

The Child Savers also actively pursued the passage of legislation that would permit the institutionalization of children, especially juvenile paupers. The goal of removing children from extreme poverty was admirable, but it resulted in transforming children into nonpersons. Children were shunted into factories, poorhouses, orphanages, and houses of refuge, where they were treated badly, with almost no attention given to their individual needs.

Under the guise of providing children with better preparation for life, the "new" institutions sometimes did children more harm than good. A case involving the Children's Aid Society illustrates this point. The Society's goal

BOX 1–3   DELINQUENCY PREVENTION
Orphan Trains

In the mid-19th century, thousands of children who were orphans, runaways, and throwaways filled New York City streets. Many of them were incarcerated or put in poorhouses. A more daring tack was taken by Reverend Charles Loring Brace, who in 1853 established the Children's Aid Society, whose purpose was to provide homeless children with shelter and education. Between 1854 and 1929, the Society ran "orphan trains" that carried approximately 250,000 abandoned children from New York to locations in the West where they were adopted by Christian farm families.

The process of finding new homes for the children was haphazard. At town meetings across the country, farming families took their pick of the orphan train riders. Children who were not selected got back on board the train and continued to the next town. The children

and those who adopted them had one year to decide whether they would stay together. If either decided not to, the child would be returned to the Society, boarded on the next train out of town, and offered to another family.

The impact of Brace's efforts on children's lives was variable. Some children thrived. Two boys became governors, one became a Supreme Court justice, and others became mayors, congressmen, or local representatives. Thousands of others did not fare so well. Many became drifters and thieves; at least one became a murderer. The vast majority of the children led ordinary and unaccomplished lives.

Source: Stephen O'Conner, *Orphan Trains* (Boston: Houghton Mifflin Company, 2001); Sandra Dallas, "Author Disputes Rosy Claims About Orphan Trains," *The Denver Post*, April 22:6 (2001). An excellent PBS video on this topic is entitled *The Orphan Trains* (1995).

was to place "unwanted" children in good foster homes in the countryside where they would learn the value of hard work and love of nature. What emerged was a profit-making organization that drafted nearly 250,000 children into indentured servitude until age 18 (see Box 1–3).[21]

Are the orphan trains a viable delinquency prevention program that should be reinstated? How does society today address the problem of orphaned, abandoned, and throwaway children? What living arrangements are provided for them?

Some of the first recorded attempts to control delinquency in the United States in a public, institutional manner took place in the 1800s. By this time childhood had come to be regarded as a period of life that deserved the care and attention its innocent nature demanded.[22] But in cities, such as New York, Philadelphia, and Boston, conflicting aspects of juvenile behavior gained public notice. Here, the young delinquent stood in sharp contrast to the purity of childhood. The Child Savers launched interventionist efforts to save delinquents, to relieve the circumstances of their development, and to guide them firmly toward the path of righteousness. This path, however, was often a winding one because of the anxieties of these well-meaning reformers. To them, delinquents were not just innocent children gone wrong; they were "bad seeds" who were capable of wreaking havoc on society. They must be restrained from activities that violated social norms, and these

Orphaned children on Mulberry Street in New York City in the 19th century.

restraints sometimes reached astonishing dimensions. As for their parents, they should be sterilized to prevent further members of the "dangerous class" from being born.

It was in this political climate that the doctrine of **parens patriae** was created. This doctrine asserted that the state is "the ultimate guardian of every child." It therefore may assume parental responsibility and intervene in family matters to protect children. As a "super-parent," the state enjoyed wide latitude in its efforts to reform the delinquent child. One of the earliest judicial expressions of *parens patriae* was fought vigorously in 1839 by a distraught father whose child had fallen victim to the "compassion" of the Philadelphia House of Refuge.

What is the purpose of having status offenses? Should chronic status offenders be arrested? Should they be punished or treated? What should their punishment or treatment be?

Mary Ann Crouse had been committed to the House of Refuge by her mother, who alleged the child was *incorrigible*.[23] The child's father disagreed. He argued that the commitment procedures had been unfair. The child herself had not been allowed to defend herself at the trial, plus she had only been accused of committing a **status offense,** an act illegal for children only, such as incorrigibility, truancy, curfew violation, and running away. The court accepted the mother's charge and committed Mary Ann to the state for guidance. Not too much has changed in the 160 years since Mary Ann's commitment. Children today still are arrested for status offenses. In 2000 more than 150,000 juveniles were arrested for curfew and loitering violations and for running away.[24]

New York House of Refuge

The first house of refuge opened in 1825 in New York State. It was yet another example of the mixture of concerns underlying the philosophy of *parens patriae*. In 1824 nearly 10,000 children under age 14 were living in poverty in New York City. Many people were not only concerned for their welfare but also were motivated out of fear "that this mass of pauperism [would] form a fruitful nursery of crime, unless prevented by the watchful superintendence of the legislature."[25] One of the main instruments that was employed as a remedy for this problem was the New York House of Refuge. Designed to save children from a life of crime, the house soon revealed an orientation toward saving society from children.

The reformers' attitudes toward delinquency were rooted in their beliefs about poverty and delinquency (see Chapter 2). Poverty was linked with idleness, which was seen as a reprehensible moral quality that led to crime. The managers of the New York House of Refuge translated this equation into a severely regimented boot camp type of existence for house inmates, where "children were marched from one activity to the next, were put on a rigid time schedule, . . . and were corporally punished for being uncooperative."[26]

Children suffered greatly at the hands of adults, whose mixture of hostility and kindness produced a peculiar atmosphere. Common to houses of refuge was an emphasis on remorse and punishment. Children accused of crimes were not only persuaded of the error of their ways; they were also made to suffer for them. Amends in the form of punishment provided the most convenient method of conversion.

The Juvenile Court

Social reformers continued to look for other solutions to the growing problem of juvenile delinquency. The most significant of these was the creation of the juvenile court in Cook County (Chicago), Illinois, in 1899.[27] Like the earlier houses of refuge, the juvenile court was to closely supervise problem children. But unlike the houses of refuge, supervision was to occur within the child's own home and within the community, not in institutions.

Outraged by the plight and the potential threat of so many needy children, the Child Savers joined hands with lawyers and penologists to establish the juvenile court. It began with an 1899 Illinois legislative act "to regulate the treatment and control of dependent, neglected, and delinquent children." This Act defined a *delinquent* as a child "under the age of 16 years who violates any law of this State or any City or Village ordinance." A *dependent* or *neglected* child was one who

> is destitute or homeless or abandoned; or dependent upon the public for support; or has not proper parental care or guardianship; or who habitually begs or receives alms; or who is found living in any house of ill fame or with any vicious or disreputable person; or whose home . . . is an unfit place for such a child; or [one] under the age of 8 years who is found peddling or selling any article or singing or playing any musical instrument upon the street or giving any public entertainment.[28]

Because the juvenile court movement was spearheaded by social workers, the court's procedures were *civil*, not criminal. Children were treated, not punished, and the judge was to be a wise and kind parent. The new court would segregate juvenile offenders from adult offenders at all procedural stages. Furthermore, the court would hire probation officers to exercise friendly supervision over children involved in informal court proceedings.[29]

The juvenile court reaffirmed and extended the doctrine of *parens patriae*.[30] This paternalistic philosophy meant that reformers gave more attention to the "needs" than to the rights of children. In their campaign to meet the needs of children, the Child Savers enlarged the role of the state to include the handling of children in the judicial system.

Juvenile Probation

In the state's expanded role as parent, one important component of the new court organization was juvenile probation.[31] Probation officers performed two crucial tasks: presentence investigation and postsentence supervision.[32] The range of their mission was enormous. According to David Rothman, "Probation officers had the tasks, incredible as they were, of correcting the child's difficulties and at the same time correcting faults in the family and in the community."[33]

The importance of the probation officer's role reflected the juvenile court's commitment to rehabilitate rather than to incarcerate young offenders whenever possible. Although institutionalization was still available for the most difficult children, probation in the child's home was more often the alternative chosen by court personnel. Like the expansion of the definition of delinquency to include status offenses, the reliance on probation mirrored the reformer's interest in rehabilitating both the child and his or her home.[34]

Ideally, probation was to extend for a indeterminate amount of time since no one could predict how long treatment would be needed. Frequent visits to the child's home, school, and neighborhood would allow the probation officer to facilitate the rehabilitation of the child and his or her family. The indeterminate probation period granted the state an active, extended role in molding children under its surveillance, necessary if the children of the immigrant poor were ever to conform successfully to middle-class standards. The ambitions of juvenile court supporters focused on transforming the child's natural environment and that of his or her family. Reforming the child's habits and attitudes in an artificially controlled setting, such as the residential institution, had become a less desirable alternative.

What Is Delinquency? Who Is a Delinquent?

Only a fraction of delinquent offenders are "caught" by police. What explains this? Do police select which delinquents they will arrest based on ascribed characteristics such as race and sex? Are "official" delinquents less intelligent than ones who are not caught?

No one can say with factuality what delinquency is and who delinquents are. This is because society's views about who children are in relation to adults is always changing. As a result, there is little agreement today among the 50 states on what behavior constitutes delinquency, except to say that **juvenile delinquency** is an action committed by a minor child that violates a state's penal code.

The principal distinction between *crime* and *delinquency* is the age of the offender. Delinquency refers to criminal acts committed by juveniles. When deciding who is a delinquent, few criminologists adopt a strict legal definition. This is because nearly all children have broken the law and had they been caught and prosecuted could have been institutionalized for one or more years (see Chapter 2). It is not instructive, however, to argue that all children are delinquents. There are measurable differences in the behavior of children. Most children are only sporadically delinquent, while others are chronic offenders (see Chapter 2).

One way of deciding who is a juvenile delinquent is to evaluate the behavior of children on a series of three continua that represent the *frequency*, *seriousness*, and *duration* of their behavior. As shown in Figure 1–1, each factor forms its own continuum and children fall at different points on each one. A **juvenile delinquent** is a child who has shown a consistency in behavior that falls toward the extreme right end of *each* continuum. Delinquents are children

Figure 1–1
Continua of Delinquency

1. *Number of Offenses (Frequency)*

   Infrequent ———————————————— Occasional ———————————————— Often
   (once or twice)   (sporadic)   (regularly)

2. *Gravity of Offenses (Seriousness)*

   Minor ——————————————————————————————————————— Major
   (status offenses)   (misdemeanor offenses)   (felony crimes)

3. *Span of Offenses (Duration)*

   Short —————————————————————————————————————— Long
   (days or weeks)   (several months)   (few years)   (many years)

Source: Adapted from Hugh D. Barlow and Theodore N. Ferdinand, *Understanding Delinquency* (New York: HarperCollins Publishers, 1992), p. 43. Copyright © 1992 by HarperCollins Publishers, Inc. Reprinted by permission.

who have committed many serious offenses over an extended period of time. They are children with a long and problematic history of involvement in crime.

Conclusions

How society defines delinquency is a reflection of the status of children. When society's beliefs about children change, so does its formal response to their misbehavior. When juveniles were thought to be miniature adults, the legal codes that applied to adults were presumed adequate for children. However, with the changes in social roles and relationships brought about by the Industrial Revolution, juveniles were seen as different from adults and their law-breaking behavior became defined as a serious challenge to the social order.

While the legal codes of the 17th and 18th centuries equated delinquency with sin, by the 19th century this view was replaced with one that forged a connection between urban poverty and crime. To a large extent, the plight of the urban adolescent, poverty, and exposure to the corrupting influences of adult criminals were responsible for many reforms near the end of the 19th century and early 20th century.

The most significant reform was the creation of the juvenile court. The juvenile court and codes that followed it carved out special areas of misbehavior (status offenses) and special conditions (dependency and neglect) that permitted court intervention and the designation of a child as delinquent.

How delinquency is defined determines how it is measured and explained. In the next chapter, measures of delinquency are discussed with special attention given to what they tell us about the nature and extent of the problem in modern society.

Key Terms

achieved status: *A status that is earned.*

ascribed status: *A status that is received at birth.*

Child Savers: *19th-century reformers who believed children were basically good and blamed delinquency on a bad environment.*

juvenile delinquency: *Behavior committed by a minor child that violates a state's penal code.*

juvenile delinquent: *A child with a long and problematic history of involvement in crime.*

juveniles: *People under age 18.*

Keating-Owen Act: *Congress passed an Act in 1916 that raised the legal work age to 14 and allowed children between 14 and 16 to work only eight hours per day.*

master status: *The status of a person that people initially react to when they interact with him or her for the first time.*

parens patriae: *A doctrine that defines the state as the ultimate guardian of every child.*

status: *A socially defined position in a group.*

status offense: *Acts that are illegal only for children, such as truancy.*

stubborn child law: *Passed in 1641, the law stated that children who disobeyed their parents may be put to death.*

Getting Connected

The Children's Defense Fund maintains a comprehensive website that includes information on current activities, publications, policies, and programs related to children.

http://www.childrensdefense.org

1. The activities of the Children's Defense Fund and the positions it takes are often seen as controversial by conservative politicians. About which kinds of CDF activities or issues might they be concerned?
2. Compare "healthy start" data for your state and one neighboring state. What could be done to change this picture?
3. Find your state's ranking on per-pupil expenditures in the public schools. Is this ranking related to juvenile delinquency in your state?

The Anne Casey Foundation is a private charitable organization dedicated to helping build better futures for disadvantaged children in the United States.

http://www.aecf.org/aechome.htm

continued

1. What is the Juvenile Detention Alternatives Initiative?

2. Using information from the KIDS COUNT page, discuss the problem of undercounting children in the decennial census.

3. According to the president of the foundation, how did children fare in the United States' economic prosperity in the 1990s? What does he propose that Americans do about this?

The goal of the Partnership for Children organization is to mobilize powerful and effective new voices to speak out for children.

http://www.pfc.org/

1. Read about the goals of the Partnership. Does your hometown have such an organization? If so, what is it like? If not, why not?

2. Check the links on the Youth Violence Prevention page. What kinds of prevention techniques does this organization advocate?

3. According to the Partnership's report card on Kansas City, what is the city's most recent grade? How would you grade your hometown using the Partnership's benchmarks?

National Center for Missing and Exploited Children is a private, nonprofit organization whose goal is to locate and recover missing children and to raise public awareness about ways to prevent child abduction, molestation, and sexual exploitation.

http://www.missingkids.com

1. Why is this website a ".com" site, rather than an ".edu" or an ".org" or a ".gov"? Does this have an impact on its credibility?

2. Some have argued that this organization misstates this serious problem, thus making it difficult to actually understand the reasons why children become missing or are exploited. Having checked out the website, what do you think?

3. Evaluate the organization's *Know the Rules* advice for teenage girls.

The Juvenile Law Center (JLC) is one of the oldest children's rights organization in the United States. The JLC operates as a nonprofit legal service, working on behalf of children who come into the juvenile court system.

http://www.jcl.org/html

1. What is a public interest law firm?

2. Explore the site's links. What is the goal of the Hamilton Fish Institute?

3. What is this organization's stand on zero-tolerance policies?

Endnotes

1. Federal Bureau of Investigation, *Crime in the United States 2000* (Washington, DC: U.S. Department of Justice, 2001).
2. Terry Spencer, "Teen Guilty of Murder in 'Wrestling'," *Rocky Mountain News*, January 26:45A (2001); Terry Spencer, "Florida Boy Puts Blame on Pro Wrestling in Beating Death," *Rocky Mountain News*, January 14:51A (2001).
3. Letty Pogrebin, *Family Politics* (New York: McGraw-Hill, 1983).
4. Charles Gill, "Essay on the Status of the American Child, 2000 A.D.," *Ohio Northern University Law Review* 17:543–579 (1991).
5. Kirsten Scharnberg and Rudolph Bush, "Girl Died After Parents Hit Her 160 Times, Court Told," *Chicago Tribune*, November 14, 2001.

6. Thomas Jacobs, *What Are My Rights?* (Minneapolis: Free Spirit Publishing, 1997).

7. Pogrebin, note 3; Richard Gelles, *Contemporary Families* (Thousand Oaks, CA: Sage Publications, 1995); Clifford Dorne, *Crimes Against Children* (New York: Harrow and Heston Publishers, 1989), p. 30.

8. Philip Greven, *Spare the Child* (New York: Knopf, 1991).

9. David Rothman, *The Discovery of the Asylum* (Boston: Little, Brown, 1970).

10. Joseph Hawes, *Children in Urban Society* (New York: Oxford University Press, 1971), p. 19.

11. Hawes, note 10.

12. Edwin Powers, *Crime and Punishment in Early Massachusetts* (Boston: Beacon Press, 1966), p. 442.

13. LaMar Empey, *American Delinquency* (Homewood, IL: Dorsey Press, 1978), p. 50.

14. George Haskins, *Law and Authority in Early Massachusetts* (New York: Archon Books, 1968).

15. *Hammer v. Dagenhart*, 247 U.S. 251 (1918).

16. Jacobs, note 6, p. 57.

17. Stephen O'Connor, *Orphan Trains* (Boston: Houghton Mifflin, 2001); John Hart, "In the School-Room," pp. 252–257 in *Work, Culture, and Society in Industrializing America*, edited by Herbert Gutman (New York: Knopf, 1976).

18. Wiley Sanders, *Juvenile Offenders for a Thousand Years* (Chapel Hill, NC: University of North Carolina Press, 1970).

19. Richard Johnson, *Juvenile Delinquency and its Origins* (Cambridge, England: Cambridge University Press, 1979), p. 83.

20. Anthony Platt, *The Child Savers* (Chicago: University of Chicago Press, 1969), p. 76.

21. O'Connor, note 17.

22. Lloyd deMause, *The History of Childhood* (New York: Peter Bedrick, 1988).

23. *Ex parte Crouse*, 4 Warton 9 (1838).

24. Federal Bureau of Investigation, note 1.

25. New York State Board of Charities, *Report of the Secretary of State in 1824 on the Relief and Settlement of the Poor* (Albany, NY: 1901), cited in Robert Bremner et al., *Children and Youth in America*, 2 volumes (Cambridge, MA: Harvard University Press, 1970).

26. Dorne, note 7, p. 28.

27. Timothy Hurley, *Origin of the Illinois Juvenile Court Law*, 3rd ed. (New York: AMS Press, 1907/1977).

28. Grace Abbott, *The Child and the State* (Chicago: University of Chicago Press, 1938), pp. 392–401.

29. Hurley, note 27.

30. Hurley, note 27, p. 56.

31. Hurley, note 27, p. 225.

32. Harvey Baker, "Proceedings of the Boston Juvenile Court," in *Preventive Treatment of Neglected Children*, Hastings Hart (New York: Charities Publication Committee, 1910), pp. 318-327.

33. David Rothman, "The Progressive Legacy," in *The Progressive Legacy and Current Reforms*, edited by LaMar Empey (Charlottesville: University of Virginia Press, 1979).

34. Ellen Ryerson, *The Best Laid Plans* (New York: Hill and Wang, 1978), pp. 444–445.

Chapter 2

Measuring Delinquency

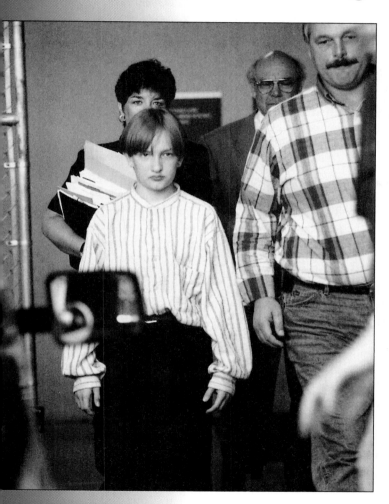

The government is very keen on amassing statistics. . . . But you must never forget that every one of the figures comes in the first instance from the village watchman, who just puts down what he damn pleases.[1]

—Sir Josiah Stamp

The English economist Sir Josiah Stamp cautions us about relying too heavily on crime statistics. This is because some juveniles are **falsely accused** (believed to have committed a crime when they did not) and others are **secret delinquents** (their crimes are not known to the police). To alleviate these problems, criminologists estimate the **prevalence** (number of juveniles committing delinquency) and **incidence** (number of delinquent acts committed) of delinquency using three sources of data: the *Uniform Crime Reports*, National Crime Victimization Survey, and self-report studies.

Uniform Crime Reports

Since 1929 the Federal Bureau of Investigation (FBI) has collected crime data from local law enforcement agencies. The data are published in an annual report entitled *Crime in the United States,* which is frequently referred to as the ***Uniform Crime Reports*** *(UCR).*[2] The *UCR* is divided into three sections:

1. Crimes known to the police. These are crimes police know about. They may be crimes reported to police or crimes police discovered on their own.

2. Number of arrests. This section of the *UCR* reports the number of arrests police made in the past calendar year. The number of arrests is not the same as the number of people arrested because some people are arrested more than once during the year. Nor does the number of arrests tell us how many crimes the people who were arrested committed because multiple crimes committed by one person may produce a single arrest, or a single crime may result in the arrest of multiple persons.

3. Persons arrested. The third section of the *UCR* reports the number of persons arrested, crimes for which they were arrested, and the age, sex, and race of those arrested.

The *UCR* Crime Index

Data for the *UCR* come from more than 17,000 police agencies who *voluntarily* participate in the program. The agencies represent over 95 percent of the U.S. population. The crime data are summarized by the FBI in a **Crime Index** (called **Part I crimes**) that consists of eight offenses: murder and nonnegligent manslaughter, forcible rape, robbery, aggravated assault, burglary, larceny-theft, motor vehicle theft, and arson.

The Index is divided into two subcategories: violent crimes and property crimes. The *Violent* Index crimes are murder and nonnegligent manslaughter, forcible rape, robbery, and aggravated assault. The *Property* Index crimes are burglary, larceny-theft, motor vehicle theft, and arson.

The *UCR* also counts the number of persons arrested for 20 additional crimes and a catchall category called "all other offenses" (which excludes traffic offenses). The non-Index offenses are called **Part II crimes** and in-

Animosity toward the police is pervasive in American society. Does this contribute to distrust of *UCR* data? What role does conspiracy theory play in the lay assessment of official measures of delinquency?

BOX 2-1   A WINDOW ON DELINQUENCY
Uniform Crime Reports Offenses

The *Uniform Crime Reports* are divided into Part I and Part II offenses. Law enforcement agencies report data on the number of Part I offenses known to them and the number of people arrested monthly to the Federal Bureau of Investigation (FBI). Police report only arrest data to the FBI for Part II offenses.

PART I OFFENSES (THE INDEX CRIMES)

1. *Murder and nonnegligent manslaughter*—The willful killing of one human being by another.
2. *Forcible rape*—the carnal knowledge of a female forcibly and against her will.
3. *Robbery*—the taking or attempting to take anything of value from the care, custody, or control of a person or persons by force or threat of force or violence and/or by putting the victim in fear.
4. *Aggravated assault*—the unlawful attack by one person upon another for the purpose of inflicting severe or aggravated bodily injury.
5. *Burglary*—the unlawful entry of a structure to commit a felony or theft.
6. *Larceny-theft*—the unlawful taking, carrying, leading, or riding away of property from the possession or constructive possession of others. Examples are thefts of bicycles or automobile accessories, shoplifting, and pocket-picking.
7. *Motor vehicle theft*—the theft or attempted theft of a motor vehicle.
8. *Arson*—Any willful or malicious burning or attempt to burn, with or without intent to defraud, a dwelling house, public building, motor vehicle or aircraft, or the personal property of another.

PART II OFFENSES

1. Simple assault
2. Forgery and counterfeiting
3. Fraud
4. Embezzlement
5. Buying, receiving, and possessing stolen property
6. Vandalism
7. Carrying and possessing weapons
8. Prostitution and commercialized vice
9. Sex offenses (except forcible rape, prostitution, and commercialized vice)
10. Drug abuse violations
11. Gambling
12. Offenses against the family and children
13. Driving under the influence of liquor and narcotics
14. Liquor law violations
15. Drunkenness
16. Disorderly conduct
17. Vagrancy
18. Suspicion
19. Curfew and loitering violations
20. Runaway violations
21. All other crimes (except traffic)

Source: Federal Bureau of Investigation, *Crime in the United States 2000* (Washington, DC: U.S. Department of Justice, 2001).

Should police exercise discretion when deciding how to report a crime? Is there any way to limit police discretion in crime reporting?

clude crimes such as prostitution, simple assault, and drug abuse violations. All Part I and Part II crimes are listed in Box 2–1.

Limitations of *UCR* Data

The *UCR* underestimates the amount of delinquency committed because it only reports *crimes known to police*. Most crime never comes to the attention of police because it is not reported.[3] Therefore, the *UCR* may tell us more about police behavior than about criminality because:

1. Police officers have considerable discretion when deciding how to record a crime. Some officers record a robbery as a robbery, and others may record it as a theft.

2. Police departments lose crime reports, accidentally or deliberately.

3. Under the *UCR*'s **hierarchy rule,** police record only the most serious crime incident. For example, the arrest of a juvenile charged with aggravated assault and possession of a controlled substance would be reported by police agencies to the FBI as an arrest for aggravated assault. When the *UCR* shows, for instance, that police arrested 105,993 juveniles for drug abuse violations in 2000, this means a drug abuse violation was the most *serious* charge in 105,993 arrests. An unknown number of additional arrests in 2000 included a drug charge as a lesser offense.[4]

4. All Crime Index offenses are presumed to be of the same seriousness. A murder is counted the same as a burglary when the crime rate is calculated.

5. The official crime rate is based only on the Crime Index offenses. Information on other serious crimes (kidnapping, for instance) are not included.[5]

The *UCR* also provides information on a few white-collar and corporate crimes, such as tax fraud, insider trading, and price-fixing. No data on other serious crimes, such as environmental crimes and child trafficking, are collected.

Significance of *UCR* Data

UCR data are popular with criminologists. They are one of only two sources of data that provide a *national estimate* of the prevalence and incidence of delinquency. Those who use them assume that the inaccuracies of *UCR* data are consistent over time and that the data accurately depict trends in delinquency.

National Crime Victimization Survey

Many scholars are skeptical of official data because of alleged biases against racial and ethnic minorities. However, NCVS data largely support official estimates of crime and delinquency. What are the implications of this for the race–crime relationship?

The *UCR* is not able to measure **hidden delinquency,** which are criminal acts the police do not know about. One way to discover them is through the **National Crime Victimization Survey** (NCVS), which asks people directly whether they have been a crime victim.

Beginning in 1973, the federal government started to generate crime victimization data by surveying citizens.[6] Each year interviews are conducted with persons age 12 and older in a nationally representative sample of about 49,000 households (about 101,000 persons). They are asked whether they have been the victim of any of seven **crimes of interest** in the past year: rape, sexual assault, robbery, assault, theft, household burglary, and motor vehicle theft. If respondents have been victimized, they are asked additional questions about the offense, including whether it was reported to police and if they knew the offender (see Box 2–2).

BOX 2–2   A WINDOW ON DELINQUENCY
Sample Questions from the National Crime Victimization Survey

Victimization studies ask juveniles directly about crimes committed against them during a specific time period. Children may be asked questions similar to those below:

1. Did you have your (pocket picked/purse snatched)?
2. Did anyone try to rob you by using force or threatening to harm you?
3. Did anyone beat you up, attack you, or hit you with something, such as a rock or bottle?
4. Were you knifed, shot at, or attacked with some other weapon by anyone at all?

5. Did anyone steal things that belonged to you from inside any car or truck, such as packages or clothing?
6. Was anything stolen from you while you were away from home, for instance at work, in a theater or restaurant, or while traveling?
7. Did you call the police during the last six months to report something that happened to you that you thought was a crime? If yes, how many times?

Source: Bureau of Justice Statistics, *Criminal Victimization in the United States 2000* (Washington, DC: U.S. Department of Justice, 2001).

Limitations of NCVS Data

The NCVS underestimates the amount of delinquency committed. One reason is that only information on seven crimes for people age 12 and older is collected. No information is collected on other serious crimes, on crimes committed against younger children, or on crimes committed by and against businesses. In addition, when people are asked questions about criminal victimization they (1) may not recall when or how many times a crime occurred, (2) may remember a crime occurring more recently than it did because the event remains vivid in their memories, or (3) may not report victimizations because they are embarrassed, the crime is unpleasant to talk about, or the crime may incriminate them in illegal activity.

Significance of NCVS Data

NCVS data have helped criminologists gain a better understanding of the seriousness of criminal victimization and the types of crime that are likely to be reported to police. From NCVS data it is known that only about 40 percent of criminal victimizations are ever reported. There are many reasons why. People may view the crime as a personal matter. Or, possibly, they fear retaliation or believe the police cannot solve the crime anyway.[7]

Self-Report Studies

Self-report studies ask juveniles directly about their law-violating behavior (see Box 2–3). In 1946, Austin Porterfield published the first self-report study.[8] He found that over 90 percent of the college students surveyed ad-

---

BOX 2–3   A WINDOW ON DELINQUENCY
Sample Self-Report Delinquency Survey

Self-report surveys ask juveniles directly about their own criminal behavior during a specific time period. Juveniles may also be asked to indicate how many of their illegal acts came to the attention of police and whether they were arrested, convicted, and institutionalized.

Now that you have read the survey, complete it for yourself. What problems did you have when answering the questions? Did you answer truthfully? Why or why not?

OFFENSE	NUMBER OF OFFENSES	NUMBER OF OFFENSES KNOWN TO THE POLICE	NUMBER OF ARRESTS	NUMBER OF CONVICTIONS
1. Murder				
2. Manslaughter				
3. Kidnapping				
4. Robbery				
5. Forcible rape				
6. Forgery				
7. Arson				
8. Burglary				
9. Shoplifting				
10. Used fake ID				
11. Pimping				
12. Prostitution				
13. Fighting				
14. Running away				
15. Window peeking				
16. Used marijuana				
17. Used cocaine				
18. Auto theft				
19. Drunk driving				
20. Vandalism				

mitted to at least one felony. The next year James Wallerstein and J. C. Wyle surveyed juveniles and found that 91 percent admitted to at least one offense punishable by one or more years in prison, and 99 percent admitted to at least one offense they could have been arrested for had they been caught.[9] In 1954 James F. Short, Jr., reported findings from the first self-report study to include institutionalized juvenile delinquents.[10] Four years later, in 1958, Short and F. Ivan Nye published a study of (1) juveniles in three Washington State communities, (2) students in three Midwestern towns, and (3) a sample of delinquents in training schools. They found (1) delinquency was widespread and (2) detected no relationship between social class and delinquency. These findings inspired more systematic research.[11] In 1976, Delbert Elliott launched the **National Youth Survey** (NYS), a nationwide self-report survey of more than 1,700 youths between the ages of 11 and 17. For 25 years this original group of respondents (now in their 30s) has reported to Elliott how often during the past 12 months (from one Christmas to the next) they have committed certain criminal acts, ranging from felony assaults to minor thefts.[12]

Limitations of Self-Report Data

Problems with self-report studies are similar to those of victimization studies. Juveniles are not always able to recall what they did and when, sometimes they embellish or simplify what happened, and other times they do not report what they did. These problems have led to the development of strategies for assessing the accuracy of what juveniles report. Three ways to do this are to:

1. Compare the self-reports with official records. Researchers compare what respondents tell them with police or court records.[13]

2. Ask knowledgeable persons about the child's delinquency. A juvenile's peers might be asked about his or her behavior. If the self-reported behavior is confirmed by a knowledgeable other, the assumption is that it probably happened.[14]

3. Use or threatened use of a polygraph test. Lie detector tests or the threat of being subjected to one have helped verify self-reports of delinquency.[15]

By using these tactics, criminologists have been able to produce reliable and valid data with the self-report method.[16]

Significance of Self-Report Data

We have learned a great deal about delinquency from self-report data. We know that over 90 percent of juveniles have committed an act that, if they had been caught and prosecuted to the full extent of the law, could have had them incarcerated.[17] Self-report data also have alerted us to just how much delinquency is hidden from the authorities. The amount of delinquency committed is between 4 and 10 times greater than what is reported in the *UCR*.[18] Finally, self-report research has produced evidence of a possible racial bias in the processing of juveniles who enter the juvenile justice system.[19]

Would you tell strangers the truth about your involvement in delinquency? If not, would you likely embellish or minimize your involvement in crime? Why would you report what you have done? Why might people lie?

Are police practices such as racial profiling rational and, moreover, necessary for the effective control of delinquency? Why or why not?

Scholars who advocate the use of self-report data sometimes suggest that there is no relationship between social class and delinquency. Is this believable? To defend your answer, create a list of affluent neighborhoods that are/are not plagued by crime and delinquency.

Delinquency Trends

Is juvenile delinquency a serious social problem? Are more children committing crime today than five years ago? Is the criminal behavior of girls becoming more like boys? Why are blacks arrested proportionally more often than whites? Are age and delinquency related? What is the relationship between poverty and crime?

How Many Children Are Arrested?

The United States has a population of around 273 million people, of which 70 million or 26 percent are **children,** persons under age 18. In 2000, 9.1 million people were arrested for *all* crimes; 1.6 million or 17 percent of those arrested were juveniles. For the eight Crime Index offenses, 28 percent of persons arrested were juveniles. The percentage of children arrested for Index crimes varied by offenses. For instance, of the 8,709 persons arrested for murder, only 9 percent or about 700 were children, whereas 53 percent (5,635) of the 10,675 persons arrested for arson were under age 18. Overall, 16 percent and 32 percent of persons arrested for Violent and Property Index crimes, respectively, were juveniles (see Table 2–1).[20]

UCR data also indicate that delinquency is a less serious problem today than it was in the immediate past. Between 1996 and 2000, the number of juvenile arrests dropped by over 15 percent and arrests of juveniles for Crime Index offenses dropped by more than 23 percent. There was a particularly substantial decrease in the number of juveniles arrested for murder and robbery (see Figure 2–1).[21]

Table 2–1   Percent of Juveniles and Adults Arrested for Crime Index Offenses

	PERCENT ARRESTED	
OFFENSE	JUVENILES	ADULTS
CRIME INDEX TOTAL	28	72
Violent Crime Index	16	84
Property Crime Index	32	68
Murder	9	91
Forcible Rape	16	84
Robbery	25	75
Aggravated Assault	14	86
Burglary	33	67
Larceny-Theft	31	69
Motor Vehicle Theft	34	66
Arson	53	47

Source: Federal Bureau of Investigation, *Crime in the United States 2000* (Washington, DC: U.S. Department of Justice, 2001), Table 41, p. 232.

Figure 2–1
Percent Change in Juvenile Arrests, 1996–2000

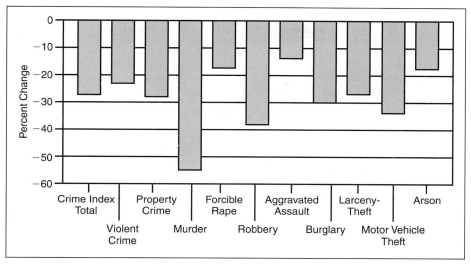

Source: Federal Bureau of Investigation, *Crime in the United States 2000* (Washington, DC: U.S. Department of Justice, 2001), Table 34, p. 222.

What do you think about the reported link between abortion and delinquency reduction discussed on the next page? Proponents might suggest that abortion is the merciful salvation from a life of delinquency. Do you agree with this logic?

There are many reasons why delinquency is declining. One reason ties the reduction to abortion (see Box 2–4). Other reasons criminologists give are discussed below.[22]

1. Economy. Reductions in delinquency have been attributed to the economy regardless of whether it is in recession or expansion. In "bad times," the economy may lead to fewer crimes because unemployed parents are more likely to be home supervising their children (see Chapter 10). In "good times," the economy provides young people with more legitimate opportunities to earn money, making it less likely that they will see crime as a necessary or desirable option.

2. Prisons. Incarcerating more offenders for a longer period of time reduces the crime rate. James Q. Wilson believes that putting people in prison is the single most important thing society can do to decrease crime. Since 1985, the U.S. incarceration rate has more than doubled, from 313 per 100,000 to 702, the highest rate in the world.[23]

3. Policing. Better policing is also sometimes cited as a reason for the drop in crime. One effective strategy is based on the "broken windows" thesis, which argues that just as a broken window left unattended is a sign nobody cares and will lead to more broken windows, ignoring small crimes such as vandalism and public urination will lead to more serious crimes being committed if they go unpunished.[24]

BOX 2–4   FACE OF DELINQUENCY
The Criminal Unborn

Between 1991 and 2000 the percentage of juveniles arrested for Crime Index offenses declined by 30 percent. Many explanations for the decline have been offered, including the economy, population changes, aggressive police practices, and increased incarceration of chronic offenders. However, no explanation is more controversial than the one offered by John Donohue III of Stanford University Law School and Steven Levitt from the University of Chicago. They attribute the decrease in crime to the 1973 *Roe v. Wade* decision that legalized abortion.

Donohue and Levitt offer evidence that legalized abortion has contributed significantly to recent crime reductions. The relationship between legalized abortion and crime is straightforward: A steep rise in abortions after 1973 has meant that many persons prone to criminal activity in the 1990s were never born. There are two reasons for this:

1. Abortion shrinks the number of people who reach the age where they are most prone to commit crimes.
2. Abortion is not random. Teenagers, unmarried women, the poor, and blacks are more likely than others to have abortions; they are also more likely to have children who are "at risk" for committing crimes later in life.

Similarly, women with unwanted pregnancies are less likely to be good parents and may harm their fetus during pregnancy by drinking alcohol and taking drugs that increase the likelihood of future criminality. Donohue and Levitt present three strands of evidence in support of their claim:

1. The precipitous drop in crime across the United States coincides with the period in which the generation affected by *Roe v. Wade* would have reached the peak of its criminal activity.
2. The five states that legalized abortion in 1970, three years before *Roe v. Wade*, were the first to experience the drop in crime.
3. States with high abortion rates from 1973 to 1976 have seen the largest decrease in crime since 1985, even after controlling for incarceration rates, racial composition, and income.

The authors conclude that current crime rates would be 10 to 20 percent higher if abortion had not been legalized. They estimate that legalized abortion may account for as much as 50 percent of the recent drop in crime. Furthermore, in terms of costs of crime, Donohue and Levitt believe that legalized abortion has saved Americans more than $30 billion annually.

Source: John Donohue III and Steven Levitt, "The Impact of Legalized Abortion on Crime," Stanford Law School, Public Law Working Paper No. 1; Stanford Law and Economics Olin Working Paper No. 204; Federal Bureau of Investigation, *Crime in the United States 2000* (Washington, DC: U.S. Department of Justice, 2001).

4. *Age.* Crime rates also change in response to changes in the age distribution of the population. The most likely people to commit crime are young males, ages 15 to 24. When there is a smaller percentage of the population in the "crime-prone years," the overall crime rate naturally decreases.[25]

5. *Crack.* The United States experienced a crack cocaine epidemic in the 1980s and early 1990s (see Chapter 4). About the same time, violent juvenile crime skyrocketed. The increase in violent delinquency was blamed on factors related to crack, such as gang turf wars and street-corner crack markets. For many reasons, such as the *younger brother syndrome,* where today's teens witnessed the ravaging effect of crack addiction on an older sibling, crack cocaine has become less popular.[26]

There is no single reason why there is less juvenile crime today than there was in the immediate past. The reduction is likely a consequence of many factors interacting with each other in unknown ways.

Is Sex Related to Delinquency?

Delinquency is predominately a male phenomenon. More boys commit delinquency and boys commit more delinquency than girls. Boys also are arrested more than girls, particularly for violent crimes. Eighty-two percent of the juveniles arrested for Violent Index crimes were boys. For murder and forcible rape, 89 percent and 99 percent of the juveniles arrested were males (see Table 2–2).[27]

But the arrest gap between the sexes is not as great today as it was. Since 1991 the sex arrest ratios for Crime Index offenses have steadily declined (see Table 2–3). In 1991 the sex arrest ratio for Violent Index crimes was 8 to 1; by 2000 it had narrowed to less than 5 to 1. A similar pattern has been observed for Property Index crimes. In 1991 the sex arrest ratio was 4 to 1; in 2000 it was 2 to 1. When specific crimes within the Index are examined separately, we see that between 1991 and 2000 an increasing percentage of the

---

Table 2–2   Percent of Juveniles Arrested for Crime Index Offenses, 2000

OFFENSE	PERCENT ARRESTED	
	BOYS	**GIRLS**
CRIME INDEX TOTAL	72	28
Violent Crime Index	82	18
Property Crime Index	70	30
Murder	89	11
Forcible Rape	99	1
Robbery	91	9
Aggravated Assault	77	23
Burglary	88	12
Larceny-Theft	63	37
Motor Vehicle Theft	83	17
Arson	88	12

Source: Federal Bureau of Investigation, *Crime in the United States 2000* (Washington, DC: U.S. Department of Justice, 2001), Table 36, p. 224.

Fifteen-year-old Daphne Abdela was a troubled product of some of New York City's best private schools. Always in trouble, she had poor self-control, was overly self-conscious about her weight, and had a drinking problem. On March 11, 1998, Daphne pleaded guilty to manslaughter in the death of a drinking companion in Central Park. As a juvenile, she received a sentence of 3 to 10 years in prison.

Table 2–3   Comparison of Sex Arrest Ratios for Crime Index Offenses for Juveniles, 1991–2000

OFFENSE	SEX ARREST RATIO		PERCENT CHANGE
	1991	2000	1991–2000
CRIME INDEX TOTAL	4:1	3:1	−25
Violent Crime Index	8:1	5:1	−38
Property Crime Index	4:1	2:1	−50
Murder	17:1	13:1	−24
Forcible Rape	49:1	81:1	+40
Robbery	11:1	10:1	−9
Aggravated Assault	6:1	3:1	−50
Burglary	11:1	7:1	−37
Larceny-Theft	3:1	2:1	−33
Motor Vehicle Theft	8:1	5:1	−38
Arson	10:1	8:1	−20

Note: To read this table, see for example, the 1991 "Sex Arrest Ratio" number for the Crime Index Total. The number is 4:1; it is at the top of the first column. It means that four boys were arrested for every one girl arrested for a Crime Index offense in 1991.

Source: Federal Bureau of Investigation, *Crime in the United States 2000* (Washington, DC: U.S. Department of Justice, 2001), Table 32, p. 220.

juveniles arrested for robbery, aggravated assault, burglary, larceny-theft, motor vehicle theft, and arson were girls.

How are boys and girls different? Do you think girls are more moral and pure than boys? Should boys and girls be punished or treated the same?

Self-report studies confirm these findings from the *UCR*. Boys admit to committing more delinquency and more boys commit delinquency than girls. Research also reports a higher sex arrest ratio (in favor of boys) for serious rather than less-serious crimes.[28] Data from the National Youth Survey also suggest that the gap in juvenile male-female behavior is closing, particularly for property offenses. According to James F. Short, Jr.:

> Research demonstrates that the decline in gender ratios for most crimes has been especially pronounced for persons under age 18. That is, arrests of young females–compared to young males–have experienced greater increases than is the case for gender comparisons of older persons, and they have been greater for property crimes than for violent crimes.[29]

A similar pattern of convergence has been reported by Roy Austin who compared the arrest ratios of male rates to female rates based on juvenile arrest data between 1963 and 1986. Austin discovered that "there was convergence of male and female arrests rates over these 22 years for total Index offenses, aggravated assault, burglary, larceny-theft, auto theft, and arson."[30]

The existing data strongly suggest that sex arrest ratios for nearly all Index crimes are shrinking. Whether this trend will continue likely depends on whether gender roles become more or less differentiated. If they become less differentiated, the behavior of males and females will become more similar. On the other hand, if sex roles become more differentiated, the present trend may reverse itself.

Is There a Link Between Race and Delinquency?

Research on race and delinquency has historically reflected larger social concerns. Throughout history, one or more oppressed groups of people have been assigned the brunt of the blame for crime. Today, much of the delinquency problem is blamed on young black males. There are a couple of reasons why.

A recent study attributes this popular perception to the news media's routine portrayal of young blacks as perpetrators of crime. The negative characterization of them has made whites fearful of being victimized by black juveniles. Twice as many whites than blacks believe that they are more likely to be victimized by a black than a white, even though whites are three times more likely to be victimized by a white than by a black.[31]

Another causal possibility is tied to cultural values. Sociologist Joe Feagin believes that the United States is a *totally* racist society.[32] Since the 1787 Constitutional Convention, whites have oppressed blacks. Along with oppression comes the presumption by whites that blacks are inferior. The promulgation of a racist ideology has devastating effects for all blacks, particularly for black children. While roughly 20 percent of America's 70 million children are poor, the percentage of poor black children is three times greater than the percentage of poor whites.[33] The impact of poverty on growing children goes far beyond malnourishment and the ruinous consequences of poor nutrition. Being poor also means these children are more likely to endure family stress and depression, have access to fewer resources for learning, and experience severe housing problems (see Figure 2–2).[34]

About 15 percent (10.8 million persons) of American children are black. There are roughly five times more white than black children in the United States. But a disproportionate percentage of children who are arrested for all Crime Index offenses, except arson, are black. When the populations of black and white juveniles are made statistically equal, the arrest disparity between them becomes apparent. For all Crime Index offenses, blacks are twice as likely as whites to be arrested. For murder and robbery, blacks are five and seven times more likely to be arrested, respectively (see Table 2–4).

Some evidence suggests that the differences in arrest rates of black and white juveniles is not because blacks commit more crime. In a study of illegal drug use among high school students, it was found that whites used cocaine at seven times the rate of blacks, used crack cocaine at eight times the rate of blacks, and used heroin at seven times the rate of blacks.[35] Self-report research has discovered that black and white juveniles admit to committing about the same amount of delinquency.[36]

Conversely, other evidence hints at the possibility that blacks are arrested more often than whites because they do commit more crimes, particularly

One week after the Lionel Tate incident (12-year-old black male murdered a 6-year-old black female) described in Chapter 1, a 15-year-old white male was sentenced to life imprisonment without parole for the murder of his 12-year-old white friend. Both incidents occurred in Florida. However, the publicity surrounding the Tate incident dwarfed the publicity of the latter incident. Why? Moreover, Reverend Al Sharpton and other civil rights leaders protested the sentencing of Tate as a human rights violation. No such protest marked the second killing. Why?

**Figure 2–2
How Poverty Matters**

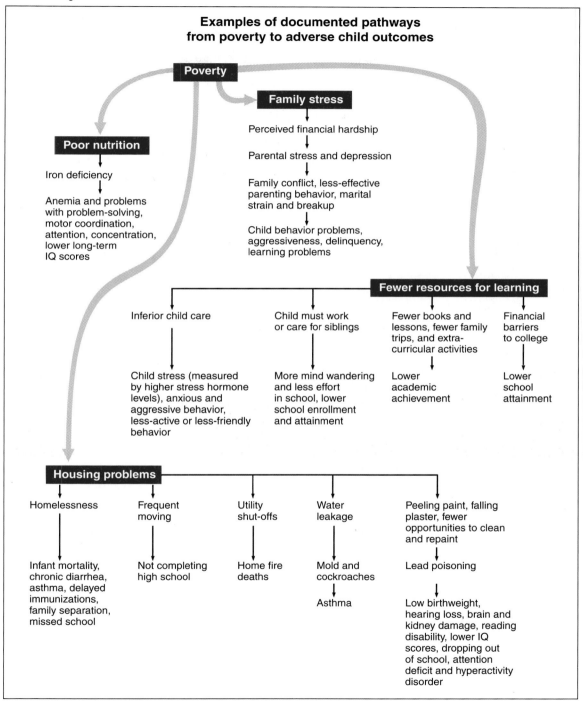

Examples of documented pathways from poverty to adverse child outcomes

Poverty

Family stress

Perceived financial hardship

Parental stress and depression

Family conflict, less-effective parenting behavior, marital strain and breakup

Child behavior problems, aggressiveness, delinquency, learning problems

Poor nutrition

Iron deficiency

Anemia and problems with problem-solving, motor coordination, attention, concentration, lower long-term IQ scores

Fewer resources for learning

Inferior child care

Child stress (measured by higher stress hormone levels), anxious and aggressive behavior, less-active or less-friendly behavior

Child must work or care for siblings

More mind wandering and less effort in school, lower school enrollment and attainment

Fewer books and lessons, fewer family trips, and extra-curricular activities

Lower academic achievement

Financial barriers to college

Lower school attainment

Housing problems

Homelessness

Infant mortality, chronic diarrhea, asthma, delayed immunizations, family separation, missed school

Frequent moving

Not completing high school

Utility shut-offs

Home fire deaths

Water leakage

Mold and cockroaches

Asthma

Peeling paint, falling plaster, fewer opportunities to clean and repaint

Lead poisoning

Low birthweight, hearing loss, brain and kidney damage, reading disability, lower IQ scores, dropping out of school, attention deficit and hyperactivity disorder

Source: Adopted from Arloc Sherman, *Poverty Matter* (Washington, DC: Children's Defense Fund, 1997), p. 23.

Table 2–4   Percent of Black and White Juveniles Arrested for Crime Index Offenses, 2000

| OFFENSE | PERCENT ARRESTED[1] | | ESTIMATED BLACK-WHITE ARREST RATIO[2] |
	BLACKS	WHITES	
CRIME INDEX TOTAL	30	67	2:1
Violent Crime Index	42	55	4:1
Property Crime Index	27	69	2:1
Murder	50	47	5:1
Forcible Rape	35	63	3:1
Robbery	56	41	7:1
Aggravated Assault	37	61	3:1
Burglary	25	73	2:1
Larceny-Theft	26	70	2:1
Motor Vehicle Theft	41	55	4:1
Arson	18	80	1:1

[1]The percentages do not add to 100 percent because arrest data for two races, American Indian and Asian American, are not included.

[2]The "Black-White Arrest Ratio" was calculated by multiplying the number of blacks arrested by 5 (since there are five times as many white juveniles as there are black children) and dividing that number by the number of white children arrested. For an example of how to interpret the "Black-White Arrest Ratio," see the "Arrest Ratio" number for the Crime Index Total. The number is 2:1. It is found at the top of the third column in the table. The number indicates that two black juveniles were arrested for every one white child arrested for a Crime Index offense in 2000.

Source: Federal Bureau of Investigation, *Crime in the United States 2000* (Washington, DC: U.S. Department of Justice, 2001); U.S. Bureau of Census, *Statistical Abstract of the United States 2000,* 120th ed. (Washington, DC: U.S. Census Bureau, 2001), Table 43, p. 235.

serious offenses.[37] A study by DeLisi and Regoli in fact concluded that *whites*, not blacks, were disproportionately arrested for some offenses.[38] In addition, other research casts doubt on the accuracy of offending rates reported by black juveniles in self-report studies. While it is true that black and white juveniles admit to committing similar amounts of delinquency, blacks may underreport their involvement in serious crimes they have been arrested for. To the extent that blacks underreport their arrests, they will appear less delinquent than they are.[39]

Is Social Class Related to Delinquency?

Research examining the social class–delinquency connection has produced mixed results. Some studies have found a direct relationship between social class and delinquency and other studies have found the relationship to be weak or insignificant.[40]

A few criminologists have tried to clarify the conflicting findings. Charles Tittle and Robert Meier think the strength of the class–crime relationship depends on *how* and *when* crime is measured. They observed that the relationship between class and crime varied from decade to decade and that self-report data yielded different results than *UCR* data.[41]

Other criminologists disagree. Michael Hindelang and his colleagues reported a consistent relationship between class and delinquency for serious offenses.[42] When Delbert Elliott and Suzanne Ageton analyzed NYS data, they found that the behavior of juveniles was very similar, except for *predatory crimes against persons* (robbery and aggravated assault). For these crimes, differences across classes were profound. For every such crime committed by a middle-class person, 2.5 such crimes were committed by a working-class youth and 3.5 by a lower-class juvenile. Elliott and Ageton concluded that the behavior of lower-class juveniles is similar to the behavior of others for "run-of-the-mill offenses" but that lower-class children commit many more serious crimes.[43]

Why are many affluent neighborhoods in the United States gated or guarded by security? Are these philanthropic gestures by the wealthy to keep the rampant delinquency in their neighborhoods from spreading to less-affluent areas? Or, are gated communities an indicator of the delinquency plaguing less-affluent areas? How would criminologists argue this?

Are Age and Delinquency Related?

A well-documented fact about delinquency is the age–crime curve: Crime rates increase during preadolescence, peak in late adolescence, and steadily decline thereafter.[44] The high point of the curve is slightly different for Violent and Property Index crime arrests. Arrests for *Violent* Index crimes peak at age 18, then steadily decline; arrests for *Property* Crime Index offenses top out at age 16 and decrease consistently thereafter. Juveniles whose behavior fits this pattern are called **adolescent-limited offenders** because their delinquency is restricted to the teenage years.[45]

This pattern, however, does not hold for all children. Some children begin and end their involvement in delinquency at earlier and later ages. Variation in offending patterns among juveniles has been observed across offense type, by sex, and by race. For instance, (1) arrests for Property Index crimes peak at age 16 while Violent Index offense arrests peak at age 18, (2) violent offending by girls peaks earlier than boys, and (3) black children are more likely than whites to continue offending into early adulthood.[46] What is constant across all categories of children is that they commit fewer crimes as they grow older.[47] This is called the **aging-out phenomenon**.

Why does crime diminish with age? What factor(s) explain the aging-out process? There are several plausible reasons:

1. People's personalities change as they mature. Once-rebellious juveniles often mature into adults who exercise self-control over their impulses.[48]

2. People become more aware of the costs of crime. They start to realize they have too much to lose if they are caught and little to gain.[49]

3. Peer influences over behavior weakens with age. As people grow older, the importance of what peers think decreases.[50]

Twelve-year-old Michael Nichols is escorted out of the Federal Courts Building followed by his father, in Fayetteville, Arkansas, on July 25, 2000. A juvenile court judge refused to allow a mental insanity defense for Nichols. Nichols is charged with attempted murder in the shooting of Prairie Grove police officer Greg Lovett.

4. For males—inasmuch as aggression is linked to the hormone testosterone—as they age the level of testosterone in their bodies decreases and so does their aggressiveness.[51]

5. Some crimes, such as strong-arm robbery and burglary, decline with age because older people lack the physical strength or agility to commit them.[52]

6. The need for money decreases. It is more difficult for children to get money than adults. As people age, their prospects for full-time employment increase.[53]

Most children eventually mature out of delinquency, although some do not. Those who do not become *chronic offenders.* These children begin offending at a very young age and continue to offend as adults. **Chronic offenders** commit many more delinquencies (frequency) of a more serious nature (seriousness) over a longer period of time (duration) than adolescent-limited offenders.

Who Are Chronic Offenders? How Many Are There?

Chronic offenders often commit their first *serious* crime before age 10 and, by 18, have achieved a lengthy police record. (See Box 2–5 for a profile of a chronic offender.) A number of major studies have been conducted on this topic.

By early adolescence, chronic juvenile offenders like Keith (discussed in Box 2–5 on the next page) have been victimizing society for nearly 10 years. In addition to common forms of delinquency, these youth are engaged in serious violence. Are juvenile offenders such as Keith hopeless? Are some juvenile delinquents not worth saving? Conversely, do all juvenile offenders deserve a second chance?

The Glueck Research   The first criminologists to study chronic offenders were Sheldon Glueck and Eleanor Glueck. In the 1930s they tracked a matched sample of 500 delinquent and 500 nondelinquent juveniles from childhood into adulthood. They discovered that children who participated in crime early in life were more likely to become adult criminals. Their data, in other words, speak to the continuity of crime over the life course. The children who were most likely to become career delinquents had strained family relations, low intelligence, and a muscular physique.[54]

Delinquency in Philadelphia   Two decades later, Marvin Wolfgang and his colleagues reported the results of a study of police records of 9,945 males born in Philadelphia in 1945.[55] Thirty-five percent of the boys had one recorded police contact (excluding traffic offenses) before their 18th birthday and over 50 percent had more than one police contact. A smaller group of 627 boys (18 percent of all male offenders, but only 6 percent of the boys in the birth cohort) were *chronic offenders:* juveniles with five or more police contacts. These boys had been arrested at younger ages than other arrestees and had committed more serious violent crimes. They accounted for 82 percent of robberies, 73 percent of forcible rapes, 71 percent of homicides, and 69 percent of aggravated assaults in the police records.

In a follow-up study, Paul Tracy, with assistance from Wolfgang and Robert Figlio, reviewed the police records of more than 27,000 children born

BOX 2–5   FACE OF DELINQUENCY
A Chronic Offender

Keith was 16 when he was sentenced to 27 years to life for robbery and murder. He had a long history of violence. He was an only child of parents who had never lived together. By age 7, he was uncontrollable and would run away from home. His mother fought with her live-in boyfriends over Keith's behavior. He was physically abused by nearly every adult male with whom he came in contact.

Problems in school led to a suicide attempt by Keith to "get back" at his mother for spanking him. Keith and a friend stole an automobile at age 12 and were arrested after they wrecked the automobile. Within days, Keith was suspended from school for assaulting a student who refused to loan him a pencil. He and a friend tortured and hanged a lamb at a nearby school. Keith was placed in a boys' home at age 13.

At the home, Keith was disruptive and hostile, and escaped several times. During one escape, he physically assaulted two girls who were 11 and 12 years old. Afterward, Keith was captured and placed in a juvenile detention center where his stay was marked by several escapes, misconduct, and fighting. Keith's final escape ended in a siege in which Keith held detention center staff and police at bay with a tire iron. The net result of all these incidents was, astonishingly, that Keith was placed on probation.

Instances of vehement tantrums, vandalism, assaults, and attempted suicide followed in an escalating pattern of violence. Keith was sentenced to 20 months in a detention facility for attacking his 21-year-old cousin with a hammer. Keith was 15 at the time. After serving one year, Keith was returned to his home, where truancy, disruptive behavior, and drug use continued. One day Keith skipped school with two of his friends. He stopped his car at a shopping center to "get some money." Keith entered a bakery, demanded money from the woman owner, and then shot her in the face when she refused to open the cash register. Keith's excuse was, "The bitch should have given me the money, it was her fault."

Source: Timothy Crowe, *Habitual Juvenile Offenders* (Washington, DC: U.S. Department of Justice, 1994), pp. 9–11.

in Philadelphia in 1958.[56] The findings from this second study paralleled the earlier one. In both studies, about 33 percent of the juveniles had at least one recorded police contact by age 18. Chronic offenders made up 7.5 percent of the 1958 cohort compared with 6.3 percent of the 1945 sample. They also accounted for a disproportionate amount of the serious violent crimes: 75 percent of forcible rapes, 73 percent of robberies, 65 percent of aggravated assaults, and 60 percent of murders.

Delinquency in Columbus   Simon Dinitz and John Conrad studied chronic offenders in a sample of 811 boys and girls born in Columbus, Ohio, between 1956 and 1958. Each child had been arrested for at least one violent crime before his or her 18th birthday (90 percent were arrested only once for a violent crime). The 811 arrestees were less than 2 percent of the 50,000 persons in their birth cohort in Columbus. Of the 811 children, only 22, or about 3 percent of the juveniles, could be classified as "serious chronic offenders."[57]

Does white, liberal guilt have any role in framing our understanding of juvenile delinquency? If so, how does it do this? If not, why do some scholars persist in blaming liberals for social problems?

The National Youth Survey   Data from the National Youth Survey also indicate that few delinquent children become chronic offenders. More than 50 percent of offenses reported by the juveniles in the NYS sample, and 83 percent of the serious crimes that were reported, were committed by just 5 percent of the juveniles surveyed.[58]

Conclusions from Cohort Studies   Studies of chronic offenders have drawn one or more of the following conclusions: (1) A small number of youths commit most of the serious crime, (2) boys commit more delinquency than girls, and (3) participation in delinquency decreases with age.

Do Chronic Offenders Become Adult Criminals?

Research on chronic offenders leaves an important question unanswered: Are chronic offenders likely to become adult criminals? Yes, they are. While

"It seems like only yesterday you were a juvenile offender."

BOX 2–6   A CROSS-CULTURAL PERSPECTIVE ON DELINQUENCY
Tracking Chronic Offenders

Police in London, England, are prepared to set up a secret database of children as young as three who they fear might grow up to become criminals. Any child who is thought to be at risk of committing crime by the police, schools, or social services, will be put on the database. Their progress will be monitored at school and on the streets by special squads of police officers and social workers, even though the children have not committed a crime and will not have been warned that they are being watched.

Officials say the register was needed because of a rise in juvenile violent crime. The idea for it grew out of a murder investigation in which detectives came across dozens of wild and unruly children who, they believed, were in danger of becoming criminals. For some of the children, street gangs provided a safer and more caring environment than their homes or schools. Many of them had been abused at home and were bullied and mugged at school and in their neighborhood.

Critics of the register want answers to some questions: What kind of behavior will cause a child to be put on the register? Who will have access to the register? Who will decide whether a child is removed from the register? While the intent of the register is to reduce crime, it may seriously violate civil liberties.

Source: David Bamber, "Naughty Children to Be Registered as Potential Criminals," online at news.telegraph.co.uk/news.

few adolescent-limited offenders become adult criminals, most chronic offenders do.[59]

When Marvin Wolfgang and his colleagues tracked 974 persons from their Philadelphia cohort through adulthood to age 30, they discovered that over 50 percent of chronic offenders were arrested at least four times between ages 18 and 30. In comparison, only 18 percent of persons with no juvenile arrests were ever arrested as adults.[60]

Because there is a strong likelihood that chronic offenders will become adult criminals, efforts are underway to identify children who are predisposed to a lifetime of crime. One controversial strategy being considered to track chronic offenders in London is discussed in Box 2–6.

Risk prediction has a long history, dating back to 1928 when Ernest Burgess completed his prediction study on parole decision making.[61] Early research on risk prediction reported chronic offenders were children with low intelligence who had a hyperactivity disorder (ADHD) and lived in poverty with a single parent who did not supervise them very well.[62] Current research on chronic offenders suggests they may suffer from a neurological defect that adversely affects their temperament, behavioral development, and cognitive abilities.[63] If this is true, it may not be possible to rehabilitate them.

Conclusions

No one can say how much delinquency is committed or how many children commit it. This is because most crime never comes to the attention of police. It is hidden from them. Criminologists therefore are forced to estimate the prevalence and incidence of delinquency by using a variety of measures such as the *Uniform Crime Reports*, National Crime Victimization Survey, and self-reports.

Some groups of children are arrested more often than others. But all children commit fewer crimes as they grow older. This does not mean all of them stop committing crime. Some children become chronic offenders. Chronic offenders have been reported to have low intelligence, suffer from hyperactivity disorder, live in poverty, be reared by single parents, and be poorly supervised. Current research on chronic offenders suggests they may suffer from a neurological defect that adversely affects their temperament, behavioral development, and cognitive abilities.

Key Terms

adolescent-limited offenders: *Juveniles whose law-breaking behavior is restricted to their teenage years.*

aging-out phenomenon: *The gradual decline of participation in crime after the teenage years.*

children: *People under age 18.*

chronic offenders: *Juveniles who continue to engage in law-breaking behavior as adults.*

Crime Index: *A statistical indicator consisting of eight offenses used to gauge the amount of crime reported to the police.*

crimes of interest: *The crimes that are the focus of the National Crime Victimization Survey.*

falsely accused: *Juveniles who are thought to have committed a crime when they have not.*

hidden delinquency: *Criminal activity that is not known to the police.*

hierarchy rule: *In the* Uniform Crime Reports, *the police record only the most serious crime incident.*

incidence: *The number of delinquent acts committed.*

National Crime Victimization Survey: *Annual survey of criminal victimization conducted by the U.S. Bureau of Justice Statistics.*

National Youth Survey: *Nationwide self-report survey of approximately 1,700 people who were between the ages of 11 and 17 in 1976.*

Part I crimes: *The eight offenses that form the Crime Index and are used to gauge the amount of crime reported to police; also referred to as* Index crimes.

Part II crimes: *Twenty-one less serious offenses included in the* Uniform Crime Reports.

prevalence: *The number of juveniles committing delinquency.*

secret delinquents: *Juveniles whose crimes are not known to the police.*

self-report studies: *Unofficial measures of crime in which juveniles are asked about their law-breaking behavior.*

Uniform Crime Reports: *Annual publication from the Federal Bureau of Investigation presenting data on crimes reported to the police, number of arrests, and number of persons arrested.*

Getting Connected

A good source of criminal justice statistics for the United States is the Bureau of Justice Statistics.

http://www.ojp.usdoj.gov/bjs

1. Compare the summary findings of the 1995 survey of campus law enforcement to what is common on *your* campus.
2. Discuss three major findings about crime victimization and age.
3. Using the NIBRS process, what kinds of information are available about sexual assault among young victims?

The *Sourcebook of Criminal Justice Statistics* is the online version of the very successful publication with the same name. The *Sourcebook* provides readers with the largest compilation of criminal justice statistics available. The site is regularly updated.

http://www.albany.edu/sourcebook

1. Using materials from Section 2, discuss teenagers' attitudes toward the main problems facing people their age.
2. Using materials from Section 2, discuss attitudes toward the treatment of juveniles who commit violent crimes.
3. Draw three inferences about juvenile delinquency from the material reported in Table 4–6.

The FBI's home page presents a lot of interesting information, including the most current statistics from the *Uniform Crime Reports.*

http://www.fbi.gov

1. Evaluate the FBI's core values.
2. Evaluate "The FBI for Kids" pages. What are their main messages?
3. Play "Special Agent Undercover." Is this game based upon stereotypes about crime and criminals?

The Justice Information Center provides users with information on crime statistics, crime prevention, and research and evaluation on juvenile delinquency. The site also provides users with links to other websites that present information on a wide range of juvenile justice issues.

http://www.ncjrs.org

1. Link to the juvenile justice pages, then to the information on female juvenile delinquency. What kinds of issues have been studied in the last five years?
2. Link to the juvenile justice pages, then to the information on conflict resolution. How might conflict resolution be related to the arts?

continued

3. Link to the juvenile justice pages, then to the information on juvenile gun violence. Discuss the Boston Gun Project's Operation Ceasefire. Would such a project be successful in your hometown?

The *Statistical Abstract of the United States* provides a comprehensive collection of statistics on social and economic conditions in the United States.

http://www.census.gov/statab/www

1. Find the business QuickFacts for your state. How does your state compare to the nation as a whole?
2. Which state has the highest resident population under the age of 18 as of July 1999? Which state has the lowest such population? What might explain these figures?
3. Which state has the lowest infant mortality rate as of July 1999? Which state has the highest? What might explain these figures?

Endnotes

1. Gwynn Nettler, *Explaining Crime*, 3d ed. (New York: McGraw-Hill Publishing Co., 1984), p. 39.
2. Federal Bureau of Investigation, *Crime in the United States 2000* (Washington, DC: U.S. Department of Justice, 2001).
3. Andrew Karmen, *Crime Victims*, 4th ed. (Belmont, CA: Wadsworth Publishing Co., 2001).
4. Samuel Walker and Charles Katz, *The Police in America*, 4th ed. (New York: McGraw-Hill Publishing Co., 2002).
5. Jeffery Reiman, *The Rich Get Richer and the Poor Get Prison*, 6th ed. (Boston: Allyn and Bacon, 2000).
6. Bureau of Justice Statistics, *Criminal Victimization in the United States 2000* (Washington, DC: U.S Department of Justice, 2001).
7. L. Edward Wells and Joseph Rankin, "Juvenile Victimization," *Journal of Research in Crime and Delinquency* 32:287–307 (1995).
8. Austin Porterfield, *Youth in Trouble* (Austin, TX: Leo Potishman Foundation, 1946).
9. James Wallerstein and J. C. Wyle, "Our Law-Abiding Lawbreakers," *Federal Probation* 25:107–112 (1947).
10. James F. Short, Jr., "A Report on the Incidence of Criminal Behavior, Arrests and Convictions in Selected Groups," *Research Studies of the State College of Washington* 22 (June):110–118 (1954).
11. James F. Short, Jr., and F. Ivan Nye, "Extent of Unrecorded Juvenile Delinquency," *Journal of Criminal Law, Criminology, and Police Science* 49:296–302 (1958).
12. Suzanne Ageton and Delbert Elliott, *The Incidence of Delinquent Behavior in a National Probability Sample* (Boulder, CO: Behavioral Research Institute, 1978); Delbert Elliott et al., *The Prevalence and Incidence of Delinquent Behavior: 1976–1980* (Boulder, CO: Behavioral Research Institute, 1983).
13. David Farrington, Rolf Loeber, Magda Stouthamer-Loeber, Welmoet Van Kammen, and Laura Schmidt, "Self-reported Delinquency and a Combined Delinquency Seriousness Scale Based on Boys, Mothers, and Teachers," *Criminology* 34:493–517 (1996); David Huizinga and Delbert Elliott, "Reassessing the Reliability and Validity of Self-Report Delinquency Measures," *Journal of Quantitative Criminology* 2:293-327 (1986); Maynard Erickson and LaMar Empey, "Court Records, Undetected Delinquency, and Decision Making," *Journal of Criminal Law, Criminology, and Police Science* 54:456–469 (1963); John Blackmore, "The Relationship Between Self-Reported Delinquency and Official Convictions Amongst Adolescent Boys," *British Journal of Criminology* 14:172–176 (1974).
14. Martin Gold, "Undetected Delinquent Behavior," *Journal of Research in Crime and Delinquency* 3:27–46 (1966).
15. John Clark and Larry Tifft, "Polygraph and Interview Validation of Self-Reported Deviant Behavior," *American Sociological Review* 31:516–523 (1966).
16. Michael Hindelang, Travis Hirschi, and Joseph Weis, *Measuring Delinquency* (Beverly Hills, CA: Sage Publications, 1981), p. 114.
17. Porterfield, note 8; Wallerstein and Wyle, note 9; Short and Nye, note 11.
18. Jay Williams and Martin Gold, "From Delinquent Behavior to Official Delinquency," *Social Problems* 20:209–220 (1972).
19. Williams Chambliss and Richard Nagasawa, "On the Validity of Official Statistics," *Journal of Research in Crime and Delinquency* 6:71–77 (1969); Leroy Gould, "Who Defines Delinquency," *Social Problems* 16:325–336 (1969); Travis Hirschi, *Causes of Delinquency* (Berkeley: University of California Press, 1969); David Huizinga and Delbert Elliott, "Juvenile Offenders," *Crime and Delinquency* 33:206–223 (1987); "Racial Equality," *Time*, August 29:50 (1988).

20. Federal Bureau of Investigation, note 2.
21. Federal Bureau of Investigation, note 2.
22. Gordon Witkin, "The Crime Bust," *U.S. News and World Report*, May 25:28–40 (1998).
23. Thomas Bonczar and Allen Beck, *Lifetime Likelihood of Going to State or Federal Prison* (Washington, DC: U.S. Department of Justice, 1997).
24. James Q. Wilson and George Kelling, "Broken Windows," *Atlantic Monthly*, March:29–38 (1982).
25. Witkin, note 22.
26. Witkin, note 22.
27. Federal Bureau of Investigation, note 2.
28. Meda Chesney-Lind and Randall Shelden, *Girls, Delinquency, and Juvenile Justice*, 2nd ed. (Pacific Grove, CA: Brooks/Cole, 2001).
29. James F. Short, Jr., *Delinquency and Society* (Englewood Cliffs, NJ: Prentice Hall, Inc., 1990), p. 115.
30. Roy Austin, "Recent Trends in Official Male and Female Crime Rates," *Journal of Criminal Justice* 21:447–466 (1993).
31. Lori Dorfman, *Off Balance* (Berkeley, CA: Berkeley Media Studies Group, 2001).
32. Joe Feagin, *Racist America* (New York: Routledge, 2000).
33. U.S. Bureau of Census, *Statistical Abstract of the United States 2000*, 120th ed. (Washington, DC: U.S. Bureau of Census, 2001).
34. Arloc Sherman, *Poverty Matters* (New York: Children's Defense Fund, 1997).
35. National Institute on Drug Abuse, *Monitoring the Future Report, 1975–1999* (Washington, DC: National Institute on Drug Abuse, 2000).
36. David Huizinga and Delbert Elliott, *Self-Reported Measure of Delinquency and Crime* (Boulder, CO: Behavioral Research Institute, 1984); Hindelang et al., note 16.
37. Delbert Elliott, David Huizinga, and Scott Menard, *Multiple Problem Youth* (New York: Springer-Verlag, 1989).
38. Matt DeLisi and Bob Regoli, "Race, Conventional Crime, and Criminal Justice," *Journal of Criminal Justice* 27:549–557 (1999).
39. Hindelang et al., note 16; Travis Hirschi, note 19; Steven Lab and Roy Allen, "Self-Report and Official Measures,"*Journal of Criminal Justice* 12:445–455 (1984); Huizinga and Elliott, note 13.
40. See Robert Sampson, "The Community," pp. 193–216 in *Crime*, edited by J. Q. Wilson and J. Petersilia (San Francisco: ICS Press, 1995).
41. Charles Tittle and Robert Meier, "Specifying the SES/Delinquency Relationship," *Criminology* 28:271–299 (1990).
42. Michael Hindelang, Travis Hirschi, and Joseph Weis, "Correlates of Delinquency," *American Sociological Review* 44:995–1014 (1979); Hindelang et al., note 16.
43. Delbert Elliott and Suzanne Ageton, "Reconciling Race and Class Differences in Self-Reported and Official Estimates of Delinquency," *American Sociological Review* 45:95–110 (1980).
44. Daniel Nagin, David Farrington, and Terrie Moffitt, "Life-Course Trajectories of Different Types of Offenders," *Criminology* 33:111–139 (1995); David Farrington, "Age and Crime," in *Crime and Justice*, Volume 7, edited by Michael Tonry and Norval Morris (Chicago: University of Chicago Press, 1983); Travis Hirschi and Michael Gottfredson, "Age and the Explanation of Crime," *American Journal of Sociology* 89:552–584 (1983).
45. Terrie Moffitt, "'Life-Course Persistent' and 'Adolescent-limited' Antisocial Behavior," *Psychological Review* 100:674–701 (1993).
46. Delbert Elliott, "Serious Violent Offenders," *Criminology* 32:1–21 (1994).
47. Lawrence Cohen and Kenneth Land, "Age Structure and Crime," *American Sociological Review* 91:170–183 (1987).
48. Marc Le Blanc, "Late Adolescence Deceleration of Criminal Activity and Development of Self- and Social-Control," *Studies on Crime and Crime Prevention* 2:51–68 (1993).
49. John Laub and Robert Sampson, "Turning Points in the Life Course," *Criminology* 31:301–325 (1993).
50. Mark Warr, "Life-Course Transitions and Desistance From Crime," *Criminology* 36:183–215 (1998).
51. David Rowe, *Biology and Crime* (Los Angeles: Roxbury Publishing Company, 2002); Diana Fishbein, *Biobehavioral Perspectives in Criminology* (Belmont, CA: Wadsworth Publishing Co., 2001).
52. James Q. Wilson and Richard Herrnstein, *Crime and Human Nature* (Chicago: University of Chicago Press, 1987), pp. 134–163.
53. Robert Agnew, "Delinquency and the Desire for Money," *Justice Quarterly* 11:411–427 (1994).
54. Sheldon Glueck and Eleanor Glueck, *Unraveling Juvenile Delinquency* (New York: The Commonwealth Fund, 1950).
55. Marvin Wolfgang, Robert Figlio, and Thorsten Sellin, *Delinquency in a Birth Cohort* (Chicago: University of Chicago Press, 1972).
56. Paul Tracy, Marvin Wolfgang, and Robert Figlio, *Delinquency Careers in Two Birth Cohorts* (New York: Plenum Publishing, 1990).
57. Simon Dinitz and John Conrad, "The Dangerous Two Percent," in *Critical Issues in Juvenile Delinquency*, edited by David Shichor and Delos Kelly (Lexington, MA: Lexington Books, 1980).

58. Franklyn Dunford and Delbert Elliott, "Identifying Career Offenders Using Self-Reported Data, *Journal of Research in Crime and Delinquency* 21:57–86 (1984).

59. Tracy et al., note 56.

60. Marvin Wolfgang, Terence Thornberry, and Robert Figlio, *From Boy to Man, From Delinquency to Crime* (Chicago: University of Chicago Press, 1987).

61. See Peter Jones, Philip Harris, Jamie Fader, and Lori Grubstein, "Identifying Chronic Juvenile Offenders," *Justice Quarterly* 18:479–507 (2001), for a discussion of risk prediction.

62. David Farrington, "Human Development and Criminal Careers," pp. 363–408 in *The Oxford Handbook of Criminology*, edited by M. Maguire, R. Morgan, and R. Reiner (New York: Oxford University Press, 1997).

63. Terrie Moffitt, "Adolescence-Limited and Life-Course Persistent Antisocial Behavior," pp. 91–145 in *Life Course Criminology*, edited by Alex Piquero and Paul Mazerolle (Belmont, CA: Wadsworth Publishing Co., 2001).

Chapter 3

Violent Youth Crime

The Nature and Extent of Youth Violence

The Role of Firearms in Youth Violence

Violence Prevention

Conclusions

Key Terms

Getting Connected

Endnotes

Is this going to take long?
I got someplace to go tonight.

—An eight-year-old Chicago boy as he was questioned by
police after shooting a classmate in the spine.[1]

In November 1995, the nation's news media reported that the just-released *Uniform Crime Reports* once again showed a decline in the crime rate, dropping 2 percent overall from the year before, while violent crime dropped 4 percent. The crime rate continued to decline over the next five years. Between 1996 and 2000, arrests of juveniles had dropped over 15 percent, with arrests for violent Crime Index offenses declining by over 23 percent.[2]

Youth violence had been steadily, and in some cases, dramatically, increasing during the 1980s, but then took a major downturn in the 1990s. By the turn of the century, juveniles were still committing violent crimes; many were still carrying and using guns; and youths continued to be victims of violent crime. And while general rates of juvenile violence were down, individual acts of violence by young, and sometimes very young, persons still made headlines, especially when the violence occurred at a school.

- "First-Graders Accused of Murder Plot: Allegedly Planned to Slay 7-Year-Old Classmate."[3]
- "Too Young to Charge."[4]
- "Twelve-Year-Old Holds Class at Gunpoint in Ohio."[5]
- "Teacher Fatally Shot by Student on Last Day of Classes."[6]
- "An Epidemic of Violence: Incidents in Schools Rise Sharply Since Santee Shooting."[7]

Concern over youth violence, whether it is statistically increasing or decreasing, remains high among politicians and most citizens. The news media has been accused of both dramatizing and overreporting juvenile violence in general and school violence more specifically. Although neighborhoods and schools are actually much safer than in recent decades, public perceptions have changed little. People continue to believe juvenile violence is a serious threat and should be dealt with severely.

The Nature and Extent of Youth Violence

More than 58,000 juveniles were arrested in 2000 for serious violent crimes. While more than 66 percent of those youths were arrested for aggravated assault, approximately 700 youths were arrested for murder and over 2,600 for forcible rape.[8] Youth gangs are responsible for a disproportionate amount of violence in large urban areas as well as in suburban and rural communities (see Chapter 12). Gang violence ranges from drive-by shootings and inter-gang fights to drug-deal rip-offs and home-intrusion robberies. And yet, even the number of youth gang homicides declined in the 1990s, with substantial decreases reported in both Los Angeles and Chicago.[9] Adolescents bring violence into the schools: Each year, approximately 5 percent of students are victims of assault, sexual assault, rape, or robbery.[10] (See Chapter 11 for additional discussion of violence in schools.)

However, most violence by juveniles occurs during the hours shortly after school. While the number of violent crimes by adults increases from 6 A.M. through the afternoon and evening hours, peaks at 11 P.M., and then drops hourly to a low point at 6 A.M., juvenile violence peaks in the afternoon between 3 P.M. and 4 P.M., the hour at the end of the school day. More than one in seven sexual assaults by juveniles occurs in the four hours between 3 P.M. and 7 P.M. on school days. And unlike other violent crimes, sexual assaults by juveniles on nonschool days are most likely to occur between noon and 1 P.M.[11]

Youth violence has increasingly been characterized by the use of guns. Large numbers of adolescents carry guns and use them for sport; to defend themselves against perceived threats; to intimidate others; to rob, kill, or injure others; and sometimes just to indulge themselves—because they feel like shooting at someone.[12] According to Susan Winfield, a Washington, D.C., Superior Court Judge,

> "There is far more gratuitous violence and far more anger, more shooting. . . . Youngsters used to shoot each other in the body. Then in the head. Now they shoot each other in the face."[13]

Trends in Youth Violence

Recall from the discussion in Chapter 2 that juveniles constituted approximately 26 percent of the U.S. population in 2000 but accounted for 28 percent of all Crime Index arrests and 16 percent of all serious violent-crime arrests. In addition, juveniles contribute 25 percent of the arrests for robbery, 9 percent of the arrests for murder, and 16 percent of the arrests for rape (see Table 2–1 in the previous chapter).[14] These figures are the lowest they have been in decades. The decline in arrests of juveniles for murder has been the most significant. As illustrated in Figure 3–1, juvenile homicide offending rates remained fairly steady from the mid-1970s to the mid-1980s. Then, between 1985 and 1993, the murder rate for juveniles ages 14 to 17 more than tripled. After dropping slightly in 1994, the next five years saw substantial declines each subsequent year. The juvenile homicide rate in 1999, for example, was nearly identical to that in 1976. The 10-year and 5-year changes in arrests of juveniles for violent crimes reflect a consistent pattern of decline (see Table 3–1). The largest declines were for murder and robbery, although arrests for rape and aggravated assault also showed double-digit change.

Other types of serious juvenile violence also peaked in the mid-1990s, and then dropped back to levels reported in the early 1970s. For example, Nancy Brener and her colleagues report that the percentage of high school students who carried a weapon at least once during the 30 days prior to the survey decreased 30 percent between 1991 and 1997; the percentage who engaged in a physical fight one or more times during the year prior to the survey decreased 14 percent; and the percentage injured in a fight declined 20 percent.[15] Curiously, the number of juveniles petitioned to the juvenile

For certain social phenomena, there is little difference between empirical reality and people's perceived reality. How do empirical and perceived realities differ when evaluating the prevalence of school crime or mass killings in high schools? Is the public foolish for believing that schools are endlessly dangerous or justified in their fears?

Figure 3–1
Homicide Offending Rates of Juveniles Ages 14-17

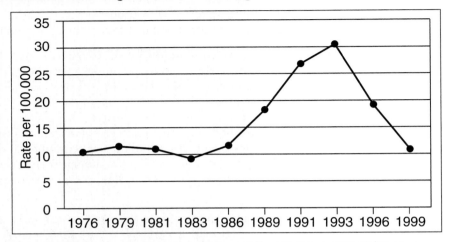

Source: Federal Bureau of Investigation, *Supplemental Homicide Reports, 1976–99* (Washington, DC: Federal Bureau of Investigation, 2001).

Criminologist Alfred Blumstein suggests that the crack-cocaine epidemic was largely responsible for urban decay evidenced by a tripling of the adolescent homicide rate between 1985 and 1993. In a larger sense, the crippling effect of the crack epidemic is much larger. Should drug barons be forced to make reparations to the inner cities that were devastated by their product? Should the government tax criminal organizations (via forfeitures) in order to reinvest in cities?

court for violent crimes actually increased by 88 percent between 1989 and 1998,[16] perhaps reflecting "get-tough" legislative changes implemented in most states in response to the dramatic increases in youth violence in the previous decade (see Chapter 14).

Alfred Blumstein believes the turning point in youth violence occurred in 1985, when homicides, assaults, and the use of guns began to chart a dramatic upward surge. He notes that all of these three factors appear to be related to the parallel increase in the distribution of crack cocaine, particularly in inner-city areas.[17] The growth of the crack markets, brought about primarily through extensive street transactions, involved the recruitment of large numbers of juveniles, especially black and Latino youths. Blumstein argues that juveniles were recruited into the drug industry because they had lower risks of punishment and they could be more easily exploited due to their sense of economic hopelessness. These youths became inclined to carry guns primarily for self-protection since they were carrying large amounts of drugs and or cash.[18] This widespread diffusion of guns into the youth subculture in neighborhoods and schools led other youths to arm themselves. As more youths carried guns, arguments and fights that in previous years would have been settled with fists soon became deadly.

The significant decline in the youth homicide rate since 1995 appears to be directly related to the decline in handgun-related homicides.[19] Explanations for this decline include the maturation of the crack market that resulted in a reduction in disputes over marketing territories, the economic expansion in the mid-1990s that provided more legitimate jobs for adolescents, and

What are the costs and benefits of having a firearm in the home, particularly where there are children? For obvious safety reasons, handguns are often stored unloaded with trigger locks. Do these safety measures effectively preclude the likelihood that a handgun would stop an intruder?

Table 3–1   Percent Change in Juvenile Arrests for Violent Crimes

OFFENSE	% CHANGE		
	1991–2000	1996–2000	1999–2000
Murder	−64.6	−54.0	−13.4
Rape	−26.4	−17.3	−5.3
Robbery	−28.8	−38.1	−4.6
Aggravated assault	−6.7	−14.7	−4.2
Total violent crime	−16.7	−23.1	−4.4

Source: Federal Bureau of Investigation, *Crime in the United States 2000* (Washington, DC: U.S. Department of Justice, 2001), pp. 220, 222, 224.

Table 3–2   Juveniles Arrested for Violent Crimes, by Sex and Race/Ethnicity, 2000

	SEX		RACE/ETHNICITY		
OFFENSE	MALE	FEMALE	WHITE	BLACK	OTHER
Murder	89.3	10.7	47.1	49.8	3.1
Rape	98.9	1.1	63.1	35.4	1.5
Robbery	90.6	9.4	41.4	56.1	2.5
Aggravated assault	77.0	23.0	60.9	36.6	2.5
Total violent crime	81.8	18.2	55.4	42.1	2.5

Source: Federal Bureau of Investigation, *Crime in the United States 2000* (Washington, DC: U.S. Department of Justice, 2001), pp. 225, 235.

police crackdowns on drug distribution.[20] According to Joan McCord and her associates, the changes in adolescent gun-related homicides also parallel changes in adolescent gun-related suicides. They note that the suicide rate for adolescents ages 15 to 19 increased by 27 percent between 1980 and 1992 and that the vast majority of these suicides were committed with guns. But as adolescent homicides began to decline, so did adolescent suicides. Furthermore, "the decrease in firearm-related suicides accounted for all the suicide decrease in this age group between 1994 and 1996."[21]

Today, as in past years, the overwhelming majority (82 percent) of youths arrested for violent crimes are males, although girls accounted for about 23 percent of those arrested for aggravated assault, 11 percent for murder, and 9 percent for robbery (see Table 3–2). Girls who murder are more likely to use knives than are boys, who tend to use guns. They are also more likely to murder family members and very young victims. For example, 24 percent of girls' murder victims were under age 3, compared to only 1 percent of boys' murder victims.[22]

White youths accounted for over half, or about 55 percent, of all youths arrested for violent Crime Index offenses. White youths were roughly 63 percent of juveniles arrested for forcible rape and 61 percent for aggravated assault, but only 47 percent of the arrests for murder and 41 percent for robbery. Black youths are most overrepresented in arrests for robbery and murder, and this pattern has been generally consistent over the past several decades.[23] While some criminologists suggest arrest data may reflect police bias in arrest decisions (see Chapter 13), the use of broader measures of delinquency, such as self-report data from the National Youth Survey, provides additional support for findings of disproportionate minority involvement in violent crime. Delbert Elliott reports that, at the peak age of offending (17 years), 36 percent of black males and 25 percent of white males reported that they had committed one or more serious violent crimes and that nearly twice as many blacks as whites continued violent offending into adulthood.[24] (See Box 3–1 for a discussion of youth violence in European countries.)

BOX 3–1   A CROSS-CULTURAL PERSPECTIVE ON DELINQUENCY
Youth Violence in European Countries

The United States is not the only country facing increases in juvenile violence. Research on recent trends in juvenile crime and violence in European Union countries suggests that the rate of juvenile violence rose sharply in the mid-1980s or early 1990s in every country studied. In some countries, the official figures increased between 50 and 100 percent. In England and Wales in 1986, for example, approximately 360 of every 100,000 youths ages 14 to 16 were "convicted or cautioned by the police" for violent crimes; in 1994 that figure had climbed to approximately 580 per 100,000.

Increases in youth violence in Germany were even higher. In 1984 the number of 14- to 18-year-olds suspected of violent crime in the former West Germany was approximately 300 per 100,000; by 1995 that figure had more than doubled to about 760 per 100,000. Rates in the former East Germany were between 60 and 80 percent higher. Even Sweden, a country that forbids parental use of physical force against their children and prohibits professional boxing, reports dramatic increases in the number of juveniles sentenced for assault since the mid-1980s.

In general, the victims of violent crimes committed by juveniles were other juveniles. In the Netherlands in 1995, young people ages 15 to 17 were four times more likely than adults to be the victims of assault. Juveniles in Germany were also more likely to be the victims of violent crime than members of other age groups. In every country, young males were far more likely than young females to be violent crime victims.

Explanations for the growth in European juvenile violent crime rates parallel those used to explain youth violence in the United States: unemployment, alcohol, drugs, availability of guns, and domestic abuse. In some countries—France and Germany, for example—the problem of unemployment was exacerbated in the early 1990s by an influx of immigrants from countries that had been under Communist rule. Immigrants who could not overcome language and culture barriers in order to find employment were more likely to engage in violent crimes than those who found jobs and became integrated into society.

German officials noted an increase in the use of alcohol and other drugs in the last decade, and firearms had become somewhat more available after the fall of the Berlin Wall than they had been in the past. While many of the German males arrested for violent crimes came from low-income households, the most common thread in their life histories is that they came from families where violence was common: they were beaten, their siblings were beaten, or one of their parents was beaten.

Sources: Christian Pfeiffer, *Trends in Juvenile Violence in European Countries* (Washington, DC: National Institute of Justice, 1998); Hanns Von Hofer, "Criminal Violence and Youth in Sweden: A Long-term Perspective," *Journal of Scandinavian Studies in Criminology and Crime Prevention* 1:56–72 (2000).

Violent Victimization of Youths

If the middle of the decade of the 1980s marked the beginning of an upsurge in juvenile arrests for violent crime, it also marked the point at which violent juvenile *victimizations* began to increase dramatically. Between 1984 and

Figure 3–2
Homicide Victimization Rates of Juveniles Ages 14–17

Source: Federal Bureau of Investigation, *Supplemental Homicide Reports, 1976-99* (Washington, DC: Federal Bureau of Investigation, 2001).

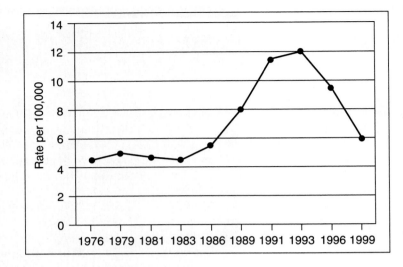

A different form of youth violence occurs when adolescent females commit infanticide. For example, in June 1997, 18-year old Melissa Drexler birthed and then strangled to death her newborn baby in a bathroom stall while attending a school dance. After the murder, she joined her classmates on the dance floor. Drexler served just 3 years of a 15-year sentence for aggravated manslaughter. Are such acts more or less egregious than school shootings? How does gender influence lethal violence?

1993, the rate of juvenile homicide victimizations increased threefold. In 1999 a total of 1,789 juveniles were homicide victims, an average of just under 5 per day, and fully 607 were age 4 or younger.[25] One 4-year-old murder victim is Emanuel Barima, who was stabbed in the neck by two brothers, one 9 years old, the other only 8. The two brothers had allegedly been teasing and bullying Emanuel's 5-year-old sister, Abigail, for months before confronting Emanuel and Abigail outside their Bronx apartment. If convicted, both young murderers could face up to 18 months in a secure juvenile correctional facility.[26] But like the juvenile homicide offending rate, the rate of homicide victimization of juveniles has declined significantly since the mid-1990s, dropping from an all-time high of 12.1 per 100,000 in 1993 to 5.9 in 1999 (see Figure 3–2). (See Box 3–2 for a discussion of the murder of very young children.)

Juveniles have higher violent victimization rates than older adults but are about as likely to be victims of serious violence as are young adults ages 20 to 24 (see Table 3–3). Male juveniles are substantially more likely than females to be victims of violent crimes, with the exception of rape and sexual assault. Serious injuries resulting from violent crimes also differ by gender. Girls were more likely than boys to have stab wounds, while boys were more likely than girls to have gunshot wounds. And girls were also more likely than boys to be injured at home rather than in a public place or at school.[27] Black youths are victims of violence at rates higher than white and Latino youths.[28] However, it is significant to note that between 1993 and 1998, the annual average violent victimization rates were highest for American Indian juveniles, lowest for Asian American youths, with victimizations of white, black, and Latino youths falling in between.[29]

Juveniles comprise about 12 percent of all crime victims reported to police, but 71 percent of all sex crime victims and 38 percent of all kidnapping

BOX 3-2   FACE OF DELINQUENCY
The Murder of Very Young Children

More very young children, those under age 6, die from homicide than from infectious diseases or cancer. Girls under age 6 are much more likely than girls ages 12 to 17 to be murdered, and white children under age 6 were nearly as likely as their teenage counterparts to be victims of homicide. Homicides of very young children rose 38 percent between 1984 and 1993, remained steady for a few years, and then declined in 1997.

However, the actual homicide rate for very young children is likely to be much higher than official statistics suggest because they are among the most difficult to document. The deaths of very young children often resemble deaths resulting from accidents and other causes. For example, a child who dies from sudden infant death syndrome (SIDS) is fairly indistinguishable from a child who has been smothered; a child who has been thrown or intentionally dropped is likely to have injuries quite similar to those of a child who died from an accidental fall.

Two characteristics distinguish homicides of very young children from other juvenile victims: Such homicides are committed primarily by family members (71 percent) and by the common use (68 percent) of "personal weapons," such as hands and feet, to batter, strangle, or suffocate victims. In addition, young girls and young boys are about equally likely to be victims of homicide (46 and 54 percent, respectively). Among very young children, those at highest risk of homicide are those under age one. Homicides of children in this group include a certain number appropriately classified as **infanticide** (homicides in which recently born children are killed by relatives who do not want the child or who are suffering from a childbirth-related psychiatric disturbance). The FBI does not provide data identifying infanticides as a distinct subgroup, although countries such as Britain and Canada have a special infanticide offense category in their national crime statistics. Furthermore, FBI data do not identify victims murdered during the first six days of life (victims of what is sometimes called neonaticide), and in 1997, there were about 70 such victims. Two-thirds of these children were murdered by mothers, one-half of whom were under age 20. Fathers were responsible for only about 1 out of 10 of these murders.

Source: David Finkelhor and Richard Ormrod, *Homicides of Children and Youth* (Washington, DC: Office of Juvenile Justice and Delinquency Prevention, 2001).

victims. Simple assault is the most commonly reported crime against juveniles, comprising 41 percent of all juvenile victimizations. Sexual assault accounts for almost one-third of preteen victimizations, more than twice the proportion for older juveniles. In incidents where offenders are able to be identified as family member, acquaintance, or stranger, most offenders against juveniles (about 80 percent) are known to the victim; only 11 percent of child victimizers are strangers. However, there are two violent crimes with relatively higher percentages of stranger perpetrators—kidnapping (24 percent) and robbery (52 percent).[30]

Table 3–3   Violent Crime Victimization by Age, Gender, and Race (rate per 1000)

CHARACTERISTIC OF VICTIM	ALL CRIMES OF VIOLENCE	RAPE/SEXUAL ASSAULT	ROBBERY	AGGRAVATED ASSAULT
AGE				
12–15	74.4	4.0	6.7	13.1
16–19	77.4	6.9	8.2	16.8
20–24	68.5	4.3	7.7	16.7
15–34	36.3	1.7	4.1	8.3
GENDER				
Male	37.0	0.4	5.0	8.7
Female	28.8	3.0	2.3	4.8
RACE				
White	31.9	1.6	3.1	6.2
Black	41.6	2.6	7.7	10.6
Latino	33.8	1.9	5.6	8.9

Source: Callie Rennison, *Criminal Victimization 1999: Changes 1998–99 with Trends 1993–99* (Washington, DC: Bureau of Justice Statistics, 2000), p. 6.

Violence in Schools

On March 8, 2000, six-year-old Kayla Rolland was shot in the neck in her first-grade classroom with a .32-caliber pistol and died a half hour later. Her killer, Dedrick Owens, was also only 6 years old and had gotten into a quarrel with Kayla on the playground the day before. Dedrick, already known as a bully at school, had found the loaded pistol lying under blankets on the floor of his home and brought it to school tucked in his pants. After shooting Kayla, Dedrick ran into a nearby bathroom and tossed the gun into a trash can. Once in police custody, Dedrick sat quietly drawing pictures after indicating to the police that he thought he had done something "naughty."[31]

Between February 1997 and December 1999, the United States witnessed a series of shockingly violent episodes taking place around the country in the nation's high schools. These events included a principal and student killed in Bethel, Alaska; three students killed and five more wounded in West Paducah, Kentucky; one teacher and five students killed in Jonesboro, Arkansas; a teacher killed and a student wounded in Edinboro, Pennsylvania; and then a teacher and 14 students killed at Columbine High School in Littleton, Colorado. Shootings in high schools, though generally rare, have been part of the school landscape during much of the second half of the 20th century. Even in the 1950s, a number of movies, such as *High School Confidential* and *Blackboard Jungle*, focused on high school violence. But before the late 1980s and early 1990s, when juvenile gun violence had risen so dramatically, shootings in schools typically involved only single victims, and students in the lower grades rarely witnessed the violence and were even

Adam Smith once said that "mercy to the guilty is cruelty to the innocent." How does this sentiment apply to incidents like the Kayla Rolland killing? What is just treatment when the perpetrators of murder are only children?

Children who attend public schools experience significantly higher rates of serious violence than children who attend private schools. Based on this information, why do some people fight school voucher programs, which empower parents to choose where their children will attend school?

more rarely the victims of violence. With the shooting of Kayla Rolland, America's elementary schools were no longer seen as inviolate islands of safety for our children. Guns were now being brought into first-grade classrooms and six-year-olds were being shot to death.

Perhaps due to the great amount of media attention given to the series of incidents involving multiple-shooting victims in schools in the late 1990s, school violence, including bomb threats and mundane incidents of bullying, seems to have replaced drive-by shootings and gang-related violence as the country's greatest concern involving the safety of its children. And yet school-associated violent deaths are very rare. Less than 1 percent of the more than 1,350 children who were murdered in the first half of the 1998–99 school year were killed at school (either on school property, at a school-sponsored event, or on the way to or from school). Furthermore, the number of multiple-victim homicides at school actually declined during the 1990s.[32] Nonfatal violent crimes against students at school , including rape, sexual assault, aggravated assault, and simple assault, declined from 144 per 1,000 students in 1992 to 101 per 1,000 in 1998. According to the 2001 national survey of school crime and safety, male and female students were about equally likely to be victims of serious violence at school. Little racial or ethnic difference was reported in terms of percentage of students threatened or injured with a weapon on school property. Not surprisingly, public schools reported significantly higher rates of serious violence than private schools.[33]

Because of lethal school violence involving the use of guns, many schools have installed metal detectors. Do you agree with such a policy? What is more important: community safety or individual civil liberty?

Recent national surveys report that school violence is associated with a variety of factors in addition to reflecting the nature and extent of violence in surrounding communities. For example, students who carry weapons to school, who have been involved in fights, who have been threatened or injured, and who skipped school because they felt unsafe in school are more likely to be involved in violence on school ground. The availability of illegal drugs in school was also associated with higher rates of school violence, even for students who did not use drugs. And the greatest likelihood of being involved in school violence was found for those students who used multiple drugs while at school.[34]

The Role of Firearms in Youth Violence

A frequently made claim by a segment of one side in the gun control debate is that "Guns don't kill people, people kill people." The implication is that guns do not act on their own; they are simply tools in the hands of people who choose to use them for carrying out violent acts. If people did not have access to guns, then they would find other deadly weapons to use. Many advocates of strict gun control take a very different view. To them, guns are, in and of themselves, evil. Guns are deadly forces that are directly responsible for the deaths or maiming of tens of thousands of people every year. If it were not for the easy availability of guns, most perpetrators would either refrain from violence altogether or, at worst, select a less deadly weapon.

While it is not the intent of this chapter to resolve the gun control debate, there is no question that juveniles have significantly greater access to guns today than in past decades and that the guns they have access to are much more deadly than in the past. While the number of arrests of juveniles for weapons violations increased by over 400 percent between 1960 and 1990, they *decreased* significantly over the decade of the 1990s (dropping over 26 percent between 1991 and 2000),[35] although they remain much higher than four decades ago. In 2000 juveniles accounted for 24 percent of all persons arrested for weapons violations. Of those juveniles arrested, 90 percent were males, 67 percent were white, and 31 percent were African American.[36] Among all age and sex groups, males at age 18 have the highest per capita arrest rates for weapons violations, followed by males at age 17.[37]

Carrying and Possessing Guns

National surveys of middle/junior high and high school students conducted in the mid-1990s reported that 18 percent of the students said they had carried a weapon during the month prior to the survey and 8.5 percent said they had carried a weapon on school property. Nationally, over 7 percent of students reported having been threatened or injured with a weapon on school property once or more during the preceding year.[38] More recent surveys indicate that, while carrying a weapon on school property declined by over a third between 1993 and 1999, nearly 10 percent of students continue to bring weapons, including guns, knives, or clubs, to school. Seventh-graders were least likely to bring a weapon to school (6.6 percent), ninth-graders were most likely (13.2 percent). Among students who brought weapons to school, two-thirds carried a knife, while only 19 percent reported bringing a gun.[39]

Pamela Wilcox and Richard Clayton surveyed over 6,000 sixth- through twelfth-grade students in 21 schools in one county in Kentucky. They found males were about 30 percent more likely than females to carry weapons to school, and that nonwhites were nearly 50 percent more likely than whites to bring weapons to school. In addition, they reported that students of lower socioeconomic status, students who have been threatened at school, students who report a variety of other problem behaviors, and students whose parents own guns were also significantly more likely to carry weapons to school.[40]

Surveys of only students may not provide the most accurate estimate of how many youths possess or carry guns on a regular basis. Many youths have dropped out of school, and substantial numbers are confined in correctional institutions. Sheley and Wright surveyed students as well as 835 male juvenile inmates in six different correctional facilities. Students were asked if they currently owned a gun, and inmates were asked if they had owned a gun at the time they were arrested. About 22 percent of the students and 83 percent of the incarcerated youths reported ownership of a gun at the time in question.[41] Tom Luster and Su Min Ho's analysis of data from the 1997 National Longitudinal Survey of Youth based on interviews with over 9,000 adolescents between the ages of 12 and 16 found 9 percent of the youth reporting having carried a handgun during the previous year. Adolescent males who engaged in other problematic behaviors, had witnessed another person being shot or shot at, or who were involved in gangs were more likely than their peers to carry handguns. Finally, Luster and Ho found that boys under age 15 who were closely monitored by their mothers, *and who respected their mothers,* were less likely to carry handguns.[42]

Getting Guns

The **Brady Bill** mandated a five-day waiting period for the purchase of handguns, while The Violent Crime Control and Law Enforcement Act of 1994 made it a federal crime for anyone to sell or transfer a handgun, or ammunition for a handgun, to a person under age 18.[43] The act also made it a crime for juveniles to possess a handgun or ammunition for a handgun, although there are certain exceptions: A youth may possess a handgun when it is used for farming, ranching, target shooting, or safety instruction provided the youth has his or her parent's written permission to have the handgun. However, most states already prohibit the sale of handguns to persons under age 21 and the sale of rifles and shotguns to persons under the age of 18.[44] Therefore, if it is clearly illegal for youths to obtain guns through legitimate channels, how do they get them?

After the Columbine High School massacre, pundits wondered if armed teachers could have averted the tragedy. This sparked considerable debate. Should teachers pack pistols in case their students attempt a violent rampage? What are the political and social obstacles to such a policy? What are the benefits of such a policy?

Is the ultimate argument for gun control that children can readily obtain them from family, friends, and their home? What are the benefits and costs of having firearms in a family home?

Sheley and Wright asked students and juvenile inmates how they had obtained the guns they possessed. More than half the students said they borrowed their guns from a family member or friend, whereas most of the juvenile inmates said they had gotten their guns from friends and street sources. Both students and inmates indicated that they felt they could obtain guns with little trouble: There was little need to steal guns or to go through normal retail outlets where a friend or family member could legally purchase a gun.[45] This is fairly consistent with a recent survey of firearm use by offenders. About 40 percent of state prison inmates age 24 or younger obtained the gun used in their current offense from family members or friends. Only 7 percent obtained a gun from a retail store.[46]

Sheley and Wright also found that most of the youths in their study (both students and inmates) lived in social worlds characterized by crime and violence. Of the juvenile inmates, 40 percent had siblings who had been incarcerated, 62 percent reported having male family members who routinely carried guns, and 84 percent indicated that they had been threatened with a gun or shot at during their lives. Half had been stabbed with a knife and more than 80 percent had been beaten up by someone. Students were only slightly less exposed to violent environments. Nearly half the students reported that male members of their households regularly carried guns, 45 percent reported having been threatened with a gun or shot at, and one-third of the students had been beaten up either at school or on the way to or from school.[47]

Guns, Gangs, and Drugs

Juvenile gangs are often associated with violence, especially violence involving guns (see Chapter 12). Walter Miller has suggested that the much greater levels of gang violence that began to emerge in the mid-1970s was largely due to the greater availability of guns.[48] However, the gang violence of the 1970s was relatively modest compared to what was to come in the late 1980s and early-to-mid-1990s as more gang members carried more lethal weapons.[49] Higher rates of gun possession and a greater willingness to use them appear highly correlated with the intensity of gang violence.[50]

William Sanders noted that among the most significant changes in the behavior of gangs in the San Diego area between 1981 and 1988 was not just that violence had increased so much but that by 1988 there was a much greater use of guns. According to Sanders, "In 1981, only about a third of the violent reported incidents involved guns, but by 1988, over half of gang situations involved some type of firearm."[51] By that year, most gang members had substituted pistols and shotguns for knives, clubs, and fists in conflict situations.

Sheley and Wright found that youths who belonged to gangs were much more likely to own and use guns than youths who did not belong to gangs. However, they caution that:

> It may not be gang membership–generally or with respect to type of gang– that increases the chances of gun-related activity. It may be, instead, that gangs attract more violent offenders and, therefore, more firearm activity.[52]

Do gangs recruit members who already own guns and know how to use them? Does gun ownership decline when boys leave gangs? Alan Lizotte and David Sheppard note that while gun ownership is clearly greater for gang members than for nongang members, "the rate of owning illegal guns was not significantly higher for future gang members than for those who did not join gangs."[53] In other words, there is no evidence to suggest that gangs intentionally recruit boys who already carry guns. Lizotte and Sheppard also found that the rate of gun ownership declined among boys who leave gangs, returning "to a level similar to that of boys who had never belonged to a gang."[54]

There is substantial research suggesting that adolescent use of drugs, especially alcohol, cocaine, and crack, is related to violent behavior.[55] Numerous studies also report a strong association between the level of adolescent drug use and the carrying and use of guns. Youths who are more deeply involved in the drug culture, who use harder drugs or use drugs more frequently, or who actively engage in the street dealing of drugs are more likely to own or carry weapons.[56] The strongest link appears to be between selling drugs and having guns: Youths who sell drugs on the street are engaged in more dangerous activity than youths who merely use drugs and, consequently, are more likely to carry handguns or to possess sawed-off shotguns.[57] However, James Howell argues that, based on his research in Seattle, adolescents who are involved in gang-based drug trafficking are not necessarily more likely to engage in violence but that involvement in drug trafficking by nongang youths does predict violence.[58]

Violence Prevention

Although youth violence has declined significantly since the mid-1990s, it remains well above levels observed in the middle of the 20th century. What can be done to ensure that youth violence continues to decline? In this final section we will consider five arenas or strategies for preventing violence by juveniles: controlling availability of guns, reducing violence in families, preventing school violence, community-based prevention programs, and treatment and get-tough approaches.

Controlling Availability of Guns

Advocates of comprehensive bans on firearms sometimes appear willing to support at least a partial ban that would prohibit the sale and possession of assault rifles and "Saturday night specials." However, Sheley and Wright believe that the emphasis on banning specific *types* of guns, such as assault rifles, only creates a distinction between "good guns" and "bad guns" and will do little to reduce overall gun availability for youths. And although they see merit in increasing the penalties for the illegal transfer of guns to minors, they are quick to point out that "most of the methods used by juveniles to ob-

Criminologist Franklin Zimring suggests that raising the price of guns and creating a scarcity of ammunition would sharply reduce the ability of youths to possess firearms. In other words, he argues that guns should be priced out of the reach of youths. Would such a policy discriminate against persons from lower socioeconomic strata?

At least in the short term, Weed and Seed programs, such as those discussed on the next page, are very effective at reducing youth violence. Weed and Seed policies require brief but intense law enforcement. Why are the policies not more widely used given their effectiveness? Is the American public reluctant to empower the police? Is the American public tolerant of youth violence and neighborhood crime?

tain guns already are against the law."[59] Sheley and Wright support a national campaign aimed at encouraging people to engage in *responsible* gun ownership (for example, keeping guns locked and secure to avoid theft). However, they caution that

> so long as guns are available to *anyone*, they will also be available to any *juvenile* or any *felon* with the means and motives to steal one or to exploit the informal network of family and friends to obtain a gun stolen by someone else [italics in original].[60]

Franklin Zimring suggests an alternative to banning firearms.[61] He notes that there is a distinct political economy of adolescents. Youths have less monetary capital, lower regard for property as capital assets, and shorter monetary attention spans than adults. Adolescents with many economic wants, therefore, can be more easily distracted from investing their capital in guns. According to Zimring, raising the price of guns and creating a scarcity of ammunition for those who possess guns would have a significant negative impact on juveniles', especially younger juveniles' decisions to spend money on guns.

Easy availability of guns may also be reduced through a variety of strategies, such as targeted enforcement operations by the police (including hot spots of gun crime and the use of gun sweeps), community-supported silent witness programs that encourage residents to report the presence of illegal guns, cooperation with the Bureau of Alcohol, Tobacco, and Firearms (ATF) to trace illegal guns, safe gun storage programs, and the creation of juvenile gun courts.[62] Box 3–3 discusses some successful approaches to getting guns off the street.

Reducing Violence in Families

A growing number of criminologists believe that the structure of the modern family and the lack of meaningful relationships between parents and children today are significant causal factors in youth violence (see Chapter 10 for a discussion of families and violence). Many families face a shortage of financial resources, time, and energy for raising children, and this situation is significantly more problematic for poor female-headed families.[63] Not having a male role model for boys creates a greater risk that boys will pick up notions of what is manly from television. Television, according to Delbert Elliott, greatly distorts the role of violence in resolving conflict. He believes that "society should promote loving, intact two-parent families as the best way of raising children."[64]

"Loving families" may be more critical for preventing violence than "intact two-parent families." Laree Slack, a 12-year-old girl was being raised in a church-going, intact two-parent family, but her parents were anything but loving. Laree's parents, Larry and Constance, became angry at Laree because she had failed to appropriately wash and put away the family's clothes one day. As punishment, Laree was ordered to "assume the position" and stand ready to be whipped. She was whipped with the same 5-foot

BOX 3–3   DELINQUENCY PREVENTION
Getting Guns off the Streets

The evidence presented in this chapter so far clearly establishes the increase in firearm crime, especially among youths. If the police could get more guns off the streets, would there be fewer firearm crimes?

The **Kansas City Gun Experiment** was designed to test this idea. For 29 weeks, from July 7, 1992, to January 27, 1993, the Kansas City Police Department focused extra patrol attention on gun-crime "hot spots" in an 80- by 10-block area of the city. The extra patrol consisted of a pair of two-officer cars, with officers assigned on a rotating basis. Four officers worked six hours of overtime each night, from 7 P.M. to 1 A.M., and two other officers worked an additional 24 nights. The overtime was funded by the Bureau of Justice Assistance Weed and Seed program.

All officers focused exclusively on gun detection, primarily through traffic stops and pedestrian checks. The experiment appears to have had a number of significant effects. Among them are the following:

- Gun seizures by police in the target area increased by more than 65 percent, while gun crimes declined in the target area by 49 percent.
- Neither the number of gun crimes nor that of guns seized changed significantly in a similar beat several miles away, where the focused patrol was not used.
- The number of drive-by shootings dropped from seven to one in the target area but doubled in the comparison beat.
- Homicides were significantly reduced in the target area but not in the comparison beat.
- Traffic stops were the most productive method of finding guns, with an average of one gun found in every 28 traffic stops.

- Two-thirds of the persons arrested for gun carrying in the target area resided outside the area.
- Before-and-after surveys of citizens showed that respondents in the target area became less fearful of crime and more positive about their neighborhood than did respondents in the comparison beat.

The Kansas City Gun Experiment was replicated in Indianapolis between 1995 and 1997 as part of that city's Weed and Seed program, but with mixed success. Directed patrols that met with greater success were more selective about which vehicles to stop and issued citations rather than warnings; they also used K–9 patrols and probation sweeps for guns.

Boston's **Operation Ceasefire** combines a direct law enforcement attack on illicit firearms found on traffickers supplying juveniles with guns and an attempt to create a strong deterrent to gang violence. The project includes:

- Expanding the focus of local, state, and federal authorities to include intrastate firearms trafficking in Massachusetts in addition to interstate trafficking.
- Focused enforcement attention on traffickers of the makes and calibers of guns most used by gang members.
- Focused enforcement attention on traffickers of guns that had short time-to-crime intervals and, thus, were most likely to have been trafficked.
- Focused enforcement attention on traffickers of guns used by the city's most violent gangs.
- Attempts to restore obliterated serial numbers of confiscated guns and subsequently investigating trafficking based on those restorations.
- Targeting gangs engaged in violent behavior.
- Delivering an explicit message that violence would not be tolerated.
- Backing up that message by "pulling every lever" legally available when violence occurred.

(continued)

(continued)

Sources: Lawrence Sherman, James Shaw, and Dennis Ro-gan, *The Kansas City Gun Experiment* (Washington, DC: U.S. Department of Justice, 1995); Shay Bilchik, *Promising Strategies to Reduce Gun Violence* (Washington, DC: Office of Juvenile Justice and Delinquency Prevention, 1999); David

Kennedy, Anthony Braga, Anne Piehl, and Elin Waring, *Reducing Gun Violence: The Boston Gun Project's Operation Ceasefire* (Washington, DC: U.S. Department of Justice, 2001).

A variety of criminologists suggest that loving, two-parent families are the best protection against juvenile delinquency and that exposure to violence or abuse in the home is one of the most important risk factors for delinquency. Why, then, did society generally mock former Vice President Dan Quayle's belief in family values? Similarly, why is former drug czar William Bennett mocked for similar "traditional" beliefs?

stretch of electrical cord Larry had used earlier on Laree's 8-year-old brother. When Laree attempted to squirm away, her father ordered Laree's two older brothers to tie her face down on a metal bed frame. Larry and Constance took turns lashing Laree. When her back began to bleed, Larry untied her and turned her over and she was whipped again on her chest and stomach. Laree suffered more than 160 lashes and was pronounced dead at the hospital a few hours later.[65]

Violence within the family has far-reaching effects on children, regardless of whether they are the direct object of the violence or not. Children who observe their parents fighting or physically punishing siblings begin to internalize these acts as "normal" techniques for resolving conflicts. Exposure to violence or abuse in the home and exposure to hostile and punitive parenting are among the most important risk factors for a child's subsequent involvement in violent behavior.[66] Stephen Baron and Timothy Hartnagel's study of the violent behavior of street youth also note that domestic violence is a significant factor in decisions to engage in violence. As Baron and Hartnagel say, "these youths also learn from their abusive home experiences that using force is a practical and effective method of gaining compliance, increasing the odds that they will use coercion to gain financial or material rewards."[67]

Parent training programs, similar to those designed to reduce delinquency generally (discussed in Chapter 10), have been found effective in reducing children's antisocial behavior. These programs teach parents specific skills in child management, problem solving, and communication. Intensive family preservation services (IFPS) can provide short-term crisis intervention for families who have aggressive or violence-involved children. For example, the Homebuilders Program sends intervention workers to a crisis family within 24 hours to provide a variety of clinical and material services. IFPS interventions typically address poor family management practices, family conflict, and the antisocial behavior of youths. Finally, marital and family therapy has been found to be effective in reducing adolescent problem behaviors, including aggressiveness and violent acting out.[68]

The Coordinating Council on Juvenile Justice and Delinquency Prevention's *Action Plan* calls for reducing adolescent violence through breaking the cycle of youth victimization, abuse, and neglect that occurs within families.

The Plan proposes strengthening families' capabilities to supervise and nurture the positive development of their children in nonviolent homes. This would involve programs aimed at providing support through assistance with effective parenting skills, home visitation, and teen-parent groups designed to prevent child abuse and neglect and to foster healthy development. The Plan further calls for enhancing local efforts to investigate and prosecute child abuse and neglect cases, strengthening child protective services by promoting interdisciplinary efforts, and strengthening at-risk families through family support services.[69]

Preventing School Violence

The playground game dodgeball has been banned from many schools because critics suggest that the game fosters aggression in boys and promotes a survival-of-the-fittest ideology. Do you agree? Did you play dodgeball as a child? Did the game have devastating short- and long-term effects?

After two students were shot to death in Santana High School in Santee, California, only two years after the Columbine High School massacre, schools around the country began to implement zero-tolerance measures in an attempt to prevent future school violence. Pottsgrove High School, just outside Philadelphia, prohibited students from driving cars to school because students might hide bombs or weapons in the trunks of the car and banned book bags, soda cans, and water bottles unless they are made of mesh or clear plastic. One Houston school requires students to enter school through a metal detector, while another Houston school suspended two third-grade boys for possessing a small pocketknife even though no one was threatened or hurt. And in Indianapolis, a 14-year-old boy was arrested after school officials heard a rumor that the boy planned to bring a gun to school the next day.[70] Other schools have suspended students for drawing pictures of guns or for turning in creative writing assignments that were too violent, and one school suspended an elementary school student for pointing a chicken nugget at a teacher during lunch and yelling "Bang!" Finally, a growing number of schools have dropped dodgeball from their gymnasiums and playgrounds after it came under attack by some women's groups who argued that it fosters aggression and future violence among players. However, few of these measures are likely to have any serious, long-term impact on school violence.

Some school antiviolence programs attempt to reduce school-related risk factors—such as academic failure, low self-esteem, low commitment to school, and problematic peer relationships—by targeting classroom organization, management practices, and instructional strategies. Many of the more promising programs include reductions in class size, nongraded elementary schools, tutoring, and computer-assisted instruction, interactive teaching, and cooperative learning.[71]

Other school programs focus primarily on in-school counseling and behavior modification. This approach involves group counseling, the use of time-out rooms, interpersonal and problem-solving skills training, moral education, value clarification, peer counseling, and intervention in the opening moves of escalating conflicts.[72] The National Resource Center for Safe Schools recommends a number of components be considered in planning for safe schools. These include developing emergency response planning, creating a positive school climate and culture, ensuring quality facilities and

In November 2001, three teens from New Bedford, Massachusetts, were arrested for conspiring to detonate explosives and create a massacre similar to the Columbine High School massacre. Why would youths want to emulate such an atrocity? Do the conditions of American high schools help produce alienated adolescents? Is "society to blame?" Or, are these disaffected offenders simply aberrant in the first place?

technology, and instituting links with mental health social services.[73] Still other programs emphasize control. Control-oriented programs are likely to entail measures such as closing off isolated areas, increasing staff supervision, installing electronic monitoring for weapons detection, removing tempting vandalism targets, requiring students to wear only see-through backpacks, and using police or private security personnel for patrol, crowd control, investigation of criminal activities, and intelligence gathering.[74]

Targeted violence in schools, or incidents in which the attacker has targeted particular persons or groups, may not be as amenable to prevention programs such as those just discussed. An intensive study of 37 school shootings, involving 41 attackers, was conducted by the U.S. Secret Service National Threat Assessment Center. They found that

1. Incidents of targeted violence at school are rarely impulsive. The attacks are typically the end result of an understandable and often discernible process of thinking and behavior.
2. Prior to most incidents, the attacker told someone about his idea and/ or plan.
3. There is no accurate or useful profile of "the school shooter."
4. Most attackers had previously used guns and had access to them.
5. Most shooting incidents were not resolved by law enforcement intervention.
6. In many cases, other students were involved in some capacity.
7. Most attackers engaged in some behavior, prior to the incident, that caused others concern or indicated a need for help.[75]

Implications for prevention of targeted school violence reflect a number of issues. For example, because the typical student engaged in school violence did not "just snap," it may be possible to gather information about intent and planning before the incident. It is also helpful to distinguish between *making* a threat and *posing* a threat; adults should attend to concerns that someone poses a threat. Because profiling is not effective for identifying students who may pose a risk of targeting violence, school officials should focus instead on a student's *behaviors* and *communications* to determine whether the student appears to be planning or preparing for an attack. It is important to discover if a student is on a path toward a violent attack. Because other students often know about incidents in advance, it is wrong to assume shooters are "loners." Thus, it is important to gather information from a potential attacker's friends and schoolmates.[76]

Community-Based Prevention Programs

Early American sociologists, such as Clifford Shaw and Henry McKay, believed that the local neighborhood and community largely determined the nature and extent of various social problems, including delinquency (see Chapter 5). This theoretical perspective within the sociological discipline led to a wide variety of community-based programs, such as the Chicago Area Project, aimed at eradicating or reducing such social ills as poverty, alcohol and drug abuse, the breakdown of the traditional family, and crime and delinquency. Today, community-based programs are targeting youth violence.

Children rarely choose where they live. Rather, they are dependent upon their parents, or their parents' fate, with regard to the particular neighborhood in which they reside. The neighborhood may be more or less safe, inhabited by the homeless, littered with graffiti, preferred by drug dealers and users, occupied by juvenile gangs, and lacking in supportive and nurturing social institutions such as a school and church. In other words, many children, through no choice of their own, face daily lives in communities that are threatening and dangerous.

Fortunately, programs are emerging in some communities to counter such problems. Individuals (such as parents, neighbors, clergy, social workers, and health care workers) as well as diverse community groups (such as community policing teams, youth development organizations, churches, schools, tenant organizations, and civic groups) are sponsoring neighborhood and community programs to reduce violence.[77] Among these programs are

- Community policing
- Safe havens for youth
- Drug-free school zones
- Neighborhood watch programs
- After-school programs sponsored by community organizations
- Job training and apprentice programs for at-risk youths

In spite of the efforts being made to reduce the availability of guns, to reduce violence in the media, to intervene in families and schools, and to create safer and more nurturing communities, many experts believe that the only way to reduce youth violence is by arresting violent youths and dealing with them formally within either the juvenile or adult justice system.

Treatment and "Get-Tough" Approaches

There is a serious dilemma facing both criminologists and policy makers when attempting to determine the "best" treatment approach or the "most effective" punishment approach for dealing with serious, violent juveniles. Unfortunately, it is extremely difficult to distinguish the causes of the behaviors of violent youths from those of nonviolent delinquent youths. Therefore, any process to select only, or primarily, violent youths for participation in a particular treatment program or for transfer to criminal court for prosecution based upon assumptions about the ability to bring about rehabilitation or deterrence is likely flawed. For example, research by Dewey Cornell points out that even very violent juveniles can be subdivided into smaller subgroups based upon the youths' prior adjustment problems. Cornell states: "Among violent offenders, youth convicted of the most serious violent crime, homicide, actually have less history of prior violence than do offenders convicted of less serious assaults."[78]

In Cincinnati, Ohio, a 54-year-old man is being charged for the murder of his high school girlfriend—a crime that occurred 38 years ago. The defendant, Michael Wehrung, admitted to the crime but suggested that his "other self" is really responsible for the killing. Wehrung believes that he should be tried as a juvenile since the crime occurred when he was 15. The Ohio Supreme Court had already ruled in a 1996 decision that takes jurisdiction away from juvenile court if a defendant is not apprehended until adulthood. This case raises an interesting question about youth violence. Here we have a case of a high school murderer who leads a successful life (executive of a roofing company) and never experiences an arrest. If you were the sentencing judge, what type of sentence would you order? Does this person deserve leniency?

Treatment Approaches   Most treatment programs for violent youths occur within locked, secure correctional facilities, although they continue to emphasize rehabilitation and early reintegration into the community. One such treatment program is the Violent Juvenile Offender (VJO) program, designed to target chronic violent male juvenile offenders in four urban areas: Boston, Detroit, Memphis, and Newark. Youths selected for the VJO program must have been adjudicated for a Part I Index felony and must have at least one prior adjudication for a serious felony. The program involves efforts aimed at "strengthening youths' bonds to prosocial people and institutions, providing realistic opportunities for achievement, employing a system of rewards for appropriate behavior and sanctions for inappropriate behavior, and individualized treatment."[79] To accomplish these goals, VJO youths are initially placed in small, secure treatment facilities and then gradually reintegrated into the community in phases. The second phase involves treatment in a community-based residential program, after which youths progress to the third phase, involving intensive supervision in the neighborhood.

Another treatment program for violent juvenile offenders is the Capital Offender Program (COP) in Texas. For a youth to be eligible for placement in COP, he or she must have committed a homicide and must not have been diagnosed as having a severe psychological disorder. COP is designed to "promote verbal expression of feelings, to foster empathy for victims, to create a sense of personal responsibility, and to decrease feelings of hostility and aggression."[80] Treatment includes group psychotherapy emphasizing role playing in which youths act out their life stories and reenact their crimes from their own perspectives and those of their victims.

Get-Tough Approaches   Many states have lowered the age for waiver of violent youths to criminal court or are making it less difficult to transfer such youths (see Chapter 14); have established determinate sentences for serious, violent youths adjudicated in the juvenile courts; and have permitted a juvenile's arrest and court record to be made available to schools and to adult criminal courts once a youth is prosecuted as an adult. In addition, some states have passed parental-liability laws whereby juveniles' parents are held in contempt of court for missing their children's court hearings.

Law enforcement, prosecutors, and the courts are coordinating efforts in a number of jurisdictions to develop new strategies for targeting violent juveniles. For example, the Salinas Police Department in California created a Violence Suppression Unit consisting of 15 officers involved in aggressive patrol focusing on violent and gun-related crimes. The Seattle Police Department established a system for tracking violent offenders and disseminating information through the department and other social service agencies to reduce the anonymity of the juveniles and refer the offenders to intervention services. A list of the 50 most violent juveniles was developed, with increased communication between police and probation, to increase surveillance of these youths and to provide for greater enforcement of their conditions of probation. In addition, enhanced prosecution for serious, violent juvenile offenders was instituted with the addition of a new full-time position in the prosecutor's office. At the same time, Seattle's Juvenile Firearms Prosecution Project provided for vertical prosecution of all juvenile firearms offenses with a Deputy Prosecutor specializing in firearm prosecutions assigned to handle all juvenile firearms offenses from initial filing of the case through juvenile sentencing. Finally, the Baltimore City Police Department's Youth Violence Task Force, working closely with the U.S. Attorney, ATF, FBI, and school police, identifies and targets gang members and violent offenders and aggressively seeks their apprehension and incarceration.[81]

Conclusions

For some criminologists, the easy availability of guns is seen as the primary cause of the increases in youth violence. Other experts point to the growing involvement of juveniles in the drug industry, especially in street dealing of crack. Still others believe that the increase in violence stems from the expansion of the urban gang problem. In any case, the intersection of teenagers, guns, drugs, and gangs is likely to provide all of the major ingredients for violence.

Is it possible to prevent youth violence? Criminologists, legislators, and policy makers differ greatly in their opinions of what the root causes of youth violence are as well as how the violence might best be responded to. Some avenues of response are getting guns out of the hands of juveniles, reducing violence in the media, strengthening families, assisting schools to teach alternatives to violence, drawing upon community resources, providing treatment for offenders, and getting tough on violent offenders. None of these approaches appears terribly promising on its own, but possibly a comprehensive strategy that combines the best features of each may more effectively control youth violence.

Key Terms

Brady Bill: *Federal legislation mandating a five-day waiting period for the purchase of handguns.*

infanticide: *Homicides in which recently born children are killed by relatives who do not want the children or who are suffering from childbirth-related psychiatric disturbances.*

Kansas City Gun Experiment: *A 1992 experiment in which the use of additional police to patrol in target areas for the exclusive purpose of gun detection significantly increased gun seizures and decreased gun crimes.*

Operation Ceasefire: *A gun prevention program in Boston involving direct law enforcement attack on illicit firearms traffickers supplying juveniles with guns.*

Getting Connected

The National Criminal Justice Reference Service maintains two pages that provide an extensive array of statistics, reports, and publications dealing with youth violence and violent victimization. They are: Juvenile Victimization

http://www.ncjrs.org/victjuv.htm

1. What kinds of partnerships are investigated in the report "Solving Youth Violence: Partnerships that Work"?
2. Link to the National Council of Juvenile and Family Court Judges. What is their stand on the role of alcohol and substance abuse in the families that come to their attention?
3. How are childhood sexual abuse and later criminal consequences related?

Violence and Victimization

http://www.ncjrs.org/jjvict.htm

1. Link to OJJDP fact sheets. What is "The 8% Solution"?
2. Link to the OJJDP fact sheets. Evaluate the "Guide to the Family and Educational Rights and Privacy Act."
3. Find the Appropriate and Effective Use of Security Technologies in U.S. Schools." What kinds of technologies are evaluated? Were any in use in your school?

The National Centers for Disease Control conducts annual surveys of adolescent behaviors, including violence. Data and reports from their annual Youth Risk Behavior Surveillance are available at their website:

http://www.cdc.gov/nccdphp/dash/yrbs/

1. Consider the YRBS report Youth Risk Behavior Trends "Risk Behaviors That Improved, 1991–1999." How does this report compare to popular stereotypes about youth behaviors?
2. Consider the YRBS report Youth Risk Behavior Trends "Risk Behaviors That Worsened, 1991–1999." How does this report compare to popular stereotypes about youth behaviors?
3. What is the purpose of Programs That Work? What kinds of adolescent health issues are addressed by these programs?

A website maintained by Streetcats and The National Childrens Coalition providing ideas and links to organizations and publications on preventing youth violence can be found at:

http://www.child.net/violence.htm

1. Link to the CRIMES COPS CROOKS website. To what kinds of sites does it link? What are some assumptions about delinquency in these sites?
2. What are Streetcats Patrols?
3. Evaluate the information about the "Handwriting and Violence" seminar.

A website maintained by Common Sense About Kids and Guns provides information, resources, and additional Web links for a variety of issues related to adolescents, guns, and violence. They can be found at:

http://www.kidsandguns.org/

1. Evaluate the organization's "Statement on Kids and Guns in the Home." How might adults in your area respond to this statement?
2. The "Common Sense Safety Tips" reflect an interesting social reality. What percent of American homes have a gun or guns? Why might these safety tips be needed?
3. What is the most recent news about kids and guns?

Endnotes

1. Quoted in Joseph Sheley and James Wright, *In the Line of Fire: Youth, Guns, and Violence in Urban America* (New York: Aldine De Gruyter, 1995), p. 1.

2. Federal Bureau of Investigation, *Crime in the United States 2000* (Washington, DC: U.S. Department of Justice, 2001), p. 222.

3. "First-Graders Accused of Murder Plot," *APBNews.com* (April 13, 2000) Online: Available http://www.apbnews.com/newscenter/breakingnews/2000/04/13/firstgrader0413_01.html.

4. "Too Young to Charge," *ABC News.com* (March 8, 2001) Online: Available http://www.abcnews.go.com/sections/us/DailyNews/shooting000301.html.

5. "Twelve-Year-Old Holds Class at Gunpoint in Ohio," *DailyNews.Yahoo.com* (March 23, 2000) Online: Available http://www.rense.com/politics6/class.htm.

6. Karin Meadows, "Teacher Fatally Shot by Student on Last Day of Classes," *Naplesnews.com* (May 27, 2000) Online: Available http://www.naplesnews.com/00/05/florida/d469705a.htm.

7. "An Epidemic of Violence: Incidents in Schools Rise Sharply Since Santee Shooting," *CNN.com* (March 8, 2001) Online: Available http://www.cnn.com/2001/US/03/08/alarming.incidents/index.html.

8. Federal Bureau of Investigation, note 2, p. 224.

9. G. David Curry, Cheryl Maxson, and James Howell, *Youth Gang Homicides in the 1990s* (Washington, DC: Office of Juvenile Justice and Delinquency Prevention, 2001), p. 1.

10. Margaret Small and Kellie Tetrick, "School Violence: An Overview," *Juvenile Justice* 8:3–12 (2001).

11. Shay Bilchik, *Violence After School* (Washington, DC: Office of Juvenile Justice and Delinquency Prevention, 1999).

12. Alan Lizotte and David Sheppard, *Gun Use by Male Juveniles: Research and Prevention* (Washington, DC: Office of Juvenile Justice and Delinquency Prevention, 2001); Sheley and Wright, note 1.

13. Quoted in Richard Lacayo, "When Kids Go Bad," *Time*, September 19:61 (1994).

14. Federal Bureau of Investigation, note 2, p. 224.

15. Nancy Brener, Thomas Simon, Etienne Krug, and Richard Lowry, "Recent Trends in Violence Related Behaviors Among High School Students in the United States," *JAMA* 282:440–446 (1999).

16. Meghan Black, *Person Offenses in Juvenile Court, 1989–1998* (Washington, DC: Office of Juvenile Justice and Delinquency Prevention, 2001), p. 1.

17. Alfred Blumstein, "Violence by Young People: Why the Deadly Nexus," *National Institute of Justice Journal* 229:2–9 (1995).

18. Alfred Blumstein and Daniel Cork, "Linking Gun Availability to Youth Gun Violence," *Law and Contemporary Problems* 59:5–18 (1996).

19. Alfred Blumstein and R. Rosenfeld, "Explaining Recent Trends in U.S. Homicide Rates," *The Journal of Criminal Law and Criminology* 88:1175–1216 (1998).

20. Joan McCord, Cathy Widom, and Nancy Crowell, eds., *Juvenile Crime Juvenile Justice* (Washington, DC: National Academy Press, 2001).

21. McCord et al., note 20, p. 45.

22. Meda Chesney-Lind, "What About the Girls? Delinquency Programming as if Gender Mattered," *Corrections Today* February:39 (2001).

23. Darnell Hawkins, John Laub, Janet Lauritsen, and Lynn Cothern, *Race, Ethnicity, and Serious and Violent Juvenile Offending* (Washington, DC: Office of Juvenile Justice and Delinquency Prevention, 2000); Matt DeLisi and Bob Regoli, "Race, Conventional Crime, and Criminal Justice: The Declining Importance of Skin Color," *Journal of Criminal Justice* 27:549–557 (1999).

24. Delbert Elliott, "Serious Violent Offending: Onset, Developmental Course, and Termination," *Criminology* 32:1–21 (1994).

25. Federal Bureau of Investigation, *Supplemental Homicide Reports, 1976–99* (Washington, DC: Federal Bureau of Investigation, 2001).

26. Amy Waldman, "Brothers, 8 and 9, Charged in Fatal Stabbing of Boy, 4," *The New York Times* (September 8, 2001) Online: Available http://www.nytimes.com/2001/09/08/nyregion/08STAB.html.

27. Harry Moskowitz, John Griffith, Carla DiScala, and Robert Sege, "Serious Injuries and Deaths of Adolescent Girls Resulting from Interpersonal Violence," *Archive of Pediatric Adolescent Medicine* 155:905 (2001).

28. Callie Rennison, *Criminal Victimization 1999: Changes 1998–99 with Trends 1993–99* (Washington, DC: Bureau of Justice Statistics, 2000), p. 6.

29. Callie Rennison, *Violent Victimization and Race, 1993–98* (Washington, DC: Bureau of Justice Statistics, 2000), p. 3.

30. David Finkelhor and Richard Ormrod, *Characteristics of Crimes Against Juveniles* (Washington, DC: Office of Juvenile Justice and Delinquency Prevention, 2000), pp. 7, 12.

31. Christy McDonald and Chris Pavelich, "First-Grader Shot Dead at School," (March 8, 2000) Online: Available http://www.ABC-NEWS.com/2000/3/8; Victoria Newton, "Face of School Killer, 6," Online: Available http://www.the-sun.uk/news/4300619.

32. Margaret Small and Kellie Tetrick, "School Violence: An Overview," *Juvenile Justice* 8:4 (2001).

33. Phillip Kaufman, Xianglei Chen, Susan Choy, Sally Ruddy, Amanda Miller, Kathryn Chandler, Michael Planey, and Michael Rand, *Indicators of School Crime and Safety, 2001* (Washington, DC: U.S. Department of Education/U.S. Department of Justice, 2001).

34. Richard Lowry, Lisa Cohen, William Modzeleski, Laura Kann, Janet Collins, and Lloyd Kolbe, "School Violence, Substance Use, and Availability of Illegal Drugs on School Property Among U.S. High School Students," *Journal of School Health* 69:347–355 (1999).

35. Federal Bureau of Investigation, note 2, p. 220.

36. Federal Bureau of Investigation, note 2, pp. 224, 225, 235.

37. Lawrence Greenfeld and Marianne Zawitz, *Weapons Offenses and Offenders* (Washington, DC: U.S. Department of Justice, 1995), p. 3.

38. Centers for Disease Control and Prevention, *Youth Risk Behavior Surveillance—United States, 1997* (Atlanta, GA: U.S. Department of Health and Human Services, 1998), p. 8.

39. Kimberly Forrest, Amy Zychowski, Wendy Stuhldreher, and William Ryan, "Weapon-Carrying in School: Prevalence and Association with Other Violent Behaviors," *American Journal of Health Studies* 16:133–140 (2000).

40. Pamela Wilcox and Richard Clayton, "A Multilevel Analysis of School-Based Weapon Possession," *Justice Quarterly* 18:509–541 (2001).

41. Sheley and Wright, note 1, p. 43.

42. Tom Luster and Su Min Ho, "Correlates of Male Adolescents Carrying Handguns Among Their Peers," *Journal of Marriage and Family* 63:714–726 (2001).

43. 103rd Congress, HR 3355, *The Violent Crime Control and Law Enforcement Act of 1994, Title XI, Sec. 110201,* Washington, DC: (U.S. Government Printing Office, 1994).

44. Sheley and Wright, note 1, p. 151.

45. Sheley and Wright, note 1, pp. 46–50.

46. Caroline Harlow, *Firearm Use by Offenders* (Washington, DC: Bureau of Justice Statistics, 2001), p. 9.

47. Sheley and Wright, note 1, pp. 27–29; Joseph Sheley and James Wright, *Gun Acquisition and Possession in Selected Juvenile Samples* (Washington, DC: U.S. Department of Justice, 1993), p. 4.

48. Walter Miller, *Violence by Youth Gangs and Youth Groups* (Washington, DC: U.S. Government Printing Office, 1975).

49. Tom Squiteri, "Gang Problem Spreads: 'Magnitude Is Startling'," *USA TODAY,* October 24:6A (1991); Carolyn Block and Richard Block, *Street Gang Crime in Chicago* (Washington, DC: U.S. Department of Justice, 1993).

50. John Hagedorn, *People and Folks: Gangs, Crime and the Underclass in a Rustbelt City* (Chicago: Lakeview Press, 1988); Martin Jankowski, *Islands in the Street: Gangs and American Urban Society* (Berkeley: University of California Press, 1991).

51. William Sanders, *Gangbangs and Drive-Bys: Grounded Culture and Juvenile Gang Violence* (New York: Aldine De Gruyter, 1994), p. 56.

52. Sheley and Wright, note 1, p. 107.

53. Lizotte and Sheppard, note 12, p. 4.

54. Lizotte and Sheppard, note 12, p. 4.

55. See for example, Ernest Abel, "Drugs and Homicide in Erie County, New York," *The International Journal of the Addictions* 22:195–299 (1987); Richard Goodman et al., "Alcohol Use and Interpersonal Violence: Alcohol Detected in Homicide Victims," *American Journal of Public Health* 76:144–149 (1986); Matti Virkkunen, "Alcohol as a Factor Precipitating Aggression and Conflict Behavior Leading to Homicide," *British Journal of Addiction* 69:149–154 (1974); Jared Tinklenberg, Patricia Murphy, and Adolf Pfefferbaum, "Drugs and Criminal Assaults by Adolescents: A Replication Study," *Journal of Psychoactive Drugs* 13:277–287 (1981).

56. See for example, James Inciardi, Ruth Horowitz, and Anne Pottieger, *Street Kids, Street Drugs, Street Crime* (Belmont, CA: Wadsworth Publishing Co., 1993); David Altschuler and Paul Brounstein, "Patterns of Drug Use, Drug Trafficking and Other Delinquency Among Inner City Adolescent Males in Washington, DC," *Criminology* 29:589–621 (1991); Alan Lizotte, James Tesoriero, Terence Thornberry, and Marvin Krohn, "Patterns of Adolescent Firearms Ownership and Use," *Justice Quarterly* 11:51–73 (1994); W. Van Kammen and R. Loeber, "Are Fluctuations in Delinquent Activities Related to the Onset and Offset in Juvenile Illegal Drug Use and Drug Dealing?" *Journal of Drug Issues* 24:9–24 (1994).

57. Terry Williams, *The Cocaine Kids* (New York: Addison-Wesley, 1989); Sheley and Wright, note 1, p. 92.

58. James Howell, *Juvenile Justice & Youth Violence* (Thousand Oaks, CA: Sage, 1997), p. 149.

59. Sheley and Wright, note 1, p. 150.

60. Sheley and Wright, note 1, p. 151.

61. Franklin Zimring, "Kids, Guns, and Homicide: Policy Notes on an Age-Specific Epidemic," *Law and Contemporary Problems* 59:34 (1996).

62. Shay Bilchik, *Promising Strategies to Reduce Gun Violence* (Washington, DC: Office of Juvenile Justice and Delinquency Prevention, 1999); David Sheppard, Heath Grant, Wendy Rowe, and Nancy Jacobs, *Fighting Juvenile Gun Violence* (Washington, DC: Office of Juvenile Justice and Delinquency Prevention, 2000).

63. Timothy Thornton, Carole Craft, Linda Dahlberg, Barbara Lynch, and Katie Baer, *Best Practices of Youth Violence Prevention: A Sourcebook for Community Action* (Atlanta: Centers for Disease Control and Prevention, 2000).

64. Quoted in Peter Caughey, "Growing Up Violent," *Summit Magazine* Fall:10 (1995).

65. Kirsten Scharnberg and Eric Ferkenhoff, "Girl Died After Parents Hit Her 160 Times, Court Told," *ChicagoTribune.Com* (November 14, 2001) Online: Available http://chicagotribune.com/news/local/chi-0111140266nov14.story.htm.

66. Laurence Steinberg, "Youth Violence: Do Parents and Families Make a Difference," *National Institute of Justice Journal* April:31–38 (2000); John Wilson, *Safe from the Start: Taking Action on Children Exposed to Violence* (Washington, DC: Office of Juvenile Justice and Delinquency Prevention, 2000).

67. Stephen Baron and Timothy Hartnagel, "Street Youth and Criminal Violence," *Journal of Research in Crime and Delinquency* 35:184 (1998).

68. Devon Brewer, J. David Hawkins, Richard Catalano, and Holly Neckerman, "Preventing Serious, Violent, and Chronic Juvenile Delinquency," in *A Sourcebook: Serious, Violent & Chronic Juvenile Offenders*, edited by James Howell, Barry Krisberg, J. David Hawkins, and John Wilson (Thousand Oaks, CA: Sage Publications, 1995), pp. 90–95.

69. Coordinating Council on Juvenile Justice and Delinquency Prevention, *Combating Violence and Delinquency: The National Juvenile Justice Action Plan* (Washington, DC: U.S. Department of Justice, 1996), pp. 9–10.

70. "Schools Cracking Down at Slightest Hints of Threats," *CourtTV.Com* (March 9, 2001) Online: Available http://www.courttv.com/news/2001/0309/threats_ap.html.

71. Brewer et al., note 68, pp. 70–74.

72. Daniel Lockwood, *Violence Among Middle School and High School Students: Analysis and Implications for Prevention* (Washington, DC: National Institute of Justice, 1997).

73. Ira Pollack and Carlos Sundermann, "Creating Safe Schools: A Comprehensive Approach," *Juvenile Justice* 8:14 (2001).

74. C. Ronald Huff and Kenneth Trump, "Youth Violence and Gangs: School Safety Initiatives in Urban and Suburban School Districts," *Education and Urban Society* 28:492–503 (1996); Randy Page and Jon Hammermeister, "Weapon-Carrying and Youth Violence," *Adolescence* 32:505–513 (1997).

75. Bryan Vossekuil, Marisa Reddy, Robert Fein, Randy Borum, and William Modzeleski, *Safe School Initiative: An Interim Report on the Prevention of Targeted Violence in Schools* (Washington, DC: U.S. Secret Service National Threat Assessment Center, 2000), pp. 3–7.

76. Vossekuil et al., note 75.

77. John Wilson and James Howell, "Comprehensive Strategy for Serious, Violent, and Chronic Juvenile Offenders," in Howell et al., note 68, pp. 36–46.

78. Dewey Cornell, "Prior Adjustment of Violent Juvenile Offenders," *Law and Human Behavior* 14:575 (1990).

79. Barry Krisberg, Elliot Currie, David Onek, and Richard Wiebush, "Graduated Sanctions for Serious, Violent, and Chronic Juvenile Offenders," in Howell et al., note 68, p. 164.

80. Krisberg et al., note 79, p. 165.

81. Bilchik, note 62.

Chapter 4

Illegal Drug Use and Delinquency

Patterns of Adolescent Drug Use

"Everybody must get stoned."

—Bob Dylan

"Just say no."

—Nancy Reagan

American culture, it could be argued, is very pro-drug. Indeed, the large Baby Boom cohort is notorious for its liberal attitudes toward drug use, and large percentages of Americans have experimented with a variety of illicit drugs. Because of these attitudes and behaviors, does the United States deserve to have a drug problem and to be embroiled in a drug war? In other words, is America reaping what it has sown regarding drugs?

Do you believe the arguments of people who suggest that legal drugs, such as caffeine, nicotine, and alcohol, are as toxic as illicit drugs? Do psychoactive and addictive properties render all drugs the same? Are licit and illicit drugs qualitatively different or are their differences mere social constructions?

The United States is a drug-oriented society. From birth until death, drugs play a varied and important role in most people's lives. Drugs are used to block the physical pain of childbirth, to keep premature babies alive, to help gain or lose weight, to help people wake in the morning and sleep at night, to reduce anxiety, stress, and depression, and to clear up faces marked by acne. In addition, drugs prevent illnesses and overcome diseases, keep cancers from spreading, and comfort people when they are dying. Air Force fighter pilots used amphetamines in the war against terrorists in Afghanistan to stay alert during long combat missions. Drugs are used to control the hyperactive behavior of students, primarily boys, in school, and drugs are the preferred method of execution in those states that use the death penalty.

Most Americans use some sort of drug on an almost daily basis—caffeine, nicotine, alcohol, and aspirin are but a few examples. Most drugs are used legally. As an adult, you can legally consume alcohol and smoke tobacco, although where you may smoke is increasingly restricted. Even children can legally drink liquid refreshments loaded with caffeine and buy aspirin over the counter. But these are not the major focus of concern when talking about the drug problem in America. The drug problem, especially for young people, involves marijuana, LSD, Ecstasy, cocaine, crack, and heroin.

Each fall, over 9 million high school students and nearly 5 million middle school students head off to schools, entering buildings where licit and illicit drugs are stashed, sold, and used. According to the National Center on Addiction and Substance Abuse at Columbia University "By the time students reach twelfth grade, 70 percent have smoked cigarettes, 81 percent have drunk alcohol and 47 percent have used marijuana. . . . Each year, 13.2 million students (ages 12 to 17) become new users of tobacco, alcohol and drugs."[1]

The problem of adolescent drug use is complex and cannot be understood apart from the broader nature of drug use in the larger society. In this chapter, we will explore the nature and extent of the drug problem facing youth, explanations of why juveniles use drugs, the relationship between drug use and delinquency, and ways we might best respond to adolescent drug use.

Patterns of Adolescent Drug Use

Prior to the 1960s, adolescent drug use was relatively rare. That changed in the 1960s as the "drug culture" burst upon the scene. Marijuana, LSD, "uppers," and "downers," initially used by college students and those in the hippie counterculture, eventually spread to the high school and junior high level. Whether it was an attraction to the lifestyle of the hippies, a simple interest in "getting high," or a growing alienation from the norms and values of conventional society, more youths began to turn on with an ever-increasing variety of drugs. The drug of choice among youths varies over time, and there is a continuous flow of new drugs and rediscovery of older drugs by each generation. According to the National Institute on Drug Abuse, today's youths are rediscovering a variety of drugs, such as LSD, methamphetamines, heroin, PCP, and cocaine, that had declined in use after their initial popularity.[2]

Measuring Adolescent Drug Use

Control theorists, with their assumption of humans' natural tendency toward deviance, would have a field day with the shocking prevalence of drug use in this country. Are control theorists correct in their assessment of human nature? Are people naturally bad?

As you may recall from Chapter 2, it is very difficult to obtain accurate estimates of delinquency. Consequently, a number of different measures (arrest data, self-report surveys, and victim surveys) are used to arrive at the most reliable estimates possible. Drug use is equally difficult to measure. Because illicit drug use is considered a "victimless crime," one in which there is no obvious "innocent" victim, the *National Crime Victimization Survey* does not inquire into drug violations (or many other similar law violations). Two good estimates of adolescent drug use come from *Uniform Crime Reports* (*UCR*) data on people arrested for drug violations and from self-report surveys on drug use, such as the University of Michigan's *Monitoring the Future* survey of high school students and the U.S. Department of Health and Human Service's *National Household Survey on Drug Abuse*.[3]

The past three decades have witnessed major shifts in juvenile drug use. Among both boys and girls, illicit drug use increased at an alarming rate between 1965 and 1974, with drug use by girls converging toward levels similar to that of boys. However, from the mid-1970s to the mid-1980s, arrests of juveniles for drug violations declined. Then, as crack cocaine use increased during the late 1980s, so did arrests of juveniles for drug offenses. Between 1991 and 2000, while overall arrests of youths rose 3.4 percent, arrests of youths for drug abuse violations increased by 145 percent, and nearly all of this increase occurred in the first half of the decade. Juvenile drug arrests actually declined 3.6 percent between 1996 and 2000.[4]

Uniform Crime Report data are far from perfect (see Chapter 2). First, with respect to drug arrests, they do not distinguish between arrests for specific kinds of drugs; for example, marijuana versus crack. Second, the *UCR* data reflect only those juveniles arrested for drug violations; and, as with most other victimless crimes, most people who use drugs do so out of sight of police and with others who are not likely to report their drug use to authorities. In other words, *UCR* data do not reflect *hidden* drug use. Thus, arrest data grossly underestimate the prevalence and incidence of adolescent drug use.

Each year the Institute for Social Research at the University of Michigan examines patterns of drug use and attitudes about illicit drugs in its survey of eighth-, tenth-, and twelfth-grade students. In 2000 the survey included 45,000 students in 435 secondary schools. A separate annual survey, conducted by the U.S. Department of Health and Human Services, is designed to measure the prevalence of illicit drug use throughout the U.S. civilian, noninstitutionalized population age 12 and older. Both of these national self-report surveys provide three different measures of drug use–**lifetime prevalence** (use of a drug at least once during the respondent's lifetime); **annual prevalence** (use of a drug at least once during the prior year); and **30-day prevalence** (use of a drug at least once during the previous month)– as well as a measure of frequency of use. Both surveys, unlike the *UCR*, provide information on the use of specific drugs.

Current Adolescent Drug Use

In 2000 more than 116,000 juveniles were arrested for drug abuse violations, accounting for nearly 13 percent of all drug arrests. Of all juveniles arrested for drug violations, 17 percent were under age 15. Juveniles were actually less likely to be arrested for liquor law violations in 2000 (91,304 arrests) and much less likely to be arrested for public drunkenness (13,222 arrests).[5] About 4 percent of 12-year-olds reported current illicit drug use, with inhalants being the clear drug of choice. Slightly over 9 percent of 14-year-olds reported they currently used illicit drugs, with marijuana their drug of choice. Nearly 17 percent of youths ages 16 to 17 reported current drug use and, like 14-year-olds, their drug of choice was marijuana.[6]

Substantial numbers of juveniles have recently been initiated into drug use. For example, the rate of new adolescent marijuana users in 1998 (81 per 1000) marked the highest level since the late 1970s. Among the estimated 471,000 persons who used heroin for the first time in the late 1990s, about one-fourth (125,000) were under age 18. Rates of adolescent initiation for other drugs vary greatly by type of drug (cocaine, 13.1 per 1000; crack, 3.6; hallucinogens, 25.9; inhalants, 28.1; alcohol, 216.8; cigarettes, 159.2).[7] Whether these youths become regular users, use only occasionally, or quit after initial use remains to be seen.

Adolescent males are significantly more likely than females to be arrested for drug offenses, with males comprising just over 85 percent of all juvenile drug arrests. However, among juveniles under age 15, only 80 percent of the arrests for drug offenses are males.[8] Although boys are arrested for drug offenses nearly nine times as often as girls, the difference, according to Joan McCord and her colleagues, may simply be the result of boys using drugs more frequently than girls in public places, thereby increasing their likelihood of being arrested.[9]

White youths (including Latinos) comprised slightly over 69 percent of all juvenile drug offense arrests in 1999, while black youths accounted for 29 percent of drug arrests. Referrals of juvenile drug offenders to the juvenile court reflect similar racial patterns: White youths accounted for 68 percent of drug cases; black youths 29 percent; and other youths 3 percent.[10] While white youths comprise the vast majority of drug arrests and court referrals at the national level, official processing of juvenile drug offenders in many large cities suggests serious disparities in the opposite direction. For example, in Illinois, blacks are 59 percent of youths arrested for drug crimes. More importantly, in

Is there any symbolic criminological meaning behind the conviction of First Daughter Jenna Bush for minor in possession of alcohol? Would Jenna Bush have been treated differently if she was not the president's child? If so, would this treatment be harsher or more lenient? How would conflict and consensus theorists answer this question differently?

Cook County (Chicago), blacks make up 95 percent of juvenile drug offenders transferred to criminal court to be tried as adults. Furthermore, 91 percent of youths admitted to Illinois State Prisons from Cook County for drug offenses were black. It should be noted that nearly two-thirds of all juvenile drug arrests in Illinois occurred in Cook County.[11]

Alcohol-related arrests reflect a significantly different pattern and one not consistent with self-report surveys or other studies of adolescent drinking patterns. Whites accounted for 92 percent of all juvenile arrests for liquor law violations and 91 percent of juvenile arrests for public drunkenness.[12] These arrest figures are interesting in that white and black high school seniors report much more similar frequencies of alcohol use. Six percent of white seniors reported heavy monthly alcohol consumption, compared to 5 percent of black seniors. White seniors are more likely, however, to be "binge" drinkers. About 36 percent of white seniors reported consuming five or more drinks in a row on one or more occasions during the two-week period prior to the survey, compared to only 12 percent of black seniors.[13]

Trends in Drug Use

During the last third of the 20th century, adolescents were using illicit drugs at rates never before seen in this or any other country. By 1975, the majority of youths (55 percent) had used an illicit drug by the time they left high school. By 1981, this figure had increased to 66 percent, but then gradually declined to 41 percent in 1992. In 2000 it had again risen to 54 percent. However, the patterns do vary somewhat depending upon the specific illicit drug (see Table 4–1).

Marijuana Use   The percentage of high school seniors reporting that they had ever tried marijuana rose during the last half of the 1970s and reached a peak in 1980, with 60 percent admitting having tried the drug at least once in

Table 4–1   Percentage of High School Seniors Reporting Ever Having Used Specific Drugs, 1975–2000

DRUG	1975	1980	1985	1990	1995	2000
Alcohol	90.4	93.2	92.2	89.5	80.7	80.3
Cigarettes	73.6	71.0	68.8	64.4	64.2	62.5
Marijuana	47.3	60.3	54.2	40.7	41.7	48.8
Tranquilizers*	17.0	15.2	11.9	7.2	7.1	8.9
Cocaine	9.0	15.7	17.3	9.4	6.0	8.6
Hallucinogens	16.3	13.3	10.3	9.4	12.7	6.9
Heroin	2.2	1.1	1.2	1.3	1.6	2.4

*Reflects only drugs used without a doctor's prescription.

Sources: Lloyd Johnston, Patrick O'Malley, and Jerald Bachman, *Monitoring the Future, 1997* (Washington, DC: U.S. Department of Health and Human Services, 1998), Table 3; Lloyd Johnston, Patrick O'Malley, and Jerald Bachman, *Monitoring the Future: National Results on Adolescent Drug Use: Overview of Key Findings 2000* (Washington, DC: U.S. Department of Health and Human Services, 2001), Table 1.

> **The lifetime prevalence of drugs, such as alcohol and marijuana, is drastically higher than the prevalence of drugs such as heroin, cocaine, and methamphetamine. Does this suggest people have a natural sense that these substances vary according to risk? Or does culture determine which drugs are most widely used?**

their lifetime. Since 1980, marijuana use by seniors steadily and significantly declined, dropping to slightly over 40 percent in 1990. Unfortunately, as with adolescent drug use generally, marijuana use rose during the 1990s. By 2000, 49 percent of the seniors reported having used marijuana at some point in their lifetime.

Cocaine Use   The percentage of high school seniors reporting having ever tried cocaine nearly doubled between 1975 and 1985 when 17 percent of seniors reported having tried cocaine. Cocaine use declined over the next 10 years, reaching a low of only 6 percent in 1995. Perhaps more importantly, the percentage of seniors reporting use of cocaine during the prior 12-month period dropped noticeably from 13 percent in 1985 to only 3.1 percent in 1992, but then rose again to 5.5 percent in 1997. The use of crack by seniors during the prior year, a figure never very high, dropped from nearly 4 percent in 1987 to 2.6 percent in 1991. However, beginning in 1993, reported crack use, like cocaine use, reflected a gradual but consistent increase, more than doubling to 4.6 percent by 1999.[14]

Other Drug Use   The use of other drugs by high school seniors followed the broad trends in adolescent drug use, generally declining between the mid-1970s and the late 1980s. While use of certain drugs continued to decline into the mid-1990s, use of other drugs began a steady increase by the early 1990s. Amphetamine and LSD use by seniors peaked in 1997 at 16.5 and 13.6 percent, respectively. Tranquilizer use had been cut by more than half by 1995, declining from 17.0 percent in 1975 to only 7.1 percent. However, its use increased after 1995, rising to 9.3 percent in 1999 before declining slightly to 8.9 percent in 2000. Heroin use by seniors has never been very

None of the eventual outcomes of hard-core drug use (pictured here) are positive. Given this, why are drugs so prevalent in U.S. society? Furthermore, why are many American attitudes toward drugs so liberal?

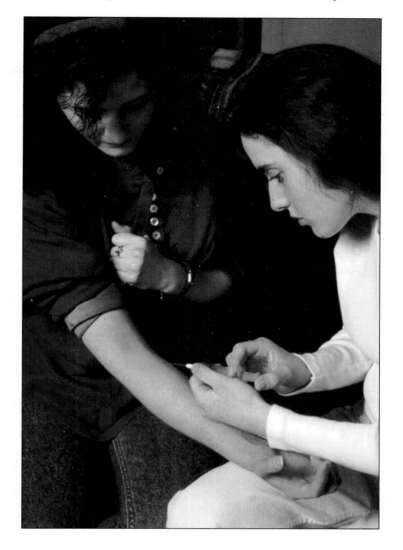

popular. However, the decade of the 1990s shows a very steady increase in its use, rising from less than 1 percent in 1991 to 2.4 percent in 2000, an increase of over 160 percent.[15]

Alcohol and Cigarette Use   While use of illicit drugs has broadly declined, alcohol use by high school seniors remained fairly steady between 1975 and 1985, although a modest decline has been observed in more recent years. Cigarette smoking by seniors also has declined, with reported lifetime prevalence dropping from about 74 percent in 1975 to just over 62 percent in 2000. Only 31 percent of seniors reported having used cigarettes during the prior 30-day period.

While drug use by high school seniors fluctuated during the 1990s, greater percentage increases occurred among eighth-graders. As noted in Table 4–2, between 1991 and 2000 lifetime use of most illicit drugs by eighth-graders nearly doubled. Use of any illicit drug increased from 18.7 percent in 1991 to 26.8 in 2000. Marijuana use increased from 10.2 percent to 20.3, while LSD use increased from 2.7 percent to 3.9. The percentage of eighth-graders ever having used cocaine increased from 2.3 to 4.5 percent, and heroin use rose from 1.2 to 1.9 percent. On a more positive note, lifetime use of alcohol by eighth-graders declined substantially, dropping from 70.1 percent in 1991 to just under 52 percent in 2000. Cigarette use, however, remained fairly steady over the decade. It is important to recognize that adolescent drug use is not confined to the United States. A discussion of drug use by juveniles in a variety of countries is found in Box 4–1.

BOX 4–1   A CROSS-CULTURAL PERSPECTIVE ON DELINQUENCY
Adolescent Drug Use in Other Countries

The use of illicit drugs by adolescents is not unique to the United States; youths around the world experiment with and use a variety of drugs in ways not too dissimilar to their American counterparts. For example, a survey of 21,000 Spanish youths ages 14 to 18 found that the use of cocaine has increased dramatically in recent years. Only 5 percent of 18-year-olds had used cocaine at least once in 1994, compared to 8.8 percent in 1998. There was a threefold increase in cocaine use by 16-year-olds during the same period, with 1.7 percent having used cocaine at least once in 1994, compared to 4.7 percent in 1998.

Over 1,700 tenth-graders in Bogota, Colombia, were surveyed in 1997. Nearly 90 percent reported having used alcohol at least once during their lifetime, and 54 percent reported they started drinking before age 12. Some 77 percent of the youths reported having used tobacco at least once during their lifetime, with 60 percent reporting tobacco use during the 30 days prior to the survey. Eleven percent of the youths reported having used marijuana at least once during their lifetime. Slightly over a third of the students reported having first used marijuana when they were 15 or 16 years old, although about 5 percent indicated they first experimented with marijuana before age 9.

The *1998 National Drug Strategy Household Survey* of nearly 1,600 Australian adolescents ages 14 to 19 reports about 45 percent of the respondents had used marijuana at least once in their lifetime, and 78 percent of that group had used it during the year prior to the survey. The use of marijuana significantly increased with age: 24 percent of 14- to 15-year-olds had tried marijuana at least once, compared to 47 percent of 16- to 17-year-olds and 63 percent of 18- to 19-year-olds. The average age of first use of marijuana was 14.6 years old. While the proportion of adolescent males having ever tried marijuana

Table 4–2   Percentage of Eighth-Graders Reporting Ever Having Used Specific Drugs, 1991–2000

DRUG	1991	1993	1995	1997	1999	2000
Any illicit drug	18.7	22.5	28.5	29.4	28.3	26.8
Marijuana	10.2	12.6	19.9	22.6	22.0	20.3
LSD	2.7	3.5	4.4	4.7	4.1	3.9
Cocaine	2.3	2.9	4.2	4.4	4.7	4.5
Heroin	1.2	1.4	2.3	2.1	2.3	1.9
Alcohol	70.1	67.1	54.5	53.8	52.1	51.7
Cigarettes	44.0	45.3	46.4	47.3	44.1	40.5

Source: Lloyd Johnston, Patrick O'Malley, and Jerald Bachman, *Monitoring the Future: National Results on Adolescent Drug Use: Overview of Key Findings 2000* (Washington, DC: U.S. Department of Health and Human Services, 2001), Table 1.

changed little between 1995 and 1998, the proportion of females reporting having ever used marijuana nearly doubled during the same period, increasing from 24.4 percent in 1995 to 45.2 percent in 1998. While many Australian youths who had tried marijuana stopped using the drug, about 21 percent of those who continued to smoke marijuana reported using it on a weekly basis and 7 percent smoke it daily.

Although both licit and illicit drug use by youths in Taiwan is substantially lower than among American youths, the Taiwanese government is concerned about its apparent increase in use and related social and health problems. A survey of approximately 2,200 13- to 18-year-olds was conducted in 1997 in a rural county in Taiwan. Seven percent of the youths reported tobacco use, 1.3 percent reported chewing betel gum, nearly 2 percent currently drank alcohol, and 0.6 percent reported illicit drug use. Males ages 13 to 15 were much more likely than females to use tobacco (8.8 percent compared to 3.2 percent), but only slightly more likely to use alcohol (3.5 percent compared to 2.2 percent) or illicit drugs (0.7 percent compared to 0.4 percent).

Smoking is considered to be the greatest substance abuse problem among adolescents in China. Almost all of the 320 million smokers in China began smoking as teenagers, with the average age of onset being before age 15. According to the *1996 National Prevalence Survey of Smoking Pattern*, most youths initially experimented with smoking out of curiosity. Chinese youths also obtain a degree of status in smoking foreign-brand cigarettes, especially Marlboro. The Chinese government is attempting to counter the "cool" image of the teenage smoker by advertising campaigns designed to portray adolescent smokers as social misfits.

Sources: Xavier Bosch, "Survey Shows Cocaine Use by Spanish Adolescents on the Rise," *The Lancet* 355:2230 (2000); Kow-Tong Chen, Chien-Jen Chen, Anne Fagot-Campagna, and K.M.V. Narayan, "Tobacco, Betel Quid, Alcohol, and Illicit Drug Use Among 13- to 35-Year-Olds in I-Lan, Rural Taiwan: Prevalence and Risk Factors," *American Journal of Public Health* 91:1130–1134 (2001); Tsung Cheng, "Teenage Smoking in China," *Journal of Adolescence* 22:607–620 (1999); Miguel Pérez and Helda Pinon-Pérez, "Alcohol, Tobacco, and Other Psychoactive Drug Use Among High School Students in Bogota, Colombia," *Journal of School Health* 70:377–380 (2000); Amanda Reid, Michael Lynskey, and Jan Copeland, "Cannabis Use Among Australian Adolescents: Findings of the 1998 National Drug Strategy Household Survey," *Australian and New Zealand Journal of Public Health* 24:596–602 (2000).

One word of caution is needed in considering findings from these surveys. The school survey (including eighth-, tenth- and twelfth-graders) does not provide information on youths who are absent from school (estimated to be about 18 percent of the enrolled students) or youths who have dropped out of high school (estimated to be about 15 percent for this survey). These two groups of students are likely to be among the most vulnerable to serious drug use.[16] The National Household Survey of 12- to 17-year-olds also underestimates serious drug use by adolescents. It does not include institutionalized youths (those incarcerated in juvenile facilities), transients (including the growing number of homeless children), and people unable to be identified through normal census identification procedures.

Changes in Adolescent Attitudes Toward Drugs

Many youths today perceive illicit drugs to be relatively dangerous or at least risky. Columbia University's national survey of 12- to 17-year-olds in 1997 provides some interesting findings (see Table 4–3). Approximately half of the youths perceived smoking one or more cigarettes per day, smoking marijuana once or twice a week, and using cocaine once a month as a great risk. About two-thirds of the youths thought that having four or five drinks nearly every day was very risky, and just over 80 percent of the youths perceived that using cocaine once or twice a day was a great risk. Perceptions of risk are not necessarily shared between parents and children. For example, a 1998 study by the Partnership for a Drug Free America reported that 33 percent of the parents surveyed thought that their children viewed marijuana as harmful, although only 18 percent of the 13- to 18-year-olds felt that smoking marijuana was risky.[17]

Of greater concern, perhaps, are the perceptions held by eighth-graders of the harmfulness of certain drugs. According to the University of Michigan study, only 48 percent of eighth-graders believed that trying crack once or twice would put them at "great risk," while 43 percent thought that use of cocaine powder once or twice was as risky. One-third of eighth-graders thought

---

Table 4–3   Perceived Risk in Drug Use by Youths Aged 12 to 17

DRUG USE	PERCEPTION OF GREAT RISK (PERCENT)
Smoke 1 or more cigarette packs per day	54.5
Smoke marijuana once a month	29.0
Smoke marijuana once or twice a week	52.6
Use cocaine once a month	49.8
Use cocaine once or twice a week	80.4
Have 4 or 5 drinks of alcohol nearly every day	65.9
Have 5 or more drinks once or twice a week	42.2

Source: U.S. Department of Health and Human Services, *Summary of Findings from the 1999 National Household Survey on Drug Abuse* (Washington, DC: U.S. Department of Health and Human Services, 2000), Table 4.6.

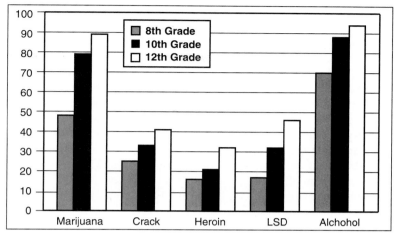

Figure 4–1
Percent of Students Reporting Drugs "Fairly Easy to Get"

Source: Lloyd Johnston, Patrick O'Malley, and Jerald Bachman, *Monitoring the Future: National Results on Adolescent Drug Use: Overview of Key Findings 2000* (Washington, DC: U.S. Department of Health and Human Services, 2001), Table 8.

that using LSD once or twice produced a great risk of harm, while less than 30 percent believed that using marijuana only once or twice was a serious risk.[18]

Although adolescents perceive drug use as carrying risks, they are also quick to report that most drugs are "fairly or very easy" to get (see Figure 4–1). Understandably, high school seniors are more likely than tenth-graders and eighth-graders to report drugs as easy to obtain. For example, while nearly 95 percent of the seniors said alcohol was "fairly easy to get," 88 percent of tenth-graders and only 71 percent of the eighth-graders so indicated. About twice as many seniors as eighth-graders report marijuana, heroin, and crack easy to obtain and seniors are three times more likely to say LSD is fairly easy to get.

Causes of Adolescent Drug Use

Later in the book we discuss a variety of theories of juvenile delinquency, ranging from early theories focusing on supernatural forces and classical and neoclassical theories emphasizing free will and choice to more deterministic theories focusing on biological, psychological, and sociological factors. At this point, we would like to briefly explore five approaches from the sociological perspective as they apply to possible causes of adolescent drug use.

Double Failure by the Individual

In strain theory (see Chapter 7), Robert Merton argued that in a competitive and materialistic society in which success through legitimate avenues is

The retreatist drug addict or alcoholic is a social type described by Merton and Cloward and Ohlin. Are retreatists living evidence that certain people simply lack the capacity to participate in society? Are retreatists useful for other members of society since they provide a point of comparison to measure life success?

attainable by relatively few individuals, those unable to achieve success may choose deviant modes of adaptation to deal with their failure.[19] An individual who chooses *retreatism* as an adaptation rejects both the cultural goal of success and the approved means to achieve success. Merton suggests that moral scruples also prevent the individual from choosing criminal means to achieve success as well. Richard Cloward and Lloyd Ohlin believe that the avoidance of illegitimate means is due not to the constraint of the person's scruples but, rather, to the lack of opportunity to utilize such means in the pursuit of success.[20] Regardless of who is right, drug use is seen as deriving from failing to "make it" in conventional society as well as failing to achieve success in the criminal world. The person has failed twice and, consequently, retreats into a world of drugs.

Learning to Use Drugs

Edwin Sutherland was among the first to suggest that delinquent behavior is learned (see Chapter 7). The idea that a youth learns delinquent or criminal behavior through an interactive process has been extended by integrating Sutherland's principles of differential association with theories of operant conditioning drawn from the field of psychology. *Social learning theory* argues that a person's behavior is the result of group-based reinforced learning situations. According to Erich Goode, adolescents learn to define behaviors as good or bad through their intimate interactions with other youths in certain groups. Different groups tend to express different norms regarding illicit drugs and differentially reward or punish the use or distribution of drugs by members of the group.[21]

Adolescent drug use, then, is positively reinforced by exposure to drug-using role models, approval of drug use by peers, and the perceived positive or pleasurable effects of the drug itself. To the extent that the individual's drug use is also not negatively reinforced either by bad effects of the drug or by statements or actions by parents, peers, or authorities, drug use will persist.

Peer pressure, particularly as it applies to adolescent drug use, denotes a negative connotation. This does not have to be the case, however. Can positive, strong-willed teens (e.g., scholars, athletes, students with vocational skills, or cheerleaders) also be role models for their peers and provide healthy pressure? Did such persons exist at your school?

Weakening of Social Controls

According to social control theory (discussed in Chapter 7), delinquency is the result of an absence or weakening of the social control mechanisms that ensure conformity. Without established social controls, people will pursue their self-interests, including pleasure. A strong social bond to conventional social institutions reduces the likelihood of deviation from normative expectations, while weakening of the bond releases the individual from the constraints of the norms.[22]

To the extent that a youth is strongly *attached* to conventional others (parents, peers, or teachers), is strongly *committed* to conventional institutions, is heavily *involved* in conventional activities, and strongly *believes* in conventional norms, he or she is unlikely to violate society's laws and use drugs. Conversely, if any of these elements of the social bond are weakened, the juvenile becomes more likely to deviate, and drug use becomes more probable.

Socialization into Drug Use by the Subculture

Another theory on adolescent drug use is that youths begin to use drugs and continue to do so because of their involvement in social groups in which drug use is encouraged. Drug subcultures vary. For many adolescents, membership in one drug subculture may bring involvement in other drug subcultures, for example, alcohol-using, marijuana-using, cocaine-using, heroin-using, or multiple drug-using subcultures.

As an adolescent's involvement in a drug-using subculture deepens, he or she becomes increasingly socialized into the values and norms of the group, and drug-using behavior is likely to ensue. Howard Becker has described the process of becoming a marijuana user through interaction with a marijuana-using subculture. For an individual to become a marijuana user, three events must occur. First, one must learn the proper technique for smoking marijuana to produce the desired effects. Second, one must learn to perceive the effects and connect them with marijuana. And third, one must define the effects of marijuana smoking as pleasurable. The smoker "has learned, in short, to answer 'Yes' to the question: 'Is it fun?' "[23]

But learning to smoke marijuana is not enough to become a regular user. One must also establish a reliable means of supply, keep the drug use secret from others who may disapprove, and neutralize moral objections to marijuana use held by conventional society. Becker suggests that fulfilling these conditions requires involvement in a group that regularly uses marijuana.

Goode believes that the socialization process within a drug subculture involves much convincing of new users that they have nothing to fear from the drug.[24] He has identified five elements critical to the person's decision to use marijuana:

1. The perception of danger or lack of danger.
2. The perception of any benefit from use of the drug.
3. The attitude toward users of marijuana.
4. The closeness to those advocating use of marijuana.
5. The closeness to those who are trying to get them to smoke marijuana.

Goode also found that heavy users of marijuana tended to be more involved with friends who also used marijuana, as well as other drugs, and who were generally more involved in the drug subculture. Bruce Johnson arrived at the same conclusion: Youths with marijuana-using friends also tended to use marijuana, to buy and sell it, and to use other drugs.[25]

Denise Kandel argues that the process of socialization into drug use is selective.[26] Among early adolescents, drug and alcohol use tends to be more situational or even accidental. The specific activities of the immediate peer group greatly influence the behavior of the individual: If the youth has close peers who drink, he or she will be more likely to drink; if the youth has close peers who are drug users, he or she will be more inclined to try drugs; and if he or she hangs out with peers who disapprove of alcohol and drug use, he or she will not be inclined to use either. In later adolescence, youths who have begun to use drugs or alcohol will gradually break away from non-drug-using peers and move toward peers who do use them.

Family Conflict and Poor Parenting

Delinquency frequently occurs as a result of dysfunctional dynamics within the home and most often in homes characterized by poverty, disruption, and conflict. It should be no surprise that the same conditions might produce drug use among children:

> Rare in the ghetto today are neighbors whose lives demonstrate that education is meaningful, that steady employment is a viable alternative to welfare and illegal pursuits, and that a stable family is an aspect of normalcy. . . . More and more families, stressed and depleted, are surrounded by others in similar straits. This concentration of the persistently poor, unskilled, alienated, unemployed, and unmarried is central to the development of children who grow up in such a setting.[27]

These children often turn to drugs. Parental failures, fighting, extreme or inconsistent discipline of children, lack of communication, physical and sexual abuse, emotional distance, and disrupted marriages all take their toll on children. Drug use may help ease the pain of criticism and serve as an escape from the fears of the next assault by an abusive parent.

Some studies have found that adolescent drug use is associated with strict or inconsistent parental discipline. Anthony Jurich and his colleagues report that adolescent drug abusers (those who used drugs nearly on a daily basis) are more likely to have parents with *laissez faire* or authoritarian patterns of discipline rather than democratic ones or to have parents who were inconsistent in their disciplinary patterns.[28] In addition, a number of studies report that parental conflict in child-rearing philosophy and inconsistent or restrictive discipline were associated with both marijuana and alcohol use among children.[29]

Emotional distance, perceived lack of love, or outright conflict with parents has also been associated with adolescent drug use. Rafaela Robles and his associates found that among Puerto Rican high school students, those who felt their parents were disgusted with them and those who were not close to their fathers were more likely to be drug users.[30] Other studies have found adolescent drug use was greater among children who perceived lower levels of parental love or negative parental attitudes expressed toward them.[31] Rick Kosterman and his colleagues found that the likelihood of adolescent initiation into marijuana and alcohol use was reduced by proactive family management practices (for example, monitoring, application of rules and discipline, and reward practices), while bonding to mother appeared to have little or no effect.[32]

Broken homes, divorce, separation, and abandonment by the father have also been correlated with adolescent drug use.[33] (See Chapter 10 for more extensive discussion of this relationship.) Research also suggests that lack of supervision by parents when children come home from school is related to adolescent drug use. For example, Peter Mulhall and his associates

Significant research findings link child abuse victimization and subsequent substance abuse. Is the drug abuse of abused children an effort to "escape" from their adverse social reality? Why or why not?

report that latchkey children (middle school youth who were home alone after school two or more days per week) were significantly more likely to have used alcohol during the prior month, to consume more alcohol, and to drink to intoxication than were nonlatchkey children. Furthermore, latchkey youth were more likely to have used marijuana and to have smoked cigarettes during the prior month.[34]

The relationship between child abuse (physical, sexual, or emotional) and the child's subsequent drug use has also been explored in recent studies. Ann Burgess and her colleagues compared a group of youngsters who had been sexually abused as children with a control group of nonabused youths. They found a strong connection between the childhood experience of sexual abuse and later drug use.[35] And a study of 145 youths confined in a detention center in a southeastern state found that both male and female youths who had been sexually abused were much more likely to be current drug users.[36]

Finally, parental use of drugs and alcohol has been found to have a direct effect on the child's likelihood of using drugs. One study found that 78 percent of parents who used marijuana also had children who were drug users,[37] while other studies have confirmed that children tend to imitate their parent's drinking habits. Parents who drank were likely to have children who also drank, while parents who abstained were likely to have abstaining children.[38] Denise Kandel and her colleagues examined parental influences on marijuana use, comparing the Baby Boom generation and their children. They found children of parents who had ever used marijuana were about three times as likely to have ever used marijuana as the children of parents who had never used the drug. The influence was similar for mothers and fathers and sons and daughters. In addition, parents who perceived little risk associated with marijuana use had children with similar beliefs, and adolescent attitudes had the strongest association with adolescent marijuana use of any of the adolescent characteristics examined in the study.[39]

Drug Use and Delinquency

Does illegal drug use cause other acts of delinquency? Conversely, does delinquency lead to drug use? What exactly is the relationship between adolescent drug use and delinquent behavior? These questions have puzzled criminologists for some time.

Drugs and Delinquency

While many studies have led criminologists and policy makers at the federal, state, and local level to believe there is a causal link between drug use and delinquency,[40] the exact nature of the relationship has not been established. Research by Scott Menard and his colleagues explored the relationship between drugs and crime from adolescence into adulthood with data from the National Youth Survey collected between 1976 and 1992. They reported that "the drug-crime relationship is different for different ages and for different stages of involvement in crime and drug use" and that "initiation of substance use apparently is preceded by initiation of crime for most individuals."[41] However, they note that in later stages of involvement the relationship becomes reciprocal. That is, adolescent involvement in serious illicit drug use appears to "contribute to continuity in serious crime, and serious crime contributes to continuity in serious illicit drug use."[42]

A number of studies confirm an association between alcohol and drug use and general patterns of delinquency, but again with no causal relationship established.[43] That is, although adolescents were found to use drugs and alcohol extensively, they often did so on a regular basis rather than using drugs only when engaging in delinquency. David Altschuler and Paul Brounstein found that although drug use and drug trafficking were correlated with other delinquent activities, "still, for every type of crime reported in the past year, only a minority of offenders reported ever using drugs while committing the crime. . . . Most youths appear to commit crime for reasons completely independent of drugs."[44] While most serious delinquents were found to be regular users of alcohol and drugs (and often more serious drugs), "the vast majority of their instances of drug and alcohol use occurred without crimes, and most crimes occurred without prior substance abuse."[45]

A slightly different conclusion has been reached by Colleen McLaughlin and her colleagues based on their study of 25 male juveniles committed to Virginia juvenile correctional facilities for murder or voluntary manslaughter between 1992 and 1996.[46] Over half of the murderers were known drug dealers, compared to less than 10 percent of all juveniles incarcerated in the state. In addition, 28 percent of the murder incidents were regarded as drug related. Perhaps more important, they found that none of the drug-related murders involved offenders who did not have some history of illicit drug use. Drug use by homicide victims was also a significant contributor to murder incidents. Victims who had recently used drugs were more likely to be killed in a drug-related incident than victims who did not use drugs.

Drugs, Delinquent Friends, and Delinquency

Some research suggests that associating with peers who are delinquent, who use drugs, or both is strongly related to both delinquency and drug use.[47] Criminologists who have examined self-report responses from a national sample of 1,725 youths ages 11 to 17 have concluded that there was a *causal* relationship between prior delinquency and involvement in delinquent peer groups and subsequent drug use. In other words, having strong bonds to delinquent peers increases the risk of both delinquency and drug use for all youths.

In addition, as youths are more involved in delinquency and drug use, they are significantly more likely to fall into long-term life trajectories involving a variety of precocious transitions. Marvin Krohn, Alan Lizotte, and Cynthia Perez report that alcohol and drug use during early adolescence increases the risk of becoming pregnant or impregnating someone, dropping

Do you think this juvenile drug dealer considers the damage that drugs are causing his neighborhood? Are drug offenses "victimless crimes?"

out of school, becoming a teenage parent, and living independently from parents. These consequences, in turn, increase the likelihood of drug and alcohol use as the youths become young adults. Krohn and his colleagues note that these youths are then greatly disadvantaged in their ability to form stable adult lives and more likely to turn to deviant lifestyles.[48]

Responding to Adolescent Drug Use

Former drug czar William Bennett was once quoted as saying that the beheading of drug dealers would be an effective anti-drug policy. Do you agree? Is this simply a conservative platitude or is there merit to extreme policies? Would the criminal justice system have greater general deterrent value if it employed more draconian techniques?

A point that is often lost in the incessant pro-drug/anti-drug dialogue is the message that would be sent by legalizing drugs. Would such a policy be an admission of defeat? Think of it this way: Murder, rape, and robbery are crimes that (like drugs) persist despite the efforts of the criminal justice system. Should we simply legalize such behaviors to avoid incarcerating our citizens? What is the moral worth of our current drug policy?

In this section we will examine four ways of responding to adolescent drug use: taking a punitive, or law enforcement, approach; utilizing programs that focus on education, prevention, and treatment; the decriminalization of certain drugs; and changing the lives and environments of adolescents.

Punitive, or Law Enforcement, Response

The punitive response to adolescent drug use may be best exemplified by the policies recommended a little over a decade ago in the Anti-Drug Abuse Act of 1988. In the introduction to the White House report describing President Bush's 1989 national drug strategy, William Bennett, then director of the Office of National Drug Control Policy, wrote:

> Anyone who sells drugs—and (to a great if poorly understood extent) anyone who uses them—is involved in an international criminal enterprise that is killing thousands of Americans each year. For the worst and most brutal drug gangsters, the death penalty is an appropriate sentence of honest justice. And for the multitude of crimes associated with trafficking and use, many of the other tough and coherently punitive anti-drug measures proposed in recent years have their place and should be employed.[49]

Bennett is quoted elsewhere as saying that *beheadings* might be the best solution for dealing with those who sell drugs to children: "Legally, it's difficult . . . But . . . [beheading] somebody selling drugs to a kid? Morally, I don't have any problem with that at all."[50]

While the Anti-Drug Abuse Act includes recommendations for education and prevention programs, the primary focus was on control of both drug dealers and users. Optimistically, the Act declares that it would be the policy of the United States government to "create a drug-free America" by 1995—a goal obviously not achieved. Legislation and guidelines were established to provide greater support for federal, state, and local law enforcement agencies and to allocate funds for the expansion of the nation's prison system.

The Anti-Drug Abuse Act had only modest success in reducing adolescent drug use as evidenced by renewed drug use in the late 1990s (see earlier discussion in this chapter). Each year, in an attempt to emphasize and strengthen federal efforts in attacking the problem of illicit drugs in the lives of juveniles, the White House Office of National Drug Control Policy produces a *National Drug Control Strategy*.[51] The 2001 plan includes more than 20 specific initiatives, ranging from early childhood substance-abuse prevention programs and safe and drug-free schools and sports initiatives to faith initiatives and specific programs aimed at prevention of use of tobacco and alcohol by youths. One of the strategies is the National Youth Anti-Drug Media Campaign, described in Box 4–2.

BOX 4–2   DELINQUENCY PREVENTION
National Youth Anti-Drug Media Campaign

The White House Office of National Drug Control Policy (ONDCP) has established a five-year campaign designed to harness the media to educate America's youth to reject illegal drugs. Tapping into advertising, television programming, movies, music, the Internet, and print media, the campaign focuses on primary prevention. The initial media campaign began in 1999 with four- to six-week advertising programs providing various specific anti-drug messages often supplemented with local coalitions and other partners amplifying these messages by adding their own messages and conducting related local events and activities.

In 2000 the Office of National Drug Control Policy launched a new "brand" for youth audiences. Advertisers and marketers have long used "branding" to create a consistent identity for a product or company and, through repeated exposure, keep the image top of mind for the consumer. The ONDCP conducted research to find out if young people would embrace the idea of an "antidrug"–something important enough in their lives to stand between them and drugs. Not only did teens and tweens find ownership and empowerment in the idea of an "antidrug" brand that reflected their own values and passions (i.e., Soccer, My Anti-Drug; Dreams, My Anti-Drug), they suggested that the brand could serve as an invitation to other youths to reflect on what their anti-drugs might be. ONDCP partnered with youth organizations nationwide in launching "my anti-drug." Through community outreach efforts, the YMCA, Future Farmers of America, Girl Scouts, and Boys and Girls Clubs were among numerous groups working with youths within their own organizations to participate.

Media initiatives also targeted multicultural audiences. For example, within the American Indian community, print advertising was developed that not only reflects the values that exist within Native culture, but also lays the groundwork for extending the campaign's prevention message within local community-based programs. During much of 2001, media campaign advertising reached 95 percent of America's youth 7.5 times a week and communicated messages in eight languages to youths and adults of various ethnic groups.

Since its inception, the media campaign's messages have become ubiquitous in the lives of America's youth and their parents. From network television advertisements to school-based educational materials, from murals to Internet websites, and from local soccer competitions to national youth organizations, the campaign's messages reach Americans wherever they are–work, play, school, worship, and home.

Source: The White House, *The National Drug Control Strategy, 2001* (Washington, DC: Office of National Drug Control Policy, 2001).

Efforts to control the drug problem have also involved a call for more extensive drug testing. But the issue of drug testing is controversial. Who should be tested? How accurate are the tests? Are tests for all illicit drugs equally accurate? Are such tests in violation of constitutional rights ensuring protection against self-incrimination and the right to privacy?

The media seizes upon various drug problems, such as the use of performance-enhancing drugs by high school athletes. At the same time, drug searches in schools teeter on Fourth and Fifth Amendment violations. Is it wrong for authorities to bring drug-detecting dogs into schools to walk the hallways? Do truly innocent people have anything to fear?

Many school districts are beginning to require drug tests of high school athletes, and a New Jersey school district recently mandated that all high school students submit to drug tests. Failure to submit to the tests may result in suspension from school.[52] The Supreme Court, in *Vernonia School District 47J v. Acton*[53] held that it was constitutional for the school district in a small Oregon community to require that all students participating in interscholastic athletics sign a form consenting to a urinalysis drug test at the beginning of the season for their sport. In addition, once each week of the season the names of the athletes are placed in a "pool" from which a student, with the supervision of two adults, blindly draws the names of 10 percent of the athletes for random testing. The Supreme Court said that the "invasion of privacy was not significant" and that student privacy rights implied by the Fourth Amendment were outweighed by the problem of drug use in the school, especially among athletes who are often looked at as "role models" by younger students or who may face injury while playing his or her sport.

The Court's position raises questions. For example, should students participating in other extracurricular activities, such as debate, marching band, or school government also be tested? Should teachers and school administrators be required to take similar drug tests? If there is a legitimate concern about possible injury due to the student's activity, then should students enrolled in certain science or vocational courses where potential danger exists with chemicals and hazardous machinery be tested? And because studies have found that first drug use often occurs prior to entering high school, should drug testing begin in middle school or even earlier? (See Chapter 11 for additional discussion on drug use in schools.)

Emile Durkheim, one of the patriarchs of sociology, viewed punishment as highly moral. How would Durkheim assess acquiescence in the drug war? Does society have an obligation to combat drug use and vice generally?

A rather different law enforcement approach is found in the efforts of the Vallejo Community Consortium in Vallejo, California, working with the Fighting Back Partnership of Vallejo to pass the 1999 Teen Party Ordinance. This ordinance authorizes the police department to recoup any costs associated with calls for service involving teenage parties where alcohol and illegal substances are used. Parents of teens are asked to repay the costs of the service calls for each reported incident. Copies of the ordinance and a pledge are mailed to the parents of all middle and high school students in the district. Parents are asked to sign the pledge, signifying that they will make their home a safe place for teens.[54]

Education, Prevention, and Treatment

In 1884 New York state passed legislation to make anti-alcohol teaching compulsory in the public schools.[55] Forty years later, Richmond Hobson, a leading prohibitionist, warned of "demonic drug pushers" seducing young children into drug addiction by such practices as hiding heroin in snow cones. Hobson eventually founded a number of national organizations for educating the public about the evils of drugs. Lectures and brochures were prepared and provided to hundreds of school systems for use during a week set aside in February as "Narcotics Week."[56] Henry Anslinger, director of the Federal Bureau of Narcotics, published a widely read article in 1937 entitled *Marijuana: Assassin of Youth*, in which he described murders, debauchery, and the seduction of innocent girls as a consequence of marijuana smoking. And in 1936 the movie *Reefer Madness*, depicting many of the same marijuana-induced behaviors, was produced under the Bureau's guidance. These efforts were attempts at "educating" the public, especially the young, about the dangers of drug use. However, in retrospect, they appear to have been little more than scare tactics, misinforming rather than informing.

Education and Prevention in School   Today, alongside law enforcement strategies, rational and informed education about the nature and effects of drugs is finding wide acceptance. Media campaigns—including cartoon characters, popular songs, and costumed actors who appear as talking brain cells—are aimed at young children between the ages of 9 and 12 in an attempt to delay their first substance abuse.[57] Parent groups and "Just Say No" clubs have been formed in many schools.

Like the anti-alcohol provision of the 1884 New York law, anti-drug education has become a standard part of school curricula. Many schools offer "refusal-skill training" or "resistance training" to students through such programs as **Drug Abuse Resistance Education (D.A.R.E.)**, begun in 1983. The D.A.R.E. program is aimed at children in kindergarten through twelfth grade and is designed to equip students with appropriate skills to resist substance abuse and gangs. The primary objectives of D.A.R.E include

- Acquiring the knowledge and skills to recognize and resist peer pressure to experiment with tobacco, alcohol, and other drugs.
- Enhancing self-esteem.
- Learning assertiveness techniques.
- Learning about positive alternatives to substance use.
- Learning anger management and conflict resolution skills.
- Developing risk assessment and decision-making skills.
- Reducing violence.
- Building interpersonal and communication skills.
- Resisting gang involvement.[58]

School-based prevention programs often combine teaching about the negative consequences of drug use with clearly stated policies on use, possession, and distribution of drugs. Anne Arundel County schools in Maryland claim to have reduced the number of school drug offenses by more than 80 percent since 1980 after implementing their anti-drug program. They present a simple and straightforward policy:

Any student caught selling or distributing drugs is immediately expelled. When a student is caught using or possessing drugs, the school notifies the police, calls his parents, and suspends him for one to five school days. In order to return to school, the student must participate in counseling and agree to participate in the district's after-school drug program. Students caught using or possessing drugs a second time are expelled.[59]

However, such programs have been criticized for reducing the school drug problem by simply adding to the already high dropout problem. In addition, a recent six-year evaluation of D.A.R.E. found it to have no long-term effects in reducing drug use.[60] Still further studies found that the "simplistic message of the $226 million program has little effect on keeping kids from abusing drugs" and that "kids who go through the program in elementary school are just as likely to use drugs later as kids who don't."[61] D.A.R.E. officials admitted the program needed to be dramatically revised. With nearly $14 million in support from the Robert Wood Johnson Foundation, the revised program was launched in six cities in the fall of 2001. Major changes include a reduction in the use of local police, lectures to students, and involving youths in more active ways.

Drug Treatment Programs   There are well over 5,000 drug treatment programs in the United States. These programs fall into one of five broad categories:

1. *Detoxification programs,* which are usually conducted on an inpatient basis and are designed to end the user's addiction to drugs.
2. *Chemical dependency units,* which are generally inpatient programs, lasting three to four weeks.
3. *Outpatient clinics,* which offer counseling and support.
4. *Methadone maintenance programs,* in which heroin addicts are treated by means of methadone, a prescribed drug that "blocks" the craving for heroin.
5. *Residential therapeutic communities,* at which drug users may spend up to 18 months in a highly structured program.

However, many programs are understaffed and underfunded and cannot meet the needs of increasing numbers of applicants. In addition, many programs treat only one type of drug problem. For example, in the late 1990s most existing programs were initially created to deal with heroin addicts, but today cocaine users outnumber heroin users by more than six to one.[62]

In providing effective drug or alcohol treatment for juveniles, programs face an additional problem that stems from the issues of consent and parental notification.[63] Most states allow treatment for drug abuse of youths without parental consent, although some states restrict services to treatment for either drug or alcohol abuse, but not both. Furthermore, a few states require that a youth's parents be notified before services are provided. Such requirements can interfere with a youth's perception of the acceptability of treatment: He or she may simply find it easier to avoid seeking care.

In spite of the criticisms of drug treatment programs, Stanley Kusnetz has identified several programs that appear to be working well for adolescents.[64] Bridgeback is an outpatient program in Los Angeles. Youths come to Bridgeback as self-referrals or as referrals from schools, community agencies, or the juvenile court (about 80 percent of all referrals). The guiding philosophy of Bridgeback is that a person learns from those with whom he or she identifies. Providing positive role models, the program also tries to help the adolescent "search for and examine basic beliefs, attitudes, and habits."[65]

On a typical day, the Woodbridge Action for Youth (WAY) program, in Woodbridge, New Jersey, treats about 15 youths between the ages of 14 and 18. Unlike the case in many other programs, abstinence from drug use is not required for participation in treatment. Instead, WAY works toward abstinence by focusing on drug-related problems that interfere with the family, school, social relationships, and the law. Family participation is required, with six months of family counseling following six to nine months of individual counseling with the youth.

The Bridge is a residential therapeutic center in Philadelphia. Its primary goal is to create an atmosphere in which clients will feel comfortable, develop peer relationships for support, take responsibility for themselves, and learn problem solving related to their personal lives. While nearly 50 percent of clients are referred by the juvenile court, self-referrals, family and school referrals, and referrals by other community agencies are common. Clients receive a minimum of 10 hours of therapy a week, with emphasis on developing awareness and life skills. Counseling is combined with an educational program that offers nearly 30 hours of classroom experience a week, as well as vocational guidance and job placement. The staff at the Bridge believe that adolescent drug users, with proper motivation and development of skills, can develop an appreciation of their personal worth, learn how to make decisions, set goals and accept consequences, and learn how to cope, behave responsibly in difficult situations, communicate more effectively with their families, and develop honest, positive, and supportive friends."[66]

Decriminalization

Many critics of current drug control strategies argue that punitive measures will fail because profits from the sale of illegal drugs are too great and the pleasurable reinforcements of using drugs are too strong. Economist Lester Thurow has stated, "If our goal is to deprive criminals of large profits from selling drugs, economic theory and history teach us that legalization is the only answer."[67] Others have called for a national 10-year experiment in which marijuana, heroin, and cocaine would be decriminalized. If the experiment fails, the country could return to present policies that are viewed as being relatively ineffective.[68]

Essentially, **decriminalization** of certain drugs involves relaxing enforcement of existing laws. For example, decriminalizing marijuana might mean that police would not make arrests for simple possession of small amounts of the drug. Possession of marijuana still technically would be illegal; the law would just not be enforced. **Legalization**, on the other hand, involves eliminating many of the laws currently prohibiting the distribution and possession of drugs, but not necessarily eliminating all regulation. Alcohol is legal, but regulated in terms of who may sell it, where it may be sold, and how old a person must be to buy it.

A cottage industry of research has accused U.S. drug policy as being racist because of the disproportionate impact on blacks and Latinos. How would a drug policy of radical nonintervention work? What would be the racial and ethnic implications of a reversal of current drug policy? Which groups would "turning a blind eye" to drugs most damage?

Advocates of decriminalization/legalization suggest that an immediate consequence of the reform would be the production of less-expensive drugs, produced and sold under government regulations and control and in accordance with standardized quality control. In other words, decriminalized drugs would contain no surprise additives or contaminants and their lower cost would reduce potential black market profits, and thus the economic attractions of importing and dealing would be eliminated. In addition, many advocates argue that many drugs currently criminalized are not as harmful as certain of the legal prescription drugs that are widely used.

However, critics of decriminalization/legalization are quick to point out that either decriminalizing or legalizing particular drugs would only increase their use and abuse. If drugs such as marijuana and cocaine were inexpensive and readily available, adolescents who currently refrain from drug use would be drawn to drugs in large numbers. Evidence for this may be found in the Alaskan experience when the Alaska Supreme Court decriminalized small amounts of marijuana for personal use in 1975. Even though marijuana remained illegal for children, the perception that marijuana was harmful decreased, and marijuana use rates among Alaskan youths increased significantly. A 1998 poll of voters conducted by the Family Research Council found that 80 percent of respondents rejected the legalization of drugs like cocaine and heroin, with 70 percent indicating strong opposition.[69]

Erich Goode believes that it may not be possible to eliminate marijuana use through legal controls such as those used in the Netherlands. Furthermore, Goode argues against any decriminalization/legalization of drugs such as cocaine and crack. He claims that both are immensely pleasurable and, therefore, are strongly reinforcing drugs that have devastating personal consequences for the user.[70] In addition, James Inciardi and Duane McBride suggest that policies to decriminalize drugs are elitist and racist because they would result in increasing levels of drug dependence in low income and minority communities: decriminalization ". . . represents a program of social management and control that would serve to legitimate the chemical destruction of an urban generation and culture."[71]

Is the overall prevalence of vice disconcerting to you? If so, why? Are vice crimes victimless? Why or why not?

But if punitive measures do not work, if education, prevention, and treatment programs are only marginally effective, and if decriminalization could possibly add to the drug problem, how should we respond to adolescent drug use?

Changing Lives and Environments

Generally, when social scientists have studied adolescent problems, they have explored a specific problem such as delinquency, drug use, running away, or teenage pregnancy in isolation from the others. However, as we stress throughout this book and as recent research has suggested,[72] these adolescent problem behaviors may well have a common origin. Therefore, adolescent drug use and programs designed to respond to it cannot be studied apart from the larger social milieu in which the child develops. Most juveniles using cocaine and crack are found in our nation's inner cities, where poverty, unemployment, homelessness, broken families, lack of hope, and a multitude of related problems are pervasive.

In an attempt to stop adolescent drug use and delinquency before they start, several programs are focusing specifically on improving children's lives and environments. Some of the following examples provide overlapping services, but each clearly makes a difference.[73]

Preschool education programs may help reduce the risks of later school failure and frustration, which often lead to drug use. The Head Start program is one of the most effective early interventions for changing childrens' lives. Children who have participated in Head Start are less likely to eventually be involved with drugs, be delinquent, quit school, or have unwanted pregnancies.[74] In Missouri, the Parents As Teachers (PAT) program sends teachers into homes of preschoolers every six weeks to educate parents about each stage of the child's development. The PAT program is now included in the Harvard Family Research Project being conducted in five states to improve family support and education. Early evaluations indicate that PAT children have better problem-solving skills and language ability than children not in the program.

Strengthening the family can have immeasurably positive consequences in the lives of children, ranging from reducing conflict and abuse to improving communication, affection, and respect. In Tacoma, Washington, Homebuilders established a team of professionals with social work, psychology, and counseling backgrounds to provide services to any family deemed by juvenile justice, child welfare, or mental health agencies to be in imminent peril of having the child removed from the home. Through intensive interventions with the family and the use of community resources, the professionals help clients regain control over their lives. The TOGETHER! project in Lacey, Washington, targets drug abuse prevention to children and families living in low-income apartment complexes. TOGETHER! rents an apartment in each complex and offers afterschool and summer programs promoting a drug-free climate for children through activities ranging from homework assistance and skills building to conflict resolution and peer pressure resistance training. Drug abuse information is disseminated to parents at family potluck dinners and informal coffee hours.[75]

Health care for adolescents, especially in the early years, is critical for establishing a foundation for success. Programs such as WIC (a supplemental food program for women, infants, and children) and Children's House (an innovative pediatric and child care program in New Haven, Connecticut) provide needed nutrition plus a combination of comprehensive health care and family support. Follow-up evaluations of the Children's House program found significant positive effects for both children and their mothers. Only 28 percent of Children's House children suffered from serious school adjustment problems compared to nearly 70 percent of children in a control group.[76]

Job training and placement are important in changing the lives of lower-class children who may often be tempted by the easy money to be had from selling drugs. One model job placement program is Jobs for Youth/Chicago (JFY). Each year nearly 1,000 youths are placed in jobs after a careful screening process. Volunteers from the local business community help them prepare for job interviews, and the JFY staff stay in contact with the youths during their first two years.

Conclusions

Drugs are widely used, and while most drug use is legal, many adolescents are involved in the use of illicit drugs. Adolescent drug use is one of the most important problems facing children today, according to recent opinion polls. In spite of declines in reported drug use during much of the 1980s, juvenile drug use has increased since the early 1990s, especially among younger adolescents.

Sociological theories suggest that the causes of adolescent drug use are varied. Strain theory posits that drug use is the result of a youth's failure to make it either in the legitimate or the illegitimate world. Social learning theory argues that adolescents learn to use drugs from peers much as they learn other forms of social behavior. According to social control theory, the weakening of social controls allows an adolescent to become involved with drugs. Subcultural socialization theories hold that involvement in a delinquent subculture in which drugs are used is likely to result in drug use by the youth.

How should society respond to adolescent drug use? A punitive response suggests hiring more police, building more prisons, and creating more severe sentences. This approach has encouraged the creation of military-style boot camps, suspension of drivers' licenses, school suspensions, eviction from public housing, and drug testing in the schools. Education, prevention, and treatment responses have become very popular. Unfortunately, few school-based education and prevention programs appear to work, and treatment programs that are effective are unable to meet the demands of the growing number of clients. Decriminalization or legalization of drugs raises many questions. Should all drugs be made legal and subject to regulation, or should only certain drugs be legalized? If the latter, which drugs? Would decriminalization or legalization of some drugs lead to greater use of those drugs by adolescents? Finally, attempts to change the lives and environments of children assume that drug use is only one facet of a larger, more complex milieu of social problems facing today's youth. Poverty, unemployment, homelessness, abuse, and lack of hope create an environment in which drug use, as well as other forms of delinquency, is likely to occur. But possible solutions to these larger problems may actually be within our reach. Among programs found to be effective are those that provide preschool education, prevent teenage pregnancy, and strengthen the family.

Key Terms

annual prevalence: *In self-report surveys, the use of a drug at least once during the prior year.*

decriminalization: *The relaxing of the enforcement of certain laws, for example, drug laws.*

Drug Abuse Resistance Education (D.A.R.E.): *A program aimed at children in kindergarten through twelfth grade, designed to equip students with appropriate skills to resist substance abuse and gangs.*

legalization: *The elimination of many laws currently prohibiting the distribution and possession of drugs, but not necessarily eliminating all regulation.*

lifetime prevalence: *In self-report surveys, the use of a drug at least once during the respondent's lifetime.*

30-day prevalence: *In self-report surveys, the use of a drug at least once during the previous month.*

Getting Connected

National statistics on drug and alcohol abuse are available at a number of websites. Two excellent sites for current data based on national surveys are:

National Center on Addiction and Substance Abuse

http://www.casacolumbia.org

1. In the FYI section of the site, take the "tweens and teens" CASA quiz.
2. In the FYI section of the site, read the checklist for parents which asks them "How good are your Parent Power skills?" Why are these "Parent Power" skills seen to be related to preventing substance abuse?
3. What is CASAWORKS for families?

The National Household Survey on Drug Abuse and other statistical studies on drug abuse are available through the U.S. Department of Health and Human Services Office of Applied Studies website:

http://www.drugabusestatistics.samhsa.gov/

1. According to this site, American Indian/Alaska Native youths aged 12 to 17 were more likely than youths from other racial/ethnic groups to smoke cigarettes during the past month. What might explain this finding?

continued

2. What is DAWN?

3. What kind of information about youth substance abuse is available through this site?

The National Institute on Drug Abuse provides statistical data, reports, and publications at their website:

http://www.nida.nih.gov

1. Link to the Sara's Quest website. Who is Sara and what is her "quest"?

2. Take the Sara's Quest challenge quiz. How knowledgeable are you?

3. What is the "Monitoring the Future" survey? How do its results compare to popular perceptions about adolescents?

Students may be interested in visiting the Office of National Drug Control Policy at their website:

http://www.whitehousedrugpolicy.gov

1. Find the site's "Media Campaign" section. Look at the latest television, print, radio, and banner ads and evaluate their potential effectiveness among adolescents in your area.

2. How are parents the "anti-drug," according to this site?

3. Who is the current director of the ONDCP? How did this person get the job?

Finally, the home website for D.A.R.E. can be located at:

http://www.dare-america.com

1. Enter the D.A.R.E. for Kids part of the site, then argue whether drug use has had an influence on American popular culture and its imagery.

2. Enter the part of the site designed for adults. What seems to be its goal?

3. On this site, is there reference to research findings critical of D.A.R.E.'s effectiveness?

Endnotes

1. Center on Addiction and Substance Abuse at Columbia University, *Malignant Neglect: Substance Abuse and America's Schools* (New York: Center on Addiction and Substance Abuse at Columbia University, 2001), p 11.

2. Lloyd Johnston, Patrick O'Malley, and Jerald Bachman, *Monitoring the Future: National Results on Adolescent Drug Use: Overview of Key Findings, 2000* NIH Publication No. 01–4923 (Bethesda, MD: National Institute on Drug Abuse, 2001), p. 4.

3. Johnston, O'Malley, and Bachman, note 2; U.S. Department of Health and Human Services, *Summary of Findings from the 1999 National Household Survey on Drug Abuse* (Washington, DC: U.S. Department of Health and Human Services, 2000).

4. Federal Bureau of Investigation, *Crime in the United States 2000* (Washington, DC: U.S. Department of Justice, 2001), pp. 220, 222.

5. Federal Bureau of Investigation, note 4, pp. 224.

6. U.S. Department of Health and Human Services, note 3.

7. U.S. Department of Health and Human Services, note 3.

8. Federal Bureau of Investigation, note 4, pp. 228, 230.

9. Joan McCord, Cathy Widom, and Nancy Crowell, eds. *Juvenile Crime, Juvenile Justice* (Washington, DC: National Academy Press, 2001), p. 57.

10. Anne Stahl, *Drug Offense Cases in Juvenile Courts, 1989–1998* (Washington, DC: Office of Juvenile Justice and Delinquency Prevention, 2001), p. 1.

11. Jason Ziedenberg, *Drugs and Disparity: The Racial Impact of Illinois' Practice of Transferring Young Drug Offenders to Adult Court* (Washington, DC: Building Blocks for Youth, 2001).

12. Federal Bureau of Investigation, note 4, p. 235.

13. Schneider Institute for Health Policy, *Substance Abuse: The Nation's Number One Health Problem* (Princeton, NJ: Robert Wood Johnson Foundation, 2001), pp. 36–37.

14. Johnston et al., note 2, Table 1 and earlier reports.

15. Johnston et al., note 2, Table 1.

16. James F. Short, Jr., *Delinquency and Society* (Englewood Cliffs, NJ: Prentice-Hall, Inc., 1990), p. 119.

17. Larry McShane, "Poll: Kids' Drug Use Underestimated," *Washington Post,* April 13, 1998, p. 2.

18. Johnston et al., note 2, Table 4.

19. Robert Merton, *Social Theory and Social Structure,* rev. ed. (New York: Macmillan Publishing Co., 1968).

20. Richard Cloward and Lloyd Ohlin, *Delinquency and Opportunity* (New York: The Free Press, 1960).

21. Erich Goode, *Drugs in American Society*, 5th ed. (New York: McGraw-Hill Publishing Co., 1998).

22. Travis Hirschi, *Causes of Delinquency* (Berkeley: University of California Press, 1969).

23. Howard Becker, *Outsiders: Studies in the Sociology of Deviance* (New York: The Free Press, 1963), p. 58.

24. Erich Goode, *The Marijuana Smokers* (New York: Basic Books, 1970).

25. Bruce Johnson, *Marijuana Use and Drug Subcultures* (New York: John Wiley & Sons, 1973).

26. Denise Kandel, "Drugs and Drinking Behavior Among Youth," *Annual Review of Sociology*, edited by Alex Inkeles (Palo Alto, CA: Annual Reviews, 1980); "Inter- and Intragenerational Influences on Adolescent Marijuana Use," *Journal of Social Issues* 30:107–135 (1974); and "Adolescent Marijuana Use: Role of Parents and Peers," *Science* 181:1067–1070 (1973).

27. Lisbeth Schorr, *Within Our Reach: Breaking the Cycle of Disadvantage* (New York: Anchor Books, 1989), p. 20.

28. Anthony Jurich, Cheryl Polson, Julie Jurich, and Rodney Bates, "Family Factors in the Lives of Drug Users and Abusers," *Adolescence* 20:143–159 (1985).

29. Alfred Friedman, "Family Factors and the Family Role in Treatment for Adolescent Drug Abuse," *Treatment Services for Adolescent Substance Abusers*, edited by Alfred Friedman and George Beschner (Washington, DC: U.S. Government Printing Office, 1985), pp. 13–30; Joan Kelly, "Children's Adjustment in Conflicted Marriage and Divorce: A Decade Review of Research," *Journal of the American Academy of Child and Adolescent Psychiatry* 39:963–973 (2000).

30. Rafaela Robles, Ruth Martinez, and Margarita Moscoso, "Predictors of Adolescent Drug Behavior," *Youth and Society* 11:415–430 (1980).

31. Mark Halebsky, "Adolescent Alcohol and Substance Abuse: Parent and Peer Effects," *Adolescence* 22:961–967 (1987); Roberta Pandina and James Schuele, "Psychological Correlates of Alcohol and Drug Use of Adolescent Students and Adolescents in Treatment," *Journal of Studies on Alcohol* 44:950–973 (1985).

32. Rick Kosterman, J. David Hawkins, Jie Guo, Richard Catalano, and Robert Abbott, "The Dynamics of Alcohol and Marijuana Initiation: Patterns and Predictors of First Use in Adolescence," *American Journal of Public Health* 90:360–366 (2000).

33. Michelle Miller, Finn-Aage Esbensen, and Adrienne Freng, "Parental Attachment, Parental Supervision and Adolescent Deviance in Intact and Non-Intact Families," *Journal of Crime & Justice* 22:1–29 (1999); Jeffrey Cookston, "Parental Supervision and Family Structure: Effects on Adolescent Problem Behaviors," *Journal of Divorce & Remarriage* 32:107–122 (1999).

34. Peter Mulhall, Donald Stone, and Brian Stone, "Home Alone: Is It a Risk Factor for Middle School Youth and Drug Use?" *Journal of Drug Education* 26:39–48 (1996).

35. Ann Burgess, Carol Hartman, and Arlene McCormack, "Abused to Abuser: Antecedents of Socially Deviant Behaviors," *American Journal of Psychiatry* 144:1431–1440 (1987).

36. Richard Dembo, Max Dertke, Lawrence Lavoie, and Scott Borders, "Physical Abuse, Sexual Victimization and Illicit Drug Use: A Structural Analysis Among High Risk Adolescents," *Journal of Adolescence* 10:13–34 (1987).

37. Fawzy Fawzy, Robert Coombs, and Barry Gerber, "Generational Continuity in the Use of Substances: The Impact of Parental Substance Use on Adolescent Substance Use," *Addictive Behavior* 8:109–114 (1983).

38. Halebsky, note 31; Ernest Harburg, Deborah Davis, and Roberta Caplan, "Parent and Offspring Alcohol Use," *Journal of Studies on Alcohol* 43:497–515 (1982); Denise Kandel, Ronald Kessler, and Rebecca Margulies, "Antecedents of Adolescent Initiation into Stages of Drug Use: A Developmental Analysis," *Journal of Youth and Adolescence* 7:13–40 (1978).

39. Kenise Kandel, Pamela Griesler, Gang Lee, Mark Davis, and Christine Schaffran, *Parental Influences on Adolescent Marijuana Use and the Baby Boom Generation: Findings from the 1979–1996 National Household Surveys on Drug Abuse* (Washington, DC: Department of Health and Human Services, 2001).

40. Stuart Greenbaum, "Drugs, Delinquency, and Other Data," *Juvenile Justice,* Spring/Summer:2–8 (1994); David Huizinga, Rolf Loeber, and Terence Thornberry, *Urban Delinquency and Substance Abuse: Initial Findings* (Washington, DC: Office of Juvenile Justice and Delinquency Prevention, 1994); Delbert Elliott, David Huizinga, and Scott Menard, *Multiple Problem Youth* (New York: Springer-Verlag, 1989).

41. Scott Menard, Sharon Mihalic, and David Huizinga, "Drugs and Crime Revisited," *Justice Quarterly* 18:295 (2001).

42. Menard et al., note 41, p. 295.

43. Cheryl Carpenter, Barry Glassner, Bruce Johnson, and Julia Loughlin, *Kids, Drugs, and Crime* (Lexington, MA: D. C. Heath, 1988); Elliott et al., note 40; James Farrow and James French, "The Drug Abuse-Delinquency Connection Revisited," *Adolescence* 21:951–960 (1986); and John Watters, Craig Reinarman, and Jeffrey Fagan, "Causality, Context, and Contingency: Relationships Between Drug Abuse and Delinquency," *Contemporary Drug Problems* 12:351–373 (1985).

44. David Altschuler and Paul Brounstein, "Patterns of Drug Use, Drug Trafficking, and Other Delinquency Among Inner-City Adolescent Males in Washington, D.C.," *Criminology* 29:589 (1991).

45. Carpenter et al., note 43, p. 220.

46. Colleen McLaughlin, Jack Daniel, and Timothy Joost, "The Relationship Between Substance Use, Drug Selling, and Lethal Violence in 25 Juvenile Murderers," *Journal of Forensic Sciences* 45:349–353 (2000).

47. Delbert Elliott, David Huizinga, and Suzanne Ageton, *Explaining Delinquency and Drug Use* (Beverly Hills, CA: Sage, 1985); Delbert Elliott and Barbara Morse, "Delinquency and Drug Use as Risk Factors in Teenage Sexual Activity," *Youth and Society* 21:32–60 (1989); Huizinga et al., note 40.

48. Marvin Krohn, Alan Lizotte, and Cynthia Perez, "The Interrelationship Between Substance Use and Precocious Transitions to Adult Statuses," *Journal of Health and Social Behavior* 38:87–103 (1997).

49. The White House, *National Drug Control Strategy, 1989* (Washington, DC: Office of National Drug Control Policy, 1989), p. 7.

50. Quoted in Daniel Lazare, "The Drug War Is Killing Us," *The Village Voice*, January 23:25 (1990).

51. The White House, *The National Drug Control Strategy, 2001* (Washington, DC: Office of National Drug Control Policy, 2001).

52. Kathryn Buckner, "School Drug Tests: A Fourth Amendment Perspective," *University of Illinois Law Review* 2:275–310 (1987).

53. *Vernonia School District 47J v. Acton*, 515 U.S. 646 (1995).

54. James Simonson and Pat Maher, *Promising Practices: Drug-Free Communities Support Program* (Washington, DC: Office of Juvenile Justice and Delinquency Prevention, 2001).

55. Thomas Szasz, *Ceremonial Chemistry: The Ritual Persecution of Drugs, Addicts, and Pushers*, rev. ed. (Holmes Beach, FL: Learning Publications, 1985), p. 192.

56. Jerry Mandel and Harvey Feldman, "The Social History of Teenage Drug Use," *Teen Drug Use*, edited by George Beschner and Alfred Friedman (Lexington, MA: Lexington Books, 1986), pp. 19–42.

57. J. Funkhouser, "Before the Cameras Turn: The Research Base of the Youth Alcohol Prevention Campaign," *Alcohol Health and Research World* 11:44–47 (1987).

58. Bureau of Justice Assistance, *Drug Abuse Resistance Education (D.A.R.E.)* (Washington, DC: U.S. Department of Justice, 1995), p. 1.

59. The White House, note 49, p. 50.

60. Dennis Rosenbaum and Gordon Hanson, "Assessing the Effects of School-Based Drug Education: A Six-Year Multilevel Analysis of Project D.A.R.E.," *Journal of Research in Crime and Delinquency* 35:381–412 (1998).

61. Claudia Kalb, "DARE Checks into Rehab," *Newsweek*, February 26:56 (2001).

62. The White House, note 51.

63. National Research Council, *Losing Generations: Adolescents in High-Risk Settings* (Washington, DC: National Academy Press, 1993), p. 96.

64. Stanley Kusnetz, "Services for Adolescent Substance Abusers," *Teen Drug Use*, edited by George Beschner and Alfred Friedman (Lexington, MA: Lexington Books, 1986), pp. 123–153.

65. Kusnetz, note 64, p. 135.

66. Kusnetz, note 64, p. 144.

67. Lester Thurow, "U.S. Drug Policy: Colossal Ignorance," *The New York Times*, May 8:29 (1988).

68. Pete Hamill, "Facing Up to Drugs: Is Legalization the Solution?" *New York* 21, August 15:20–27 (1988).

69. The White House, note 51.

70. Goode, note 21.

71. James Inciardi and Duane McBride, "The Case Against Legalization," *The Drug Legalization Debate*, edited by James Inciardi (Newbury Park, CA: Sage Publications, 1991), p. 65.

72. See John Donovan and Richard Jessor, "Structure and Problem in Adolescence and Young Adulthood," *Journal of Consulting and Clinical Psychology* 53:890–904 (1985); D. Wayne Osgood, Lloyd Johnston, Patrick O'Malley, and Jerald Bachman, "The Generality of Deviance in Late Adolescence and Early Adulthood," *American Sociological Review* 53:81–93 (1988).

73. James Baker and Regina Elam, "Programs That Can Make a Difference," *Newsweek*, September 11:28 (1989); Schorr, note 27.

74. Schorr, note 27.

75. Simonson and Maher, note 54.

76. Schorr, note 27, p. 167.

Explaining Delinquency

In Section 2, theories of delinquency that have guided scholarship and policy development during most of the 20th century are discussed. Some of the theories are specific to juveniles while others apply to both children and adults. To help guide your reading, the major premise and juvenile justice policy applications of each group of theories are summarized in the table at the end of this introduction.

In Chapter 5, two groups of theories are reviewed. The first, supernatural theory, is based on beliefs in demons, witches, and evil spirits that consume a person's body and control his or her behavior. Such an understanding is just the opposite of the second perspective, the Classical School of criminology, which emerged during the Enlightenment of the 17th and 18th centuries. Classical theory, on the other hand, blames delinquency on freely chosen actions of pleasure-seeking adolescents. Juveniles are assumed to be rational, intelligent people who choose to commit crime.

Chapters 6 through 8 examine biological, psychological, and sociological theories. Instead of suggesting that behavior is the result of free will (choice), these theories attribute delinquency to factors over which children have no control.

Chapter 6 critiques biological and psychological theories. Biological theories range from the 19th century work of Cesare Lombroso, who saw delinquents as throwbacks to an early stage of human development, to explanations based on an analysis of the relationship between genes and the environment. Psychological theories are often measured against the work of Sigmund Freud. Deficient personality, low intelligence, psychopathy, positive and negative reinforcements, and learning disorders have all been put forth as causes of crime.

Chapter 7 discusses three groups of sociological theories: cultural deviance, strain, and social control. Cultural deviance theories examine a child's interactions with social, cultural, and ecological factors that lead to delinquency; strain theories argue that blocked opportunities push children into delinquency; and social control theories assume people are inherently amoral and do not naturally conform to group values and norms.

Critical theories are discussed in Chapter 8. Three perspectives are examined: labeling, conflict, and radical. Labeling theories blame delinquency

Overview of Criminology Theories and Their Policy Applications

THEORY*	MAJOR PREMISE	POLICY APPLICATION†
Supernatural theory (5)	Crime is caused by other-world powers or spirits.	Trial by battle or trial by ordeal
Classical and neoclassical (5)	Children commit crimes because they anticipate more benefits from violating the law than from conformity.	Fixed-time sentences, shock probation, boot camps
Biological theories (6)	Crime is caused by some biological deficiency inside of the offender.	Segregation; sterilization
Psychoanalytic theory (6)	Crime is caused by an overdeveloped or underdeveloped superego.	Psychotherapy
Behavioral theory (6)	Criminal behavior is a learned response that has been strengthened because of the reinforcements it produces.	Aversion therapy; token economies
Cultural deviance theory (7)	Crime is caused by disorganization, which hinders the ability of neighborhoods to monitor children.	Chicago Area Project
Strain theory (7)	Crime is caused by society telling children what to seek without providing them with the means to do so.	Project Head Start
Social control theory (7)	Juveniles who are not bonded to society are free to violate its rules.	Programs that integrate children into mainstream society, such as the Police Athletic League
Labeling theory (8)	Crime is caused by societal reactions to behavior, which include exposure to the juvenile justice system.	Diversion programs; decriminalization of offenses
Conflict theory (8)	Crime is caused by imbalances in power and status.	Social programs that equalize relations among children, such as Project Head Start

*The chapter where each theory is discussed is shown in parentheses.

†Social policies often derive from more than one theory. The objectives of Project Head Start, for example, are to reduce strain and to make relations among children more equal. Its origin can be traced to both strain and conflict theories.

on the interactions between individuals and other people or groups. The unequal distribution of the power to define behaviors as delinquent, the inability of some youths to resist the application of stigmatizing labels, and the process by which juveniles may move from unwitting or spontaneous acts to behavior associated with more organized social roles and delinquent identities are among the concerns explored by these theories. Conflict and radical theories assess the relationship among economic, social, and political factors and how they interact to produce delinquency.

Female theories of delinquency are discussed in Chapter 9. A significant criminological reality is that nearly all theories of delinquency have been built around patterns of male delinquency and may not necessarily apply well when trying to explain why girls commit law-violating behavior. After a brief examination of the development of female gender roles and identities, the chapter discusses biological and developmental theories, sociological theories, critical and feminist theories, and differential oppression theory in terms of their relevance and applicability to female delinquency.

Chapter 5

Supernatural, Classical, and Neoclassical Theories

The unexamined life is not worth living.

—Socrates

Just as the unexamined life is not worth living, reporting crime data without carefully examining their meaning is of little value. Data by themselves tell us very little without a framework to interpret them. Simply knowing that more delinquency is committed than is reported to police, or that males commit more crime than females, does not tell us very much.

The causes of delinquency have been studied for more than 200 years. During this time, **theories** or integrated sets of ideas that explain and predict why and when children break the law have emerged. The reason they are discussed at length in this text is because *ideas have consequences.* The general public, criminologists, and state and federal legislators use theories (usually without knowing it) when they develop or vote on crime control policies. Many of the proposals for delinquency prevention in the 1994 Crime Control Bill were based on theories discussed in this and the following chapters. For example, the "three strikes and you're out" legislation is based on principles of Classical School theory that argues for specific deterrence through incapacitation.

Over the years, delinquency has been blamed on many factors, including heredity and lead poisoning (Chapter 6), neighborhood and community (Chapter 7), childhood oppression (Chapter 8), and sex stereotyping (Chapter 9). There is not much agreement among criminologists on what is the best theory. Consider the case of Harold (Peewee) Brown:

> Over a four-year period, from the age of 11 to 15, Peewee was arrested 15 times on charges ranging from sodomy to assault. . . . He now admits that those arrests were for only a small number of his crimes. For example, he said when he was 13 he shot and killed a man on a street corner in Brooklyn, but was never caught. He added that he seriously wounded at least six others and committed countless other robberies.[1]

Why are some children, like Peewee, chronic offenders while many others are not? Does the devil reside in their bodies? Do they choose to commit crime? Are their genes defective? Do they have an under- or overdeveloped superego? Does their neighborhood "push" them into crime?

How should society react to habitual offenders like Peewee? Should they be given an exorcism? Forced to take therapeutic drugs? Be incarcerated? Be sterilized? Undergo psychotherapy? Receive job training?

There are no correct answers to any of these questions. What you think the right answer is depends on whether you believe behavior is the result of free will, supernatural forces, nature (heredity), nurture (environment), or some combination of these.

Supernatural Theory

Supernatural theories blame delinquency on demonic possession. In the Middle Ages (500–1500 A.D.) people believed criminals were possessed by the devil.[2] This idea declined in popularity in the 18th century, when there

Most scholars would suggest that linking exorcisms and witchcraft to crime is nonsense. Do you agree? Does scientific theory do a better job of explaining crimes, such as murder, rape, and abduction? Is there something "devilish" about these behaviors that inspires unorthodox practices such as exorcisms?

In the mid-1980s, Richard Ramirez was convicted of 15 homicides and over 40 other serious felonies and sentenced to death. Ramirez insisted that he was possessed by the devil and was merely fulfilling his evil responsibilities. Does the idea of evil have any credibility today?

was an emphasis on rational thinking and free will. But even today remnants of this theory are found. In 1949 a 13-year-old boy was believed to be possessed by the devil and was given an exorcism.[3] In 1995 Eric Star Smith stabbed and beheaded his 14-year-old son while driving on the interstate highway because he thought the boy was under the devil's spell.[4] In 2000 the Union Public School District No. 9 in Tulsa, Oklahoma, suspended 15-year-old Brandi Blackbear for three weeks for putting a hex on a teacher.[5] Yet, supernatural explanations are not taken too seriously because they cannot be scientifically tested. Since the cause of crime is otherworldly (the devil), it is nothing that can be observed and measured. Thus, modern crime theories are based on conditions and events that can be observed and measured. These theories are called **natural explanations**, the first of which were constructed in the 18th century by the Classical School.

Classical School Theory

Do people have free will? Are they rational? Intelligent? Do people seek to maximize pleasure and minimize pain? If you answered yes to these questions, you likely will agree with the cause of crime expressed in theories by **Classical School** criminologists. They believe people are rational, intelligent beings who exercise **free will** or the ability to make choices. People calculate the costs and benefits of their behavior *before* they act. Crime results from imagining greater gains from breaking the law than from conformity. In the same way, children who skip school first determine the likelihood of getting caught against the potential fun they will have. Similarly, juveniles who rape weigh the pleasure they imagine they will have against being arrested, prosecuted, convicted, and sent to prison. Because behavior is a conscious decision people make, they must be held accountable for their actions and their consequences.[6]

Cesare Beccaria

The leading figure of the Classical School was Cesare Beccaria. He formulated his ideas about crime control during the 18th century when criminal justice systems throughout Europe were cruel and ruthless and exercised a callous indifference for human rights. People were punished for crimes against religion, such as atheism and witchcraft, and for crimes against the state, such as criticizing persons in power. Worse yet, "offenders" were rarely told why they were being punished. No one was exempt; any person could be hauled off to jail at any time for any reason. Wealthy persons were spared the most torturous and degrading punishments, which were reserved for common folks who were sometimes burnt alive, whipped, mutilated, or branded.[7]

These conditions inspired Beccaria to write *On Crimes and Punishments*, where he laid the groundwork for a system of criminal justice that focused on humanity, consistency, and rationality.[8] He suggested the following:

1. Social action should be based on the utilitarian principle of the greatest happiness for the greatest number.
2. Crime is an injury to society, and the only rational measure of crime is the extent of the injury.
3. Crime prevention is more important than punishment. Laws must be published so that the citizenry can understand and support them.
4. In criminal procedure, secret accusations and torture must be abolished. There should be speedy trials, and accused persons should have every right to present evidence in their defense.
5. The purpose of punishment is to prevent crime. Punishment must be *swift*, *certain*, and *severe*. Penalties must be based on the social damage caused by the crime. There should be no capital punishment. Life imprisonment is a better deterrent. Capital punishment is irreparable and makes no provision for mistakes.
6. Imprisonment should be widely used, but prison conditions should be improved through better physical quarters and by separating and classifying inmates as to age, sex, and criminal histories.[9]

On Crimes and Punishment is one of the most influential papers ever written. It became the basis for the 1791 criminal code of France and for ideas such as (1) people are innocent until proven guilty, (2) people cannot be forced to testify against themselves, (3) people have the right to counsel and to confront their accusers, and (4) people have the right to a speedy trial by a jury of their peers, as found in the U.S. Constitution.

Jeremy Bentham

Bentham suggested that the punishment should fit the crime. Does the U.S. criminal justice system do this for serious felonies? Should legal condemnation and punishment match the barbarity of certain crimes?

A second leading pioneer in criminal justice reform in the 18th century was the English economist Jeremy Bentham. He based his ideas about crime on the belief that people sought out pleasure and avoided pain. The correct punishment was one that produced more pain than the pleasure the offender received from committing the crime. The punishment must thus "fit the crime." Therefore, no single punishment was always best; rather a variety of punishments should be used.

Bentham's ideas radically transformed the 19th century English penal code, known then as "The Bloody Code," since people were executed for crimes such as stealing turnips, associating with gypsies, and damaging fish ponds.[10] Between 1820 and 1861, the number of capital crimes in the code was reduced from 222 to 3, for murder, treason, and piracy.

Neoclassical School Theory

The Classical School ultimately failed because of its own rigidity. It did not take into account *why* people commit crime. Instead, all people were held *equally* responsible for their behavior. Those who committed similar crimes received identical punishments. The Classical School focused on the criminal *act* (the crime) and not the *actor* (why it was committed). But, in reality, people are not the same. Children, the insane, and the incompetent are not as responsible for their behavior as adults, the sane, and the competent. The idea that there are real differences among people led to the development of the **Neoclassical School**.

Mitigating Circumstances

During the Jim Crow era, exclusively white juries routinely viewed race as a mitigating circumstance for white defendants, particularly if the victim was black. As a consequence, these juries often refused to convict white defendants, and serious miscarriages of justice occurred. How can race ever be used to mitigate a crime?

Neoclassical School reformers were sympathetic to what the Classical School wanted to accomplish. They agreed that people were rational, intelligent beings who exercised free will. But they also thought some crimes were caused by factors beyond the offender's control. **Mitigating circumstances**, such as age or mental condition, sometimes influence the choices that are made and affect a person's ability to form criminal intent or *mens rea* (guilty mind). This is why children under age seven cannot legally commit a crime–they are presumed to be not capable of having a guilty mind.[11]

Individual Justice

Permitting the introduction of mitigating circumstances at criminal trials triggered the development of **individual justice**, the idea that criminal law must reflect differences among people and their circumstances. Individual justice gave rise to a series of important developments including the insanity defense, inclusion of expert witnesses, and a new explanation for crime that blamed it on conditions that were in place *before* the act. The cornerstone of this new way of thinking about crime was *scientific determinism*, which gave rise to the Positive School of criminology, whose theories are discussed in Chapters 6, 7, and 9.

Modern Classical School Theory

James Q. Wilson's "wicked people exist" passage has been dismissed as ranting, rightist ideology by some criminologists. But, criminologists, as professors, generally occupy a social class position that is largely protected from serious crime and delinquency. Do many criminologists dismiss Wilson's views because they simply never encounter "wicked people" in their everyday lives? If criminal victimization were more randomly distributed, would criminologists harbor more conservative crime-control beliefs?

In the 1960s criminologists started to question the effectiveness of reha-bilitation. A flurry of evaluation studies of rehabilitation programs con-cluded that *some* treatment works *some* of the time for *some* offenders in *some* settings.[12] This unconvincing endorsement of the rehabilitation model led to the proposal that criminals be punished. One advocate was James Q. Wilson, who said:

> Wicked people exist. Nothing avails except to set them apart from innocent people. And many people, neither wicked nor innocent, but watchful, dissembling, and calculating of their chances, ponder our reaction to wickedness as a clue to what they might profitably do.[13]

Society needs to punish crime. If crime is not punished, then people "on the fence" will think crime pays and possibly commit it (see Box 5–3).

Around this same time, criminologists were busy constructing new theo-ries. One has been called **rational choice theory**, which claims delinquents are rational people who make calculated choices regarding what they are go-ing to do *before* they act. Offenders collect, process, and evaluate information about the crime and make the decision whether to commit it after they have weighed the costs and benefits of doing so.[14] Crime, in other words, is a well-thought out decision. Offenders decide where to commit it, who or what to target, and how to execute it.

Research has found many offenders do select a specific location to com-mit a crime. For example, Bruce Jacobs found that crack cocaine street deal-ers liked to operate in the middle of a long block because they could see everything in both directions.[15] Offenders also have been found to pick crime targets after they scrutinize the behavior of potential victims.[16] Criminals also learn how to avoid arrest. Successful crack cocaine dealers know where to hide drugs on their person, in the street, and at home.[17]

An explanation that is similar to rational choice theory is **routine activ-ities theory**, which focuses on the *crime target* or anything an offender wants to take control of, whether it is a house to break into or a bottle of beer to shoplift.[18] Before a crime will occur, however, three elements must come to-gether: motivated offenders; suitable targets; and an absence of people to de-ter the would-be offender. Crime thus increases when there are vulnerable targets (e.g., keys left in the ignition) and only a few people to protect them (e.g., police).[19]

BOX 5–3   A WINDOW ON DELINQUENCY
Does Crime Pay?

Classical School criminologists believe people weigh the costs and benefits of committing crime *before* they act. The crime rate is high because, for many people at least, the benefits of committing crime outweigh the costs or even the likelihood of incurring costs.

One way of measuring the cost of crime is to estimate the actual punishment received, which can be calculated by multiplying the following probabilities:

- Being arrested for a crime after it is committed.
- Being prosecuted if arrested.
- Being convicted if prosecuted.
- Going to prison if convicted.

The product of this calculation is then multiplied by the median time served for an offense. For example,

- 7 percent of all burglaries (reported and unreported) result in arrest.
- Of those arrested, 87 percent are prosecuted.
- Of those prosecuted, 79 percent are convicted.
- Of those convicted, 25 percent go to prison.
- Average period of confinement in prison for burglary is 13 months.

Thus, a potential burglar has only a 1.2 percent probability of actually going to prison. Once in prison, burglars are incarcerated for an average of about 13 months. Because more than 98 percent of burglaries never result in prison sentences, the actual average sentence served for each burglary is less than 5 days—an amount of time many potential burglars might consider easily outweighed by the benefits of the burglary.

The expected time served in prison for other serious crimes can be similarly calculated: murder, 1.8 years; rape, 60 days; robbery, 23 days; arson, 6.7 days; aggravated assault, 6.4 days; larceny/theft, 3.8 days; motor vehicle theft, 1.5 days.

Some research suggests that as the expected punishment for serious crimes decreases, the amount of serious crime increases. The expected punishment for serious crime today is one-third of what it was in 1950, and the Crime Index offense rate has increased by nearly five times.

Sources: Reprinted by permission of the National Center for Policy Analysis, 12655 N. Central Expressway, Suite 720, Dallas, TX 75243, (214) 386–6272, from *NCPA Policy Backgrounder #123*, Morgan Reynolds, "Why Does Crime Pay?" (December 1992). Also see Morgan Reynolds, "Does Punishment Deter?" *NCPA Policy Backgrounder #148* (Dallas, TX: National Center for Policy Analysis, 1998); and Morgan Reynolds, "Crime and Punishment in America: 1998," *NCPA Policy Backgrounder #219* (Dallas, TX: National Center for Policy Analysis, 1998).

Two problems with these theories are that they (1) do not identify the factors that motivate offenders and (2) overlook factors that cause the criminalization of some behavior (smoking marijuana) and not other behavior (drinking alcohol).[20] Nonetheless, the theories do draw attention to the fact that every crime is a unique event. Crime may have as much to do with situational factors and free will as it does with the offender's psychology.

15-year-old Charles Bishop committed suicide by crashing this stolen plane into a building in Tampa, Florida. Bishop left a suicide note expressing support for Osama Bin Laden and the September 11, 2001, terrorist attacks on the United States. What does this episode suggest about the rationality of people who commit crime? Generally speaking, are criminals rational thinkers or people caught in the passions of the moment?

Should the opinions of expert witnesses (persons with Ph.D., M.D., or J.D. degrees who publish scientific studies) outweigh the opinions of lay persons? In your opinion, how frequently do personal biases contaminate the detached, scientific judgments of expert witnesses?

Are Offenders Rational?

Are juvenile offenders rational? Do rational people murder their friends?[21] Do they stab to death a 10-year-old child walking home from school?[22] Do they drop a playmate from a 14th-floor window because he would not steal some candy?[23] Juveniles have committed all of these acts.

Research on whether offenders are rational has produced mixed results. Studies have found that street criminals, prostitutes, thieves, drug dealers and users, burglars, robbers, serial killers, and rapists[24] do calculate the risks of getting caught. However, some of these same offenders have been discovered exercising less rationality than might been expected.[25] Kenneth Tunnell studied the motivations of chronic property offenders and concluded that

1. They do not consider the legal consequences of their behavior.
2. They focus on rewards and not risks, believing they will not get caught.
3. They do not consider the law, arrest, or imprisonment."[26]

Compare the general tone of classical and neoclassical theories to more sociological explanations of delinquency. Why is the latter approach championed by sociologists? Do sociologists ever want to admit that individuals might be bad, or at least, do bad things?

In addition, Ronald Akers thinks the concept of rationality is itself problematic.[27] If to be rational means to have full and accurate access to all potential outcomes of behavior, classical theories are unrealistic because such predictable situations do not exist. If to be rational means to make a decision based on the available information, then offenders only have *limited* rationality. With limited rationality, the emphasis upon free will and autonomy, which is the cornerstone of the classical argument, is lost. The information that is available may be faulty or the individual's assessment of the situation may be incorrect. People may not be as free to choose between alternative courses of action as these theories suggest.

Are Crimes Rational?

Under some circumstances, predatory crimes like robbery are rational. But what about "bizarre" crimes such as personal crimes of violence? Are these crimes rational? It is tempting to blame them on biological impulses and psychological delusions. But violence may be rational in circumstances where offenders believe it will produce rewards. When rival gangs fight, the reward is reputation. Boyfriends assault girlfriends to win arguments. Children murder classmates to stop being bullied. Violence may be an effective way to get what someone wants. It helps people get what they want.[28]

This idea has been tested in research evaluating the interactions of victims and offenders. Situational factors and incremental choices made by victims and aggressors interact in ways that cause violence to occur or to be averted.[29] Criminologists who contend violence is irrational may only be revealing a general lack of understanding of the "contexts, motivations, options, and decision-making processes that lead to offending."[30] Once we have full information, we may find violent offenders are more rational than we think.

Why is so much credence accorded to the role of mental health in delinquent decision making? Should equal credence be given the role of physical health? Just as many object to punishing or executing persons with low IQs or mental instability, could the same logic apply to delinquents who suffer from allergies, influenza, AIDS, or cancer?

Are Offenders Amoral?

Another reason given for why juveniles sometimes make bad choices is their lack of morality and not whether they are rational. James Q. Wilson thinks juveniles who behave badly do so because they have not had a sense of morality instilled into them:

> The moral relativism of the modern age has probably contributed to the increase in crime rates. . . . It has done so by replacing the belief in personal responsibility with the notion of social causation and by supplying to those marginal persons at risk for crime a justification for doing what they might have done anyway.[31]

This way of thinking is supported by Hans Eysenck, who blames juvenile violence on parental and societal permissiveness. How young people are reared today has produced a serious problem: They have not developed a conscience because they have not been taught to connect their misbehavior with a negative outcome.[32] Delinquency is the price we pay for society and parents not doing their job.

Juvenile Justice Policy Applications

The Classical School advises society to respond to delinquent offenders in one of two ways: either through the *justice model* or the *utilitarian punishment model.*

Even if people are not evil, wicked, or otherwise contaminated with supernatural spirits, certain individuals (e.g., serial killers or career criminals) continually and seriously victimize society. Do such individuals simply deserve to be killed?

The Justice Model

In . . . *We Are the Living Proof* . . ., David Fogel introduced the **justice model**, an idea that promotes fixed-time sentences, abolishment of parole, and use of prisons to punish offenders.[33] Fogel suggested that *indeterminate sentences,* or sentences of varying time lengths, be abolished since the courts cannot discriminate between offenders who can be reformed from those who cannot. A more fair system would be one in which people who committed like crimes received similar punishments.

Fogel's thinking is grounded in **retribution**, the idea that criminals deserve to be punished because of the social harm they have caused. Punishment is their *just desert.* Underlying retributive philosophy is that punishment be based on the seriousness of the crime and culpability of the offender. In addition, when sentencing offenders it is wrong to take into account their needs. Sentences should only reflect the penalties criminals deserve for breaking the law.

Critics of the justice model complain that it panders to a correctional policy of despair rather than hope.[34] There also is not much support that the justice model leads to a more humane and impartial criminal justice system. To the contrary, some state legislatures have established determinant sentencing as a way to create more punitive sentences.[35]

One of the more memorable elements of the film *Scared Straight* is the frank manner in which inmates discuss the realities of prison rape and other degradations. In fact, many of the juvenile delinquents suggested that they were deterred by even the remote possibility of being sexually assaulted. Should policy makers exaggerate the prevalence of prison rape and degradation in order to increase the deterrent effects of imprisonment? Would this policy be effective?

The Utilitarian Punishment Model

While both the utilitarian punishment and justice models hold offenders responsible for their behavior, they do so for different reasons. The **utilitarian punishment model** punishes offenders to protect society. According to Ernest van den Haag:

> If a given offender's offenses are rational in the situation in which he lives—if what he can gain exceeds the likely cost to him by more than the gain from legitimate activities he does—there is little that can be "corrected" in the offender. Reform will fail. It often fails for this reason. What has to be changed is not the personality of the offender, but the cost–benefit ratio which makes his offense rational. The ratio can be changed by improving and multiplying his opportunities for legitimate activity and the benefits they yield, or by decreasing this opportunity for illegitimate activities, or by increasing their cost to him, including punishment.[36]

Van den Haag and others assume that *punishment deters crime.* If they are right, it should be possible to prevent crime by punishing offenders more harshly. Support for this idea has steadily increased partly in response to research findings published by Morgan Reynolds. He calculated the risk of *actual* punishment for each Crime Index offense and found that the likelihood of a person who commits a serious crime of serving prison time is very, very low. (See Box 5–3.)

The origin of several delinquency prevention policies are based on the utilitarian punishment model. Three examples are discussed below; two rely on incarceration. The common thread that binds them is that each one tries to make offenders fearful of the consequences of crime.

In *shock probation*, offenders are supposed to experience fear through a short period of incarceration preceding probation. In *boot camps*, offenders

Boot camp instructors use physical coercion, verbal abuse, and harsh discipline to help delinquent youths understand the consequences of their misdeeds. Are criminal justice boot camps necessary due to the failure of many American families? How does this harsh approach reconcile with neoclassical thought?

are drilled and tormented for 60 to 90 days. And in *Scared Straight,* juveniles attend presentations at adult prisons where hardened convicts and lifetime inmates yell and scream threats of assault and rape at them, letting them know what will happen if they come to prison.[37] Research evaluating the effectiveness of these programs has generally found that none of them are very successful at deterring chronic juvenile offenders (see Chapter 15).

Conclusions

Theories answer the questions of why and when something will happen. They are important to us because *ideas have consequences.* In the Middle Ages, the most popular theories blamed delinquency on supernatural or evil powers. This idea lost luster during the Enlightenment of the 18th century with the emergence of the Classical School.

Classical School theorists believe people are rational, intelligent beings who exercise free will. They commit crime because they imagine it to be in their best interests. Classical theorists also think punishment deters crime and that the best punishment is one that is certain, swift, and severe.

The Classical School failed because of its own rigidity. It ultimately gave way to the Neoclassical School. This school introduced the ideas of mitigating circumstances and individual justice, and laid the groundwork for a new explanation of crime based on scientific determinism.

In the next chapter we will begin discussing theories of the Positive School of criminology. All Positive School theories blame delinquency on conditions that come before the actual act. These theories assume free will has nothing to do with why juveniles break the law. Rather, delinquency is determined by antecedent conditions that are in place before it occurs. It is the job of the criminologist to discover what the conditions are that cause crime to occur in the first place.

Key Terms

Classical School: *Perspective that assumes people are rational, intelligent beings who exercise free will and choose to commit criminal behavior.*

free will: *People choose one course of action over another.*

indeterminate sentence: *A sentence with a minimum and maximum number of years.*

individual justice: *The criminal law must reflect differences among people and their circumstances.*

justice model: *A corrections philosophy that promotes flat or fixed-time sentences, abolishment of parole, and use of prison to punish offenders.*

mitigating circumstances: *Factors that may be responsible for an individual's behavior, such as age, insanity, and incompetence.*

natural explanations: *Theories based on data that exist in the real world.*

Neoclassical School: *Advises us to consider mitigating circumstances when determining culpability.*

rational choice theory: *Delinquents are rational people who make calculated choices regarding what they are going to do before they act.*

retribution: *Punishment philosophy based on society's moral outrage or disapproval of a crime.*

routine activities theory: *Focus on the crime target, which is anything an offender wants to take control of.*

supernatural theory: *Theory based on beliefs in demons, witches, evil spirits, and gods.*

theories: *Integrated sets of ideas that explain and predict phenomena.*

utilitarian punishment model: *Offenders must be punished to protect society.*

Getting Connected

The Bentham Project is dedicated to the life and writings of the utilitarian philosopher Jeremy Bentham (1748–1832). This site provides a forum for debate and discussion of Bentham's studies and ideas.

http://www.ucl.ac.uk/Bentham-Project/

1. What are the aims of the Bentham Project?
2. According to the project, at what age did Bentham begin to learn Latin?
3. What is the Auto-Icon?

The National Center for Policy Analysis (NCPA) is a research institute that functions primarily as a think tank. One of the center's specialties is the examination of crime and delinquency. The site is regularly updated.

http://www.ncpa.org/studies/s229/s229.html

1. According to the NCPA, what is the main reason that crime has gone down in the last decade? Do you agree with this analysis?
2. What is "expected punishment"? How is this related to utilitarian ideas?
3. This site argues that a "get tough on criminals" approach works well. How does keeping prisoners behind bars lower their costs to society?

The concepts of hedonism and utilitarianism are explored in some detail at the following site.

http://www.utilitarianism.com/bentham.htm

1. What is the "hedonic calculus" and what might be its use in the writing of criminal laws?
2. How does Bentham's definition of "pleasure" differ from John Stuart Mill's?
3. What is the importance of education in Bentham's notion of social change?

continued

Even in the 21st century people continue to examine the supernatural causes of behavior. One site devoted to such exploration is Deliriumsrealm.

http://www.deliriumsrealm.com

1. Find "A Gallery of Demons." In the section on Judeo-Christian demons, find information on the Book of Enoch. What is the role of angels in this work?

2. In the section on Judeo-Christian demons, find Beelzebub. What are his powers? What does he look like?

3. In the section on Judeo-Christian demons, find Satan. What is the difference between Satan in the Old Testament and in the New Testament?

The Internet Encyclopedia of Philosophy offers users a good discussion of the philosophy of Cesare Beccaria (1738–1794). Of special interest is the discussion of Beccaria's view on capital punishment.

http://www.utm.edu/research/iep/b/beccaria.htm

1. What is Beccaria's stand on capital punishment? Does he see it to be an effective deterrent?

2. What are the three best ways to prevent crime?

3. What is the purpose of punishment? How does Beccaria relate his arguments about crime and punishment to the existence of the social contract?

Endnotes

1. Dena Kleiman, "At 15, Truant Ends a Trail of Crime with a Slaying," *New York Times*, February 28:1, 44 (1982).
2. Frank Tannenbaum, *Crime and Criminality* (New York: Columbia University Press, 1938).
3. This incident was the basis for the movie, *The Exorcist*.
4. Eddie Pells, "Dad Believed Sons Possessed," *The Denver Post*, July 24:3B (1995).
5. Donna Leinwand, "School Denies Sanctioning Teen for Hex," *USA Today*, October 28:1B (2000). Also see the American Civil Liberties Union website at http://www.aclu.org/court/blackbear_complaint.html
6. John Hewitt and Bob Regoli, "Holding Serious Juvenile Offenders Responsible," *Free Inquiry in Creative Sociology* (in press, 2002).
7. Leon Radzinowicz, *Ideology and Crime* (New York: Columbia University Press, 1966).
8. Cesare Beccaria, *On Crimes and Punishments*, translated by Henry Paolucci (Indianapolis, IN: Bobbs-Merrill, 1764/1963).
9. Harry Elmer Barnes and Negley Teeters, *New Horizons in Criminology*, 3rd ed. (Englewood Cliffs, NJ: Prentice Hall, 1959), p. 322.
10. Michael Radelet, "More Trends Toward Moratoria on Executions," *Connecticut Law Review* 33:845–860 (2001).
11. Frank Miller, Robert Dawson, George Dix, and Raymond Parnas, *The Juvenile Justice Process*, 3rd ed. (Mineola, NY: The Foundation Press, 1985).
12. Robert Martinson, "What Works? Questions and Answers About Prison Reform," *The Public Interest* 35:22–54 (1974); Douglas Lipton, Robert Martinson, and Judith Wilks, *The Effectiveness of Correctional Treatment* (New York: Praeger Publishers, 1975); William Bailey, "Correctional Outcome: An Evaluation of 100 Reports," *Journal of Criminal Law, Criminology, and Police Science* 57:153–160 (1966); Hans Eysenck, "The Effects of Psychotherapy," *International Journal of Psychiatry* 1:99–144 (1965).
13. James Q. Wilson, *Thinking About Crime*, rev. ed. (New York: Basic Books, 1983), p. 128.
14. Ronald Clarke and Derek Cornish, "Modeling Offender's Decisions," in *Crime and Justice*, Volume 7, edited by Michael Tonry and Norval Morris (Chicago: University of Chicago Press, 1985), p. 145.
15. Bruce Jacobs, "Crack Dealers' Apprehension Avoidance Techniques," *Justice Quarterly* 13:359–81 (1996).

16. Matthew Robinson, "Lifestyles, Routine Activities, and Residential Burglary Victimization," *Journal of Criminal Justice* 22:27–52 (1999).
17. Bruce Jacobs and Jody Miller, "Crack Dealing, Gender, and Arrest," *Social Problems* 45:550–66 (1998).
18. Lawrence Cohen and Marcus Felson, "Social Change and Crime Rate Trends," *American Sociological Review* 44:588–608 (1979); also see Ronald Clarke and Marcus Felson, *Routine Activity and Rational Choice* (New Brunswick, NJ: Transaction Books, 1993); Marcus Felson, *Crime and Everyday Life*, 3rd ed. (Thousand Oaks, CA: Pine Forge Press, 2002).
19. Andrew Buck, Simon Hakim, and George Rengert, "Burglar Alarms and the Choice Behavior of Burglars," *Journal of Criminal Justice* 21:497–507 (1993); Kenneth Tunnell, *Choosing Crime* (Chicago: Nelson-Hall, 1992), p. 105.
20. Ronald Clarke and Derek Cornish, "Rational Choice," pp. 23–42 in *Explaining Criminals and Crime,* edited by Raymond Paternoster and Ronet Bachman, (Los Angeles: Roxbury Publishing Company, 2001); Marcus Felson, "The Routine Activity Approach," pp. 42–46 in *Explaining Criminals and Crime,* edited by Raymond Paternoster and Ronet Bachman, (Los Angeles: Roxbury Publishing Company, 2001).
21. Dick Foster, "Two Teens Charged in Triple Slaying in Guffey, *Rocky Mountain News,* March 10:5A (2001).
22. "British Hold 4 Youths in Killing of Boy," *New York Times,* June 26:A8 (2001).
23. Debbie Howlett, "Chicago Tot's Young Killers Test System," *USA Today,* November 28:3A (1995).
24. Lisa Maher, "Hidden in the Light," *Journal of Drug Issues* 26:143–73 (1996); Neal Shover, *Great Pretenders* (Boulder, CO: Westview Press, 1996); John Petraitis, Brian Flay, and Todd Miller, "Reviewing Theories of Adolescent Substance Use," *Psychological Bulletin* 117:67–86 (1995); Jacobs, note 15; Paul Cromwell, James Olson, and D'Aunn Avary, *Breaking and Entering* (Beverly Hills, CA: Sage Publications, 1991); Richard Wright and Scott Decker, *Burglars on the Job* (Boston: Northeastern University Press, 1994); Eric Hickey, *Serial Murderers and Their Victims*, 2nd ed. (Pacific Grove, CA: Brooks/Cole, 1995); Janet Warren, Roland Reboussin, Robert Hazlewood, Andrea Cummings, Natalie Gibbs, and Susan Trumbetta, "Crime Scene and Distant Correlates of Serial Rape," *Journal of Quantitative Criminology* 14:231–45 (1998).
25. Cromwell, Olson, and Avary, note 24; Shover, note 24; Wright and Decker, note 24.
26. Kenneth Tunnell, "Choosing Crime," *Justice Quarterly* 7:673–690 (1990).
27. Ronald Akers, "Rational Choice, Deterrence, and Social Learning Theory in Criminology," *Journal of Criminal Law and Criminology* 81:653–676 (1990).
28. J. Tedeschi and R. Felson, *Violence, Aggression and Coercive Actions* (Washington, DC: American Psychological Association, 1994).
29. L. Kennedy and D. Forde, *When Push Comes to Shove* (Albany, NY: State University of New York Press, 1998).
30. Clarke and Cornish, note 20.
31. James Q. Wilson, *The Moral Sense* (New York: The Free Press, 1993).
32. Hans Eysenck, *Crime and Personality*, 4th ed. (London: Routledge and Kegan Paul, 1977); Hans Eysenck and G. Gudjonsson, *The Causes and Cures of Criminality* (New York: Plenum Press, 1989).
33. David Fogel, . . .*We Are the Living Proof* . . . (Cincinnati: Anderson Publishing Co., 1975).
34. Fogel, note 33.
35. Todd Clear, John Hewitt, and Robert Regoli, "Discretion and the Determinant Sentence," *Crime and Delinquency* 24:428–445 (1978).
36. Ernest van den Haag, *Punishing Criminals* (New York: Basic Books, 1975), p. 59.
37. Paul Gendreau and Robert Ross, "Revivification of Rehabilitation," *Justice Quarterly* 4:349–408 (1987); James Finkenauer, *Scared Straight*, 2nd ed. (Englewood Cliffs, NJ: Prentice Hall, 1996).

Chapter 6

Biological and Psychological Theories

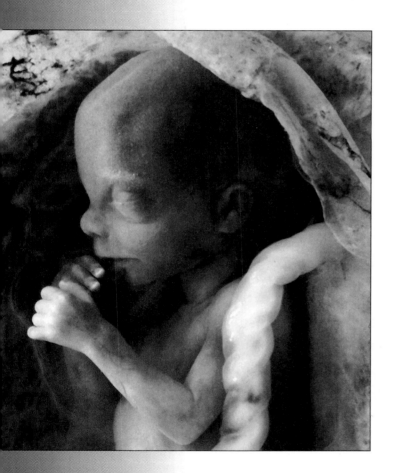

**The fault, dear Brutus, is not in our stars
But in ourselves, that we are underlings.**

—*William Shakespeare,* Julius Caesar

In *Descent of Man,* Darwin suggested that humans and animals were not as different as people thought. Does crime represent animalistic, primal urges? Why or why not?

The century between Beccaria and Bentham and the emergence of the Positive School marked a shift in thinking about crime from a focus on the *act* to the *actor.* Charles Darwin was largely responsible for this change. In *On the Origin of Species,* he argued that God had not created all the species of animals and that people had evolved from lower forms of life over millions of years.[1] Then, in *Descent of Man,* Darwin suggested that God had not made people in his own image and that there were few differences between people and animals.[2]

The Scientific Study of Crime

These ideas captured the attention of 19th century scholars who formed the Positive School of criminology. They believed crime was caused by factors that are in place *before* the crime occurs. It is presumed that the behavior was *determined* by something and it was their job to discover what it was. Free will had nothing to do with what people did (see Chapter 5).

In this chapter and the following one, positive theories of crime from the disciplines of biology, psychology, and sociology are discussed. While these theories share a common method for producing data, they disagree about which factors explain criminality.

Biological Theories

Biological theories locate the causes of crime inside the person. Over the past 150 years, these theories have proposed many reasons why people commit crime. One early explanation examined the role of physical appearance.

Physical Appearance and Crime

Cesare Lombroso was the first to connect crime to human evolution. He believed you could tell how highly evolved someone was by looking at him or her. Criminals were **atavistic** or throwbacks to an earlier, more primitive stage of human development. They more closely resembled their apelike ancestors in traits, abilities, and dispositions. Because criminals were not as highly evolved, they possessed **stigmata** or distinctive physical features, such as an asymmetrical face, an enormous jaw, large or protruding ears, and a receding chin. By default, criminals also were not able to obey the complex rules and regulations of modern society and needed to be confined in restrictive environments, such as prisons.[3]

A student openly laughed when told that sociologists generally dismiss the relationship between biology and crime. She said, biology explains most human behavior because humans are biological organisms. Do you agree with her?

One criminologist who did not agree with Lombroso was Charles Goring who compared the physical measurements of 3,000 English convicts on 43 traits with similar measurements taken from a sample of university students.[4] He found *no* evidence of a physical type of criminal. Goring's conclusion stood unchallenged until 1939 when Harvard anthropologist Earnest Hooton revealed that Goring had ignored his own data that actually refuted his argument (and supported Lombroso's theory). Upon reexamining Goring's data, Hooton found relative differences between criminals and nonoffenders.[5]

Body Type and Crime

In 1949 William Sheldon suggested there was a relationship between body build and temperament.[6] He believed the human body consisted of three components:

1. *Endomorphy*–soft roundness
2. *Mesomorphy*–square masculinity and skeletal massiveness
3. *Ectomorphy*–linearity and frailty

Each component is more or less present in all people. Sheldon tested this idea by typing people using a seven-point scale for each component. Every individual received a three-digit score that represented his or her body type. For instance, someone who scored 1–7–1, would be an extreme mesomorph.

Next, Sheldon developed a corresponding temperament for each body type. **Endomorphs** are relaxed, comfortable, extroverted "softies"; **mesomorphs** are active, assertive, and lust for power; and **ectomorphs** are introverted, overly sensitive, and love privacy (see Figure 6–1).

Sheldon typed the bodies of 200 incarcerated juvenile offenders and 4000 male college students. He discovered that the delinquents were generally more mesomorphic and less ectomorphic. (No significant differences were detected between the groups on endomorphy.)[7] This finding lead Sheldon to conclude that there was a relationship between mesomorphy and delinquency.

Other criminologists have also examined the relationship between mesomorphy and delinquency. Sheldon Glueck and Eleanor Glueck compared the body types of 500 delinquents and 500 nondelinquents. They also found that delinquents were more likely than nondelinquents to be mesomorphs.[8] Similar findings were reported by Juan Cortes and Florence Gatti who typed 100 delinquents and 100 high school students. Fifty-seven percent of the delinquents and only 20 percent of the nondelinquents were highly mesomorphic.[9] These findings lead James Q. Wilson and Richard Herrnstein to suggest that constitutional factors such as mesomorphy predispose some children toward delinquency.[10] They think a propensity toward crime has biological roots, or to put it differently: "Individuals differ at birth in the degree they are at risk for criminality."[11]

Even if there is an association between *body type* and *delinquency* is it because of *temperament?* Possibly mesomorphs are more effective in acting out their frustrations and desires than more delicately built children. Or maybe being muscular enables some children to be admitted to gangs that engage in delinquent acts. Or perhaps since masculinity allows someone to more easily

In *Crime and Human Nature,* Wilson and Herrnstein state that individuals differ at birth in the degree they are at risk for criminality. If they are correct, what are the implications of this for juvenile justice policy? Is there any hope for rehabilitation for persons who score high on innate criminality?

**Figure 6–1
Sheldon's types of
human physique.**

Source: William Sheldon,
*The Varieties of Human
Physique* (New York: Hafner
Publishing, 1963.) Used
with permission.

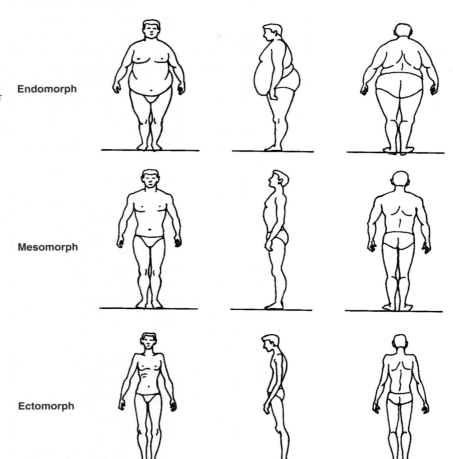

Endomorph

Mesomorph

Ectomorph

dominate others, it encourages the use of violence and threats. Or muscular-
ity may be a sign of masculinity and physical toughness, so boys with mus-
cles feel they need to play the role of the "tough guy." It is also possible that
juvenile justice officials, particularly police, regard mesomorphy in children
as a sign of danger and react differently toward these children than they do
toward more fragile-looking youngsters.

Heredity and Crime

In the late 19th century people believed that criminality was inherited. Crime
was blamed on a substance called "germ-plasm" that caused people to have
"bad blood." Once a person committed a crime, that fact was encoded in her
or his germ-plasm. When they procreated, their "bad blood" was transmitted
to their children (see Box 6–1).[12]

BOX 6-1   A WINDOW ON DELINQUENCY
Genes, Environment, and Behavior

Neither heredity nor the environment determines behavior. Genes act on behavior within the context of a particular environment. The effect of the environment on behavior depends on the hereditary characteristics of the person on which it acts.

How do genes and environment interact to produce behavior? Two possibilities are illustrated in the figure below. Segment (a) presents the basic argument that heredity determines behavior. Segment (b) shows the interactive relationship between heredity and environment.

Genes are associated with different behavioral outcomes (B1, B2 . . . Bn) that depend on environment (E1, E2 . . . En). For example, children born with Down's syndrome have a specific genetic inheritance. While the genotype has remained the same for every Down's syndrome child, the behavior of Down's syndrome children is different today than it was in the past.

What has changed is the environment Down's syndrome children are being raised in. The genotype that causes Down's syndrome has not changed. Today, many more children afflicted with Down's syndrome are receiving therapy, and when this is coupled with advancements in medicine, what these children can accomplish is remarkably different from what was thought possible.

Sources: Gregory Carey, "Genetics and Violence," in *Understanding and Preventing Violence,* ed. by Albert Reiss, Jr., Klaus Miczek, and Jeffrey Roth (Washington, DC: U.S. Department of Justice, 1994); Robert Sapolsky, "A Gene for Nothing," *Discover* (October): 40–46 (1997); Marc Peyser and Anne Underwood, "Nature or Nurture," *Newsweek* (Spring/Summer Special Edition): 60–63 (1997); Thomas Bouchard, Jr., "Genes, Environment, and Personality," *Science* 264:1700–1701 (1994).

The relationship between genes and environment

Source: Richard Lerner, *Human Development,* 2d ed. (New York: Random House, 1986), p. 84. Copyright © 1986 by Random House, Inc. Used with permission.

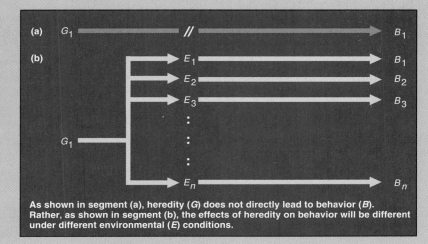

As shown in segment (a), heredity (*G*) does not directly lead to behavior (*B*). Rather, as shown in segment (b), the effects of heredity on behavior will be different under different environmental (*E*) conditions.

Scholastic tests such as the SAT are criticized for being culturally biased and geared toward the upper class. Dinesh D'Souza has reported that blacks who come from families earning more than $60,000 a year score lower on math and verbal tests than whites and Asians who come from families earning less than $10,000 per year. What does this evidence suggest about the social class biases of the SAT?

Would IQ tests be as controversial if blacks routinely outperformed whites? If so, why? If not, what does this suggest about the criticism of IQ tests in the first place?

IQ and Delinquency   The earliest studies to examine the relationship between heredity and crime centered on **intelligence**, which is the ability to learn, exercise judgment, and be imaginative. The first standardized IQ test was developed in 1905 by Alfred Binet and Theophile Simon.[13] In 1912 the German psychologist W. Stern introduced the notion of an "intelligence quotient" or *IQ*. Stern suggested that every person had a mental age that could be represented by an *IQ score,* which is the ratio of his or her mental age multiplied by 100 and divided by his or her chronological age.[14] The "average" ability for any age is 100, the level at which both the mental age and the chronological age are the same.[15] In 1916 Stanford University psychologist Lewis Terman revised the Binet-Simon test and renamed it the Stanford-Binet Intelligence Test.[16]

Historical Studies   Over the years some inflated and inflammatory claims have been made about the relationship between intelligence and crime.[17] In one early study, Henry Goddard administered intelligence tests to prison and jail inmates and discovered that 70 percent were "feeble-minded."[18] This extremely high percentage of low-intelligence inmates led the public, social reformers, and state legislators to conclude that low intelligence predisposed people to commit crime.

This idea stood unchallenged for more than a decade. Studies disputing it started to appear in the 1920s when the United States Army began administering IQ tests to its draftees. These tests revealed that their IQ scores were on the edge of "moronity," with an average mental age of 13, about the same as that of prisoners.[19] Then, in 1926, in a study comparing more than 1,500 delinquent males with a group of male nondelinquents, John Slawson discovered (1) *no* relationship between IQ and criminality and (2) IQ tests were culturally biased (see Box 6–2).[20] Subsequent research confirmed his conclusions. In 1928 Barbara Burks examined the intelligence of children of mentally deficient parents and discovered that when they were placed in foster homes with a nurturing environment, their performance on IQ tests reached "normal" levels.[21] A few years later Otto Klineber detected a dramatic increase in the IQ scores of black children who migrated from the South and attended schools in New York City.[22]

Contemporary Studies   Today, criminologists rather consistently report a link between IQ and delinquency, leading Murray and Herrnstein to conclude that low-IQ people are more prone to criminal behavior.[23] Travis Hirschi and Michael Hindelang reported the IQ of the average delinquent to be about eight points lower than nondelinquents.[24] Intelligence has also been tied to the type of crime someone is likely to commit. Bribers, embezzlers, and forgers generally have higher IQs than auto thieves, burglars, and substance abuse offenders, who are more intelligent than offenders who assault, murder, and rape.[25] Low IQ seems to predispose people to spontaneous and impulsive violent offending, while a high IQ is associated with crimes requiring more thoughtful planning and foresight.[26]

BOX 6-2   FACE OF DELINQUENCY
Cultural Bias and IQ Tests

Since John Slawson's pioneering work on cultural bias in IQ testing, concerns have been raised that intelligence tests are biased against racial and ethnic minorities. One example of a biased question from a standardized test used to estimate IQ in California (WISC-R test) is:

What should you do if you find a wallet in a store? Children earn 2 points for saying, "Find out who it belongs to and return it," or "Give it to the store owner or police officer." They receive 1 point for saying, "Try to find the owner." Juveniles receive no points if they say, "Make believe you didn't see it."

Critics of the test claim there is a problem with both the question and how it is scored. What is obviously the right answer to many children, may not be for some inner city black children who might reasonably fear that if they pick up the wallet they may be accused of stealing it.

What accounts for the relationship between IQ and delinquency? Are delinquents and nondelinquents biologically different from each other? Psychologist Adrian Raine has found that offenders are more likely to suffer from brain dysfunction as a result of birth complications, environmental toxins, and head injuries, which contribute to problem behaviors and having a low IQ.[27] Relatedly, early brain damage has been found to cause cognitive deficiencies that produce an array of endless problems for children, such as school failure and low self-esteem, which lead to delinquency.[28]

Twin Studies   One way to evaluate the impact of heredity on behavior is to study twins. There are **monozygotic twins** (MZ) or identical twins, who have identical DNA and come from one fertilized egg; and **dizygotic twins** (DZ) or fraternal twins, who come from two separate eggs fertilized at the same time. Fraternal twins are no more alike genetically than nontwin siblings. If there is a genetic factor in delinquency, MZ twins should be more alike than DZ twins. This similarity is called *concordance*, which occurs when both twins share a characteristic. For example, if one twin is delinquent and the other twin also is delinquent, concordance exists with respect to delinquency. Conversely, if one twin is delinquent and the other is not, this is called *discordance*.[29]

In 1929 Johannes Lange published the first study of twins and criminality.[30] He examined 37 twin pairs: 13 MZ twins and 17 DZ twins (7 pairs could not be classified). In each pair at least one twin had been in prison. In 10 of the 13 MZ pairs, the other twin had also been in prison, while in only two of the 17 DZ pairs had both twins served prison sentences.

Researchers have found that MZ twins have similar levels of criminality. Is the role between biology and human behavior minimized by criminologists trained in the sociological tradition?

Researchers have found that biology matters when explaining delinquency. The biological perspective is counter to the belief systems of sociologists who point to social processes and human development in explaining delinquency. Do criminologists have a vested interest in promulgating a certain perspective for the sake of their careers?

Heinrich Kranz expanded upon Lange's work when he evaluated the behavior of 32 MZ, 43 same-sex DZ, and 50 different-sex DZ pairs in which at least one twin had been in prison. Kranz reported a high degree of concordance between the criminal histories of MZ twins; moderate concordance for same-sex DZ twins; and very little concordance for different-sex DZ twins.[31]

The most comprehensive twin study was completed in 1974 in Denmark by Karl Christiansen.[32] He identified 3,586 twin pairs born between 1870 and 1920 who were listed in the Danish Twin Register. Christiansen reviewed police records and court documents for each twin set. A total of 926 twins belonging to 799 of the pairs had committed at least one criminal offense. He computed the criminal concordance rates for the sample and found much greater concordance between crime and the criminal careers of MZ twins than for DZ twins.

Research in the United States affirms Christiansen's findings. David Rowe found the concordance rates for self-reported delinquency among MZ twins was much higher than they were for DZ twins. MZ twins have also been discovered to have more delinquent friends than DZ twins do. These findings persuaded Rowe to conclude that genes predispose some children to select friends who are delinquent.[33]

Before we conclude that genes cause crime, we must consider other possible explanations. For instance, it is possible that the higher concordance rates for MZ twins are the result of their being raised in more similar environments than DZ twins are. MZ twins also are more likely to pick the same friends, are more closely attached to and dependent on each other, choose more similar occupations, and are generally cooperative while DZ twins are typically competitive.[34] In addition, because MZ twins look alike, they often are treated alike. It is also plausible that the reason MZ twins are more likely to engage in delinquency is because they do it together. Their delinquency can be traced to the simplest explanation: They spend a lot of time together.[35]

Adoption Studies   The impact of heredity on behavior can also be assessed by studying adoptees. Adopted children usually have little or no contact with their biological parents. Therefore, to the extent that their behavior resembles the behavior of their *biological* parents, an argument can be made that genes influence behavior.

Barry Hutchings and Sarnoff Mednick compared the criminal records of 662 adopted sons with criminal records of their biological and adoptive fathers.[36] When both the biological *and* adoptive fathers had a criminal record, 36 percent of the sons were criminal; when only the biological father had a criminal record, 22 percent of the sons were criminal; when only the adoptive father was criminal, 12 percent of the sons were criminal; and when neither of the fathers were criminal, only 10 percent of the sons had a record.

In 1987 Mednick and his associates matched the court convictions of 14,427 male and female adoptees with the court convictions of their biological mothers and fathers and their adoptive mothers and fathers. They found that the criminality of the child was more closely related to the criminality of the biological parents.[37] Follow-up research has produced similar findings.[38] In a Swedish study of nearly 900 male adoptees, it was reported that the criminal histories of children were more similar to those of their biological parents than to their adoptive parents.[39]

Research in the United States has reported similar findings. In 1972 Crowe analyzed arrest records of 52 adoptees who had been separated from their incarcerated biological mothers. He compared them to a group of adoptees whose biological mothers had no criminal record. Crowe discovered that the adoptees of the "criminal" mothers were about five times more likely than the adoptees of "noncriminal mothers" to have an arrest record.[40] He also found that adoptees with "criminal mothers" were more likely than adoptees with "noncriminal mothers" to be diagnosed with antisocial personalities.[41] Both Cadoret[42] and Rowe[43] have reported comparable findings.

Adoption studies are better than twin studies at separating the effects of heredity and environment. However, adoption studies are plagued by two problems.

First, the existing studies use different definitions of criminality. In some studies criminality is defined as having an antisocial personality, while other studies operationalize it in terms of engaging in benign problem behaviors such as cigarette smoking, and a few studies define crime on the basis of arrest, conviction, and incarceration records.[44]

Second, children in adoption studies have spent varying amounts of time with their biological parents *before* they were adopted. It has been reported that the more time children spend with their biological parents *before* they are adopted, the more likely they will develop personality disorders and have a criminal record.[45]

Brain Function

The brain is the most important organ in the human body. In fact, *behavior is under the control of the brain.* Only recently have criminologists realized that people's brains are different in their structure and chemistry. A growing body of research indicates that criminality may be linked to differences in brain structure in parts of the brain that affect people's ability to exercise self-control (frontal lobe) and respond to environmental changes (temporal lobe). Similarly, brain chemistry has been tied to criminality. It is now well established that some brains produce more or less chemicals than others. For example, a brain may produce too little *serotonin.* A deficiency in this neurotransmitter has been coupled with impulsivity, aggression, and violent offending.[46]

In addition to an increased likelihood of committing violence, another possible consequence for children with brains that produce too little serotonin is **Attention Deficit/Hyperactivity Disorder** (ADHD), the most common neurobehavioral disorder of childhood. ADHD was discovered in the 1930s by a physician in Providence, Rhode Island, who was studying the causes of delinquency. While doing his research, he stumbled upon a way to calm rowdy boys. By giving them stimulants he was able to help them focus their attention in school.[47] With that discovery, the first generation of drugs to treat ADHD was born.

Before we get ahead of ourselves, you should be able to recognize the symptoms of ADHD. They include inattention and hyperactivity that cause difficulty in school, poor relationships with family and peers, and low self-esteem.[48] Children with ADHD are more than just fidgety, they are "driven by a motor" all the time. They run, jump, climb everywhere, constantly lose things, and have difficulty following through on simple instructions.[49] Frequently they are depressed, have speech and language impediments, and learning disabilities.[50]

No one knows how many children have ADHD. One estimate is that somewhere between 3 and 8 million children have ADHD, which is three times more common in boys. ADHD in girls, however, may be as common as it is among boys but is underdiagnosed because girls with ADHD have developed more acceptable coping strategies than boys have. Rather than being rebellious, ADHD girls are often inattentive and thus are *mis*diagnosed as lazy or spacey when they are not.[51]

ADHD symptoms usually appear before age four, but children often are not diagnosed with ADHD until they enter school where they talk excessively, interrupt teachers, and commit physically dangerous acts.[52] But it is not easy to determine whether a child has ADHD or something else. One study found that more than half the children who received medication for ADHD did not have the disorder.[53]

Children with ADHD are difficult to parent and educate because of their consistently disruptive behavior. Should ADHD children be medicated to control their behavior? What are the benefits and costs of medicating children?

Research has found that ADHD children are often aggressive. Might the use of drugs such as *Ritalin* reduce school violence?

The cause of ADHD is unknown. It has been tied to heredity, prenatal stress, neurological damage, food allergies, and family turmoil.[54] It also has been reported the brains of ADHD children are smaller than the brains of non-ADHD juveniles.[55] Research also has found that ADHD children are more likely to be involved in other problem behaviors throughout their lives.[56] They are arrested, adjudicated delinquent, and become adult criminals more often than non-ADHD children.[57]

John Satterfield found that children with ADHD were 25 times more likely than non-ADHD children to be institutionalized. It is not difficult to imagine the problems ADHD children pose for teachers. How much of the blame for public school malaise do ADHD children deserve?

Nondelinquents with ADHD have been found to have better cognitive functioning and verbal skills than ADHD delinquents, who have more cognitive defects than non-ADHD delinquents. When John Satterfield compared 150 ADHD children, and 88 normal children, he found that ADHD children were more likely to be arrested for a serious crime and were 25 times more likely to be institutionalized for antisocial behavior.[58]

Many clinics in the United States treat ADHD children. The most common treatment is the prescribing of stimulants such as *Ritalin*, an amphetamine that has a paradoxical effect on ADHD children. Instead of speeding them up, psychotropic medications slow them down, allowing them to focus on learning tasks and calming their hyperactivity.

Skeptics, though, think the "ADHD problem" has largely been created by drug companies that reap huge profits from its existence.[59] The money spent treating ADHD children is astronomical. In 2000 physicians wrote more than 20 million prescriptions each month for *Ritalin* and similar drugs. Sales of these drugs in 2000 were $758 million, 13 percent more than in 1999.

What worries experts more than the money drug companies generate on sales of *Ritalin* and related drugs is that these stimulants may cause severe damaging side effects in children, such as neurological tics, loss of appetite, depression, sleep problems, and moodiness.[60] Research indicates that children metabolize medications differently than adults and that their brains develop at a much more rapid rate. Some studies have demonstrated that the maturing neurotransmitter system in children's brains is so sensitive to drugs that the drugs may cause permanent changes in adult life.[61]

Skeptics also wonder why 90 percent of the world's *Ritalin* is consumed in the United States. Is there something biologically different about American children? Do they really suffer from so many more behavioral problems than children who live elsewhere? Are American adults less tolerant of the behavior of children than adults in foreign countries? These questions are important to ask, particularly at a time when children are being legally drugged more than ever.

Chemical Poisoning

Few people blame delinquency on environmental toxins and chemicals. While chemicals do not cause children to commit crime, they indirectly affect behavior by interfering with the ability of the brain to perceive and react to the environment. One particular toxin that has been repeatedly found to alter brain functioning and cause changes in behavior in children is lead.

Lead gets into the bodies of children in different ways. They may ingest it through dust particles travelling in the air or by eating sweet-tasting lead-based paints peeled or chipped from walls. (Lead-based paint was banned in the U.S. in 1978 but is still found in many older homes.) A recent discovery found the wrappers of a popular Mexican candy sold throughout the United States to be highly contaminated with lead. The lead from the wrappers seeped into the candy and, when eaten by children, would go into their bloodstream.[62]

Once lead enters a child's body, it makes its way into the bloodstream, then into soft body tissue (which includes the brain and kidneys), and finally into the hard tissue (bones and teeth).[63] Children are more susceptible to low levels of lead poisoning than adults because their nervous systems are developing faster, they are exposed to more lead, and their lead absorption rate is higher. A high percentage of the lead children absorb is not eliminated from their bodies for 20 or more years (see Box 6–3).

Lead not only damages a child's internal organs, it also has been connected to behavioral problems such as delinquency.[64] For instance, in a study of 900 boys, Deborah Denno found lead poisoning to be a primary predictor of delinquency and life-persistent criminality.[65] Herbert Needleman and his colleagues also reported a connection between lead poisoning and delinquency.[66] They discovered that children with high levels of bone lead were more aggressive, self-reported more delinquency, and exhibited more

Chemical toxins, such as leaded paint, are a significant health risk to children. Leaded paint is still prevalent in dilapidated apartments throughout the United States. What are the implications for the social development of children exposed to such paint? Do you think exposure to leaded paint has any relationship to involvement in delinquency?

BOX 6–3   FACE OF DELINQUENCY
Poisoned Schools

Children are society's most powerless people. They are exposed to many dangers they can do nothing about. One place where they face danger is at school. We are not talking here about the school violence discussed in Chapter 3. Rather, we are speaking of the pesticides that are applied on school grounds and hazards from new schools that are built on or near land contaminated by chemicals.

An increasing amount of scientific evidence suggests that exposure to chemicals harms children in numerous ways, including asthma, cancers, lower IQs, and learning disabilities. The Environmental Protection Agency (EPA), for example, has recently determined that the pesticide *Dursban*, a common pesticide used to control termites, poses significant health risks to children. Chemicals like *Dursban* harm the nervous, hormone, reproductive, and immune systems of growing children, which may lead to their being hyperactive, slow to learn, disruptive in school, and afflicted with certain types of cancer.

Children are more susceptible to environmental toxins than adults because they are growing more rapidly and their immune systems are less able to handle toxins. In many schools the lives of children are endangered on a daily basis from exposure to toxins. This is because schools:

1. Are built on contaminated land or near an industrial, commercial, or municipal site (e.g., chemical plant, airport, freeway, or landfill) that daily releases toxic chemicals into the air and surrounding community.
2. Spray toxic pesticides to kill pests that subsequently contaminate carpets and floors and leave pesticide residue behind in the sprayed areas.
3. Apply weed killer and toxic fertilizers throughout schoolgrounds, exposing children to residues as they play sports and use playground equipment.
4. Are poorly maintained, which provides a habitat for pests, molds, and allergies, and allows toxic residues to accumulate.

There also are no federal guidelines regulating where schools can be built. Only California has a policy that guides the location of new schools. In the other 49 states, cash-strapped school districts build new schools on whatever land they can afford. Many new schools have been proposed for locations on old industrial land that has been poisoned with toxic chemicals. Other schools have been proposed near industrial plants that release toxins on a daily basis. Too many existing schools are already located on poisoned sites.

Sources: Poisoned Schools (Falls Church, VA: Center for Health, Environment and Justice, 2001) (The full report is available at www.childproofing@chej.org or by telephoning 703–237–2249); Tamara Henry, "Schools on Contaminated Ground, Groups Says," *USA Today*, March 19:6D (2001).

attention difficulties. These findings were similar to those reported by Needleman, where lead poisoning was found to interfere with school performance.[67]

Children in society are differentially exposed to lead poisoning. The children most susceptible to lead poisoning are poor black children. The environments in which these children live and attend school are the ones

Thousands of criminals were involuntarily sterilized prior to *Skinner v. Oklahoma* (1942). Could such a policy exist today? Would controlling the reproductive behavior of criminals have an effect on the crime rate?

most heavily contaminated with lead and other toxins. Research has found that poor black children are eight times more likely than affluent whites to have high levels of lead in their blood.[68]

Juvenile Justice Policy Applications

Policies based on biological theories suggest that criminal offenders should be isolated or sterilized, both of which neutralize the cause of crime. The United States has a long history of sterilizing offenders. Between 1911 and 1930, more than 30 states passed laws that required sterilization for certain crimes. Before the law was changed in 1942 in *Skinner v. Oklahoma*,[69] tens of thousands of people had been sterilized. Behind the nation's sterilization policy was the idea that crime could be controlled if "bad genes" were not transmitted from one generation to the next.

Psychological Theories

BOX 6–4 THEORY IN A NUTSHELL

Sigmund Freud

Freud believed the personality develops in a series of stages. If a person becomes fixated at any one stage, conflict with the other stages is likely. Conflict may also derive from an over- or underdeveloped superego, which causes maladaptive behaviors, such as juvenile delinquency.

Psychological theories of crime emerged late in the 19th century. Over the next several decades, diverse streams of thought developed. Two groups of psychological theories have impacted our thinking about delinquency more than any others. These are the psychoanalytic and behavioral perspectives.

Psychoanalytic Theory

Psychoanalytic theory can be traced to Sigmund Freud, who believed the personality consists of three parts: the *id*, *ego*, and *superego* (see Box 6–4).[70] The **id** is present at birth. It consists of blind, unreasoning, instinctual desires and motives. The *id* represents basic biological and psychological drives; it does not differentiate between fantasy and reality. The *id* also is antisocial and knows no rules, boundaries, or limitations. If the *id* is left unchecked, it will destroy the person. The **ego** grows from the *id* and represents the problem-solving dimension of the personality; it deals with reality, differentiating it from fantasy. It teaches children to delay gratification because acting on impulse will get them into trouble. The **superego** develops from the *ego* and is the moral code, norms, and values the child has acquired. The *superego* is responsible for feelings of guilt and shame and is more closely aligned with the conscience.

In mentally healthy children, the three parts of the personality work together. When the parts are in conflict, children may become maladjusted and ready for delinquency.

Psychoanalytic Theory and Delinquency   Freud did not write specifically about delinquency. Others took his ideas and applied them to the study of crime.[71] Their theories have blamed delinquency on a child having either an underdeveloped or overdeveloped *superego*.

In the case of the underdeveloped *superego*, the socialization process has been inadequate or incomplete. The *superego* is too weak to curb the impulses and drives of the *id*. The child's behavior becomes a direct expression of the *id*—for example, "If you want something steal it." But delinquent behavior may also be indirect. Socialization inhibits the open expression of unacceptable urges, but that does not mean they disappear; they may merely become unconscious. In this way, delinquent behavior may be a symbolic expression of unconscious impulses. That is why, for example, an adolescent with an unresolved Oedipus complex may "murder" his father in a figurative way, like forging checks drawn on his bank account or killing a person who represents the authority of his father such as a police officer.

Sometimes delinquent behavior is the result of too much socialization, which produces an overdeveloped *superego*. Impulses and urges of the *id* may elicit strong disapproval from the *superego*. This ongoing conflict causes the *ego* to experience guilt and anxiety. But since the *ego* knows that punishment must follow crime, the *ego* will lead the child to a commit crime to minimize guilt. To ensure punishment, the *ego* will unconsciously leave clues.

Evaluation of Psychoanalytic Theory   There are three recurring criticisms of psychoanalytic theory. First, no evidence exists of a causal link between a subjective internal state of mind and delinquent behavior. Second, it is arguable whether the personality consists of an *id*, *ego*, and *superego*. No scientific evidence indicates that any or all of the elements are present. Third, no test accurately predicts the hypothesized relationship between early childhood experiences and future behavior.

Behavioral Theory

Behaviorists think children learn conformity and deviance from the punishments and reinforcements they receive in response to their behavior. Reinforcements and punishments can be either positive or negative. A **reinforcement** is anything that increases the likelihood of a behavior reoccurring. A **punishment** decreases the probability of a behavior being repeated.

B. F. Skinner   The most widely acclaimed behaviorist is B. F. Skinner, who believed that *environment shapes behavior*.[72] Skinner thought children learn which aspects of their environment are pleasing and which ones are painful (see Box 6–5). Their behavior is the result of the consequences it produces. His research with pigeons demonstrated that organisms act on their environment to elicit a response through **operant conditioning**, a type of learning where subjects do something and connect what they do to the response they receive. Children will *repeat rewarded behavior and abort punished behavior*.

**BOX 6–5
THEORY IN A
NUTSHELL**

B. F. Skinner

Skinner argues that behavior is a consequence of the reinforcements and punishments it produces. Delinquents have had delinquency reinforced (and not punished) by others, either intentionally or unintentionally.

Social learning theorists would say that this child is likely to become a cigarette smoker. If individuals learn behaviors by watching and mimicking others, why do delinquents seem to "learn" various forms of deviance but reject conventional behaviors that they also observe?

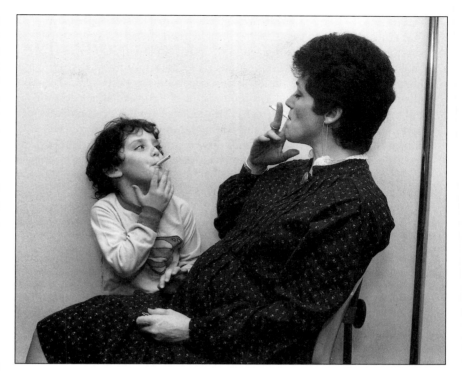

BOX 6–6 THEORY IN A NUTSHELL

Albert Bandura

Bandura thinks that children learn how to behave from others who they model and imitate. Delinquent behavior is learned from direct, face-to-face interaction or by observing others in person or symbolically in literature, films, television, and music.

Albert Bandura   Albert Bandura expanded on Skinner's ideas and developed a *theory of aggression* where he said children learn by modeling and imitating others.[73] Children learn to be aggressive from their experiences. They learn aggression in different ways; for example, by observing arguing parents, seeing their peers fight, and watching television and motion picture violence. From their observations, children may learn that aggression is sometimes acceptable and produces the desired outcome (see Box 6–6).

Bandura's most significant work focused on the relationship between mass media and aggression. He asked nursery school-age children to watch a film that showed an adult hitting a large inflated Bobo doll with a hammer. Then he showed the children one of three different endings to the film. In one ending, a second adult rewarded the actor for an "outstanding" performance. In the second ending, the second adult scolded and spanked the actor. In the third ending, the second adult behaved in a neutral manner toward the actor, providing neither reward nor punishment. An equal number of children watched each of the endings. After seeing the film, the children were placed in separate rooms with many of the same toys they had been seen in the film, including the Bobo doll. Hidden observers recorded each child's behavior. More aggressive behavior was observed among children who watched the film ending that showed aggressive behavior being rewarded. Bandura concluded that children learn aggression by observing and imitating others.

Behaviorists believe that children learn aggression by observing and imitating others. However, the behaviorists cannot explain from where certain manifestations of aggression arise. For example, do delinquents commit murder-rape-kidnapping because they witnessed their parents fighting?

Behavioral Theory and Delinquency   Children seek pleasure and avoid pain. They learn what is appropriate behavior by repeating acts that are rewarded (Skinner) and by observing and imitating others (Bandura). Behavioral theory raises an important question related to delinquency: Is there a relationship between media violence and crime?

Criminologists have studied this question for more than 70 years. In 1933 Herbert Blumer concluded from conversations with young people that movies did influence their behavior.[74] Decades later the evidence suggests that they still do. For instance in 1979, shortly after release of *The Warriors*, three murders were committed that bore striking resemblances to acts in the film.[75] Roughly 20 deaths have been blamed on *The Deer Hunter*. One incident involved a teenager who died after shooting himself with a .38-caliber handgun while playing Russian roulette, just as in the movie.

The would-be assassin of President Reagan, John Hinckley, Jr., identified with Travis Bickle, the character played by Robert De Niro in *Taxi Driver*. After seeing the film 15 times, Hinckley became obsessed with Jodie Foster, who played the teenage prostitute. In *Taxi Driver*, Bickle entertained the thought of assassinating a political candidate and stopped only after the plan had failed.[76]

Four days after watching *Born Innocent*, three teenage girls attacked a nine-year-old girl on a California beach and raped her with a bottle, just as it was done in the movie. The victim's mother filed an $11 million negligence suit against NBC, accusing the company of being responsible for the rape. The Supreme Court ruled that networks are not liable for damages unless they willfully seek to induce violence.

Other reports of violence have been linked to *Boyz N' the Hood*, *Natural Born Killers*, *Money Train*, *Juice*, *Scream*, *Scream II*, and *The Man in the Iron Mask*; and two television series, *South Park* and *Jackass*. When *Boyz N' the Hood* was released in July 1990, two people were killed and more than 30 injured near or outside movie theaters. Research has linked *Natural Born Killers* to at least 100 murders, and Senator and 1996 Republican nominee for president Robert Dole suggested that Columbia Pictures should share the blame for the torching of New York City subway clerk Harry Kaufman, the victim of a copycat crime from a scene in *Money Train*.[77] Following the premier of *Juice*, a movie about four black juveniles, including one who gets involved in a robbery that ends in murder, violence broke out at theaters across the country. For instance, in Chicago a 16-year-old was shot and killed by a stray bullet from a fight between two boys waiting for tickets to the last show. In Philadelphia an 18-year-old was paralyzed from the chest down after he was shot coming out of the movie. In New York City a 16-year-old was stabbed in a theater during a quarrel with another teenager.[78] More recently, two teens obsessed with *Scream* and *Scream II* were convicted of murder. They stabbed their victim 45 times with four knives and a screwdriver. In the movies, victims were knifed by killers obsessed with horror movies.[79] Finally, a nine-year-old girl re-enacting a scene from *The Man in the Iron Mask* hanged herself with a shoelace.[80] Newscasters have also blamed at least one school shooting on Comedy Central's television

Many people believe that the media causes crime. Should the media be censored to protect against inflaming deranged fans? Or, would such a policy be fruitless since virtually anything can serve as the inspiration to violence for a madman?

Most children play video games and are exposed to violence on television. Yet, the vast majority do not become violent delinquents. Why?

show *South Park*, and MTV's *Jackass* was blamed when a 13-year-old Connecticut boy laid himself across a barbecue grill and suffered severe burns.[81]

A consistent stream of data suggests a link between children seeing violent entertainment and their behaving aggressively. Of more than 3,500 published studies on the topic, all but 18 of them have reported a positive association between media exposure and violent behavior.[82] An esteemed panel of social and behavioral scientists recently concluded that the evidence points "overwhelmingly to a causal connection between media violence and aggressive behavior" in children.[83] Viewing violent entertainment affects children in at least one of three ways:

1. Children see violence as an effective way to settle conflicts;
2. Children become emotionally desensitized toward violence in real life;
3. Entertainment violence feeds a perception that the world is a violent and mean place and increases the fear of victimization.[84]

But other factors may be equally or more responsible for juvenile violence. Some experts think juvenile violence is more a consequence of family breakdown, peer influences, and the proliferation of guns in society than media violence.[85] There also is not much data showing that media violence has a long-term effect on children's behavior.[86] Its impact may be very short-lived. That is probably why of the millions of children who regularly see violence, only a few act violently. It could be that *already* aggressive youths watch television shows and movies that affirm behavior they *already* are committing.

Evaluation of Behavioral Theory   Behavioral theory pays too little attention to how mental processes affect behavior. It is also arguable whether human behavior can be predicted from studies with pigeons. Behavioral theory also does not adequately explain why more children do not commit delinquency when they know the possible gains.[87] And, if media violence has a strong impact on behavior, why are levels of personal violence low? Finally, behavioral theory dismisses the possibility that free will influences behavior.[88]

Juvenile Justice Policy Applications

Two strategies for preventing delinquency have evolved from psychological theories. Both are widely practiced today.

Psychotherapy   If children's instinctual drives are not controlled, they will experience internal conflicts that will manifest themselves in delinquent behavior. Delinquency is a symptom of deep-seated psychological problems. Offenders need psychotherapy to gain an understanding of the cause of their emotional disturbance.

The use of psychoanalytic theory in juvenile justice peaked in the 1950s, when influential groups such as the United States Children's Bureau, the World Health Organization, and the United States Senate championed psychoanalysis as a correctional technique. In turn, these and other groups seized upon the psychoanalytic idea that it was possible to identify "predelinquents" before they committed crime. (Today these children are called "at-risk" youths.) Prevention programs were developed for children in need. The creation of antidelinquency programs marked the beginning of the *child-guidance movement*, the goal of which was to neutralize latent delinquency in the preadolescent.[89]

Antabuse is a drug that induces vomiting and severe nausea if taken in combination with alcohol. Many criminal defendants are ordered to take Antabuse as a condition of bond or probation. The rationale is that many crimes are the outcome of alcohol use, and if alcohol can be viewed as an unpleasant experience, then many people will choose to not ingest it.

Is Antabuse a good idea? Does it raise civil liberty issues? Should the criminal justice system force sobriety onto individuals?

Behavior Modification   The theories of B. F. Skinner and Albert Bandura blame delinquency on a child's interactions with his or her environment. Social policies based on their theories teach children alternative ways of living. One therapy is **behavior modification**, a method for changing behavior through conditioning.

Behavior modification was widely practiced in the 1960s and 1970s to treat maladaptive behaviors such as overeating, drug use, alcoholism, and smoking. Two behavior modification techniques used then and still practiced today are *aversion therapy* and *operant conditioning*.

Aversion therapy teaches children to connect unwanted behavior with punishment. Juvenile alcohol offenders may be required to receive treatment where they must ingest a drug that causes nausea or vomiting if they drink alcohol. The idea behind the therapy is that they will connect drinking with unpleasantness and stop drinking to avoid the ill effect.

Operant conditioning uses rewards to reinforce desired behavior and punishment to abort behavior. One example of using operant conditioning in juvenile reformatories is the **token economy**, a system of handing out points that can be exchanged for privileges such as watching TV and punishing behavior by taking those same privileges away.

Conclusions

The biological and psychological theories of delinquency discussed in this chapter represent more than 150 years of thinking. Characteristic of all the theories is that behavior is determined by something inside the child.

Biological theories blame delinquency on heredity. The cause may be, for example, faulty brain chemistry. Psychological theories, on the other hand, tell us all children have the capacity to commit crime. What separates biological from psychological theories are the factors they use to explain delinquency.

Biological and psychological theories are heavily criticized. Biological theories do not specify very clearly the specific behavior they want to explain. It is not enough to explain something called antisocial behavior. After all, not all "antisocial" behaviors are dysfunctional and not all legal behaviors are moral or acceptable. Similar criticisms have been made about psychological theories. They are difficult to test because their main concepts are so loosely defined. Hence, the relationship between, for example, an antisocial personality and delinquency has not received strong empirical support. For some children, personality is a major determinant of whether they will commit delinquency and, for others, it does not matter very much.

Both biological and psychological theories assume that the causes of delinquency are someplace inside the child. Flaws, defects, or deficiencies in her or his biological or psychological makeup account for delinquent behaviors. By the early 20th century, sociologists started to develop delinquency theories that highlighted the role of social forces. In Chapter 7 three groups of sociological theories are reviewed: cultural deviance, strain, and social control theories.

Key Terms

atavistic: *Criminals are a throwback to a more primitive stage of development.*

Attention Deficit/Hyperactivity Disorder (ADHD):   *The most common neurobehavioral childhood disorder.*

behavior modification: *A therapeutic technique to change behavior through operant conditioning.*

dizygotic twins (DZ):   *Fraternal twins; develop from two eggs fertilized at the same time.*

ectomorphs: *Introverted, overly sensitive people with a lean and fragile physique.*

ego: *Problem-solving dimension of the personality.*

endomorphs: *Relaxed, extroverted people, with round and soft physiques.*

id: *Represents the basic drives of the personality.*

intelligence: *The ability to learn, exercise judgment, and be imaginative.*

mesomorphs: *Active, assertive people with muscular physiques.*

monozygotic twins (MZ):   *Identical twins; develop from one fertilized egg.*

operant conditioning: *A type of learning in which an animal associates its behavior with rewards and punishments.*

punishment: *Anything that decreases the probability of behavior reoccurring.*

reinforcement: *Anything that increases the probability of behavior reoccurring.*

stigmata: *The distinctive physical features of born criminals.*

superego: *Develops from the ego and represents the moral code of the personality.*

token economy: *A system for distributing and withdrawing privileges to control behavior.*

Getting Connected

An excellent source of information on childhood lead poisoning is sponsored by the Alliance to End Lead Poisoning.

http://www.aeclp.org

1. What are some of the policy solutions suggested by the Alliance? Are any already in use in your area?
2. Does the site address the relationship between childhood lead poisoning and juvenile delinquency?
3. Why are lawsuits sometimes advised in the fight to end childhood lead poisoning?

The American Psychoanalytic Association is a good source of information on the theories and therapeutic methods originally developed by Sigmund Freud.

http://apsa.org

1. What is the special nature of child and adolescent psychoanalysis?
2. How does this organization answer the question: "Who Can Benefit from Psychoanalysis?"
3. How might psychoanalysis benefit juvenile delinquents, according to the information on this site?

Established in 1987, the B. F. Skinner Foundation is dedicated to publishing significant literary and scientific works in the analysis of behavior.

http://www.bfskinner.org

1. Find "A Brief Survey of Operant Behavior." Why is positive reinforcement more effective than negative reinforcement in encouraging students to study?
2. What did Skinner learn about a cat in a box? How could the outcome of this experiment apply to juvenile delinquency?
3. In what kinds of settings might behavior modification be useful in dealing with juvenile delinquency?

Twinsworld is dedicated to providing information for and about twins.

http://www.twinsworld.com

1. What is T.W.I.N.S. and why is the organization needed, according to this site?

2. Scroll through the list of "links." What seem to be the major issues of interest to twins and their families? Are there links addressing the issue of twins and delinquency?

3. What kinds of movies involve twins? How are the movies rated by the site's raters?

AdoptINFO provides information, research opinion, and policy documents related to adoption and issues facing adoptive families.

http://www.cyfc.umn.edu/Adoptinfo

1. Does this site include any information on research findings about the link between juvenile delinquency and adoption?

2. What are the goals of the Child Welfare League?

3. Visit the "Facts about Children and the Law" link. What is the role of foster care in the juvenile justice system?

Endnotes

1. Charles Darwin, *On the Origin of Species* (London: John Murray, 1859).
2. Charles Darwin, *The Descent of Man* (London: John Murray, 1871).
3. Marvin Wolfgang, "Pioneers in Criminology: Cesare Lombroso," *Journal of Criminal Law, Criminology, and Police Science* 52:361–369 (1961).
4. Charles Goring, *The English Convict* (London: His Majesty's Stationary Office, 1913).
5. Earnest Hooton, *The American Criminal* (Westport, CT: Greenwood Press, 1939/1969).
6. William Sheldon, *Varieties of Delinquent Youth* (New York: Harper & Row, 1949).
7. Sheldon, note 6.
8. Sheldon Glueck and Eleanor Glueck, *Physique and Delinquency* (New York: Harper & Row, 1956).
9. Juan Cortes and Florence Gatti, *Delinquency and Crime* (New York: Seminar Press, 1972).
10. James Q. Wilson and Richard Herrnstein, *Crime and Human Nature* (New York: Simon and Schuster, 1985).
11. Wilson and Herrnstein, note 10.
12. Janet Katz and William Chambliss, "Biological Paradigms," in *Exploring Criminology*, edited by William Chambliss (New York: Macmillan Publishing Co., 1988).
13. Barbara Burks, "The Relative Influence of Nature and Nurture Upon Mental Development," in *Yearbook*, Part 1 (Washington, DC: National Society for the Study of Education, 1928).
14. Derek Cornish and Ronald Clarke, *The Reasoning Criminal* (New York: Springer-Verlag, 1986).
15. Carl Murchison, *Criminal Intelligence* (Worcester, MA: Clark University Press, 1926).
16. Geoffrey Cowley, "Testing the Science of Intelligence," *Newsweek*, October 24:56–57 (1994).
17. Cowley, note 16.
18. Henry Goddard, *Feeblemindedness* (New York: Macmillan Publishing Company, 1914).
19. Murchison, note 15.
20. John Slawson, *The Delinquent Boys* (Boston: Budget Press, 1926).
21. Burks, note 13.
22. Otto Klineber, *Negro Intelligence and Selective Migration* (New York: Columbia University Press, 1935).
23. Charles Murray and Richard Herrnstein, *The Bell Curve* (New York: The Free Press, 1994).
24. Travis Hirschi and Michael Hindelang, "Intelligence and Delinquency," *American Sociological Review* 42:571–586 (1977).
25. Wilson and Herrnstein, note 10.

26. Anthony Walsh, "Cognitive Functioning and Delinquency," *International Journal of Offender Therapy and Comparative Criminology* 31:285–289 (1987).

27. Adrian Raine, P.A. Brennan, and S.A. Mednick, "Birth Complications Combined with Early Maternal Rejection at Age 1 Year Predispose to Violent Crime at Age 18 Years," *Archives of General Psychiatry* 51:984–988 (1994); Albert Reiss and J.A. Roth, *Understanding and Preventing Violence* (Washington, DC: National Academy Press, 1993).

28. Hirschi and Hindelang, note 24.

29. David Rowe, *Biology and Crime* (Los Angeles: Roxbury Publishing Company, 2002).

30. Johannes Lange, *Crime as Destiny* (London: Allen & Unwin, 1929).

31. Heinrich Kranz, *Lebensschicksale Kriminellen Zwillinge* (Berlin: Springer, 1936).

32. Karl Christiansen, "A Preliminary Study of Criminality Among Twins," in *Biosocial Basis of Criminal Behavior*, edited by Sarnoff Mednick and Karl Christiansen (New York: Gardner Press, 1977).

33. David Rowe, "Genetic and Environmental Components of Antisocial Behavior," *Criminology* 24:513–532 (1986); David Rowe and B. Gulley, "Sibling Effects on Substance Abuse and Delinquency," *Criminology* 30:217–223 (1992).

34. Dennis Stott, *Delinquency* (New York: SP Medical and Scientific Books, 1982).

35. Steffen Odd Dalgaard and Einar Kringlen, "A Norwegian Twin Study of Criminality," *British Journal of Criminology* 16:213–232 (1976).

36. Barry Hutchings and Sarnoff Mednick, "Criminality in Adoptees and Their Adoptive and Biological Parents," in Mednick and Christiansen, note 32.

37. Sarnoff Mednick, W. Gabrielli, and Barry Hutchings, "Genetic Factors in the Etiology of Criminal Behavior," in *The Causes of Crime*, edited by Sarnoff Mednick, Terri Moffitt, and Susan Stack (Cambridge, MA: Cambridge University Press, 1987).

38. Patricia Brennan, Sarnoff Mednick, and Jan Volavka, "Biomedical Factors in Crime," in *Crime*, edited by James Q. Wilson and Joan Petersilia (San Francisco: Institute for Contemporary Studies, 1995).

39. Michael Bohman, C. Robert Cloninger, Soren Siguardson, and Anne-Liss von Knorring, "Predisposition to Petty Criminalistics in Swedish Adoptees," *Archives of General Psychiatry* 39:1233–1241 (1982).

40. R.R. Crowe, "The Adopted Offspring of Women Criminal Offenders," *Archives of General Psychiatry* 27:600–603 (1972).

41. R.R. Crowe, "An Adoptive Study of Psychopathy," in *Genetic Research in Psychiatry*, edited by Ronald Fieve, David Rosenthal, and Henry Brill (Baltimore: Johns Hopkins University Press, 1975).

42. R.J. Cadoret, "Psychopathology in Adopted-Away Offspring of Biological Parents with Antisocial Behavior," *Archives of General Psychiatry* 35:176–184 (1978).

43. David Rowe, "Genetic and Cultural Explanations of Adolescent Risk Taking and Problem Behavior," pp. 109–126 in *Adolescent Problem Behavior* edited by R. Ketterlinus and M. Lamb (Mahwah, NJ: Lawrence Erlbaum Associates, 1994).

44. Rowe, note 43; G. Walters and T. White, "Heredity and Crime," *Criminology* 30:595–613 (1989).

45. Daniel Curran and Claire Renzetti, *Theories of Crime*, 2nd ed. (Boston: Allyn and Bacon, 2001).

46. Diana Fishbein, *Biobehavioral Perspectives in Criminology* (Belmont, CA: Wadsworth Publishing Co., 2001); Terrie Moffitt, G.L. Brammer, Avshalom Caspi, J.P. Fawcett, M. Raleigh, A. Yuwiler, and Phil Silva. "Whole Blood Serotonin Relates to Violence in an Epidemiological Study," *Biological Psychiatry* 43:446–457 (1998); D. Niehoff, *The Biology of Violence* (New York: Free Press, 1999).

47. Alice Park, "More Drugs to Treat Hyperactivity," *Time*, September 10:63 (2001); David Rowe, C. Stever, L.N. Giedinghagen, J.M. Gard, H. Cleveland, S.T. Terris, J.H. Mohr, S. Sherman, A. Abramowitz, and I.D. Waldman, "Dopamine DRD4 Receptor Polymorphism and Attention Deficit Hyperactivity Disorder," *Molecular Psychiatry* 3:419–426 (1998).

48. American Psychiatric Association, *Diagnostic and Statistical Manual for Mental Disorders*, 4th ed. (Washington, DC: American Psychiatric Association, 1994).

49. Mona Charen, "Attention Deficit a Real Problem," *Rocky Mountain News*, March 8:45A (2001).

50. G.J. August, G.M. Realmuto, A.W. MacDonald III, S.M. Nugent, R. Crosby, "Prevalence of ADHD and Comorbid Disorders Among Elementary School Children Screened for Disruptive Behavior," *Journal of Abnormal Child Psychiatry* 24:571–595 (1996).

51. M. Green, M. Wong, D. Atkins, *Diagnosis of Attention Deficit Hyperactivity Disorder* (Rockville, MD: U.S. Department of Health and Human Services, 1999); Kimberly Sanchez, "Slowly, ADHD Gender Gap Closes," at www.healthy.excite.com/living_better_content/her/article/1689.51339.

52. American Psychiatric Association, note 48.

53. Charen, note 49.

54. Leonore Simon, "Does Criminal Offender Treatment Work?," *Applied and Preventive Psychology* (Summer 1998); Stephen Faraone et al., "Intellectual Performance and School Failure in Children with Attention Deficit Hyperactivity Disorder and Their Sibling," *Journal of Abnormal Psychology* 102:616–623 (1993).

55. Karen Thomas, "Cause of Attention Deficit?" *USA Today*, November 9:10 (1995).

56. Karen Stern, "A Treatment Study of Children with Attention Deficit Hyperactivity Disorder," *OJJDP Fact Sheet #20* (May 2001); Terrie Moffitt, "Juvenile Delinquency and Attention Deficit Disorder," *Child Development* 61:893–910 (1990).

57. M.L. Wolraich, J.N. Hannah, T.Y. Pinnock, A. Baumgaetel, and J. Brown, "Comparison of Diagnostic Criteria for Attention Deficit Hyperactivity Disorder in a County-Wide Sample," *Journal of American Academy of Child and Adolescent Psychiatry* 35:319–324 (1996); M.L. Wolraich, J.N. Hannah, T.Y. Pinnock, A.Baumgaetel, and J. Brown, "Examination of DSM-IV Criteria for Attention Deficit Hyperactivity Disorder in a County-Wide Sample," *Journal of Developmental and Behavioral Pediatrics* 19:162–168 (1998).

58. John Satterfield, "Childhood Diagnosis and Neurophysiological Predictors of Teenage Arrest Rates," in *The Causes of Crime*, edited by Sarnoff Mednick, Terri Moffitt, and Susan Stack (Cambridge, MA: Cambridge University Press, 1987).

59. Peter Conrad and Joseph Schneider, *Deviance and Medicalization* (St. Louis: Mosby, 1980).

60. Monte Whaley, "Moving Beyond Drugs to Fix Attention Woes," *The Denver Post*, November 18:29A (2001); Nancy Shute, Toni Locy, and Douglas Pasternak, "The Perils of Pills," *U.S. News & World Reports*, March 6:45–50 (2000).

61. Shute et al., note 60.

62. "Lead-wrapped Lollipop Poses Health Hazard," *The Denver Post*, April 27:15A (2001).

63. Karen Florini, George Krumbhaar, Jr., and Ellen Silbergeld, *Legacy of Lead* (Washington, DC: Environmental Defense Fund, 1990).

64. Geoffrey Cowley, "Children in Peril," *Newsweek* Special Issue, Summer:18–21 (1991).

65. Deborah Denno, "Sociological and Human Developmental Explanations of Crime," *Criminology* 23:711–741 (1985).

66. Herbert Needleman, Julie Riess, Michael Tobin, Gretchen Biesecker, and Joel Greenhouse, "Bone Lead Levels and Delinquent Behavior," *Journal of American Medical Association* 275:363–369 (1996).

67. Herbert Needleman, Alan Schell, David Bellinger, Alan Leviton, and Elizabeth Allred, "The Long-Term Effects of Exposure to Low Doses of Lead in Children," *New England Journal of Medicine* 322:83–88 (1990); Herbert Needleman and Constantine Gatsonis, "Low-Level Lead Exposure and the IQ of Children," *Journal of the American Medical Association* 263:673–678 (1990).

68. Stanley Eitzen, "Problem Students," *Phi Delta Kappan*, April:584–590 (1992).

69. *Skinner v. Oklahoma*, 316 U.S. 535 (1942).

70. Sigmund Freud, *The Standard Edition of the Complete Psychological Works of Sigmund Freud* (London: Hogarth Press, 1925).

71. Franz Alexander and William Healy, *Roots of Crime* (New York: Knopf, 1935); August Aichhorn, *Wayward Youth* (New York: Viking Press, 1936); Kate Friedlander, "Latent Delinquency and Ego Development," pp. 205–215, *Searchlights on Delinquency*, edited by Kurt Eissler (New York: International University Press, 1949); Fritz Redl and David Wineman, *Children Who Hate* (New York: The Free Press, 1951).

72. B.F. Skinner, *The Behavior of Organisms* (New York: Appleton, 1938); B.F. Skinner, "Are Theories of Learning Necessary?" *Psychological Review* 57:211–220 (1950); B.F. Skinner, *Science and Human Behavior* (New York: Macmillan Publishing Co., 1953).

73. Albert Bandura, *Social Learning Theory* (Englewood Cliffs, NJ: Prentice Hall, 1977).

74. Herbert Blumer, *Movies, Delinquency, and Crime* (New York: Macmillan Publishing Co., 1933).

75. Scott Snyder, "Movies and Juvenile Delinquency: An Overview," *Adolescence* 26:121–132 (1991).

76. Snyder, note 75.

77. Snyder, note 75.

78. Premiere of 'Juice' Sparks Violence in at Least 8 States," *Rocky Mountain News*, January 19:3 (1992); Dick Foster, "Officials Fear Movie Inspired Kids' Crime," *Rocky Mountain News*, March 17:8A (1995); "Does Crime Imitate Art?" *Rocky Mountain News*, November 30:57A (1995).

79. "Movie-obsessed Murderers Convicted," *Daily Camera*, July 12:11A (1999).

80. "Child Dies in Apparent Movie Re-enactment," *Daily Camera*, November 16:2A (1999).

81. Diane Eicher, "TV Tempest That Never Dies," *The Denver Post*, June 10:2001:1K, 12-13K; Matt Sebastian, "Panel Looks at Reality, TV," *Daily Camera*, April 8:8C (1998).

82. Eicher, note 81.

83. Ann Oldenburg, "TV, Films Blamed for Child Violence," *USA Today*, July 26:9D (2000).

84. Oldenburg, note 83.

85. Oldenburg, note 83.

86. Jonathon Freedman, "Effect of Television Violence and Aggression," *Psychological Bulletin* 96:227-246 (1984); Jonathan Freedman, "Television Violence and Aggression: A Rejoinder," *Psychological Bulletin* 100:372-378 (1986).

87. Michael Nietzel, *Crime and Its Modification* (Elmsford, NY: Pergamon Press, 1979).

88. J. Robert Lilly, Francis Cullen, and Richard Ball, *Criminological Theory*, 3rd ed. (Thousand Oaks, CA: Sage Publications, 2002).

89. Lilly et al., note 88.

Chapter 7

Cultural Deviance, Strain, and Social Control Theories

Poverty urges us to do and suffer anything that we may escape from it, and so leads us away from virtue.

—Horace

Biological and psychological theories blame delinquency on factors *inside* of children. This view of crime was challenged in the early 20th century by sociologists, who said criminality was caused by factors *outside* of the child. This chapter reviews three groups of sociological theories: cultural deviance, strain, and social control. Cultural deviance theories blame delinquency on rapid social change, which weakens neighborhood controls on children; strain theories assume that children are inherently good, and commit delinquency only when they are under extreme pressure; and social control theories suggest that children are amoral—without obstacles thrown in their path, they will likely commit crime.

Cultural Deviance Theory

Cultural deviance theories were popular in the early 20th century. They state that children do not *really* commit deviant acts. Their behavior may be considered deviant by larger society but it is compatible with the behavior in their neighborhood. In this view, what society calls delinquency is actually *conformity* to norms frowned upon by "outsiders" but not by "insiders."[1]

Clifford Shaw and Henry McKay

Clifford Shaw and Henry McKay blame delinquency on the *neighborhood* where a child lives. They hypothesized that delinquency rates would decline the farther one moved from the center of the city, called the **zonal hypothesis,** and tested this idea by dividing Chicago into five concentric circles or zones. At the center was the Loop, the downtown business district where property values were highest (Zone I). Beyond the Loop was the zone of transition (Zone II), containing an inner ring of factories and an outer ring of "first-settlement colonies, of rooming-house districts of homeless men, of resorts of gambling, bootlegging, sexual vice, and of breeding places of crime."[2] Zones III and IV were suburban residential areas, and Zone V extended beyond the suburbs. They found delinquency rates were highest in the first two zones and declined steadily as one moved farther away from the city center (see Figure 7–1).

Neighborhoods and Delinquency   Shaw and McKay had a ready explanation for their findings. Neighboring railroad, stockyards, and industry made Zone II the least desirable residential area, but also the cheapest. Therefore, people naturally gravitated to this area if they were poor, as many immigrants to the United States were. But what did these findings say about the cause of delinquency? Shaw and McKay interpreted the findings in cultural and environmental terms. Delinquency rates in neighborhoods remained stable regardless of the race or ethnicity of people who lived there. Areas high in delinquency at the turn of the century were high 30 years later, even though the original residents had passed away or moved. Shaw and McKay explained their finding in the following way (see Figure 7–2).

**BOX 7–1
THEORY IN A
NUTSHELL**

**Clifford Shaw
and Henry
McKay**

Shaw and McKay argued that run-down areas of cities create social disorganization, fostering cultural conflicts that allow delinquency to become a tradition.

1. *Run-down areas create social disorganization.* Cities such as Chicago were expanding industrially, their populations were expanding, and segregation was forcing new immigrants into the slums. These immigrants were not familiar with the city's geography or culture; they arrived with different languages and work experiences; and they immediately faced new and overwhelming problems including poverty, disease, and confusion.

2. *Social disorganization fosters cultural conflicts.* In low-delinquency areas of the city, there typically was agreement among parents on which values and attitudes were the "right" ones, with general consensus on the importance of education, constructive leisure, and other child-rearing issues. These conventional values were reinforced by local institutions such as the PTA, churches, and neighborhood centers. But no such consistency prevailed in high-delinquency areas. The norms of a variety of cultures existed side by side, creating a state of normative ambiguity, or anomie (or cultural conflict). This condition was aggravated by the presence of individuals who promoted a nonconventional lifestyle and defined behaviors such as theft as an acceptable way to acquire wealth.

Figure 7–1
Zones of Delinquency in Chicago, 1900–1933

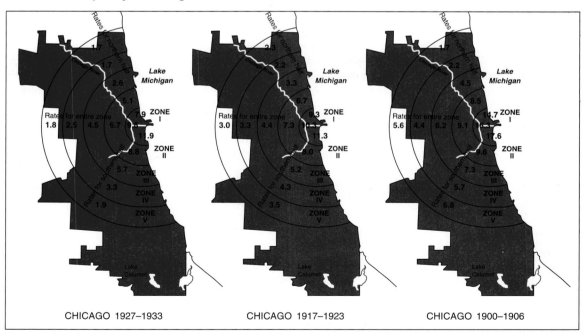

Source: Clifford Shaw and Henry McKay, *Juvenile Delinquency in Urban Areas* (Chicago: University of Chicago Press, 1969:69). Used with permission.

This value system could count on the support of criminal gangs, rackets, and semilegitimate businesses.

3. *Cultural conflict allows delinquency to flourish.* Children raised in low-socioeconomic, high-delinquency rate areas were exposed to both conventional and criminal value systems. They saw criminal activities and organizations in operation daily. Successful criminals passed on their knowledge to younger residents, who then taught it to even younger children. Delinquency became a tradition in certain neighborhoods through a process of **cultural transmission,** in which criminal values are passed from one generation to the next.

4. *Allowed to flourish, delinquency becomes a full-time career.* Children dabbled in delinquency very early in life, perhaps by age 5 or 6. Initial offenses were trivial, but their acts became increasingly serious, and delinquencies often became group efforts.

Even in the worst neighborhoods in the United States, the majority of the residents are law-abiding people, suggesting that *individual* flaws explain delinquency. How would sociologists, psychologists, and biologists differently address this issue?

Evaluation of Shaw and McKay's Theory   There are three serious problems with Shaw and McKay's theory. First, high-delinquency rate neighborhoods may not be disorganized. It is arguable whether these neighborhoods are disorganized or whether they are just organized differently than other neighborhoods. The idea that there may be a **differential social organization** among neighborhoods was suggested by Edwin Sutherland. According to Sutherland, children in high-delinquency rate neighborhoods come into regular contact with values that support criminality.[3] But that does not make neighborhoods disorganized, just that they are organized differently than other neighborhoods.

Second, Shaw and McKay only explain the neighborhood–crime relationship for a specific historical period. When Robert Bursik, Jr., reexamined delinquency rates in Chicago over an extended period of time, he observed an uneven pattern contrary to what Shaw and McKay had asserted about crime being stable across neighborhoods.[4]

Third, Shaw and McKay did not explain *non*delinquency in high-delinquency rate neighborhoods. In these neighborhoods, most children are not delinquents. This suggests the possibility that neighborhoods do not establish criminal traditions and values that are passed from one generation to the next.[5]

Figure 7–2
Mapping Delinquency Theory: Clifford Shaw and Henry McKay

| RAPID SOCIAL CHANGE | → | WEAK COMMUNITY CONTROLS | → | HIGH-DELINQUENCY AREAS | → | DELINQUENCY TRADITIONS | → | DELINQUENCY |

If immersion in gang life is a central component of childhood socialization, is there any social policy that can preclude gang involvement? What are the probable life chances of this child? Who is most to blame if this child becomes a gang-affiliated juvenile delinquent?

Economist Thomas Sowell rejects the cultural deviance approach. Sowell contends that cities could build new housing with amenities in disorganized areas and within six months the new facilities would be bastions of delinquency. Are traditionally "bad" neighborhoods simply bad because of the hoodlums living there?

Despite these criticisms, studies testing Shaw and McKay's theory and reformulations of it have found support for the basic premise that neighborhoods influence criminality. There is strong evidence of a relationship between "neighborhood disadvantage" (which includes the percentage of persons living below the poverty line, unemployment rates, proportion of single-parent households) and crime.[6] However, some research has reported the neighborhood disadvantage–crime association is affected by other factors such as friendship networks, attachment of residents to family and schools, and involvement of residents in community activities.[7] For instance, DeLisi and Regoli reported that feelings of neighborhood safety varied by a person's level of attachment to the neighborhood.[8] Another variable that affects the neighborhood disadvantage–crime relationship is *collective efficacy*, which is the "mutual trust among neighbors combined with willingness to intervene on behalf of the common good, specifically to supervise children and maintain public order."[9] Robert Sampson and his colleagues found that the degree of collective efficacy in a neighborhood is a better predictor of the violent crime rate than either poverty or racial composition.[10]

Edwin Sutherland

Edwin Sutherland has had an extraordinary influence on our thinking about delinquency. His most important contribution is the **theory of differential association**, where he described the process children go through to *become* delinquent.

Delinquency is inversely related to educational attainment, IQ, and, it could be argued, learning. Why do delinquents have difficulty applying the precepts of learning to conventional phenomena but no problem learning crime?

The Theory of Differential Association   The theory of differential association consists of nine principles:

1. Delinquent behavior is learned.
2. Delinquent behavior is learned in interaction with others through a process of communication.
3. Learning takes place in intimate groups.
4. In intimate groups children learn techniques for committing crime, as well as the appropriate motives, attitudes, and rationalizations.
5. The specific direction of motives and drives is learned from definitions of the legal code as being favorable or unfavorable.
6. A child becomes delinquent because of an *excess* of definitions favorable to violation of law over definitions unfavorable to violation of law. Definitions favorable to the violation of law are learned from both criminal and noncriminal persons.
7. The tendency toward delinquency will be affected by the *frequency, duration, priority,* and *intensity* of learning experiences.
8. Learning delinquent behavior involves the same mechanisms involved in any other learning.
9. Criminal behavior and noncriminal behavior are expressions of the same needs and values.[11]

Sutherland does not think delinquency is inherited. Rather it is learned in the same way as is any other behavior—from interaction with significant others. In their interactions children learn *how* and *why* to commit delinquency. But just because children are exposed to criminal attitudes does not mean they will become delinquent. For that to happen, they must learn how to *define* particular situations as ones in which it is okay to behave criminally. Children learn how to define situations from their associations. However, associations are not all equal. They vary in their *frequency, duration, priority,* and *intensity*. Associations that occur more often (frequency), are long-lasting (duration), take place early in life (priority), with people the child respects (intensity), will have the greatest influence on a child's behavior.[12]

**BOX 7–2
THEORY IN A
NUTSHELL**

**Edwin
Sutherland**

In differential association theory, Sutherland told us delinquent behavior is learned from intimate others. Delinquents are children who have learned an excess of definitions favorable to the violation of law over definitions unfavorable to the violation of law.

Evaluation of Sutherland's Theory   Sutherland's theory has been criticized on a number of fronts. First the theory is difficult to test.[13] For instance, the number of definitions a child has received from significant others favorable or unfavorable to the violation of law can never be known. Also, the time sequence Sutherland proposes is problematic.[14] Does differential association or delinquency come first? Delinquency may occur first, and only later do delinquent youths select other delinquents as associates. Sutherland thinks associates are chosen first and that they socialize (or influence) one another into becoming delinquent. Sutherland also assumes that children passively accept their environments. He thinks their behavior is *only* the product of the ratio of differential associations. More probable is

According to differential association theory, members of white hate organizations such as the Ku Klux Klan and members of minority gang subcultures have a commonality: Both learn deviance through primary relationships. Do you agree? Are Klan members and gang members similarly the victims of their social circumstances?

In 2000 in Marietta, Georgia, 25 males aged 12 to 25 abducted, molested, and gang-raped a 13-year-old mentally disabled girl over a period of 12 hours. The boys also videotaped the savagery. Do any of the criminological theories in this chapter explain such an act?

that children interact with their environment; each helps to shape the other (see Chapter 6).[15] The impact of media violence on behavior may also be greater than Sutherland thought (see Chapter 6).[16] Finally, the theory may be too simple. Sutherland only vaguely describes how learning takes place. This limitation has inspired others to reformulate the theory. One reformulation was crafted by Robert Burgess and Ronald Akers. They restated differential association theory in terms of principles of behaviorism, explaining how behavior is learned through operant conditioning (see Chapter 6).[17] They think rewarded behavior will be repeated and behavior that is punished will be squelched.

Differential association theory has had a significant impact on how criminologists think about delinquency. Of special note is that the theory forces them to ask difficult questions:

1. Why among children with comparable opportunities do only some commit crime?
2. Why in high-delinquency rate neighborhoods are many children law-abiding?
3. Why do middle- and upper-class children participate in delinquency?

Whether the answers to these questions are found in differential associations or in some other theory is arguable. What is not debatable is that these questions energized criminologists to pursue the study of delinquency in a more systematic way.

Walter Miller

Walter Miller explained lower-class male gang delinquency.[18] He started with the idea that lower-class boys learned values that contradict those of mainstream society. Miller hypothesized that boys developed sex-role problems in response to (1) living in female-based households and (2) having internalized values that set them apart from middle- and upper-class persons.

Female-Based Households, Focal Concerns, and Sex-Role Problems   The lower-class has a unique family structure, characterized by female-headed households and serial monogamy. Women run the household and have many husbands and lovers. This family structure alienates young boys, leading them to join all-male peer groups. In these all-male peer groups, the lower-class culture is created and transmitted.

Lower-class culture revolves around six **focal concerns**:

1. *Trouble* is the most important concern. Getting into and staying out of trouble are major preoccupations of lower-class people. Children are judged (assigned status) by how well they do this.
2. *Toughness* is a physical prowess that is often displayed through "machismo" (lack of sensitivity and treating women as "sex objects" and conquests).
3. *Smartness* is the ability to avoid being outfoxed. It refers to "street smarts," or the ability to take advantage of the weaknesses of others.
4. *Excitement* is the search for thrills, danger, or risk that often occurs as a result of excessive drinking, fighting, gambling, and promiscuous sexual relationships.
5. *Fate* is the lower-class belief that life is controlled by forces beyond their control. These forces are not religious ones (see Chapter 5), but refer to whether someone is naturally lucky or unlucky.
6. *Autonomy* describes the resistance of lower-class people to having their lives controlled by any others. Often you hear them say: "No one's gonna push me around" and "He can shove this job up his ass." Curiously, however, the actual behavior of lower-class people contradicts the cultural value of autonomy. Typically they seek out jobs in restrictive settings where they are told what to do and when to do it, because they identify strong controls with being cared for.

BOX 7–3
THEORY IN A NUTSHELL

Walter Miller

Miller blamed delinquency on two features of the lower-class culture: focal concerns and female-based households. Together they produce sex-role problems for boys. Because boys need to learn to become men and cannot learn to be a man from a woman, they join together and form a gang. They achieve status in the gang by living up to focal concerns, some of which lead to delinquency.

Figure 7–3
Mapping Delinquency Theory: Walter Miller

These focal concerns *are not* totally unique to the lower-class, but they are more significant to it than they are to the middle and upper classes.

Strong identification with these values is why boys break the law. Children participate in delinquency because they must live-up to the standards of their neighborhood, regardless of what "outsiders" think about what they are doing.[19] For instance, the focal concern of *toughness* may mean the juvenile must fight when disrespected; possessing street smarts (*smartness*) may lead to drug dealing; and *excitement* may result in the excessive use of drinking, gambling, or illegal drugs. (See Figure 7–3.)

The music of many rap artists reflects lower-class focal concerns. Did the allegiance to a gangster lifestyle cost rap singers Tupac Shakur and Notorious BIG their lives?

Evaluation of Miller's Theory   Miller's theory has been heavily criticized. Research suggests that the values held by gang delinquents are not endorsed by the majority of lower-class youth.[20] Second, Miller implies that middle-class values have a negligible impact on lower-class children. This is unlikely given that lower-class children are exposed every day to middle-class images in school and in the media. Third, the evidence on the relationship between fatherlessness and delinquency is mixed. Some studies have reported a strong relationship between them, while others have not (see Chapter 10).[21]

Strain Theories

Strain theories assume that children are basically good. Only under pressure (strain) do they deviate. Pressure for deviance comes from their having internalized society's goals, such as being successful, and wanting to achieve them. But many cannot become successful by conforming to society's rules. Out of desperation, they turn to crime.[22]

Robert Merton

Robert Merton blames delinquency on conformity to conventional cultural values. American society has (1) *cultural goals* that are regarded as worth striving for and (2) *institutionalized means* or approved ways of reaching these goals. The main goals in society are the acquisition of wealth and status. The socially approved ways to achieve them are by getting a good education, job

Males are more involved in delinquency than females, even though, as this photo attests, many girls are raised in socially disorganized neighborhoods. Why are girls less involved in delinquency than boys? Are girls more resistant to negative neighborhood influences and social disorder? If not, does this reduce the salience of cultural and strain theories?

Figure 7–4
Mapping Delinquency Theory: Robert Merton

| CULTURAL GOALS + LEGITIMATE MEANS | → | DIFFERENTIAL ACCESS TO LEGITIMATE MEANS | → | BLOCKED ACCESS TO CULTURAL GOALS | → | STRAIN | → | DELINQUENCY |

Table 7–1   Merton's Modes of Adaptation

MODES OF ADAPTATION	CULTURAL GOALS	INSTITUTIONALIZED MEANS
Conformity	Accept	Accept
Innovation	Accept	Reject
Ritualism	Reject	Accept
Retreatism	Reject	Reject
Rebellion	Reject prevailing goals and means and substitute new ones	

Source: Adapted from Robert Merton, *Social Theory and Social Structure*, rev. ed (New York: Macmillan Publishing Co., 1968).

training, and career advancement. However, for many children access to legitimate means is blocked. Doors to good jobs are not open to them, which creates a problem since they desire wealth and status. This situation produces pressure to deviate (see Figure 7–4) and children will resolve this conflict in different ways (see Table 7–1).

Adaptations to Strain   The most common way to adapt to strain is through *conformity*. Most children who are blocked from achieving success continue to ascribe to the society's cultural goals and believe in the legitimacy of its institutionalized means.

But some do not. For example, *innovators* embrace the cultural goals but turn to illegitimate means to achieve them. *Ritualists* accept institutionalized means but reject the cultural goals. *Retreatists* reject both cultural goals and the legitimate means. They are people who are "in society but not of it." These children become society's psychotics, pariahs, outcasts, vagrants, vagabonds, drunks, and drug addicts.[23] Finally, there are *rebels*. They reject *both* the goals and the means and substitute new ones. They want to change the existing system. The Earth Liberation Front and the Freemen in Montana are examples of groups who have adapted to strain through rebellion.

Evaluation of Merton's Theory   Merton assumes children commit delinquency only when their backs are against the wall. Delinquency can

Many crimes are not committed for pecuniary gain. For example, some armed robbers commit their crimes to obtain drugs. Rarely do they commit crime to pay rent, buy basic living supplies, or meet obligations to creditors. Are most juveniles who commit property crimes *really* economically motivated?

thus be prevented by eliminating conditions that generate strain. As palatable as this idea sounds, there are problems with it.[24]

Merton, for example, does not identify which juveniles among those denied legitimate means will commit delinquency. Nor does he say much about the relationship between strain and delinquency. Why do some children who should be terribly frustrated not commit delinquency while seemingly less frustrated juveniles do? He also understates the unique qualities of the child by exaggerating the homogeneity and solidarity of social class and social structure. And he does not explain how the distribution of goals and means originally came about. What is it in American society that explains how cultural goals and accessibility to institutionalized means are distributed? Finally, Merton does not tell us why some children commit one kind of crime while others choose a different type, or become alcohol or drug abusers, or become affected by mental disorders.

But at least two criminologists think these criticisms are not valid. Margaret Farnworth and Michael Leiber argue that Merton's critics really tested not his theory but their own *mis*interpretation of it. Farnworth and Leiber correctly suggest that how the variable "strain" is operationalized will determine what a study's findings will be.[25] While the validity of these criticisms will continue to be debated, Merton did motivate others to construct theories of their own. One who did was Albert Cohen.

Albert Cohen

In 1955 Albert Cohen published *Delinquent Boys*, where he explained why urban, lower-class boys commit delinquency.[26] Cohen began by identifying characteristics of delinquents. They are malicious, negativistic, nonutilitarian, versatile, loyal, and cannot defer gratification. Next, he explained how they became this way.

The Middle-Class Measuring Rod   Americans judge children in different ways. Most people evaluate them in terms of a particular set of values that Cohen calls the **middle-class measuring rod**. These values are ambition, accepting responsibility, seeking achievement, being industrious, exercising rationality, being considerate and courteous to others, controlling physical aggression, not wasting time, and respecting property. All children are expected to abide by these values. But doing so is not so easy for some children. Whereas most middle-class children may live up to them effortlessly, lower-class children may not be taught these standards (or not taught them well) and have difficulty adopting them.

Status-Frustration Theory   In school, children are judged by their ability to follow middle-class values. Children who do not follow them lose status and are looked down upon by the teacher and fellow students. Boys who become frustrated by their low status unite and form a delinquent subculture

Figure 7–5
Mapping Delinquency Theory: Albert Cohen

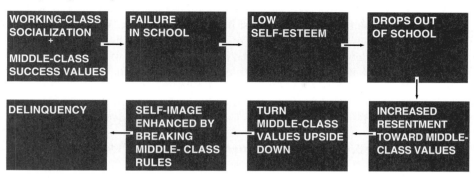

with a set of values that reject middle-class values. By making a complete change—from accepting middle-class values to rejecting them—these children gain status in the eyes of their peers. But once they adopt their new code, they lose any respect they had in the larger society; and once delinquent, they cannot turn back.

Cohen blames delinquency on (1) the frustration children experience because of their low status and (2) their inability to live up to middle-class standards. Delinquency is the consequence of children expressing their frustration toward middle-class norms and institutions (see Figure 7–5).

Evaluation of Cohen's Theory   The most striking criticism of Cohen's work is the lack of evidence supporting his central assumption that lower-class delinquents reject middle-class values. They do not seem to. Lee Rainwater found that lower-class boys shared middle-class values but "stretched" them to fit their circumstances. Rainwater also discovered that lower-class children "will live up to" the middle-class norms if they possibly can.[27] Relatedly, David Downes reported that the typical response of delinquents to frustration is not to reject middle-class values but to disassociate from them.[28] Similarly, Steve Box found that many lower-class boys never internalize the status criteria of school and teachers in the first place, always being distant from them.[29]

Richard Cloward and Lloyd Ohlin

In 1960, in *Delinquency and Opportunity*, Richard Cloward and Lloyd Ohlin also designed a theory to explain lower-class male delinquency.[30] They blamed it on the disparity between what children are taught to want and what is available to them. Children joined delinquent gangs to achieve success, but because their legitimate path is blocked, they turn to illegitimate means in the form of delinquency.

Lower-class children who want to make money but stay with their lower-class friends are the most likely to join a gang. When a lower-class boy believes he will not achieve financial success, he may blame his failure on society or on himself. If he blames society, he will see its rules as illegitimate and attribute his failure to unfair and discriminatory practices. He thus may join a gang whose rules are regarded by its members as the only legitimate rules. Once boys realize they are isolated from the rest of society, they become closer, more cohesive, and more dependent on one another.

Delinquent Subcultures   Cloward and Ohlin identified three delinquent subcultures. The type of subculture that develops in a neighborhood is a reflection of its social organization. A *criminal subculture* develops in stable neighborhoods that provide children with illegitimate opportunities to become successful criminals. In these communities: (1) there are successful adult criminals who serve as role models, (2) there is an integration of age levels (which enables younger people to learn from older juveniles how to commit crime, and (3) there is cooperation between offenders and legitimate people in the neighborhood (such as bail bondsmen, lawyers, and politicians).

Next is the *conflict subculture.* It is found in disorganized slums, where a lot of migration produces social and cultural rootlessness and conflict. Children in these neighborhoods have only a few opportunities to be successful. The adult criminals who live there are abject failures. There is no integration of different age levels because the adult offenders have no useful knowledge to pass on. There also is little cooperation between offenders and legitimate members of the community because local lawyers and politicians have nothing to gain by associating with and assisting "losers." In addition, the adult criminals here have neither the ability nor the inclination to help neighborhood delinquents reduce their violent activity. The absence of legitimate and illegitimate opportunities frustrates children, and they vent their frustrations by turning to violence.

Finally, there is the *retreatist subculture.* Some children want to succeed in the criminal or conflict subculture but cannot. They also cannot meet the requirements of the conventional culture. They are *double failures*, finding it impossible to succeed at anything they do. Eventually, they give up and turn to drugs or alcohol.

Becoming Delinquent   Cloward and Ohlin blame delinquency on pressures to succeed and on the obstacles lower-class children face. If legitimate opportunities for success were available, they would not turn to crime. But just as there are differences in the availability of legitimate opportunities, there also are differences in the availability of illegitimate opportunities. Not

BOX 7–5 THEORY IN A NUTSHELL

Richard Cloward and Lloyd Ohlin

Cloward and Ohlin identified legitimate and illegitimate opportunity structures. In both systems, opportunity is limited and differentially available depending on the child's position in society. Lower-class juveniles have greater opportunities for acquisition of delinquent roles through their access to deviant subcultures and greater opportunity for carrying them out once they are acquired.

Figure 7–6
Mapping Delinquency Theory: Richard Cloward and Lloyd Ohlin

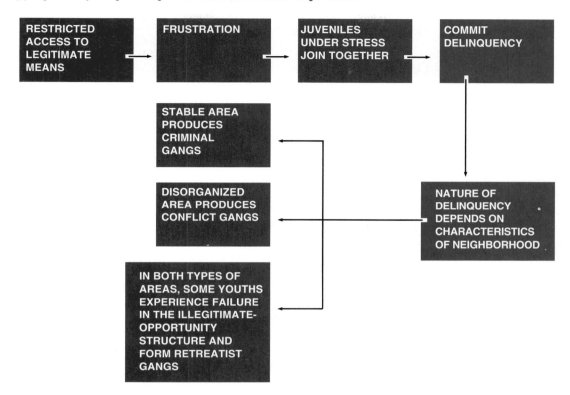

everyone who wants to be a college professor can be one, just as not everyone who wants to be a drug dealer or prostitute can do it very well (see Figure 7–6).

Evaluation of Cloward and Ohlin's Theory   Delinquents are more likely than nondelinquents to believe that opportunities to be successful are limited.[31] They also believe that they have more illegitimate opportunities available to them than nondelinquents.[32] But, even so, the assimilation of the lower-class into the larger society may be impossible. There may be too few opportunities or too little room for lower-class people in the existing system. A capitalist economy requires a large number of people to fill boring, empty, dead-end, low-paying jobs. It also is arguable whether gangs are as organized or as specialized as Cloward and Ohlin think they are. More likely is that delinquents are generalists who commit a variety of criminal acts.[33]

Is it wasteful to channel resources to retreatists such as transients, drug addicts, and hobo-alcoholics? Are retreatists worthy of public sympathy and policy monies? Is it inevitable that some individuals simply will not succeed in life?

General strain theory
is nuanced and not
overly simplistic. Do
theories need to be so
complex? Do the
strengths and weak-
nesses of individuals
best explain variation
in delinquency? Why
are some people so
resilient and others
so likely to succumb
to external forces?

Robert Agnew

In 1992 Robert Agnew added a twist to the work of Merton, Cohen, and Cloward and Ohlin in his *general strain theory* that increased the number of conditions that produced frustration for children.[34]

Types of Strain

According to Agnew, there are three general sources of strain. Frustration may be produced by the following:

1. *Failure to achieve positively valued goals.* This type of strain may result from doing poorly on an exam or not performing well in a sporting event.
2. *Denial of previously attained achievements.* This type of strain may stem from being fired from a job or being "dumped" by a boyfriend or a girlfriend.
3. *Exposure to negative stimuli.* An example of a social interaction that may produce this type of strain is being picked on by classmates or receiving a speeding ticket.

Strain triggers a negative emotion but it does not always lead to delinquency.[35] In other words, the relationship between strain and delinquency is indirect, not direct. Only *some* children who experience strain will commit crime.[36] How children react to strain depends on particular *conditioning factors* such as their self-esteem, intelligence, social support, coping strategies, problem-solving skills, and associations with conventional and delinquent peers. Conditioning factors provide children with the tools to imagine alternative reactions and solutions to the strain. For instance, some children will respond to strain by ignoring or minimizing the event, while others will blame themselves or others for what happened. The type of strain, who the strain is blamed on, the intensity of the strain, the emotion the strain evokes, affects how children will react (see Figure 7–7).

Evaluation of Agnew's Theory   Because Agnew's theory is new, it has not been widely tested. Existing tests, however, have generally supported it. Raymond Paternoster and Paul Mazerolle detected a positive association between strain and both drug use and delinquency.[37] Studying males and females, Mazerolle,[38] John Hoffman and Susan Su,[39] and Agnew and Timothy Brezina,[40] discovered a relationship between delinquency and interpersonal strain. Working alone, Brezina found that for some children participation in delinquency reduced strain and lessened the impact of negative feelings associated with it.[41] In a related study, Brezina discovered that the emotion of anger intervenes in the relationship between strain and delinquency. This finding is consistent with results reported by Agnew[42] and Mazerolle and Alex Piquero,[43] who discovered that anger increases the likelihood of delinquency. Finally, while Lisa Broidy's research generally supports the theory, she found that the relationship among strain, emotion, and crime varies by the cause of the strain. For example, persons who experienced

BOX 7–6
THEORY IN A
NUTSHELL

Robert Agnew

Agnew thinks there are many sources of strain and each one triggers a negative emotion. Whether strain leads to delinquency depends on certain conditioning factors the children possess, such as coping skills and intelligence. Children, for instance, who are less intelligent or who have few coping skills are more likely to see crime as a solution.

Figure 7–7
Mapping Delinquecy Theory: Robert Agnew

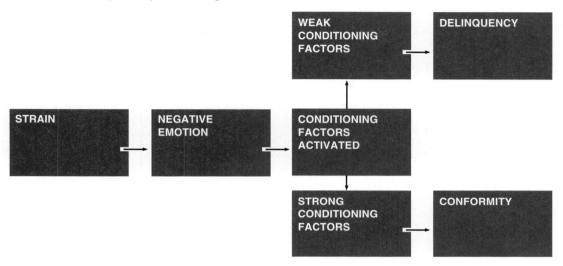

strain because of "lack of fairness" and "stressful life events" were more likely to respond with anger than individuals whose strain was caused by "blocked goals."[44]

Social Control Theory

Social control theories assume that children are amoral. Without controls on their behavior, they are inclined to break the law. Delinquency is thus expected behavior. What needs to be explained is why most children obey society's rules most of the time (see Figure 7–8).

David Matza

David Matza thinks delinquency theories exaggerate the differences between delinquents and nondelinquents.[45] He believes delinquents are normal in all respects except in belonging to a subculture that teaches them it is all right to be delinquent. Matza also believes that if delinquents were really committed to their misdeeds, they would participate in delinquency nearly all of their waking hours. But even chronic offenders spend most of their time involved in conventional, nondelinquent activities. Matza also feels many delinquents know that what they did was wrong and feel sorry for it. If he is right, then why do they do it? Matza says it is because they pick up cues from other children that lead them to believe delinquency is acceptable and that they are the only ones who do not do it. Fear of being called a "chicken" makes some juveniles reluctant to back out of a delinquent escapade.

Figure 7–8
Mapping Delinquency Theory: Social Control Theory

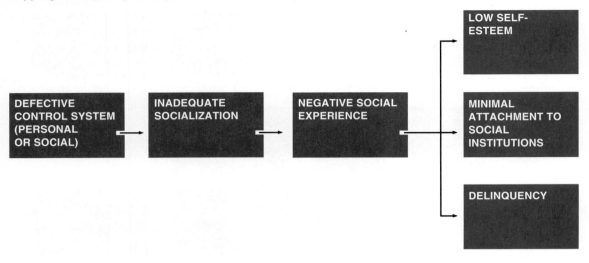

Techniques of Neutralization   Because delinquents feel bad for what they did, they absolve themselves of guilt by turning to one of five **techniques of neutralization**.[46] These are

1. *Denial of responsibility.* Juveniles will deny being responsible for their illegal acts. They may say, "The alcohol made me do it."
2. *Denial of injury.* Delinquents may believe that even though what they have done was illegal, it was not immoral because no one was seriously injured. Shoplifting may be rationalized in this way.
3. *Denial of victim.* Sometimes juveniles deny the seriousness of their behavior by saying that what they did was right under the circumstances. For example, beating someone up may be explained away by saying: "He had it coming."
4. *Condemnations of condemners.* Children may shift blame from their own illegal behavior to the behavior of others. They will criticize those who condemn them. For instance, children may rationalize the legitimacy of their illegal drug use by saying that some police are also involved in the drug trade.
5. *Appeal to higher loyalty.* Sometimes juveniles justify their illegal behavior by claiming that they were committed in deference to a high authority such as a moral or religious belief, the gang, or a racial or ethnic group.

While techniques of neutralization can be used as post-event explanations of delinquent behavior, Matza thinks they are in place *before* the delinquent act takes place. They ready a child for delinquency by reducing the effectiveness of social controls.

BOX 7–7
THEORY IN A NUTSHELL

David Matza

Matza thinks juveniles are neither committed nor compelled to delinquency, and delinquents feel guilty about their misdeeds. To feel better about themselves, they turn to *techniques of neutralization* to reduce guilt and justify their behavior.

Social control theory assumes that people are naturally prone to engage in delinquency. The control perspective suggests that human beings are selfish, bad, or at worst, evil. What evidence can you use to support this dark evaluation of human nature?

Evaluation of Matza's Theory   Research testing Matza's theory has produced mixed results. Some evidence supports the idea that delinquents believe in conventional values and their involvement in delinquency decreases as they get older, a process called the **aging-out phenomenon** or maturational reform (see Chapter 2).[47] On the other hand, some of Matza's other major propositions run contrary to research findings.[48] Michael Hindelang did not find support for the idea that delinquents disapprove of delinquency but go along with it only because they believe their friends expect them to.[49] Travis Hirschi found evidence to support three of the five techniques of neutralization (denial of responsibility, denial of injury, and condemnation of condemners), but was not able to determine whether these rationalizations came before delinquency or were post-event justifications for it.[50]

Travis Hirschi

Travis Hirschi is not surprised that children commit deviance. He expects them to unless obstacles are thrown in their path by a disapproving society.[51]

Social Bonding Theory   At the core of Hirschi's theory is the **bond** or the glue that connects children to society. The bond consists of four elements: attachment, commitment, involvement, and belief.

1. *Attachment* is an emotional element. It describes the extent that a child is tied to other people. A child's most important attachments are those to his or her parents, school, and peers. The stronger the child's attachments, the less likely it is he or she will commit delinquency.
2. *Commitment* is a rational component of the bond. It refers to the extent that children are invested in conventional activities. Commitment controls juveniles because they know getting into trouble will hurt their chances of becoming successful.[52]
3. *Involvement* is the amount of time a child spends in conventional activities. If these occupy a youth's entire day, delinquency cannot take place. Involvement in conventional activities was viewed as a means of preventing delinquency as early as Biblical times, when sages counseled that "idle hands are a devil's workshop."
4. *Belief* in the moral validity of conventional norms is the fourth component of the social bond. Some children believe more strongly in the legitimacy of society's rules. Those who do are less likely to commit delinquencies.

BOX 7–8
THEORY IN A NUTSHELL

Travis Hirschi

Hirschi asks, "Why do juveniles conform?" He says it is because of their bond to society, which consists of four elements: attachment, commitment, involvement, and belief. Children with a strong bond to society are less likely to commit delinquency because they have something to lose.

Evaluation of Hirschi's Theory   For every child, each component of the social bond forms its own continuum. When the continua are merged, they offer an indicator of how strongly the child is connected to society. The stronger the bond, the less likely the youth will deviate. A lot of research has tested Hirschi's theory. The following assessment is divided into research supporting the theory and research opposing it.

Warm, healthy family relationships are perhaps the best way to ward off delinquency. What are some of the numerous ways that fatherhood equips youngsters, particularly boys, to engage in successful endeavors?

Supporting Research   Studies examining the relationship between attachment and delinquency have found that juveniles with a strong attachment to parents are less likely to be delinquent.[53] As for peer attachments, the better connected a boy is to his peers, the less delinquent he will be.[54] But what about closeness to delinquent peers? Close ties to delinquent peers does not make a child any more or less delinquent than he already is.[55] Regarding commitment, children who are more heavily invested in conventional activities are less likely to be delinquent.[56] Involvement does not seem to have much impact on delinquency. This is because delinquency is not a full-time job. It requires so little time that anyone, no matter how involved they are in conventional activities, can find time for delinquency if they want to.[57] Belief in the moral validity of law does reduce the likelihood of committing crime.[58]

Opposing Research   A few studies shed doubt on some of Hirschi's claims. Marvin Krohn and James Massey found that commitment is a better predictor of delinquency than either attachment or belief.[59] Hirschi's theory

Some criminologists have found that persons with low self-control are more likely to participate in delinquent behaviors. What does this suggest about the chances of rehabilitation or positive change for delinquents?

also predicts female delinquency better than it predicts male delinquency and is a better predictor of minor delinquencies than serious offenses.[60] Randy LaGrange and Helen White reported that the influence of the social bond on delinquency changes over time.[61] In his research, Agnew discovered that social bonding variables explain only 1 or 2 percent of future delinquency.[62] These studies suggest that the impact of the social bond on delinquency is variable over time and juvenile populations.

Michael Gottfredson and Travis Hirschi

In 1990 Michael Gottfredson and Travis Hirschi published a theory of crime that departed significantly from Hirschi's earlier work. In their book, *A General Theory of Crime*, the idea of individual self-control took center stage.

Self-Control and Delinquency   This theory is based on a simple explanation: Children commit delinquency when the opportunity is available because crime is gratifying.[63] But why do some children break the law and others do not? Gottfredson and Hirschi think delinquents cannot resist the easy, immediate gratification that accompanies delinquency because they have low self-control.[64] They are "impulsive, insensitive, physical (as opposed to mental), risk-taking, short-sighted, and non-verbal."[65]

The origin of low self-control is found in childhood experiences, specifically in poor child-rearing practices (see Chapter 10). Parents who are attached to their children, supervise them closely, recognize when their children are exhibiting a lack of self-control, and punish bad behavior promote self-control in their children.[66] These children become adolescents with the self-control necessary to resist easy gratification and develop the will to succeed in school and later in the job market.[67]

Evaluation of Gottfredson and Hirschi's Theory   There have been many tests of the relationship between low self-control and delinquency.[68] A large body of research rather consistently supports the core proposition of the theory: Low self-control increases the likelihood of criminal behavior.[69] Studies have also reported a strong association between low self-control and self-reported delinquency, law-violating behavior, and chronic offending.[70]

Critics of the theory complain that it

1. Minimizes the importance of biological factors.[71]
2. Pays too little attention to individual differences among children, which will affect how they are parented.[72]
3. Predicts male delinquency better than female delinquency.[73]
4. Ignores power differentials that influence criminal offending.[74]

Finally, if Gottfredson and Hirschi are right, not much can be done to prevent delinquency. If, indeed, the cause of delinquency is faulty parenting, there really is not much the juvenile justice system can do to overcome what was done to the child over many years.[75]

Juvenile Justice Policy Applications

In West Palm Beach, Florida, police have installed stereo systems that play classical music 24 hours per day in crime-ridden neighborhoods. Since the policy, crime has decreased. Delinquents despise the policy and initially destroyed the stereo equipment. Does this example demonstrate that neighborhoods and their delinquency rates can be altered by ecological change? Or, does this example show that bad apples (delinquents) can spoil the barrel (neighborhood)?

The theories discussed in this chapter blame delinquency on factors outside of the child. The aim of policies based on these theories is to change the relationship between the child and his or her environment.

Cultural Deviance Theory

Social policies based on the cultural deviance theories of Shaw and McKay and Miller are similar. Those derived from Sutherland are somewhat different.

Shaw and McKay and Miller say that neighborhoods generate crime. The most comprehensive policy application of their theories is the Chicago Area Project (CAP). Started in 1932 and still in operation today, CAP attacks delinquency in three ways: direct service, advocacy, and community involvement. Community residents work with CAP to keep children out of trouble, help them when they get into trouble, and keep the neighborhood clean. Research assessing the effectiveness of area projects such as CAP have reported that in communities where these projects have operated for many years, incidents of crime and delinquency have decreased.[76]

Many social policies have been based on Sutherland's differential association theory. Some of these policies are aimed at rewarding prosocial

What is the purpose of programs like Head Start? Does the very existence of such a program validate the theoretical ideas of cultural deviance, strain, and control theorists? Why or why not?

The Denver Police Activities/Athletic League is one example of law enforcement agencies reaching out to the community. How can the police and community residents benefit from such a link? Do healthy police-community relations reduce delinquency?

behavior, discouraging the assignment of stigmatizing labels such as "delinquent," promoting the diversion of youth from the juvenile justice system whenever possible, and establishing programs that de-isolate or reintegrate offenders into community life.[77] The policies that are based on cultural deviance theories share the common goal of changing a child's social environment in ways that make it easier for the youth to be integrated into mainstream society.

Strain Theory

Delinquency can be prevented if children are provided with legitimate opportunities to be successful. One example of a program that does this is Project Head Start, started in 1965. At the heart of the program is the notion that poor children fail in school because they enter school ill prepared. Project Head Start readies them for school. Since its inception, more than 19 million children have participated in Head Start. Today, with an annual budget in excess of 6 billion dollars, Head Start programs in all 50 states are helping almost 1 million children.[78]

Contrary to periodic good-news reports in daily newspapers, scholarly evaluations of Head Start consistently point in a different direction. Children show initial improvement, but gains made in the first grade begin to evaporate by third grade and virtually disappear by sixth grade.[79]

Social Control Theory

Policies based on social control theories try to reattach or reconnect children to their parents (and other adults) and to schools by involving them in conventional activities. One way of doing this is by having families and neighborhoods actively participate in the lives of children. For example, programs sponsored by the Police Athletic League provide children with positive experiences with other youths and with law enforcement officers. By working together, stronger ties will be developed between adults and children, and children become more committed to the rules of society.

Conclusions

This chapter has reviewed theories from three schools of sociological thought. Cultural deviance theories were the first to reject biological and psychological theories of delinquency. These theories shifted attention to considering the role of the environment, particularly the child's neighborhood. Strain theory distinguished itself from cultural deviance theory by claiming that there is no unique lower-class culture. There is one culture in the United States and it emphasizes wealth and status. But not all people are able to achieve success because the legitimate means to it are restricted to the middle- and upper-classes. Thus, lower-class people are more likely to give up the chase for these goals or go about achieving them in illegal ways. In contrast, social control theory argues that children are amoral and that without controls on their behavior they will deviate. These theories ask "Why do children conform?," not "Why do children deviate?" They answer the question by turning to the strength of the bond that connects the child to parents, school, and peers.

In the next chapter, critical theories of delinquency are discussed. These theories look at power differences among people and how differences in power may produce delinquency.

Key Terms

aging-out phenomenon: *The gradual decline of participation in crime after the teenage years.*

bond: *The glue that connects a child to society.*

cultural transmission: *The process by which criminal values are transmitted from one generation to the next.*

differential social organization: *Neighborhoods are differentially organized.*

focal concerns: *The values that monopolize lower-class consciousness.*

middle-class measuring rod: *The standard teachers use when they assign status to students.*

techniques of neutralization: *Rationalizations given to explain delinquent behavior.*

theory of differential association: *A learning theory explaining the process children go through to become delinquent.*

zonal hypothesis: *Rates of delinquency decline the farther one moves from the center of the city.*

Getting Connected

The National Association of Midnight Basketball Leagues is an intervention program that helps young adults by offering them an alternative to cruising the streets during the late-night, high-crime hours.

http://www.highfiveamerica.com/volunteer.htm

1. What are the four specific objectives of High Five America?
2. What does the acronym REECH stand for? How effective has this program been?
3. Does your community have a midnight basketball league? If so, describe it. If not, discuss whether the experience of High Five America might be replicated in your town.

Many of the theories discussed in this chapter examine the origin of youth gangs. An excellent source of information on this topic is the Documents on Gangs and Youth website.

http://www.ericcass.uncg.edu/virtuallib/gangs/gangsbook.htm

1. Find "Youth Gang Homicides in the 1990's." Did the number of gang homicides increase or decrease in the early to mid-1990's?
2. Link to the "secondary student level," then to "Is Your Child in a Gang?" What are the warning signs of gang involvement, according to the Sacramento Police Department? Do these warning signs apply in your hometown?
3. According to the Sacramento police, how should parents discourage their children from joining gangs?

Crime Prevention Programs provide information on community service programs designed and led by youths. The goal of the programs is to provide opportunities for young people to bond with their communities.

http://www.ncpc.org/3you4dc.htm

1. Link on the Teen Alert! page. What can teens do to prevent crime?
2. Find information about McGruff the Crime Dog. Was McGruff active in your community?
3. How can teens educate one another about crime, according to this site?

Project Head Start is based on the notion that poor children more often fail in school because they enter school ill-prepared. The goal of Head Start is to get them ready for school. For information on Project Head Start visit:

http://www.headstartinfo.org

1. How can parents and family members become active partners in Head Start programs?
2. Head Start programs are never fully funded; many children who qualify to attend cannot. How does this site discuss the issue of funding?
3. Does the information on this site support the idea that Head Start is a good delinquency prevention tool?

In 2000 the U.S. Congress passed the National Police Athletic League Act, which intends to improve academic and social outcomes for at-risk youth by providing police-sponsored activities during nonschool hours. Review the Act at:

http://www.feds.com/basic_svc/public_law/106-367.htm

1. What is PAL?

2. According to this act, what kinds of activities must a PAL chapter provide for youth in its community in order to qualify for funding?

3. What assumptions about the nature and extent of juvenile delinquency form the context for this legislation?

Endnotes

1. Travis Hirschi, *Causes of Delinquency* (Berkeley: University of California Press, 1969).
2. Clifford Shaw and Henry McKay, *Juvenile Delinquency in Urban Areas* (Chicago: University of Chicago Press, 1942); Clifford Shaw and Henry McKay, *Juvenile Delinquency in Urban Areas: Revised Edition* (Chicago: University of Chicago Press, 1969).
3. Edwin Sutherland, *Principles of Criminology* (Philadelphia: Lippincott, 1947).
4. Robert Bursik, Jr., "Delinquency Rates as Ecological Change," in *The Social Ecology of Crime*, edited by James Byrne and Robert Sampson (New York: Springer-Verlag, 1986); Robert Bursik, Jr., "Urban Dynamics and Ecological Studies of Delinquency," *Social Forces* 63:393–413 (1984); Gerald Suttles, *The Social Construction of Communities* (Chicago: University of Chicago Press, 1972).
5. Donald Shoemaker, *Theories of Delinquency*, 4th ed. (New York: Oxford University Press, 2000).
6. Paul Bellair, "Social Interaction and Community Crime," *Criminology* 35:677–703 (1997); F. Peeples and Rolf Loeber, "Do Individual Differences and Neighborhood Context Explain Ethnic Differences in Juvenile Delinquency?," *Journal of Quantitative Criminology* 10:141-157 (1994).
7. Dennise Gottfredson, R. McNeill, III, and Gary Gottfredson, "Social Area Influences on Delinquency," *Journal of Research in Crime and Delinquency* 28:197–226 (1991).
8. Matt DeLisi and Bob Regoli, "Individual Neighborhood Attachment and Perceptions of Neighborhood Safety," *American Journal of Criminal Justice* 24:181–188 (2000).
9. Robert Sampson, S. Raudenbush, and F. Earls, *Neighborhood Collective Efficacy—Does It Help Reduce Violence?* (Washington, DC: National Institute of Justice, 1998), p. 1.
10. Sampson et al., note 9.
11. Sutherland, note 3.
12. Robert Stanfield, "The Interaction of Family Variables and Gang Variables in the Etiology of Delinquency," *Social Problems* 13:411–417 (1966).
13. Ruth Kornhauser, *Social Sources of Delinquency* (Chicago: University of Chicago Press, 1978); Hirschi, note 1.
14. B. Costello and P. Vowell, "Testing Control Theory and Differential Association," *Criminology* 37:815–842.
15. Joseph Rogers and M.D. Buffalo, "Fighting Back," *Social Problems* 22:101–118 (1974).
16. S. Bok, *Mayhem* (Reading, MA: Addison-Wesley, 1998).
17. Robert Burgess and Ronald Akers, "A Differential Association-Reinforcement Theory of Criminal Behavior," *Social Problems* 14:128–147 (1966).
18. Walter Miller, "Lower-Class Culture as a Generating Milieu of Gang Delinquency," *Journal of Social Issues* 14:5–19 (1958).
19. Miller, note 18, p. 12.
20. John Braithwaite, *Crime, Shame, and Reintegration* (New York: Cambridge University Press, 1989).
21. B. B. Whiting, "Sex Identity Conflict and Personal Violence," *American Anthropologist* 67:123–140 (1965); Roy Austin, "Race, Female Headship, and Delinquency," *Justice Quarterly* 9:585–608 (1992); Roy Austin, "Race, Father-Absence, and Female Delinquency," *Criminology* 15:487–504 (1978).

22. Hirschi, note 1.
23. Robert Merton, *Social Theory and Social Structure*, rev. ed. (New York: Macmillan Publishing Co., 1968).
24. Albert Cohen, "The Sociology of the Deviant Act," *American Sociological Review* 30:5–14 (1965); Francis Cullen, *Rethinking Crime and Deviance* (Totawa, NJ: Rowman and Allanheld Publishers, 1984); William Simon and John Gagnon, "The Anomie of Affluence," *American Journal of Sociology* 82:356–376 (1976).
25. Margaret Farnworth and Michael Leiber, "Strain Theory Revisited," *American Sociological Review* 54:263–274 (1989); Scott Menard, "A Developmental Test of Mertonian Anomie Theory," *Journal of Research in Crime and Delinquency* 32:136–174 (1995).
26. Albert Cohen, *Delinquent Boys* (New York: The Free Press, 1955).
27. Lee Rainwater, "The Problem of Lower-Class Culture," *Journal of Social Issues* 26:133–148 (1970).
28. David Downes, *The Delinquent Solution* (London: Hutchinson, 1966).
29. Steven Box, *Deviance, Reality and Society* (London: Holt, Rinehart and Winston, 1981).
30. Richard Cloward and Lloyd Ohlin, *Delinquency and Opportunity* (New York: The Free Press, 1960).
31. Stephen Cernkovich, "Value Orientations and Delinquency Involvement," *Criminology* 15:443–458 (1979); Susan Datesman, Frank Scarpitti, and R. Stephenson, "Female Delinquency," *Journal of Research in Crime and Delinquency* 12:107–123 (1975); Jeffery Seagrave and Douglas Hastad, "Evaluating Three Models of Delinquency Causation for Males and Females," *Sociological Focus* 18:1–17 (1985).
32. James F. Short, Jr., and Fred Strodtbeck, *Group Process and Gang Delinquency* (Chicago: University of Chicago Press, 1965).
33. Michael Gottfredson and Travis Hirschi, *A General Theory of Crime* (Palo Alto: Stanford University Press, 1990).
34. Robert Agnew, "Foundation for a General Theory of Crime,"*Criminology* 30:47–87 (1992).
35. Lisa Broidy, "A Test of General Strain Theory," *Criminology* 39:9–33 (2001).
36. Agnew, note 34, p. 66.
37. Raymond Paternoster and Paul Mazerolle, "General Strain Theory and Delinquency," *Journal of Research in Crime and Delinquency* 31:235–263 (1994).
38. Paul Mazerolle, "Gender, General Strain, and Delinquency," *Justice Quarterly* 15:65–91 (1998).
39. John Hoffman and S. Susan Su, "The Conditional Effects of Stress on Delinquency and Drug Use," *Journal of Research in Crime and Delinquency* 12:107–123 (1997).
40. Robert Agnew and Timothy Brezina, "Relational Problems With Peers, Gender, and Delinquency," *Youth and Society* 29:84–111 (1997).
41. Timothy Brezina, "Adapting to Strain," *Criminology* 34:39–60 (1996).
42. Timothy Brezina, "Adolescent Maltreatment and Delinquency," *Journal of Research in Crime and Delinquency* 35:71–99 (1998).
43. Paul Mazerolle and Alex Piquero, "Linking Exposure to Strain with Anger," *Journal of Criminal Justice* 26: 195–211 (1998).
44. Broidy, note 35.
45. David Matza, *Delinquency and Drift* (New York: The Free Press, 1964).
46. Gresham Sykes and David Matza, "Techniques of Neutralization," *American Sociological Review* 22:664–670 (1957).
47. Short and Strodtbeck, note 32; Barry Krisberg, *The Gang and the Community* (San Francisco: R & E Associates, 1975); Scott Briar and Irving Piliavin, "Delinquency, Situational Inducements, and Commitments to Conformity," *Social Problems* 13:35–45 (1965); William McCord, Joan McCord, and Irving Zola, *Origins of Crime* (New York: Columbia University Press, 1959).
48. Richard Ball, "Development of a Basic Norm Violation," *Criminology* 21:75–94 (1983); Michael Hindelang, "The Commitment of Delinquents to their Misdeeds," *Social Problems* 17:502–509 (1970); Shoemaker, note 5.
49. Michael Hindelang, "Moral Evaluations and Illegal Behavior," *Social Problems* 21:370–385 (1974).
50. Hirschi, note 1.
51. Hirschi, note 1.
52. Jackson Toby, "Social Disorganization and Stake in Conformity," *Journal of Criminal Law, Criminology, and Police Science* 48:12–17 (1957).
53. Velmer Burton, Francis Cullen, T. David Evans, R. Gregory Dunaway, Sesha Kethinene, and Gary Payne, "The Impact of Parental Control on Delinquency," *Journal of Criminal Justice* 23:111–126 (1995); Robert Agnew, "Social Control Theory and Delinquency," *Criminology* 23:47–61 (1985); Delbert Elliott, David Huizinga, and Suzanne Ageton, *Explaining Delinquency and Drug Use* (Beverly Hills, CA: Sage Publications, 1985); Rachelle Canter, "Sex Differences in Self-Reported Delinquency," *Criminology* 20:373–393 (1982); Michael Hindelang, "Causes of Delinquency," *Social Problems* 20:471–487 (1973).
54. Michael Hindelang, Travis Hirschi, and Joseph Weis, *Measuring Delinquency* (Beverly Hills, CA: Sage Publications, 1981).
55. Eric Linden and James Hackler, "Affective Ties and Delinquency," *Pacific Sociological Review* 16:27–46 (1973).
56. Linden and Hackler, note 55.
57. Hirschi, note 1.

58. John Hepburn, "Testing Alternative Models of Delinquency Causation," *Journal of Criminal Law and Criminology* 67:450–460 (1976); Matthew Silberman, "Toward a Theory of Criminal Behavior," *American Sociological Review* 41:442–461 (1976); Michael Wiatrowski, David Griswold, and Mary Roberts, "Curriculum Tracking and Delinquency," *American Sociological Review* 47:151–160 (1982); Michael Wiatrowski, David Griswold, and Mary Roberts, "Social Control Theory and Delinquency," *American Sociological Review* 46:525–541 (1981).

59. Marvin Krohn and James Massey, "Social Control and Delinquent Behavior," *Sociological Quarterly* 21:529–543 (1980).

60. Krohn and Massey, note 59.

61. Randy LaGrange and Helen White, "Age Differences in Delinquency," *Criminology* 23:19–45 (1985).

62. Agnew, note 53.

63. Travis Pratt and Francis Cullen, "The Empirical Status of Gottfredson and Hirschi's General Theory of Crime," *Criminology* 38:931–964 (2000).

64. Gottfredson and Hirschi, note 33.

65. Gottfredson and Hirschi, note 33, p. 90.

66. Ronald Akers, "Self-Control as a General Theory of Crime," *Journal of Quantitative Criminology* 7:201–211 (1991).

67. Pratt and Cullen, note 63.

68. Velmer Burton, Jr., T. David Evans, Francis Cullen, Kathleen Olivares, and R. Gregory Dunaway, "Age, Self-Control, and Adults' Offending Behaviors," *Journal of Criminal Justice* 27:45–54 (1999); John Gibbs, Dennis Giever, and Jamie Martin, "Parental Management and Self-Control," *Journal of Research in Crime and Delinquency* 35:40–70 (1998); T. Evans, Francis Cullen, Velmer Burton, R. Gregory Dunaway, and Michael Benson, "The Social Consequences of Self-Control," *Criminology* 35:475– 501 (1997).

69. David Brownfield and Ann Marie Sorenson, "Self-Control and Juvenile Delinquency," *Deviant Behavior* 14:243–264 (1993); Velmer Burton, Jr., Francis Cullen, and Gregory Dunaway, "Reconsidering Strain Theory," *Journal of Quantitative Criminology* 10:213–229 (1994); Harold Grasmick, Charles Tittle, Robert Bursik, Jr., and Bruce Arneklev, "Testing the Core Empirical Implications of Gottfredson and Hirschi's General Theory of Crime," *Journal of Research in Crime and Delinquency* 30:5–29 (1993); Carl Keane, Paul Maxim, and James Teevan,"Drinking and Driving, Self-Control, and Gender," *Journal of Research in Crime and Delinquency* 30:30–36 (1995); Daniel Nagin and Raymond Paternoster, "Enduring Individual Differences and Rational Choice Theories of Crime," *Law and Society Review* 27:467–496 (1993); M. Polakowski, "Linking Self- and Social Control with Deviance," *Journal of Quantitative Criminology* 10:41–78 (1993); John Gibbs and Dennis Giever, "Self-Control and Its Manifestations Among University Students," *Justice Quarterly* 12:231–255 (1995).

70. Gibbs et al., note 68; Michael Polakowski, "Linking Self- and Social-Control with Deviance," *Journal of Quantitative Criminology* 10:41–78 (1994); Matt DeLisi, "It's All in the Record," *Criminal Justice Review*, 26:1–16 (2001).

71. Grasmick et al., note 69.

72. Hugh Barlow, "Explaining Crimes and Analogous Acts, Or the Unrestrained Will Grab at Pleasure Whenever They Can," *Journal of Criminal Law and Criminology* 82:229–242 (1991).

73. Pratt and Cullen, note 63.

74. Pratt and Cullen, note 63.

75. DeLisi, note 70.

76. Richard Lundman, *Prevention and Control of Juvenile Delinquency* (New York: Oxford University Press, 2002); Anthony Sorrentino and David Whittaker, "The Chicago Area Project—Addressing the Gang Problem," *FBI Law Enforcement Bulletin* 63:8–12 (1994); "Philadelphia Settles with Estates of MOVE Members," *Jet*, February 17:40 (1997); Solomon Kobrin, "The Chicago Area Project," *Annals of the American Academy of Political and Social Sciences* 332 (March): 19–29 (1959); Steven Schlossman, Gail Zellman, and Richard Shavelson, *Delinquency Prevention in South Chicago* (Santa Monica, CA: Rand, 1984).

77. Albert Cohen, Alfred Lindesmith, and Karl Schussler, *The Sutherland Papers* (Bloomington, IN: Indiana University Press, 1956), pp. 8–10.

78. For current information on Project Head Start see www.headstartinfo.org.

79. Dinesh D'Souza, *The End of Racism* (New York: The Free Press 1995) p. 455.

Chapter 8

Labeling, Conflict, and Radical Theories

The community cannot deal with people whom it cannot define. . . . The young delinquent becomes bad because he is defined as bad and because he is not believed if he is good.

—Frank Tannenbaum

Children, partly because they are relatively powerless, are subject to being labeled by adults who wield greater power. Frank Tannenbaum argued that the society actually produces delinquents through "a process of tagging, defining, identifying, segregating, describing, emphasizing, and evoking the very traits that are complained of . . . .The person becomes the thing he is described as being."[1] The theories discussed in this chapter explore the nature of the labeling process, the role of conflict, differential power, and influence in creating and enforcing the criminal law, and the consequences of how adults exert power and oppress children.

Labeling Theory

If labels have such formidable power, why don't parents label their children as "gifted," "intelligent," or "athletic?" In turn, why don't youth affix a positive label to themselves and then allow the self-fulfilling prophecy to occur?

While cultural deviance, strain, and social control theories assume that deviance leads to social control, **labeling theory** assumes that social control leads to deviance. Labeling theorists believe that human nature is malleable and that personality and behavior are products of social interaction. Yet, labeling theorists are less concerned with influences that might instigate initial deviant acts than they are with the stigmatizing effects of the juvenile justice system upon those it labels delinquent. Labeling theorists, therefore, emphasize the power of the social response, especially in the form of formal social control, to produce delinquent behavior. Their concern is that publicly or officially "labeling someone as a delinquent can result in the person *becoming the very thing he is described as being.*"[2] See Box 8–1, for a brief discussion of how the effects of labeling may have contributed to Willie Bosket becoming one of New York State's most dangerous prisoners.

Frank Tannenbaum

Frank Tannenbaum rejected the **dualistic fallacy**—the idea that delinquents and nondelinquents are two fundamentally different types of people.[3] According to Tannenbaum, criminologists previously attributed undesirable qualities, such as atavistic physical features and intellectual inferiority, to delinquents, which led to antisocial behavior. However, such accusations are not well founded; he believed that delinquents are instead rather well adjusted to their social groups (see Box 8–2).

Is labeling theory simply an academic excuse to absolve delinquents of guilt and responsibility? If so, how does this occur?

Tannenbaum argues that delinquent activity begins as random play or adventure. Children do not think of their play as constituting delinquency, but a play group may later evolve into a delinquent gang as a result of conflict between the group and the community. Adults in the community may be annoyed with the group (which perhaps is considered too noisy) and try to subdue or crush it. This usually fails, however, and the children become more defiant, turning to fellow gang members for support. When conflict between a gang and the community breaks out, both sides resort to name-calling.

BOX 8-1   FACE OF DELINQUENCY
The Case of Willie Bosket

At the age of 26, Willie Bosket stabbed prison guard Earl Porter in the visiting room at Shawangunk state prison in New York. At his trial for the attempted murder of the guard, Willie explained his violent behavior as a direct product of having been labeled a delinquent at an early age and being institutionalized in the state's juvenile and adult correctional systems for most of his life since age nine. Acting as his own defense counsel, he stated to the jury: "Willie Bosket has been incarcerated since he was nine years old and was raised by his surrogate mother, the criminal justice system . . . . This being the case, Bosket is only a monster created by the system he now haunts." It is a strong claim for the effects of labeling. However, in Willie's case it is difficult to disentangle the causes and effects of the labels.

At age six, Willie was already a troublemaker in school, throwing temper tantrums, hitting teachers, fighting with other students, and playing hooky. When he was eight years old and in second grade, he threw a typewriter out of a school window, nearly hitting a pregnant teacher. By nine years of age, Willie was experimenting with sex with neighbor girls. Police reports on Willie at the time included purse snatching, auto theft, threatening other children with a knife, and the setting of a number of fires; most of his crimes were never reported to the police. His first appearance in Family Court came as the result of his mother filing a PINS (Person in Need of Supervision) petition, which at that time was a status offense. The judge ordered Willie placed at the Wiltwyck School for Boys.

Willie's disruptive and violent behavior over the next few years led him to be moved from institution to institution, including both psychiatric and correctional facilities. At age 11 he was sent to the Highland School for Children where he was soon punished for throwing a chair at another boy and attacking a supervisor with a broom.

At age 14, Willie's placement expired and he was sent home. Over the next few months he was arrested five times, mostly for minor robberies and burglaries, but received no serious sanctions for any of the crimes. According to Fox Butterfield, "By the age of 15, Willie claimed he had committed two thousand crimes, including two hundred armed robberies and twenty-five stabbings." Three months after Willie turned 15, he went on a robbing and killing spree in the New York subways, resulting in the murder of two subway passengers and the serious wounding of a motorman. Although Willie was only 15 years old, the judge sentenced him to the maximum allowed under the current state law: commitment to an initial period of five years with the Division of Youth Services, and then a transfer to the adult system until he turned 21. Willie was eventually convicted as an adult of an assault and sentenced to prison where additional assaults on guards resulted in his being convicted of being an habitual offender, which carried a sentence of 25 years to life.

Labeling theory argues that it is the label that causes the problem behavior. The person becomes, as Tannenbaum suggests, the thing he or she has been described as being, and that labeling, processing, and institutionalizing individuals only promotes recidivism, as Lemert claims. Is Willie Bosket a monster created by the juvenile justice system? Or was the labeling and official processing of Willie only a response to his violent behavior?

Source: Fox Butterfield, *All God's Children: The Bosket Family and the American Tradition of Violence* (New York: Avon Books, 1995).

Willie Bosket is one of the most notorious career criminals in recent history. Prior to his arrest for double homicide at age 15, Bosket reported that he had committed hundreds of armed robberies and approximately 25 stabbings. Do such violent juvenile offenders deserve any compassion from the juvenile and criminal justice systems?

BOX 8–2 THEORY IN A NUTSHELL

Frank Tannenbaum

Tannenbaum sees delinquents as well-adjusted people. Delinquent behavior is behavior so labeled by adults in a community. Adults, who have more power than children, are able to have children labeled "delinquent." Once children are labeled delinquent, they become delinquent.

Adults call the youths' activity "delinquent" or "evil," and insist that the activity should no longer be tolerated.[4] Thus, calling a child "delinquent" makes it more likely that he or she will accept the description and live up to it. Labeling and stereotyping lead children to isolate themselves from the rest of the community and to associate with others similarly identified. Tannenbaum feels the community expects the labeled youth to act according to the label and is unlikely to believe the child has turned over a new leaf regardless of the individual's efforts at change.[5] See Figure 8–1 for an illustration of this process.

Figure 8–1
Mapping Delinquency Theory: Labeling Theory

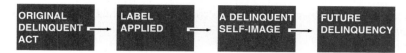

Edwin Lemert

Edwin Lemert developed the ideas of *primary* and *secondary* deviation. **Primary deviation** is deviance that everyone engages in occasionally; it is "rationalized, or otherwise dealt with as [part of] a socially acceptable role. Under such circumstances, normal and [deviant] behaviors remain strange and somewhat tensional bedfellows in the same person."[6] This can change, however, and the person may step into a deviant or delinquent role. This role and the definition of oneself as a delinquent are affected by several factors: how much delinquency the person commits, how visible such acts are to the community, how serious others' reactions are, and how aware the delinquent is of their reaction. If the delinquency is highly visible and societal reaction is very obvious and negative, the youth will see him- or herself differently and it will be difficult for the individual to hold onto past self-images and roles. The youth must choose new roles, which may be more or less deviant than the old ones. If the roles are more deviant, the adolescent has reached the stage Lemert calls secondary deviation: "When a person begins to employ his deviant behavior or a role based upon it as a means of defense, attack, or adjustment to the overt and covert problems created by . . . societal reaction to him, his deviation is secondary."[7] **Secondary deviation** involves a long process, a dynamic relationship between the person's deviation and society's reaction to it. If the adolescent is eventually stigmatized, efforts to control him or her will shift from informal to formal legal ones and he or she will be redefined as delinquent:

> The sequence of interaction leading to secondary deviation is roughly as follows: (1) primary deviation; (2) social penalties; (3) further primary deviation; (4) stronger penalties and rejections; (5) further deviations . . . ; (6) crisis reached in the tolerance quotient, expressed in formal action by the community stigmatizing of the deviant; (7) strengthening of the deviant conduct as a reaction to the stigmatizing and penalties; and (8) ultimate acceptance of deviant social status and . . . the associated role.[8]

Lemert said that not all youths labeled "delinquent" accept these roles; how receptive they are to such labels depends on their social class. If a youth comes from a family where the parents are powerless and poor, he or she is more likely to accept the assigned delinquent role. Lower-class parents may be frustrated by their situation and disturbed by inner conflicts. They may be quick to label their children bad or worthless, overreacting to qualities in

Crime and delinquency are overwhelmingly intraracial phenomena. However, when interracial crime does occur, whites are much more likely to be victimized by minorities. Why are these "normal" crimes not labeled as hate or bias-motivated crime?

their children that remind them of traits they despise in themselves. This leads them to reject their children and, when trouble occurs, to turn them over to community agencies such as the juvenile court. Once the child arrives in juvenile court, the individual's character and deviant behavior are redefined by the court and related agencies.[9]

Lemert believes that having a juvenile court record formally establishes the youth's status as a deviant and segregates him or her from the community. Jail experience and contacts advance this process, further ensuring that the juvenile will think of him- or herself as truly delinquent. Lemert takes it for granted that institutions fail to rehabilitate. He believes, rather, that they promote the opposite: recidivism (see Box 8–3).

Howard Becker

In the 1960s, there was a new intellectual ferment. A charismatic young president, John F. Kennedy, had entered the White House; a new focus on civil rights also emerged, followed by student protests a few years later. In sociology, labeling theory assumed new prominence and popularity; it was antiestablishment, liberal, unconventional, and "hip." Its guru during the 1960s was Howard Becker, who achieved fame with two books, *Outsiders* and *The Other Side*.[10]

Deviants, according to Becker, are not a homogeneous group. Some who are labeled deviant have not broken any rule (they have been **falsely accused**), and others have broken many rules but have not been caught or officially labeled (they are **secret deviants**) (see Chapter 2). As a result, criminologists study people who have little in common.

Becker studied how people acquire their labels, suggesting that whether an activity is considered deviant depends on *how people react to it*, not on the nature of the activity itself. That is, behavior is neither moral nor immoral in and of itself. Rules are not always enforced regularly or consistently; some are even allowed to lapse completely.[11]

Next, Becker considered the *process of becoming deviant*. The first step is to commit a deviant act (even if it is unintentional). The juvenile may have no idea that others call what he or she did "deviant." The next step is to get caught—which puts the spotlight on the person and his or her behavior. Now the youth acquires a new status or label as a "slut," a "mental," or a "juvenile delinquent." The labeled person is presumed likely to engage in deviant behaviors repeatedly. Police will round up suspects (including this person) if a similar act occurs in the community at some later time. People expect the delinquent to commit other offenses, too. Thus, the stigma (negative label) becomes generalized; juveniles accused of one kind of deviance are expected to lie, cheat, and steal as well (see Box 8–4).

Delinquency is a **master status**; that is, " . . . a status that takes precedence over all other statuses or characteristics of the individual."[12] The status of "delinquent" will carry the greatest weight in the minds of others (see Chapter 1). This may be self-fulfilling: The juvenile labeled "delinquent"

BOX 8–4
THEORY IN A NUTSHELL

Howard Becker

Becker believed that acquiring a label depends on how other people react to the behavior and not the behavior itself. Becker saw the process of becoming a deviant in terms of a series of stages that lead to the person's deviance becoming a master status, that feature of the person that is most important to him or her as well as to others.

From the labeling theory perspective, what might happen if this child perceives that he is a troublemaker? Why should elementary school teachers be especially delicate in disciplining young children?

BOX 8–5
THEORY IN A
NUTSHELL

Edwin Schur

Schur thinks the best we can do for children is to leave them alone. He emphasized three elements of the labeling process: stereotyping, retrospective interpretation, and negotiation. To the extent that these three elements work together to get the adolescent caught up in the deviant role, that role becomes increasingly difficult to disavow.

Whose interests are best served by radical nonintervention policies? Is it more important to protect delinquents from a deviant label or to protect society from delinquency?

may not be heavily involved or interested in delinquency but may be pressured because of labeling to sever ties with conventional people and turn to illegal activities to survive. The label may also cause conventional people to sever ties with the youth. Thus, deviance becomes a consequence of other people's reactions, not a simple continuation of the original deviant act.

The final step in the process is for the delinquent to join an organized group or gang, where each member knows how to rationalize delinquency; for example, to regard their victims as unworthy people (con artists call their victims "suckers"). Delinquents learn reasons to continue their participation in delinquency, and these tips on how to commit acts and avoid capture are passed along to others.

Edwin Schur

Edwin Schur has made a number of significant contributions to labeling theory in his analysis of the labeling process and his recommendations for reducing juvenile delinquency through *radical nonintervention*.[13] According to Schur, the labeling process involves stereotyping, retrospective interpretation, and negotiation. He argues that *stereotyping* of youths is rampant in juvenile courts, with officials typing youths taken into custody in ways that best fit the minimal information available. For example, a youth from a single-parent family may be viewed as unlikely to be given adequate supervision and control at home, and therefore he or she is best served by being institutionalized (see Box 8–5).

Schur suggests that the juvenile justice system is particularly susceptible to inappropriate *retrospective interpretation* of youths due to the vagueness of formal definitions of delinquency.[14] When examined with a cynical eye, almost every child's background has something that may suggest future trouble and delinquency.

Schur takes a rather tolerant view of delinquency, arguing that most of it is insignificant and benign—not violent, aggressive, or harmful to other people; therefore, punishment is unnecessary, as are most delinquency laws. These laws are actually counterproductive, producing more delinquency than they deter. Society should permit the widest possible diversity of behavior and not require individuals to adapt to certain standards. Only very serious violations should be brought to the attention of the courts. If a youth is adjudicated delinquent, he or she should not be committed to a correctional facility but rather diverted to a less coercive and stigmatizing program. Schur's call for this policy of **radical nonintervention** is very simple: "Leave kids alone whenever possible."[15]

John Braithwaite

In his extension of labeling theory, John Braithwaite explores the nature and impact of shaming, which is one form of labeling. Shaming takes two forms: disintegrative and reintegrative. According to Braithwaite, **disintegrative shaming**, a form of negative labeling by the juvenile justice system consistent with traditional labeling notions, is counterproductive and tends to stigmatize and exclude targeted youths, thereby tossing them into a "class of outcasts."[16] Juveniles marked as delinquents or predelinquents have legitimate avenues to membership in conventional society severely restricted. Consequently, they turn to others similarly situated and collectively develop delinquent subcultures.

Reintegrative shaming, on the other hand, involves expressions of community disapproval, ranging from mild chastisement to formal sanctions by the court, followed by indications of forgiveness and reacceptance into the community of responsible law-abiders. The emphasis is upon a condemnation of the act rather than on the actor. According to Daniel Curran and Claire Renzetti, "reintegrative shaming actually reaffirms the offender's morality; the disappointment stems from the fact that a 'good person' would do something wrong."[17]

Evaluation of Labeling Theory

Several early studies have identified a link between the labeling of a child as a juvenile delinquent and subsequent development of a deviant identity.[18] A very notable study of two juvenile gangs by William Chambliss vividly illustrates this link.[19] One gang ("the Saints") consisted of eight members from respectable families. The second gang ("the Roughnecks") consisted of six boys from lower-class families. Chambliss observed these gangs "in action" and found that they lived up to their reputations in the community. Each gang (and its members) defined themselves as they perceived others saw them. The Saints, who never thought of themselves as delinquents, never saw anything wrong with what they did. They passed off their delinquency as mere "pranks." The Roughnecks, on the other hand, were seen by the police and school officials as a "bad bunch of boys." In turn, they flaunted their delinquency and described themselves as delinquents. However, Charles Tittle and Robert Meier argue that there is very little evidence suggesting that offenders subjected to receive the strongest controls are more likely to be recidivists.[20]

Many other studies fail to support the claims of labeling theory. Charles Thomas and Donna Bishop found no evidence that sanctioning offenders pushes them toward acceptance of a deviant label.[21] Steven Burkett and Carol Hickman found that official processing of youths charged with marijuana offenses affected changes in girls' identities (but not boys), although the identity changes in the girls did not lead to recidivism.[22] Jack Foster and his colleagues reported that youths who had been officially labeled did not feel it made much of a difference.[23] Labeling, in other words, did not seem to have much effect on their self-esteem or on what they thought was possible for them to achieve. In comparing official delinquents with nondelinquents, John Hepburn discovered that arrest record had no direct influence on self-identification.[24]

Other research has proven more supportive of the labeling perspective. Research by David Ward and Charles Tittle led them to conclude that labeling through the application of informal sanctions " . . . significantly affects the

Do some delinquents deserve to be shamed and ostracized because of their illegal behavior? Isn't it helpful for society to have a "class of outcasts" as a stern reminder of what is appropriate and lawful behavior?

likelihood that an offender will develop a deviant identity and that such identities significantly affect the likelihood of recidivism."[25] Support for this position is found in the work of Karen Heimer and Ross Matsueda who note that delinquency is produced by interactions between the youth and a referenced delinquent group or conventional others, such as parents, in which such factors as motives, norms, attitudes, and gestures coalesce into self-reflected delinquent identity.[26] Similarly, Mike Adams has found that negative labeling of youths who associate with delinquent peers is more likely to lead to increased delinquency.[27] Heimer has also argued that structural gender inequality affects "the meaning that actors give to themselves, situations, and behaviors such as delinquency."[28] A youth's definitions of situations as favorable or unfavorable to delinquency are affected by significant others and reference groups he or she considers in the process of role-taking, and these others and groups are shaped by the youth's gender. According to Heimer, the delinquency "gender gap emerges in part because inequality teaches girls to express their motivations through behavior that differs from that of boys." In short, it is the *meaning* of behavior that varies across gender.[29] These observations about role-taking behavior may also apply to boys. For example, Dawn Bartusch and Ross Matsueda found that the negative effects of informal labels are greater for boys than for girls, especially for boys with strong self-identities as males.[30]

In terms of labeling and social reaction, labeling theorists think some youths participate in delinquency in response to the problem of having an official record. Studies completed in the 1980s provide additional support for this notion. Malcolm Klein found that among similarly charged delinquents who were either randomly released, referred to court, or diverted, those who received the least severe disposition (randomly released) were least likely to commit a future delinquent act.[31] Likewise, Michael Miller and Martin Gold observed that youths whose delinquencies were detected were more likely to commit future delinquencies.[32]

However, some research produced findings quite the opposite of what labeling theorists predict. A variety of studies have found that youths sent to juvenile court have lower rates of future delinquency than those handled less severely.[33] In other words, formal intervention decreases the likelihood of future offending. These findings would support a deterrence theory of delinquency but fail to produce evidence favorable to the labeling perspective.

Juvenile Justice Policy Applications

The one overriding finding from research on labeling is that an official label seems more likely to have a negative effect when applied to not-so-serious offenders. Official labeling does not have much of an impact on more serious delinquents. In the minds of these youths, the official label may be just one facet of their life to which they have become acclimated. Labeling theory also suggests that formal intervention by the juvenile justice system only serves to instill deviant self-identification and thereby increases delinquency.

The logical policy implications of such a theory would be to either (1) ignore delinquent acts or (2) react informally, diverting the individual away from the juvenile justice system. In other words, whatever the juvenile justice system might do, it should do less: that is, decline to formally intervene in the lives of children unless absolutely necessary and to divert youths at every possible stage in the juvenile justice process.

Such an approach may require, in the terms used by Edwin Schur, policies of *radical nonintervention.*[34] That is, he argues that we have overcriminalized youths, we bring too many into the juvenile justice system, and the enforcement of unnecessary laws is counterproductive. Therefore, we should consider fully removing status offenses (and related violations of court orders produced by such offenses) from the system. We also should remove all but the most serious juvenile offenders from the nation's juvenile corrections system.

Diversion programs at both the police and court level should be used whenever possible. The use of police diversion programs, such as Big Brother or Big Sister and Police Athletic League (PAL) Clubs have been extensively developed around the country. Court diversion provides a variety of alternatives ranging from informal adjustment and mediation to referral of adolescents to Youth Service Bureaus and Community Youth Boards. A number of diversion programs also exist at the correctional stage. For example, wilderness programs, such as Vision Quest, Outward Bound, the Stephen French Youth Wilderness Program, and the Florida Associated Marine Institute, combine fitness, survival skills and personal challenges as alternatives to secure institutional placements.[35]

While diversion programs continue to exist today, they are not nearly as popular as they were at their peak in the mid-1970s. The lack of empirical evidence in support of the theory and concerns over diversion actually "widening the net" and bringing *more* youths into the system raised serious questions as to its usefulness (see Chapter 14). Labeling theory and diversion policies were clearly on the decline by the late-1970s. As Akers notes:

> After the mid-1970s, Becker himself essentially gave no further attention to the theory. Indeed, he claimed that he had been only "minimally" involved in the study of deviance and that he had never intended to create a labeling theory at all.[36]

The one variation in labeling theory that appears to be most appealing to policy makers today may be that of John Braithwaite and his advocacy of reintegrative shaming. Three practical policy implications may be derived from Braithwaite's work:

1. Expressing the community's disapproval of the delinquent act through the use of informal agencies or institutions of social control;
2. Integrating the repentant role with rehabilitation programs; and
3. Increasing media coverage of not only the delinquent acts of juveniles, but also of individual juvenile offenders who may then be held up as examples of successful reform following their delinquencies.[37]

Mentoring an adolescent, like the Big Brother program pictured here, can be a rewarding experience for adults and reduce the likelihood of delinquency for youths. However, most Americans do not mentor at-risk youths? Why?

Braithwaite's ideas also have been drawn upon extensively by restorative justice programs bringing the offender, victim, and community together to respond to less serious forms of delinquency (see Chapter 15).

Conflict Theory

Conflict theory challenges the assumptions of social disorganization, strain, and social control theories that society is organized around functionally interdependent elements (institutions, roles, statuses, values, and norms), that existing social arrangements are normal and natural, and that societal norms reflect consensus. These assumptions view delinquency as behavior identified and prohibited by law because it violates consensual norms and values of society. Instead, **conflict theory** views conflict within society as normal and rejects the idea that society is organized around a consensus of values and norms.[38] Conflict theorists believe that in its normal state, society is held together by force, coercion, and intimidation. The values and norms of different groups are often the basis of conflicting interests between those groups. Law, therefore, represents the interests held by groups that have obtained sufficient power or influence to determine the legislation.[39] Conflict theory of the Marxist mode suggests that capitalism is the essential root of crime and that repressive efforts by the ruling class to control the ruled class produce delinquency.[40]

Karl Marx and Friedrich Engels

**Is the existence of an
underclass inevitable?
Are some people
simply unwilling to
conventionally partici-
pate in society and
instead choose to
lead lives of vice and
delinquency?**

Writing in the latter half of the 19th century, Karl Marx and Friedrich Engels argued that the character of every society is determined by its particular mode of economic production. The primary conflict in society is between the material forces of production and the social relations of production. By *material forces of production*, they meant the ability of a society to produce material goods. The concept of *social relations of production* refers simply to relationships among people, especially those relationships based upon property, and the manner in which material goods produced are distributed. The primary relationship in industrialized societies reflects the incompatible economic interests of the owners of the means of production (the *bourgeoisie*) and people who sell their labor (the *proletariat*). The inevitable class conflict between these two groups also produces (both directly and indirectly) the conditions for delinquency.[41]

Because the bourgeoisie controls the means of production, it also can control all aspects of social life, even the production of ideas. Included in the production of ideas would be those that create the criminal law along with ideological or philosophical beliefs that become the basis for policies of law enforcement. According to Marx and Engels, law and its enforcement are simply tools of the powerful designed to protect their own economic interests. The police, courts, and correctional system of society operate to control the working class (see Box 8–6). Behaviors prohibited by criminal law or selectively enforced by the police and courts reflect acts or values that threaten the interests of the dominant class (see Figure 8–2 for an illustration of this process).

Marx and Engels offered, at best, a very modest explanation of crime and delinquency. According to Paul Hirst, Marx and Engels believed that crime was largely the product of a demoralized working class. It was part of human nature to work and be productive, and yet capitalist societies created large surplus populations of unemployed and underemployed workers. Over time, unproductiveness leaves the individual demoralized and vulnerable to crime and vice. Marx and Engels called criminals and their juvenile counterparts the lumpenproletariat, the "dangerous class," and a "parasite class living off productive labor by theft, extortion and beggary, or by providing 'services' such as prostitution and gambling. Their class interests are diametrically opposed to those of the workers. They make their living by picking up the crumbs of capitalist relations of exchange."[42]

Not all conflict theory is based on strictly economic competition between classes or the unequal distributions of economic resources. The work of Thorsten Sellin and George Vold (discussed below) explored the nature of group conflict in socially heterogeneous societies. Generally, the groups in such societies reflect associations based on common interests, such as the pursuit of goals or the protection of vested interests (power, wealth, and status).

Figure 8–2
Mapping Delinquency Theory: Conflict Theory

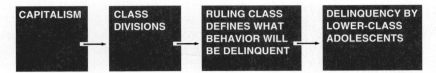

Thorsten Sellin

Thorsten Sellin distinguished between *crime norms* (norms found in the criminal law) and *conduct* or *group norms* (norms specific to localized groups that may or may not be consistent with crime norms).[43] **Crime norms** refer to rules that prohibit specific conduct and provide punishments for violations.[44] **Conduct norms**, on the other hand, reflect the values, expectations, and actual behaviors of groups in everyday life. Conduct norms can be specific to particular groups, may be shared by many diverse groups, and may conflict with each other. Conduct norms are not necessarily the norms found in criminal law, and at times may directly conflict with crime norms (see Box 8–7).[45] As societies become more heterogeneous and complex, the likelihood that group norms will conflict with crime norms increases. In turn, delinquency rates will be higher in neighborhoods with the greatest diversity of group norms. Sellin, for instance, believed that urban neighborhoods with a variety of recently arrived immigrant groups living in close proximity would have a higher level of delinquency than suburban neighborhoods where residents had little contact with "outsiders." Sellin's emphasis on the normative conflict that arises in disorganized neighborhoods is thus consistent with the thinking of Shaw and McKay, discussed in Chapter 7.

George Vold

George Vold argues that human nature leads people into groups–that is, people by nature are group-oriented.[46] Groups form because common interests draw people together. As new interests arise, new groups are created. However, "groups come into conflict with one another as the interests and purposes they serve tend to overlap, encroach on one another, and become competitive."[47] This competitiveness generates a continuous struggle to maintain or even enlarge the position of one's own group relative to others. This conflict may eventually lead to the creation of new laws. "Whichever group interest can marshal the greatest number of votes will determine whether there will be a new law to hamper and curb the interests of the opposing group."[48]

Not surprisingly, group members who supported the new law are more likely to obey it and call for its strict enforcement, while people who opposed it would be less sympathetic to it and, consequently, more likely to violate it. Minority groups, the poor, and even some majority groups with little power or influence have little impact on the legislative process. Therefore, behaviors reflecting their interests are more likely to be legislated as criminal by groups with the necessary influence.[49]

Robert Regoli and John Hewitt

Robert Regoli and John Hewitt developed a microconflict explanation of delinquency called **differential oppression theory**.[50] They argue that delinquency is the culmination of a process that begins at conception and evolves through adolescence. What is unique about their perspective is the idea that delinquents and their delinquencies are a product and that adults are the producers (see Box 8–8).

Regoli and Hewitt believe that children, because of their social and legal status, have little power to affect their social world. Compared to adults, children have limited resources available to manipulate others. From a resource standpoint, adults are at a considerable advantage in controlling children and can be said to be more "free" than children. Compared to parents and teachers, children are relatively powerless and must submit to the power and authority of these adults. When this power is exercised to prevent the child from attaining access to valued resources or to prevent the child from developing a sense of self as a subject rather than an object, it becomes oppression.[51]

Oppressive acts against children vary widely and depend upon the social context. The primary objectives in the oppression of children are to "isolate" and "control" their development under the guise of "knowing and doing what is for their own good."[52] But this is only a rationale for adults to intervene in the lives of children, to establish and maintain an order in the relationship advantageous to adults. While there are occasions when adults exercise their power over children out of sincere concern for the child's welfare, often the adult's use of power over children "for their own good" is little more than a pretext to make the lives of adults more convenient. (For example, making a child go to bed early gives parents time for themselves.)

Children usually accept their status as oppressed persons because it is a social reality that pervades our society: The perception of children as oppressed is constantly reinforced by their submersion in the reality of oppression. Paulo Freire describes how oppressors can create images of oppressed groups as dependent and threatening to the social order:

> For the oppressors it is always the oppressed (whom they obviously never call "the oppressed" but—depending on whether they are fellow countrymen or not—"those people" or the "blind and envious masses" or "savages" or "natives" or "subversives") who are disaffected, who are "violent," "barbaric," "wicked," or "ferocious" when they react to the violence of the oppressors.[53]

It takes little effort to substitute the following images of children (as the oppressed) into the preceding quote: "hoods," "hoodlums," "punks," "disrespectful," "problem children," and "delinquent." As children internalize the image of the oppressor and adopt the oppressor's guidelines and rules of

Source: FEIFFER © 1989 JULES FEIFFER. Reprinted with permission of UNIVERSAL PRESS SYNICATE. All rights reserved.

behavior, they become fearful of exploring the nature of their own freedom and autonomy.

The theory of differential oppression is organized around four principles (see Figure 8–3):

1. *Adults emphasize order in the home and school.* Every day, children are forced to obey rules designed to reinforce adult notions of "right and wrong" behavior. These rules derive from adults' ideas about how children should behave. Because adults believe that the rules are for a child's own good, when a young person violates a rule, adults will defend the rule's legitimacy.

2. *Adults see children as inferior subordinate beings and as troublemakers.* To the extent that children are seen as people who pose a threat to the established order, they must be controlled. "Good" children show deference in almost all interactions with adults. A child who asserts that he or she is not inferior or who questions the rules that define the social order in which adults and children exist is seen as threatening adult control.

3. *The imposition of adult conceptions of order on children may become extreme to the point of oppression.* Adults' desire to establish order in the home and school often leads to oppressive acts directed at children. Sometimes the coercion and force take the form of abuse and neglect, which diminishes the parent-child relationship and ultimately the child's respect for even legitimate authority. The child who comes to view the use of authority by adults at home or school as a coercive tool promoting the interests of adults at the expense of children will tend to see the exercise of authority by store owners or the police as equally suspect.

4. *Oppression leads to adaptive reactions by children.* The oppression of children produces at least four adaptations: passive acceptance; exercise of illegitimate coercive power; manipulation of one's peers; and retaliation.

Figure 8–3
Mapping Delinquency Theory: Differential Oppression Theory

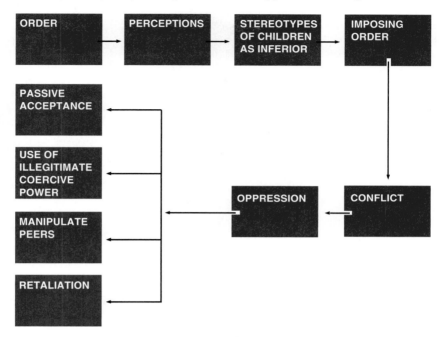

The first adaptation involves *passive acceptance* of one's status and subsequent obedience—an obedience built upon fear. It is similar to the passive acceptance of the slave role, adaptations of prison inmates, and the learned helplessness of battered women. Children who accept their inferior position often develop a negative conception of (learn to hate) those who exercise power over them. By learning to hate but repressing the hatred, further negative consequences such as alcoholism, drug addiction, and low self-esteem may occur later.

A second adaptation is the *exercise of illegitimate coercive power.* According to Jack Katz, many adolescents are attracted to delinquency because it helps them establish a sense of autonomy and control.[54] David Matza suggests that for many youths, because "an infraction is among the few acts that immediately and demonstrably make things happen . . . it may serve well as a symbol of restored potency."[55] This response may take one or more of a variety of forms ranging from sexual misbehavior to illicit use of drugs or alcohol to common crime.

A third form of adaptation involves *manipulation of one's peers* in an attempt to gain social power. Through manipulation of others within the peer group, a child who has experienced oppression by adults may acquire a

Differential oppression theory suggests that adults consider children subordinate to them. Does this picture support such a claim? Do you think that this father would point his finger in the face of an adult to handle a dispute?

sense of strength and control or a degree of empowerment not otherwise felt. Gerald Marwell suggests that

> at any given point of time this potential [for social power] lies primarily in the opinions of the actor held by those with whom one interacts. If one is thought strong, one, by and large, is strong, or at least, may use "strength" to manipulate others.[56]

Unfortunately, many adults define the child's involvement in the peer group as problematic itself and may react by exercising even greater control over the child's interaction with others.

The fourth adaptation is *retaliation*. Children may retaliate by striking back at both the people and the institutions they blame for causing their oppression. Much school vandalism occurs because a student is angry at a teacher or principal. Some children may strike directly at their parents, assaulting or even killing them. Others try to hurt their parents by turning inward—by becoming psychotically depressed or committing suicide. (See Figure 8–3 for an illustration of this process.)

Evaluation of Conflict Theory

Conflict theories have been criticized on a number of grounds. For example, Jackson Toby believes that conflict theories are nothing more than rehashings of the traditional liberal approach of helping the underdog.[57] He claims that most crime is for profit and luxury, not merely for survival.[58] Conflict theories have also been accused of relying too heavily on historical and theoretical approaches that fail to produce testable hypotheses. Statements or postulates offered tend to be untestable; they are not subject to scientific verification and instead must be accepted as a matter of faith.[59] In addition,

Francis Allen[60] and David Shichor[61] state that conflict theories oversimplify and overemphasize the political and economic nature of juvenile delinquency.

J. A. Sharpe[62] analyzed patterns of law violations in England between the 15th and 19th centuries and concluded that there was little evidence to support the claims of conflict theorists that crime and delinquency increased with the development of capitalism.

Ronald Akers has taken conflict theory to task for portraying modern society as too heterogeneous for the general population to arrive at any significant value consensus. Instead of viewing society as a precarious balancing of crisscrossing, conflicting, and competing interest groups, Akers believes that "society is also held together by the larger or smaller number of widely supported values, common assumptions, and images of the world. This is a chief factor in providing some continuity and unity in a diversified society."[63] Akers also notes that most delinquency cannot be explained by group conflict inasmuch as most delinquency is intragroup in nature—that is, committed by members within the group against other members within the group.

Donald Shoemaker is very critical of conflict theorists' claims of a direct link between capitalism and delinquency. Such a link is questionable because (1) delinquency is widespread in the middle- and upper-middle classes; (2) juveniles appear to have little concern for their status in the economic system; (3) racial and ethnic factors have as much or more influence on crime and delinquency as social class factors do; and (4) there is a failure to demonstrate "a necessary connection between capitalism per se and industrial or demographic conditions within a society."[64]

Research connecting the more extreme forms of oppression of children (including beatings, sexual abuse, hitting, slapping, screaming, ridicule, verbal insults, and serious neglect and deficiencies in child care) to subsequent delinquency is substantial.[65] Among recent studies illuminating this relationship are Cary Heck and Anthony Walsh's analysis of data from a sample of 489 white male adolescents on probation in Idaho[66] and Cathy Widom and Michael Maxfield's study of childhood abuse as a predictor of both juvenile delinquency and subsequent adult criminality.[67] Heck and Walsh found that, even when controlling for type of family structure, verbal IQ, family size, and birth order, maltreatment was the most significant predictor of violent delinquency and was one of the more powerful predictors of both property offending and minor misbehaviors. They note a modest significant relationship between youths from homes broken by desertion and minor delinquency. Perhaps more importantly, they found that "delinquents from homes broken by desertion were the most maltreated and the most delinquent."[68]

The research by Widom and Maxfield is interesting because it updates data initially collected on the abuse-offending relationship in 1988 with new data collected in 1994. Their study followed 1,575 cases from childhood through young adulthood and included a study group of 908 substantiated cases of childhood abuse or neglect and a comparison group of 667 children,

Part of the undeniable allure of conflict theory is that subordinated groups are disproportionately involved in delinquency. The glaring exception to this is sex: Males are much more delinquent than females. Does this suggest that biology is more important than sociology in explaining delinquency?

Since the poor and racial and ethnic minorities are vastly over represented among crime victims, then the greatest beneficiaries of tough juvenile and criminal justice systems are the poor and racial and ethnic minorities. Why don't conflict or radical theorists acknowledge this?

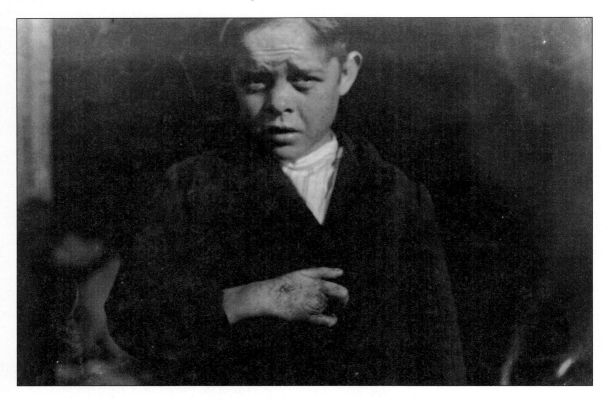

This early 20th century child-laborer lost two fingers in an industrial accident. Payment compensation of just $1 released his employer from any responsibility for the accident. Does this photo convey how far the United States has progressed in its treatment of children? If so, is conflict theory an academic anachronism? If not, are there current examples of the flagrant abuses of children?

not officially recorded as abused or neglected, matched on sex, age, race, and family socioeconomic status. According to Widom and Maxfield:

> Those who had been abused or neglected as children were more likely to be arrested as juveniles (27 percent versus 17 percent), adults (42 percent versus 33 percent), and for a violent crime (18 percent versus 14 percent. . . . The abused and neglected cases were younger at first arrest, . . . committed nearly twice as many offenses, . . . and were arrested more frequently.[69]

Patterns of increased risk for violent offending differed slightly by sex and race. For example, childhood victimization increases the risk for participation in violence for females, while for males there is an increase in frequency of violent arrests. And while white abused and neglected children were no more likely to be arrested for a violent crime than their nonabused and nonneglected counterparts, abused and neglected black children showed significantly increased rates of violent crime arrests compared to nonabused and nonneglected black children.[70]

Juvenile Justice Policy Applications

Criminological conflict theories have had very little direct impact on either juvenile justice policy or broader social policy.[71] Federal and state legislative bodies have, understandably, been hesitant to consider policy changes that would require a restructuring of the larger society along socialist lines. Similarly, they have generally balked at dramatically redefining crime to either include broadly accepted business and economic practices associated with capitalism or to exclude "revolutionary" crimes of the economically or socially deprived or marginalized underdog. On the other hand, conflict theories have contributed in many ways to the discourse within criminology and the larger society on the need to reduce structural inequalities (for example, those based on economic, social, racial, and gender differences) and to eliminate discriminatory practices within the juvenile and adult justice systems. Finally, differential oppression theory has led to calls for adults to refuse to define children as objects and instead to empower children with the essential fundamental constitutional rights adults enjoy. At a minimum, seriously abused and neglected children should be quickly removed from dangerous and threatening home environments and placed in foster care or group homes designed to provide loving and supportive adult care and supervision.

Radical Theory

Contemporary radical theories of delinquency are largely based in Marxist or neo-Marxist theories that continue to focus on class conflict, power differences, and the negative effects of capitalism as an economic system. This section will briefly look at two variations in radical theory.

Mark Colvin and John Pauly

Mark Colvin and John Pauly's "integrated structural-Marxist" theory argues that serious delinquency is the result of the reproduction of coercive control patterns tied to the relationship between production and class structure in capitalist societies.[72] According to Colvin and Pauly, the actual or objective structure of social relationships is "grounded in the process of material production under capitalism."[73]

Colvin and Pauly believe that coercive control patterns that exist for lower-class parents in the workplace are reproduced in the home, shaping the parents' behavior as they interact with each other and their children. Parents, holding jobs that are inferior, tightly controlled, lacking in personal authority, and regulated by superiors through coercive means reproduce these control patterns in the home. This leads to the increased alienation of the child from authority in general. In addition, the use of coercive controls in the home, including physical punishments, tends to weaken the bond between parent and child. Thus, class-related socialization patterns within the home ultimately produce delinquent or conforming behavior.

Left Realism

Left realism evolved as a reaction to Marxist and neo-Marxist romanticized views of crime and delinquency committed by the working class, the poor, and the downtrodden as mere "struggles for survival" and rebellions against capitalist oppression. Early left realists such as Jock Young[74] believed that radical and critical criminologists, whom they referred to as "left idealists," were too extreme in their writings about both the causes of crime and policies for its control or elimination. Left realists recognize that much working-class delinquency is not done out of an attempt to survive, but because they, like the wealthy, want to enjoy luxuries. More importantly, they emphasize that the poor, workers, and the underclass in general are not only victimized by crimes of powerful capitalists, but as often or more often they are victims of street crime and street gangs in their own neighborhoods.[75] For left realists, the calls for the dismantling of capitalism or disarming of the police are not only politically naïve, they are likely to lead criminologists and policy makers to "overlook the reality of pain and suffering generated by criminal offenders who victimize their fellow human beings, usually the poor and powerless."[76]

Evaluation of Radical Theory

The "integrated structural-Marxist" theory of Colvin and Pauly has been most severely criticized for its failure to clearly establish any link between capitalism, coercive norms in the workplace, disciplinary practices by parents in the home, and delinquency. Recent tests of Colvin and Pauly's theory have found only modest support for their claims. Studies by Steven Messner and Marvin Krohn and by Sally Simpson and Lori Elis have found that the basic relationship between social class and delinquency is largely structured by gender.[77] These researchers suggest that traditional gender controls in the home interact with workplace controls to produce more rigid discipline and control for girls than for boys.

Left realists have been criticized for a variety of weaknesses. Curran and Renzetti note that critics have found left realism theory neglectful of gender issues, especially violence against women, and that they have taken "too simplistic a view of communities, overlooking the fact that there are often racist and sexist divisions within neighborhoods that put groups in conflict over 'community concerns and priorities.' These problems could be worsened through 'community control' of decision making."[78]

Simply because we can explain behavior does not mean that we should excuse behavior. Are social scientists and the general public too concerned with the background of delinquents to effectively control their illegal behavior?

Do the popularity and applicability of critical theories guarantee ineffective crime policy? Is it possible to get tough on crime using theories described in this chapter? If so, how can effective crime policies be devised?

Juvenile Justice Policy Applications

Similar to our discussion of policy applications derived from conflict theories, radical theories have had very little impact on policies aimed at controlling or reducing juvenile delinquency. Left realists stress support for participatory democracy, job development, and social activism or intervention in crime-ridden neighborhoods and reductions in police surveillance and heavy-handed, get-tough-on-crime policies that disproportionately focus attention on minorities and the poor. Calls for studying the root causes of crime, establishing victim restitution or compensation programs, and control of police excesses appear to be little more than the liberal reform policies advocated since the early 1960s.

Conclusions

Critical theories are relatively new explanations that have been popularized during the last third of the 20th century. Unlike strain and social control theories, critical theorists have little interest in the immediate causes of individual delinquency, being more concerned with reactions to behavior and imbalances in power that stem from social arrangements. Such theories, therefore, often tend to side with the adolescent and view the juvenile justice system in a critical light.

Labeling theory assumes that social control efforts produce more serious problem behavior, especially juvenile delinquency. The social response to acts socially defined as delinquent results in individuals engaging in such acts being labeled as delinquents. It is the interactional process and impact of the response and label that is of greatest interest to labeling theorists. If there are solutions to the problem of delinquency, they are to be found in the juvenile justice system doing less, not more.

Conflict explanations of delinquency generally assume that social order in contemporary, heterogeneous societies is maintained through coercion, force, and confrontation. These theories stress the effects of economic and political power, influence, and group or vested interests on the development and enforcement of law. Solutions to delinquency from the conflict perspective largely focus on major social and economic structural changes designed to eliminate discriminatory laws and legal processes and to equalize wealth and power.

Differential oppression theory assumes that children develop in an arena of oppression. This oppressive environment has consequences for who and what children are in relation to adults. Adult attempts to impose their sense of order within the home or school on children whom they perceive to be inferior leads to maladaptive responses by children, including delinquency. Differential oppression theory, then, argues that the solution to delinquency lies not so much in reforming the juvenile or changing the juvenile justice system, but in changing existing adult perceptions of children: Children must be seen as equally valuable, autonomous, and independent human beings.

Finally, radical theories, such as Colvin and Pauly's "integrated structural-Marxist" theory emphasize the impact of coercive control patterns in the workplace on how parents socialize and discipline their children. The replication of these control patterns in the home leads to alienation, to weakening of the bonds between parent and child, and eventually to delinquency. Left realists have attempted to move Marxists and extreme radical criminologists closer to more traditional liberal crime reduction policies, having recognized that street crime is a problematic reality not easily done away with through broadside attacks on capitalism and the largely consensual legal order.

Key Terms

conduct norms: *Rules that reflect the values, expectations, and actual behaviors of groups in everyday life. They are not necessarily the norms found in the criminal law.*

conflict theory: *A perspective that argues that society is held together by force, coercion, and intimidation and that the law represents the interests of those in power.*

crime norms: *Rules that prohibit specific conduct and provide punishments for violations.*

differential oppression theory: *A theory that argues delinquency is the culmination of a process that begins at conception and evolves through adolescence; the more a child is oppressed, the greater the likelihood he or she will become delinquent.*

disintegrative shaming: *A form of negative labeling by the juvenile justice system that stigmatizes and excludes targeted youths, tossing them into a class of outcasts.*

dualistic fallacy: *The idea that delinquents and nondelinquents are two fundamentally different types of people.*

falsely accused: *Juveniles who are thought to have committed a crime when they have not.*

labeling theory: *A perspective that assumes that social control leads to deviance; how behavior is reacted to determines whether it is defined as deviant.*

master status: *The status of an individual that people react to first when they see or meet him or her for the first time.*

primary deviation: *Deviant behavior that everyone engages in occasionally.*

radical nonintervention: *An approach to juvenile justice whereby police and the courts would, whenever possible, "leave kids alone."*

reintegrative shaming: *The expression of community disapproval of delinquency, followed by indications of forgiveness and reacceptance into the community.*

secondary deviation: *Deviant behavior based on the youth's taking on and accepting the deviant role as part of his or her identity.*

secret deviant: *Offenders whose deviant behavior is hidden from others.*

Getting Connected

Howie's Home Page, maintained by Howard Becker himself, is filled with recent writings and biographical information and is available at:

http://soc.ucsb.edu/faculty/hbecker/

1. What seem to be Becker's reasons for having a web page? How is his discussion about this related to his ideas about deviance?
2. What links does Becker think might be interesting to his page's visitors? Visit one or two to see if you agree.
3. Who are Becker's sociological heroes? What might have made them heroic to him?

A series of Working Papers from the Reintegrative Shaming experiments conducted by Larry Sherman and Heather Strong and based on the theoretical work of John Braithwaite are available at:

http://www.cjcentral.com/rise

1. What IS the right kind of shame for crime prevention?
2. How is the victim's perspective different in restorative justice practice?
3. How does a restorative justice perspective affect an offender's respect for the law?

The Marx and Engels Internet Archive is a compendium of thinking and writing covering the origins of Marxist theory. It can be found at:

http://www.marxists.org/archive/marx/index.htm

1. Consider several quotations from Marx's writings. Do they provide any insight on the causes of delinquency?
2. Read the V.I. Lenin biography of Marx. How are Marx's life and his political philosophy related?
3. Read the V.I. Lenin biography of Engels. How are Engels's life and his political philosophy related?

The Division of Critical Criminology of the American Society of Criminology maintains a website that will help guide you to a variety of theoretical and policy concerns from the critical perspective.

http://www.critcrim.org

1. Link to "critcrim issues." What are they? Might studying any of them improve one's understanding of juvenile delinquency? Is there a critical criminology of juvenile delinquency?
2. Link to "peacemaking criminology," then to "What Works." What kinds of ideas seem to "work" in delinquency prevention?
3. What is the difference between the American Society of Criminology and the Academy of Criminal Justice Sciences?

Additional information about Alice Miller, who has contributed so much to our understanding of the oppression of children, can be found at:

http://www.naturalchild.com/alice_miller/

1. Read Alice Miller's "Letter to College Students of All Nations." How might you write to her in response?
2. Read Alice Miller's "Letter to Children and Adolescents of All Nations." What action might this letter inspire its readers to take?
3. Research the United Nations Convention on the Rights of the Child. Why has the United States not signed?

Endnotes

1. Frank Tannenbaum, *Crime and the Community* (New York: Columbia University Press, 1938), pp. 19–20.
2. Donald Shoemaker, *Theories of Delinquency*, 4th ed. (New York: Oxford University Press, 2000), p. 196.
3. Tannenbaum, note 1.
4. Tannenbaum, note 1, pp. 17–18.
5. Tannenbaum, note 1, p. 20.
6. Edwin Lemert, *Social Pathology* (New York: McGraw-Hill Publishing Co., 1951), p. 75.
7. Lemert, note 6, p. 75.
8. Lemert, note 6, p. 76.
9. Lemert, note 6, pp. 70–71.
10. Howard Becker, *Outsiders* (New York: The Free Press, 1963); Howard Becker, *The Other Side* (New York: The Free Press, 1964).
11. Becker, note 10, 1963, pp. 12–13.
12. Daniel Curran and Claire Renzetti, *Theories of Crime*, 2nd ed. (Boston: Allyn and Bacon, 2001), p. 174.
13. Edwin Schur, *Radical Nonintervention* (Englewood Cliffs, NJ: Prentice-Hall, Inc., 1973); Edwin Schur, *Labeling Deviant Behavior* (New York: Harper & Row, 1971).
14. Schur, note 13, 1973, p. 123.
15. Schur, note 13, 1973, p. 155.
16. John Braithwaite, *Crime, Shame and Reintegration* (Cambridge: Cambridge University Press, 1989), p. 55.
17. Curran and Renzetti, note 12, p. 179.
18. See for example, Robert Emerson, *Judging Delinquents* (Chicago: Aldine, 1969); Aaron Cicourel, *The Social Organization of Juvenile Justice* (New York: John Wiley & Sons, 1976); Carl Werthman, "The Function of Social Definitions in the Development of Delinquent Careers," *Becoming Delinquent*, edited by Peter Garabedian and Don Gibbons (Chicago: Aldine, 1970); and Francis Palamara, Francis Cullen, and Joanne Gersten, "The Effects of Police and Mental Health Intervention on Juvenile Deviance: Specifying Contingencies in the Impact of Formal Reaction," *Journal of Health and Social Behavior* 27:90–106 (1986).
19. William Chambliss, "The Saints and the Roughnecks," *Society* 11:24–31 (1973).
20. Charles Tittle and Robert Meier, "Specifying the SES/Delinquency Relationship," *Criminology* 28:271–299 (1990).
21. Charles Thomas and Donna Bishop, "The Effect of Formal and Informal Sanctions on Delinquency," *Journal of Criminal Law and Criminology* 75:1222–1245 (1984).
22. Steven Burkett and Carol Hickman, "An Examination of the Impact of Legal Sanctions on Adolescent Marijuana Use: A Panel Analysis," *Journal of Drug Issues* 12:73–87 (1982).
23. Jack Foster, Simon Dinitz, and Walter Reckless, "Perceptions of Stigma Following Public Intervention for Delinquent Behavior," *Social Problems* 20:202–209 (1972).
24. John Hepburn, "The Impact of Police Intervention Upon Juvenile Delinquents," *Criminology* 15:235–262 (1977).
25. David Ward and Charles Tittle, "Deterrence or Labeling: The Effects of Informal Sanctions," *Deviant Behavior* 14:43–64 (1993).
26. Karen Heimer and Ross Matsueda, "Role-Taking, Role Commitment, and Delinquency: A Theory of Differential Social Control," *American Sociological Review* 59:365–390 (1994); Ross Matsueda, "Reflected Appraisals, Parental Labeling, and Delinquency: Specifying a Symbolic Interactionist Theory," *American Journal of Sociology* 97:1577–1611 (1992).
27. Mike Adams, "Labeling and Differential Association: Towards a General Social Learning Theory of Crime and Deviance," *American Journal of Criminal Justice* 20:147–164 (1996).
28. Karen Heimer, "Gender, Race, and the Pathways to Delinquency: An Interactionist Explanation," in *Crime and Inequality*, edited by John Hagan and Ruth Peterson (Stanford, CA: Stanford University Press, 1995), p. 140.
29. Heimer, note 28, p. 167.
30. Dawn Bartusch and Ross Matsueda, "Gender, Reflected Appraisals, and Labeling: A Cross Group Test of an Interactionist Theory of Delinquency," *Social Forces* 75:145–177 (1996).
31. Malcolm Klein, "Labeling Theory and Delinquency Policy," *Criminal Justice and Behavior* 13:47–79 (1986).
32. Michael Miller and Martin Gold, "Iatrogenesis in the Juvenile Justice System," *Youth and Society* 16:83–111 (1984).
33. See for example, Alexander McEachern and Rita Bauzer, "Factors Related to Dispositions in Juvenile Justice Police Contacts," in *Juvenile Gangs in Context*, edited by Malcolm Klein (Beverly Hills, CA: Sage Publications, 1967); Lawrence Sherman and Richard Berk, "The Specific Deterrent Effects of Arrest for Domestic Assault," *American Sociological Review* 49:261–271 (1984); and Douglas Smith and Patrick Gartin, "Specifying Specific Deterrence," *American Sociological Review* 54:94–106 (1989).

34. Schur, note 13.
35. Albert Roberts, "Wilderness Experiences: Camps and Outdoor Programs," in *Juvenile Justice: Policies, Programs, and Services*, 2nd ed., edited by Albert Roberts (Chicago: Nelson-Hall, 1998), pp. 327–346.
36. Ronald Akers, *Criminological Theories: Introduction, Evaluation, and Application*, 3rd ed. (Los Angeles: Roxbury Publishing Co., 2000) p. 135.
37. Curran and Renzetti, note 12, p. 179.
38. William Chambliss, *Criminal Law in Action*, 2nd ed. (New York: John Wiley & Sons, 1984), p. 76.
39. Akers, note 36, pp. 166–167.
40. Shoemaker, note 2.
41. Karl Marx and Friedrich Engels, *Capital* (New York: International Publishers 1867/1967).
42. Paul Hirst, "Marx and Engels on Law, Crime and Morality," in *Critical Criminology*, edited by Ian Taylor, Paul Walton, and Jock Young (London: Routledge & Kegan Paul, 1975).
43. Thorsten Sellin, *Culture and Conflict in Crime* (New York: Social Science Research Council, 1938).
44. Sellin, note 43, p. 21.
45. Sellin, note 43, p. 3.
46. George Vold, *Theoretical Criminology* (New York: Oxford University Press, 1958).
47. George Vold and Thomas Bernard, *Theoretical Criminology*, 3rd ed. (New York: Oxford University Press, 1986), p. 272.
48. Vold and Bernard, note 47, p. 273.
49. Vold and Bernard, note 47.
50. Robert Regoli and John D. Hewitt, *Delinquency in Society* (New York: McGraw-Hill Publishing Co., 1991); Robert Regoli and John D. Hewitt, *Delinquency in Society*, 2nd ed. (New York: McGraw-Hill Publishing Co., 1994).
51. Gerald Marwell, "Adolescent Powerlessness and Delinquent Behavior," *Social Problems* 14:35–47 (1966).
52. Alice Miller, *For Your Own Good* (New York: Farrar, Straus, & Giroux, 1984).
53. Paulo Freire, *Pedagogy of the Oppressed* (New York: Continuum, 1990), p. 41.
54. Jack Katz, *Seductions of Crime* (New York: Basic Books, 1988), p. 9.
55. Marwell, note 51, p. 41.
56. Marwell, note 51, p. 40.
57. Jackson Toby, "The New Criminology is the Old Sentimentality," *Criminology* 16:515–526 (1979).
58. Charles Tittle, Wayne Villemez, and Douglas Smith, "The Myth of Social Class and Criminality," *American Sociological Review* 43:643–656 (1978); Tittle and Meier, note 20.
59. Arnold Binder, Gilbert Geis, and Bruce Dickson, *Juvenile Delinquency* (New York: Macmillan Publishing Co., 1988).
60. Francis Allen, *The Crimes of Politics* (Cambridge: Harvard University Press, 1974).
61. David Shichor, "The New Criminology: Some Critical Issues," *British Journal of Criminology* 20:1–19 (1980).
62. J. A. Sharpe, *Crime in Early Modern England, 1550–1750* (London: Longmans, 1984).
63. Akers, note 36, p. 162.
64. Shoemaker, note 2, p. 221.
65. See for example, Cathy Widom, "Child Abuse, Neglect, and Violent Criminal Behavior," *Criminology* 27:251–271 (1989); Carolyn Smith and Terence Thornberry, "The Relationship between Childhood Maltreatment and Adolescent Involvement in Delinquency," *Criminology* 33:451–477 (1995); Barbara Kelly, Terence Thornberry, and Carolyn Smith, *In the Wake of Childhood Maltreatment* (Washington, DC: Office of Juvenile Justice and Delinquency Prevention, 1997); Timothy Brezina, "Adolescent Maltreatment and Delinquency: The Question of Intervening Processes," *Journal of Research in Crime and Delinquency* 35:71–99 (1998); K. M. Thompson and R. Braaten-Antrim, "Youth Maltreatment and Gang Involvement," *Journal of Interpersonal Violence* 13:328–345 (1998);and David Wolfe, Katreena Scott, Christine Wekerle, and Anna-Lee Pittman, "Child Maltreatment: Risk of Adjustment Problems and Dating Violence in Adolescence," *Journal of the American Academy of Child and Adolescent Psychiatry* 40: 282 289 (2001).
66. Cary Heck and Anthony Walsh, "The Effects of Maltreatment and Family Structure on Minor and Serious Delinquency," *International Journal of Offender Therapy and Comparative Criminology* 44:178–193 (2000).
67. Cathy Widom and Michael Maxfield, *Update on the "Cycle of Violence"* (Washington, DC: National Institute of Justice, 2001).
68. Heck and Walsh, note 66, p. 178.
69. Widom and Maxfield, note 67, p. 3.
70. Widom and Maxfield, note 67, p. 4.
71. J. Robert Lilly, Francis Cullen, and Richard Ball, *Criminological Theory: Context and Consequences*, 3rd ed. (Thousand Oaks, CA: Sage Publications, 2002).
72. Mark Colvin and John Pauly, "A Critique of Criminology," *American Journal of Sociology* 89:513–551 (1987).
73. Colvin and Pauly, note 72, p. 513.

74. Jock Young, "The Tasks Facing a Realist Criminology," *Contemporary Crisis* 11:337–356 (1987).

75. Curran and Renzetti, note 12, pp. 197–198.

76. Akers, note 36, p. 210.

77. Steven Messner and Marvin Krohn, "Class, Compliance Structures, and Delinquency: Assessing Integrated Structural-Marxist Theory," *American Journal of Sociology* 96:300–328 (1990); Sally Simpson and Lori Elis, "Is Gender Subordinate to Class? An Empirical Assessment of Colvin and Pauly's Structural Marxist Theory of Delinquency," *Journal of Criminal Law and Criminology* 85:453–480 (1994).

78. Curran and Renzetti, note 12, p. 199.

Chapter 9

Female Delinquency Theories

Criminology, like most academic disciplines, has been concerned with the activities and interests of men.

—Allison Morris[1]

For over a century, the study of delinquency has focused almost exclusively on the behavior of males. In part, this reflects the simple reality that male law violating exceeds that of females in both frequency and seriousness (see Chapter 2). But it also reflects the fact that criminology, as a discipline, has been dominated by men who see the world through their own eyes. In addition, the vast majority of people who create laws, who prosecute and defend offenders, and who administer the juvenile corrections systems have been, and still are, males.

How might our under-standing and concep-tualization of delinquency differ if females had histori-cally dominated crim-inology instead of males? Do male and female criminologists study delinquency differently? If so, why?

The United States has traditionally been a patriarchal society. **Patriarchy** refers to "a social, legal, and political climate that values male dominance and hierarchy."[2] Patriarchy affects not only social structures (including the family and the economy), relationships, and definitions of appropriate social roles, but also how people, both males and females, perceive the world around them. Gender stratification as a product of patriarchy has led to unconscious assumptions about female and male behavior and misbehavior. According to Joanne Belknap, "Patriarchy and its privileges, then, remain as part of the defining quality of the culture and thus of criminology and crime processing."[3]

To the extent that patriarchy extends into the academic arena of criminological research and writing, the delinquent behaviors of girls and the causes of those behaviors have largely been invisible. While sex is the most statistically significant factor in predicting delinquency, criminologists have rarely shown much concern in including girls in their samples. Belknap states that:

> When the researchers did include girls in their samples, it was typically to see how girls fit into boys' equations. That is, rather than include in the study a means of assessing how girls' lives might be different from boys' lives, girls' delinquency has typically been viewed as peripheral and unnecessary to understanding juvenile offending and processing.[4]

When females have been studied as delinquents, it has nearly always been in comparison to males: why girls are less delinquent than boys, why girls commit less serious crimes, and how the causes of female delinquency differ from those of male delinquency.

In this chapter we will try to avoid falling into the trap of making comparisons between female and male delinquents. To this end, we will begin by examining how patriarchy and gender stratification affect the lives of girls as they grow up. Such an examination is critical for understanding the nature of female delinquency and the appropriateness of explanations put forth to explain it.

Growing Up Female

In Charlotte Brontë's 19th-century novel *Jane Eyre*, the young protagonist paces the roof of Thornfield Hall, frustrated over the contrast between her confined existence and the possibilities that lie in the larger world:

> Women need exercise for their faculties and a field for their efforts as much
> as their brothers do; they suffer from too rigid a restraint, too absolute a
> stagnation, precisely as men would suffer; and it is narrow-minded in their
> more privileged fellow-creatures to say that they ought to confine them-
> selves to making puddings and knitting stockings, to playing on the piano
> and embroidering bags.[5]

The frustration that came from realizing the unfair situation she and other women faced in life because of their sex was not unique to Jane Eyre. In generation after generation, young girls have experienced the same frustration after realizing the same unfairness. Somehow, their place in society has been defined as being different from that of boys. But Jane Eyre's sense of a self-identity as a female was perhaps more consciously formed than that of many other young girls, and such an awareness may, in part, explain why some girls feel more frustration than others over their defined place in society.

Throughout most of human history, girls have grown up in societies that have viewed them as being "inferior" to boys. The pervasiveness of the belief that girls are inferior is illustrated by Jean Stafford in her novel *The Mountain Lion*. Ralph, at age 11, already senses his superiority to his nine-year-old sister, Molly:

> It was natural for her to want to be a boy (who *wouldn't!*) but he knew for a
> fact that she couldn't be. Last week, he had had to speak sharply to her
> about wearing one of his outgrown Boy Scout shirts: he was glad enough for
> her to have it, but she had not taken the "Be Prepared" thing off the pocket
> and he had to come out and say brutally, "Having that on a girl is like drag-
> ging the American flag in the dirt."[6]

What accounts for Jane Eyre's confinement to an existence less fulfilling than that of the men of her community or for Ralph's assumption of his superiority over his sister? The differences between girls and boys suggested in the two extracts above reflect widely held perceptions of the superiority of boys over girls. The relegation of girls to more restricted lives also reflects patriarchal society, in which males have managed to maintain control over females. For both girls and boys, one's sense of self, and of oneself in relation to others, is highly influenced by society's perceptions of gender roles. In patriarchal societies, then, growing up female is quite different from growing up male and has significant implications for how girls confront their lives. Box 9–1 provides a look at one consequence of preferential treatment of boys in India.

The Development of Girls' Gender Roles

Creating **gender-role identities** begins at birth (or even at the fetal stage, given ultrasound identification of the child's sex) with the announcement of "It's a girl!" or "It's a boy!" Almost immediately, in describing their infants, parents start using typical gender stereotypes. In one study parents described

BOX 9–1   A CROSS-CULTURAL PERSPECTIVE ON DELINQUENCY
Preferential Treatment of Boys in India

It is true that in patriarchal societies, such as the United States, boys receive preferential treatment over girls. This fact is reflected in a variety of ways, one being that the study of American delinquency has focused almost exclusively on the behavior of boys.

But the situation of boys receiving preferential treatment over girls is not unique to the United States. For example, in contemporary Indian society, female fetuses are targeted for abortion at a much higher rate than male fetuses. Advances in ultrasound technology have made it possible for pregnant women in India to determine the sex of their fetus for about $11. Because boys are more valued than girls in India, increasing numbers of women are aborting female fetuses because family elders want boys, not girls. The reason: Boys are important because they have to look after all the property.

Early figures from the 2001 census indicate that female fetuses are regularly being aborted, continuing a trend that started in the 1980s. The number of girls per 1,000 boys dropped in 2001 to 927 from 945 in 1991 and 962 in 1981. The fall in the ratio of girls to boys over the past decade has been the most pronounced in the richest states where more people can afford ultrasound tests and abortions are more easily obtained.

Source: Celia Dugger, "Female Fetuses Targeted for Abortions in India," *The Denver Post,* April 22:16A (2001).

Data from international studies indicate that boys are more involved in delinquency than girls in all countries. What are the implications of this for those who argue that gender-role identities and gender socialization explain delinquency? In your opinion, what percentage of delinquency is explained by socialization and what percentage is explained by biological factors?

boy babies as being firm, large-featured, alert, and strong, while girl babies were characterized as delicate, fine-featured, soft, and small.[7] Parents also respond to toddlers differently on the basis of the child's sex. They discourage rough-and-tumble play by girls and doll play by boys. They listen to girls and respond to them more attentively when girls are gentle or talk softly, but they attend more to boys when boys demonstrate assertiveness. Parents encourage dependence in girls and independence in boys.[8] By age four or five, children have become aware of their gender and the behaviors appropriate to it.[9]

Girls' gender roles are reinforced through toys and games in early adolescence. Boys frequently are given toys that encourage creativity and manipulation, such as construction and chemistry sets, while girls are given toys that encourage passivity and nurturance, such as stuffed animals and dolls. Girls are more likely to play in small, unstructured groups; their games tend to have few rules and emphasize cooperation rather than competition. Boys, on the other hand, typically play in larger groups, often teams; their games have more complex rules and often emphasize cooperation to facilitate competing.[10]

Going to school provides both girls and boys with opportunities to learn the *four* R's: reading, 'riting, 'rithmetic, and (gender) roles. Conscious and unconscious patterns of interaction between teachers and students as well as the formal and informal activities of girls and boys in school encourage stereotyped gender roles. Girls receive reinforcement from teachers for being passive, verbal, and dependent, while boys are encouraged to explore, examine how things work, and be independent.[11]

Schools also provide avenues to develop self-esteem. For boys, the avenues are being tough, developing a good body build, participating in sports (including competition and aggressiveness), being cool (not showing emotions), and being good at something (sports, school, cars, and sex, for example). The avenues for building self-esteem in girls have traditionally been more problematic: being pretty, being popular, being liked as sociable and pleasant, and being preoccupied with body weight (which may lead to anorexia or bulimia).[12]

The socialization into sex-appropriate gender roles for adolescents is also reinforced in the home. In traditional family arrangements, girls are kept more dependent and cloistered through closer supervision and more restrictive rules. Parents encourage girls to stay at home or in close proximity to their mothers, to avoid risks, and to fear social disapproval.[13] Girls generally join groups later than boys, are less likely than boys to have a regular meeting place outside the home, and are less likely to belong to single-sex groups at all.[14] Parents typically encourage boys, on the other hand, to be independent, aggressive, and group-oriented, and they allow boys to date earlier than girls, to stay out later than girls with their friends, to be left alone at home, and to participate in organized activities.[15]

Girls' Identities

What are the effects of these gender-role socialization patterns on girls' identities and self-esteem? The patterns lead many girls to identify with traditional female roles, anticipate economic dependence and a more restricted adult status, and accept political, social, and sexual privileges secondary to those of boys. Such socialization creates narrower boundaries of opportunities for girls than for boys and instills in them a self-perception of powerlessness and dependence.[16] Girls also learn "that to be feminine includes the prescription to be nurturant,"[17] and therefore they focus on relationships. Carol Gilligan suggests that girls are raised to identify with the primary caretaker, the mother, and therefore experience a strong bonding relationship that becomes a model for the rest of their lives.[18] But this emphasis on relationships, or "making connections," encourages in adolescent girls the development of a "morality of response," or "care," which emphasizes the creation and maintenance of interdependence and responsiveness in relationships.[19] An alternative view on these arguments is presented in Box 9–2.

Girls, then, begin to operate very early within a network of intimate interpersonal ties that reinforce a more nurturing and caring role. And because girls are more likely to define themselves relationally, they do not develop the same precise and rigid ego boundaries common to boys.[20] According to Erik Erikson, "Much of a young woman's identity is already defined in her kind of attractiveness and in the selective nature of her search for the man (or men) by whom she wishes to be sought."[21]

Inadequate parental socialization may produce children with low self-control. Based on the disproportionate role of women in parenting and nurturing, are they to blame for children having low self-control? Or, are "dead-beat" dads the main culprits for children with low self-control?

BOX 9–2   A WINDOW ON DELINQUENCY
Is it a Problem for Girls if Boys are Boys?

Eight-year-old Joseph loves to play tag at his school, West Annapolis Elementary, but can no longer play the game during recess because it is now banned by the school's "no touching" policy. The Cleveland Avenue Elementary School in Atlanta intentionally designed *out* the playground when it was recently built. In 1998, the elementary schools in Atlanta eliminated recess and rules stating "no running and no jumping" are enforced. Boys are frequently punished for engaging in what has traditionally been considered normal play activity. Philadelphia elementary schools have replaced the traditional recess with "socialized recesses" where girls, but especially boys, are closely monitored as they play in assigned structured activities. Michael Gurian, author of *The Good Son* says: "If Huck [Finn] and Tom [Sawyer] were in today's schools, they would be labeled ADD, having attention deficit disorder, and drugged." And Thomas Sowell writes: "The old saying, 'boys will be boys' has long since become obsolete in schools across the length and breadth of this country . . . [with] programs to prevent boys from acting the way boys have always acted before."

Is normal youthful male exuberance no longer tolerable? Does the distinct preference of boys for engaging in active play and games with "body contact, conflict, and clearly defined winners and losers" suggest some gender aberration in need of correction? Is "rough-and-tumble" play by boys that includes running, jumping, wrestling, play fighting, and chasing one another a sign of inherent male aggression? With contemporary concerns about bullying and school violence, it is understandable that a more cautious eye is turned on boys who pose real threats in their physical play. However, Christina Hoff Sommers believes that much of the writing of feminists, such as Carol Gilligan, have misinterpreted and misstated normal gender differences in young children. She questions Gilligan's claims that girls' voices are silenced in school and that schools patronize and marginalize girls while permitting boys to dominate both the classroom and the playground. Sommers argues that Gilligan wants to fundamentally restructure authority "by making changes that will free boys from the masculine stereotypes that bind them." Is it really necessary to rescue boys from the "myths of boyhood" in order to ensure that girls' voices are heard and for girls to be protected from violent victimization?

Sources: Kimberly Marselas, "City School Bans Students from Playing Tag," Online, available at http:www.hometownannapolis.com (March 26, 2001); Chuck Colson, "No Running, No Jumping: The War Against Boys in Our Schools," Online, available at http://Upstairs.weblogger.com/discuss/msgReader$7 (September 15, 2000); Thomas Sowell, "The War Against Boys," *Jewish World Review* Online, available at http://www.jewishworldreview.com/cols/sowell061500.asp (June 15, 2000); Michael Gurian, *The Good Son: Shaping the Moral Development of our Boys and Men* (New York: Penguin, 2000); Christina Hoff Sommers, *The War Against Boys: How Misguided Feminism is Harming Our Young Men* (New York: Simon & Schuster, 2000).

In a three-year study of 100 girls, ages 15 and 16, in London, Sue Lees explored some of the problems of identity for adolescent girls. Lees found that a girl's sexuality is central to the way she is judged in everyday life.

To speak of a woman's reputation is to invoke her sexual behavior, but to speak of a man's reputation is to refer to his personality, exploits, and his standing in the community. For men sexual reputation is, in the main, separated from the evaluation of moral behavior and regarded as private and incidental.[22]

While a boy's social standing is typically enhanced by his sexual exploits, a girl's standing can be destroyed by simple insinuations; therefore, she is often required to defend her sexual reputation to *both* boys and girls. The use of slang terms and insults, such as *slut* or *whore*, functions to control the activities and social reputations of girls. A girl need not actually have slept with a boy to have her reputation threatened. As one girl commented: "When there're boys talking and you've been out with more than two you're known as the crisp they're passing around . . . . The boy's alright but the girl's a bit of scum."[23]

One widely held norm is that males are expected never to use violence against women. Despite this, why are domestic violence and misogyny so prevalent?

The possibility of being labeled "bad" or a "slut" is a form of "moral censure" reflecting dominant perceptions of departure, or potential departure, from male conceptions of female sexuality. More importantly, such terms are applied to "any form of social behavior by girls that would define them as autonomous from the attachment to and domination by boys."[24] Consequently, girls are steered into acceptable or "legitimate" forms of sexual and social behavior characterized by having a steady boyfriend, being in love, and, eventually, getting married. In many ways, a girl's apparent sexual behavior is seen as a barometer, testing her capacity to learn appropriate codes of social conduct with boys.[25]

To what extent are delinquencies among girls acts of rebellion against the constraints of these restricting and oppressive sex roles imposed in adolescence? If they are not revolts, what may account for girls' involvement in delinquency? When they do violate the law, why are their delinquencies generally less serious, and how might we account for the increasing involvement of girls in delinquent behavior (recall the discussion in Chapter 2)? Finally, how adequate are male-oriented criminological theories in explaining female delinquency? In the next section we will discuss theories of female delinquency.

Theories of Female Delinquency

As noted at the beginning of this chapter, criminology as a discipline has, by and large, been the domain of males. It thus should be no surprise that explanations of female delinquency essentially reflect male perceptions of females. For the most part, these perceptions evolved from beliefs about innate or biological differences between males and females. Even when sociological explanations of delinquency became mainstream, theories were largely developed from studies of boys; girls were still viewed as "naturally" less delinquent. The relative inattention given to female delinquency was also due in part to the fact that most criminological theory has been policy driven; that is, because males made up most of the delinquent population in the courts and correctional institutions, policies designed to respond to delinquency sought out theories that dealt primarily with boys.

As more women entered the field of criminology during the past two decades, they brought with them a greater interest in female delinquency, its nature and causes, and how its origins may differ from those of male delinquency. In this section we will examine biological and psychological theories of female delinquency, consider how sociological theories may apply to girls, and look at the more recent feminist and critical theories.

Will female involvement in delinquency ever match or exceed male involvement? Which social factors might facilitate or prevent this from occurring?

Biological and Psychological Theories

Although the earliest explanations of delinquency located its causes in demons and, later, in free will, they did not make causal distinctions on the basis of the sex of the delinquent. It was not until the rise of positivistic criminology, with its early emphasis on biological and psychological causes of behavior, that female law violators were seen as uniquely "different" from male criminals (see Chapter 5).

Lombroso and Ferrero's "Atavistic Girl"   In *The Female Offender,*[26] published in 1895, Cesare Lombroso and William Ferrero applied to females the principles of Lombroso's earlier work on the male criminal. Inasmuch as criminals were viewed as "throwbacks," or atavistic by their nature, the female criminal was also seen as biologically distinct and inferior to noncriminal women. Lombroso and Ferrero believed that women were lower on the evolutionary scale than men and therefore closer to their "primitive" origins. Consequently, female criminals were not as visible as their male counterparts and showed fewer signs of degeneracy than males.

According to Lombroso and Ferrero, women are naturally more child-like, less intelligent, lacking in passion, more maternal, and weak—characteristics that make them less inclined to commit crimes. Women also share other traits with children: their moral sense is deficient and they are "revengeful, jealous, [and] inclined to vengeances of a refined cruelty."[27] However, because "women are big children; their evil tendencies are . . . more varied than men's, but generally . . . latent. When . . . awakened and excited they produce results proportionately greater."[28] Therefore, when a woman does turn to crime she is "a monster," as "her wickedness must have been enormous before it could triumph over so many obstacles."[29]

For Lombroso and Ferrero, women's criminality is a product of their biology, but this biology also keeps most women from crime. To the extent that woman's nature is antithetical to crime, and with criminality seen as a characteristic more common to men, the female criminal not only is an abnormal woman, but is biologically more like a man, only "often more ferocious."[30] It should be noted that Lombroso and Ferrero believed that most female delinquents were only "occasional criminals," as were most male delinquents. The

Aileen Wuornos is a serial killer awaiting execution on Florida's death row. She was a career criminal prostitute who robbed and murdered at least six men. Given the sheer exceptionality of serial killing among females, does Wuornos deserve extra condemnation? Should girls who engage in extreme forms of delinquency be punished differently than males?

physical features of these occasional female delinquents did not appear to reflect any atavistic degeneration and their basic moral character was essentially the same as that of their "normal sisters."[31]

Freud's "Inferior Girl"   Sigmund Freud saw female delinquency arising primarily out of the anatomical inferiority of women and their inability to deal adequately with the Electra complex, which emerges during the Oedipal stage of development (between age 3 and 6).[32] Freud believed that when girls realize they have no penis, they sense that they are being punished because boys have something important they have been denied. Consequently, they develop *penis envy*, which results in an inferiority complex. Envy, and a desire for revenge, lead the girl to "act out" as she attempts to compensate for her inferiority. In addition, Freud believed that promiscuous sexual behavior by girls, and eventually prostitution, grow out of the Oedipal stage of development and repression of early sexual love for the parent of the opposite sex.

Thomas's "Unadjusted Girl"   In *The Unadjusted Girl*, published in 1923, W. I. Thomas postulated that males and females are biologically different.[33] Although both males and females are motivated by natural biological instincts leading to "wish fulfillment," how they approach the fulfillment of the wishes differs. Thomas identified four distinct categories of wishes:

1. the desire for new experience;
2. the desire for security;
3. the desire for response; and
4. the desire for recognition.

Thomas believed that women by nature have stronger desires for response and love than men and that they are capable of more varied types of love as demonstrated by maternal love, a characteristic atypical of males. This intense need to give and receive love often leads girls into delinquency, especially sexual delinquency, as they use sex as a means to fulfill other wishes.

However, Thomas did not believe girls were inherently delinquent. Rather, their behaviors are the result of choices circumscribed by social rules and moral codes designed to guide people's actions as they attempt to fulfill their wishes. Girls, more than boys, are limited by their gender roles in society and consequently are more likely to become demoralized and frustrated as they perceive deprivations.[34]

The origins of female delinquency, according to Thomas, are found in the girl's impulsive desire to obtain "amusement, adventure, pretty clothes, favorable notice, distinction and freedom in the larger world. . . . Their sex is used as a condition of the realization of other wishes. It is their capital."[35] Unfortunately, such impulsive behavior is also likely to drive girls into the arms of boys who will take advantage of them, frequently leading to pregnancy, prostitution, and eventual ruin.

Pollak's "Deceitful Girl"   In *The Criminality of Women*, published in 1950, Otto Pollak argued that women are actually as criminal as men but their criminality is hidden or "masked."[36] The masking of their crimes and delinquencies is a result of "natural" physiological differences in the sexes, as well as the tendency of males to overlook or excuse offenses by women.

Pollak believed that the physiological nature of women makes them more deceitful than men. With less physical strength than men, women must resort to indirect or deceitful means to carry out crimes or to vent their aggression; women also are more likely to be "instigators" and men "perpetrators" of crime.[37] Pollak further argued that social norms force women to conceal their menstruation each month and to misrepresent or conceal information regarding sex from their children, at least for some time. According to Pollak, social norms "thus make concealment . . . in the eyes of women socially required and commendable . . . , condition[ing] them to a different attitude toward veracity than men."[38]

In Pollak's view, lower rates of crime and delinquency among females reflect men's deference and protective attitude toward women, whereby female offenses are generally overlooked or excused by males (a premise known as the **chivalry hypothesis**). Male victims of female delinquencies, police officers, prosecutors, judges, and juries, Pollak suggested, are hesitant to report, arrest, prosecute, or convict women. Thus, the actual rate of female delinquencies is much higher than official statistics reported.

Recent Biological and Developmental Explanations   The idea that girls' behavior is largely controlled by their biology, physiology, or sexuality continued to appear in studies for some time, although today it is rare to find expressions of the "natural" inferiority of girls in criminological literature. Instead, many of the more recent studies from this perspective suggest that girls' biological nature interacts with social forces, usually those found in the family.

Gisela Konopka's *The Adolescent Girl in Conflict*,[39] published in 1966, was strongly influenced by the work of Freud. Like Freud, Konopka believed that much female delinquency is driven by girls' sexuality. The origins of a girl's problem behavior are found in negative experiences in the family. As a result of the absence of warmth and love in the home, the girl develops emotional instability, uncertainty, loneliness, and low self-esteem. Her loneliness leads her to seek acceptance and love from others in a group whose members can lose themselves anonymously or to engage in "a highly romanticized love relationship" with a boy.[40] Unfortunately, in many boy-girl relationships, the girl is willing to take a great deal of abuse and exploitation (especially sexual exploitation) if she is required to "prove" her love in order to keep the boy's attention.[41] But as the relationship proves to be superficial and short term and the girl experiences additional disapproval from her family, her self-esteem slides further, resulting in increased loneliness and further sexual delinquencies.

In *Delinquency in Girls*,[42] published in 1968, John Cowie and his associates describe female delinquency as being dominated by sexual misbehaviors.

Romantic, primary relationships are an important and essential part of healthy human development. How might these relationships contribute to delinquency? Are females or males more susceptible to delinquent influences from their partner? Why?

They argue that female delinquents are unhappy and that "their unhappiness is commonly related to disturbed emotional relationships with the parents."[43] Delinquent girls tend to come from families characterized by low moral standards, poor discipline, conflict, and disturbed family relations. In addition, delinquent girls are more likely than delinquent boys to have pathological psychiatric problems, to have impaired physical health, and "to be oversized, lumpish, uncouth, and graceless with a raised incidence of minor physical defects."[44] The fact that girls are less likely than boys to be delinquent is accounted for, in part, by girls being more timid and lacking in enterprise.

The idea that girls are led to sexual delinquencies because of dysfunctional families and unsatisfactory peer relations is also presented in Clyde Vedder and Dora Somerville's *The Delinquent Girl*.[45] Feeling unloved and disapproved of by family and peers, girls are likely to engage in sexual delinquency to gain acceptance and love. Official female delinquency, according to Vedder and Somerville, is dominated by five offense categories: running away, incorrigibility, sexual offenses, probation violation, and truancy (listed in order of decreasing frequency). They suggest that running away and incorrigibility are typically the less "serious" charges filed when such behavior is actually nearly always linked to sexual misbehaviors. To "protect" the girl, officials are more likely to charge her with the more innocuous offense, thus masking the true extent of sexual delinquency among girls.[46]

The most recent attempts to link biological and physiological factors to female delinquency have stressed the effects of hormonal differences between girls and boys. Normally, males produce six times as much testosterone and twice as much androgen as females. Females, on the other hand, produce estrogen in excess of males. These hormonal differences appear to be associated with many of the basic masculine and feminine characteristics of males and females and may have some effect on gender-role behavior. A number of researchers have reported higher levels of testosterone among violent female offenders than among those considered nonviolent.[47] While hormonal changes in females linked to the premenstrual phase of the menstrual cycle (known as *premenstrual syndrome* or PMS) may increase irritability, no connection has been found between irritable modes and aggressive behavior and many of the changes in mood may actually be due to other factors, such as stressful external events.[48]

Sociological Theories

Biological and developmental theories of female delinquency continued to dominate the literature long after theories of male delinquency had shifted to the role of social forces. Their popularity reflected the lingering belief, even among many sociologists, that biological differences between females and males were deterministic of their social behaviors as well. In this section we examine the ideas of several theorists whose work influenced the development of major bodies of criminological theory.

Sociological theories of delinquency from the 1920s through the 1960s stressed male patterns of behavior almost exclusively. Misbehavior by girls was treated as extraneous, marginal, and irrelevant. In his 1927 study of gangs, for example, Frederic Thrasher devoted only slightly more than one page to the five or six female gangs he found. He attributed the relative absence of girl gangs to the fact that the traditions and customs underpinning socially approved patterns of girls' behaviors are contrary to the activities of gangs. The few girls who did become involved in gangs were accounted for in stereotypic and simplistic terms: "The girl *takes the role of a boy* and is accepted on equal terms with the others. Such a girl is probably a tomboy in the neighborhood."[49]

Clifford Shaw and Henry McKay's studies of the impact of social disorganization on delinquency included analyses of more than 60,000 male delinquents in Chicago.[50] While Shaw and McKay noted the persistence of high delinquency rates in particular zones of the city and argued that these rates were linked to characteristics of the community rather than to the groups of people living in them, they made only brief reference to female delinquency. Delinquency was implicitly defined as a part of the male domain. Whether female delinquency was also a product of social disorganization was not explored.

Robert Merton's strain theory also fails to address the issue of female crime and delinquency.[51] No attempt was made by Merton or his followers to apply his typology of adaptations to women, even though interesting but contradictory implications for females could have been derived from his work. For example, Ruth Morris suggests that the goals of women are fundamentally *relational* (for example, marriage, family, friends, love), in contrast to the material goals typically pursued by men. She argues that because most women have lower material aspirations and their goals are more accessible, they do not experience the same stressful conditions as men and therefore are less likely to turn to delinquency.[52] On the other hand, Allison Morris argues that women do have aspirations similar to men (for example, jobs, education, and money) but are denied the same opportunities to achieve them. If this is so, it would follow that female rates of crime and delinquency should actually be higher than the rates for men.[53]

Like Shaw and McKay and Merton, Walter Miller appears to have been unconcerned with explaining female delinquency in his classic 1958 article on lower-class culture and gang delinquency, although he did give them some attention in an article on "The Molls" written some 15 years later.[54] His analysis of the "focal concerns" of the lower class is limited to male adaptations and assumes that such aspirations are exclusive to the lower class. That is, these definitions of "masculinity" are exclusive to the lower class rather than common to all social classes. Eileen Leonard suggests that Miller's focal concerns are not particularly relevant to females (even in the lower class): "Given their different location in society, they [girls] are unlikely to be as concerned as males about trouble, toughness, smartness, excitement, fate, and autonomy."[55] Leonard further suggests that if lower-class males and females did have the same focal concerns and if these concerns alone explained the development of delinquent subcultures, their delinquency rates would be similar.

Albert Cohen explicitly defined the problem of delinquency and the development of the delinquent subculture as a male phenomenon. Still, he devoted 11 pages to a discussion of why his work *did not* apply to girls.[56] According to Cohen, boys and girls have different adjustment problems requiring different solutions. The delinquent subculture develops largely as a response to the problems faced by boys and is not an appropriate response for dealing with the problems of girls arising from the female role. Boys, Cohen says, are most interested in their own achievements compared with those of other boys; girls are more interested in their relationships with boys. According to Cohen, "It is within the area of these relationships . . . that a girl finds her fulfillments *as a girl*. It is no accident that 'boys collect stamps, girls collect boys.'"[57] Cohen does recognize the existence of female delinquency, but he defines it primarily as sexual delinquency. According to Cohen, "sex delinquency is one kind of meaningful response to the most characteristic . . . problem of the female role: the establishment of satisfactory relationships with the opposite sex."[58] In a feminist critique of Cohen's work, Ngaire Naffine states:

> The message from Cohen is manifest. Men are the rational doers and achievers. They represent all that is instrumental and productive in American culture. Women's world is on the margins. Women exist to be the companions of men and that is their entire lot. . . . While men proceed with their Olympian task of running all aspects of the nation, women perform their role of helpmate.[59]

Richard Cloward and Lloyd Ohlin's work on delinquency and opportunity focused exclusively on male delinquency produced by the frustrations associated with the unequal distribution of both legitimate and illegitimate opportunities.[60] Females are important only as they contribute to the difficulties boys have in developing a clear masculine image.[61] Boys, in their attempts to establish themselves as males in female-dominated homes and schools, often experience strain:

> Engulfed by a feminine world and uncertain of their own identification, they tend to "protest against femininity. This protest may take the form of robust and aggressive behavior, and even of malicious, irresponsible, and destructive acts.[62]

Because girls are seen as having no difficulty in adapting to their own prescribed female roles within this feminine world, they do not experience this strain. The fact that girls also experience similar unequal distributions in opportunities and that some girls *do* become delinquent was apparently of no interest to Cloward and Ohlin.

Edwin Sutherland offered his theory of differential association in 1939 as a general theory of crime that explains all types of law-violating behaviors.[63] However, he made no reference to females or to how differential association may account for their lower rates of delinquency. This is particularly significant given the widespread influence of Sutherland and his position as the so-called father of American criminology. The implication in his work is that, compared with boys, girls encounter more anticriminal patterns and are exposed to fewer criminal associations and definitions favorable to violation of law. Some years later, Sutherland noted that the differences in rates of male and female delinquency are explained by differential associations: "Parents and other intimate associates define one kind of propriety for girls and another for boys, and exercise one kind of supervision over girls and another over boys."[64] Sutherland presumably believed that girls who do become delinquent have less parental supervision and thus develop the same kind of delinquent associations as those developed by delinquent boys.

While Sutherland did not specifically test the impact of differential associations on gender differences in delinquency, other criminologists have. Numerous studies have looked at how girls' association with delinquent friends affects their likelihood of engaging in delinquency.[65] For example, Kristan Erickson and her colleagues conducted a longitudinal analysis of gender differences among students from six high schools in California and three high schools in Wisconsin. They found a significantly greater positive effect of having delinquent friends on subsequent delinquency for males than for females.[66] Karen Heimer and Stacy De Coster, using data from the National Youth Survey, found that girls "learn fewer violent definitions than boys, on average, although the impact of violent definitions on violence is equal across gender."[67] Finally, Xiaoru Liu and Howard Kaplan's longitudinal analysis of a sample of 2,753 junior and senior high school students in Houston, Texas, found that, while females and males engaged in similar levels of minor delinquencies, exposure to delinquent peers was more positively associated with delinquency for males than for females.[68]

Travis Hirschi's notion of the *social bond*, reflecting a social control perspective, provides a framework for explaining differences in rates of female and male delinquency, although Hirschi himself never explored this possibility.[69] Hirschi's explanation of delinquency was developed from his analysis of a sample of about 4,000 boys; girls were intentionally excluded from the analysis. Coramae Mann has commented on this exclusion:

> Travis Hirschi stratified his samples of race, sex, school, and grade. He included 1,076 black girls and 846 nonblack girls; but in the analysis of his data Hirschi admits "the girls disappear," and he adds, "Since girls have been neglected for too long by students of delinquency, the exclusion of them is difficult to justify. I hope I return to them soon." He didn't.[70]

Because social control theory appears to be one of the most powerful explanations of juvenile delinquency generally (see Chapter 7), it is understandable that criminologists would soon test its application for explaining female delinquency. For example, Rachelle Canter found that girls had stronger bonds to their parents than did boys, although this attachment had a greater inhibitory effect on delinquency for boys.[71] Other studies have observed that boys are more likely than girls to be negatively influenced by their attachments to delinquent friends and are subsequently more likely than girls to engage in delinquency and substance abuse.[72] Although Bobbi Jo Anderson and her colleagues found no differences in boys' and girls' attachment to their parents, gender differences in attachment to peers and school appeared to reduce the severity of delinquency among girls.[73]

In an extension of social control theory, Michael Gottfredson's and Travis Hirschi's *A General Theory of Crime* posits that delinquency is more likely to occur among youth: who lack self-control and this is equally true for girls and boys.[74] However, Gottfredson and Hirschi argue, as noted earlier in this chapter, that there are clear gender differences in delinquency and that these differences "appear to be invariant over time and space."[75] The explanation for this difference is found in the substantial gender differences in self-control resulting from early childhood socialization. Girls are socialized to be less impulsive and less risk-taking than boys and more sensitive and verbal (rather than physical), more resistant to temptations, and more obedient. It is this difference in socialization, rather than differences in levels of attachment or parental supervision (as suggested in social bond theory), that accounts for gender differences in frequency and seriousness of delinquency.[76] Recent tests of the general theory provide support for the argument that differences in *self-control* largely account for the gender differences in delinquency: boys exhibit lower self-control than do girls and this has direct effects on delinquent behavior.[77]

Writing from the labeling perspective, Edwin Schur argues that women are negatively labeled with great regularity as "aggressive," "bitchy," "hysterical," "fat," "homely," and "promiscuous." According to Schur,

Edwin Schur argues that females are regularly labeled as "aggressive," "bitchy," "hysterical," or "promiscuous." With such an assortment of negative labels, shouldn't women be more involved in delinquency? Is the female ability to nullify negative labels a testament to women or another piece of evidence contradicting labeling theory?

BOX 9–3   FACE OF DELINQUENCY
Sexual Labeling and Control of Girls

Although adolescent girls and boys frequently engage in harmless bantering, kidding, and joking with each other, all too often the informal verbal interactions take on an insidious, demeaning, and manipulative flavor designed to facilitate boys' control of girls. Mark Fleisher suggests that the use of insulting terms in the verbal dueling of girls and boys in the Freemont area in Kansas City helps to establish social hierarchies, allows for the release of tensions without violence, and defines group membership and friendships. "Boys call girls by the standard list of insulting terms, including *bitch, rotten bitch, stank bitch, pussy, cunt,* and *slut,* among others. Girls retaliate with a vengeance, shouting, 'bastard,' 'prick,' 'pussy,' 'bitch,' 'little dick,' . . . among others. Girls call one another by the standard list of insults." The seeming equality of insults, however, masks the actual inequalities in the relationships. According to Fleisher:

> Girls think about relationships as moral contracts; boys don't. Beyond the street rhetoric of the gang, girls' implicit construction of rela-

tionships, especially with boys, includes fairness, reciprocity, and equality. . . . In what they perceive to be long-term relationships, girls feel an inherent responsibility toward the boys with whom they are involved, but the boys feel neither reciprocity nor fairness nor equality.

Elijah Anderson's study of the informal street code that guides interactions between boys and girls in the inner city of Philadelphia reflects a similar pattern of control in relationships. While many girls "offer sex as a gift" in their attempt to gain a boy's attention, boys define the exchange as only a means to enhance their self-esteem. According to Anderson, "The girls have a dream, the boys a desire. The girls dream of being carried off by a Prince Charming who will love them . . . . The boys often desire either sex without commitment or babies without responsibility for them." The boys want to "score" with as many girls as possible—the more girls he has sex with, the higher his esteem in the eyes of his male peers. "But the young man not only must 'get some'; he also

Judgments such as these, and the social reactions that accompany them, represent a very potent kind of deviance-defining. They may not put the presumed "offender" in jail, but they do typically damage her reputation, induce shame, and lower her "life chances."[78]

Through the process of labeling, an informal form of social control over females is maintained. Earlier in this chapter we discussed how the development of girls' identities worked to keep women in their "place" and how girls were devalued through use of such terms as *slut* or *whore.* See Box 9–3 for a discussion of sexual labeling and control of girls. According to Schur, "When women are effectively stigmatized, that reinforces their overall must prove he is getting it. This leads him to talk about girls and sex with any other young man who will listen." Labels may also be used to control boys. If his peers suspect him of becoming too committed to a girl, they are likely to sanction him with "demeaning labels such as 'pussy,' 'pussy-whipped,' or 'house-husband.'"

Many of the interviews Mark Totten conducted with 90 Canadian boys ages 13 to 17 in Ottawa, Ontario, reflected the boys' willingness to use demeaning labels to control girls. Steve, a 15-year-old, responded to Totten's question "Do you like girls?"

> No, not really . . . I think most of them are stupid bitches. I'll call them bitch, slut, whore all the time. They're always trying to show me up—make me look stupid, like a goof. . . . It's all about knowing your place in society. Some girls do, but most girls don't know what they're supposed to do. . . . We all think that girls should do what we want them to. And it pisses us off when they don't. So I've seen some of them when they've hit girls. And all the time we are just joking around, calling them names—slut, cunt, whore, bitch, fat cow— we all do it.

When boys label girls in this manner as part of their oppression and control of girls, it should not be surprising that boys also express an attitude of negative fatalism with regard to future generations of girls. Philippe Bourgois spent five years studying the neighborhood culture of the crack trade in East Harlem. Getting girls pregnant seemingly produced some ambivalence. Many boys took pride in noting how many girls they had impregnated. Luis, for example, bragged about getting a number of girls pregnant in just a nine-month period, but then referred to them as "holes out there." The ambivalence came from thinking about the possibility of the pregnancy producing a daughter. According to one youth, "That's why I wouldn't never want to have a daughter, if I was to get my girl pregnant. I couldn't handle the fact of having a baby, and then I have to see her being a ho'." And an 11-year-old commented about his mother's pregnancy: "He told us he hoped his mother would give birth to a boy 'because girls are too easy to rape.'"

Sources: Elijah Anderson, *Code of the Street: Decency, Violence, and the Moral Life of the Inner City* (New York: W.W. Norton, 1999); Philippe Bourgois, *In Search of Respect: Selling Crack in El Barrio* (New York: Cambridge University Press, 1995); Mark Fleisher, *Dead End Kids: Gang Girls and the Boys They Know* (Madison, WI: University of Wisconsin Press, 1998); Mark Totten, *Guys, Gangs, & Girlfriend Abuse* (Peterborough, Ontario: Broadview Press, 2000).

subordination and makes it more difficult for them to achieve desired goals."[79] Furthermore, the differential enforcement of status offenses for girls can be seen as punishment for "violating or threatening to violate gender-related norms."[80]

Of course, it is also possible that labeling theory may help account for gender differences in official rates of delinquency. Joanne Belknap suggests that

> the possibility that girls may be less likely than boys to be labeled or viewed as delinquent might also help explain their lower rates. Or perhaps women-girls are labeled more harshly for some crimes, while men-boys are discriminated against for others.[81]

Marxist-Feminist Theories

Marxist-feminist theories combine the notions of patriarchal male dominance in the home and interpersonal relationships with male control of the means of production. In such an environment, the criminal justice system "defines as crimes those actions that threaten this capitalist-patriarchal system."[82] For example, James Messerschmidt argues that in societies characterized by patriarchal capitalism, male owners or managers of capital control workers and men control women. Thus, under patriarchal capitalism, women experience *double marginality:* Women are subordinate to both capitalists and men.[83]

Messerschmidt suggests that girls are less likely to be involved in serious delinquencies for three reasons: (1) Most crimes are "masculine" in nature; physical strength, aggressiveness, and external proofs of achievement are facets of the male personality. (2) Because women are subordinate and less powerful, they have fewer opportunities to engage in serious crimes. And (3) males control even illegitimate opportunities, and females are relegated to subordinate roles even in criminal activities.[84] When women do engage in crime, their criminal activity tends to be a response to their subordinate and powerless position in patriarchal capitalist society. Such activity may take the form of *privatized resistance* (alcoholism, drug abuse, or suicide) or of *accommodation* (generally less serious economic crimes including shoplifting, embezzlement, and prostitution).[85]

Ronald Akers has raised important questions about Messerschmidt's general reliance on the patriarchal social structure as an explanation of all types of crimes committed by both females and males. Akers believes that, for the theory to truly be testable, it would be necessary to be able to measure the specific nature and impact of patriarchy in different parts of society, as well as to examine the relationship of gender inequalities and male and female crime patterns within a cross-cultural perspective.[86] One such test, conducted by Darrell Steffensmeier, Emilie Allan, and Cathy Streifel, involved the examination of arrest data for homicide and major and minor property crimes in a wide range of societies.[87] Steffensmeier and his colleagues found that neither "gender inequality" nor "female economic marginality" was related to female-male arrest ratios in different societies. They noted, instead, that arrest ratios were more significantly related to the degree to which women had access to consumer goods and to the general formalization of social control within the societies. Akers concludes that these findings provide very little support for Messerschmidt's claim that patriarchal inequalities produce the gender differences in crime patterns.[88]

Power-control theory, developed by John Hagan and his associates, argues that girls engage in less delinquency because their behavior is more closely monitored and controlled by parents (especially the mother) in patriarchal families.[89] In *patriarchal families* the father works outside the home and has control over others, while the mother stays at home and raises the children. Because the father has a higher control position than the mother, he maintains control over both the wife and the children in the home. *Egalitarian families*, on the other hand, are characterized by a lack of gender differences

Female behavior, including delinquent behavior, has historically been defined by stereotypical conceptions of femininity. Does this photo invoke any delinquent imagery? If so, why?

in the consumption and production spheres. Both parents work and have control positions outside the home, and both share child rearing responsibilities within the home. Parental control is redistributed so that the control over daughters is more like that over sons, and daughters, like sons, are prepared to enter the production sphere and given greater opportunities for risk taking. This differential treatment leads boys in such families, more so than girls, to engage in greater risk taking, and, consequently, delinquency.

However, Meda Chesney-Lind and Randall Shelden suggest that this is "essentially a not-too-subtle variation of the **liberation hypothesis**, that women's liberation directly led to increases in female criminality. Now, mother's liberation or employment causes daughter's crime."[90] They argue there is no evidence to support Hagan's claim that as women's participation in the labor force increases, so too will female delinquency. It should be noted, however, that Roy Austin's analysis of labor force participation, divorce rates, and female arrests for minor, major, and occupational offenses does lend support to the claim that female liberation is associated with an increase in female criminality.[91]

Numerous tests of power-control theory have been conducted over the past two decades, with rather inconsistent findings. For example, Simon Singer and Murray Levine analyzed data from 705 high school youth and 560 parents and found that, consistent with power-control theory, parents exerted less control over boys than girls and mothers tended to exert greater control over girls. However, they also found that boys were more delinquent than girls in egalitarian households, which is contrary to the theory's predictions.[92] Merry Morash and Chesney-Lind, found, in their analysis of the 1981 National Survey of Children, that sex differences in delinquency were present regardless of patriarchal or egalitarian family structures.[93] While Hagan and his associates assumed that single-parent families were sufficiently similar to his classification of egalitarian families, other researchers questioned the assumption. Michael Leiber and Mary Ellen Wacker examined data from two samples of juveniles living in single-mother households in Washington and Iowa. While associations with delinquent peers were related to delinquency, they found no support for power-control theory.[94] Finally, Christopher Uggen examined the relationship between parents' perceptions of their workplace power and control and the delinquencies of their children. He found that "Parental power and control in the workplace increases the rate of arrest among males and decreases it among females. Maternal authority position, in contrast, dramatically raises the risk of arrest among females and reduces this risk among males."[95]

Daniel Mears and his colleagues suggest that sex differences in delinquency are more appropriately explained by how girls and boys are differentially affected by the same criminogenic factors due to differences in their moral development. They argue that "the primary socialization of women instills moral values that strongly discourage behavior that hurts or harms others."[96] Thus, moral evaluations by females counteract criminogenic conditions, such as dysfunctional family organization, poverty, and exposure to delinquent friends. Not only are boys more likely than girls to have delinquent friends, it appears that boys also are more likely than girls to be strongly affected by their delinquent peers. According to Mears and his associates, this "reflects the greater effect of moral evaluations in counteracting peer influence among females."[97]

While many feminist criminologists have called for the development of a "feminist" theory of female delinquency, no clearly articulated theory has emerged. The work of Chesney-Lind and Morash may come closest.[98] Girls' lower involvement in delinquency is explained by the emphasis placed on their developing nurturing relationships. Morash and Chesney-Lind argue that children, female or male, who identify with a nurturing parent who cares for others are likely to develop identities built on an ethic of care and concern for others rather than identities conducive to harming others. They also note that men can take on nurturing roles and—since sons can identify just as easily with a nurturing father as with a nurturing mother—can thus promote prosocial behavior in boys.[99]

Feminists acknowledge that girls do become delinquent. Chesney-Lind says that female delinquency is accounted for by the gender and sexual scripts in patriarchal families that lead girls, more than boys, to be victims of family-related sexual abuse. In patriarchal societies, male-female relationships are unequal, and young women are defined as sexual objects and seen

In May 2001, the U.S. Supreme Court ruled that hospitals cannot join forces with police to drug-test pregnant women for narcotics use without their permission. A sizable research literature has found that perinatal drug use has serious negative consequences for children, including delinquency. Is this a blatant example that U.S. adults could care less about the welfare of children?

as sexually attractive by older men. Girls become more vulnerable to both physical and sexual abuse because of norms that give males control over females and keep them at home where victimizers have greater access to them. Furthermore, victimizers, usually males, can call upon official agencies of control to keep girls at home. The juvenile court has historically been willing to uncritically support parental control and authority over daughters. Girls who react to abuse by running away from home are often returned to their parents by juvenile authorities. If girls persist in running away, the court may then incarcerate them. Girls who successfully run away often find themselves unable to enroll in school or to obtain reasonable jobs and may then be forced into the streets, where their survival may depend on petty crimes such as theft, panhandling, or prostitution.[100]

Differential Oppression Theory

Differential oppression theory (see Chapter 8) also provides a framework for understanding why girls become delinquent as well as why they are less inclined to delinquency than males. Differential oppression theory argues that adults oppress children as they attempt to impose and maintain adult conceptions of social order. Children are perceived as objects, devalued and defined as inferior to adults, and consequently experience a sense of powerlessness and marginality. Adults impose their social order on children frequently through oppressive means. But oppression falls on a continuum, ranging from simple demands for obedience to rules designed for the convenience of adults to the physical or sexual abuse of children. Adults' perceptions of children as inferior, subordinate, and troublemakers allow adults to rationalize their oppressive acts. Generally, the more oppressed the child is, the more likely she or he will become delinquent.

Girls in patriarchal societies, however, are **doubly oppressed:** they are oppressed as children *and* as females (recall that earlier Messerschmidt argued that females experience *double marginality*: their being oppressed by both patriarchs and capitalists). Adult conceptions of the *girl as child* (inferior, subordinate, troublemaker) lead to oppressive acts by adults that alienate the girl and lead her into adaptive reactions as she attempts to become a "subject" instead of an "object." These adaptive reactions are the same general modes of reaction to oppression that all children may express and include:

1. passive acceptance of one's status;
2. manipulation of peers to gain power;
3. exercise of illegitimate coercive power; and
4. retaliation.

Girls experiencing adult oppression may passively accept their inferior status as children and conform while learning to resent those who exercise power over them. They may react by manipulating peers, which may result in sanctions by adults. They may instead exercise illegitimate coercive power, which may involve drugs or alcohol. They may also try to "make things happen" through participation in juvenile gangs, prostitution, or by acts of common

Proportionately low female involvement in delinquency seriously challenges most criminological theories. Do female offenders require separate theorization? Are feminist scholars the only ones who can adequately theorize about female delinquency? Why might scholars be unwilling to develop "separate but equal" explanations for delinquency based on sex?

Domestic violence is pervasive in the United States. Thousands, perhaps millions, of females suffer frequent abuses, harassment, and indignities from their husbands and male partners. Do you agree that long-term abuse should be used as a legal defense for females charged with domestic homicide?

crime such as shoplifting. Or, they may retaliate by striking back at the people or institutions they blame for their oppression (e.g., assaults against parents or siblings as representatives of their parents, assaults against boyfriends, or school vandalism or attacks on teachers). Retaliation may also take the form of suicide attempts.

Adult conceptions in patriarchal societies of the *girl as female* (relational, nurturing, and passive) lead to oppression reinforcing her traditional gender role and, subsequently, to the girl's identity as "object." Treated as an "object," a girl may adapt by developing an identity through relationships with boys; she does not have to "prove" her own worth as long as she is "related" to a proven person. Consequently, her delinquencies may be indirect and relational. Being defined as a female "object" may also reinforce the identity of the girl as "sexual object." In this case, adaptations may take the form of sexual delinquencies and prostitution.

But oppression of girls as females also carries with it a reinforcement of more domestic, passive, relational, and nurturing roles that often exclude them from the outside world of male street–peer groups. Girls are not only more closely monitored and kept closer to home, they are encouraged to identify with their mothers and to concentrate on building and maintaining relations. In addition, girls learn to anticipate economic dependence and the need to develop intimate interpersonal ties through which a sense of value and self-esteem may be gained. At the same time, they are discouraged from pursuing independent acts and risk-taking activities. As girls develop identities that reinforce positive, prosocial, and nurturing relations with others stressing caring and fairness, they are less likely to engage in behaviors harmful to others.

Differential oppression theory, as applied to female delinquency, builds on earlier work stressing differences in socialization patterns of girls and boys and views the role of socialization of adolescent girls within the context of oppression. While male adolescents experience the oppression of being a child, female adolescents experience the double oppression of being a female child. The socialization of girls not only leads to their being less likely to engage in delinquency in general, but also to their likelihood of engaging in particular forms of delinquency.

Juvenile Justice Policy Applications

In the opening of this chapter, we noted that criminological theorizing about delinquency has long focused on male, rather than female, delinquency. The same criminological gaze through male eyes has led to a marginalizing or minimizing of policies and programs aimed at preventing or treating female delinquency. Recognizing this, Meda Chesney-Lind argues that "girls involved in the juvenile justice system are particularly invisible in terms of programming."[101] According to Chesney-Lind, most programs offered for females are based on stereotypes of "girls' issues," such as teen pregnancy, sexual abuse, or gang violence, and thus tend to focus on intervention in the lives of girls already in trouble rather than on prevention for girls who are at risk of involvement in delinquency.

There are approaches that Chesney-Lind believes may be effective, including policies and programs designed to protect girls from physical and sexual violence, to reduce the risk of HIV-AIDS and pregnancy, to deal with unemployment and job training, to locate safe and affordable housing, to assist in managing family problems and stress, and to develop a sense of empowerment. Finally, Chesney-Lind suggests that programs for at-risk girls "need to create separate time and space for girls, separate from boys, so that issues related to sexism will not be overshadowed by boys' more disruptive behavior."[102]

Conclusions

The study of delinquency over the past century has focused almost exclusively on male behavior. The marginal treatment of females in the literature reflects the realities of a patriarchal society in which males control the sexuality and labor of women. Girls grow up in a society in which they are presumed to be "inferior" to boys and are socialized into sexually stereotypic gender roles beginning at birth.

Early explanations of female delinquency stressed the biological and developmental differences between the constitutional makeup of females and that of males: Female delinquents were seen as atavistic, inferior, unadjusted, and inherently deceitful. More recent biological and developmental theories have explored girls' emotional problems and differences in hormonal levels as factors leading to delinquency.

Early sociological theories shifted attention from individual characteristics or flaws to the role of social forces in delinquency. Although they tended to ignore the existence of female delinquency or saw it as only marginal and irrelevant in explaining the real problems of delinquency, more recent tests of many of the theories appear to provide partial explanations for gender differences in patterns of delinquency. Marxist and feminist theories, stressing the effects of patriarchy and capitalism in society on females, have focused attention on the role of control and supervision of girls in limiting their activities, including delinquency.

Finally, differential oppression theory emphasizes the impact of the double oppression girls face: oppression as children and oppression as females. These modes of oppression account for both the lower rates of female delinquency as well as the particular adaptive reactions of girls to oppression, which often include delinquency.

Key Terms

chivalry hypothesis: *The belief that lower rates of crime and delinquency among females reflect men's deference and protective attitude toward women whereby female offenses are generally overlooked or excused by males.*

doubly oppressed: *The notion that adolescent girls are oppressed both as children and as females.*

gender-role identities: *Individual identities based on sexual stereotypes.*

liberation hypothesis: *The belief that changes brought about by the women's movement triggered a wave of female crime.*

patriarchy: *A social system that enforces masculine control of the sexuality and labor power of women.*

power-control theory: *A theory that emphasizes the consequences of the power relations of husbands and wives in the workplace on the lives of children.*

Getting Connected

Findings and reports from the Florida Delinquent Girls Reseach Project are available online at:

http://www.djj.state.fl.us/RnD/FDGRP/

1. What is the mission of this research project?
2. What are "deep end" female juvenile offenders? Why are they the focus of this research?
3. In what way does this kind of research increase our knowledge of female delinquency?

Numerous research reports and government publications about female delinquency and girls in the juvenile justice system can be obtained through the following sites:

http://www.ncjrs.org

1. Find the names of three of the NCJRS's juvenile justice publications which specifically target females. How does "female delinquency" seem to be defined in these publications?
2. What are the implications of "adolescent motherhood" for the juvenile justice system?
3. Look through the list of publications related to juvenile substance abuse. To what extent are female juveniles addressed as a group with special needs?

http://www.ncjrs/ojjdp

1. Link to "Highlights," then to "New Publications." Read "Protecting Children in Cyberspace: The ICAC Task Force Program." Is gender discussed specifically in this article?
2. The site lists and describes upcoming OJJDP conferences. Which ones address female delinquency?
3. What is the OJJDP's JUMP program? Is there a JUMP program or similar activity in your hometown? Could girls benefit from being part of a JUMP program?

http://www.ojp.usdoj.gov/bjs

1. Find the site's information on victims of violent crime, by gender. What is the relationship of gender and this kind of victimization?
2. Link to the OJJDP from this site and then to the site of the Child Welfare League of America. How does this organization address female delinquency?
3. Check the latest BJS press releases. To what extent is female delinquency a focus of attention?

The Girls Inc. movement began during the Industrial Revolution in New England as a response to the needs of a new class of young working girls and women. You can visit their website at:

http://www.girlsinc.org/

1. What is the Girls' Bill of Rights? How does it address issues of gender stereotyping discussed in the textbook?

2. What kinds of legislation does this organization advocate?

3. What is a "strong" girl? a "smart" girl? a "bold" girl? Would developing these qualities help insulate girls from juvenile delinquency?

Endnotes

1. Allison Morris, *Women, Crime and Criminal Justice* (Oxford: Basil Blackwell, 1987), p. 1.
2. Joanne Belknap, *The Invisible Woman: Gender, Crime, and Justice,* 2nd ed. (Belmont, CA: Wadsworth, 2001), p. 13.
3. Belknap, note 2, p. 14.
4. Belknap, note 2, p. 6.
5. Charlotte Brontë, *Jane Eyre,* edited by Richard Dunn (New York: Norton, 1971), p. 96.
6. Jean Stafford, *The Mountain Lion* (New York: Harcourt, Brace & World, 1947), p. 30.
7. Jeffrey Rubin, Frank Provenzano, and Zella Luria, "The Eye of the Beholder: Parents' Views of Sex of Newborns," *American Journal of Orthopsychiatry* 44:512–519 (1974).
8. Marie Richmond-Abbot, *Masculine & Feminine: Gender Roles over the Life Cycle*, 2nd ed. (New York: McGraw-Hill Publishing Co., 1992), p. 69.
9. Beverly Fagot, "The Child's Expectations of Differences in Adult Male and Female Interactions," *Sex Roles* 11:593–600 (1984); Bernice Lott, *Women's Lives: Themes and Variations in Gender Learning* (Pacific Grove, CA: Brooks-Cole Publishing Co., 1987).
10. Doreen Kimura, "Sex Differences in the Brain," *Scientific American Presents*, Special Issue: "Men: The Scientific Truth About Their Work, Play, Health, and Passions" 10:26–31, Summer Quarterly (1999).
11. Myra and David Sadker, *Failing at Fairness: How America's Schools Cheat Girls* (New York: Scribners, 1994).
12. Peggy Orenstein, *SchoolGirls: Young Women, Self-Esteem, and the Confidence Gap* (New York: Doubleday, 1994).
13. Jeanne Block, *Sex Role Identity and Ego Development* (San Francisco: Jossey-Bass, 1984); Pamela Richards and Charles Tittle, "Gender and Perceived Chances of Arrest," *Social Forces* 51:1182–1199 (1981).
14. Merry Morash, "Gender, Peer Group Experiences, and Seriousness of Delinquency," *Journal of Research on Crime and Delinquency* 23:43–67 (1986).
15. Robert Bursik, Jr., Don Merten, and Gary Schwartz, "Appropriate Age-Related Behavior for Male and Female Adolescents: Adult Perceptions," *Youth and Society* 17:115–130 (1985).
16. Teresa LaGrange and Robert Silverman, "Low Self-Control and Opportunity: Testing the General Theory of Crime as an Explanation for Gender Differences in Delinquency," *Criminology* 37:44 (1999).
17. Richmond-Abbot, note 8, p. 84.
18. Carol Gilligan, *In a Different Voice: Psychological Theory and Women's Development* (Cambridge: Harvard University Press, 1983).
19. Carol Gilligan, Nona Lyons, and Trudy Hanmer, *Making Connections: The Relational Worlds in Adolescent Girls at Emma Willard School* (Cambridge: Harvard University Press, 1990), p. 40.
20. Nancy Chodorow, *The Reproduction of Mothering* (Berkeley: University of California Press, 1978).
21. Erik Erikson, *Identity, Youth and Crisis* (New York: Norton, 1968), p. 283.
22. Sue Lees, "Learning to Love: Sexual Reputation, Morality and the Social Control of Girls," in Maureen Cain, *Growing Up Good: Policing the Behavior of Girls in Europe* (Newbury Park, CA: Sage Publications, 1989) p. 19.
23. Lees, note 22, p. 24.
24. Lees, note 22, p. 25.
25. Annie Hudson, " 'Troublesome Girls': Towards Alternative Definitions and Policies," in Cain, note 22, p. 207.
26. Cesare Lombroso and William Ferrero, *The Female Offender* (New York: Appleton, 1899).
27. Lombroso and Ferrero, note 26, p. 151.
28. Lombroso and Ferrero, note 26, p. 151.
29. Lombroso and Ferrero, note 26, p. 152.
30. Lombroso and Ferrero, note 26, p. 150.

31. Lombroso and Ferrero, note 26, pp. 193-195.
32. Sigmund Freud, *A General Introduction to Psychoanalysis* (New York: Boni and Liveright, 1924).
33. W. I. Thomas, *The Unadjusted Girl* (New York: Harper & Row, 1923).
34. Thomas, note 33, p. 71.
35. Thomas, note 33, p. 109.
36. Otto Pollak, *The Criminality of Women* (New York: Barnes and Company, 1950).
37. Pollak, note 36, p. 18.
38. Pollak, note 36, p. 10.
39. Gisela Konopka, *The Adolescent Girl in Conflict* (Englewood Cliffs, NJ: Prentice-Hall, Inc., 1966).
40. Konopka, note 39, p. 94.
41. Konopka, note 39, p. 97.
42. John Cowie, Valerie Cowie, and Eliot Slater, *Delinquency in Girls* (London: Heinemann, 1968).
43. Cowie et al., note 42, p. 45.
44. Cowie et al., note 42, pp. 166–167.
45   Clyde Vedder and Dora Somerville, *The Delinquent Girl,* 2nd ed. (Springfield, IL: Charles C. Thomas, 1975).
46   Vedder and Somerville, note 45, p. 145.
47. James Dabbs, Robert Frady, Timothy Carr, and Norma Besch, "Saliva Testosterone and Criminal Violence in Young Prison Inmates," *Psychosomatic Medicine* 49:174–182 (1987); James Dabbs, Barry Ruback, Robert Frady, Charles Hooper, and David Sgoutas, "Saliva Testosterone and Criminal Violence Among Women," *Personality and Individual Differences* 9:269–275 (1988).
48. See for example, Desmond Ellis and Penelope Austin, "Menstruation and Aggressive Behavior in a Correctional Center for Women," *Journal of Criminal Law, Criminology, and Police Science* 62:388–395 (1971); S. Golub, *Periods: From Menarche to Menopause* (Newbury Park, CA: Sage, 1992); and E.A. Hardie, "Prevalence and Predictors of Cyclic and Noncyclic Affective Change," *Psychology of Women Quarterly* 21:299–314 (1997).
49. Frederic Thrasher, *The Gang* (Chicago: University of Chicago Press, 1927), p. 228.
50. Clifford Shaw and Henry McKay, *Social Factors in Juvenile Delinquency* (Chicago: University of Chicago Press, 1931); *Juvenile Delinquency in Urban Areas* (Chicago: University of Chicago Press, 1942).
51. Robert Merton, "Social Structure and Anomie," *American Sociological Review* 3:672–682 (1938).
52. Ruth Morris, "Female Delinquencies and Relational Problems," *Social Problems* 43:82–88 (1964).
53. Morris, note 52, pp. 6–8.
54. Walter Miller, "Lower-Class Culture as a Generating Milieu of Gang Delinquency," *Journal of Social Issues* 14:5–19 (1958); "The Molls," *Society* 7:3–35 (1973).
55. Eileen Leonard, *Women, Crime, & Society* (New York: Longmans, 1982), p. 134.
56. Albert Cohen, *Delinquent Boys: The Subculture of the Gang* (New York: The Free Press, 1955), pp. 137–147.
57. Cohen, note 56, p. 142.
58. Cohen, note 56, p. 147.
59. Ngaire Naffine, *Female Crime: The Construction of Women in Criminology* (Sydney, Australia: Allen and Unwin, 1987), pp. 11–12.
60. Richard Cloward and Lloyd Ohlin, *Delinquency and Opportunity* (New York: The Free Press, 1960).
61. Cloward and Ohlin, note 60, p. 49.
62. Cloward and Ohlin, note 60, p. 49.
63. Edwin Sutherland, *Criminology,* 4th ed. (Philadelphia: Lippincott, 1947).
64. Edwin Sutherland, "Prevention of Juvenile Delinquency," *The Sutherland Papers,* edited by Albert Cohen, Alfred Lindesmith, and Karl Schuessler (Bloomington, IN: Indiana University Press, 1956), p. 133.
65. See for example, S.M. Clark, "Similarities in Components of Female and Male Delinquency: Implications for Sex-Role Theory," in *Interdisciplinary Problems in Criminology,* edited by Walter Reckless and Charles Newman (Columbus, OH: Ohio State University Press, 1964); Michael Hindelang, "Age, Sex and Versatility of Delinquent Involvement," *Social Problems* 18:522–535 (1971); Peggy Giordano "Girls, Guys, and Gangs: The Changing Social Context of Female Delinquency," *Journal of Criminal Law and Criminology* 69:126–132 (1978); and Jeanette Covington, "Self-Esteem and Deviance: The Effects of Race and Gender," *Criminology* 24:105–138 (1986).
66. Kristan Erickson, Robert Crosnoe, and Sanford Dornbusch, "A Social Process Model of Adolescent Deviance: Combining Social Control and Differential Association Perspectives," *Journal of Youth and Adolescence* 29:395–425 (2000).
67. Karen Heimer and Stacy De Coster, "The Gendering of Violent Delinquency," *Criminology* 37:277–312 (1999).
68. Xiaoru Liu and Howard Kaplan, "Explaining the Gender Difference in Adolescent Delinquent Behavior: A Longitudinal Test of Mediating Mechanisms," *Criminology* 37:195–215 (1999).
69. Travis Hirschi, *Causes of Delinquency* (Berkeley: University of California Press, 1969).
70. Coramae Mann, *Female Crime and Delinquency* (Montgomery, AL: University of Alabama Press, 1984), p. 263.

71. Rachelle Canter, "Family Correlates of Male and Female Delinquency," *Criminology* 20:149–166 (1982).

72. See for example, Delbert Elliott, David Huizinga, and Scott Menard, *Multiple Problem Youth: Delinquency, Substance Use, and Mental Health Problems* (New York: Springer-Verlag, 1989); Erickson et al., note 66; Joan McCord "Problem Behaviors," in *At the Threshold,* edited by Shirley Feldman and Glen Elliott, (Cambridge, MA: Harvard University Press, 1993); and Julie Wall, Thomas Power, and Consuelo Arbona, "Susceptibility to Antisocial Peer Pressure and its Relation to Acculturation in Mexican-American Adolescents," *Journal of Adolescent Research* 8:403–448 (1993).

73. Bobbi Jo Anderson, Malcolm Holmes, and Erik Ostresh, "Male and Female Delinquents' Attachments and Effects of Attachments on Severity of Self-Reported Delinquency," *Criminal Justice and Behavior* 26:435–452 (1999).

74. Michael Gottfredson and Travis Hirschi, *A General Theory of Crime* (Stanford, CA: Stanford University Press, 1990).

75. Gottfredson and Hirschi, note 74, p. 145.

76. Gottfredson and Hirschi, note 74, p. 148–149.

77. See for example, LaGrange and Silverman, note 16, and Bradley Wright, Avshalom Caspi, Terrie Moffitt, and Phil Silva, "Low Self-Control, Social Bonds, and Crime: Social Causation, Social Selection, or Both?" *Criminology* 37:479–514 (1999).

78. Edwin Schur, *Labeling Women Deviant: Gender, Stigma, and Social Control* (New York: Random House, Inc., 1984), p. 3.

79. Schur, note 78, p. 8.

80. Schur, note 78, p. 12.

81. Belknap, note 2, p. 45.

82. George Vold, Thomas Bernard, and Jeffrey Snipes, *Theoretical Criminology*, 4th ed. (New York: Oxford University Press, 1998), p. 278.

83. James Messerschmidt, *Capitalism, Patriarchy, and Crime: Toward a Socialist Feminist Criminology* (Totowa, NJ: Rowman & Littlefield, 1986).

84. Messerschmidt, note 83, pp. 42–43.

85. Messerschmidt, note 83, p. 44.

86. Ronald Akers, *Criminological Theories*, 3rd ed. (Los Angeles: Roxbury Publishing Co., 2000), p. 232.

87. Darrell Steffensmeier, Emilie Allan, and Cathy Streifel, "Development and Female Crime: A Cross-National Test of Alternative Explanations," *Social Forces* 68:262–283 (1989).

88. Akers, note 86, p. 233.

89. John Hagan, A. R. Gillis, and John Simpson, "The Class Structure of Gender and Delinquency: Toward a Power-Control Theory of Common Delinquent Behavior," *American Journal of Sociology* 90:1151–1178 (1985); John Hagan, John Simpson, and A. R. Gillis, "Class in the Household: A Power-Control Theory of Delinquency," *American Journal of Sociology* 92:788–816 (1987); John Hagan, A.R. Gillis, and John Simpson, "Clarifying and Extending a Power-Control Theory of Gender and Delinquency," *American Journal of Sociology* 95:1024–1037 (1990); and Bill McCarthy, John Hagan, and Todd Woodward, "In the Company of Women: Structure and Agency in a Revised Power-Control Theory of Gender and Delinquency," *Criminology* 37:761–788 (1999).

90. Meda Chesney-Lind and Randall Shelden, *Girls, Delinquency, and Juvenile Justice*, 2nd ed. (Belmont, CA: West-Wadsworth, 1998), p. 120.

91. Roy Austin, "Women's Liberation and Increases in Minor, Major, and Occupational Offenses," *Criminology* 20:407–430 (1982).

92. Simon Singer and Murray Levine, "Power-Control Theory, Gender, and Delinquency: A Partial Replication with Additional Evidence on the Effects of Peers," *Criminology* 26:627–647 (1988).

93. Merry Morash and Meda Chesney-Lind, "A Reformulation and Partial Test of the Power Control Theory of Delinquency," *Justice Quarterly* 8:347–377 (1991).

94. Michael Leiber and Mary Ellen Wacker, "A Theoretical and Empirical Assessment of Power Control Theory and Single-Mother Families," *Youth & Society* 28:317–350 (1997).

95. Christopher Uggen, "Class, Gender, and Arrest: An Intergenerational Analysis of Workplace Power and Control," *Criminology* 38:835–862 (2000).

96. Daniel Mears, Matthew Ploeger, and Mark Warr, "Explaining the Gender Gap in Delinquency: Peer Influence and Moral Evaluations of Behavior," *Journal of Research in Crime and Delinquency* 35:263 (1998).

97. Mears et al., note 96, p. 263.

98. Morash and Chesney-Lind, note 93; Meda Chesney-Lind, "Girls' Crime and Woman's Place: Toward a Feminist Model of Female Delinquency," *Crime and Delinquency* 35:5–29 (1989).

99. Morash and Chesney-Lind, note 93, p. 351.

100. Chesney-Lind and Shelden, note 90, pp. 35–43.

101. Meda Chesney-Lind, "What About the Girls? Delinquency Programming as if Gender Mattered," *Corrections Today,* February (2001), p. 44.

102. Chesney-Lind, note 101, p. 44.

The Social Context of Delinquency

In previous sections we examined the nature of juvenile delinquency as it has come to be defined, measured, and explained. How delinquency is defined and measured largely determines how we go about explaining it. The theories and explanations that evolve, however, must also connect to the social reality of delinquency. This section, then, examines juvenile delinquency within its societal context.

Juvenile delinquency is closely tied to those social groupings or institutions where children spend most of their time—within the family, in school, and with friends. Chapter 10 examines the forces in today's family that directly or indirectly contribute to a child's delinquency. The traditional functions of the family, socializing of children, inculcating moral values, regulating sexual activity, and providing material, physical, and emotional security, as well as the traditional structure of the family, have undergone substantial change during the past 40 years. Many of the changes have caused increased tension, anxiety, and conflict within the family. Single-parent families, working mothers, and inadequate parenting skills have been identified as contributing in one way or another to delinquency. So, too, have the problems of divorce, including custody battles, forced visitation, and failure to pay court-ordered support for noncustodial children. To whatever extent basic parenting skills and structural change within families impact the likelihood of delinquency, current research is rather consistently suggesting that there are even greater effects produced by familial maltreatment of children.

Children spend close to half their waking hours in school. Chapter 11 explores how schools are not only locations of adolescent crime, but may directly or indirectly contribute to the problem of youth crime. Although violent crime has declined in schools in recent years (in spite of the horrific, but rare, mass killings such as that at Columbine High School in Colorado), students and teachers are still victimized. Bullying has recently gained national attention as a possible correlate, if not cause, of school violence. And schools continue to grapple with the problems associated with both high rates of dropouts and troublesome students who stay in school. To what extent do the built-in stresses and conflicts of the schooling process, the temptations and pressures of peers, and the enforcement of school rules, with sanctions ranging from suspensions to corporal punishment, contribute to disruptive behaviors and more serious delinquencies?

Chapter 12 looks at juvenile delinquency within the context of peer activity, especially the gang. Are children more likely to violate norms and laws when with their friends? Are juvenile gangs simply more formal and violent expressions of more normal school and neighborhood peer groups? Why do juveniles form gangs? How do the cultural experiences of Asian Americans, Blacks, Latinos, and numerous other groups affect the development of juvenile gangs? Although criminologists ponder the difficulties in defining gangs, local law enforcement and politicians often draw upon statutory definitions to support get-tough approaches to gang suppression. Might intervention and prevention policies provide a more effective long-term solution to the gang problem?

Chapter 10

Family and Delinquency

**Nobody's family can hang out the sign, "Nothing the matter
here."**

—*Chinese Proverb*

The family is the most critical social institution. The earliest and most important stages of a child's socialization occur within the family. The family is largely responsible for instilling in children important moral and religious values and understandings about right and wrong. However, as the Chinese proverb states, no family is perfect; nobody's family can claim they do not have problems. Family problems, however, vary greatly in both type and magnitude. The problems of some families may be minor and produce only small consequences for family members. Other families may experience greater problems and the impact on members may be significant. One common problem related to families is juvenile delinquency.

The family has long been considered to play an important role in producing or reducing delinquency. For example, in 1915 Douglas Morrison wrote that " . . . among social circumstances which have a hand in determining the future of the individual it is enough for our present purpose to recognize that the family is chief."[1] Just how do families contribute to the delinquent behavior of their children? In this chapter, after discussing traditional functions of the family, we will explore the possible effects of varying family structures, family dynamics, and parenting styles on delinquency.

Traditional Functions of the Family

Traditionally, the family has performed four principal functions: the socialization of children, the inculcation of moral values, the reproduction and the regulation of sexual activity, and the provision of material, physical, and emotional security.

The Socialization of Children

The family is the first and most important social unit to affect children; it is the first social world the child encounters. **Socialization** is the process through which children learn the ways of a particular society or social group so that they can function within it. Individuals learn the attitudes, behaviors, and social roles considered appropriate for them from already-socialized individuals, typically parents and other family members.[2] Through the socialization process in families, the personalities, values, and beliefs of children are initially shaped. But families are not isolated groups. Rather, they exist within a larger social and cultural context and will reflect the family's particular class, ethnic, racial, religious, political, and regional characteristics. This means that a child's socialization is somewhat selective, depending on the background and contextual experiences of his or her particular family.[3]

Inculcation of Moral Values

One of the most critical aspects of socialization is the development of moral values in children. Moral education, or the training of the individual to be inclined toward the good, involves a number of things, including the rules—the

In June 2001, a case of child abuse shocked the world. Police discovered that an eight-year-old girl was confined by her own parents to a urine-and feces-filled closet for four years. The child weighed only 25 pounds. What would be an appropriate punishment for the parents? Will the abused child likely become delinquent because of this extreme maltreatment? If so, should this horrific treatment be used to mitigate her potential future delinquency?

do's and don't's—and the development of good habits.[4] Although the church and school complement the family in both teaching and setting examples of moral behavior, it is in the family where the development of moral virtue or good character is effectively formed or left unformed.[5] Robert Coles puts it this way:

> Good children are boys and girls who in the first place have learned to take seriously the very notion, the desirability, of goodness—a living up to the Golden Rule, a respect for others, a commitment of mind, heart, soul to one's family, neighborhood, nation—and have also learned that the issue of goodness is not an abstract one, but rather a concrete, expressive one: how to turn the rhetoric of goodness into action, moments that affirm the presence of goodness in a particular lived life.[6]

Similarly, the Children's Defense Fund, actively working in partnership with the religious community, advocates that every child deserves a moral start in life, meaning that children should be "taught the enduring values of honesty, hard work, discipline, respect for self and others, responsibility, and of doing unto others as they'd have done to themselves."[7]

Emile Durkheim believed the integrative function of religion was crucial for maintaining social order. Social cohesion was enhanced through shared values and norms generally originating from religious practice. When parents view religion as important, communicate religious values and practices to their children, and involve their children in religious activities, inclinations toward delinquency are reduced. Religious beliefs, according to Bruce Chadwick and Brent Top, have long been understood to be the foundation for moral behavior and thus, "the more religious a person is, the less likely he or she will be to participate in delinquent or criminal behaviors."[8]

Criminologist John DiIulio is spearheading efforts to help the church resurrect the most embattled inner cities and prevent delinquency. Will this be helpful? Given the effective role of religion in reducing delinquency, why is society generally intolerant of the Christian Right?

There is much evidence that an adolescent's moral sense or personal religiosity (variously measured by religious participation and affiliation) is negatively related to delinquency. There have been well over a hundred published studies in the last half century examining the relationship between religion and delinquency, all but a handful failing to report a negative relationship.[9] For example, a recent study by Byron Johnson and his colleagues examined the impact of religiosity on over 2,300 at-risk black juveniles living in poverty tracts in Boston, Chicago, and Philadelphia.[10] They found that church attendance, even after controlling for background and other nonreligious variables, such as secular bonding and informal social controls through the family and school, "has an independent effect on nondrug crime, drug use, and drug dealing among the disadvantaged youth."[11]

Interestingly, the most frequently cited work on this topic is "Hellfire and Delinquency" published in 1969 by Travis Hirschi and Rodney Stark. They reported that there was no link between religiosity (church and Sunday school attendance and belief in Hell) and delinquent behavior. The popularity of the study's findings "that religion fails to guide teenagers along the

Children with a strong family and religious background are dually protected from the allures of delinquency. What values and beliefs does religion inculcate?

straight and narrow was soon enshrined in undergraduate textbooks."[12] Subsequent research, however, consistently found strong negative effects of religion on delinquency. Stark accounts for the relative uniqueness of their findings as a product of their study being done in the Far West where there is very low religious involvement compared to other regions of the country. Studies conducted in the East, South, Midwest, and Mountain states have consistently found an adolescent's religiosity, especially when reinforced by family and peer religiousness, to have a preventative effect on delinquency.[13] Today, Stark is not hesitant to state: "Other things being equal, religious individuals will be less likely than those who are not religious to commit deviant acts."[14]

Reproduction and Regulation of Sexual Activity

Should parents be held legally responsible when producing juvenile delinquents? If so, what punishments are appropriate?

The family has been the traditional social unit for sexual reproduction.[15] The family teaches children society's norms about sexual conduct—what is acceptable and what is unacceptable. In the family, children learn at what age, with whom, and under what circumstances they may engage in sexual relationships. Children also learn in the family about the consequences of sexual activity; that is, if pregnancy occurs, who is responsible for the care and maintenance of the infant and how such care should be provided.

Provision of Material, Physical, and Emotional Security

Families traditionally have been the primary providers of the material well-being of their members. The family clothes, feeds, and provides shelter. Parents or older siblings provide supervision and monitoring of younger children to ensure their safety and obedience. In addition, the family provides for the physical security of its members, and the mere presence of family members in the home functions to protect the family from potential thieves, vandals, and burglars.[16] Finally, the family provides emotional security to its members through giving encouragement, support, and unconditional love.

Is sexual behavior during adolescence intrinsically delinquent? Do real differences exist between gender and sexual behavior? Has the juvenile justice system appropriately criminalized the sexuality of female adolescents?

The world, however, is not perfect, and many families fail miserably at achieving one or more of these goals. Families, unfortunately, often transmit values that promote violence or criminality and undermine the development of positive self-concepts among its members. Too often, families fail to inculcate moral values or virtues in their young. Too many families fail to teach proper sexual conduct, either by instruction or by direct example. And too many families fail to provide adequate material, physical, and emotional security to its members when parents divorce or fail to marry in the first place or when they engage in disreputable or criminal behavior, thereby ignoring the primary needs of the children. Such failures of the family are not new, but there is much evidence that recent changes in the family have significantly contributed to the problem behaviors, including delinquency, of so many children today.[17]

The Changing Family

A number of changes in the American family during the past few decades have prompted both controversy and debate over the meaning and implications of the trends. In 1970, 85 percent of children under age 18 lived with both mother and father; by 2000, only 71 percent of children lived with both parents (see Figure 10–1).[18] Demographers predict that over half of all children born in the 1990s will spend a portion of their childhood in families with only one parent.[19] Of the nearly 20 million children currently living with only one parent, 84 percent live in families headed by women, while 16 percent are in families headed by men.[20] Over two and a half million children live with neither parent, with about half of these children living with grandparents, about 21 percent living with other relatives, and about 22 percent living with nonrelatives. Nearly half of the children living with nonrelatives live with foster parents. In addition, over 3 million children live with a parent or parents who are cohabiting.[21]

Figure 10–1
Percentage of children under age 18 living with both parents, 1970–2000

Source: U.S. Bureau of the Census, *Current Population Reports, No. 71,* 2000, and earlier reports (Washington, DC: U.S. Government Printing Office, 2001).

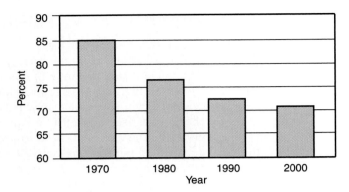

Single-Parent Families

What might account for this increase in **single-parent families**? Linda Gordon and Sara McLanahan point out that in 1900 only about 5 percent of all children in single-parent homes were living with a parent who was divorced or had never married. Most of the parents in these homes were widowed.[22] However, by the early 1990s

> only about 5 percent of all female-headed households with children had experienced the death of the father; about 37 percent had experienced parental divorce; and in 36 percent of these homes, the parents had never married [the remaining 22 percent of the households were classified as "married, spouse absent."][23]

Nearly 1 million American teenagers become pregnant each year. About 40 percent abort their pregnancies. The birthrate for teenagers ages 15–17 in 1999 was 28.7 per 1000, down from its all-time high of 38.7 per 1000 in 1991. Teenage birthrates vary by race and by state. For example, in 1999 the birthrate for white, non-Latino teenagers was 17.1, for black teenagers 52.1, and for Latino teenagers 61.2. Vermont and New Hampshire had the lowest teen birth rates (11.4 and 13.1 respectively) while Mississippi and Washington, DC, had the highest rates (47.2 and 65.5 respectively). Most teenage births are to *unmarried* teenagers. Although the birthrate for unmarried teenagers has fallen since 1994, births to unmarried girls ages 15–17 accounted for 87.5 percent in 1998, while 96.6 percent of births to girls under 15 years of age were unmarried.[24]

Single-parent families are not evenly distributed across racial and ethnic groups. Today, approximately 23 percent of white children, 37 percent of Latino children, and 65 percent of black children are being raised by a single parent.[25] Single-parent families also are disproportionately at or near the poverty level: The poverty rate for single-parent families is approximately five times higher than for two-parent families. Nine percent of children in two-parent families live in poverty, while 46 percent of children in female-headed families are at or below the poverty level.[26] And although race and

Conflict explanations of delinquency are often criticized for being too conspiratorial, particularly in relation to the effect of race on delinquency. How do the various data on the disintegration of the black family impact delinquency? Which is a greater explanation of black crime: criminal justice system biases or family disintegration?

The crime problem would be insurmountable without the efforts of mothers. Are policy makers doing enough to strengthen families to reduce the likelihood of delinquency?

ethnicity are clearly related to poverty, such dramatic differences in family poverty rates are not a function of race or ethnicity. Only 12 percent of black children living with their married parents in 1998 were living in poverty, while 55 percent of black children living in female-headed households that same year were in poverty.[27]

Teenage mothers are three times more likely than other teenagers to drop out of school, and they will earn less money than unmarried mothers who did not have their first child until they were in their twenties. They are also likely to spend longer periods of time living in poverty. Travis Hirschi points out, however, that the teenage mother herself should not be targeted as the primary problem. According to Hirschi, "In my view, the teenage mother is not the problem. . . . The problem is the mother without a husband. Her children are likely to be delinquent, and she is likely to have more of them."[28] He argues that there should be two parents for every child and that delinquency can be reduced by improving the quality of child-rearing practices. This means strengthening the bonds not only between parents and children but also between husbands and wives (see Box 10–1 for a discussion about absent parents and the failure to pay child support).

What about teenage fathers? What are the consequences of fatherhood for adolescent boys? Terence Thornberry and his colleagues have studied the relationship between teenage fatherhood and delinquent behavior.[29] Somewhere between 2 and 7 percent of male teenagers are fathers, and the

BOX 10–1   A WINDOW ON DELINQUENCY
Nonresident Parents and the Failure to Pay Child Support

While teenage mothers are more likely than older mothers to be single, the difficulties and consequences of raising children without fathers in the household are common for both younger and older mothers. As so much research has shown over the years, when the father does not reside in the household the children tend to suffer in a variety of ways: economically, emotionally, cognitively, and behaviorally. Many experts believe that the economic stresses produced by the absence of fathers directly contributes to the other problems. As one means of reducing these stresses, the law requires nonresident fathers to pay child support (in a small percentage of cases, nonresident mothers are required to pay support). But only a small percentage of those who owe child support actually comply with the law. Over 80 percent of the families owed child support in California get no payments. In 1998, California children were owed more than $8 billion in unpaid child support.

Does payment of child support really make that much difference in a child's life? Is the payment of child support by nonresident fathers beneficial to children in any way other than the contribution of money? Recent research suggests that there are many benefits. Payment of support can positively influence parent–child and mother–father relationships. It is positively related to the amount of contact and visitation between absent fathers and their children. It reduces reliance on more stigmatizing sources of income such as welfare. It is positively related to cognitive development and academic success of the children. And, finally, payment of child support is positively associated with fewer problem behaviors of children.

While state and local agencies have the primary responsibility for enforcing child support laws, the federal government is playing an increasingly important role as greater numbers of nonresident fathers move from state to state. The Child Support Recovery Act creates a federal offense for (1) traveling in interstate or foreign commerce with the intent to evade a child support obligation, if the obligation has remained unpaid for longer than one year or is greater than $5,000, and (2) the willful failure to pay a past due child support obligation for a child who resides in a state other than that in which the noncustodial parent resides, if the obligation has remained unpaid for longer than one year or is greater than $5,000; the willful failure to pay a past due obligation may qualify as a felony if it has remained unpaid for longer than two years or is greater than $10,000.

The Department of Justice at the federal level and the Office of Child Support Enforcement in many states and counties maintain "Most Wanted" Child Support Evaders websites with photographs and information about some of the worst of the "Deadbeat Parents." For example, the Kentucky and Georgia "Most Wanted Child Support Evaders" websites can be found at the following locations: http://www.law.state.ky.us/childsupport/wanted.htm; http://www2.state.ga.us/Departments/DHR/CSE/mw.htm.

Sources: Barbara Grob and Amy Dominquez-Arms, "Working Families," [Online] Available:http://www.childrennow.org/economics/CostOfFailure-PR.html (October 12, 1998); Laura Argys, H. Elizabeth Peters, Jeannie Brooks-Gunn, and Judith Smith, "The Impact of Child Support on Cognitive Outcomes of Young Children," *Demography* 35:159–173 (1998); Paul Amato and Joan Gilbreth "Nonresident Fathers and Children's Well-Being: A Meta-Analysis," *Journal of Marriage and the Family* 61:557–473 (1999); Child Support Recovery Act, Title 18, United States Code, Sec. 228.

rate of teen fatherhood stood at 23 per 1,000 in 1996. Black teenagers are more likely to be fathers than are white or Latino teenagers. Teen fatherhood is also associated with growing up in poverty and hanging out with friends who engage in delinquency and other problem behaviors. Like teenage mothers, teenage fathers experience many negative educational, financial, social, health, and other developmental consequences. Interestingly, boys who become teenage fathers are also likely to engage in a variety of other problem behaviors, such as status offenses, disruptive school behavior, and illicit drug use. According to Thornberry and his colleagues,

> Young fathers tended to be troubled young men who were significantly more likely than their matched controls to have engaged in varied serious acts of delinquency in the year of fatherhood and in the year after. . . . They were more likely than nonfathers to have had a court petition alleging delinquency, to be drinking alcohol frequently, to be involved in drug dealing, or to have dropped out of school.[30]

Unfortunately, teen fathers are unlikely to be in a position to provide financial, emotional, or other parental support for their children, and thus are likely to be poor role models. As Thornberry and his associates note: "Their legacy to their children is likely to be one of socioeconomic disadvantage, poorer health, and poorer education, among other hardships."[31]

Children in poor, single-parent families, especially those headed by teenage mothers, clearly face special difficulties. They are more likely to experience chronic psychological distress, to engage in health-compromising behaviors (including drug and alcohol use, cigarette smoking, and unprotected sex), to perform less well academically, to be expelled or suspended from school, to drop out of school, to suffer from mental illness, to commit suicide, to have trouble getting along with their peers, and to start their own single-parent families.[32] And Jeffrey Grogger points out that the sons of adolescent mothers are nearly three times more likely to be incarcerated at some point in their 20s than the sons of mothers who delay childbearing until they are in their early 20s.[33] But not all children being raised in single-parent homes live in poverty, nor are all born to unmarried or teenage mothers. Many children are being raised by a divorced parent. The process and consequences of divorce on children may have negative effects independent of the mother's age or economic status.

It is not unusual for intact families to be fraught with conflict between husbands and wives or for a pervasive silence to be cast over the members as each attempts to avoid provoking outbursts in others. Frequently, relations improve after divorce or separation. However, much current research suggests that both the structural reality of single parenting as a consequence of divorce and the very process of going through divorce produce adverse consequences for the children in the family.[34] According to Michael Rutter, the breaking up of a family by divorce or desertion is significantly more likely to have adverse effects on the children than is the breaking up by the death of one of the parents.[35]

Each year about 2 percent (nearly 1.2 million families) of all married couples get divorced, and more than half involve children under the age of 18.[36] Those who divorce and then remarry are even more likely to find the subsequent marriage falling apart, and multiple divorces are harder on the children. Children who have experienced multiple divorces are more likely to report higher levels of anxiety and depression, to have worse academic records, and eventually to have more troubled marriages of their own than are children who have experienced a single divorce or children whose families remain intact. Frank Furstenberg, Jr. and Andrew Cherlin estimate that 15 percent of all children in divorced families will see the parent they live with remarry and redivorce before they reach the age of 18.[37]

Single Parents, Divorce, and Delinquency

The relationship between single-parent families and delinquency has been widely studied.[38] Much research exists reporting that children from single-parent families are more likely to become delinquent than children from two-parent families. For example, Ann Goetting noted that only 30 percent of the children arrested for homicide in Detroit between 1977 and 1984 lived with both parents.[39] Edward Wells and Joseph Rankin's analysis of 50 studies led them to conclude that the effect of the single-parent family on delinquency is real and consistent, but of relatively low magnitude; the effect is greater for minor offenses, weaker for serious offenses.[40] Furthermore, Michelle Miller and her colleagues surveyed about 500 students in 11 public schools and report that adolescents in single-parent families are more likely to engage in both serious and minor delinquencies than are youths in two-parent families.[41]

Explanations offered to explain the greater likelihood of delinquency for children from single-parent families include suggestions that single parents can less-effectively supervise their children (one can do less than two);[42] children in single-parent families grow up too fast;[43] single mothers give adolescents greater say in what they can do or give too early autonomy, thus reducing control over youths;[44] and children from single-parent families are more susceptible to peer pressure.[45]

On the other hand, there exists a body of research that suggests that the most important determinant of whether a child will be involved in delinquency is the quality of the parent-child relationship rather than family structure alone (the nature and impact of parenting are discussed later in this chapter).[46] For example, a recent study of nearly 2,500 middle and junior high school students in Dade County, Florida, reported that a strong attachment between parent and child significantly reduced the likelihood of delinquency, while family structure had only a weak indirect effect.[47] In addition, Marc Zimmerman and his colleagues studied the effects of family structure and parental attachment among 254 black male adolescents from a large East Coast city. They report that regardless of family structure, time spent

Given the colossal implications of divorce on delinquency and the maladjustment of children, should divorce become a criminal offense? If there were criminal consequences of getting divorced, how would the American family change? Would delinquency increase or decrease?

with father and perception of father's emotional support were associated with lower levels of delinquency and marijuana use.[48]

The Impact of Divorce on Children   What impact does the breakup of a family have on children? Mavis Hetherington reports that in the year following the breakup, children in single-parent families are more likely to suffer psychological distress, but in the long run they cope more successfully than children in intact families where parents do not get along.[49] She sees three major effects of divorce on women that heavily affect children: They are overloaded from both work and child rearing, face financial strain, and are likely to be socially isolated.

Divorce also may produce "family wars," in which relatives and friends pick sides and attempt to "win" by attacking the former spouse. Children are caught in the middle, often being defined as victims or expected to accept new definitions of the former spouse. In either case, the stress produced for the child may manifest itself in many ways. Some studies have found a relationship between father absence and a host of social and emotional ills, including decreased school performance and self-control and increased rates of psychological disturbance, drug use, gang affiliation, and involvement in violent crime.[50]

Judith Wallerstein and Joan Kelly studied families in the early stages of breaking up, after 18 months apart, and after 5 years.[51] In the first period, both parents typically felt the pinch of a lower standard of living and were depressed and lonely. Mothers were also overburdened by having to juggle bread-winning and homemaking roles and had to stay up late to do so. Children were often upset and thoroughly opposed to the divorce. Children became more angry, aggressive, and unruly during this initial stage of the breakup, partly because of their deteriorating relationship with their mother. Eighteen months later, some mothers were still depressed, but parent-child relations were healing and children themselves improved, with fewer feeling deprived or lonely. At the five-year point, conditions were slightly worse than at 18 months. Among children, there was increased evidence of anger and depression.

Judith Wallerstein and Sandra Blakeslee published results from a study in which 60 families and 131 youths were interviewed at 1-, 5-, 10-, and 15-year intervals after divorce in an attempt to discover both short- and long-term effects of divorce.[52] After five years, one-third of the children were doing well, but another third were significantly worse off, suffering both academic and psychological difficulties. Some specific consequences of divorce on children are the result of the diminished capacity of parents to supervise in almost all dimensions of child rearing. In the process of divorce, parents spend less time with their children and are less responsive to their needs. Wallerstein and her colleagues recently published their findings from follow-up interviews with these same 131 subjects, now 25 years after divorce. Reflections by some of these subjects on the effects of having to make court-ordered visits with noncustodial parents are presented in Box 10–2.

BOX 10–2   FACE OF DELINQUENCY
Court-Ordered Visitations

Numerous studies confirm that most children are adversely affected by the divorce of their parents and the struggle of the custodial parent to provide for the well-being of the children in the absence of the other parent. But do court-ordered visitations with the noncustodial parent aggravate the adjustment difficulties of child? Paula was only four years old when her parents separated. Her father reentered her life when she was eight, and got a court to grant him rights to regular visitation. By the time Paula was 13, she had accumulated a police record of drug use, public drinking, and theft. She had also become sexually active with two 17-year-old boys. How much of her delinquency might be attributed to the consequences of court-ordered visits with her father? Are court-ordered visits always in the child's best interests?

Judith Wallerstein and her colleagues have studied the effects of divorce on children (and parents) for over 25 years. Paula was just one of the many children who reported that being subjected to court-ordered visitations made them feel like "nonpersons" with no right to express opinions or preferences or to question the visitation arrangements imposed on them. Thousands of children, many as young as eight or nine, make lengthy and complicated plane trips by themselves to comply with the court's orders. While Paula did not have to fly to visit her father, the court did require that she visit her dad for two weekends each month, that holidays be rotated every other year, and that Paula reside with her father during the month of July. According to Wallerstein, "The visiting schedule was set up on the basis of a compromise meeting the demands of both parents.

Working Mothers and Latchkey Children

Most women participate full time or part time in the labor force today. Three-fourths of married women with children between the ages of 6 and 17 are employed; 79 percent of single mothers with children in this same age group are employed. But mothers with much younger children are also working outside the home. In 1999, 10.3 million women with children under age 6 were employed: This includes 61 percent of married women and 67 percent of single women with children under age 6.[53] Some criminologists ask whether there is a connection between women in the labor force and delinquency.

Research has found one definite effect of mothers being in the labor force—they have less time to spend with their children. But Russell Hill and Frank Stafford report that college-educated working mothers try hard to compensate: They cut down on time spent sleeping and relaxing more than they cut down on time spent with their children.[54] The same authors also note that by the time children reach adolescence, parents in general spend

The wishes and needs of [Paula] were never consulted or considered."

The courts and parents rarely discuss with children how they will spend time on their visits. Little, if any, thought is given to how visits might cut into the child's social life or friendships, or how they may disrupt school activities, including participating in sports or doing homework. Paula's visits with her father generally involved her spending the weekend watching television or videos or accompanying her father on his errands. Sometimes she was left in his apartment when he went out on dates. Paula dreaded the month-long visit during July. "When summer comes, all the other kids in my class look forward to it. . . . I hate July. It's terrible for me. Last July I cried the whole month and thought, why am I being sentenced? What crime did I commit?"

> Years later, Paula reflected on the court-ordered visits. She said: "I hated it there. I don't think it's good for children to spend two weekends with one parent and then go back to the other home. It's really hard. When you're a child, you're trying to discover who you are and

to have friends. Their plan was totally disruptive to me. My friends got so they wouldn't even invite me on the weekends I was home."

When Wallerstein asked Paula "How did you manage?" Paula replied, "I would pretend all weekend to myself that I wasn't really there."

Instead of building relationships, court-ordered visitation frequently brings further deterioration. Wallerstein notes that most of the children in her study who were required to make court-ordered visits "were very angry at the parent they had been ordered to visit. All rejected the parent whom they were forced to visit when they got older."

While no easy solution is likely to be found, it seems only reasonable that the courts, at a minimum, should allow children the right to participate in developing the plans that will affect their lives and to recognize that children change and that court-ordered visitation for very young children should be reviewed each year and modified as the child's life changes.

Source: Judith Wallerstein, Julia Lewis, and Sandra Blakeslee, *The Unexpected Legacy of Divorce: A 25 Year Landmark Study* (New York: Hyperion, 2000), pp. 174–187.

---

only an hour or two per week in nurturing them and thus, under these circumstances, there is little difference between working and nonworking mothers in the time they give. Therefore, having less time to spend with her children does not necessarily mean that the mother is failing to perform her role adequately. Keith Melville states that "when working mothers derive satisfaction from their employment and do not feel guilty about its effects, they are likely to perform the mother's role at least as well as non-working women."[55]

Studies examining the effects of mothers' employment on children and their development have produced mixed results. For example, Matthijs Kalmijn reports that mothers who work in high-status jobs lead to positive school effects for their children: Sons and daughters do better academically, are more likely to complete high school, attend college, and eventually graduate.[56] And studies by Jay Belsky and David Eggebeen found that a variety of measures of adjustment, such as behavior problems, insecurity, and sociability, reflected no negative effects of employment of mothers.[57]

"Latchkey" child is a negative connotation. Why? Are latchkey programs beneficial to the children in the program and to their working parents? What role does social class play in the national perception of latchkey children?

Travis Hirschi's comparison of sons of homemakers, women who worked part time, and women who worked full time found that 20 percent of sons of full time working mothers, 17 percent of sons of part-time workers, and 16 percent of sons of homemakers were delinquent. With differences this small, we can safely say that there is at most only a weak relationship between delinquency and mothers' employment status.[58] Additional researchers have also reported that the two factors were unrelated.[59] Thus, there is little evidence showing that working mothers play much of a role in their children's delinquency.

But what about working fathers? Between 80 and 90 percent of married and single fathers with children are employed.[60] In the past, traditional gender roles guided fathers into bread-winning rather than into child rearing and caregiving roles, which were considered the primary domains of mothers. However, David Popenoe notes that with the majority of mothers now in the labor force, "men are being asked to return to domestic roles. Fathers are badly needed as comprehensive childrearers on an equal basis with mothers."[61] But conflicts between father's and mother's employment schedules not only reduce the time fathers have available for caregiving, competing schedules also contribute to increased stress and role conflict between husbands and wives. Only when fathers work different schedules than their wives are they more likely to provide care for their children.[62]

Have latchkey children received an unfair reputation? Doesn't the latchkey process force children to become independent human beings? Would granting children autonomy be a good or a bad thing?

When both mothers and fathers are employed outside the home with overlapping schedules, most children are faced with the prospect of coming home to empty houses. The number of **latchkey children,** that is, children who regularly care for themselves without adult supervision after school or on weekends, has increased dramatically. About 12 percent of children ages 5 to 12 and 41 percent of children age 12 to 14 spend substantial amounts of time at home alone while their parent or parents are at work.[63] Many experts feel that latchkey children, especially those in their teenage years, are more susceptible to opportunities for getting involved in delinquent situations. See Box 10–3 for a discussion of what the YMCA is trying to do to reduce problems associated with teenagers who are unsupervised after school.

Laurence Steinberg thinks latchkey children face a variety of subtle fears and worries, such as exposure to dangers while alone and increases in their susceptibility to peer pressure.[64] They have less adult supervision and are therefore more vulnerable to peer pressure to engage in delinquent acts. Latchkey children are likely to "find other [children] who are coming home to empty houses. They create a peer-group culture, and it's likely to be an ugly culture—a culture of destroy, of break, of acting-out."[65]

Latchkey children exist because many families cannot survive unless both parents are employed outside the home. Consequently, latchkey children are disproportionately from the working class. Are criminologists projecting their views of appropriate parenting in lamenting the latchkey child? In other words, is the latchkey child only a problem for middle class parents who can afford to stay at home?

In a study of behavioral consequences of leaving children in self-care, Jean Richardson found that students who spent 11 or more hours a week in self-care were twice as likely to use alcohol, tobacco, and marijuana as children of the same age whose after-school time was supervised.[66] A recent national longitudinal study on adolescent health of more than 12,000 middle and high school students conducted by Michael Resnick and his associates found that the presence of parents at home at key times during the day (early morning, after school, evening meal, and at bedtime) provided moderate protection against emotional distress for children, reduced the frequency of use of alcohol and marijuana, and delayed adolescents' initiation of sexual intercourse.[67]

With the numerous problems posed by self-care, it is understandable that many parents turn to child-care providers. In 1999, more than 50 percent of children under eight years of age were cared for on a regular basis by caregivers other than parents. About 75 percent of children under age five were in

BOX 10–3 DELINQUENCY PREVENTION
After-School Programs for Unsupervised Teens

The average teen in the United States is unsupervised after school two days per week for up to five hours. Nearly 60 percent of teens are left without supervision by a parent or other adult at least one day per week after school, and nearly 40 percent are left unsupervised three or more days. Older teens (17 and 18 years old) are more likely than younger teens to lack adult supervision after school at least one day per week (67 percent versus 52 percent). And teens from single-parent households are left unsupervised for more days per week than teens from two-parent homes (an average of 2.2 days versus 1.7 days).

Teens who are unsupervised after school are more likely to engage in delinquency or other activities that put them at risk than supervised teens. They are more likely to drink alcohol, smoke cigarettes, and engage in sex, and twice as likely to skip school and three times more likely to use marijuana or other drugs.

Participation in after-school activities appears to not only reduce risky behavior and delinquency but to have a positive effect on grades. Nearly 80 percent of teens who engage in after-school activities get grades of "A" or "B," but only half of teens who do not participate in such activities get such high grades. Teens who do not engage in after-school activities are five times as likely to be "D" students as those who do participate. More than one-third of teens who do not participate in after-

school activities drink alcohol and get in trouble at school, compared to only about one-fourth of teens who do engage in after-school activities.

In response to these findings, the YMCA has launched its Teen Action Agenda designed to double the number of teens served through its after-school and other programs by 2005. The Teen Action Agenda's goals are to build skills and values; improve teens' health practices, educational development, and character; help teens become contributing members of their communities; and place committed, caring adults in long-term relationships with the youth. Each local YMCA chapter will offer at least one program in each of the following key areas: (1) education, career, and life skills; (2) health, safety, and well-being; and (3) leadership and service learning. Specific activities include

- mentoring programs
- computer literacy classes
- basketball leagues
- drug prevention programs
- writing and literary arts centers
- teen leadership clubs
- recycling and environmental projects

To learn more about the YMCA and its Teen Action Agenda, go to their website at www.ymca.net.

Source: Office of Juvenile Justice and Delinquency Prevention Fact Sheet, *The YMCA's Teen Action Agenda* (Washington, DC: U.S. Department of Justice, 2001).

some sort of child care arrangement during a typical week, with 55 percent cared for by nonrelatives. Preschoolers spent an average of 28 hours per week in child care.[68] But children who spend a large amount of time in daycare may be more likely to develop behavioral problems than children who spend less time or children cared for only by parents.[69] According to Jay Belsky, 17 percent of children who spend over 30 hours a week in nonparental child care are more demanding, more noncompliant, and more aggressive, compared to only 6 percent of children who spend less than 10 hours a week. They are also more likely to engage in hitting, bullying, explosive behavior, and to demand a lot of attention. The solution may be problematic. Some critics argue that instead of reducing the time spent in childcare, *high-quality* child care should be expanded. According to a 1995 University of Colorado study, only 8 percent of day-care facilities were determined to be "high-quality" operations. What distinguished "high-quality" child care? They provided intense, personal attention over an extended period of time—the same thing that real mothers do. Thus, instead of expanding child care, other critics argue that mothers should be urged to work less and spend more time with their children.[70]

Parenting in Families

While the relationships among broken homes, absent fathers, and working mothers have been extensively studied, research findings are inconsistent. Perhaps delinquency has more to do with family process than with family structure, an idea proposed by F. Ivan Nye more than 40 years ago.[71] The link between family process variables and delinquency is examined next.

Parenting Skills

A standard assumption is that married adults automatically know how to be good parents. Presumably there is some universal common sense transmitted from one generation to the next. Yet perhaps parents of chronic delinquents not only do *not* know how to parent effectively but in many cases do not care—many may have almost no affection for their children.

Effective parenting depends on many things. The quality of parenting (as well as interactions within the family) changes as a child's misbehavior or delinquency increases over time. Often parents become angry and short-tempered with a child who consistently gets into trouble or disillusioned when they find they cannot believe what the child tells them. Over time, parent-child conflicts may escalate, or the relationship between parent and child may become more distant and alienated. In circumstances where the child's antisocial behavior is directed against the parents, many parents are less able to exercise reasonable parental authority and may even abdicate parental responsibilities altogether.[72]

Gerald Patterson found the type of deviance children engage in most is the type parents tolerate most. In the case of children who steal, for example:

> Many of the parents maintained that since they had never actually seen their child steal, they could not prove that their child had stolen, and therefore could not punish the child. In numerous instances, someone else had actually seen the child steal, but the child's "story" would be accepted by the

parents, who would then rise to the child's defense and accuse others of picking on the child. As the parents used the word "steal," it could be used as a label only if it could be proven, which was usually impossible; ergo the child did not really steal, ergo no punishment could be applied.[73]

James Snyder and Gerald Patterson have identified two divergent disciplinary styles that characterize families with delinquent children: enmeshed and lax. Parents who practice the *enmeshed* style are overly inclusive in what they define as problematic behavior. Even trivial misbehaviors by the child result in sharp parental reactions ranging from cajoling to verbal threats. But enmeshed parents "fail to consistently and effectively back up these verbal reprimands with nonviolent, nonphysical punishment . . . [and] inadvertently provide more positive consequences for deviant child behavior."[74] At the other extreme, parents who engage in the *lax* style tend to be very underinclusive in what they define as excessive or antisocial behavior.

Problem solving and negotiating disagreements or conflict are ways to forestall violence. Snyder and Patterson believe that parental violence often erupts at the end of a chain of events that began with a trivial incident like the child "sneaking" candy or food. To avoid such violence, parents must learn to break the chain and learn techniques of negotiating a settlement before minor matters get out of hand. (See Box 10–4 for more on family intervention strategies to reduce delinquency.)

It is arguable, however, whether Patterson's prescription can be effective for all parents. Travis Hirschi thinks not, noting four problems with Patterson's approach:

Corporal punishment is often criticized. However, is it possible that spanking is an effective means of anticipatory socialization for children? Does parental spanking send the message that behavior has consequences? In this sense, does spanking prepare youths for facing the legal consequences of their delinquency?

> The parents may not care for the child (in which case none of the other conditions would be met); the parents, even if they care, may not have the time or energy to monitor the child's behavior; the parents, even if they care and monitor, may not see anything wrong with the child's behavior; finally, even if everything else is in place, the parents may not have the inclination or the means to punish the child.[75]

Hirschi also reminds us that families with more children face greater strain on parental resources such as time and energy. And single-parent families (usually headed by a female) are strained even more:

> The single parent . . . must devote a good deal to support and maintenance activities that are at least to some extent shared in the two-parent family. Further, she must do so in the absence of psychological or social support. As a result, she is less able to devote time to monitoring and punishment, and is more likely to be involved in negative, abusive contacts with her children.[76]

Parental Supervision

Patterson's rules of parenting also note the need for effective parental supervision, such as establishing a set of "house rules" and clearly communicating them. House rules should cover whom the child associates with, places

BOX 10–4   DELINQUENCY PREVENTION
Reducing Delinquency by Strengthening Families

As this chapter has already illustrated, juvenile delinquency is greatly affected by the family environment, including structures and dynamics of parenting. Much research has established the importance of improving families and parenting practices as a means of combating delinquency. In an attempt to identify the most effective methods or practices for providing parents with the critical skills needed to strengthen families and promote resilience to delinquency in high-risk youth, the Office of Juvenile Justice and Delinquency Prevention launched its strengthening America's Families Initiative in the mid-1980s. Evaluations of more than 500 family-focused prevention strategies were reviewed in 1999 to identify those deemed most effective. Among those strategies regarded as exemplary models are the following:

- **The Incredible Years: Parents, Teachers, and Children Training Series** The parent-training curriculum of this series, designed for parents of children ages 3 to 12, focuses on strengthening parents' monitoring and disciplinary skills and building their confidence. The curriculum includes an 11-week basic program that uses videotapes depicting real-life situations. Parents meet in groups and cover topics such as Helping Children Learn, The Value of Praise and Encouragement, Effective Limit Setting, and Handling Misbehavior.
- **Strengthening Families Program** This 14-week family skills training program is designed to reduce risk factors for substance abuse and other problem behaviors. The program includes three separate courses: Parent Training, Children's Training, and Family Life Skills Training. Families with children ages 6 to 10 attend the program as a family. The parents and children attend separate sessions for the first hour of the program and then

come together as a family for the second hour to practice the skills they have learned. Parents learn strategies for effective family communication, problem solving, and limit setting while children learn about communication, social skills, and ways to resist peer pressure.

- **Prenatal and Early Childhood Nurse Home Visitation Program** This program is designed to improve the health and social functioning of low-income first-time mothers and their babies. Nurse home visitors develop a supportive relationship with the pregnant mother and family and provide them with information on personal and environmental health, maternal roles, life course development, and the value of support from family and friends. The home visits continue until the child reaches age two, with the frequency of visits varying depending on the child's age.
- **Multisystemic Therapy (MST)** The primary goals of this intensive home-based family treatment are to reduce rates of antisocial behavior in youths ages 10 to 18, reduce out-of-home placements, and empower families to resolve difficulties. Goals are developed in collaboration with the family, and family strengths are used as levers for change. MST treats factors in the youth's environment that are contributing to behavior problems in addition to addressing individual characteristics of the youth such as poor problem-solving skills, academic difficulties, or association with deviant peers.

Sources: Rose Alvarado and Karol Kumpfer, "Strengthening America's Families," *Juvenile Justice* 7:8–18 (2000); Carolyn Webster-Stratton, *The Incredible Years Training Series* (Washington, DC: Office of Juvenile Justice and Delinquency Prevention, 2000); Virginia Molgaard, Richard Spoth, and Cleve Redmond, *Competency Training: The Strengthening Families Program: For Parents and Youth 10–14* (Washington, DC: Office of Juvenile Justice and Delinquency Prevention, 2000); Stephen Bavolek, *The Nurturing Parenting Programs* (Washington, DC: Office of Juvenile Justice and Delinquency Prevention, 2000).

considered off limits, curfews, and when the child should be home from school. Parents must be aware of the child's performance in school as well as school attendance, the possibility of drug or alcohol use, and the activities the child is involved in with friends. "Good supervision . . . indirectly minimizes the adolescents' contact with delinquency–promoting circumstances, activities, and peers."[77]

Common sense suggests that unsupervised children are more likely to participate in delinquency, and substantial research confirms the relationship. For example, Grace Barnes and Michael Farrell studied a sample of 699 adolescents and their families and found that high parental monitoring, when combined with high parental support, was the key factor in preventing delinquency.[78] Jaana Haapasalo and Richard Tremblay examined aggressiveness in samples of more than 1,000 boys in Montreal in an attempt to predict which boys would become "fighters" and which would be "nonfighters." They concluded that nonfighters appeared to be the most supervised and that low levels of supervision were associated with higher levels of fighting.[79]

Does the national concern for unsupervised youths suggest that we think children lack human agency? Does society deny the humanity of children by constantly treating them as nonsentient babies?

Although the findings from a variety of studies report poor parental supervision to be a significant contributor to delinquency,[80] Sung Jang and Carolyn Smith suggest that parental supervision and delinquency is reciprocally related.[81] Their analysis of data from 838 urban adolescents led them to conclude that although parental supervision has a significant negative impact on delinquency, the impact of supervision tends to vary over time with its influence declining as adolescents mature. They also found that weak parental supervision not only promotes delinquency, but to the extent that the child is delinquent, his or her participation in delinquency then further leads to an erosion in the perception of effective parental supervision.[82]

Positive parenting involves interactions between parent and child that have positive effects on interpersonal, academic, and work skills for the child and that reinforce conventional values and norms. Positive parenting requires a consistent approach to the child, as well as positive feedback when the child behaves as desired.

Parenting Styles

The preceding discussion suggests that the style of parenting influences the behavior of children. According to Diana Baumrind, there are two critical aspects of parents' behavior toward children: parental responsiveness and parental demandingness. *Responsiveness* is the degree to which parents are supportive of the needs of their children. *Demandingness* is the extent to which parents demand age-appropriate behavior from children.[83]

Parents will vary on each dimension. They can be supportive and demand much (*authoritative*) or rejective and demand much (*authoritarian*). Similarly, parents can be supportive and demand very little (*indulgent*) or rejective and demand little (*indifferent*). A description of these four parenting styles follows (see Table 10–1):

Table10-1   Parental Styles

		DEMANDING	
		HIGH	LOW
SUPPORTIVE	HIGH	1	3
	LOW	2	4

1. **Authoritative parents** are warm but firm. They set standards for the child's conduct but form expectations consistent with the child's developing needs and capabilities. They place a high value on development of autonomy and self-direction but assume the ultimate responsibility for their child's behavior. Authoritative parents deal with their child in a rational, issue-oriented manner, frequently engaging in discussion and explanation with their children over rules and discipline.

2. **Authoritarian parents** place a high value on obedience and conformity, tending to favor more punitive, absolute, and forceful disciplinary measures. These parents are not responsive to their child and project little warmth and support. Verbal give-and-take is uncommon in authoritarian households, because authoritarian parents believe that the child should accept without question the rules and standards established by the parents. They tend not to encourage independent behavior and, instead, place importance on restricting a child's autonomy.

3. **Indulgent parents** behave in responsive, accepting, benign, and more passive ways in matters of discipline. They place relatively few demands on the child's behavior, giving the child a high degree of freedom to act as he or she wishes. Indulgent parents are more likely to believe that control is an infringement on the child's freedom that may interfere with healthy development. Instead of actively shaping their child's behavior, indulgent parents view themselves as resources the child may or may not use.

4. **Indifferent parents** are fairly unresponsive to their child and try to minimize the time and energy they must devote to interacting with the child or responding to the child's demands. In extreme cases, indifferent parents may be neglectful. They know little about their child's activities and whereabouts, show little interest in their child's experiences at school or in his or her friends, and rarely consider the child's opinion when making decisions. The child is typically ignored except when making demands on parents, which often results in hostile or explosive responses toward the child.

Elijah Anderson describes parenting styles of inner city black families using a rather different framework.[84] In his study of informal rules of interaction (what he refers to as the "code of the street") among members of a lower-income minority neighborhood on the near northwest side of Philadelphia, Anderson observed two distinct family types, each with its own pattern of parenting, coexisting in strained tension. The parenting styles of these "decent" and "street" families are discussed in Box 10–5.

BOX 10–5   A WINDOW ON DELINQUENCY
Decent Families and Street Families: Parenting Children in the Inner City

Sociologists have long known that not all children in poor inner-city neighborhoods with high-rates of delinquency are equally likely to become involved in criminal or violent behavior. Some children, growing up in the same apartment building, or the same block, and attending the same school become delinquent while others do not. Elijah Anderson believes that family differences, especially differences in parenting styles, account for a large part of these varying outcomes. One thing nearly all residents of such neighborhoods have in common is an alienation from mainstream America as a result of their daily financial struggles. But, Anderson argues, there are degrees of alienation represented by two polar types of families he calls "decent" and "street" families.

According to Anderson, decent families are characterized by a concern for the future and a work ethic aiming at building a good life. Holding more closely than street families to mainstream values, decent families reinforce hard work, saving money, and raising children to make something of themselves. The role of the "man of the house" reflects the traditional high value placed on male authority. In exchange for his protection of family members from threats, the husband-father "expects to rule his household and to get respect from the other members, and he encourages his sons to grow up with the same expectations."

Decent parents are more likely to be strict in child rearing and discipline, and they teach their children to respect authority and lead moral lives. While corporal punishment tends to be used in disciplining children, spankings are typically accompanied with explanations. Decent parents also express their love and concern for their adolescent children by discouraging any "loose" behavior, such as staying out late, being aggressive, or using drugs, that would be viewed as street behavior.

Street families, often having developed a deep-seated bitterness at the "system" as a result of racial discrimination and the absence of well-paying jobs, are more invested in the code of the street and are more likely to aggressively socialize their children into the values and norms of the street. This includes a lack of consideration for others and a very superficial understanding of and commitment to family and community. Anderson says that many street parents engage in self-destructive behaviors and expose their children to conflict and mayhem. Street children "come up hard." Their adult family role models are likely to be short-tempered, angry, verbally abusive, and physically aggressive. Children, victimized by the conflict and violence in their homes, learn to fight at a young age, not only in defense, but as a means for dealing with those who cross them.

Source: Elijah Anderson, *Code of the Street: Decency, Violence, and the Moral Life of the Inner City* (New York: W.W. Norton, 1999), pp. 35-49.

Parental Attachment

Another way parents influence the behavior of children is through emotional closeness. Presumably, children who like their parents will generally respect their wishes and stay out of trouble. Research supports the conclusion that the children least likely to turn to delinquency are those who feel loved, identify with their parents, and respect their parents' wishes. On the other hand, delinquents tend to lack a supportive relationship with their fathers, have minimal supervision of their activities, are closer to their mothers, and come from broken homes. Strongly attached children also are more likely to have more open communication with parents, and youths who have problems communicating with either parent or who communicate less frequently are more likely to engage in serious forms of delinquency.[85]

Likewise, parental love may reduce delinquency because it is something children do not want to lose. Randy LaGrange and Helen White found this to be true especially for juveniles in middle adolescence.[86] They suggest that attachment to a positive role model is important because it functions as a "psychological anchor" to conformity. For some adolescents, the attachment to parents is reflected in their family pride. That is, establishment of a positive family identity appears to significantly reduce levels of delinquency for white and black youths.[87]

Finally, the positive effects of attachment vary somewhat in single and intact families. Michelle Miller and her colleagues found that attachment to mothers and fathers in intact families was negatively related to delinquency. However, in single-mother households, parental attachment was negatively related to serious delinquency, but was inconsistently predictive of minor delinquency.[88]

Maltreatment of Children

Differential oppression theory, discussed in Chapter 8, suggests that adults in general, and parents in particular, attempt to establish and maintain order and social control in the home in ways that are broadly oppressive of children. In more rigid and authoritarian families, when children violate the rules they are punished, often severely. Its more severe form, **maltreatment**, includes physical and sexual abuse, physical neglect, lack of supervision, emotional maltreatment, educational maltreatment, and moral-legal maltreatment. In response to such maltreatment, a child is likely to develop a sense of powerlessness and impotency, leading to negative and often harmful adaptations–frequently, delinquency and adult criminality.

How extensive is the maltreatment of children, and what are its consequences? In 1999 about 3 million cases of child abuse or neglect were reported to the various state child protective services. Sixty percent of these cases were referred for investigation and slightly fewer than one-third of the investigated cases resulted in a disposition of either substantiated or indicated child maltreatment. About 60 percent of the estimated 826,000 victims of maltreatment suffered neglect, while 21 percent suffered physical abuse, and just over 11 percent were sexually abused. The highest victimization rates by age were for children under four years old (13.9 per 1,000) and rates declined as age increased. Victimization rates by race-ethnicity varied from a low of 4.4 per 1,000 for Asian-Pacific Islander children to 25.2 for black children. About 1,100 children died of abuse and neglect. Children younger than a year old accounted for 43 percent of the fatalities, and 86 percent were younger than six years of age.[89]

The nonlethal consequences of maltreatment are also serious. John Lemmon's study of a cohort of 632 male juveniles from low-income families reported a significant impact of maltreatment on initiation and continuation of delinquency.[90] The maltreated boys had significantly higher scores on all measures of delinquency, were more likely than their nonmaltreated counterparts to be referred to the juvenile court, and were more likely to be

Given the immediate and long-term consequences of suffering physical abuse as a child, should the penalties for various forms of child abuse and neglect be made more severe?

The short- and long-term consequences of dire child abuse, neglect, and maltreatment are very serious. Should notorious incidents of child abuse be punishable by death? Would sterilizing the parents who commit horrible acts of child abuse or incest be appropriate? If not, why not?

adjudicated delinquent. The maltreated group comprised the overwhelming majority of youths in the juvenile justice system, accounting for 84 percent of those youths receiving placement dispositions and 78 percent of those transferred to criminal court for prosecution. The maltreatment group also accounted for most of the serious delinquencies by juveniles: 78 percent of aggravated assaults, 83 percent of robberies, and 86 percent of weapons offenses. Male delinquents who had been maltreated were significantly more likely to be persistent and violent offenders, while nonmaltreated delinquents tended to be routine, infrequent offenders.[91] See Box 10–6 for a discussion of how Sweden's anti-spanking law affected rates of child abuse in that country.

John DiIulio is a strong supporter of families and parental involvement in children's lives, but he notes that

> I have never seen a kid who was violent and remorseless and had criminally violated others in a heinous way who was not himself or herself also terribly sinned against—severely abused and neglected, growing up in genuinely dire conditions of material deprivation, having absolutely no positive adult-child relationship in their lives.[92]

BOX 10–6   A CROSS-CULTURAL PERSPECTIVE ON DELINQUENCY
Has Sweden's Anti-Spanking Law Reduced Child Abuse?

Approximately two-thirds of Americans approve of spanking, down from 74 percent in 1946. College-educated parents are twice as likely to disapprove of spanking than are those who didn't complete high school, and whites are about twice as likely to disapprove of spanking as are blacks. Many anti-spanking advocates express concern that spanking children produces a variety of psychological and behavioral problems, including delinquency. Other anti-spankers are concerned that spanking a child is just the beginning of a slide down the slippery slope toward more serious forms of child abuse. For example, recent surveys report that nearly 20 percent of parents admit hitting their children on their bottoms with brushes, belts, or sticks, while

another 10 percent report spanking their children with "hard objects." In addition, about two-thirds of mothers with children under six years of age report spanking them at least three times a week.

In 1979, Sweden passed the first law prohibiting parents from spanking their children in a major effort to reduce child abuse. Five other countries soon followed, passing similar laws (Austria, Cyprus, Denmark, Finland, and Norway). Did Sweden's anti-spanking law actually reduce child abuse? Most of the evidence to date suggests that it did not. Robert Larzelere, director of residential research at Boys Town in Nebraska, has examined all of the published studies evaluating the Swedish spanking ban and concludes that "it has made little change in

(continues)

(continued)

problematic forms of physical punishment." While significantly fewer Swedish parents spanked their children or hit them with an object than American parents, more serious forms of physical punishment occurred more frequently in Sweden during the year after the ban than in the United States. Furthermore, Swedish police records indicate that reported child abuse of children under the age of seven actually increased 489 percent from 1981 to 1994.

Larzelere also reports that "the rate of beating a child up was three times as high in Sweden as in the United States, the rate of using a weapon was twice as high, and the overall rate of very severe violence was 49% higher in Sweden than the United States average." Moreover, "the rate of pushing, grabbing, or shoving was 39% higher in Sweden than the average rate in the United States." Larzelere concludes that although parents in Sweden were significantly less likely than American parents to spank their children, they were also significantly more likely to use physical aggression and to engage in child abuse than their American counterparts.

Larzelere believes that parents need to be empowered with "milder, effective disciplinary tactics" incorporating limited spanking. He and other experts argue that it is not so much whether parents spank their children, but *how* they spank them that makes a difference. Most "limited spanking" advocates argue that children under two years of age should never be spanked because the risk of serious physical injury is too great and that spanking adolescents may actually increase their misbehaviors. Spanking, they believe, is most effective with children between the ages of two and six, that spankings should be done in private to reduce humiliation, never done in anger, and applied only with an open hand on the child's bottom.

Sources: John Lyons and Robert Larzelere, "Where is Evidence that Non-Abusive Corporal Punishment Increases Aggression?" Paper presented at the XXVI International Congress of Psychology, Montreal, August 18, 1996; Lynn Rosellini, "When to Spank," Online, Available at http://Usnews.com/usnews/issue/980413/13span.htm (April 13, 1998); J.E. Durrant, "Evaluating the Success of Sweden's Corporal Punishment Ban," *Child Abuse & Neglect* 5:435–448 (1999); Robert Larzelere, "Child Abuse in Sweden," Online, Available at http://people.biola.edu/faculty/paulp/sweden2.html (April 25, 2001).

Conclusions

Probably few people would agree that the family has no effect at all on whether a child becomes delinquent. But what is the nature of that effect? What aspects of the family are most significant in this arena? Is it the inculcation of moral values? Is it the structure of the family? Is it working mothers? Or does it have more to do with parenting styles and degree of supervision? This chapter has explored these issues and presented what often appear to be conflicting findings from research.

Studies suggest that the relationship between divorce and single-parent families and delinquency exists but that it is strongest for girls and for trivial offenses. However, this finding may be misleading. Possibly, the relationship between broken or single-parent homes and delinquency may seem weak because these variables are separated by a number of important intervening variables. In other words, the absence of one parent may affect delinquency by producing weak attachments between the parent and child. Related work examines the relationship between mothers' working outside the home and delinquency. A small relationship has been detected. Research indicates that latchkey children suffer more from loneliness than from temptations of peer-influenced delinquency.

Parenting skills have a considerable effect on delinquency. Patterson's techniques for making children more conforming to conventional norms include reinforcing conformity and providing sane punishment for transgressions. But reinforcement alone is not enough, Patterson discovered, particularly with very problematic children. Research shows that parents can be taught how to be more effective and, in turn, their children's misbehavior will decline.

Child maltreatment, including abuse and neglect, is extensive. Nearly 3 million cases of abuse and neglect are reported each year, and about 1,100 children die each year as a result of maltreatment. The maltreatment of children also creates an oppressive environment that produces a variety of negative outcomes, including drug use, teen pregnancy, low academic achievement, emotional problems, *and* juvenile delinquency.

While the family is the most critical social institution, children may actually spend more time in direct interaction with other children and adults in another major social institution—the school. For at least nine months every year, from age 5 (or even younger) until about age 18, children spend nearly half their waking hours in school. Does this time in school deter or contribute to problem behaviors in children? The next chapter will explore the relationship between school and delinquency.

Key Terms

authoritarian parents: *Parents who place a high value on obedience and conformity, tending to favor more punitive, absolute, and forceful disciplinary measures.*

authoritative parents: *Parents who are warm but firm; they set standards of behavior for their child and highly value the development of autonomy and self-direction.*

indifferent parents: *Parents who are rather unresponsive to their child and may, in extreme cases, be neglectful.*

indulgent parents: *Parents who are more responsive, accepting, benign, and passive in matters of discipline and place few demands on their child.*

latchkey children: *Children who regularly care for themselves without adult supervision after school or on weekends.*

maltreatment: *Severe mistreatment of children, including physical and sexual abuse, physical neglect, lack of supervision, emotional maltreatment, educational maltreatment, and moral-legal maltreatment.*

single-parent families: *Families composed of children and one parent who is divorced or widowed or who was never married.*

socialization: *The process through which children learn the ways of a particular society or social group so that they can function within it.*

Getting Connected

Current statistics on families and children can be found at the following websites:

The Statistical Abstract of the United States

http://www.census.gov/statab/www/

1. In the 2001 Statistical Abstract of the United States, find Table 68. Compare marriage and divorce rates in the year you were born with the most current year. What has changed? What might explain these changes?
2. In the 2001 Statistical Abstract of the United States, find Table 71. Discuss any changes in birthrates among females in the "delinquency" age group.
3. In the 2001 Statistical Abstract of the United States, find Table 69. How has family income fared in the last twenty years? Is family income related to race or ethnicity?

U.S. Department of Health and Human Services

http://www.os.dhhs.gov

1. Get information on child care, then review the HHS Fact Sheet "HHS Child Care Programs." Which programs funded by this federal agency might be most effective in addressing juvenile delinquency?
2. Get information on fatherhood, then review the HHS Fact Sheet "HHS Fatherhood Initiative." What is this initiative? Is it related to delinquency prevention?
3. Get information on family assistance, then link to the Office of Family Assistance. What is TANF and how does it assist families?

A number of family and child advocacy groups maintain useful websites. Two of them are

The Children's Defense Fund and Children Now.

http://www.childrensdefense.org

1. Find the Parents Resource Network and link on the CDF resources. Evaluate the ten ways in which parents can "stand for children" every day. Would implementing these ten ideas have an impact on juvenile delinquency?
2. Find the Parents Resource Network and link on the national resources. Choose an issue area, then evaluate whether information available on these links might help reduce juvenile delinquency.
3. According to CDF national data, how much does it cost to raise a child?

http://www.childrennow.org

1. What is the "Fair Play" video game study?
2. Discuss three findings of the "Fair Play" study which are closely related to family issues.
3. Does your state have groups or activities similar to this organization's "working families" concerns?

The National Clearinghouse on Child Abuse and Neglect Information provides current information on the nature and extent of child maltreatment. They can be found at:

http://www.calib.com/nccanch/

1. What is Child Abuse Prevention Month?
2. What kinds of resources are in the child abuse prevention "tool kit"?
3. According to this site, what are some solutions to the child abuse problem?

Endnotes

1. Douglas Morrison, *Juvenile Offenders* (New York: D. Appleton and Co., 1915), p. 121.
2. Frederick Elkin and Gerald Handel, *The Child and Society: The Process of Socialization*, 4th ed. (New York: Random House, 1984).
3. Craig Calhoun, Donald Light, and Suzanne Keller, *Sociology*, 7th ed. (New York: McGraw-Hill, 1997), pp. 132–133.
4. William Bennett, *The Book of Virtues* (New York: Simon & Schuster, 1993), p. 11.
5. James Q. Wilson, *On Character* (Washington, DC: AEI Press, 1991), pp. 30, 108.
6. Robert Coles, *The Moral Intelligence of Children* (New York: Random House, 1997), p. 17.
7. The Children's Defense Fund, "Every Child Deserves a Moral Start" (Washington, DC: CDF Reports, March, 1998).
8. Bruce Chadwick and Brent Top, "Religiosity and Delinquency Among LDS Adolescents," *Journal for the Scientific Study of Religion* 32:52 (1993).
9. See, for example, Charles Tittle and Michael Welch, "Religiosity and Deviance: Toward a Contingency Theory of Constraining Behavior," *Social Forces* 61:653–682 (1983); D. Brownfield and M. Sorenson, "Religion and Drug Use Among Adolescents: A Social Support Conceptualization and Interpretation," *Deviant Behavior* 12:259–276 (1991); Brent Benda and R. Corwin, "Religion and Delinquency: The Relationship After Considering Family and Peer Influence," *Journal for the Scientific Study of Religion* 36:81–92 (1997); Byron Johnson, Spencer Li, David Larson, and M. McCullough, "A Systematic Review of the Religiosity and Delinquency Literature: A Research Note," *Journal of Contemporary Criminal Justice* 16:32–52 (2000).
10. Byron Johnson, David Larson, Spencer Li, and Sung Jang, "Escaping from the Crime of Inner Cities: Church Attendance and Religious Salience Among Disadvantaged Youth," *Justice Quarterly* 17:377–391 (2000).
11. Johnson et al., note 10, p. 388.
12. Rodney Stark and William Bainbridge, *Religion, Deviance, and Social Control* (New York: Routledge, 1997), p. 69.
13. See, for example, Brent Benda, "An Examination of a Reciprocal Relationship Between Religiosity and Different Forms of Delinquency Within a Theoretical Model," *Journal of Research in Crime and Delinquency* 34:163–186 (1997); John Cochran, P. B. Wood, and B. Arneklev, "Is the Religiosity-Delinquency Relationship Spurious? A Test of Arousal and Social Control Theories," *Journal of Research in Crime and Delinquency* 31:92–123 (1994); R. Fernquist, "A Research Note on the Association Between Religion and Delinquency," *Deviant Behavior* 16:169–175 (1995); Paul Higgins and Gary Albrecht, "Hellfire and Delinquency Revisited," *Social Forces* 55:952–958 (1977).
14. Stark and Bainbridge, note 12, p. 7.
15. J. Ross Eshleman, *The Family: An Introduction*, 8th ed. (Boston: Allyn and Bacon, 1997), pp. 323–324.
16. Travis Hirschi, "The Family," in *Crime*, edited by James Q. Wilson and Joan Petersilia (San Francisco: ICS Press, 1995), pp. 128–129.
17. Hirschi, note 16.
18. U.S. Census Bureau, *Current Population Reports* (Washington, DC: U.S. Bureau of the Census, 2001); U.S. Census Bureau, *Current Population Reports*, pp. 20–450, and earlier reports (Washington, DC: U.S. Census Bureau, 1997).
19. Barbara Kantrowitz and Pat Wingert, "Unmarried, with Children," *Newsweek,* May 28:48 (2001).
20. U.S. Census Bureau, note 18.
21. Federal Interagency Forum on Child and Family Statistics, *America's Children: Key National Indicators of Well-Being 2000* (Washington, DC: U.S. Government Printing Office, 2000), p. 7.
22. Linda Gordon and Sara McLanahan, "Single Parenthood in 1900," *Journal of Family History* 16:97, 100–101 (1991).
23. David Blankenhorn, *Fatherless America: Confronting our Most Urgent Social Problem* (New York: Basic Books, 1995), pp. 23, 239.
24. Stephanie Ventura, Sally Curtin, and T.J. Mathews, *Variations in Teenage Birth Rates, 1991–98: National and State Trends* (Washington, DC: U.S. Department of Health and Human Services, 2000); Sally Curtin and Joyce Martin, *Births: Preliminary Data for 1999* (Washington, DC: U.S. Department of Health and Human Services, 2000); Stephanie Ventura and Christine Bachrach, *Nonmarital Childbearing in the United States, 1940–99* (Washington, DC: U.S. Department of Health and Human Services, 2000).
25. Federal Interagency Forum on Child and Family Statistics, note 21, p. 6
26. Federal Interagency Forum on Child and Family Statistics, note 21, p. 14.
27. Federal Interagency Forum on Child and Family Statistics, note 21, p. 14.
28. Hirschi, note 16, p. 138.
29. Terence Thornberry, Evelyn Wei, Magda Stouthamer-Loeber, and Joyce Van Dyke, *Teenage Fatherhood and Delinquent Behavior* (Washington, DC: Office of Juvenile Justice and Delinquency Prevention, 2000).

30. Thornberry, et al., note 29, pp. 5–6.

31. Thornberry, et al., note 29, p. 7.

32. Maxine Seaborn Thompson and Margaret Ensminger, "Psychological Well-Being Among Mothers with School Age Children," *Social Forces* 67:715–730 (1989); James Q. Wilson, *The Moral Sense* (New York: The Free Press, 1993), p. 176; K. Alison Clarke-Stewart, Deborah Vandell, and Kathleen McCartney, "Effects of Parental Separation and Divorce on Very Young Children," *Journal of Family Psychology* 14:304–326 (2000).

33. Jeffrey Grogger, "Incarceration-Related Costs of Early Childbearing," in *Kids Having Kids: Economic Costs and Social Consequences of Teen Pregnancy*, edited by Rebecca Maynard (Washington, DC: The Urban Institute Press, 1997), p. 253.

34. Lisa Borrine, Paul Handa, and Nancy Brown, "Family Conflict and Adolescent Adjustment in Intact, Divorced, and Blended Families," *Journal of Consulting and Clinical Psychology* 59:753–755 (1991); Joan Kelly, "Children's Adjustment in Conflicted Marriage and Divorce: A Decade Review of Research," *Journal of the American Academy of Child and Adolescent Psychiatry* 39:963–973 (2000).

35. Cited in Wilson, note 5, p. 72.

36. National Center for Health Statistics, *Monthly Vital Statistics Report*, 43(9), Supplement, DHHS Publication No. 95 1120 (Hyattsville, MD: Public Health Service, 1995).

37. Susan Chira, "Multiple Divorce Hard on Kids," *The Denver Post*, March 19:16A (1995).

38. See for example, David Demo and Alan Acock, "The Impact of Divorce on Children," *Journal of Marriage and the Family* 50:619–648 (1988); George Thomas, Michael Farrell, and Grace Barnes, "The Effects of Single-Mother Families and Nonresident Fathers on Delinquency and Substance Abuse in Black and White Adolescents," *Journal of Marriage and the Family* 58:884–894 (1996); Edward Wells and Joseph Rankin, "Families and Delinquency: A Meta-Analysis of the Impact of Broken Homes," *Social Problems* 38:71–93 (1991); Roy Austin, "Race, Female Headship, and Delinquency: A Longitudinal Analysis," *Justice Quarterly* 9:585–607 (1992).

39. Ann Goetting, "Patterns of Homicide Among Children," *Criminal Justice and Behavior* 16:63–80 (1989).

40. Wells and Rankin (1991), note 38.

41. Michelle Miller, Finn-Aage Esbensen, and Adrienne Freng, "Parental Attachment, Parental Supervision and Adolescent Deviance in Intact and Non-Intact Families," *Journal of Crime & Justice* 22:1–29 (1999).

42. Jeffrey Cookston, "Parental Supervision and Family Structure: Effects on Adolescent Problem Behaviors," *Journal of Divorce & Remarriage* 32:107–122 (1999).

43. Sadi Bayrakal and Teresa Kope, "Dysfunction in the Single-Parent and Only-Child Family," *Adolescence* 25:1–7 (1990).

44. Sanford Dornbusch, J. Merrill Carlsmith, Steven Bushwall, Philip Ritter, Herbert Leiderman, Albert Hastorf, and Ruth Gross, "Single Parents, Extended Households, and the Control of Adolescents," *Child Development* 56:326–341 (1985).

45. Laurence Steinberg, "Single Parents, Stepparents, and the Susceptibility of Adolescents to Antisocial Peer Pressure," *Child Development* 58:269–275 (1987).

46. John Laub and Robert Sampson, "Unraveling Families and Delinquency," *Criminology* 26:355–380 (1988); Ross Matsueda, "Testing Control Theory and Differential Association," *American Sociological Review* 47:489–504 (1982).

47. Jan Sokol-Katz, Roger Dunham, and Rick Zimmerman, "Family Structure Versus Parental Attachment in Controlling Adolescent Deviant Behavior: A Social Control Model," *Adolescence* 32:199–215 (1997).

48. Marc Zimmerman, Deborah Salem, and Kenneth Maton, "Family Structure and Psychosocial Correlates Among Urban African-American Adolescent Males," *Child Development* 55: 1598–1613 (1995).

49. Mavis Hetherington, *Review of Child Development Research* (New York: Russell Sage Foundation, 1977); Mavis Hetherington and Ross Parke, *Contemporary Readings in Social Psychology* (New York: McGraw-Hill Publishing Co., 1981); Mavis Hetherington and Ross Parke, *Child Psychology* (New York: McGraw-Hill Publishing Co., 1979).

50. Nicholas Davidson, "Life Without Father," *Policy Review* 51:40–44 (1990).

51. Judith Wallerstein and Joan Berlin Kelly, *Surviving the Breakup* (New York: Basic Books, 1980).

52. Judith Wallerstein and Sandra Blakeslee, *Second Chances* (New York: Ticknor and Fields, 1989).

53. U.S. Bureau of Census, note 18, Reports No. 653 and 655.

54. Russell Hill and Frank Stafford, "Parental Care of Children," *Journal of Human Resources* 15:219–239 (1979).

55. Keith Melville, *Marriage and the Family Today*, 4th edition (New York: Random House, 1988), p. 352.

56. Matthijs Kalmijn, "Mother's Occupational Status and Children's Schooling," *American Sociological Review* 59: 257–275 (1994).

57. Jay Belsky, "Parental and Nonparental Child Care and Children's Socioemotional Development: A Decade in Review," *Journal of Marriage and the Family* 52:885–903 (1990); Jay Belsky and David Eggebeen, "Early and Extensive Maternal Employment and Young Children's Socioemotional Development: Children of the National Longitudinal Survey of Youth," *Journal of Marriage and the Family* 53: 1083–1110 (1991).

58. Travis Hirschi, *Causes of Delinquency* (Berkeley, CA: University of California Press, 1969).

59. Mary Gray Riege, "Parental Affection and Juvenile Delinquency in Girls," *British Journal of Criminology* 12:55–73 (1972); Prodipto Roy, "Adolescent Roles," *The Employed Mother in America*, edited by F. Ivan Nye and Lois Wladis Hoffman (Chicago: Rand McNally, 1963).

60. U.S. Bureau of Census, note 18, Report No. 655.

61. David Popenoe, *Life Without Father: Compelling Evidence that Fatherhood and Marriage are Indispensable for the Good of Children and Society* (New York: The Free Press, 1996), p. 6.

62. April Brayfield, "Juggling Jobs and Kids: The Impact of Employment Schedules on Fathers' Caring for Children," *Journal of Marriage and the Family* 57:321–332 (1995).

63. "Middle-School Kids Battle for the Right to Stay Home Alone," *The Wall Street Journal* (Sept. 1, 1999), p. B1.

64. Laurence Steinberg, "Latchkey Children and Susceptibility to Peer Pressure," *Developmental Psychology* 22:433–439 (1986).

65. Susan Byrne, "Nobody Home," *Psychology Today* 10:40–47 (1977).

66. Lawrence Kutner, "Parents of Latchkey Children Need to Make the Most of an Undesired Situation," *The New York Times*, October 19:B6 (1989).

67. Michael Resnick et al., "Protecting Adolescents from Harm: Findings from the National Longitudinal Study on Adolescent Health," *JAMA* 278:823–865 (1997).

68. Federal Interagency Forum on Child and Family Statistics, note 21, p. 10; U. S. Census Bureau, *Who's Minding the Kids? Child Care Arrangements* (Washington, DC: U.S. Bureau of the Census, 2000), p. 2.

69. Valerie Strauss, "New Studies Prompt New Worries on Child Care," *The Washington Post* (April 30, 2001), p. A1; Marilyn Elias, "Day Care Linked to Aggression," *USA Today* (April 19, 2001), p. 1A; Barbara Kantrowitz, "A New Battle Over Day Care," *Newsweek* (April 30, 2001), 38.

70. Richard Lowry, "Nasty, Brutish, and Short: Children in Day Care—and the Mothers Who Put Them There," *National Review*, May 28:36–42 (2001).

71. F. Ivan Nye, *Family Relationships and Delinquent Behavior* (New York: John Wiley & Sons, 1958).

72. Rolf Loeber, *Families and Crime* (Washington, DC: U.S. Department of Justice, 1988).

73. Gerald Patterson, "Children Who Steal," *Understanding Crime*, edited by Travis Hirschi and Michael Gottfredson (Beverly Hills, CA: Sage Publications, 1980), p. 82.

74. James Snyder and Gerald Patterson, "Family Interaction and Delinquent Behavior," *Handbook of Juvenile Delinquency*, edited by Herbert Quay, (New York: John Wiley & Sons, 1987), p. 221.

75. Travis Hirschi, "Crime and the Family," *Crime and Public Policy*, edited by James Q. Wilson (San Francisco: Institute for Contemporary Studies Press, 1983), p. 55.

76. Hirschi, note 75, p. 62.

77. Patterson, note 73, p. 227.

78. Grace Barnes and Michael Farrell, "Parental Support and Control as Predictors of Adolescent Drinking, Delinquency, and Related Problem Behaviors," *Journal of Marriage and the Family* 54:763–776 (1992).

79. Jaana Haapasalo and Richard Tremblay, "Physically Aggressive Boys from Ages 6 to 12: Family Background, Parenting Behavior, and Prediction of Delinquency," *Journal of Consulting and Clinical Psychology* 62:1044–1052 (1994).

80. See for example, Robert Sampson and John Laub, "Urban Poverty and the Family Context of Delinquency: A New Look at Structure and Process in a Classic Study," *Child Development* 65:523–540 (1994); Patrick Heaven, "Family of Origin, Personality, and Self-Reported Delinquency," *Journal of Adolescence* 17:445–459 (1994); Cookston, note 42; Miller et al., note 41.

81. Sung Jang and Carolyn Smith, "A Test of Reciprocal Causal Relationships Among Parental Supervision, Affective Ties, and Delinquency," *Journal of Research in Crime and Delinquency* 34:307–336 (1997).

82. Jang and Smith, note 81.

83. Diana Baumrind, "Parental Disciplinary Patterns and Social Competence in Children," *Youth and Society* 9:239–276 (1978); Diana Baumrind, "The Influence of Parenting Style on Adolescent Competence and Substance Use," *Journal of Early Adolescence* 11:56–95 (1991); Diana Baumrind, "Parenting Styles and Adolescent Development," *The Encyclopedia of Adolescence*, edited by Richard Lerner, Anne Petersen, and Jeanne Brooks-Gunn (New York: Garland Publishing Company, 1991).

84. Elijah Anderson, *Code of the Street: Decency, Violence, and the Moral Life of the Inner City* (New York: W.W. Norton & Co., 1999).

85. Robert Sampson and John Laub, *Crime in the Making: Pathways and Turning Points Through Life* (Cambridge, MA: Harvard University Press, 1993); Richard Clark and Glenn Shields, "Family Communication and Delinquency," *Adolescence* 32:81–92 (1997); Karla Klein, Rex Forehand, Lisa Armistead, and Patricia Long, "Delinquency During the Transition to Early Adulthood: Family and Parenting Predictors from Early Adolescence," *Adolescence* 32: 61–79 (1997); Bobbi Anderson, Malcolm Holmes, and Erik Ostresh, "Male and Female Delinquents' Attachments and Effects of Attachments on Severity of Self-Reported Delinquency," *Criminal Justice and Behavior* 26:435–452 (1999).

86. Randy LaGrange and Helen White, "Age Differences in Delinquency," *Criminology* 23:19–45 (1985).
87. Linda Weber, Andrew Miracle, and Tom Skehan, "Family Bonding and Delinquency: Racial and Ethnic Influences Among U.S. Youth," *Human Organization* 54: 363–372 (1995).
88. Miller et al., note 41, p. 21.
89. U.S. Department of Health and Human Services, *Child Maltreatment 1999* (Washington, DC: U.S. Government Printing Office, 2001).
90. John Lemmon, "How Child Maltreatment Affects Dimensions of Juvenile Delinquency in a Cohort of Low-Income Urban Youths," *Justice Quarterly* 16:357–376 (1999).
91. Lemmon, note 90, p. 372-373.
92. John DiIulio, "With Unconditional Love," *Sojourners* 26:16 (1997).

Chapter 11

Schools and Delinquency

"School sucks."

—Emily, 15-year-old high school student

On countless occasions students have told us "school sucks." When we ask what sucks about school, they tell us it is the principal, teachers, coaches, students, cafeteria, library, athletic teams, cheerleaders, mascot, band, and the parking lot. Something else they say sucks about school is the crime.

School Crime and Safety

Crime committed in our nation's schools continues to be a concern.[1] Even though school crime has decreased in recent years, theft and violence at school can still lead to disruptive and threatening environments, adversely affecting student academic performance. In 1999, students were victims of roughly 2.5 million nonfatal crimes (theft plus violent crime) at school. About 880,000 of these were violent crimes such as rape, sexual assault, robbery, and aggravated and simple assaults. The victims were evenly distributed between males and females. (See Chapter 3 for a discussion of fatal student victimizations in schools.)

Student Victimization

Students are victims of a wide range of nonfatal offenses in school, including threats and injuries, bullying, exposure to hate words and hate graffiti, and having property stolen or deliberately damaged. Oftentimes, in some schools, these violations are committed by street gang members (see Chapter 12). Street gangs can be very disruptive to schools. They create fear among students and increase the level of violence in schools.

Between 1995 to 1999, the percentage of students who reported street gangs at their schools decreased. In 1995, 29 percent of students reported street gangs being present in their schools. By 1999, this percentage had fallen to 17 percent. In part, the decline in the percentage of street gangs in schools is the result of policies and programs such as those reviewed in Box 11–1.

One reason that schools are characterized by delinquency is that they warehouse people ages 14 through 18. These are the most criminogenic ages. Thus, is a school-delinquency connection inevitable given the age effect?

Weapons   Every year, students are threatened or injured with a weapon while they are on school property. The percentage of students who are victimized in this way provides an important measure of how safe schools are and how this is changing over time. The percentage of students who were threatened or injured with a weapon on school property has remained constant in recent years. In 1993, 1995, 1997, and 1999, about 7 to 8 percent of students reported being threatened or injured with a weapon such as a gun, knife, or club on school property (see Figure 11–1). In each survey year, males were more likely than females to report being threatened or injured with a weapon on school property. For example, in 1999, 10 percent of males reported being threatened or injured in the past year, compared with 6 percent of females. There were no racial/ethnic differences in the percentages of students being threatened or injured with a weapon on school property in 1999.

BOX 11–1   A WINDOW ON DELINQUENCY
Combating Gangs

There are street gangs in about 29 percent of our schools. Street gangs are often involved in drugs, weapons trafficking, and violence. Their presence in schools can be very disruptive to the school environment. Schools have responded in a variety of ways to combat gangs. Some school districts have established specific regulations that govern the dress or behavior of youth by barring specific types of dress, activities, or property (for example, pagers) from school grounds. One common rule aimed at gang members is the prohibition of gang attire or colors or hairstyle. Some schools have adopted school uniforms as an alternative to clothing prohibitions. There also is court precedent for schools' outlawing gang members. Schools may extend the bar to gang membership to the barring of gang symbols, hand signals, or other actions furthering gang interests, such as recruitment of new members on school grounds.

Nonpunitive school responses include education and training programs designed to increase youth resistance to gangs, peer mentoring, and the development of vocational skills and creation of future job opportunities as clear and realistic alternatives to the perceived benefits of membership in a gang. For example,

Project BUILD (Broader Urban Involvement and Leadership Development) on Chicago's North Side provides a series of 12 classroom sessions in the local schools, informing students about the dangers and consequences of gang membership. In addition, the BUILD prevention staff invite at-risk students to participate in after-school athletics and job-skills training workshops, as well as a variety of social and recreational activities. Early evaluations suggest that students involved in the BUILD program are significantly less likely to be recruited into street gangs. Another school-based antigang program, Se Puede ("You Can") in San Juan, Texas, aims to prevent at-risk middle school youths from becoming involved with gangs, gun violence, and drugs and to improve their academic performance by providing counseling, positive alternatives and role models, lessons on substance abuse and violence, and monthly weekend camping experiences in which small groups of students learn survival skills and develop relationships with mentors.

Sources: James Howell, *Youth Gang Programs and Strategies* (Washington, DC: Office of Juvenile Justice and Delinquency Prevention, 2000); *Olesen v. Board of Education,* 676 F. Supp. 821 (N.D. Ill 1987); David Thompson and Leonard Jason, "Street Gangs and Preventive Interventions," *Criminal Justice and Behavior* 15:323–333 (1988).

Bullying   Negative acts by students carried out against other students repeatedly over time is called **bullying**. It contributes to a climate of fear and intimidation in schools. There are four types of bullying that regularly take place on school property:

1. *Physical bullying,* which involves hitting, kicking, spitting, pushing, and taking personal belongings;
2. *Verbal bullying,* which includes taunting, malicious teasing, name calling, and making threats;

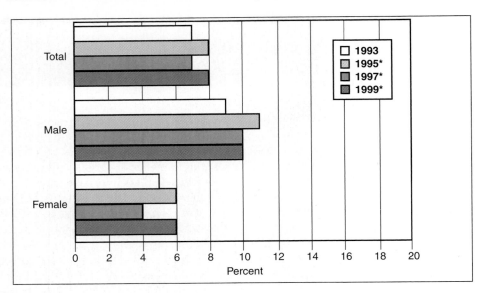

Figure 11–1

Percentage of students who reported being threatened or injured with a weapon on school property during the last 12 months, 1993, 1995, 1997, and 1999

Source: Phillip Kaufman, Xianglei Chen, Susan Choy, Katharin Peter, Sally Ruddy, Amanda Miller, Jill Fleury, Kathryn Chandler, Michael Planty, and Michael Rand, *Indicators of School Crime and Safety: 2001* (Washington, DC: U.S. Departments of Education and Justice, 2001).

3. *Emotional bullying,* which encompasses spreading rumors, manipulating social relationships, or engaging in social exclusion, extortion, or intimidation; and

4. *Sexual bullying,* which involves harassment and actual abuse.[2]

Bullying occurs every day in school and most bullying never comes to the attention of school officials. The National Institute of Child Health and Human Development (NICHD) estimates that about 17 percent of school-aged children have been bullied "sometimes" or "weekly," 19 percent had bullied others "sometimes" or "weekly," and 6 percent had both bullied and been bullied. According to one calculation, nearly 2 million children are bullied at least once a week and about the same number of children bully others just as often.[3] While boys and girls are equally likely to be bullied, they are bullied differently. Girls tend to be the victims of rumors, innuendo, and character assassination, whereas boys are usually physically bullied.[4]

Bullying has long- and short-term consequences for both those who are bullied and bullies. Children who are bullied often feel lonely, have trouble making friends, and do not get along well with classmates. Sometimes they are insecure, embarrass easily, have low self-esteem, and are fearful of

Tracking is often maligned for its effects on student self-esteem. However, should bullies be permitted to constantly interact with and victimize other students? Should bullies be placed in separate schools resembling boot camps?

Bullying has been cited as a cause of school violence. Is bullying taken more seriously now than in prior eras? What characteristics increase the likelihood that a child will be bullied in school?

attending school. The impact of chronic childhood bullying often follows them into adulthood where they face substantial risks of suffering from depression, schizophrenia, and committing suicide.[5]

Children who bully are also affected by their own behavior. Bullying is typically only one of their problems. They also may abuse animals, vandalize buildings, shoplift, drop out of school, fight, and use illegal drugs and alcohol (see Box 11–2). According to Dan Olweus and Susan Limber, bullies are more likely to be chronic offenders and adult criminals (see Chapter 2). They also found that 60 percent of boys who bullied in grades 6 through 9 were convicted of at least one crime as adults, compared with 23 percent of boys who did not bully. More striking is that 40 percent of boys who bullied had three or more convictions by age 24, compared with only 10 percent of boys who did not bully.[6]

Hate Words and Hate Graffiti   Related to bullying are hate words and hate graffiti. A student's exposure to hate-related words and symbols at school can increase feelings of vulnerability. An environment in which students are confronted with discriminatory behavior is not conducive to learning and creates a climate of hostility.

Is bullying a genuine social problem or a minor nuisance that many people experience at some point in their lives? Which way has bullying been presented recently? For example, do you believe that bullying contributed to the shooting at Columbine High School?

BOX 11-2   A WINDOW ON DELINQUENCY
Animal Abuse and Youth Violence

There has been a resurgence of interest in the relation between animal cruelty and violent crime among juvenile offenders. Every state has a law prohibiting animal cruelty. While the language of the laws varies from state to state, animal cruelty is generally defined as "socially unacceptable behavior that intentionally causes unnecessary pain, suffering, or distress to and/or death of an animal."

As with other forms of abuse, animal cruelty varies in its frequency, severity, and duration, and ranges from the developmentally immature teasing of animals (e.g., a toddler pulling on a kitten's tail) to serious animal torture (e.g., setting a cat on fire).

Criminologists believe animal abuse and violent behavior toward humans share common characteristics: Both types of victims are living creatures, have a capacity for experiencing pain, can display physical signs of their pain, and may die as a result of inflicted injuries.

It has been reported in research that animal abuse may be characteristic of the developmental histories of between 25 and 67 percent of violent offenders. Other research has reported that juveniles who abuse animals share common life experiences. In two recent studies, for example, animal abuse has been linked to corporal punishment. It has been found that children who are physically and sexually abused are much more likely to hurt animals.

Attending to animal abuse is not a panacea for dealing with the challenges of identifying and addressing youth violence. Violent behavior in children is multidimensional and multidetermined, and its developmental course is still the subject of concerted research investigation. However, animal abuse has received insufficient attention as being one of the "red flags," warning signs, or sentinel behaviors that could help identify youths at risk for perpetrating interpersonal violence and youths who have themselves been victimized.

Source: Frank Ascione, *Animal Abuse and Youth Violence* (Washington, DC: U.S. Department of Justice, 2001).

In 1999, about 13 percent of students reported that someone at school had used hate-related words against them. Specifically, they were called a derogatory word having to do with their religion, sex, race/ethnicity, disability, size, or sexual orientation. In addition, about 36 percent of students were exposed to hate-related graffiti at school.

Students in urban, suburban, and rural schools were equally likely to report being the victim of hate-related words and to have seen hate-related graffiti. Girls were more likely than boys to be targets of derogatory words and were also more likely to report seeing hate-related graffiti at their school. About 14 percent of females report being called hate words in 1999 compared with 12 percent of males. About 39 percent of girls in 1999 had seen hate-related graffiti compared with 34 percent of males.

Black students are more likely than white or Latino students to be called hate words. About 17 percent of black students have reported they have been the targets of derogatory words compared with 13 percent of white students and 12 percent of Latino students. Students of all racial/ethnic groups are equally likely to report hate-related graffiti at school.

Stolen and Damaged Property   Students also have their personal property stolen or deliberately damaged at school. While less harmful than attacks on students themselves, such crimes have financial consequences and can divert students' attention from their studies as well as contribute to perceptions of schools as unsafe places.

About one-third of all students in grades 9 through 12 said that someone had stolen or deliberately damaged their property, such as their car, clothing, or books, on school property during the last 12 months. Boys are more likely than girls to report being victims of theft or deliberate property damage on school grounds. About 40 percent of boys compared to 28 percent of girls have had their property stolen or deliberately damaged.

Consequences of Student Victimization   One consequence of an unsafe school environment is the fear it instills in students. Students who fear for their own safety may not be able or ready to learn. Concerns about vulnerability to attacks by others at school may also have a detrimental effect on the school environment and learning. Between 1995 and 1999, there were decreases in the percentages of students feeling unsafe while they were at school. In 1995, 9 percent of students sometimes or most of the time feared they were going to be attacked or harmed at school, while in 1999 this percentage fell to 5 percent. However, in both years, larger percentages of (1) black and Latino students than whites and (2) students in urban than in suburban or rural schools feared being attacked at school.

Another consequence of crime in school is that students begin to perceive specific areas in the school as unsafe. In trying to ensure their own safety, they begin to avoid these areas. Changes in the percentage of students avoiding areas in school may be a good barometer of how safe schools are, at least in the minds of students who attend these schools.

Between 1995 and 1999, there was a decrease in the percentage of students who avoided one or more places in school, from 9 percent in 1995 to 5 percent in 1999. Despite this decline, this percentage still represents over 1 million students in 1999 who reported avoiding some areas in school out of fear for their own safety.

Teacher Victimization

Students are not the only persons targeted for crime at school. Teachers are also the victims of violence and theft. In addition to the personal toll such violence takes on teachers, those who worry about their safety may have difficulty teaching and may leave the profession altogether.

Four students and one teacher were killed and several others were wounded, such as teacher Sara Lynette Thetford (pictured), during a rampage at Westside Middle School in Jonesboro, Arkansas. Should the young perpetrators of lethal violence be punished as juveniles or adults? Would either sanction help protect against future incidents of lethal school violence?

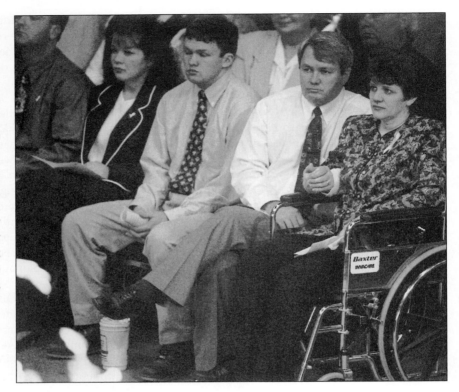

Over the 5-year period from 1995 to 1999, teachers were the victims of approximately 1,708,000 nonfatal crimes at school, including 1,073,000 thefts and 635,000 violent crimes (rape or sexual assault, robbery, aggravated assault, and simple assault). On average, this translates into 342,000 nonfatal crimes per year, or 79 crimes per 1,000 teachers per year. Among the violent crimes against teachers during this five-year period, there were about 69,000 serious violent crimes, including rape or sexual assault, robbery, and aggravated assault. On average, this translates into 14,000 serious violent crimes per year.

Some teachers are more likely than others to be crime victims. For example, from 1995 through 1999:

1. High school and middle school teachers were more than twice as likely as elementary school teachers to be victims of violent crime.
2. High school and middle school teachers were also about twice as likely as elementary school teachers to be victims of property crimes.
3. Male teachers were more than twice as likely as female teachers to be victims of violent crime.

Furthermore, teachers are differentially victimized depending on the location of the school in which they teach. From 1994 through 1998, urban teachers were more likely to be victims of violent and property crimes than either teachers in rural or suburban schools.

Do Schools Have a Stay-In or a Dropout Problem?

All forms of crime and violence contribute to a climate of fear and intimidation in schools that can make learning and teaching very difficult. Criminologists have come up with a number of ways of making the school environment more conducive to learning (see Box 11–3). Some suggest that students need to be offered parenting classes and provided with family support services.[7] Others blame the problem on schools being too large and impersonal with too many pupils in each classroom.[8] A more controversial recommendation is offered by Jackson Toby.

The Stay-In Problem

According to Toby, schools are unsafe because they have a *stay-in problem*, not a dropout problem. "Stay-in" students earn bad grades (F's and D's), disrupt classes, and interfere with the education of children who go to school to be educated. In describing an interview with a young man named Joe, Toby tells us about the type of student who causes the stay-in problem:

> "I like school," Joe said. I was surprised. Most delinquents I had known hated school and did poorly in their schoolwork. "What did you like about it?" I asked. He told me about sitting in the lunchroom with his gang and having food fights, about "making out" in the halls with his girlfriends, . . . about harassing a young, inexperienced teacher. . . . "What about your classes?" I asked. "Did you like them?" "Yeah," he replied. "I liked gym." Did he like English, math, or anything else in the curriculum? "No," he replied, smiling. "They weren't in my curriculum.[9]

Criminologist Jackson Toby has unique views on school delinquency; namely, he believes that too many disruptive students are permitted to remain in school when they should be encouraged to drop out. Do American schools have a "stay-in" problem?

Joe was a perpetual disruption to the education of other students. While a school can tolerate a few students like Joe, when there are many like him the education of all students will be compromised. Toby thinks schools must get rid of students like Joe and suggests how to do it:

1. Lower the age students can quit school from 16 to 15.
2. Abolish rules that tie Aid to Families with Dependent Children (AFDC) to continued school enrollment.
3. Create a subminimum wage for teens that would give them the opportunity to work in the legal job market.[10]

Toby's critics believe that if his proposals were implemented, the number of children dropping out of school would increase, which would lead to more delinquency.[11]

BOX 11-3   DELINQUENCY PREVENTION
Preventing School Crime and Violence

Nearly every school district in the United States has a dropout prevention program. One program with impressive results is in New York City. Students with good attendance records who demonstrate good behavior are given jobs upon graduation. Jobs can have an enormously stabilizing influence on youngsters whose lives are in turmoil.

Another type of dropout prevention program is more punitive. In West Virginia, juveniles who drop out of school are denied a driver's license. If a student misses 10 consecutive days or 15 total days during a semester, the state may revoke his or her license unless the student can prove economic hardship. The license is restored when the student returns to school and pays a $15 fine. Since implementation of the law in 1988, the dropout rate in West Virginia has declined by 15 percent.

The Bullying Prevention Program has been able to reduce school bullying. The program targets children in elementary, middle, and junior high schools. To implement the program, students complete anonymous questionnaires that determine the scope of the problem and who is primarily responsible for it. Teachers are also interviewed about bullying. In the classroom, bullying is discussed. A school conference day is scheduled to highlight the seriousness of bullying.

From information received through the student questionnaires, school bullies are identified. Teachers, administrators, and school counselors talk to known bullies and to their parents.

Another school improvement strategy is Values in Action, a character education program that teaches students seven core values including responsibility and perseverance. At the Emperor Elementary School in San Gabriel, California, classroom teachers display "integrity trees" to honor students' good deeds. And children at the school formally pledge to show respect and compassion for others. Character education in public schools was popular in the 1920s. During the 1960s and 1970s, it faded in public education as teachers were reluctant to impose values on students. Today, many educators once again see themselves as having a responsibility to stand for civic virtues and willingly display moral values such as honesty and caring.

Sources: James Larson, "Violence Prevention in the Schools," *Social Psychology Review* 23:151–164 (1994); "Employment Strategies for Dropout Prevention," *Education Week*, January 27:28 (1988); B. Drummond Ayres, "West Virginia Reduces Dropouts by Denying Them Driver's License," *The New York Times*, May 12:1, 12 (1989); Karen Peterson, "When School Hurts," *USA Today*, April 10:6D (2001); Martha Groves, "Character Joins Curriculum," *The Denver Post*, May 6:2001 (29A).

The Dropout Problem

About 3,000 students drop out of school every school day.[12] And the decision to drop out may have a serious effects on the life of the child. Dropouts have fewer job prospects, make less money, and are more likely to be unemployed than youths who stay in school.[13] The Bureau of Labor Statistics reports that about 6 percent of workers with a high school diploma were in poverty in

Many adolescents detest school and view it as a perfunctory step prior to entering the work force. Should the United States make a greater effort to encourage work participation from children indifferent to school? Should youths have to pass a GED exam prior to officially leaving school?

1999, considerably lower than the proportion of those unemployed who dropped out of high school (14.3 percent). High school dropouts also are more likely to depend on welfare, experience unstable marriages, and be incarcerated than those who complete their schooling.[14]

But does dropping out of school lead to delinquency? Does dropping out turn a law-abiding juvenile into a delinquent? While dropouts do have higher crime rates than juveniles who continue their schooling, their rates also were higher before they left school.[15] Data on whether dropping out of school increases or decreases the likelihood of future criminality are mixed. Delbert Elliott and Harwin Voss found that delinquency *decreased* after troubled children dropped out. They reasoned that this was because school was causing them to experience stress and frustration.[16] On the other hand, Terence Thornberry reported that dropping out of school *increased* the likelihood of later crime.[17] These conflicting findings led Roger Jarjoura to probe more deeply into the reasons children drop out. Jarjoura hypothesized that why a child dropped out of school would be related to future delinquency. He found that students who quit school because of family problems, financial reasons, or poor grades were not any more involved in delinquency after leaving school than before. But students who were expelled from school increased their involvement in drug abuse and theft after dropping out. In other words, sometimes dropping out of school leads to more delinquency and other times it does not.[18]

Schools, Children, and Rules

Because schools today find themselves struggling to promote a climate that fosters learning first and foremost, students are often required to obey a wide range of rules and regulations. The student handbook children receive when they enter secondary school is roughly the same across the nation. It lists the rules students are expected to obey and the consequences for violating them. For example, in many schools students cannot

- smoke or possess tobacco products;
- bring toys to school (e.g., frisbees);
- wear their hair in any style; or
- use disrespectful or abusive language.

Students who violate a school rule will be disciplined (see Box 11–4). The most common form of discipline is removing the student from the activity or specific area for a "timeout." For more serious violations, students may be required to have their parents sign and return a discipline form. If a student continues to misbehave, the principal, teacher, student, and parents will have a conference. Sometimes students are expelled or suspended from school. And, in some school districts, in some states, students may be physically punished.

BOX 11–4   A WINDOW ON DELINQUENCY
Serious Consequences for Breaking School Rules

Students in school must obey many different rules. In some instances, children may make a minor mistake that has serious consequences, as the following examples illustrate.

- Three baseball bats left over from a pickup game got Joseph Piper suspended from school for possessing dangerous weapons. He and a friend were drinking in the parking lot at the school's homecoming dance when an administrator ordered that the car be searched for alcohol. In the process of searching the vehicle for alcohol, the baseball bats were discovered. The principal wanted Joseph to be expelled for the rest of the school year, but a hearing officer denied his request. However, believing he would never catch up after missing seven weeks, Joseph dropped out. He now works full time bagging groceries. He plans to take automotive classes in the fall and begin working toward his general equivalency diploma.
- Seven-year-old Seamus Morris liked lemon drops. But when a friend took them from the first-grader's backpack and gave them to others at school, Seamus was suspended for a half-day. School officials called the drops an "unknown substance" and called paramedics to check children who had sampled the organic candy. For weeks thereafter, older children at the school teased the little boy and called him a "pill-pusher." His grades suffered. His mother reported that Seamus "would come home after school and crawl under his bed and cry. . . . We're changing school districts this summer."
- Eleven-year-old Shanon Coslett made a mistake when she picked up her mother's lunch box and took it to the charter school she attended. She did not know the lunch box contained a paring knife, and she did not know she would be expelled after she found the knife and told a teacher. School district officials overturned the expulsion after the fifth-grade honor student missed two days of school. But Shanon soon transferred to another school. The family had received hate mail accusing them of setting up Shanon's expulsion and creating a national uproar solely to defame the charter school. "It was very traumatic for her," said Shanon's mother. Shanon cried many mornings when she was dropped off at her new school.
- A 10-year-old girl repeatedly asked a certain boy on the playground whether he liked her. He complained to a teacher and the school threatened to suspend the girl, citing the school's policy of zero tolerance for sexual harassment.

Sources: John Derbyshire, "The Problem with Zero," *National Review*, May 28:46 (2001); Cathy Cummins, "'Busted' Students Try to Cope," *Rocky Mountain News*, June 14:4A, 26A (1998).

Suspension and Expulsion

Students are suspended or expelled from school for violating school rules or for having a dangerous health condition, such as lice (see Box 11–5). Students who face suspension have specific legal rights. In 1976, in *Goss v. Lopez*, the Supreme Court ruled that students who may be suspended for 10 or more days must receive a hearing.[19] However, at the hearing they do not have the right to an attorney or the right to cross-examine and confront witnesses. Within 24 hours following a suspension, the principal must provide the student's parents with a written statement describing the reason why the child

BOX 11–5   FACE OF DELINQUENCY
Alice

Lice cavort across little Alice's scalp like children in a playground. "The shampoo doesn't help," her mother explains, as seven-year-old Alice scratches through her long brown hair. "You have to pick them out with your fingers." Lice are the cause of Alice's bigger problem: a first-grader, she has been absent from school for 30 consecutive days.

That's why Cathy Luevano has come to Alice's home. Luevano is the school district's truant officer. "We need to figure something out," Luevano tells Alice's mother. "In order for Alice to go on to second grade, she needs to be [in school]." The state law requires that children attend school from age 7 until they turn 16. But state law also bars Alice from attending school until her lice are gone, as they are easily passed among children.

Alice lives in a basement apartment. Outside, dumpster divers work the trash. Inside the building, the halls are strewn with cigarette butts and sunflower seed shells. In the apartment, garbage overflows the trash container and clothing is strewn around the bedroom.

Alice's mother is 22. Alice is the oldest of six children, four of whom live in the apartment. Two others live with relatives. While Luevano talks to the mother, children grab cereal from a box with their fists and dump it into bowls. Milk comes from a gallon container that sits in the refrigerator next to a liter of Seagram's 7 and a 12-pack of Budweiser.

The mother says she shampooed Alice's hair three days ago. "That bottle was full," the mother says, bringing out a half-full prescription bottle of anti-lice shampoo. "I did everything. I threw their clothes away. I threw their mattress away. . . . . Everything's been done. They just keep coming back."

But Luevano observes that the prescription is almost three months old and that the children's clothes are all over the floor in the bedroom. "It's been 30 days with lice," Luevano says in frustration. Turning to Alice, she asks, "Don't you miss your friends?" Alice shakes her head and begins to sob. "Don't cry, sweetheart," Luevano says.

"I told you they're going to send someone," the mother says to Alice. Speaking to the back of Alice's head, Luevano tells the child, "You have to go to school—you need your education." "Did you know she can take you away from me because you don't go to school?" the mother says, bringing on even bigger sobs from the girl. Finally, Alice stops crying. "Can I play Nintendo?" she asks. While Alice plays, Luevano explains to the mother that lice are breeding in the clothes on the floor. She tells the mother to wash the clothes and then keep them in a laundry bag. She promises to contact a social worker and arrange for additional medical treatment. "I've learned not to sit down," Luevano explains as she walks back to her car. "You can get lice right off the furniture."

Source: Berny Morson, "The Truant Officer," *Rocky Mountain News*, April 2:38A–39A (1995).

was suspended. The principal must also make a reasonable effort to hold a conference with the parents before the student is readmitted to school.

Students who face expulsion are guaranteed a more exhaustive list of rights than students who may only be suspended. Students who face expulsion have a right to a hearing, the right to know the qualifications of the hearing examiner, and the right to appeal the decision to the school superintendent or school board. Some children are more likely to be suspended than others. Of the more than 3 million children suspended from school every year, over 30 percent are black, even though only 17 percent of the total student population nationwide is black. In fact, nearly 1 in 8 black children are suspended every year, while only 1 of 30 white students are suspended annually.[20]

Corporal Punishment

Corporal punishment is the infliction of pain as a penalty for a student who violates a school rule.[21] Teachers and other school officials hitting students for breaking school rules has a well-documented history. In fact, in 17th-century Jesuit schools it was expected that teachers would hit students. Serious student offenders were "stripped in front of the whole community and beaten until they bled."[22] Whipping was a teaching aid. One student complained, "My master . . . beat me horribly; he used to seize me by the ears and lift me off the ground."[23]

Corporal punishment was also widely practiced in the colonial era. Disobedient students were tied to the whipping post and beaten. Violence against students was justified on the basis of an assertion in the Old Testament attributed to Solomon in the "Book of Proverbs": "He that spareth his rod hateth his son; but he that loveth him chastiseth him betimes."[24] Thus, the "right thing to do" was for teachers to physically punish unruly students.[25]

By the end of the 19th century and into the early 20th century, discipline problems in schools were a daily occurrence. Teachers tried to control students through threats, intimidation, and beatings. One 19th-century schoolmaster kept a detailed record of the punishments he had administered during his 50 years of teaching. These included:

> 911,527 blows with a cane; 124,010 blows with a rod; 20,989 blows with a ruler; 136,715 blows with the hand; 12,235 blows on the mouth; 7,905 boxed ears; 115,800 raps on the head; 22,763 *nota belles* with Bible, grammar, or other books; 777 kneelings on peas; 1,707 instances of holding up the rod; 613 kneelings on a triangular block of wood.[26]

Today, corporal punishment in schools is prohibited in every industrialized nation except the United States, Canada, and one state in Australia. The U.S. Supreme Court has ruled twice on corporal punishment in schools. In 1975 in **Baker v. Owen** the Court decided that teachers could administer reasonable corporal punishment for disciplinary purposes.[27] In 1977 in **Ingraham v. Wright**, the Court added that corporal punishment does not violate the cruel and unusual punishment clause of the Eighth Amendment.[28]

Many students in previous generations attended schools that used corporal punishment. For most students, the threat of paddling is an effective means of social control. But for some bullies and other delinquents, paddling may be viewed as a status symbol of achievement. Should paddling be used more widely in the United States? Why or why not?

Should schools be able to use corporal punishment on students in efforts to control their behavior? Would such a policy be accepted where you attended high school? If not, why?

Table 11–1   Paddlings in American schools, 1998

In the United States, 457,754 students were subjected to corporal punishment in 1998. Twenty-seven states and the District of Columbia now have prohibited all corporal punishment in public schools. Data for the remaining 23 states are listed below.

Alabama	45,610	Mississippi	49,859
Arizona	346	Missouri	9,717
Arkansas	40,811	New Mexico	2,935
Colorado	0	North Carolina	7,080
Delaware	95	Ohio	903
Florida	12,850	Oklahoma	18,581
Georgia	27,559	Pennsylvania	90
Idaho	17	South Carolina	5,426
Indiana	2,482	Tennessee	36,477
Kansas	20	Texas	81,323
Kentucky	2,584	Wyoming	56
Louisiana	19,986		

Source: U.S. Department of Education, 2001.

Every year nearly 500,000 students are physically punished by teachers, principals, coaches, and bus drivers. About 5,000 children are beaten so badly they require medical attention. (You can see photos of students who required medical attention at www.nospank.com.) Furthermore, more than 90 percent of the reported incidents of corporal punishment in schools nationwide occurred in only 10 states (see Table 11–1).[29] Blacks and males are hit most often. Boys, who comprise 51 percent of the student population, receive 80 percent of the beatings administered at schools. Similarly, blacks constitute about 17 percent of the students nationwide, but are hit 40 percent of the time.[30]

> Corporal punishment has been linked to increased aggression, depression, school and emotional problems, and delinquency. Does spanking produce these other behavioral outcomes or are children who receive spanking precisely the types of children who are involved in delinquency and other negative behaviors?

Twenty-three states allow corporal punishment. In the other 27 states, it has been decided that the long-term consequences of hitting children outweigh the short-term benefit that may be realized. Research examining the effect of corporal punishment has found that it may lead to more serious problems for the child, the school, and other students through increased aggression and depression.[31]

Today there is a national movement to ban corporal punishment in public schools. But there is stiff opposition to doing so. In a recent national opinion poll, 48 percent of the respondents answered yes when asked: "Do you agree with teachers' being allowed to inflict corporal punishment?" (44 percent of the sample said no, and 8 percent voiced no opinion.)[32] However, the movement to stop corporal punishment in public schools is moving forward. Twenty years ago more than 1.5 million students were paddled annually; today, only about 500,000 are hit. In addition, in the mid-1980s, corporal punishment was illegal in just five states; today it is banned in 27 states and, in 11 states where it is allowed, it is prohibited in many school districts.[33]

But does corporal punishment deter unwanted behavior? Only a few studies have attempted to answer this question. The general conclusion from those that have is that:

> Corporal punishment is of limited effectiveness and has potentially deleterious side effects. . . . The more children are spanked, the more anger they report as adults, the more likely they are to spank their own children, the more likely they are to approve of hitting a spouse, and the more marital conflict they experience as adults.[34]

Psychologist Ralph Welsh has added that corporal punishment produces fear and anger in students. When the fear subsides, the anger remains. Angry students are more likely to strike out at whomever and whatever they blame for their pain and suffering.[35]

Schools, Children, and Law

Sometimes school rules and policies are challenged by the American Civil Liberties Union, parents, and students. When they are, there is always the possibility of legal action and, on occasion, a case being decided by the Supreme Court. In this section we will review a few of the more important judicial rulings on the rights of students in schools.

Searches and Seizures

School officials may legally search students and their lockers without consent. While this may seem to violate the Fourth Amendment, it does not. The standard is lowered for searches in schools to protect and maintain a proper educational environment for all students. This was the decision reached in **Thompson v. Carthage School District**.[36] Ramone Lea was expelled from Carthage High School after school officials found crack cocaine in his coat pocket while looking for guns and knives reported to be on school grounds. The district court awarded $10,000 to Lea in damages for "wrongful expulsion" because the search had violated his Fourth Amendment rights. The Carthage School District appealed the ruling to the U.S. Court of Appeals, which concluded that under the circumstances the search was constitutionally reasonable.

School officials may also search student lockers because the school owns both the locks and lockers. Students "borrow" them to store clothes, school books, supplies, and personal items necessary for school. Lockers cannot be used to store items that interfere with any school purpose. Therefore, lockers and their content are subject to search to ensure they are being properly used.

Should schools be able to use dogs to search for contraband such as explosives and drugs? Are such measures unnecessary forms of social control or viable steps toward preventing delinquency?

Do school administrators have too much or too little control over the student body? Is the school coercive and therefore problematic?

A search of all lockers is called a **sweep search**, which can be ordered whenever a principal believes an inspection of lockers is necessary for any one of the following reasons:

1. Interference with a school purpose or an educational function
2. Physical injury or illness
3. Damage to property
4. Violation of state law or school rules
5. Disposal of confiscated contraband
6. Involvement of law enforcement officials
7. Locker cleaning

Contrary to the *probable cause* requirement of the Fourth Amendment, the decision to search lockers is based on the less restrictive notion of *reasonableness* and school officials' interpretation of what reasonableness is. The "reasonable suspicion doctrine" was created in ***New Jersey v. T.L.O.*** (1985), when the Court ruled that school officials can conduct warrantless searches of individuals at school on the basis of reasonable suspicion.[37]

The decision in *T.L.O.* was affirmed in ***Vernonia School District 47J v. Acton*** (1995).[38] In *Acton,* the Court held that students participating in school athletic activities must submit upon request to an involuntary drug test (urinalysis). The *Acton* ruling thus allows schools to "seize" the urine of particular students to "search for" chemical traces of unlawful drugs, without any evidence of grounds for suspicion that drug testing is warranted.

Many people are uncomfortable with the Pledge of Allegiance because God is invoked. How has the debate over the pledge changed after the terrorist attacks of September 11, 2001? Should schools inculcate moral-religious messages into students? Why or why not?

Free Speech

No one has absolute free speech. The guarantee of free speech in the First Amendment is a relative one and no one can say what they want, when they want, wherever they want, without consequence. But the free speech students have in schools is more restricted than the free speech of adults.

One early Supreme Court ruling on the free speech of students was issued in 1943. In **West Virginia State Board of Education v. Barnette**, the Court held that the free speech rights of students were violated when they were required to salute the flag while reciting the Pledge of Allegiance (see Box 11–6).[39]

Twenty-six years later, in 1969 in **Tinker v. Des Moines Independent Community School District**, the Supreme Court revisited the issue of students' free expression.[40] In *Tinker*, several students who wore black arm bands to school in protest of the Vietnam War were suspended. (The school claimed that their behavior violated the dress code policy.) The Court ruled in favor of the students, stating that their dress "neither interrupted school activities nor sought to intrude in the school affairs or the lives of others."

The Gates siblings were suspended from their Briggsdale, Colorado school for three days for violating a school policy banning "exaggerated hair coloring and styles." Does such a policy infringe on the children's right to free speech?

BOX 11–6   A WINDOW ON DELINQUENCY
Religion, Schools, and Students

The relationship among religion, schools, and students has evolved over the past 60 years. The Supreme Court has heard many cases where at issue is the First Amendment of the Constitution. With respect to religion, the First Amendment states:

> Congress shall make no law requiring an establishment of religion, or prohibiting the free exercise of religion . . . .

On occasion the Court has struggled with how to interpret this Amendment. For example, in 1940 in *Minersville School District v. Gobitis*, the Court decided that a school district could require students to salute the American flag. Three years later in *West Virginia State Board of Education v. Barnette*, the Court reversed the earlier decision.

There are many other instances where the Court has been asked to establish the boundaries that govern the relationship among religion, schools, and students. Some of the more notable Court decisions on this topic are the following:

1948 In *McCollum v. Board of Education*, the Court disallowed the practice of having religious education take place in public school classrooms during the school day.

1962 In *Engel v. Vitale*, the Court ruled it was unconstitutional for a school to require students to recite school prayers.

1968 In *Epperson v. Arkansas*, the Court found the state law prohibiting the teaching of evolution to be unconstitutional.

1980 In *Stone v. Graham*, the Court ruled a Kentucky law requiring the posting of the Ten Commandments in each public school classroom in the state to be unconstitutional.

1985 In *Wallace v. Jaffree*, the Court found that an Alabama law requiring that each day begin with a one-minute period of "silent meditation or voluntary prayer" was unconstitutional.

1992 The Court ruled in *Lee v. Weisman* that the graduation prayer during a high school graduation was unconstitutional.

2000 In *Santa Fe School District v. Doe*, the Court held that official student-led prayers before a high school football game was unconstitutional.

These rulings are based on the Court's interpretation of the First Amendment, which guarantees that the government will not coerce any person to support or participate in religion or its exercise.

Sources: Minersville School District v. Gobitis, 310 U.S. 586 (1940); *West Virginia State Board of Education v. Barnette,* 319 U.S. 624 (1943); *McCollum v. Board of Education,* 333 U.S. 203 (1948); *Engel v. Vitale,* 370 U.S. 421 (1962): *Epperson v. Arkansas,* 393 U.S. 97 (1968); *Stone v. Graham,* 449 U.S. 39 (1980); *Wallace v. Jaffree,* 472 U.S. 38 (1985); *Lee v. Weisman,* 505 U.S. 577 (1992); *Santa Fe School District v. Doe,* 168 F.3d 806 (2000).

There are some limits on a student's right to free expression. In 1986 in **Bethel School District No. 403 v. Fraser**, the Court ruled that schools may prohibit vulgar and offensive language.[41] In this case, a student named Fraser gave the following endorsement for a student government candidate:

I know a man who is firm in his pants, he's firm in his shirt, his character is firm–but most of all, his belief in you, the students of Bethel, is firm. Jeff Kuhlman is a man who takes his point and pounds it in. He doesn't attack things in spurts–he drives hard, pushing and pushing until finally he succeeds. Jeff is a man who will go to the very end–even the climax, for each and every one of you. So vote for Jeff for ASB vice-president; he'll never come between you and the best our high school can be.[42]

The day after the speech, Fraser was suspended for three days and his name was removed from the graduation speaker ballot. Once Fraser had exhausted the school district's appeal process, he filed suit, claiming his free speech rights under the First Amendment had been violated. After two favorable lower-court decisions, the Supreme Court reversed the decision, stating that while adults possess "wide freedom" to engage in offensive speech making "it does not follow . . . that . . . the same latitude must be permitted to [school] children to engage in similar speech. . . ."[43]

Shortly after *Fraser*, in 1988 in **Hazelwood School District v. Kuhlmeier**, the Court decided that school administrators could regulate the content of student publications in public schools, but only if it served an educational purpose.[44] The *Hazelwood* case involved a disagreement between students and school officials over administrative censorship of two pages in the school's student-run newspaper. (Students in private schools do not have First Amendment protection against censorship by their teachers and principals, who are not government employees.) The topics the students had written about were important to them: teenage pregnancy and divorce. The Court held that "censorship will only be prohibited in school-sponsored activities when school officials have no valid educational purpose for their action."

The Court's decision in *Hazelwood* was widely protested on the basis that it constituted an unreasonable form of censorship. Critics complained that censorship does not enhance the education of young journalism students unless the purpose is to teach them not to report on unpopular issues. Students, however, have taken it on themselves to circumvent the censorship imposed upon them by *Hazelwood* by establishing independent student Web publications that are not under school control.[45] (For examples of alternative school publications see: www.alternet.org/wiretapmag and www.void.oblivion.net/ ~ugpapers.)

Conclusions

There is an extensive body of literature on the decline of American public schools. Anxiety over schools is relatively recent, following a long period during which education was thought to be one of our nation's greatest strengths. There is a growing concern with school crime, bullying, hate words and graffiti, and teacher victimization. Every year about 2.5 million students are crime victims. Countless others are bullies or are bullied. And in many schools, there are street gang members.

Many ways have been suggested to improve schools. On one hand, some criminologists believe schools could be improved if it were easier for students to drop out. On the other hand, there are many programs in place designed to keep students in school. But the more salient issue is whether dropping out of school leads to more crime and delinquency. Research addressing that issue has produced mixed results. Finally, in schools today, students have few rights with regard to clothes they may wear, searches and seizures of lockers, and their freedom of speech.

Key Terms

Baker v. Owen: Teachers can administer reasonable corporal punishment for disciplinary purposes.

Bethel School District No. 403 v. Fraser: Schools may prohibit vulgar and offensive language.

bullying: Negative acts by students carried out against other students repeatedly over time.

corporal punishment: The infliction of pain as a penalty for violating a school rule.

Goss v. Lopez: Students who may be suspended for 10 or more days must receive a hearing.

Hazelwood School District v. Kuhlmeier: School administrators can regulate the content of student publications in public schools for educational purposes.

Ingraham v. Wright: Corporal punishment does not violate the cruel and unusual punishment clause of the Eighth Amendment.

New Jersey v. T.L.O.:   School officials can conduct warrantless searches of individuals at school on the basis of reasonable suspicion.

sweep search: A search of all lockers.

Thompson v. Carthage School District: School officials may legally search students and their lockers without consent.

Tinker v. Des Moines Independent Community School District: Students have the right of free expression as long as their behavior does not interrupt school activities or intrude in the school affairs or the lives of others.

Vernonia School District 47J v. Acton: Students participating in school athletic activities must submit upon request to an involuntary drug test (urinalysis).

West Virginia State Board of Education v. Barnette: Students do not have to salute the flag while reciting the Pledge of Allegiance.

Getting Connected

Communities in Schools operates an excellent website for additional information on bullying and conflict resolution at:

http://www.cisnet.org

1. What is the CIS philosophy?
2. CIS argues that children need a "chance to give back." What kinds of programs provide this opportunity? Is "giving back" related to delinquency prevention?
3. Is your community part of the CIS network?

Information about corporal punishment of children in America's schools can be found at the website of the Center for Effective Discipline.

http://www.stophitting.com

1. What is "SpankOut Day USA"? Would your community support such an event?
2. Find the corporal punishment in schools materials, then find the "Facts About Corporal Punishment" page. How does the United States compare to other nations on the issue of corporal punishment in schools?
3. What are the main arguments against corporal punishment in schools? What kinds of alternative discipline methods does this organization advocate?

A very good source of information on contemporary issues and debates in education can be found at the website sponsored by the National Education Association (NEA).

http://www.nea.org/index.html

1. Describe two of the partnership activities the NEA has developed that could be effective in preventing delinquency.
2. Find the parents' page "Keeping Kids Out of Trouble During After-School Hours."
    What does the NEA suggest that schools should do?
3. Find the NEA's "Discipline That Works" page. Evaluate the recommendations given to parents.

Information about school dropouts can be found at a website maintained by the National Dropout Prevention Center.

http://www.dropoutprevention.org

1. Discuss three of the "effective strategies" for dropout prevention that this organization advocates.
2. According to the site's "Stats and Facts," what are the most frequent explanations that people give for dropping out of school?
3. What is the compulsory school age requirement in your state? Should it be higher? lower?

A source of information on the latest developments in school safety efforts and antiviolence programs is provided by a site entitled Safe Schools.

http://www.safeschools.org/index.html

1. Who founded the NASS? Why?
2. What kinds of services does the NASS provide?
3. What are S.A.F.E. Teams? Could such a team be effective in your area's high school?

Endnotes

1. This discussion draws heavily on Phillip Kaufman, Xianglei Chen, Susan Choy, Katharin Peter, Sally Ruddy, Amanda Miller, Jill Fleury, Kathryn Chandler, Michael Planty, and Michael Rand, *Indicators of School Crime and Safety: 2001* (Washington, DC: U.S. Departments of Education and Justice, 2001).

2. Nels Ericson, *Addressing the Problem of Juvenile Bullying* (Washington, DC: U.S. Department of Justice, 2001); Tonja Nansel, Mary Overpeck, Ramani Pilla, June Ruan, Bruce Simons-Morton, and Peter Scheidt, "Bullying Behaviors Among US Youth," *Journal of the American Medical Association* 289:2094–2100 (2001); Karen Peterson, "When School Hurts," *USA Today*, April 10:6D (2001).

3. Nansel et al., note 2.

4. Nansel et al., note 2; Rolf Loeber and Magda Stouthamer-Loeber, "Juvenile Aggression at Home and at School," pp. 94–126 in *Violence in American Schools,* edited by Delbert Elliott et al. (New York: Cambridge University Press, 1998).

5. Ericson, note 2.

6. Dan Olweus and Susan Limber, *Blueprints for Violence Prevention: Bullying Prevention Program* (Book 9)(Boulder, CO: University of Colorado, 1999).

7. "Seeking Safety from Violence," *USA Today Magazine*, December:11 (1994).

8. "Downsizing Our Schools," *Rocky Mountain News*, March 25:2B (2001).

9. Jackson Toby, "Crime in the Schools," in *Crime and Public Policy*, edited by James Q. Wilson (San Francisco: Institute for Contemporary Studies, 1983); Jackson Toby, "Crime in American Public Schools," *The Public Interest* 58:18–42 (1980).

10. Teresa Lindeman, "Retailers Find Seniors Make Good Workers," *Daily Camera*, June 15:6 (1998); Jackson Toby, "Of Dropouts and Stay-Ins," *The Public Interest* 95:3–13 (1989).

11. Terence Thornberry, "The Effect of Dropping Out of High School on Subsequent Criminal Behavior," *Criminology* 23:3–18 (1985); Myriam Baker, Nady Sigmon, M. Elaine Nugent. *Truancy Reduction* (Washington, DC: U.S. Department of Justice, 2000).

12. Children's Defense Fund, *The State of America's Children, 2001* (Washington, DC: Children's Defense Fund, 2001).

13. Bureau of Labor Statistics, *A Profile of the Working Poor* (Washington, DC: U.S. Department of Labor, 2001).

14. Baker et al., note 11.

15. Toby, note 9; Ellen Flax, "New Dropout Data Highlights Problems in the Middle Years," *Education Week*, September 30:1, 21 (1989).

16. Delbert Elliott and Harwin Voss, *Delinquency and the Dropout* (Lexington, MA: Lexington Books, 1974).

17. Thornberry, note 11.

18. Roger Jarjoura, "Does Dropping Out of School Enhance Delinquency Involvement?," *Criminology* 31:149–172 (1993).

19. *Goss v. Lopez*, 419 U.S. 565 (1976).

20. Anjetta McQueen, "Black Students Suspended More Often," *Rocky Mountain News*, June 15:59A (2000).

21. Irwin Hyman, *Reading, Writing, and the Hickory Stick* (Lexington, MA: Lexington Books, 1991).

22. Philipe Ariès, *Centuries of Childhood* (New York, Knopf, 1962), p. 190.

23. Ariès, note 22.

24. Proverbs 13:24.

25. H. Falk, *Corporal Punishment* (New York: Columbia Teachers College, 1941).

26. Joan Newman and Graeme Newman, "Crime and Punishment in the Schooling Process," in *Violence and Crime in the Schools*, edited by Keith Baker and Robert Rubel (Lexington, MA: Lexington Books, 1980).

27. *Baker v. Owen*, 395 F.Supp. 294 (1975).

28. *Ingraham v. Wright*, 430 U.S. 651 (1977).

29. Jodi Wilgoren, "Paddling Opponents Get Change in Teacher Liability Amendment," *New York Times*, May 11:A26 (2001); Mary Beth Marklein, "More Educators Sparing the Rod," *USA Today*, June 6:9D (1997).

30. "Paddling Becoming Uncommon at School," *USA Today*, July 12:2D (2000); Steven Shaw and Jeffery Braden, "Race and Gender Bias in the Administration of Corporal Punishment," *School Psychology Review* 19:378–383 (1990).

31. Murray Strauss and Julie Stewart, "Corporal Punishment by American Parents," *Clinical Child and Family Psychology Review* 2:55–70 (1999); Murray Strauss, David Sugarman, and Jean Giles-Sims, "Spanking by Parents and Subsequent Antisocial Behavior of Children," *Archives of Pediatric Adolescent Medicine* 151:761–767 (1997); Murray Strauss, *Beating the Devil Out of Them* (San Francisco: Jossey-Bass Publishers, 1994).

32. Nat Hentoff, "U.S. Schools Still Legalize Abuse," *Rocky Mountain News*, August 21:29A (1995); Murray Strauss, Demie Kurtz, Donileen Loseske, and Joan McCord, "Discipline and Deviance," *Social Problems* 38:133–154 (1991).

33. Hyman, note 21.

34. John Lang, "Suits Take a Swing at Paddling," *Rocky Mountain News*, May 2:2A, 58A (1998); "End Legal Child Abuse: Stop School Paddling," *USA Today*, July 18:14A (1994).

35. Ralph Welsh, "Delinquency, Corporal Punishment, and the Schools," *Crime and Delinquency* 24:336–354 (1978).

36. *Thompson v. Carthage School District*, 87 F3d 979 (1996).

37. *New Jersey v. T.L.O.*, 469 U.S. 325 (1985).

38. *Vernonia School District 47J v. Acton*, 515 U.S. 646 (1995).

39. *West Virginia State Board of Education v. Barnette*, 319 U.S. 624 (1943).

40. *Tinker v. Des Moines Independent Community School District*, 393 U.S. 503 (1969).

41. *Bethel School District No. 403 v. Fraser*, 478 U.S. 675 (1986).

42. "Supreme Court Reverses *Fraser*," *SPLC Report*, Fall:3–4 (1986), p. 3.

43. *Bethel School District No. 403 v. Fraser*, 478 U.S. 675 (1986), p. 682.

44. *Hazelwood School District v. Kuhlmeier*, 484 U.S. 260 (1988).

45. Jeffery Selingo, "Student Writers Try to Duck the Censors by Going Online," *The New York Times*, June 7:D6 (2001).

Chapter 12
Gang Delinquency

" 'You have to make your mark, make your name be known,' he said. 'Unfortunately, once you get the taste of blood, it's no big thing if you have to smoke someone again.' "[1]

Gang behavior, especially gang violence, was thought to have subsided somewhat during the late 1990s. However, whether it is in Denver, Los Angeles, Newark, or Memphis, gang activity appears to remain a serious problem. All too often a young male enters a gang as a way to make his mark, get a name, and build his reputation as a "bad" character. At the same time, many more youths, both boys and girls, join gangs simply for the social satisfactions derived from being part of a group. In this chapter, we will look closely at the nature of group delinquency, the emergence of the contemporary gang problem, types and characteristics of gangs, gang violence, and how communities and schools organize to respond to gangs.

Peers and Group Delinquency

Do youths usually engage in delinquent acts alone or with others? If delinquency is principally the work of isolated individuals, then perhaps it ought to be the province of psychiatrists and psychologists. If, on the other hand, most delinquent activities are carried out in groups, then sociologists might have more appropriate explanations to offer.

In 1967 Paul Lerman published a study of boys ages 10 to 19 living in low-income neighborhoods in New York City. He found that fewer than 10 percent of the boys who engaged in delinquency belonged to a named group or gang; for younger boys, ages 10 to 13, the figure was especially low. Most of the boys involved in delinquency said they usually spent their time alone or with just one or two others.[2] This early association with delinquent peers outside of gangs, however, is a significant predictor of later gang entry.[3] Lerman thus sees delinquency as an activity typically done in pairs or trios—not in gangs. James F. Short, Jr., challenged Lerman's argument by noting that many gang members pair off and commit offenses with each other but still remain part of the larger gang. And when the gang travels outside its territory or faces a hostile confrontation with another gang, many members band together rather than splinter off into separate pairs or trios.[4]

Other criminologists have looked into the group nature of delinquency. Studies in the early part of the 20th century overestimated the amount of delinquency that could be attributed to groups.[5] These studies relied on official data, and the police were more likely to arrest and refer youths to court if they congregated in packs. To counter this bias, Michael Hindelang turned to self-report data to estimate group delinquency rates (see Chapter 2). He found that some offenses are more likely than others to be committed with associates; using marijuana and getting drunk, for instance, are primarily social activities.[6] But a few crimes are more often engaged in alone (such as carrying a weapon). For a discussion of group delinquency in the Netherlands, see Box 12–1.

When gang membership is a known factor in group offending, clear differences in delinquency rates between gang and nongang members have been reported. Studies by Finn-Aage Esbensen and his colleagues have

BOX 12–1   A CROSS-CULTURAL PERSPECTIVE ON DELINQUENCY
Group Delinquency in the Netherlands

For many Dutch youths, hanging around or street loitering is a preferred leisure activity. Many youths hang around in small groups and engage in troublemaking, nuisance, or intimidating behavior. More often than not, these youths are not terribly involved in crime, but when they are, they tend to commit their crimes in groups rather than alone. Recent surveys in the Netherlands indicate that the majority of delinquencies involve co-offenders. Delinquencies most often committed with others include vandalism, followed by drug violations, intimidation, aggression, shoplifting, bicycle theft, and other thefts. Younger adolescents are more likely to commit crimes with co-offenders than are older youths. And girls are more likely than boys to commit crimes with others, especially for such crimes as shoplifting and bicycle theft. Youths who commit crimes together are most likely to be friends, followed by classmates and neighborhood youths. If not engaging in delinquencies with friends, girls are most likely to co-offend with classmates, while boys co-offend with neighborhood youths.

More criminally involved youth groups also hang out and loiter and it is understandable that the public and authorities often lump all street youth groups together. There are important differences according to Alfred Hakkert, who has divided local youth groups into "nuisance groups," "trouble-making groups," "criminal groups," and "gangs." All of these groups engage in a variety of similar behaviors, including hanging out in groups in doorways or sidewalks, getting in the way of passersby, playing loud music, and making impudent remarks.

Nuisance groups are the least problematic, tending to simply annoy or intimidate people, especially older people, by their mere presence or incivility in encounters on the street. *Trouble-making groups* often engage in minor delinquencies, such as bicycle theft, vandalism, shoplifting, and drug use. *Criminal youth groups*, on the other hand, are likely to participate in more serious offenses, such as robberies, burglaries, auto theft, and drug dealing. Finally, *youth gangs*, organized expressly to engage in criminal activities, are involved in extortion, serious property crimes, violent thefts, and drug dealing.

Source: Alfred Hakkert, "Group Delinquency in The Netherlands: Some Findings from an Exploratory Study," *International Review of Law Computers & Technology* 12:453–474 (1998).

indicated that prevalence rates and individual offending are greater for both male and female gang members than for their nongang counterparts.[7] Terence Thornberry and his associates report that, although gang members did not appear to have higher rates of delinquency or drug use prior to entering the gang, once they were members their rates became significantly greater than nongang youths.[8] Sara Battin and her colleagues report that gang members have higher rates of offending compared to nongang adolescents and that "belonging to a gang predicted court-reported and self-reported delinquency above and beyond the contribution of having delinquent peers . . . and above and beyond prior delinquency."[9]

Youths often engage in delinquency while immersed in a group setting when they would not commit crime alone. Why? What role does "peer pressure" play in producing group or gang delinquency?

Finally, the Rochester Youth Development Study examined the portion of delinquency in the community that could be attributed to gang members as opposed to nongang youths.[10] About one-third of the youths reported being members of a street gang at some time prior to the end of high school. Those youths who belonged to gangs, however, account for the lion's share of delinquent acts, especially the more serious acts. Gang members account for 86 percent of the serious delinquent acts, 69 percent of the violent delinquent acts, and 70 percent of the drug sales. The study concludes that involvement in gangs substantially increases the likelihood of involvement in delinquency, particularly serious delinquency.

A slightly cautionary note about the findings just reported is suggested by Tom Winfree and his associates. They conclude that, among youths, having a progang attitude and a predisposition toward violence, especially group-context violence, may be a more important delinquency factor than actual gang membership. No difference was found between gang and nongang youths in theft crimes, other property crimes, and even drug crimes, although gang members were more likely to be involved in violent offenses.[11] However, the distinctions between gang and nongang youth groups are more problematic than it might appear at first. What makes a youth group a gang? What are the appropriate criteria for classifying a youth as a gang member? We turn to these issues in the next section.

Gangs and Gang Delinquency

For people working in the juvenile justice system and for social scientists as well, concern about juvenile delinquency has historically centered around gangs. But the notion of "gang" itself has been poorly understood, defined, and measured. In this section we will examine various ways of defining gangs and the diversity of characteristics associated with gangs and gang members.

Problems in Defining Gangs

In the early 20th century the term *gang* was frequently associated with groups in socially disorganized and deteriorated inner-city neighborhoods: It was applied to youths who engaged in a variety of delinquencies ranging from truancy, street brawls, and beer running to race riots, robberies, and other serious crimes.[12] Frederic Thrasher, in his 1927 study of more than 1,300 delinquent gangs in Chicago,[13] noted that while no two gangs are exactly alike, delinquent gangs do possess a number of qualities that set them apart from other social groups. The gang, according to Thrasher,

> is characterized by the following types of behavior: meeting face to face, milling, movement through space as a unit, conflict, and planning. The result of this collective behavior is the development of tradition, unreflective internal structure, *esprit de corps*, solidarity, morale, group awareness, and attachment to a local territory.[14]

This image of gangs stressed youth groups as being localized and territory-based, with social organization and traditions and with group awareness and morale fostered through conflict with authorities and other gangs. While Thrasher's work set the tone for much of the subsequent writing on gangs for many decades, it is important to note that he does not include in his definition of a gang delinquent or law-violating behavior. For Thrasher, delinquent gangs were only one type of youth group.[15]

By the 1950s the image of the gang increasingly focused on large groups of urban boys engaged primarily in violent conflict, fighting each other in battles or "rumbles" over territory or status, much like the Sharks and the Jets in the musical and movie *West Side Story*. The gang, from this perspective, suggests a slightly broader definition:

> [The gang is] a friendship group of adolescents who share common interests, with a more or less clearly defined territory, in which most of the members live. They are committed to defending one another, the territory, and the gang name in the status-setting fights that occur in school and on the streets.[16]

By the 1980s police, politicians, and many criminologists began to emphasize the organization and illegal activities of gangs. According to Walter Miller,

> A **youth gang** is a self-forming association of peers, bound together by mutual interests, with identifiable leadership, well-developed lines of authority, and other organizational features, who act in concert to achieve a specific purpose or purposes which generally include the conduct of illegal activity and control over a particular territory, facility, or type of enterprise.[17]

But the characteristics in Miller's definition do not fit all youth groups identified as gangs by either the police or criminologists. Some groups are involved in illegal activities; some are not. Some claim territory; some do not. Some use and/or sell drugs; many do not. Some engage in drive-by shootings; most do not. And some are highly organized with identifiable leadership, while others are not.[18]

Such variations have not prevented some state legislatures and police agencies from developing very narrow and specific definitions of gangs. For example, the Street Terrorism Enforcement and Prevention Act (STEP) (section 186.22) of the California penal code defines the "criminal street gang" as

> any ongoing organization, association, or group of three or more persons, whether formal or informal, having as one of its primary activities the commission of one or more of the criminal acts enumerated in paragraphs (1) to (8), inclusive, of subdivision (e), which has a common name or common identifying sign or symbol, whose members individually or collectively engage in or have engaged in a pattern of criminal gang activity.[19]

The criminal acts specifically included in the code include aggravated assault, robbery, homicide or manslaughter, drug trafficking, arson, victim or

Is the *esprit de corps* of gangs one of deliberate failure? Given the criminal involvement of gangs, is the entrée into gang life equivalent to volunteering for a life of failure?

witness intimidation, and shooting into an inhabited dwelling. This definition gives police and prosecutors a basis for arresting any youth who actively participates in a criminal street gang (regardless of whether the youth holds formal membership in the gang) as long as the youth knows that the gang is involved in illegal activities and willfully promotes, furthers, or assists in any felonious criminal conduct by members of that gang.

However, most states do not have legislatively determined definitions of juvenile gangs. Consequently, law enforcement agencies (and criminologists) generally select their own criteria for defining a gang, and this means there continues to be a basic lack of consensus. The 1998 National Youth Gang Survey asked law enforcement agencies across the country to rank six gang characteristics according to their importance as criteria in defining a youth gang.[20] Although none received an overwhelming majority of votes as most important, "commits crimes together" was clearly the most important criterion, receiving a first-place ranking by 50 percent of the responding law enforcement agencies. The next most important characteristic, "has a name," was ranked most important by only 19 percent (see Table 12–1).

Scholars frequently disagree over the appropriate definition of gangs. Is this simply a semantic issue? Are gangs, by implicit definition, a negative, criminal phenomenon?

Similar to the problem of defining a gang is the problem of defining "gang-related" activity. The spread of gang violence (discussed later in this chapter) has complicated the problem of determining which activities are gang-related. Cheryl Maxon and Malcolm Klein report that different urban police and sheriffs' departments use different definitions of what constitutes a gang-related crime. More than half of the law enforcement agencies responding to the 1998 National Youth Gang Survey indicated that they use a **member-based definition**–a crime in which a gang member or members are either the perpetrators of the crime, regardless of the motive–while nearly a third use a **motive-based definition**–a crime committed by a gang member or members in which the underlying reason is to further the interests and activities of the gang. About 11 percent said they used some

Table 12–1   Criteria Used by Law Enforcement Agencies to Define a Youth Gang: Top Choices

GANG CHARACTERISTIC	PERCENT OF AGENCIES SELECTING AS MOST IMPORTANT CRITERION
Commits crimes together	50
Has a name	19
Hangs out together	10
Claims a turf or territory of some sort	9
Displays/wears common colors or other insignia	8
Has a leader or several leaders	7

Source: National Youth Gang Center, *1998 National Youth Gang Survey* (Washington, DC: Office of Juvenile Justice and Delinquency Prevention, 2000), p. 40.

other definition.[21] For example, the Los Angeles Police and Sheriff Departments use *member-based definitions* for designating crimes as gang-related. The criteria include the following:

1. When incidents involve participants, suspects, or victims who are identified gang members or associates.
2. When a reliable informant identifies an incident as gang activity.
3. When an informant of previously untested reliability identifies an incident as gang activity and it is corroborated by other attendant circumstances or independent information.
4. When a homicide, attempted murder, assault with a deadly weapon, rape, kidnapping, shooting at inhabited dwellings, battery on a police officer, or arson is reported and the suspect or victim is on file as an active gang or associate gang member.
5. When the investigation reveals that the incident involves a gang member, although neither the victim nor the suspect is known [to each other] to be an active or associate gang member.
6. When victims are gang members.[22]

The Chicago Police Department, on the other hand, uses a *motive-based definition*, which is more restrictive. For example, a homicide is considered gang-related "only if it occurs in the course of an explicitly defined collective encounter between two or more gangs (a 'gang fight')."[23] Furthermore, criminal activity by gang members, individually or collectively, that is unrelated to intergang encounters is not defined as "gang-related." For the Chicago police, there must be a gang-related motive to be defined as gang-related.[24]

Joining Gangs and Getting Out of Gangs

Some youths grow up in families in which older brothers, sisters, fathers, or possibly even grandfathers are or were gang members, and thus their entry into gang life is essentially just a part of adolescent socialization. From a very young age, it is expected that they will eventually become a gang member. Most youths who join gangs are influenced or encouraged by forces external to the family. Martín Jankowski suggests that there are six main reasons for joining a gang. They include *material incentives* (gang membership increases the likelihood of making money); *recreation* (gangs provide entertainment and a chance to meet girls); *refuge* or *camouflage* (the gang offers anonymity); *physical protection* (gangs provide personal protection from predatory elements, including other gangs, in high-crime neighborhoods); *a time to resist* (the gang provides opportunities to resist living lives similar to their parents); *commitment to community* (gang membership provides the opportunity to demonstrate a form of local patriotism and dedication to protecting the neighborhood).[25]

Many youths will stay in the gang into early or even middle adulthood, although most drift in and out of gangs over the years. Some will join other organizations, such as social clubs or organized crime groups; some go to prison; some die as a result of violence or drug use; and some get a job, get married, have children, and find the demands of gang membership incompatible with the new demands of family and job. While gang mythology maintains the belief that once a youth joins a gang he or she is in for life, reality is substantially different. Leaving a gang may be risky, especially for youths who have special knowledge of serious crimes committed by gang members. Most youths who leave gangs simply quit without being required to give a reason for the decision.[26]

Characteristics of Gangs

When Walter Miller asked the police, juvenile officers, social workers, and other experts to define gangs, they agreed that gangs had the following traits: organization, leadership, turf, cohesiveness, and purpose.[27] But do all gangs exhibit these characteristics? Decades of research have produced inconsistent answers.

Are the rationales youths provide for joining gangs merely excuses? Why do the majority of youth in gang-infested neighborhoods choose not to join? How does the phrase "birds of a feather flock together" apply to delinquent gangs?

Organization The organizational structures of gangs have varied widely over time, from city to city, and even within cities. An example of a highly organized gang can be found in the Vice Lords in Chicago in the 1960s.

> The most important element in the new organizational scheme was the creation of an administrative body called the "board" to deal with matters affecting the entire Vice Lord Nation. Further, regular weekly meetings were instituted with representatives from all the subgroups present. Finally, membership cards were printed with the Vice Lords' insignia—a top hat, cane, and white gloves.[28]

The Vice Lords, however, appear to be atypical. James F. Short, Jr., suggests that most gangs fall somewhere in the middle between crowds and mobs on the one hand and ordinary organizations on the other.[29] Lewis Yablonsky argues that violent gangs are not even groups; they are "near-groups."[30] Such near-groups fit the needs of their members, whose social abilities are so rudimentary that they cannot meet the minimal demands of a more organized or stable group.

Gene Muehlbauer and Laura Dodder's analysis of a suburban gang, *The Losers*, noted that its structure centered on a core group of about 10 to 12 members. These members were the nucleus of the gang and all other members were defined in relationship to this core.[31] Alternatively, some gangs become so large that they are unable to function effectively as a total unit; consequently, they divide into groupings called "cliques." In their study of Latino gangs in California, Robert Jackson and Wesley McBride report that cliques are based primarily on age but sometimes on a specialty. In some gangs, for instance, there is a clique that specializes in violence, and most of the "shooters" (gunmen) in the gang belong to that clique.[32] Often, such cliques have a number of members who are not only capable of violence but also seek it out.

Hundreds of gang-affiliated youths are murdered each year based on the neighborhood in which they were raised, the type and color of clothing they wear, and the hand signals they employ. Does this suggest a fundamental breakdown in our civilization?

Joan Moore also noted age-grading in Chicano youth gangs in barrios in Los Angeles, El Paso, and San Antonio. The age cohorts, or **klikas**, appear to form every two years or so and become "salient lifelong membership and reference groups for some, but not all, members of the gang."[33] Finally, John Hagedorn has noted that the gangs he studied in Milwaukee were organized around age-graded groups having their own internal structure and subgroups.[34]

Leadership   Most gangs have clearly established leaders, although, like any organizational structure, this has varied over time and location. In the militaristic, or Mafia-style, model of gang leadership, the top authority position "is analogous to that of the highest ranking officer in a military unit; below him are lieutenants, sublieutenants, and so on. Decisions originating in higher echelons are transmitted through the ranks by a chain-of-command system."[35]

A second type of ideal leader is charismatic, ruling by force of his or her personality. This leader is usually older and stronger than, and is revered by, the gang's members. In the violent gangs studied by Lewis Yablonsky, leaders seemed to be self-appointed and often emotionally unstable. These leaders would occasionally manipulate other gang members into aggressive or violent actions just to satisfy their own emotional needs. By a combination of charisma and intimidation, the leaders of violent gangs tended to be more permanent in their positions, while turnover among the general membership was high.[36]

For Barry Krisberg, the only distinctive feature of gang leaders is their superior verbal ability.[37] In the black gangs he studied, this verbal facility, or "gift of the gab," enabled leaders to capture the attention of other members. Jackson and McBride observed that leadership roles in Latino gangs do not carry formally recognized positions. Instead,

> no one is elected to posts such as president, vice-president or warlord. . . . Leadership positions are not usually assumed by any one individual on a permanent basis, but by any member who has demonstrated unique qualities of leadership needed by a gang at a particular moment. For example, if a gang is attacked by a rival group, the victim gang looks to the most experienced fighter available at the moment within its own group, to coordinate the retaliation raid.[38]

Leadership varied greatly among the gangs Hagedorn studied in Milwaukee. In most cases, the youth's "reputation or ability to fight was the main criterion for a leader . . . [while in other cases] someone was the leader because they knew most about gangs. . . . Some even disputed there ever was a leader."[39] In gangs whose leaders were identified, "titles" were rarely used.

Turf   According to Irving Spergel, *turf,* or territoriality, involves two components, identification and control.[40] Many urban gangs identify with particular neighborhoods, parks, housing projects, or schools. At one time, crossing turf boundaries and entering another gang's territory, often clearly marked by graffiti, involved taking serious risks. However, automobiles have increased the mobility of teenagers, and slum districts have been sliced up by highways and urban renewal, blurring the old dividing lines. In addition, identification with specific turf has been drastically altered for many gang members, largely because of frequent relocation of gang members' family residences.[41]

Cohesiveness   Are gangs very close, tight-knit organizations with loyal members bound to one another by mutual friendship and common interests? Early writers thought so. Thrasher, for instance, depicted gangs as filled with happy-go-lucky youngsters, with the gang performing positive functions such as providing status for members.[42] Modern writers are sometimes equally romantic. Waln Brown claims that gangs provide very close relationships between people who will help each other in a crisis. He quotes a gang member to support his argument:

> Me and my homies are tight, we're blood. I know I can count on them, and they know they can count on me. If I need some clothes one of my homies will help me get them. After all, if I'm looking cheap it makes them look bad . . . and if it comes to a fight, I know my homies will be there. They stone bad and they don't let nobody get over on any of us.[43]

But many criminologists disagree. Malcolm Klein says that the gang members he observed were "dissatisfied, deprived, and making the best of an essentially unhappy situation."[44] James F. Short, Jr., and Fred Strodtbeck say that gang members fail at school, on the job, and elsewhere; these failures, along with other social disabilities, make gang members anxious and insecure about their status, and such insecurities are heightened by constant challenges and insults by other gang members.[45] Klein adds that there are good reasons why gangs are not cohesive: The gang has few if any group goals; the membership is constantly in a state of flux, turning over rapidly; and group norms are practically nonexistent.[46]

Gang members have normal adolescent problems, but in more extreme form. The gang member "tends to be a caricature of the adolescent—more shy, more dependent on his peers, more ambivalent about appropriate role behaviors."[47] Peggy Giordano and Stephen Cernkovich reported that, compared with nondelinquent counterparts, members of delinquent groups were more likely to share privacies with one another and equally likely to feel they could "be themselves" with their friends. They were no less likely than nondelinquents to believe they can trust their friends and be trusted by their friends.[48]

Purpose   Delinquent gangs have been often thought to exist for the purpose of committing offenses. Purpose is a state of mind that is difficult for gang researchers to measure; it is easier to study behavior—the extent to which gangs engage in offenses. Researchers have found that gang members spend most of their time on pursuits other than crime, mostly just whiling away their time.[49]

Hagedorn confirms this perception of gang activities. He notes that primary gang activity in Milwaukee revolved around "partying and hanging out."[50] Geoffrey Hunt and his colleague's study of ethnic youth gangs in Northern California also reports that "hanging around," "kicking back," and especially drinking were "commonplace and integral part[s] of everyday life among gang members."[51] Fighting was seen as an activity more typical of one stage in the development of the gang. Constant fighting, whether with other gangs or as a form of conflict with authorities, especially the police, occurred early and helped structure the gang. As gang members grew older, their inclination was to decrease the fighting and increase the partying.

The Contemporary Gang Problem

In the 1970s, only 19 states reported gang problems. By the late 1990s, all 50 states and the District of Columbia had reported gang problems. Nearly 4,000 cities, towns, villages, and counties indicated that they were experiencing some form of gang problem.[52] The states with the largest number of gang-problem cities in 1998 were California, Illinois, Texas, and Florida. (Figure 12–1 shows the top 10 states by number of cities reporting gang problems.)

Traditionally, gang problems have been a big-city phenomenon. But gang problems are by no means confined to large cities. One of the most striking changes between 1970 and 1998 was the increase in the growth of gang problems in smaller communities. While 100 percent of cities with

Figure 12–1
Top 10 States Reporting Gang Problems

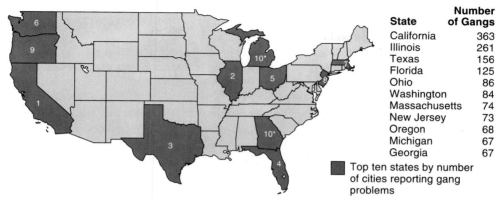

State	Number of Gangs
California	363
Illinois	261
Texas	156
Florida	125
Ohio	86
Washington	84
Massachusetts	74
New Jersey	73
Oregon	68
Michigan	67
Georgia	67

■ Top ten states by number of cities reporting gang problems

* Michigan and Georgia tied for 10th both reporting 67

Source: Walter Miller, *The Growth of Youth Gang Problems in the United States: 1970–98* (Washington, DC: Office of Juvenile Justice and Delinquency Prevention, 2001), p. 60.

populations of 250,000 or more reported gang problems in 1998, 43 percent of cities with populations between 10,000 and 25,000 and 27 percent of cities with populations between 2,500 and 10,000 also reported gang problems.[53]

The Spread of Gangs

Walter Miller has identified seven reasons offered by law enforcement, criminologists, and policy makers for the dramatic spread of gangs over the past three decades.[54]

1. *Drugs*   According to a number of law enforcement officials, the expansion of illegal drug markets increased the solidarity of existing gangs, offered incentives for the creation of new gangs, and promoted the development of widespread networks of drug-trafficking gangs.

2. *Immigration*   Major waves of immigration during the past 25 years have brought in many groups of Asians, Southeast Asians, and Latin Americans whose children have formed gangs in the tradition of Irish, Jewish, and Slavic immigrant groups during the 1800s.

3. *Gang Names and Alliances*   In the 1980s, the pattern of adopting a common name and claiming a federated relationship with other gangs became increasingly common. Hundreds of small local gangs adopted the names or claimed alliance with well-known gangs such as the Crips, Bloods, Latin Kings, and Gangster Disciples. In the mid-1990s, more than 1,100 gangs in 115 cities around the country used either Bloods or Crips in their names.

4. *Migration*   Some experts believe gangs that exhausted drug markets or faced violent competition from other drug-dealing gangs in a particular community simply left that area and transferred operations to new markets in communities with little existing gang presence.

5. *Government Policies*   During the 1960s, some policy makers viewed urban youth gangs as representing an untapped reservoir of potential leadership for improving the quality of life for residents in low-income communities. These officials advocated recognizing gangs as legitimate community groups and enlisting them in social reform efforts. Over a million dollars in federal funds were allocated to urban gangs in Chicago and New York by the Office of Economic Opportunity as part of the federal war on poverty.

6. *Female-Headed Households*   This explanation suggests that the increase in female-headed households and absence of stable adult male role models created identity problems for male adolescents who then turned to gangs for their sense of place and values.

7. *Gang Subculture and the Media*   Gangs have become "hot" market items in movies, novels, television, and music. The media portrayed gang members as macho, hip, cool, and victims of racism, police brutality, and government oppression, and the gang subculture became viewed in a glamorous and rewarding lifestyle.

Cultural figures, such as Malcolm X, Eldridge Cleaver, and Ice-T, as well as the mainstream media often portray gang-affiliated delinquents as political prisoners of various forms of governmental oppression. Do you think this perspective is correct?

However, Cheryl Maxon believes that the most common reason for the spread of gangs into smaller communities is that gang members often simply move with their families to suburbs or other traditionally safer areas to improve the quality of life and to be near relatives and friends.[55] Other studies suggest that the recent appearance of gangs in communities that had not previously had gang problems is not the result of "migrated" gang members but, rather, is the result of the development of loosely organized cliques of age-graded neighborhood adolescents who are growing up in areas characterized by declining local economic conditions and growing poverty.[56]

Racial and Ethnic Variations in Gangs

As noted earlier, gangs differ significantly in their organization and structure, leadership, cohesiveness, purpose, and sense of turf. Older perceptions of gangs as similar kinds of youth groups must be reconsidered in light of the ethnic and racial diversity of gangs today.

What does the word "wannabe" mean in reference to gangs? Have you heard this term applied to gangs with white or Asian members? To suburban gangs? To rural gangs? Regardless of their involvement in delinquency and violence, why might certain peer groups not be taken seriously?

Black Gangs   The most notable, and most widespread, of the contemporary black gangs are the Bloods and the Crips. These gangs have become essentially confederations of smaller sets or subsets. Sets are generally organized around neighborhoods and typically have between 20 and 30 members, although a few of the larger sets may have more than 100 members.

Black gangs have little, if any, formal structure: "Leadership is usually collective, and internal organization is rudimentary . . . Most sets are as casually organized as a pickup basketball game."[57] But what these gangs lack in organizational structure, they make up in violence. Much of the violence stems from traditional rivalry and competition over turf, although fights may start from something as minor as wearing a red hat in a Crips neighborhood

likely to evaluate potential members through a process of "kicking back" or "hanging around" that could last from a few months to a year: "If during this period, the potential recruit could show that he 'was down' then he became accepted as a member."[71] Hunt and his colleagues conclude that the everyday life of Southeast Asian gang members is actually rather similar to that of other California gangs and that these gang members "like other groups make a variety of attempts to deal with and transcend the mundane."[72]

Gang Violence

Two significant differences between contemporary youth gangs and those of earlier decades are that many of today's gangs are exceptionally violent and much of that violence occurs within school settings (see Chapter 11). In some instances, gangs have taken effective control of urban high schools. Gang violence and other gang activities in public schools had reached startling levels by the mid-1970s. Gang operations have been identified at all three levels of schools, including elementary, junior high or middle school, and senior high. Serious assaults—shootings, stabbings, beatings—have been directed by gang members against other gang members, teachers, and fellow students.

However, most gang violence occurs *outside* school settings. Violence perpetrated by members of youth gangs in major cities began to rise dramatically in the mid-1970s and continued into the early 1990s. Walter Miller attributes the growth of gang violence during this period largely to a single factor: the gun. By the mid-1970s, many youth gangs were giving up their traditional zip guns, chains, and knives and turning to revolvers, shotguns, and semiautomatic rifles. Miller predicted that the problem would become worse, more violent, and more confrontational with law enforcement agencies. His prediction was correct. Youth gang homicides clearly increased.[73] While gang-related killings in major gang cities totaled 633 in 1980, Chicago and Los Angeles alone accounted for more than 1,000 gang homicides in 1994.[74]

The last half of the 1990s witnessed a *decline* in gang violence, especially gang homicides. Forty-nine percent of the nation's 237 largest cities reported a decrease in gang homicides between 1996 and 1998. A total of 15 percent reported no change, and only a third reported an increase. Overall, gang homicides for these cities declined from 1,293 in 1996 to 1,061 in 1998. Substantial declines were also reported in the two cities with the highest rates of gang homicides. In 1998, Chicago reported only 180 gang homicides, while Los Angeles reported 173. Their combined number of 353 is far below the 1,000 gang homicides in 1994 noted above.[75]

Drugs and Drug Dealing by Gangs

Are juvenile gangs extensively involved in drug trafficking, and are drug-dealing gangs more likely to be involved in other forms of serious delinquency? C. Ronald Huff reports that his study of four communities in Colorado, Ohio, and Florida found that gang members were "extensively involved in drug sales, especially cocaine and marijuana . . . [and] gang

At its height, gangs were responsible for hundreds of homicides each year. In cities such as Los Angeles and Chicago, gang members murdered one to two fellow youths every day. How might the media or academic portrayal of gang-affiliated youths contribute to the problems they pose?

members sell significantly more cocaine than nongang youths."[76] However, gang involvement in the drug trade appears to vary greatly by ethnicity and locale. Black gangs are more involved in drug trafficking than Latino, Asian, or white gangs.[77] Jeffrey Fagan notes that in Los Angeles, while Chicano gangs sell small quantities of marijuana, the crack and cocaine trade is dominated by black gangs; in New York, the crack sales that emerged after 1986 did not seem to be controlled or dominated by any particular group of street gangs.[78]

The National Youth Gang Center surveyed over 1,000 police and sheriffs' departments and reported that 43 percent of the drug sales in their jurisdictions involved gang members, although the degree of involvement varied extensively (only about a fourth of gang members selling drugs were seen as doing so at a "high" level and nearly half were involved at a "low" level). Although gangs are involved in drug dealing, respondents indicated that gangs did not control or manage most of the drug distribution in their jurisdictions.[79]

Malcolm Klein takes serious issue with both law enforcement officials and criminologists who overemphasize the gang-drug connection. Klein argues that drug gangs and *street gangs* are not the same.[80] More importantly, most street gangs, he argues, simply do not have the necessary leadership, cohesiveness, sense of loyalty and secretiveness, or narrow focus on the mechanics of drug sales. Rather, Klein says that typical street gangs

> tend to have shifting leadership, intermediate levels of cohesiveness, frequently broken codes of honor, and very versatile and independent criminal involvements. Gangs are lousy mechanisms for drug distribution.[81]

James Inciardi and his colleagues studied drug use and serious delinquency in Miami, Florida, and found that only about 5 percent of the street youths in their sample had ever been involved in gangs. Most youths involved in drug distribution saw little reason to belong to gangs. As one 17-year-old youth said:

> The gangs in this town are just not where it's at. They're kid stuff. Most of 'em are just "tag crews," markin' up the buildings with graffiti, bein' macho about when and where the next fight'll be, and struttin' for the ladies. . . . If you want to make some money, ya don't have time for that shit.[82]

Female Gang Delinquency

It is difficult to obtain reliable estimates of the number of female gang members. Recent studies suggest that girls may comprise anywhere from 4 to 38 percent of all gang members.[83] While the majority of gang boys are in all-male gangs, most girls who join gangs join mixed gangs (which tend to be dominated by boys), female gangs affiliated with male gangs, or independent female gangs.[84] Gang girls are much more likely to be involved in delinquency, especially serious delinquency, than are nongang females. In general, gang girls commit fewer violent crimes than gang boys and are more inclined to commit property crime and status offenses.[85] And like males who join gangs, girls' involvement in crime increases with gang membership and tends to decline after leaving the gang.[86]

Based on in-depth interviews with 27 female gang members in St. Louis, Jody Miller and Scott Decker noted that, although girls are less often involved in violent crime than are boys, fully 85 percent of the girls reported having hit someone with the idea of hurting them.[87] Finn-Aage Esbensen and his colleagues surveyed nearly 6,000 eighth-graders in 42 different schools. A total of 623 students (10.6 percent) reported being gang members, including 237 females. While gang boys reported more delinquencies than the girls, "39 percent of the gang girls report attacking someone with a weapon, 21 percent indicate that they have shot at someone . . . 78 percent have been involved in gang fights, and 65 percent have carried hidden weapons."[88] Gang girls are much less likely to be victims of violence than are gang boys, although much more likely than nongang females. Their lower rates of violent victimization are attributed to a number of factors: Gang boys tend to exclude them from potentially violent activities, girls' peripheral status as gang members reduces the likelihood of their being targets of violence by rival gang members, and girls are protected by male gang members against predatory males in the community.[89]

What types of activities characterize the lives of gang members? Are these activities conducive to successful or criminal lifestyles?

Females, like their male counterparts, are generally initiated into gangs through a process of being "beaten in" or being required to assault a rival gang member or to participate in a serious crime. Some girls are tattooed with gang symbols while others may be "blessed in" by gang members praying over the girl. More problematic are initiations where a girl is "sexed in" (the girl is required to have intercourse with multiple male gang members.) Girls who are sexed into a gang are at much greater risk for continued sexual mistreatment and exploitation and are generally viewed by male and female gang members as weak, promiscuous, and subject to contempt and disrespect.[90]

The reasons girls join gangs are varied, although many girls seem to look to the gang as an escape from family problems. Joan Moore and John Hagedorn report that in the Latino gangs they studied in Los Angeles, girls were more likely than boys to come from families that were abusive. The parents of gang girls were also more likely to be alcoholic or heroin users.[91] Jody Miller also reports that gang girls are more likely to come from very dysfunctional families. For example, 71 percent of the gang girls in her study reported serious family problems, such as violence, drug addiction, and drug or alcohol abuse, compared to only 26 percent of nongang girls.[92] Anne Campbell's study of mixed-gender gangs in New York City suggests that girls generally join gangs to escape the isolation they experienced in their families while growing up. The girls she studied looked to the gang for a sense of belonging, for loyalty in relationships, and for unconditional acceptance.[93]

Geoffrey Hunt and his colleagues report a rather different relationship between gang girls and their families. Based on interviews with 47 Hispanic gang members representing 23 different gangs, they noted that gang girls maintain strong ties to family members, especially mothers, sisters, and other female relatives, and that these family connections are significant elements of social support. In many ways, gangs are seen as extensions of their families. These girls had grown up around gangs and gang activities and gangs were simply part of their daily lives. Fully 96 percent of the girls said they had family members who had been, or were currently, members of gangs.[94]

Finally, in her study of Hispanic female gangs in California, Mary Harris found that girls became members of gangs in a manner similar to joining other teenage groups. They were not pressured or coerced into membership but entered gangs through friendships and family ties. Once in the gang, the girl soon took on the attitudes of other gang members, including the willingness to fight, to be "bad," to be "tough," and to use drugs. And although she may have entered the gang through family ties, the gang soon became the girl's primary reference group, demanding stronger loyalty than either family or school.[95] But fighting or engaging in potentially violent confrontations are not the dominant activities of gang girls any more than of gang boys. Rather, most gang girls (and boys) spend the greater part of their time together simply hanging out watching television, listening to the radio, playing music, video games, or cards, or drinking 40s or smoking marijuana.[96]

Gang Suppression, Intervention, and Prevention Strategies

A number of strategies for responding to the problem of youth gangs have evolved over the past 80 years.[97] These strategies include *neighborhood mobilization* approaches popular in the 1920s and 1930s, *social intervention* programs popular in the 1940s and 1950s, programs aimed at *creating social and economic opportunities* for inner-city and at-risk youths used in the 1960s, the emergence of *suppression efforts* used in the 1970s and 1980s, and *intervention and prevention* strategies common in the 1990s.

While suppression strategies continue to dominate the field today, many intervention and prevention programs are being pursued in schools and communities around the country. For many gang experts, suppression strategies combined with intervention programs appear to be the most promising approaches.[98]

Suppression

A number of states have responded to the growing gang problem by revising existing laws or by establishing entirely new legislation aimed at both gang members and gang behaviors. The use of existing laws allows authorities to charge gang youths with basic criminal offenses—crimes against persons, property, and public order—as well as to use conspiracy laws to target gang members who may not have been physically present during the commission of a crime. In some states, conviction for a gang-related crime may limit the range of possible sentences or may carry an automatic maximum sentence (see Box 12–2 for a discussion of some of the ways prosecutors are using the law to control gangs). At the federal level, the Violent Crime Control and Law Enforcement Act of 1994 included provisions allowing federal prosecutors to try juvenile gang members as adults if "the juvenile played a leadership role in an organization, or otherwise influenced other persons to take part in criminal activities, involving the use or distribution of controlled substances or firearms."[99]

Police gang suppression strategies involve a variety of activities. According to a Bureau of Justice Assistance report on urban street gang enforcement, the key elements in police gang suppression involve understanding the nature and scope of the community gang problem, gathering information and intelligence into a comprehensive database, and developing strategies that will ultimately incapacitate gang leaders and the most violent and criminally involved members and associates.[100]

One of the most common strategies is the neighborhood "sweep" in which a large number of officers sweep through a neighborhood, arresting and detaining known or suspected gang members. Another strategy involves "hot spot targeting" of known gang members and their hideouts. Police select

BOX 12–2   DELINQUENCY PREVENTION
Using the Law to Get Tough on Gangs

As the gang problem continues to grow in the United States, an increasing number of states and local communities are turning to new antigang legislation or to new interpretations of existing statutes to crack down on gangs and gang members. Included in these efforts are the use of the Federal Racketeer Influenced and Corrupt Organization (RICO) Act and the Street Terrorism Enforcement and Prevention (STEP) Acts, based on the RICO model; the creation of Safe School Zones; and the use of injunctions and public congregation ordinances.

The RICO Act was signed into law in 1970 and was used for nearly two decades to fight the Mafia and other adult organized-crime groups. Today, however, prosecutors are turning to the RICO laws as a weapon against entrenched youth gangs partly because these laws allow prosecutors to charge gang members for simply being part of a criminal enterprise. This means that the more insulated and protected higher-level leaders of gangs can be prosecuted for the criminal activities of street-level members.

STEP Acts use a pattern of specified crimes as the basis for increasing sentences of youths convicted of gang-related crimes and mandating the forfeiture of a street gang's assets. Typically, the Acts link definitions of "criminal street gang," "pattern of criminal gang activity," and "participation in a criminal street gang." According to the California STEP Act, criminal gang activity is the commission of one or more of seven predicate offenses on two or more separate occasions, while a criminal street gang is defined as an ongoing group that has as one of its primary activities the commission of one or more of the predicate crimes

certain gangs for intensive or saturated surveillance and harassment in an effort to apply pressure and send a message of deterrence. During 1996 and 1997, the Dallas Police Department conducted its Antigang Initiative targeting five areas of the city that were home to seven of the city's most violent gangs. The suppression strategy included saturation patrols/high visibility patrols in target areas in which suspected gang members were stopped and frisked, aggressive curfew enforcement whenever suspected gang members were encountered, and aggressive enforcement of truancy laws and regulations. An evaluation of the program found that gang-related violence decreased in both target and control areas, although the decrease was more substantial in targeted areas (57 percent versus 37 percent).[101]

Another suppression strategy involves the creation of specialized prosecutor programs to target gangs.[102] Prosecutor gang units generally use a vertical prosecution process in which one attorney or a small group of attorneys is assigned to gang cases and is responsible for handling them from inception to sentencing. For example, in Riverside County, California, prosecutors operate a program in which 10 attorneys are on call to handle gang-related murder cases. When these cases arise, the prosecutor's office does not wait

To avoid gang violence, should prison populations be segregated based on gang affiliation? Would such a policy be construed as acquiescence to the criminal element?

and also has a common name or common identifying sign or symbol. Participation in a criminal street gang is considered a separate offense to avoid violating constitutional rights of free association. By keeping precise records pertaining to gang incidents, the police assist prosecutors in targeting gang participants.

Some states, such as Illinois, have enacted Safe School Zone laws that enhance penalties for certain weapons violations that occur within 1,000 feet of a school, public housing property, or a public park. Violations include possessing a silencer or machine gun or carrying a pistol, revolver, stun gun or taser, firearm, or ballistic knife when hooded, robed, or masked. However, a federal Safe School Zone law prohibiting the mere possession of a gun within 1,000 feet of a school was deemed unconstitutional by the U.S. Supreme Court in 1995.

Local governments also have begun to wage a turf war against gangs using a variety of ordinances including curfew laws, antiloitering laws, and civil injunctions. In addition, some courts are using nuisance-abatement injunctions against street activities of gang members, effectively prohibiting their congregating in public space. For example, the San Fernando, California, city council passed an ordinance prohibiting active gang members with recent histories of violent crime from entering its Las Palmas Park. Violation of the ordinance could result in a citation and a fine of up to $250. However, the Supreme Court, in *Chicago* v. *Morales*, held that a Chicago antiloitering law targeting gang members by prohibiting the gathering of two or more people in any public place was unconstitutional and vague. The Court stated that "in this instance the city has enacted an ordinance that affords too much discretion to the police and too little notice to citizens who wish to use the public streets."

Sources: Jamilah Owens and Robert Boehmer, "New Antigang Laws in Effect" (Chicago: Illinois Criminal Justice Information Authority, 1993); Matthew Purdy, "Using the Racketeering Law to Bring Down Street Gangs," *The New York Times*, October 19:A1, B5 (1994); Claire Johnson, Barbara Webster, and Edward Connors, *Prosecuting Gangs: A National Assessment* (Washington, DC: National Institute of Justice, 1995); Malcolm Klein, *The American Street Gang: Its Nature, Prevention and Control* (New York: Oxford University Press, 1995), p. 184; *U.S.* v. *Lopez* 514 U.S. 549 (1995); *Chicago* v. *Morales* 527 U.S. 41 (1999).

for them to work their way through the system. Rather, attorneys assigned to the gang unit go out to the streets with the police to interview victims and witnesses and talk to gang members.[103]

Operation Hardcore, begun in 1979, is a gang suppression program of the Los Angeles Prosecutor's Office that uses vertical prosecution in gang cases to increase conviction rates. In addition, Operation Hardcore provides for specialized training of police for issuing gang warrants and for testifying as expert witnesses, the use of witness protection programs, requests for high bail, and the elimination of plea bargaining.[104] According to Klein, other gang prosecution programs around the country include:[105]

- Transfers to adult court for juvenile gang members
- Forfeiture of cars used in drive-by shootings
- Enhanced penalties for crimes committed near schools
- Enhanced penalties for graffiti writing
- Prosecution for gang recruitment
- Prosecution for criminal conspiracy under federal RICO and similar state laws in cases of drug sales and other applicable crimes

Many police departments around the country have initiated "street sweeps" of suspected gang members in an effort to combat delinquency. Are such programs effective in controlling gang delinquency? Do you think that such policies aggravate or enhance police/community relations?

Intervention and Prevention

However, not all gang experts believe that the gang problem should be viewed in an "us versus them" context or that policy responses should be focused exclusively on suppression. Some criminologists suggest that gangs and the problems they present are best considered within their social, economic, and cultural context. For example, John Hagedorn argues that the growth of gangs in "rustbelt cities," such as Milwaukee, are largely the product of the emerging black urban underclass.[106] Growing unemployment, poverty, and the flight from the cities by both whites and upwardly mobile blacks have left the underclass behind in the inner city. As the poverty of the minority underclass increases, old gangs reposition themselves, new gangs emerge, and gangs generally get stronger, drawing from the increasing number of school dropouts and under- or unemployed youths looking for the only jobs in town.[107] Moreover, the social organization of the community, the social cohesion, friendship ties, and willingness to establish and participate in informal social controls are negatively affected by joblessness. According to William Julius Wilson,

> Neighborhoods plagued by high levels of joblessness are more likely to experience low levels of social organization: the two go hand in hand. High rates of joblessness trigger other neighborhood problems that undermine social organization, ranging from crime, gang violence, and drug trafficking to family breakups and problems in the organization of family life.[108]

Hagedorn stresses the need to develop urban policies directed at the problems that create gangs in the first place. This means creating jobs that pay adequate wages and improving educational opportunities for the urban underclass. Toward this end, he suggests that gang members should be brought in as participating members in any meaningful programs. This may even involve the hiring and training of former gang members as staff and consultants in the development of new programs.[109]

Many communities have turned to intervention and prevention programs that target youths before they join gangs. Contemporary approaches evolved out of programs developed during the late 1960s and early 1970s, in which street workers (also known as "detached workers") were assigned by social service agencies to work directly with gang members.[110] Current programs target at-risk youths in the community who have not yet joined gangs; they are intended to help youths develop positive social relationships and find alternatives to gang participation. These programs use combinations of community-, school-, and family-based strategies, including

- Youth outreach programs
- Establishment of community centers
- Employment and training assistance
- School dropout services
- Multicultural training for teachers
- Family intervention and training
- Substance abuse counseling
- Conflict mediation programs
- Recreational activities[111]

The Boys & Girls Clubs of America (BGCA) have developed a program designed to reach at-risk youth and divert them from gang involvement. Their Gang Prevention Through Targeted Outreach program involves a combination of structured recreational, educational, and life skills programs geared to enhance communication skills, problem-solving techniques, and decision-making abilities. In addition, the BGCA maintains detailed records on each youth, including participation in program activities, school attendance, and contact with the justice system. This information allows caseworkers to reward prosocial behavior or to take proactive measures in the event the youth engages in behaviors likely to lead to gang involvement.[112]

Some police departments are working with local neighborhoods to "design out" gang-related violence. That is, they use the deceptively simple tactic of traffic barriers to block automobile access to certain streets. Operation Cul de Sac (OCDS) was an experiment conducted by the Los Angeles Police Department after they determined that the majority of drive-by shootings and violent gang encounters occurred in clusters on the periphery of neighborhoods linked to major thoroughfares. The police closed all major roads leading to and from the identified hot spots by placing standard cement K-rails

Fraternities and sororities on university campuses meet many of the criteria for gangs. What sorts of deviance and delinquency do Greek organizations engage in at your educational institution? Why aren't fraternities called gangs? Do class, race, and ethnic characteristics impact the manner in which we conceptualize gangs?

(freeway dividers) at the end of the streets that led directly to these roads, thus producing the cul-de-sacs. The barriers effectively changed the situations in which gangs perceived opportunities to carry out "hit-and-run" violent crimes. The number of homicides and assaults in the OCDS area fell significantly during the two years the program was operating, but rose after it ceased operations. Advocates view this approach as an important example of situational crime prevention.[113]

Conclusions

Much of the research on the relationship between peers and delinquency centers around gangs. There is a mythology about gangs that depicts them as organized and cohesive, with strong leadership and an orientation to protecting their turf. Criminologists have found that, by and large, these characteristics do not accurately describe what most gangs are or do. Some researchers have found that gangs do appeal to minorities and lower-class youths in large cities, that gang members tend to have important problems as adolescents, and that they learn to cope by being aggressive, even against other members in the gang. Additionally, recent studies suggest that gang violence is increasing at a serious rate and that much of the current gang violence is related to competition in drug markets.

While legislative, law enforcement, and community strategies to combat gangs have varied greatly over the past 80 years, there is little evidence that they have been able to stem the tide of gangs. Like delinquency in general, gang delinquency ultimately brings youths into contact with the police, the courts (both juvenile and criminal), and the correctional system. Section 4 of this book, therefore, explores each of the components of the justice system and how they respond to juvenile delinquency.

Key Terms

klikas: *Age cohorts within Latino gangs.*

member-based definition: *Defining a crime as gang-related when a gang member or members are either the perpetrators or the victims, regardless of the motive.*

motive-based definition: *Defining a crime as gang-related when committed by a gang member or members in which the underlying reason is to further the interests and activities of the gang.*

youth gang: *A group of youths willing to use deadly violence to claim and protect territory, to attack rival gangs, or to engage in criminal activity.*

Getting Connected

The Office of Juvenile Justice and Delinquency Prevention provides an extensive list of reports and publications about juvenile gangs available over the Internet. They can be found at:

http://www.ncjrs.org/jjgangs.htm

1. How is "youth gang" defined in the 1999 National Youth Gang Survey? How does this definition compare to those discussed in the textbook?
2. According to the 1999 survey, to what extent are youth gang members actually "youths"?
3. According to the 1999 survey, is the gang problem staying the same, getting better, or getting worse?

http://www.ncjrs.org/works/chapter3.htm

1. What are the main causes of gang membership?
2. Explain why "traditional social intervention programs, whether agency-based, outreach or street work, or crisis intervention, have shown little effect or may even have worsened the youth gang problem," according to this article.
3. One of the main goals of this article is to review the problems of evaluating crime prevention strategies. Why is it so difficult to evaluate "what works" in reducing gang-based crime?

The National Youth Gang Center maintains a website with data, literature reviews, and a survey of gang programs at:

http://www.iir.com/nygc

1. Review recent gang-related legislation in your state. Compare it to that in a neighboring state. Are the gang issues similar?
2. Read some of the municipal curfew codes included in this site. How might curfews address a city's gang problem?
3. Read the Albuquerque, New Mexico Anti-Gang Recruitment Ordinance. Do you think this will be an effective way to fight gang recruitment?

Gangsinformation.com provides extensive links useful to gang investigators, researchers, and students. It also includes many links to gang-maintained websites and can be found at:

http://www.ganginformation.com

1. Link on the websites of several gang investigators associations. What kinds of gangs seem to be their focus?
2. Explore several of the gang sites. How do the gangs define themselves? Would they be of interest to the investigators associations?
3. Why do gangs have websites?

A personally maintained website devoted to sharing information on street gangs, especially those in L.A. County, can be found at:

http://www.streetgangs.com

1. What are some of the cultural differences between Blood, Crip, Hispanic, and White gang graffiti, according to this site?
2. What are gang injunctions? How are they used in the Los Angeles area?
3. What are the homies figures and why are they controversial?

Endnotes

1. Quoted in Sarah Huntley, "Gang Violence Appears on Rise," *Rocky Mountain News*, August 18:3B (2001).
2. Paul Lerman, "Gangs, Networks, and Subcultural Delinquency," *American Journal of Sociology* 73:63–71 (1967).
3. Benjamin Lahey, Rachel Gordon, Rolf Loeber, Magda Stouthamer-Loeber, and David Farrington, "Boys Who Join Gangs: A Prospective Study of Predictors of First Gang Entry," *Journal of Abnormal Child Psychology* 27:261–276 (1999).
4. James F. Short, Jr., "Comment on Lerman's 'Gangs, Networks, and Subcultural Delinquency,'" *American Journal of Sociology* 73:513–515 (1967).
5. See Clifford Shaw and Henry McKay, *Social Factors in Juvenile Delinquency* (Washington, DC: U.S. Government Printing Office, 1931); William Healy and Augusta Bronner, *New Light on Delinquency and Its Treatment* (New Haven, CT: Yale University Press, 1936).
6. Michael Hindelang, "With a Little Help from Their Friends: Group Participation in Reported Delinquent Behavior," *British Journal of Criminology* 16:109–125 (1976).
7. Finn-Aage Esbensen and David Huizinga, "Gangs, Drugs, and Delinquency in a Survey of Urban Youth," *Criminology* 31:565–589 (1993); Finn-Aage Esbensen, David Huizinga, and Anne Weiher, "Gang and Non-Gang Youth: Differences in Explanatory Factors," *Journal of Contemporary Criminal Justice* 9:94–111 (1993).
8. Terence Thornberry, Marvin Krohn, Alan Lizotte, and Deborah Chard-Wierschem, "The Role of Juvenile Gangs in Facilitating Delinquent Behavior," *Journal of Research in Crime and Delinquency* 30:55–87 (1993).
9. Sara Battin, Karl Hill, Robert Abbott, Richard Catalano, and J. David Hawkins, "The Contribution of Gang Membership to Delinquency Beyond Delinquent Friends," *Criminology* 36:105–106 (1998).
10. Terence Thornberry and James Burch, "Gang Members and Delinquent Behavior," *Juvenile Justice Bulletin* (Washington, DC: Office of Juvenile Justice and Delinquency Prevention, 1997), pp. 2–3.
11. L. Thomas Winfree, Larry Mays, and Teresa Vigil-Backstrom, "Youth Gangs and Incarcerated Delinquents: Exploring the Ties Between Gang Membership, Delinquency, and Social Learning Theory," *Justice Quarterly* 11:229–253 (1994); L. Thomas Winfree, Teresa Vigil Backstrom, and Larry Mays, "Social Learning Theory, Self-Reported Delinquency, and Youth Gangs," *Youth & Society* 26:147–177 (1994).
12. Frederic Thrasher, *The Gang: A Study of 1,313 Gangs in Chicago* (Chicago: University of Chicago Press, 1927).
13. Thrasher, note 12.
14. Thrasher, note 12, p. 57.
15. Finn-Aage Esbensen, L. Thomas Winfree, Ni He, and Terrance Taylor, "Youth Gangs and Definitional Issues: When Is a Gang a Gang, and Why Does It Matter," *Crime & Delinquency* 47:105–130 (2001).
16. Joan Moore, "Gangs and the Underclass: A Comparative Perspective," in *People and Folks: Gangs, Crime and the Underclass in a Rustbelt City*, edited by John Hagedorn (Chicago: Lake View Press, 1988), p. 5.
17. Walter Miller, "Gangs, Groups, and Serious Youth Crime," in *Critical Issues in Juvenile Delinquency*, edited by David Shichor and Delos Kelly (Lexington, MA: Lexington Books, 1980), p. 121.
18. Ruth Horowitz, "Sociological Perspectives on Gangs: Conflicting Definitions and Concepts," in *Gangs in America*, edited by C. Ronald Huff (Newbury Park, CA: Sage Publications, 1990), p. 45.
19. California Penal Code, Section 186.32.
20. National Youth Gang Center, *1998 National Youth Gang Survey* (Washington, DC: Office of Juvenile Justice and Delinquency Prevention, 2000).
21. National Youth Gang Center, note 20, p. 25.
22. Cheryl Maxon and Malcolm Klein, "Street Gang Violence: Twice as Great, or Half as Great?" in Huff, note 18, pp. 75–76.
23. Maxon and Klein, note 22, p. 77.
24. Cheryl Maxon and Malcolm Klein, "Defining Gang Homicide: An Updated Look at Member and Motive Approaches," in *Gangs in America*, 2nd ed., edited by C. Ronald Huff (Thousand Oaks, CA: Sage, 1996), pp. 3–20.
25. Martin Jankowski, *Islands in the Street: Gangs and American Urban Society* (Berkeley: University of California Press, 1991), pp. 40–47.
26. Randall Shelden, Sharon Tracy, and William Brown, *Youth Gangs in American Society*, 2nd ed. (Belmont, CA: Wadsworth, 2001), p. 75.
27. Walter Miller, "American Youth Gangs," in *Current Perspectives on Criminal Behavior*, edited by Abraham Blumberg (New York: Knopf, 1981), pp. 291–320.

28. R. Lincoln Keiser, *The Vice Lords* (New York: Holt, Rinehart and Winston, 1969), p. 8.
29. James F. Short, Jr., "Collective Behavior, Crime, and Delinquency," in *Handbook of Criminology*, edited by Daniel Glaser (Chicago: Rand McNally, 1974), pp. 403–449.
30. Lewis Yablonsky, "The Delinquent Gang as a Near-Group," *Social Problems* 7:108–117 (1959).
31. Gene Muehlbauer and Laura Dodder, *The Losers: Gang Delinquency in an American Suburb* (New York: Praeger Publishers, 1983), pp. 73–74.
32. Robert Jackson and Wesley McBride, *Understanding Street Gangs* (Costa Mesa, CA: Custom Publishing Co., 1985).
33. Joan Moore, *Homeboys* (Philadelphia: Temple University Press, 1978).
34. John Hagedorn, *People and Folks: Gangs, Crime and the Underclass in a Rustbelt City* (Chicago: Lakeview Press, 1988).
35. Miller, note 27, p. 297.
36. Lewis Yablonsky, *The Violent Gang* (New York: Macmillan Publishing Co., 1962). See also Lewis Yablonsky, *Gangsters* (New York: New York University Press, 1997).
37. Barry Krisberg, *The Gang and the Community* (San Francisco: R&E Research Associates, 1975).
38. Jackson and McBride, note 32, p. 34.
39. Hagedorn, note 34, pp. 92–93.
40. Irving Spergel, "Youth Gangs: Continuity and Change," in *Crime and Justice: A Review of Research*, Vol. 12, edited by Michael Tonry and Norval Morris (Chicago: University of Chicago Press, 1990), pp. 208–211.
41. Hagedorn, note 34, p. 135.
42. Thrasher, note 12.
43. Waln Brown, "Black Gangs as Family Extensions," *International Journal of Offender Therapy and Comparative Criminology* 22:41 (1978).
44. Malcolm Klein, *Street Gangs and Street Workers* (Englewood Cliffs, NJ: Prentice Hall, Inc., 1971), p. 91.
45. James F. Short, Jr. and Fred Strodtbeck, *Group Process and Gang Delinquency* (Chicago: University of Chicago Press, 1965).
46. Klein, note 44.
47. Klein, note 44, p. 83.
48. Peggy Giordano and Stephen Cernkovich, "Friendships and Delinquency," *American Journal of Sociology* 91:1170–1202 (1986).
49. Klein, note 44, p. 123.
50. Hagedorn, note 34, pp. 94–95.
51. Geoffrey Hunt, Karen Joe, and Dan Waldorf, "Drinking, Kicking Back and Gang Banging: Alcohol, Violence and Street Gangs," *Free Inquiry in Creative Sociology* 24:126 (1996).
52. National Youth Gang Center, note 20; Walter Miller, *The Growth of Youth Gang Problems in the United States: 1970–98* (Washington, DC: Office of Juvenile Justice and Delinquency Prevention, 2001).
53. National Youth Gang Center, note 20, p. 10.
54. Miller, note 52.
55. Cheryl Maxon, *Gang Members on the Move* (Washington, DC: Office of Juvenile Justice and Delinquency Prevention, 1998).
56. Richard Zevitz and Susan Takata, "Metropolitan Gang Influence and the Emergence of Group Delinquency in a Regional Community," *Journal of Criminal Justice* 20:93–106 (1992); Hagedorn, note 34.
57. George Hackett, "The Drug Gangs," *Newsweek*, March 28:23 (1988).
58. James Vigil, *Barrio Gangs: Street Life and Identity in Southern California* (Austin, TX: University of Texas Press, 1988), p. 5.
59. Moore, note 33, p. 34.
60. Vigil, note 58, p. 130.
61. Vigil, note 58, pp. 163–164.
62. Vigil, note 58, p. 120.
63. Ko-lin Chin, *Chinese Subculture and Criminality: Nontraditional Crime Groups in America* (Westport, CT: Greenwood Press, 1990).
64. Delbert Joe and Norman Robinson, "Chinatown's Immigrant Gangs: The New Young Warrior Class," *Criminology* 18:341–344 (1980).
65. Karen Joe, "Myths and Realities of Asian Gangs on the West Coast," *Humanity & Society* 18:3–18 (1994).
66. Vicki Torres, "Foot Soldiers Add Violent Twist to Asian Street Gangs," *Los Angeles Times*, August 13:A26 (1993).
67. James Vigil and Steve Yun, "Vietnamese Youth Gangs in Southern California," in Huff, note 18, pp. 146–162.
68. Phelan Wyrick, *Vietnamese Youth Gang Involvement*, OJJDP Fact Sheet (Washington, DC: Office of Juvenile Justice and Delinquency Prevention, 2001).

69. Malcolm Klein, *The American Street Gang: Its Nature, Prevalence, and Control* (New York: Oxford University Press, 1995), p. 109.

70. Geoffrey Hunt, Karen Joe, and Dan Waldorf, "Culture and Ethnic Identity Among Southeast Asian Gang Members," *Free Inquiry in Creative Sociology* 25:9–21 (1997).

71. Hunt et al., note 70, p. 18.

72. Hunt et al., note 70, p. 19.

73. James Howell, "Youth Gang Homicides: A Literature Review," *Crime and Delinquency* 45:208–241 (1999).

74. James Howell, *Youth Gangs*, OJJDP Fact Sheet (Washington, DC: U.S. Department of Justice, 1997).

75. G. David Curry, Cheryl Maxson, and James Howell, *Youth Gang Homicides in the 1990s*, OJJDP Fact Sheet (Washington, DC: Office of Juvenile Justice and Delinquency Prevention, 2001).

76. C. Ronald Huff, *Comparing the Criminal Behavior of Youth Gangs and At-Risk Youths* (Washington, DC: National Institute of Justice, 1998), p. 4.

77. Cheryl Maxon, K. Woods, and Malcolm Klein, "Street Gang Migration: How Big a Threat?" *National Institute of Justice Journal* 230:26–31 (1996).

78. Jeffrey Fagan, "Gangs, Drugs, and Neighborhood Change," in Huff, note 24, p. 49.

79. James Howell and Debra Gleason, *Youth Gang Drug Trafficking* (Washington, DC: Office of Juvenile Justice and Delinquency Prevention, 1999).

80. Klein, note 69, p. 41.

81. Klein, note 69, p. 42.

82. James Inciardi, Ruth Horowitz, and Anne Pottieger, *Street Kids, Street Drugs, Street Crime: An Examination of Drug Use and Serious Delinquency in Miami* (Belmont, CA: Wadsworth Publishing Co., 1993), p. 115.

83. Finn-Aage Esbensen and David Huizinga, "Gangs, Drugs, and Delinquency in a Survey of Urban Youth," *Criminology* 31:565–589 (1993); Irving Spergel, *The Youth Gang Problem* (New York: Oxford University Press, 1995); John Moore and Craig Terett, *Highlights of the 1996 National Youth Gang Survey* (Washington, DC: Office of Juvenile Justice and Delinquency Prevention, 1998); Finn-Aage Esbensen, Elizabeth Deschenes, and Thomas Winfree, "Differences Between Gang Girls and Gang Boys: Results from a Multisite Survey," *Youth & Society* 31:27–53 (1999).

84. Jody Miller and Rod Brunson, "Gender Dynamics in Youth Gangs: A Comparison of Males' and Females' Accounts," *Justice Quarterly* 17:419–448 (2000).

85. Joan Moore and John Hagedorn, *Female Gangs: A Focus on Research* (Washington, DC: Office of Juvenile Justice and Delinquency Prevention, 2001), p. 5.

86. Jody Miller and Scott Decker, Young Women and Gang Violence: Gender, Street Offending, and Violent Victimization in Gangs," *Justice Quarterly* 18:115–140 (2001).

87. Miller and Decker, note 86.

88. Esbensen et al., note 83, p. 41.

89. Miller and Brunson, note 84; Miller and Decker, note 86.

90. Jody Miller, *One of the Guys: Girls, Gangs, and Gender* (New York: Oxford University Press, 2001); Miller and Brunson, note 84; Moore and Hagedorn, note 85.

91. Joan Moore and John Hagedorn, "What Happens to Girls in the Gang?" in Huff, note 24, p. 207.

92. Miller, note 90, p. 37.

93. Anne Campbell, *The Girls in the Gang* (New York: Basil Blackwell, 1984), p. 266.

94. Geoffrey Hunt, Kathleen MacKenzie, and Karen Joe-Laidler, "'I'm Calling My Mom': The Meaning of Family and Kinship Among Homegirls," *Justice Quarterly* 17:1–31 (2000).

95. Mary Harris, "Cholas, Mexican-American Girls, and Gangs," *Sex Roles* 30:289–301 (1994).

96. Miller, note 90, p. 84.

97. Irving Spergel et al., *Gang Suppression and Intervention: Problem and Response, Research Summary* (Washington, DC: Office of Juvenile Justice and Delinquency Prevention, 1994).

98. Catherine Conly, Patricia Kelly, Paul Mahanna, and Lynn Warner, *Street Gangs: Current Knowledge and Strategies* (Washington, DC: U.S. Department of Justice, 1993), pp. 27–28.

99. *Violent Crime Control and Law Enforcement Act of 1994, Title XV* (Washington, DC: U.S. Government Printing Office, 1994).

100. Bureau of Justice Assistance, *Urban Street Gang Enforcement* (Washington, DC: U.S. Department of Justice, 1997), pp. 7–8.

101. James Howell, *Youth Gang Programs and Strategies: Summary* (Washington, DC: Office of Juvenile Justice and Delinquency Prevention, 2000), p. 24.

102. Claire Johnson, Barbara Webster, and Edward Connors, *Prosecuting Gangs: A National Assessment* (Washington, DC: National Institute of Justice, 1995), p. 5.
103. Johnson et al., note 102.
104. Klein, note 69, p. 173.
105. Klein, note 69, p. 175.
106. Hagedorn, note 34.
107. Anne Campbell, "Gangs, Supergangs, and Kids on the Corner," *The New York Times Review*, February 5:36 (1989).
108. William Julius Wilson, *When Work Disappears: The World of the New Urban Poor* (New York: Alfred Knopf, 1997), p. 21.
109. Hagedorn, note 34, pp. 167–168.
110. Klein, note 69.
111. Spergel et al., note 97, p. 14; Conly et al., note 98, pp. 33–35.
112. Finn-Aage Esbensen, *Preventing Adolescent Gang Involvement* (Washington, DC: Office of Juvenile Justice and Delinquency Prevention, 2000).
113. James Lasley, "Designing Out" *Gang Homicides and Street Assaults* (Washington, DC: National Institute of Justice, 1998).

The Juvenile Justice System

This final section examines the American juvenile justice system and how it responds to children identified as delinquents. During the last two decades of the 19th century and the early years of the 20th century, the child-saving movement defined juvenile delinquency as a social problem.

This new social problem was to be dealt with by a new, completely separate complex juvenile justice system. This produced major reforms in police department organization and policies, including new units dedicated to dealing with juvenile offenders and new procedures for arresting, booking and holding juveniles in custody. In addition, a separate juvenile court system was created for the adjudication of delinquents, including status offenders and dependent and neglected children. The new court viewed juvenile offenders as in need of treatment, rather than punishment, and probation soon became the default disposition. But not all juvenile offenders were placed on probation; an increasing number were placed in new correctional institutions intended to provide rehabilitation through schooling, vocational training, and counseling.

In Chapter 13, the historical role of police, legal limitations placed on police, the role of police in the formation of juvenile delinquency, and how police discretion affects which juveniles become officially identified as delinquents are examined.

Chapter 14 examines the modern juvenile court and explores the processing of juveniles through the court, detention, eventual disposition, aftercare, and due process issues in the juvenile court. In addition, the chapter explores the transfer process whereby a juvenile may be waived to adult criminal court for prosecution.

Approximately 100,000 children were housed in state correctional facilities on any given day in the late 1990s. Chapter 15 explores issues related to contemporary correctional practices—the nature of the U.S. correctional system for juveniles and which youths are most likely to be incarcerated, how long they stay, and what happens to them while there. Differences in the treatment of youths in correctional facilities—differences based on race, class, and particularly sex—raise serious questions about juvenile corrections today.

In the final analysis, the most severe sanction the state can impose on an offender is death. The United States is one of only a few countries that executes people who committed their crimes when they were juveniles. While the debate continues over whether people should be executed, 73 people convicted of crimes when they were juveniles sat on death row in 2001.

Chapter 13
Police and Delinquency

Revised Miranda Warning You have the right to remain silent. You also have the right to swing first. However, if you choose the right to swing first, any move you make can and will be used as an excuse to beat the shit out of you. You have the right to have a doctor present. If you cannot afford a doctor, one will be appointed for you. Do you understand what I just told you, you asshole!

—*Anonymous*[1]

A student who was a police officer told us about the "revised" Miranda warning. He said many of his fellow officers fully endorsed it and carried a card in their wallet with the revised warning written on it. What he told us confirms what criminologists have suspected for a long time: Police hold beliefs that separate them from the public.[2] Many are secretive, defensive, and distrustful of outsiders and "see themselves as the pragmatic guardians of the morals of the community . . . the 'thin blue line' against the forces of evil."[3]

Policing in the United States

Policing in the United States is done differently today than it was in the past. In the American colonies, when settlers lived in widely scattered villages, the *parish-constable system* of policing was used.[4] This was the type of police system the colonists were familiar with in England. Two of its distinctive features were the **watch and ward**, which allowed the constable to draft any male into service to guard the town at night and, the **hue and cry**, a loud call for help that was shouted by the constable or by one of the watchmen when they confronted more resistance than they could handle. The parish-constable system worked very well in the beginning, when there was little crime, and when the crime that did exist was minor.

Once the colonists settled in towns, such as Boston in 1630 and Philadelphia in 1682, they felt a greater need for police protection. Police operations became more formalized. However, the changes that were made did very little to prevent crime, which flourished well into the next century.[5]

In the 19th century a "new" police system evolved during the Industrial Revolution when municipal governments were forced to find fresh ways to manage highly diverse populations. Old-time Americans were fearful of the strangers on the streets, many of whom spoke foreign languages and practiced different customs and religions. They also were concerned about the spiraling number of poor and dependent people and the worsening crime problem. The fear of crime, coupled with the feeling of a decaying society, set the stage for police reform.

Since the colonial era, American policing has been the responsibility of males. Why? Does sex influence the ability to police society? Since males overwhelmingly commit crime, is it appropriate that police officers are also disproportionately male? How might feminist criminologists address these questions?

Turning to England for models of effective policing, the public endorsed the idea the government must assume responsibility for the social well-being of its citizens. The practical consequence of implementing this idea was the creation of police forces with paid full-time uniformed officers who assumed a wide range of duties, ranging from lighting the gas lamps in the evening to monitoring elections and apprehending criminals. By 1870, all big cities in the United States had full-time police departments.

It was not until the early 20th century that police departments created juvenile units. When they did, opportunities in policing became available for women, who had previously been excluded from the profession. In 1905 Portland, Oregon, hired the first female officer, Lola Baldwin. A few years later, New York City and Washington, D.C., hired women to look after "runaway, truant, and delinquent children, [and to] check on amusement parks, dance halls, and disorderly houses, and otherwise discourage youngsters from pursuing criminal careers."[6] By 1924 most urban police departments had established juvenile bureaus. This trend continued into the 1940s and 1950s, largely in response to an outbreak of delinquent gang activity (see Chapter 12). Today, nearly all police departments allocate a portion of their resources to delinquency prevention (Box 13–1).

Police, Children, and the Law

The most important Supreme Court decision affecting the rights of juveniles is actually a case about an adult. In 1966 in **Miranda v. Arizona**, the Supreme Court issued a ruling that forever changed *all* police-citizen interactions.[7] The *Miranda* case still raises many interesting questions. Who was Ernesto Miranda? What crime did he commit? Did the police treat Miranda fairly? Were his rights violated?

On the night of March 2, 1963, in Phoenix, Arizona, 18-year-old Barbara Ann Johnson was walking to a bus when she was assaulted by a man who shoved her into his car, tied her hands and ankles, and drove to the outskirts of the city where he raped her. He then drove Johnson to a street near her home, let her out of the car, and asked her to say a prayer for him.

Johnson immediately telephoned the police. Soon thereafter police picked up Ernesto Miranda and asked him whether he would *voluntarily* talk with them about the incident. Miranda agreed and was taken to the police station, where he *willingly* participated in a lineup and was identified by Johnson as the rapist.

Ernesto Miranda, a seriously disturbed man with pronounced sexual fantasies, was a 23-year-old eighth-grade dropout with a police record dating from when he was age 14. During police interrogation, two Phoenix police officers told Miranda that Johnson had identified him as the rapist. At that point, Miranda agreed to prepare a written confession, in which he described the incident and stated that his confession was voluntary and that he had given it with full knowledge of his legal rights. He was charged with kidnapping and rape.

Ernesto Miranda was a career criminal who committed dire offenses such as rape and kidnapping. Nevertheless, Miranda is a martyr in the annals of jurisprudence. Does the United States' system of law hold unsavory characters as sacrosanct because of the implications of their legal cases? If so, is this problematic?

When the case went to trial, Miranda's court-appointed attorney, Alvin Moore, questioned the officers about their interrogation of his client. Both officers stated that at no time during the two-hour interrogation had either of them advised Miranda of his legal right to have counsel present during police questioning.[8] Nevertheless, and over Moore's objection, the trial judge allowed Miranda's written confession to be admitted into evidence. Miranda was found guilty, convicted, and sentenced to 20 to 30 years in prison for each offense. The case was appealed to the Arizona Supreme Court, which upheld the decision of the lower court. The case was subsequently appealed to the U.S. Supreme Court, where Miranda's new attorney, John Flynn,

BOX 13–1   DELINQUENCY PREVENTION
Getting Tough on Delinquency

Police departments have launched delinquency prevention programs since the beginning of the 20th century. From the first Police Athletic League programs in the 1920s to the more recent DARE programs, police have attacked delinquency on many fronts, as illustrated by the following programs.

- In St. Louis, police officers knock on selected doors and tell startled parents: "We think your child has a gun. Fill out this form, and we will come in and get it." No one is arrested and no one goes to jail. What police are asking is legal. What they want is for parents to exercise their legal right to let police search their minor child's room without a warrant.
- In Indianapolis, police practice drive-by enforcement. Special teams of officers are deployed into high-crime areas with a free-ranging mandate to stop vehicles and stop and frisk citizens to find firearms. A small-scale version of this program was introduced in Kansas City, and gun-related crime was cut in half.
- In Lawrence, Massachusetts, a program to stop drug dealing in one neighborhood has been operating for more than two years. To keep drug

customers out of the neighborhood, police have "sealed off" the area by closing four streets with roadblocks and setting up a checkpoint at the only intersection. Neighborhood residents have been given yellow passes that allow them to come and go freely. Nonresidents who enter the neighborhood are stopped and given cards warning that the area is under police surveillance. Police also record the license plate numbers of nonresidents' cars and send letters to the vehicles' owners telling them that their car was stopped at a police checkpoint.

Delinquency prevention programs like these have been applauded and criticized. Many citizens like the results the programs generate; namely, less crime and a feeling of a safer neighborhood. But critics complain the tactics are too aggressive and violate constitutional rights. What is your opinion? Under what circumstances do the ends justify the means?

Sources: "'Whatever It Takes' to Stop Crime," *The Denver Post,* February 12:17A (1995); John Larrabee, "Mass. Town's Roadblock to Crime," *USA Today,* December 23:3A (1992).

asked the Court to decide whether "the confession of a poorly educated, mentally abnormal, indigent defendant, not told of his right to counsel, which was not requested, can be admitted into evidence over specific objection based on the absence of counsel." On June 13, 1966, the Court announced its decision. In a 5-to-4 vote, Chief Justice Earl Warren expressed the majority opinion that Miranda's rights to protection from self-incrimination under the Fifth Amendment and to counsel under the Sixth Amendment had been violated.[9]

One year later, in 1967, in the case of **In re Gault**, the Court directed police to change their practices with respect to how *juvenile* suspects we treated.[10] In *Gault*, the Court extended to juveniles *many* of the same protections that had been established for adults in *Miranda*, including the right against self-incrimination and the right to counsel (see Chapter 14).

Search and Seizure

Every crime is like a jigsaw puzzle with a few missing pieces. Police *search* for the missing pieces by investigating the premises or suspects they believe are linked to them. Related to the search is the *seizure*, where people or objects relating to the crime are taken into custody.[11] The **exclusionary rule** of the Fourth Amendment protects people from unreasonable searches and seizures.[12] If police produce evidence illegally, it will not be admissible in court (see ***Mapp v. Ohio***).[13] However, when a suspect is arrested, police may search the suspect and, to a limited extent, the immediate area he or she occupies. This is known as the **one-arm's length rule**. It was established in 1969 in ***Chimel v. California***.[14]

Arrest

The same law of arrest applies to adults and juveniles. To make a legal arrest, the police must have **probable cause**, which is a set of facts that would lead a reasonable person to believe a crime has been committed and the person to be arrested committed it. In *misdemeanor cases*, police can arrest a person *only* if the crime is committed in their presence (called the *in-presence requirement*). In *felony cases*, police may make an arrest (1) if they observe the crime in progress or (2) if they have knowledge a felony crime has occurred and have probable cause for believing a particular person committed it.

Booking

The most significant difference in the rights of adult and juvenile suspects occurs at **booking**, which is the official recording of a person into detention after arrest. Once suspects are booked, they are photographed and fingerprinted, and samples of their handwriting, voice, and blood are taken.[15] This information becomes part of the alleged offender's permanent record.

In most states police cannot fingerprint and photograph children. Juveniles, however, may be fingerprinted and photographed on court order and then only for identification or investigative purposes (to determine whether a youth's fingerprints match ones found at the crime scene, for example). Juvenile records may also be destroyed when a case is closed. If the records exist in the police department after the child has reached the age of majority (usually 18), the records may be erased through an *expungement order*, which must be issued by a judge to a police department, instructing it to destroy file material relating to the juvenile's arrest history.

Interrogation

During police questioning, juveniles have the right to:

1. *Remain silent.* Any statement the youth makes will be used as evidence against him or her.
2. *Have an attorney present.* If the youth cannot afford an attorney, one will be provided at public expense.

One issue that may develop when police interrogate juveniles is whether children can *waive* their rights. In *People v. Lara* in 1967, the Court decided that whether children are capable of waiving their rights will be determined by evaluating the *totality of the circumstances* of the case or by looking at the "whole picture."[16] The validity of a waiver depends on the child's age, education, intelligence, and on circumstances surrounding the interrogation such as methods and length of police questioning.[17] The Court's position went further in *Fare v. Michael C.*, where it held that a child asking police to speak to a probation officer was not equivalent to his requesting to speak to an attorney.[18] *Only* a request to speak to an attorney invokes the juvenile's *Miranda* rights.

Lineups

In a police lineup adults and juveniles have similar protections. Children have a right to counsel at lineups *after* they are charged with a crime. If this right is violated, any information produced at the pretrial identification stage of the process will likely be inadmissible in court under the exclusionary rule.[19]

Children and adults also have similar due process rights.[20] What separates children and adults is that police may take juveniles into custody for a much wider range of offenses, such as curfew violations, running away, and truancy (see Chapter 1). Police also have more latitude when deciding what to do with children, especially when the child is accused of committing a minor crime. This raises the issue of police discretion, which is the topic of the next section.

Police Discretion

When police suspect a juvenile of a crime, they can handle the matter informally or refer the child to juvenile court, criminal court, or to a welfare agency. While the decision should be made on the basis of legal criteria, sometimes it is not. Police may be influenced by *non*legal factors. In describing police encounters with poor black juveniles, Werthman and Piliavin concluded that:

> Street life in a typical [black] ghetto is perceived [by police] as an uninterrupted sequence of suspicious scenes. Every well-dressed man or woman standing aimlessly on the street during hours when most people are at work is carefully scrutinized for signs of an illegal source of income; every boy wearing boots, black pants, long hair, and a club jacket is viewed as potentially responsible for some item on the list of muggings, broken windows, and petty thefts that still remain to be cleared; and every hostile glance at the passing patrolman is read as a sign of possible guilt.[21]

What has changed in the 35 years since this research was published? Are relations between police and poor black children still defined by structured

Police officers are disproportionately cynical and harbor punitive, distrustful views of society. Why? Do the negative and sometimes depressing social circumstances that police face influence their perspective?

conflict? Is police use of discretion different today than it once was? Sandra Browning and her colleagues studied these questions and found that blacks today still believe "they are personally and vicariously hassled by the police . . . police surveillance is discriminatory . . . [and] clear racial differences exist in whom police officers watch and stop."[22] Their conclusion reinforces one drawn by Doug Smith who found that suspects police encountered in lower-class neighborhoods were more likely to be arrested than those police stopped in middle- or upper-class areas.[23]

Policing is a largely reactive, not proactive, endeavor. Thus, allegations that the police discriminate against blacks by actively patrolling minority neighborhoods are largely anecdotal.

How does the offender-victim dyad and the substance of official and victimization data address the issue of police bias against blacks?

However, as shown in Table 13–1, today police handle cases involving juveniles in a more formal, legalistic, follow-the-book manner than they did in the past. For instance, in 1972, 45 percent of the juveniles taken into police custody were handled informally *within* the department and released. By 1999, the percentage of children handled informally and released dropped to 23 percent.[24] But does one legal or nonlegal factor affect the arrest decision more than the others? Next, we will answer that question.

Legal Factors

The three legal factors of offense seriousness, prior arrest record, and presence of evidence have a profound influence on the arrest decision. However, each one affects it differently. Next, the research on each factor is examined.

Offense Seriousness   Juveniles who commit serious crimes are more likely to be arrested than ones who commit minor offenses. This is the

Table 13–1   Police Dispositions of Children in Custody, 1972–1999 (in percent)

YEAR	REFERRED TO JUVENILE COURT JURISDICTION	HANDLED WITHIN DEPARTMENT AND RELEASED	REFERRED TO CRIMINAL OR ADULT COURT	REFERRED TO OTHER POLICE AGENCY	REFERRED TO WELFARE AGENCY
1972	50.8	45.0	1.3	1.6	1.3
1973	49.5	45.2	1.5	2.3	1.4
1974	47.0	44.4	3.7	2.4	2.5
1975	52.7	41.6	2.3	1.9	1.4
1976	53.4	39.0	4.4	1.7	1.6
1977	53.2	38.1	3.0	1.8	3.0
1978	55.9	36.6	3.8	1.8	1.9
1979	57.3	34.6	4.8	1.7	1.6
1980	58.1	33.8	4.8	1.7	1.6
1981	58.0	33.8	5.1	1.6	1.5
1982	58.9	32.5	5.4	1.5	1.6
1983	57.5	32.8	4.8	1.7	3.1
1984	60.0	31.5	5.2	1.3	2.0
1985	61.8	30.7	4.4	1.2	1.9
1986	61.7	29.9	5.5	1.1	1.8
1987	62.0	30.3	5.2	1.0	1.4
1988	63.1	29.1	4.7	1.1	1.9
1989	63.9	28.7	4.5	1.2	1.7
1990	64.5	28.3	4.5	1.1	1.6
1991	64.2	26.1	5.0	1.0	1.7
1992	62.5	30.1	4.7	1.1	1.7
1993	67.3	25.6	4.8	0.9	1.8
1994	63.2	29.5	4.7	1.0	1.7
1995	65.7	28.4	3.3	0.9	1.7
1996	68.6	23.3	6.2	0.9	0.9
1997	68.9	24.6	6.8	0.8	1.1
1998	69.2	22.2	6.8	0.9	1.0
1999	69.2	22.5	6.4	1.0	0.8

Source: Ann Pastore and Kathleen Maguire, *Sourcebook of Criminal Justice Statistics, 2000* (Washington, DC: Bureau of Justice Statistics, 2001).

conclusion reached by Robert Terry from a study of police dispositions of more than 9,000 juvenile offenses.[25] In a related study, Donald Black and Albert Reiss divided offenses into four types and found that the likelihood of being arrested increased with offense seriousness.[26]

Police, however, do not always respond to serious crimes in the same way. They determine how they will handle a case based on three criteria. If

The juvenile justice system is actually extremely lenient. Most crimes never come to the attention of the police. Many charges are reduced to facilitate plea agreements. Offenders are often given chances with intermediate sanctions before facing institutional placement. Prison terms are routinely reduced because of overcrowding. Imagine that none of this occurred. Would a truly efficient and nonlenient juvenile justice system differentially impact youth based on their sex, race, and social class??

they believe the offense was sophisticated (rather than amateurish), premeditated (rather than spontaneous), malicious (rather than mischievous), they are more likely to arrest and refer the child to juvenile court rather than handle it informally.[27]

Prior Arrest Record   Police are more likely to arrest children who have a prior arrest record. Terry found that a juvenile's prior arrest record was a very strong predictor of police action. In his study, first-time offenders constituted 38 percent of juveniles arrested but only 7 percent of the juveniles referred to juvenile court. At the other extreme were juveniles with five or more previous arrests. They constituted 20 percent of arrests but more than 66 percent of juvenile court referrals.[28]

Based on observations of police-juvenile encounters in two cities, Aaron Cicourel concluded that having a prior arrest record often turned an otherwise trivial event into a serious one.[29] He also discovered that a youth's prior arrest record became a more important factor when decisions were made at the police station rather than on the street. Patrol officers often lack the necessary information to take prior arrest record into account. Patrol officers may also view past-offense history as irrelevant, since their primary concern is handling the situation they face in the least troublesome manner.[30]

Presence of Evidence   Not much attention has been given to how the presence of evidence influences police decision making. Black and Reiss examined the role of evidence and discovered that in patrol work there are two ways suspects are connected with a crime: (1) police see the suspect commit the crime or (2) a citizen informs the police about a crime and who did it. In about half of the situations that Black and Reiss researched, police witnessed the offense. Citizens provided testimonial evidence in an additional 23 percent of the cases. The remaining cases lacked any evidence of criminal conduct. Therefore, in roughly 75 percent of the routine police-juvenile contacts, police were provided with evidence sufficient to link a suspect to a crime. In these situations, 13 percent of the suspects were arrested. In the citizen-testimony situations, 19 percent of the suspects were arrested. In only one-half of 1 percent of cases was a suspect arrested when there was no situational evidence available.[31] These arrest percentages illustrate the discretion police have when deciding what to do with juvenile suspects even when they have persuasive evidence that the youth committed a crime.

Nonlegal Factors

Nonlegal factors have nothing to do with the crime, but influence the decision police make anyway. Below, several nonlegal factors are discussed with regard to how they may affect the arrest decision.

Race   Race has received more attention than any other nonlegal factor. Recall from Chapter 2 that studies examining the relationship between a suspect's race and police disposition reported a mixed bag of results. Some studies concluded that race mattered and other studies found it did not matter very much. Today, however, criminologists generally believe police do treat black and white children differently for comparable offenses.[32]

Proportionally more black than white juveniles are arrested.[33] There are several reasons why and each may be related to racial profiling as it is discussed in Box 13–2. For example, police departments assign more patrol officers to black neighborhoods than to white ones.[34] Police also stop and question black youths at a higher rate than they do white juveniles.[35] In addition, police think black juveniles are more likely to be involved in serious criminal activity than whites.[36] These practices and beliefs on the part of police generate feelings of hostility among black children. In turn, black juveniles are more likely than white youths to interact with police in a more antagonistic manner, which leads to their being arrested more often.[37]

Offender's Attitude   In 1963 Howard Becker noted that citizens who were disrespectful of police were more likely to be arrested.[38] Piliavin and Briar tested this idea over a nine-month period by observing police-juvenile encounters. They found that police decisions were based on character cues that emerged from interactions with juveniles. Among the cues police observed were the juvenile's age, race, grooming, dress, and demeanor. A juvenile's demeanor was a principal predictor of outcome in 50 to 60 percent of the cases.[39]

Aaron Cicourel also examined the role of demeanor. He determined that police initially try to establish a "trust" relationship with the child. They interpret the child's demeanor as evidence of the youth either accepting or rejecting their trust. Failure to show the proper demeanor (deference to authority, contriteness, politeness) was viewed by police as a violation of trust and resulted in a more punitive disposition.[40]

In a related study, Black and Reiss classified juveniles' demeanor as "very deferential," "civil" (expressing moderate and realistic amounts of respect), or "antagonistic." Excluding felonies, the arrest percentages for encounters where suspects were very deferential was 17 percent; for those where suspects were civil, 12 percent; and for those when suspects behaved antagonistically, 18 percent. When Black and Reiss's findings are compared to those reported by Piliavin and Briar, some striking differences in the percentages of juveniles arrested within similar demeanor categories are noted. Whereas Black and Reiss reported 18 percent of their "antagonistic juveniles" were arrested, Piliavin and Briar found nearly four times that many arrests for "uncooperative juveniles." Only 4 percent of the "cooperative juveniles" in Piliavin and Briar's study were arrested, compared with 13 percent of the combined "civil and deferential suspects" in the Black and Reiss sample.[41]

One explanation for the incompatible findings is that the researchers produced their data in different ways. Black and Reiss relied on assessments by 36 trained observers while Piliavin and Briar observed the interactions themselves. In addition, Black and Reiss observed regular patrol officers and Piliavin and Briar watched specialized juvenile officers.

BOX 13–2   A WINDOW ON DELINQUENCY
Racial Profiling

About half of all black men say they have been victims of racial profiling. Police justify racial profiling on the basis of arrest statistics that suggest blacks are more likely than whites to commit crime. Studies of racial profiling, however, indicate they are not. For example, in Maryland, 73 percent of those stopped and searched on a section of Interstate 95 were black, yet state police reported that equal percentages of the whites and blacks who were searched, statewide, had drugs or other contraband.

Racial profiling exists because the United States may be a racist society. Joe Feagin thinks people are born, live, and die within a racist system. He states:

Each major part of a . . . person's life is shaped by racism. [A] person's birth and parents are shaped by racism, since mate selection is limited by racist pressures against interracial marriage. Where one lives is often determined by the racist practices of landlords, bankers, and others in the real estate profession. The clothes one wears and what one has to eat are affected by access to resources that varies by position in the racist hierarchy. When one goes off to school, her or his education is shaped by contemporary racism–from the composition of the student body to the character of

the curriculum. Where one goes to church is often shaped by racism. . . . Even getting sick, dying, and being buried may be influenced by racism. Every part of the life cycle . . . [is] shaped by the racism that is integral to the foundation of the United States (Feagin, 2000:2).

If Feagin is correct, children of color have always been and will be victims of racial profiling. As it was in the past, whites today presume black children to be lazy, ignorant, lecherous, and delinquent, whereas white children are seen as industrious, literate, virtuous, and law-abiding. One consequence of these beliefs is that the children are treated differently. To the extent police hold these views, they will also react to the children in different ways. It is sad that in the 21st century the behavior of children is still filtered through a lens darkened by a racist ideology that permeates all social institutions, including law enforcement.

Sources: David Cole and John Lamberth, "The Fallacy of Racial Profiling," *The New York Times*, May 13:13 (2001); Joe Feagin, *Racist America* (New York: Routledge, 2000); William Helmreich, *The Things They Say Behind Your Back* (New Brunswick, NJ: Transaction Books, 1997); Tomas Almaguer, *Racial Fault Lines* (Berkeley, CA: University of California Press, 1994).

Until recently, the idea that a child's demeanor influenced the arrest decision stood unchallenged. However, in 1994, David Klinger argued that the suspect's demeanor does not exert an independent impact on the arrest decision. According to Klinger, the problem with earlier studies is they did not control for hostile behavior that occurred *after* the arrest and therefore could not have influenced the arrest.[42]

Social Class   Several criminologists have examined the impact of social class on police disposition of juveniles. Some research reports that police treat poor and wealthy youths similarly for comparable offenses, while other studies reach the opposite conclusion.[43] Terence Thornberry found that social class had a strong effect on police dispositions that did not go away when controlling for offense seriousness or prior record.[44]

Aaron Cicourel also found social class to be related to police referrals of juveniles to court. But as he explained, social class operates *indirectly* on the likelihood of court referral. Juveniles from middle- and upper-class homes fared much better *after* coming into contact with police because their families could mobilize resources to minimize their involvement with the juvenile justice system. Alternatively, parents of lower-class juveniles often felt that police and probation officers should intervene and help them control their children.[45]

Sex   Conventional wisdom tells us that a suspect's sex makes a difference in police dispositions. Some studies find that girls are treated more leniently than boys and other research does not. Thomas Monahan reported that (1) police treated female suspects more leniently and (2) police were more likely to arrest girls than boys for sex offenses.[46] Subsequently, research has investigated one or the other of these findings.

Delbert Elliott and Harwin Voss also concluded that girls were treated more leniently,[47] a finding that has been confirmed by Gail Armstrong[48] and Meda Chesney-Lind.[49] But Katherine Teilman and Pierre Landry found that police responded more harshly to girls who committed relatively minor status offenses, such as running away and incorrigibility.[50] Similarly, Ruth Horowitz and Ann Pottiger found that girls who committed serious felonies were less likely to be arrested than boys but were more likely than males to be arrested for less serious crimes.[51]

What happens to boys and girls *after* they have been arrested? Do girls receive preferential treatment at the police station? Early work examining these questions showed that girls were treated more harshly.[52] They were more likely to be referred to juvenile court or to have their case turned over to a social service agency. However, Teilman and Landry have observed a trend toward equality in police responses to girls and boys charged with status offenses.[53]

Age   Criminologists have studied the relationship between an offender's age and police disposition. Nathan Goldman found that older youths were more likely to be referred to juvenile court. Juveniles under age 10 were referred to court 21 percent of the time; those between ages 10 and 15, 30 percent; and adolescents 15 to 18 years old, 46 percent. In accounting for this referral pattern, Goldman proposed two possibilities. First, the offenses of very young children were typically less serious. Second, some police officers considered the offenses of young children as normal childhood escapades requiring informal rather than formal actions; others thought that formal system processing would do more harm than good; still other officers were too embarrassed to assume a police role in cases where the offender did not fit the stereotypical mold of a criminal menace to society.[54]

> Extralegal factors have been found to influence the treatment individuals receive from criminal justice personnel. Such findings are often presented as evidence of a biased justice system. However, demographic, personality, and behavioral characteristics also influence treatment. Is the justice system held to an unrealistic utopian ideal of equality that other social institutions are not? If not, why?

Police officers have wide discretionary powers. The police may informally process delinquents to avoid officially involving them in the juvenile justice system. Do informal sanctions or scare tactics work? Is the process of being handcuffed so visceral that delinquents are "scared straight?"

The majority of a police officer's time is spent serving the community, not performing law enforcement. Have our attitudes toward and appreciation of police officers changed since the terrorist attacks of September 11, 2001? Why or why not?

Similarly, Alexander McEachern and Rita Bauzer reported that when offense seriousness was held constant, the proportion of court petitions requested varied with age, ranging from a low of four percent for juveniles under age 10 to a high of 41 percent for people ages 17 to 18. Police records from Santa Monica, California, also indicated that petition rates were higher for older children.[55]

Bodine's analysis of over 3,000 juvenile dispositions showed that for both first-time and repeat offenders, the percentages of children referred to court were smaller for younger juveniles than for older ones.[56] Being young was more likely to reduce the possibility of referral for first-time offenders but not for recidivists. Police apparently will give young children a break if they do not have a prior record of delinquency.

Structure and Organization of Police Departments   James Q. Wilson studied how the social organization of a police department affects decisions officers make.[57] Wilson hypothesized that how police handle juveniles was predominately affected by the department's organization, community attachments, and social norms. He tested this idea in a study of the juvenile bureaus in Western City and Eastern City. Western City was a more professional force, while the Eastern City department was more of a fraternal one.

The Western City department was highly bureaucratized; organizational rules were numerous and specific; supervision was tight. Officers were likely to treat all juveniles according to a strict interpretation of departmental rules. In contrast, the Eastern City police department lacked systematic rules to guide officer decision making concerning juveniles, and supervision of their processing was minimal. Officers handled juvenile suspects primarily on the basis of personal judgment, taking into consideration individual and situational differences.

Although earlier research had indicated that department policy does not ensure consistent decision making among officers, Wilson's study suggests that when there is both centralized management and close supervision, departmental policy will more likely be adhered to by officers in the field. Richard Sundeen has tested whether it is.[58] He found that in departments with high bureaucratic control, the greater the policy emphasis on counsel and release dispositions, the higher the rate of counsel and release. In departments characterized by low bureaucratic control, policy emphasis had little impact on disposition rates.

Police Diversion

After police decide to take a child into custody, they must decide what to do with the juvenile. They have several options, ranging from giving the child a stern warning to referring the juvenile to court. Of the children police took

Traditionally, female delinquents were afforded "chivalry" by the justice system, that is, their delinquency was overlooked by paternalistic police and courts. The exception to this occurred when female delinquents violated traditional gender roles. Such behavior warranted harsher treatment from the justice system. Has this viewpoint of female delinquency changed? Why?

into custody in 1999, 69 percent were referred to juvenile court, 6 percent were referred to criminal court, 1 percent were referred to a child welfare agency, and the remaining 23 percent were handled within the department and released.[59] Police thus decide to divert the child from formal entry into the juvenile justice system in about one-fourth of the cases they encounter.

Internal Diversion

The most basic form of internal diversion is *diversion without referral*. In these cases, police warn, counsel, and release the child without taking any formal action. In contrast, there is *diversion with referral*, where a youth is referred to a program administered by an agency other than the juvenile justice system. Diversion with referral usually takes one of four forms.

An *internal referral* or an in-house diversion is the referral of a case from one branch of the police department to another branch better equipped to handle it. In-house programs can be organized in different ways. In some departments, an officer administers the program and supervises a team of full-time professional counselors (usually civilians). In a variation of this approach, an officer serves as an administrator and directs the efforts of a team of volunteer counselors. Typical internal referral programs include community volunteer programs, recreation programs, and probation programs.

The goal of *community volunteer programs* is to identify and recruit citizens to provide assistance to problem youths. The citizens serve as Big Brothers or Big Sisters or by providing educational tutoring or employment opportunities. Police officers are responsible for identifying and developing liaisons with the citizens. Volunteers are trained in the objectives of the diversion program (for instance, counseling about drugs and alcohol) and receive additional training in child development and in crisis intervention techniques.

Recreation programs are found in many large and medium-size police departments. Athletic activities—Police Athletic League programs, for example—attempt to channel the energy of delinquent youths into socially constructive activities. These programs are based on the assumption that if youths are exposed to the benefits of sportsmanship, playing by the rules, and healthy competition, they will internalize these values and apply them to other spheres of life. It is believed that by having the police directly involved in these programs, relations between police and juveniles will be improved.

Diversionary *probation programs* are designed to teach children that they must stay out of trouble. Children who are assigned to a probation program must report to police officers on a regular basis. The purpose of the meetings is to allow the juvenile to inform the police of his or her activities since the last visit and to receive encouragement, advice, or warning (as warranted) from the officers. Children who violate the conditions of the program are referred to juvenile court.

External Diversion

External diversion programs are an alternative to processing the child through the juvenile justice system. *External referrals* involve the diversion of youths to programs outside the police agency. Police departments use four criteria to decide whether to refer a youth to a community service agency: acceptability, suitability, availability, and accountability.[60]

1. Acceptability.   Police officers have a tendency to stereotype certain service agencies as soft, lenient, coddling, and permissive. Free clinics, runaway shelters, and crisis centers are generally viewed with suspicion by police. Police see these programs as catering to the vices of youths rather than controlling or preventing them.

El Camino School in Los Angeles is innovative in their approach to delinquency rehabilitation: Young offenders work with severely disabled children. Do you think that such programs force delinquents to acknowledge the many advantages they enjoy in life?

2. Suitability.   Many community service agencies are unsuitable for use by the police. An agency may accept only certain cases, or its policies and practices may conflict with those of police. Other practical considerations that affect suitability are restrictive costs, long waiting lists, and insufficient personnel. Furthermore, many service agencies are open only between 9 A.M. and 5 P.M., making it difficult for police to fully utilize their services.

3. Availability.   Over the years, various recommendations have been made in an attempt to provide community resources where none exist. There are two problems that may arise regarding such resources. First, availability of resources is no guarantee of quality. Second, there is often a low level of resource awareness among police. For instance, when Malcolm Klein interviewed officers in six California cities on the availability of community resources, he found that they had little knowledge about what was available.[61]

4. Accountability.   The appropriateness of a referral can never be fully known without formal procedures for follow-up. By actively soliciting comments from referral agencies, police are better equipped to make future referrals and improve communication with service agencies. Better communication, in turn, improves coordination and the ability of agencies to respond to police needs.

Conclusions

The first American police departments were modeled after the English police. They included constables and a night watch. By the middle of the 19th century, nearly all big cities had established police departments that closely resembled those we see today.

The decision to arrest a juvenile suspected of a crime is based on many factors. Some of the factors are legal and others are nonlegal. Characteristics of the juvenile, offense seriousness, and the community where the offense occurred all affect how an officer will respond to a situation. Research on this topic leads to three conclusions:

1. Police departments vary considerably in their policies and practices with respect to release or referral of juveniles.
2. Police handling of serious offenses is based primarily on legal criteria.
3. For minor crimes, the arrest decision is based principally on the preference of the complainant.

The decision to arrest a child is the most important decision as it gets the juvenile justice process started. At a minimum, an arrest may lead to a tainted reputation. In the worst case, adjudication and confinement may follow. When police take a child into custody, they must decide what to do next and they choose among alternative actions. Children may be referred to juvenile court for processing; they can be handled informally within the department; or they can be referred to an agency outside the juvenile justice system. The decision police make is based on many criteria including offense seriousness and the availability of appropriate community resources.

Key Terms

booking: *The official recording of a person into detention after arrest.*

Chimel v. California: *Established the one-arm's length rule: Once a suspect is arrested, police may search the suspect and the immediate area he or she occupies.*

exclusionary rule: *Evidence police produce illegally is not admissible in court (see Mapp v. Ohio).*

hue and cry: *A loud call for help shouted by colonial police when they were in need of assistance.*

In re Gault: *Juveniles may not be denied basic due process rights in juvenile adjudicatory hearings.*

Mapp v. Ohio: *Applied the exclusionary rule to state courts.*

Miranda v. Arizona: *Established the right to protection from self-incrimination under the Fifth Amendment and the right to legal counsel under the Sixth Amendment.*

one-arm's length rule: *Once a suspect is arrested, police may search the suspect and the immediate area he or she occupies (see Chimel v. California).*

probable cause: *A set of facts that would lead a reasonable person to believe a crime has been committed and the person to be arrested committed it.*

watch and ward: *A system of policing that allowed a constable to draft any male into service to guard the town at night.*

Getting Connected

Law Enforcement Links provides users with the opportunity to connect to many other websites that focus on varied aspects of policing.

http://www.leolinks.com

1. Review the list of "What's COOL" sites. What is "cool"?
2. What kinds of sites are available for police and family support?
3. Read several of the United States officers' home pages, then compare them to homepages of officers in other nations.

The Police Guide is a very large website. A wide range of topics are discussed, including ones affecting police work with juveniles.

http://www.policeguide.com

1. What is the purpose of this site?
2. Link to the "faqs" page. Test your knowledge of police lore.
3. Search the site for "juvenile delinquency." What is the result?

One of the most influential police associations in the world is the International Association of Chiefs of Police. This group provides information and direction to police agencies worldwide on a variety of topics, including delinquency prevention.

http://www.amdahl.com/ext/iacp

1. What is the goal of the IACP's Juvenile Justice Committee?
2. Link on Publications, then on the Youth Violence Summit Recommendations. Evaluate the recommendations which are related to law enforcement.
3. Who may be a member of the IACP?

The goal of the Law Enforcement Family Support Program is to prevent and treat the negative effects of stress experienced by law enforcement officers. To the extent stress affects police officer decision making, this program helps to facilitate the fair and impartial treatment of juvenile offenders.

http://www.register.aspensys.com/nij/lefs/welcome.html

1. Link to "grant awards." Has a CLEFS program been funded in your state? If so, what have been its goals?
2. When was the "C" added to the existing "LEFS" program? Why was it added?
3. Is working with juveniles a source of stress?

Information on community policing efforts aimed at preventing delinquency can be found at the website maintained by the Community Policing Consortium.

http://www.communitypolicing.org

1. How is community policing defined by the consortium? What are its main benefits?
2. According to the "About Community Policing" page, what is the difference between a "community member" and a "civilian"?
3. How has COPS enhanced school safety?

Endnotes

1. Told to us by an anonymous student.
2. Egon Bittner, *The Functions of the Police in Modern Society* (Washington, DC: National Institute of Mental Health, 1970).
3. Robert Carter, "The Police View of the Justice System," in *The Juvenile Justice System*, edited by Malcolm Klein (Beverly Hills, CA: Sage Publications, 1976), p. 131.
4. The discussion of police history relies heavily on David Johnson, *American Law Enforcement* (St. Louis: Forum Press, 1981); James Richardson, *The New York Police* (New York: Oxford University Press, 1970); Samuel Walker and Charles Katz, *The Police in America*, 4th ed. (New York: McGraw-Hill Publishing Co., 2002).
5. Arthur Cole, "The Irrepressible Conflict, 1850–1865," in *A History of American Life*, Vol. 7, edited by Arthur Schlesinger and Dixon Fox (New York: Macmillan Publishing Co., 1934), pp. 154–155.
6. Robert Fogelson, *Big-City Police* (Cambridge, MA: Harvard University Press, 1977).
7. *Miranda v. Arizona*, 384 U.S. 436 (1966).
8. *Escobedo v. Illinois*, 378 U.S. 478 (1964).
9. *Miranda v. Arizona*, note 7.
10. *In re Gault*, 387 U.S. 1 (1967).
11. *Payton v. New York*, 445 U.S. 573 (1980); *United States v. Mendenhall*, 466 U.S. 544 (1984); *Florida v. Bostick*, 489 U.S. 1021 (1991).
12. Two differences between adult law and juvenile law make it easier for police to search a child suspect. First, children may be arrested for status offenses, such as running away, truancy, and incorrigibility. Second, parents may give police permission to search the rooms and possessions of their minor children [*Vandenberg v. Superior Court*, 8 Cal.App.3d 1048 (1970)].
13. *Mapp v. Ohio*, 367 U.S. 643 (1961).
14. *Chimel v. California*, 395 U.S. 752 (1969).
15. *Gilbert v. California*, 388 U.S. 263 (1967); *United States v. Wade*, 388 U.S. 218 (1967); *United States v. Euge*, 444 U.S. 707 (1980).
16. *People v. Lara*, 67 Cal.2d 365 (1967).
17. *West v. United States*, 399 F.2d 467 (5th Cir. 1968).
18. *Fare v. Michael C.*, 439 U.S. 1310 (1978). Also see: *Moran v. Burbine*, 475 U.S. 412 (1986); *Colorado v. Connelly*, 479 U.S. 157 (1986); *Davis v. United States*, 512 U.S. 452 (1994).
19. *Gilbert v. California*, note 15; *United States v. Wade*, note 15; *In re Holley*, 107 R.I. 615 (1970).
20. Mark Stafford, "Children's Legal Rights in the U.S.," *Marriage & the Family Review* 21:121–140 (1995).
21. Carl Werthman and Irving Piliavin, "Gang Members and the Police," in *The Police: Six Sociological Essays*, edited by David Bordua (New York: John Wiley & Sons, 1967), p. 56.
22. Sandra Lee Browning, Francis Cullen, Liqun Cao, Renee Kopache, and Thomas Stevenson, "Race and Getting Hassled by the Police," *Police Studies* 17:1–11 (1994).
23. Douglas Smith, "The Neighborhood Context of Police Behavior," in *Crime and Justice*, Vol 8, edited by Albert Reiss and Michael Tonry (Chicago: University of Chicago Press, 1986).
24. Ann Pastore and Kathleen Maguire, *Sourcebook of Criminal Justice Statistics, 2000* (Washington, DC: Bureau of Justice Statistics, 2001).
25. Robert Terry, "Discrimination in the Handling of Juvenile Offenders by Social-Control Agencies," *Journal of Research in Crime and Delinquency* 4:218–230 (1967).
26. Donald Black and Albert Reiss, "Police Control of Juveniles," *American Sociological Review* 35:63–77 (1970).
27. Nathan Goldman, *The Differential Selection of Juvenile Offenders for Court Appearance* (New York: National Council on Crime and Delinquency, 1963).
28. Terry, note 25.
29. Aaron Cicourel, *The Social Organization of Juvenile Justice* (New York: John Wiley & Sons, 1976), p. 119.
30. Black and Reiss, note 26; Irving Piliavin and Scott Briar, "Police Encounters with Juveniles," *American Journal of Sociology* 70: 206–214 (1964).
31. Black and Reiss, note 26.
32. Douglas Smith and Christy Visher, "Street-Level Justice," *Social Problems* 29:167–177 (1981); Stephen Mastrofski, Robert Worden, and Jeffrey Snipes, "Law Enforcement in a Time of Community Policing," *Criminology* 33:539-563 (1995); Robert Worden and S. Myers, *Police Encounters with Juvenile Suspects*, Unpublished paper Commissioned by the Panel of Juvenile Crime Prevention, Treatment, and Control (1999); Ronet Bachman, "Victim's Perceptions of Initial Police Responses to

Robbery and Aggravated Assault," *Journal of Quantitative Criminology* 12:363-390 (1996); David Huizinga and Delbert Elliott, "Juvenile Offenders," *Crime and Delinquency* 33:206-223 (1987).

33. Federal Bureau of Investigation, *Crime in the United States, 2000* (Washington, DC: U.S. Department of Justice, 2001).

34. Samuel Walker, Cassia Spohn, and Miriam DeLone, *The Color of Justice*, 2nd edition (Belmont, CA: Wadsworth Publishing Co., 2000).

35. John Boydstun, *San Diego Field Interrogation* (Washington, DC: The Police Foundation, 1975).

36. Black and Reiss, note 26.

37. Werthman and Piliavin, note 21.

38. Howard Becker, *Outsiders* (New York: The Free Press, 1964).

39. Piliavin and Briar, note 30, p. 210.

40. Cicourel, note 29.

41. Black and Reiss, note 26.

42. David Klinger, "Demeanor or Crime?," *Criminology* 32:475–493 (1994); David Klinger, "More on Demeanor and Arrest in Dade County," *Criminology* 34:61–82 (1996); David Klinger, "Bringing Crime Back In," *Journal of Research in Crime and Delinquency* 33:333–336 (1996); David Klinger, "Quantifying Law in Police-Citizen Encounters," *Journal of Quantitative Criminology* 12:391–415 (1996).

43. Robert Terry, "The Screening of Juvenile Offenders," *Journal of Criminal Law, Criminology, and Police Science* 58:173–181 (1967); George Bodine, "Factors Related to Police Dispositions of Juvenile Offenders," paper presented at the annual meeting of the American Sociological Association, 1964.

44. Terence Thornberry, "Race, Socioeconomic Status, and Sentencing in the Juvenile Justice System," *Journal of Criminal Law and Criminology* 64:90–98 (1973).

45. Cicourel, note 29.

46. Thomas Monahan, "Police Dispositions of Juvenile Offenders," *Phylon* 31:91–107 (1970).

47. Delbert Elliott and Harwin Voss, *Delinquency and Dropout* (Lexington, MA: Lexington Books, 1974).

48. Gail Armstrong, "Females under the Law—Protected but Unequal," *Crime and Delinquency* 23:109–120 (1977).

49. Meda Chesney-Lind, "Judicial Paternalism and the Female Status Offender," *Crime and Delinquency* 23:121–130 (1970).

50. Katherine Teilman and Pierre Landry, "Gender Bias in Juvenile Justice," *Journal of Research in Crime and Delinquency* 18:47–80 (1981).

51. Ruth Horowitz and Ann Pottieger, "Gender Bias in Juvenile Justice Handling of Seriously Crime-Involved Youth," *Journal of Research in Crime and Delinquency* 28:75–100 (1991).

52. Meda Chesney-Lind and Randall Shelden, *Girls, Delinquency, and Juvenile Justice,* 2nd ed., (Pacific Grove, CA: Brooks/Cole Publishing Co., 1998).

53. Teilman and Landry, note 50.

54. Goldman, note 27.

55. Alexander McEachern and Rita Bauzer, "Factors Related to Dispositions in Juvenile Police Contacts," in *Juvenile Gangs in Context*, edited by Malcolm Klein (Englewood Cliffs, NJ: Prentice-Hall, Inc., 1967).

56. Bodine, note 43.

57. James Q. Wilson, *Varieties of Police Behavior* (Cambridge, MA: Harvard University Press, 1968).

58. Richard Sundeen, "A Study of Factors Related to Police Diversion of Departmental Policies and Structures, Community Attachment and Professionalization of the Police," doctoral dissertation, University of Southern California (1972).

59. Pastore and Maguire, note 24.

60. Malcolm Klein, "The Explosion in Police Diversion Programs," in *The Juvenile Justice System*, edited by Malcolm Klein (Beverly Hills, CA: Sage Publications, 1976).

61. Klein, note 60.

Chapter 14
The Juvenile Court

If the formalities of the criminal adjudication process are to be superimposed upon the juvenile court system, there is little need for its separate existence. Perhaps the ultimate disillusionment will come one day, but for the moment we are disinclined to give impetus to it.

—*McKeiver v. Pennsylvania, 403 U.S. 528 (1971)*

The origins of the American juvenile court were discussed in Chapter 1; this chapter examines the transformation of the court through the 20th century. One of the most significant changes in this transformation was the movement away from the court's traditional paternalistic and protectionist view of children to one that took an increasingly adversarial and punitive approach to dealing with them.

Less than a decade after Illinois had established its juvenile court in 1899, 10 more states and the District of Columbia had followed suit. By 1925 all but two states had passed juvenile codes and created special juvenile courts. When Wyoming established a juvenile court in 1945, the list was complete.[1] But creating the juvenile court system was much easier than making it work. In many cities, juvenile courts did not function to achieve their prescribed tasks. In practically all states, reformatories and penal institutions continued to be filled with hundreds of children; in many jurisdictions where detention homes had not been provided for court use, children were still confined in jails, often with adult criminals, to await hearings. The report from one juvenile court made clear that children were being handled just as they had been before the new system. The report stated that "65 were sent to jail; 40 were placed in a chain gang; 12 were sent to a reformatory and 1 to an orphanage; 156 were fined; 156 were placed on probation."[2]

Although the juvenile courts began to employ more full-time professional probation officers, their effectiveness was hindered by large caseloads that hampered complete investigation and treatment.[3] One consequence was that juvenile offenders made only infrequent appearances at their probation officer's station. These visits replaced the idealized home visits and were usually far too hurried and superficial to promote a meaningful exchange between the adult supervisor and the young offender.

From the juvenile court's inception, youths accused of serious offenses were left in the adult criminal system. According to Sanford Fox, developments in the treatment of juvenile offenders—from the house of refuge movement to the juvenile court's establishment to the concerns in the 1970s with removing status offenders from the court system—have focused on "petty offenses and salvageable offenders."[4]

By the 1980s much of the attention and concern of the court had shifted to the growing number of serious juvenile offenders and the watchwords became secure detention, punishment, deterrence, and waiver to criminal court. Although the juvenile court has experienced upheavals and controversies as well as varied reform movements over the years, it is still the mainstay of society's attempt to control delinquent and wayward youths (see Box 14–1 for a brief discussion of the juvenile courts in France).

The Processing of Juvenile Offenders

What happens to children who are brought into the juvenile court system? Typically a case flows through the system by first being reported to police,

BOX 14–1   A CROSS-CULTURAL PERSPECTIVE ON DELINQUENCY
Juvenile Justice in France

Following developments in the United States by nearly a half century, the Order of 2 February 1945 "On Delinquent Youth" established the contemporary juvenile court in France. It provided for specialized "juvenile judges" and held that the primary responsibility of the court was to educate and reform delinquents. Like its American counterpart, the French juvenile court gave the judge great power and authority in examining youth brought to the court and in determining appropriate dispositions. The 1945 Act enabled judges to inquire into the "material and moral status" of the youth's family, the child's character, school behavior and academic achievement, and past record of delinquency. In addition, judges could order psychological and medical examinations.

Hearings are not public, and except for the child and his or her parents, there are few people in attendance. Those typically involved in the hearing include the judge, two magistrate assistants, a prosecutor or deputy prosecutor, a defense attorney (either appointed or hired by the family), the court clerk, and possibly a social case worker. In minor cases, judges hold hearings in their chambers. If the child is determined to be delinquent, the judge can select from a variety of dispositions including returning the child to his or her home, formally cautioning the child, placing the child on probation, or placing the child in a special school for delinquents or in another type of specialized children's home.

Catherine Blatier surveyed juvenile courts in four representative jurisdictions including Paris, St. Etienne, Gap, and Rennes. Her research, covering the years 1990–1994, indicates that most cases brought before the French juvenile courts involve simple thefts. Nearly 75 percent of the cases involved theft, car or moped theft, or aggravated theft. Fewer than 8 percent involved violent crimes and only 1 percent were drug-related. Boys committed over 90 percent of the cases brought to the juvenile courts; nearly half of the youths were 17 or 18 years old; only about a third of both boys and girls committed their crimes alone.

Reflecting the nonpunitive approach of the French courts, dispositions during the five years studied suggest that very few juveniles are placed in custodial situations. Blatier notes that for first-time offenders, 5 percent of the youths were acquitted or discharged, 35 percent of the recommendations involved a warning, 13 percent were left in the care of the family or guardian, 25 percent received formal or informal probation, 8 percent were required to pay compensation, 6 percent were only fined, 5 percent were placed in care, and only 3.4 percent of the youths received a sentence of institutional confinement. Second-time offenders were treated much more harshly, with 55 percent placed in institutions.

Like the United States during the period between the 1960s and 1990s, France is beginning to face more frequent and more serious delinquent behavior by its youth. These offenders are also getting younger. However, French law prohibits the incarceration of children under the age of 16, and with children as young as 10 committing serious crimes, law makers might begin to consider some of the "get tough" measures that many experts argue helped reduce serious juvenile delinquency in the United States in the late 1990s.

Source: Catherine Blatier, "Juvenile Justice in France: The Evolution of Sentencing for Children and Minor Delinquents," *British Journal of Criminology* 39:240-252 (1999).

Most scholars, citizens, and juvenile justice practitioners would agree that serious violent repeat juvenile offenders are the real concern, not youths involved in petty normal delinquency. Should the juvenile justice system be used exclusively for youths engaging in minor offenses? Should intractable juvenile delinquents always be prosecuted and punished as adults?

who then refer it to the court (over 85 percent of all referrals to the court come from law enforcement agencies). Then it is processed by the juvenile court intake department, formally charged by the prosecutor, tried in a court hearing, and the youth possibly assigned to some form of correctional activity. At any point in this flow a case may be diverted, dismissed, or terminated in some other way, returning the child to the outside world.

Arrest

While adult law violators are arrested by police, juvenile offenders have traditionally been "taken into custody," reflecting the civil rather than criminal nature of the juvenile court. States vary in their procedural rules regarding the arrest of juveniles. Many states do not require arrest warrants as they would with adults in similar circumstances.[5] And, whether juveniles are only taken into custody or formally arrested, authorities must provide them with the same fundamental constitutional protections that apply when arresting adults, such as probable cause and protections against unreasonable search and seizure (see Chapter 13).

Police are generally the first to make a formal determination on whether to process the juvenile. They also exercise much discretion, and not all eligible youths are formally arrested. If police decide to arrest a child, subsequent actions are then largely determined by legal statutes. In some states, police are required to notify a probation officer or other official designated by the juvenile court; in other states, police are required to notify only the child's parents. But whenever a juvenile is taken into police custody, he or she typically goes to the police station for initial screening and possible interrogation, after which police decide whether to terminate the case, divert it to an alternative program (for example, the use of Teen Courts, examined in Box 14–2), or refer it to juvenile court for formal intake.

Court Intake

A striking feature of juvenile justice is the nomenclature used by the system. Youths are literally treated with "kid gloves." Does this reflect an implicit belief in labeling theory among juvenile justice practitioners?

Courts with juvenile jurisdiction handle an estimated 1,755,000 delinquency cases each year. Juvenile cases involving crimes against the person increased nearly 100 percent during the 10-year period between the late 1980s and the late 1990s, while property offense cases increased by 19 percent, drug law violation cases by 125 percent, and cases involving public order offenses by 67 percent. These delinquency cases were referred to the courts by a variety of sources, including law enforcement agencies, social service agencies, schools, parents, probation officers, and victims. However, about 85 percent of all delinquency cases were referred by law enforcement.[6]

Once referred to the court, juveniles go through a case-screening process called **intake**. Intake procedures are designed to screen out cases that do not warrant a formal court hearing, such as the following:

1. Cases involving matters over which the court has no jurisdiction.
2. Cases in which the evidence against the child is insufficient.

BOX 14–2   DELINQUENCY PREVENTION
Teen Court

Recent estimates suggest that as many as 675 teen courts are now operating in the United States. These increasingly popular (more than two-thirds have been in existence fewer than five years) alternatives to formal juvenile court appearance enjoy broad community support, although research has raised questions about their effectiveness in reducing recidivism.

While there are variations in how teen courts are structured and operate, most adhere to a model in which youths are responsible for most of the process. Juveniles typically function as prosecutors, defense attorneys, court clerks, bailiffs, and jurors. In a limited number of teen courts, a youth "judge" may be responsible for selecting the disposition, although most "judges" are adults drawn from the local legal community. Most teen courts do not determine the guilt or innocence of the defendant. Acceptance into the teen court program is predicated on the youth having first admitted guilt for the charged offense. The teen court has the responsibility of questioning the youth about the circumstances of the offense and determining an appropriate disposition.

Teen courts are typically used for younger juveniles, those with no prior arrests, and those charged only with less serious law violations. Nearly 40 percent of teen courts accept only youths who have never previously been arrested, almost all (98 percent) never or rarely accept youths with prior felony arrests, and 91 percent never or rarely accept youths who have prior referrals to the juvenile court. Offenses most often handled by teen courts include theft (primarily shoplifting), minor assaults, disorderly conduct, alcohol or marijuana possession or use, school disciplinary problems or truancy, and traffic violations.

With the goal of holding young offenders accountable for their behavior, teen courts use a system of graduated sanctions. The most typical dispositions include the payment of restitution or performance of community service. However, some teen courts require offenders to write formal apologies to their victims, to serve on subsequent teen court juries, or to attend classes designed to improve their decision-making skills, enhance their awareness of victims, and deter them from future thefts or traffic violations.

While proponents of teen courts claim great benefits, evaluations of the effectiveness of teen courts in reducing recidivism provide little support. Most of the positive claims about teen courts are based on anecdotal data and expressed satisfaction of parents and program administrators rather than on rigorous evaluation studies using control group experimental designs. Thus, it is impossible to test the assumption that recidivism outcomes are due to teen court rather than to other factors (for example, selection bias). Interestingly, two of the three published studies that use reasonably appropriate comparison groups found little or no difference between youths participating in teen court and those who did not. The third study reported teen court participants were less likely than the comparison group to reoffend

(continued)

(continued)

within 12 months (24 percent versus 36 percent). But reducing recidivism may not be the only reason to support teen courts. According to Paige Harrison and her colleagues, teen courts are less expensive than juvenile courts, the community service hours put in by young offenders benefit nonprofit organizations, and, ultimately, it could well be assumed that having nonserious juvenile offenders attend teen court is better than doing nothing at all.

Sources: Jeffrey Butts and Janeen Buck, *Teen Courts: A Focus on Research* (Washington, DC: Office of Juvenile Justice and Delinquency Prevention, 2000); Kevin Minor, James Wells, Irina Soderstrom, Rachel Bingham, and Deborah Williamson, "Sentence Completion and Recidivism Among Juveniles Referred to Teen Courts," *Crime and Delinquency* 45:467–480 (1999); Paige Harrison, James Maupin, and G. Larry Mays, "Teen Court: An Examination of Processes and Outcomes," *Crime and Delinquency* 47:243–264 (2001).

Should juvenile offenders be legally evaluated by a jury of their peers? Generally, should juvenile offenders be held legally responsible for their conduct, regardless of their chronological or mental age?

3. Cases that are not serious enough to require juvenile court adjudication.
4. Cases in which the youth or his or her family have already compensated the victim.
5. Cases that should be waived to criminal court (see discussion on transferring juveniles later in this chapter).

The intake department may also order social history investigations, medical or psychological diagnoses, or other studies that might be used to determine the suitability of juvenile court involvement. Informal hearings, adjudications, and probation supervision are frequently administered at the intake level, without referral to a judge.

While most state statutes on intake are deliberately broad, some jurisdictions have formulated specific guidelines for intake officials to consider when deciding whether to file a petition or to adjust a case informally. The seriousness of the offense is perhaps the most important element considered. A number of courts specify that certain offenses may not be adjusted or, more generally, that no felony offense may be adjusted. The range of available adjustments at the intake stage is limited only by the availability of resources in the community and the imagination of the intake staff. If a child has been referred on a minor charge and the intake worker determines that court intervention is not necessary, but feels the child needs to be impressed with the seriousness of his or her actions, the worker may lecture the child. To make the warning more impressive, the youth may be taken before a judge in his or her chambers for a stern reprimand.

The intake process often selects **informal adjustment** for cases that may best be handled through discretionary nonjudicial dispositions. One approach to informal adjustment is the use of a summary disposition in which the child is either simply warned, required to participate in a community service program, make restitution, apologize to the complainant, or is referred to a diversion program (a number of diversion alternatives available to the court are discussed in Box 14–3). Another approach to informal adjustment is the use of **informal probation**, in which the child is supervised by a probation officer for a period typically of three to six months and is expected to comply with probationary conditions similar to that of court-ordered probation. Informal adjustment is widely used. For example, in 1996 the Texas juvenile courts disposed of about 48 percent of all referrals to the juvenile court through informal adjustments.[7]

Problems with informal probation have arisen, however, since supervision of the child by probation personnel is conducted in much the same way as supervision of adjudicated children. If children and their parents are unfamiliar with juvenile court procedures, they sometimes agree to informal probation, not realizing they have the right to a court hearing before the probation staff has any sanctioned authority over their behavior and that their admission of guilt, which is a requirement for diversion, will become part of their formal juvenile record.

Perhaps more problematic at intake is that in many jurisdictions, statements made by juveniles during interviews with a probation or intake officer may be admissible later in the adjudication hearing. Although courts have held that juveniles have no constitutional right to counsel during the informal intake process, a few states, such as Washington, have established a statutory right to counsel for juveniles at intake.[8]

BOX 14–3   DELINQUENCY PREVENTION
Diversion of Juveniles from the Juvenile Justice System

Diversion of juveniles within the juvenile justice system may occur at any of a number of points, from the police officer's decision to handle a complaint informally to the court's placement of a youth on informal probation. In any of these situations, diversion is intended to suspend or terminate the official handling of juveniles in favor of some informal or unofficial alternative.

The formal juvenile court process can be suspended prior to the filing of a petition to permit the juvenile to be handled informally by community agencies, a process called informal adjustment. In other words, diversion is designed to allow youths to avoid formal court processing and adjudication and the stigma that typically accompanies formal action. First-time offenders charged with minor misdemeanors, repeat status offenders, or youth already participating in a community-based treatment program are generally considered good candidates for diversion programs.

Most diversion programs offer innovative approaches to treatment and rehabilitation. Early programs, such as Project Crossroads in Washington, DC, combined counseling, vocational training, and academic development opportunities for first-time offenders with no prior convictions and facing charges for a nonviolent offense. Sacramento's Project 601 aimed to reduce court costs and recidivism rates by combining crisis intervention and counseling for juveniles identified as truants, habitual runaways, or incorrigibles.

Current diversion programs may involve mediation, in which meetings are scheduled among the complainant, the juvenile, and a neutral hearing officer who facilitates communication between the disputants and helps them reach a mutually acceptable resolution to

Filing the Petition   If intake procedures result in a decision to submit the child to a formal court hearing, a **petition** is filed. A petition sets forth the specific charge that a delinquent act has been committed. It serves to notify the child of the claims made about his or her misconduct. The petition is the counterpart of an indictment in criminal prosecutions and a complaint in civil litigation with the petition requesting either an adjudicatory or waiver hearing. Approximately 57 percent of delinquency cases result in the filing of a petition.[9]

The prosecutor at this stage evaluates the case in terms of its legal adequacy. In any case in which a juvenile is alleged to qualify for prosecution in the juvenile court, the prosecutor submits a petition to the court. If the prosecutor decides not to file the petition, that decision is regarded as final and the case is dismissed. If the prosecutor does file the petition, it is usually followed by a report by the intake officer on the behavior patterns and social history of the juvenile.

the conflict. Youth Service Bureaus, very popular during the 1970s and early 1980s, provided diversion programs ranging from drop-in centers and temporary shelter for runaways to crisis hotlines and school outreach programs. Community youth boards are informal hearing boards that determine which, if any, services should be provided to children referred by schools, police, the juvenile court, parents, or the children themselves. While some boards only accept status offender referrals, others allow referral of all juvenile offenders.

Diversion programs may also be designed to provide alternatives to formal placement in a correctional institution. Wilderness programs grew out of both the Civilian Conservation Corps forestry camps of the 1930s and 1940s and the Outward Bound program created in Wales during World War I. These programs were designed to help merchant seamen gain confidence and achieve success in meeting physical challenges and to develop a sense of group pride. Contemporary wilderness programs attempt to take streetwise youths, with their well-developed skills at conning and manipulating people, and place them in a setting where they cannot avoid taking responsibility. The goal of these programs is to increase youths' self-respect through self-discipline and through overcoming both physical and psychological challenges encountered in individual and group efforts.

Are diversion programs effective? Advocates argue that such programs reduce court caseloads and costs, reduce the time staff spend in case processing, and reduce the time the juvenile is involved in the juvenile justice system. Critics, on the other hand, argue that diversion may actually increase the number of cases sent to the juvenile court as diverted youths are typically drawn from a group traditionally released by police or probation staff without further action, a process known as net-widening. Critics also note that diversion from juvenile justice processing raises fundamental issues of fairness: selection for diversion may be arbitrary or biased; procedural rights may be overlooked or ignored; eligibility requirements may violate due process; and long-term effects may hinder the juvenile's return to society.

Detention

Juvenile **detention** is the temporary confinement of children within a physically restricting facility pending filing of a petition, awaiting of adjudication or disposition hearings, or implementation of disposition. If a youth is brought to the detention facility by the police after having been taken into custody, intake probation officers must then determine whether the youth should be released or detained. If the juvenile is to be detained, then a petition must be filed and a detention hearing scheduled within 48 to 72 hours.[10]

Most states require prompt notification of parents if the child is placed in detention. Preventive detention of juveniles is practiced for three reasons: (1) to protect the child, (2) to protect society from further lawbreaking by the child, and (3) to assure that the child will appear at subsequent hearings.[11] For example, Alabama requires that a child taken into custody be released except in situations where:

- The child has no parent, guardian, custodian, or other suitable person able and willing to provide supervision and care for such child;
- The release of the child would present a clear and substantial threat of a serious nature to the person or property of others where the child is alleged to be delinquent;
- The release of such child would present a serious threat of substantial harm to such child; or
- The child has a history of failing to appear for hearings before the court.[12]

Juveniles also may be detained for evaluation purposes and while awaiting placement in a long-term correctional or treatment facility. And like adults detained in jail, the mere fact of being detained increases the likelihood of being adjudicated delinquent and receiving a more severe disposition.[13]

In recent years, both federal and state courts have held that a juvenile may not be detained pending trial on charges of delinquency without a prompt determination of probable cause. However, in 1984 the Supreme Court reversed this ruling in *Schall v. Martin.*[14] The justices upheld a New York statute authorizing the pretrial detention of an accused juvenile who, if released, may pose a "serious risk" by committing the equivalent of an adult crime. While the statute provides for a detention hearing, a formal finding that there is probable cause to believe that the youth committed the offense for which he or she was arrested is not required prior to his or her detention. (The *Schall* case is discussed in the next section.)

Approximately 19 percent of all delinquency cases brought before the juvenile court result in detentions prior to disposition.[15] In 1997 a total of 326,800 juveniles were held for some period of time in public detention facilities. Of the detained delinquency cases, 12 percent were related to drugs, 23 percent involved public order offenses, 27 percent involved crimes against the person, and 38 percent involved property crimes.[16] In addition to the nearly 327,000 youths detained for delinquency, about 9,400 juveniles were detained for status offenses in which no delinquency charges were filed.

Disparities in Detention   Race and sex disparities exist in detention as they do in arrest decisions (discussed in Chapter 13) and, as will be seen in later discussions in this chapter, in adjudications, dispositions, and waivers. These disparities or overrepresentations raise serious questions and, for many people, suggest the possibility of race and sex discrimination. But over-representation may stem from factors other than discrimination. Factors relating to the seriousness and volume of crime, prior record, and life circumstances—such as dropping out of school or living with a single parent—may influence the decisions of police, intake officers, and juvenile court judges. Thus, to fully understand the causes of disparities at different stages of the juvenile justice process would require much more information than most studies provide. Few studies control for offense seriousness, whether the

Nearly 10,000 youth are detained annually for status offenses. While this appears to be excessive, the juvenile justice system might protect chronic runaways from dangerous home environments. On occasion, juvenile detention centers are healthier places than homes. Does the *parens patriae* doctrine still apply to juvenile justice? *Should* the doctrine still apply to juvenile justice?

On any given day, many juveniles are housed in adult jails. Would such an experience deter youths from delinquency? Alternately, does confinement in adult jails needlessly expose children to adult privations?

child is charged with a felony or misdemeanor, the number of charges, or prior arrests and adjudications, let alone family and school circumstances. For example, when Frazier and Bishop looked at the impact of race and controlled for sex, age, prior record, and seriousness of offense, they found minorities more likely to have formal petitions filed, although race did not appear to negatively affect decisions at later stages in the process.[17] While the actual causes of disparities or overrepresentation based on race and sex continue to be debated, there is no question that blacks and females are treated differently by the juvenile justice system.

Race   Secure detention was nearly twice as likely in cases involving black youths compared to cases involving white youth, even after controlling for general offense category. For example, in 1997, 15 percent of delinquency cases involving white youths included detention at some point between referral and disposition, while among cases involving blacks the figure was 27 percent.[18] The most striking differences were among cases involving drug offenses and crimes against the person (see Figure 14–1). Detention was used in 14 percent of drug cases involving white youths, in 38 percent of cases involving black youths, and in 16 percent of cases involving youths of other races. White youths were also significantly less likely to be placed in detention in cases involving crimes against the person. For example, detention was

**Figure 14–1
Delinquency Cases
Detained by Race,
1997**

Source: Melissa Sickmund,
*Offenders in Juvenile Court,
1997* (Washington, DC:
Office of Juvenile Justice
and Delinquency
Prevention, 2000), p. 7.

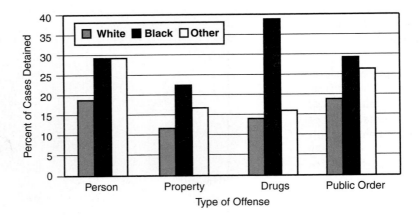

Female delinquents often benefit from their proportionately low involvement in delinquency by receiving more lenient treatment. Should the justice system respond similarly to other groups based on their general involvement in delinquency? For example, do minorities receive worse treatment because of their proportionately higher offending rates?

ordered in only 19 percent of cases involving white youths but in 28 percent of cases involving minority youths.[19] Finally, the use of detention for delinquency cases involving black juveniles increased at a significantly greater rate than for white youths during the 10 years between 1987 and 1996 (71 percent versus 18 percent).[20]

Sex   Of juveniles charged with a delinquency offense, males were more likely than females to be held in detention. Overall, 20 percent of male delinquency cases involved detention in 1997, compared to 15 percent of female cases.[21] Furthermore, the use of detention has increased more rapidly for girls than for boys. Between 1988 and 1997, the use of detention in delinquency cases involving girls grew by 65 percent compared to only 30 percent for boys.[22] Regardless of the general offense category, detention was used more often for cases involving male juveniles (see Figure 14–2). However, girls were more likely than boys to be detained for minor offenses such as status offenses, public disorder, and traffic offenses. In addition, girls are more likely than boys to be placed in detention for probation and parole violations.[23]

Court Hearings

While juvenile court proceedings have historically been less adversarial than those in adult criminal court, in recent decades they have taken on many characteristics of the adversarial system. As a result of Supreme Court decisions and get-tough legislation by states, there has been a noticeable convergence between juvenile and adult court proceedings, with hearings in the juvenile court now rather adversarial in nature. However, according to Barry Feld, juvenile courts tend to operate with two competing conceptions of adolescents. On the one hand, juveniles continue to be regarded as "children" and not given all the same protections adults receive. On the other hand,

**Figure 14–2
Delinquency Cases
Detained by Sex,
1997**

Source: Gillian Porter,
*Detention in Delinquency
Cases, 1988–1997*
(Washington, DC: Office of
Juvenile Justice and
Delinquency Prevention,
2000), p. 1.

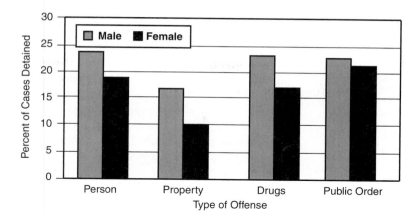

juveniles are increasingly being held criminally responsible for their "adult-like" crimes. Thus, Feld believes that young offenders "receive the worst of both worlds."[24]

There are three critical kinds of court hearings facing juvenile offenders. These are the *adjudication hearing*, the *disposition hearing*, and the *waiver hearing*. The first two of these hearings are discussed next, while the waiver hearing is discussed later in this chapter.

The Adjudication Hearing   An **adjudication hearing** determines whether the child committed the offense of which he or she is accused. In delinquency cases the required standard of evidence is proof beyond a reasonable doubt, the same as that needed to sustain a criminal charge in an adult court. Hearsay is inadmissible at the adjudication hearing. The juvenile has the right to confront and cross-examine witnesses and is entitled to the due process safeguards of adequate, timely, and written notice of the allegations and sufficient time to formulate a response. The right to refuse to testify is also ensured under the Fifth Amendment. The juvenile is entitled to counsel to protect his or her legal rights.

To be valid, confessions must be voluntary, corroborated by someone other than an accomplice, and preceded by the *Miranda* warning, which includes the right to (1) remain silent, (2) have an attorney present during questioning, and (3) have an attorney provided free of charge if the youth cannot afford to hire one. If the juvenile waives these rights, any statement he or she makes may be used in court against him or her. Generally, this warning is also given to the juvenile's parents so that they may assist in protecting their child's constitutional rights. After hearing all the evidence, the court may dismiss or continue the case or sustain the petition. If the petition is sustained, the court sets a date for the disposition hearing, or the judge may ask for the social investigation report and make an immediate disposition of the case.

The Disposition Hearing   The *disposition hearing* has retained many of the informal aspects that characterized the juvenile court system prior to the *Kent* and *Gault* decisions, which are discussed in the next section. The judge, the probation officer, the prosecutor, the defense attorney, and the child's parents typically discuss available options. Hearsay evidence and opinions are admissible at this stage. Depending on community resources, the judge may have a considerable range of disposition alternatives, ranging from dismissal to commitment to a state or local correctional facility. (Diversion alternatives available to the court are discussed in Box 14–3.)

The judge may, to obtain more information, withhold disposition and continue the case; or the court may release the child into the custody of his or her parents or place the child on probation. If probation is the disposition, then the juvenile may be referred to the probation department for formal or informal supervision. A child may also be removed from the custody of his or her parents and placed under the court's authority. The child may then be placed in a public or private facility or foster home.

The **disposition hearing** is the equivalent of the sentencing stage of the criminal court process: It is at this hearing that the court decides what disposition will best serve the child. The disposition decision is the most important aspect of a juvenile court case. At this point, the juvenile court sets forth a treatment plan to meet the child's particular needs.

Disposition decisions are made in regard to a relatively small number of juveniles, and youths who are evaluated for various disposition outcomes have already been processed through several decision points. In 1997, for example, nearly 1.8 million juveniles were referred to the juvenile court.[25] This represents an increase of 48 percent over the number of court referrals in 1988. Of the referred cases, 57 percent were petitioned to the juvenile court for an adjudicatory hearing (see Figure 14–3). Roughly 8,400, or 1 percent, of the petitioned cases were waived to criminal court, 41 percent were nonadjudicated, and 58 percent were adjudicated as delinquent. The majority of adjudicated delinquents were placed on probation (55 percent), while only 28 percent resulted in out-of-home placements (for example, a boot camp, ranch, privately operated facility, group home, or correctional institution).

Disparities in Adjudications and Dispositions   As noted earlier, some scholars and critics have expressed concern regarding possible sex and racial disparities in court adjudications and dispositions.[26] While unjustified disparities (direct or indirect discrimination) in particular communities have been reported in the literature, the national statistics are less alarming. In 1997 males accounted for 77 percent of all delinquency cases handled by the juvenile courts, and cases involving males were more likely than cases involving females to be adjudicated (59 percent to 53 percent respectively). Of petitioned youths, 59 percent of whites and 55 percent of blacks were adjudicated.[27]

> Few crimes result in arrest, a small number of cases progress through the courts, and many cases are simply dismissed. Why is the justice system so lenient or ineffective?

Figure 14–3
Juvenile Court Processing of Delinquency Cases, 1997

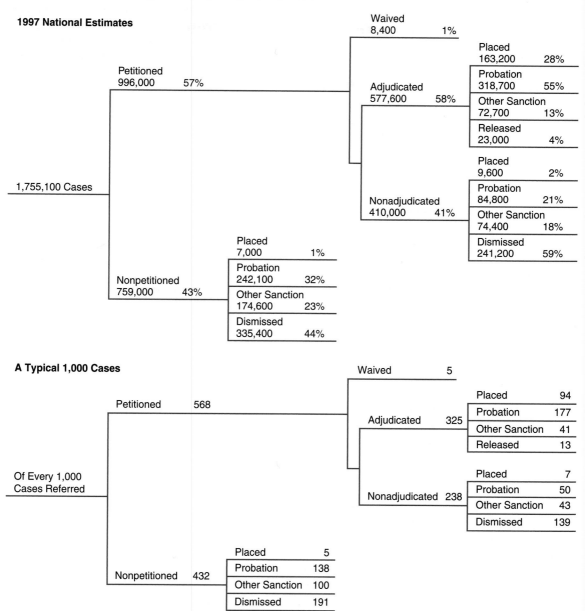

Source: Charles Puzzanchera, Anne Stahl, Terrence Finnegan, Howard Snyder, Rowen Poole, and Nancy Tierney, *Juvenile Court Statistics, 1997* (Washington, DC: U.S. Department of Justice, 2000), p. 9.

Minor discrepancies also appear in dispositions (see Table 14–1). Adjudicated cases involving males are more likely to result in out-of-home placement than cases involving females (30 percent versus 22 percent) and less likely to involve probation (54 percent versus 60 percent). Adjudicated cases involving black youths are only slightly less likely to result in probation than those involving white youths (53 percent versus 55 percent), but more likely to involve out-of-home placements (32 percent versus 26 percent).

And, as noted earlier, national court statistics are typically compiled without controlling for the seriousness or context of the crime, the criminal histories of youths, the amount of harm or loss to victims in the current offense, or the youth's family or school situation. To the extent that disparities exist that cannot be explained by legally relevant factors, race and sex considerations may play a part in the court decisions. Such concerns, in addition to the general concerns over the processing of juveniles, are best addressed by ensuring that the basic due process rights of all citizens accused of crimes apply to youths in juvenile court. But not all rights do apply, and those that do have been extended only since the mid-1960s. These concerns will be discussed in the next section.

Table 14–1   Percent of Dispositions of Adjudicated Delinquency Cases

	Out-of-Home Placement	Formal Probation
All cases	28	55
OFFENSE		
Person	30	56
Property	26	57
Drugs	24	56
Public order	33	49
AGE		
15 or younger	28	57
16 or older	29	52
SEX		
Male	30	54
Female	22	60
RACE		
White	26	56
Black	32	53
Other	29	51

Source: Charles Puzzanchera, Anne Stahl, Terrence Finnegan, Howard Snyder, Rowen Poole, and Nancy Tierney, *Juvenile Court Statistics, 1997* (Washington, DC: U.S. Department of Justice, 2000), pp. 15, 16, 19, 21, 25, 31.

Due Process Issues in the Juvenile Court

In this section, we examine the Supreme Court cases that have produced stronger safeguards of individual rights in juvenile court processing (see Figure 14–4). The decisions in these cases are not grounded solely in legal considerations. Rather, the Court has closely examined an accumulated body of research about how the juvenile justice system really works.

The Right to Due Process

The issue of whether juveniles are protected in delinquency hearings by basic due process guarantees was first considered in ***Kent v. United States*** (1966),[28] which involved a juvenile court judge's decision to waive jurisdiction and transfer a case from juvenile to criminal court without a hearing. Sixteen-year-old Morris Kent was accused of robbery, housebreaking, and rape. After an initial hearing, the juvenile court judge decided to waive Kent to adult court, without giving reasons for the waiver. Kent was tried, found guilty, and sentenced to 90 years in prison. The defense appealed on the

Figure 14–4
Juvenile Justice and the Supreme Court

Source: Howard Snyder and Melissa Sickmund, *Juvenile Offenders and Victims: A National Report* (Washington, DC: U.S. Department of Justice, 1995), p. 81.

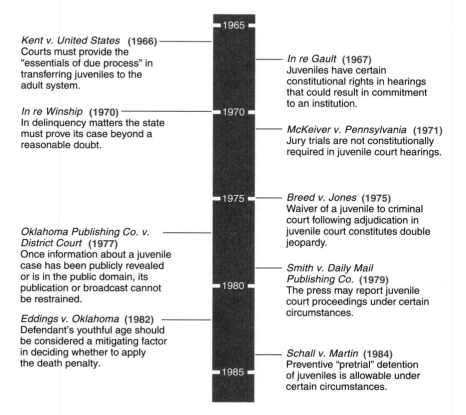

Kent v. United States **(1966)**
Courts must provide the "essentials of due process" in transferring juveniles to the adult system.

In re Winship **(1970)**
In delinquency matters the state must prove its case beyond a reasonable doubt.

Oklahoma Publishing Co. v. District Court **(1977)**
Once information about a juvenile case has been publicly revealed or is in the public domain, its publication or broadcast cannot be restrained.

Eddings v. Oklahoma **(1982)**
Defendant's youthful age should be considered a mitigating factor in deciding whether to apply the death penalty.

1965

1970

1975

1980

1985

In re Gault **(1967)**
Juveniles have certain constitutional rights in hearings that could result in commitment to an institution.

McKeiver v. Pennsylvania **(1971)**
Jury trials are not constitutionally required in juvenile court hearings.

Breed v. Jones **(1975)**
Waiver of a juvenile to criminal court following adjudication in juvenile court constitutes double jeopardy.

Smith v. Daily Mail Publishing Co. **(1979)**
The press may report juvenile court proceedings under certain circumstances.

Schall v. Martin **(1984)**
Preventive "pretrial" detention of juveniles is allowable under certain circumstances.

Why don't emotions run high when debating the legal rights of juveniles?

grounds that the juvenile judge should not have waived Kent to adult court without a hearing and that Kent's attorney should have been provided access to reports and presented with statements of reasons for the waiver.

In a 5-to-4 vote, the Supreme Court overturned Kent's conviction. The Court stated that since Kent could face the death penalty in adult court compared to only a maximum of five years in juvenile court, the waiver was of "critical importance" to him. Therefore, he should have been entitled to have access to all reports on him, a hearing, and a statement of reasons if he was to be waived. The Court further stated that not letting Kent's attorney look at the reports was the same as a denial of counsel. In *Kent*, the Court ruled that a hearing is necessary before a case in juvenile court can be waived to criminal court and that such a hearing should be guided by the "essentials of due process." *Kent* set the stage for **In re Gault** (1967).[29]

Even today, the elements of *Gault* can still shock. Gerald Gault, a 15-year-old boy, was arrested and charged with making lewd phone calls to a woman in the neighborhood. At the initial hearing, the complainant did not appear and no transcript or record of the hearing was made. At a second hearing, with the complainant still not present, the judge found Gault to be delinquent and he was committed to the state industrial school for a period of five years. No appeal was permitted for juveniles, so the defense filed a writ of *habeas corpus,* which was denied. On appeal to the Supreme Court, the defense stated that the juvenile court erred because the defendant had been denied the basic rights of due process guaranteed by the Fourteenth Amendment.

The U.S. Supreme Court overturned the verdict in a 9-to-0 decision, stating that due process rights should be applied to juveniles. If Gault had been an adult, the maximum penalty would have been two months in jail. However, as a delinquent, he faced a possible maximum of six years in an institution. While the juvenile court is intended to help the child by its informality, it did not do so in this case. The Court decided that the juvenile court system would be enhanced, not hindered, by the granting of certain due process rights to juveniles. Throughout the incident, both police and the court acted with almost no regard for due process. Whatever was done was justified by the doctrine of *parens patriae*: It was all for the "best welfare" of the child. Gerald Gault's "welfare" required that he be committed to the Arizona Industrial School for an indeterminate sentence. Under usual court procedure, this commitment would end at age 21. Therefore, Gerald Gault, who was 15, could have been deprived of liberty for six years!

Justice Fortas, writing the majority opinion for the Court, was unimpressed by any appeal to *parens patriae*. He argued that "the basic requirements of due process and fairness" must be satisfied in juvenile proceedings. Fortas summed up his position by saying, "Neither the Fourteenth Amendment nor the Bill of Rights is for adults only."[30] From this premise he proceeded to challenge the very essence of the juvenile court's operation. The court's position that its activities worked for the good of the child was shown to be suspect, and its procedure, in fact, violated fundamental rights. In Fortas's own words, "Under our Constitution, the condition of being a boy does not justify a kangaroo court."[31]

Fortas argued that the proper goal of the juvenile court would not be impaired by constitutional requirements. In fact, he felt that the essentials of due process would express a fair and responsive attitude toward the juvenile. Fortas then set out the essentials of due process and described how they should apply to the adjudicatory hearing in a juvenile proceeding:

1. The juvenile has a right to counsel and to court-appointed counsel, if necessary.
2. With the aid of counsel, the child can present his or her defense and confront witnesses, who must present testimony under oath through cross-examination.
3. The child also has the right to confront his or her accuser as well as a right against self-incrimination. Since his or her freedom is at stake, this right has a special urgency.
4. To make use of the available elements of defense, the child has a right to timely notice of the charges against him or her.

The spectrum of rights elaborated in the *Gault* decision is impressive. However, the ruling has noticeable limitations. The *Gault* decision is restricted to the adjudicatory hearing, at which guilt or innocence is determined. It does not extend, for instance, to the court intake hearing, at which the initial decision to invoke juvenile court jurisdiction is made; nor does it affect the final stage of the process, the disposition hearing, at which the decision about what to do with the child is made.

Right to Counsel

Gault established that in adjudication proceedings the Court must notify both the juvenile and his or her parents of their right to retain counsel and, if indigent, to have court-appointed counsel. However, the Court did not specify whether the right to counsel extends to other hearings, such as disposition hearings or proceedings involving nondelinquency cases. While most state juvenile codes now provide children with a statutory right to counsel, it appears that few states ensure effective legal counsel in delinquency proceedings. Barry Feld notes that many jurisdictions fail to appoint counsel or even to notify youths and their parents of the right to counsel. For example, "in Minnesota throughout the 1980s and early 1990s, the majority of all juveniles appeared without counsel" although the rates varied significantly from county to county, "ranging from nearly 100 percent in a few counties to less than 5 percent in several others." He also reports that lawyers represented 37 percent to 52 percent of the juveniles in delinquency and status offense cases in three states surveyed during the mid-1980s.[32]

Much has been written about the disadvantages faced by indigent defendants. Is justice a commodity? Does the juvenile justice system have any obligation to compensate for the poverty of its defendants?

Even when juveniles are represented by counsel, there are serious concerns regarding the quality and effectiveness of counsel. Jane Knitzer and Merril Sobie studied defense counsel performance in New York juvenile courts and report inadequate representation in 45 percent of the observed hearings. In 5 percent of the observations, counsel had not met with the child, and in 35 percent of the observations, there was little or no contact or discussion between the youth and counsel during the hearings.[33] And Janet Ainsworth reports that many attorneys in juvenile proceedings fail to contest prosecutor's claims, provide "lackadaisical defense efforts," rarely call defense witnesses, and provide only perfunctory cross-examination of prosecution witnesses.[34] Most attorneys say overwhelmingly large caseloads for court-appointed counsel in juvenile courts make effective representation difficult, if not impossible. Feld reports that delinquency caseloads in Washington State often run as high as 500, and that in Minnesota, delinquency caseloads of urban public defenders commonly run between 600 and 800. It should not be surprising that high caseloads make it difficult for attorneys to adequately prepare, file motions, or even interview juveniles prior to hearings.[35]

Burden of Proof

Three years after *Gault*, the Court dealt with the question of "whether proof beyond a reasonable doubt is among the 'essentials of due process and fair treatment' required during the adjudicatory stage when a juvenile is charged with an act which would constitute a crime if committed by an adult" in **In re Winship** (1970).[36] Samuel Winship, a 12-year-old boy, was accused of stealing $112 from a woman's pocketbook. The juvenile court judge stated that the evidence did not provide for a verdict of guilty beyond a reasonable doubt but that there was a preponderance of evidence indicating that the juvenile had committed the act. Winship was found delinquent and placed in a training school for an initial period of 18 months, which could be extended until Winship reached the age of 18. The defense appealed on the ground that juveniles should have to be proven guilty beyond a reasonable doubt according to due process guarantees in the Constitution.

In a 6-to-3 vote, the Supreme Court decided that juveniles have the constitutional right to be convicted only when there is proof beyond a reasonable doubt. The Court's reasoning was that even though juvenile court proceedings are civil and not criminal in nature, the juvenile still holds the risk of losing his individual freedom and there should not be a reasonable doubt of his guilt. Justice William Brennan delivered the opinion of the Court. In addition to affirming that "civil labels and good intentions" do not render due process safeguards unnecessary, the Court rejected the argument that "the protection of proof beyond a reasonable doubt would risk destruction of beneficial aspects of the juvenile process." Chief Justice Burger dissented, stating "Since I see no constitutional requirement of due process sufficient to overcome the legislative judgment of the States in this area, I dissent from further strait-jacketing of an already overly-restricted system. . . . The juvenile system requires breathing room and flexibility in order to survive.[37]

The issue of burden of proof is also relevant in arguing whether younger adolescents should be charged or petitioned for criminal acts. For example, California law presumes that a child under age 14 is incapable of committing a crime, but this presumption is rebuttable. This is known as the *infancy defense*. But should a child under age 14 be held to the same standard of criminal responsibility as older and more experienced adolescents and adults? In a 1994 decision, the California Supreme Court held that the state needed only to show "clear proof," not proof beyond a reasonable doubt, that at the time a minor committed a crime he or she knew it was wrong in order to proceed with a delinquency petition.[38]

Jury Trial

The issue of whether juveniles have a right to a jury trial in delinquency cases was reviewed by the Supreme Court in *McKeiver v. Pennsylvania* (1971).[39] Proponents argued that children convicted by the juvenile court are subject to incarceration. Therefore, since a jury trial is a constitutional right afforded people accused in criminal proceedings in which their liberty is at issue, juveniles should have the same right since their liberty also is at stake. Joseph McKeiver, a 16-year-old, was arrested after he and three other juveniles chased 20 to 30 youths and stole 25 cents from them. McKeiver was charged with robbery, larceny, and receiving stolen property. At the adjudication hearing, McKeiver's request for a jury trial was denied. Even though the testimony of two of the victims was inconsistent, McKeiver was found delinquent and was placed on probation. The defense appealed on the grounds that his Sixth Amendment right to a jury trial had been denied.

The Supreme Court, in a 9-to-0 decision, stated that juveniles do not have a right to a jury trial. The judges reasoned that juveniles are not guaranteed every constitutional right, that a jury trial would make a juvenile proceeding fully adversarial, and that a jury trial is not necessary in order to have a fair hearing. Writing the majority opinion, Justice Harry Blackmun expressed fear that the introduction of juries would "remake the juvenile proceedings into a fully adversary process and [would] put an effective end to what [had] been the idealistic prospect of an intimate, informal protective proceeding."[40]

The Court decided that a jury trial is an adult right that is not essential in juvenile proceedings. In fact, the majority played down the value of the jury in any trial, whether juvenile or criminal. The jury trial does not ensure competence in the fact-finding function of the proceedings. In the context of the juvenile proceeding, the right to a jury trial could be a distinctly negative factor, since it carries with it the traditional delay, formality, and clamor of the adversary system. The majority felt that the states should be allowed to have jury trials in their own juvenile proceedings if they wished, but that such a decision would in no way be based on constitutional mandate.

Because *McKeiver* did not prohibit states from allowing trials for juveniles, 11 states now permit jury trials if juveniles request them. Two states permit the judge to order a jury trial, and in one state habitual offenders may be granted jury trials.[41] In 1999, the Appellate Court of Illinois held that a juvenile charged with first-degree murder and tried in the juvenile court may not be denied a jury trial. In this case, G.O., a 13-year-old was arrested and charged in the shooting death of Rafael Kubera. His attorney requested a jury trial and was denied because the statute under which he was charged provided for jury trials only when a juvenile is facing a determinant sentence. G.O. was found delinquent and committed to the Department of Corrections until age 21. The Court reasoned that because G.O. was neither eligible for parole nor good-time credit, the sentence was punitive and determinant and the youth should have been afforded a jury trial.[42]

Double Jeopardy

In **Breed v. Jones** (1975),[43] the Supreme Court unanimously ruled that the Fifth Amendment's prohibition against **double jeopardy** forbids criminal prosecution of a juvenile after he or she has been tried in juvenile court for the same offense. Gary Jones, a 17-year-old, was accused of robbery. In this case, Gary Jones was made a ward of a California court on the basis of evidence showing that he had committed the robbery he had been charged with, and he was ordered detained pending a disposition hearing. On the date of the hearing, the court announced that because Jones was "not . . . . amenable to the care, treatment and training program available through the facilities of the juvenile court" it intended to waive jurisdiction and transfer the case to the criminal court. In adult court, Jones was tried and found guilty of robbery. Jones's attorney appealed on the ground that Jones's Fifth

Amendment rights had been violated because the juvenile hearing plus the adult trial constituted double jeopardy.

The U.S. Supreme Court, in a 9-to-0 opinion, held that the two procedures did constitute double jeopardy, and the ruling overturned the adult court's verdict. The Court's reasoning was that a juvenile runs the risk of losing his freedom in a juvenile court for many years and therefore is put in jeopardy, thus making a second trial double jeopardy. In addition, if transferal to adult court after a juvenile court hearing were possible, the juvenile would likely be uncooperative in the criminal court proceeding, thus making it more adversarial.

The Right to Bail and Preventive Detention

The Eighth Amendment guarantee that "excessive bail shall not be required" is well established for adults charged with crimes. But what about juveniles? Should the juvenile courts use a different system for release and supervision prior to an adjudication hearing? States vary in how they handle this issue. For example, Nebraska law allows for juveniles to be granted "bail by bond in such amount and on such conditions and security as the court, in its sole discretion, shall determine." Hawaii law states that "Provisions regarding bail shall not be applicable to children detained . . . except that bail may be allowed after a child has been transferred for criminal prosecution pursuant to waiver of family court jurisdiction." And the Georgia statute maintains that "All juveniles subject to the jurisdiction of the juvenile court and alleged to be delinquent or unruly, on application of the parent or guardian, shall have the same right to bail as adults."[44]

In *Schall v. Martin* (1984), the Supreme Court held that "the protection of society is an important goal in itself, and thus, preventive detention of juveniles is permissible." Did we really need the U.S. Supreme Court to determine that public safety is a societal goal? Do the juvenile and criminal justice systems place the protection of the accused over the protection of the masses?

Gregory Martin, a 14–year-old, was accused of robbery and assault. He was detained for 15 days prior to his adjudication hearing because the judge considered him to be at risk of committing an additional crime. At the hearing, he was found guilty and placed on probation. Martin then brought a class action suit, claiming that the court's policy of preventive detention violated the due process clause of the Fourteenth Amendment. The U. S. Supreme Court, in **Schall v. Martin** (1984),[45] held that preventive detention of juveniles was constitutional and articulated three primary justifications for its use. These include:

1. the legitimate and compelling state interest in protecting the community from crime;
2. protecting the juvenile from his or her own "folly" and the consequences of criminal activity; and
3. preventing the child from absconding.

Preventive detention of juveniles was determined to be constitutional when the Court upheld a New York statute authorizing the pretrial detention of an accused juvenile who, if released, may pose a "serious risk" by committing the equivalent of an adult crime. In the majority opinion, the Court held that:

- while the statute provided for a detention hearing, a formal finding that there was probable cause to believe that the youth committed the offense for which he or she was arrested was not required prior to his or her detention;
- the protection of society is an important goal in itself, and thus, preventive detention of juveniles is permissible;
- the juvenile justice system has no obligation to *treat* juvenile offenders; and
- preventive detention was justified for juveniles because, "children, by definition, are not assumed to have the capacity to take care of themselves." They are assumed to always be subject to the control of someone (their parents, guardians, or the state).[46]

Public Access to Juvenile Court Proceedings and Records

The cases discussed in the previous section focused on fundamental due process issues in the juvenile court. Although these decisions brought significant changes in terms of court procedure, they did not open the courts to the public. Most states continue to have limited public access to juvenile court proceedings and juvenile records, and many states maintain confidentiality of juveniles' names. However, public and political expressions of concern over the increasingly serious nature of juvenile crime have led to significant changes in recent years. The Supreme Court even noted in *Breed v. Jones* that individuals face deprivations in both the adult and juvenile systems and that "in terms of potential consequences, there is little to distinguish an adjudicatory hearing . . . from a traditional criminal prosecution."[47] To what extent should juvenile courts lose their special protections of confidentiality and consequently thrust youths into the public spotlight?

Right to Public Hearings
Since 1985 state legislatures have made significant changes in how information about juvenile offenders is treated by the justice system. By 1996, 22 states provided for open hearings for certain cases (typically when the youth is charged with a serious or violent offense or if the youth is a chronic offender). These changes range from allowing people or agencies with a "legitimate interest" to attend hearings to permitting the media to attend and publish stories about the proceedings.

Confidentiality of Juvenile Records
Nearly all states have statutes specifying circumstances in which juvenile records may be made available to the public. Under these statutes, juvenile records pertaining to certain crimes or cases may be made part of the public

record or made public in some other way. The crimes specified are typically violent or otherwise serious offenses, but sometimes more minor crimes are included. In some states, by statute, the records of any public court proceedings are available to the public. In several states, the court is required to release the names of juveniles adjudicated delinquent for committing serious offenses or repeat offenses, as well as the nature of the crimes involved. A few states also allow victims or other people potentially in danger from the youth to access the court record or at least to be informed of the youth's name and address and the outcome of the case.[48]

Media Involvement

Nearly 80 percent of the states permit the release of certain juveniles' names and/or photographs to the media. A few states forbid publication of the juvenile's name or other identifying information, but do not prohibit the presence of the media at hearings, and at least eight states allow the media to be present at hearings and to publish information about them (though not information identifying the juvenile). This approach is particularly popular with people who contend that private hearings make abuses of authority by the juvenile court judge more likely. They believe that allowing the media to monitor hearings effectively restrains the abuse of power.

Supreme Court decisions have largely eroded the state's power to limit publication of lawfully obtained information. In *Davis v. Alaska* (1974),[49] the Court ruled that a lower court had erred in issuing a protective order prohibiting cross-examination of a juvenile about his prior juvenile court involvement and present probation status. The lower court's order was based on a state statute protecting the anonymity of juvenile offenders. The Supreme Court held that the defendant's Sixth Amendment right to confront witnesses must prevail over the state's interest in protecting juveniles from adverse publicity.

In *Oklahoma Publishing Co. v. District Court* (1977),[50] the Court struck down a state court injunction prohibiting the media from publishing the name or photograph of an 11-year-old boy being tried before a juvenile court. Despite a state statute closing juvenile hearings to the public, the judge had permitted reporters and other members of the public to attend an initial hearing. Afterward, the juvenile court attempted to block publication of information obtained at the hearing. The Supreme Court, however, held that once information is "publicly revealed" or "in the public domain," its publication or broadcast cannot be restrained.

In *Smith v. Daily Mail Publishing Co.* (1979),[51] the Supreme Court further eroded the principle that the media must not disclose the identity of a juvenile. In West Virginia, a statute prohibited newspapers from publishing, without a written court order, the name of any child in connection with a juvenile court proceeding. But three radio stations and two newspapers carried identifying information about a 14-year-old boy who shot and killed a classmate at school. The state sought to justify its statute on the grounds that it would protect the anonymity of the juvenile offender and further the child's rehabilitation as a result. The Supreme Court ruled that when information is lawfully obtained, the state cannot prohibit its publication.

Destruction of Records

More than one-half of the states have provisions that permit destruction of certain juvenile court records. These statutes generally allow for the sealing or destruction of social-history files or arrest records. Docket sheets and official court files are maintained, although they may be sealed or placed in a restricted area. Many people argue for complete destruction of all juvenile records, contending that unless the records are destroyed, certain information will inevitably "leak" and harm the youth. However, others argue that total destruction of these records may place a juvenile in a more vulnerable position. After all, the conduct that brought a juvenile to court may be less serious than the label attached to his or her behavior.

Some argue that when an adult is facing a criminal charge, his or her juvenile record should not be considered. This argument reasons that misbehavior as a juvenile must be viewed in the context of immature adolescence, which is the basis for the juvenile court's informal response to youths' offenses. Treating a juvenile record as part of the person's adult prior record redefines his or her delinquency as criminality. However, an increasing number of states have moved to restrict the expungement or sealing of juvenile records or to forbid entirely those restrictions on information about youths adjudicated delinquent. In a number of states, not only is the destruction or sealing of juvenile records prohibited, the law now requires that the juvenile record be taken into account in determining sentencing of an adult.

Should juvenile records be considered by criminal justice systems until persons reach age 25? Does society have an obligation to remember the chronic delinquencies of youthful adult offenders? If so, why?

The Transfer of Serious Offenders to Criminal Court

There is no doubt that very young people are committing more serious and violent crime than in the past. To many people the nature of youth violence today appears senseless, vicious, spontaneous, and broadly threatening, and the public and policy makers increasingly believe that handling such serious, violent youths in the juvenile justice system is not the answer to the problem. The old system, emphasizing treatment and concern for offender privacy, is believed not only to be outmoded but to be dangerous in terms of community safety. Consequently, an increasing number of juveniles are transferred to criminal court for prosecution as adult offenders.

In response to demands for getting tough and holding serious juvenile offenders responsible, many states have made changes making it easier for juveniles to be tried as adults. Changes include the following:

- Lowering the age for waiver (dropping the minimum age for waiver from 15 to 14, for example).

On one hand, American society oppresses innocent children by fundamentally denying or limiting their humanity. On the other hand, the juvenile justice system tenuously punishes serious youthful offenders because of an overriding sense of compassion. Are these contrasts reconcilable?

- Expanding the list of crimes eligible for waiver.
- Establishing "presumptive waiver" provisions requiring that certain offenders be transferred unless they can prove they are suitable for juvenile rehabilitation.
- Excluding certain offenses from juvenile court jurisdiction, such as violent crimes against the person.
- Adding prior record provisions making certain repeat offenders eligible for waiver.
- Requiring that once an offender is waived from juvenile court or is convicted in criminal court, all subsequent cases are under criminal court jurisdiction.
- Lowering the maximum age of juvenile court jurisdiction (from 18 to 16 or 15, for example), thus allowing criminal courts to prosecute younger offenders without the need for the waiver process.[52]

Even Congress, when it passed its crime control legislation in 1994, lowered the minimum age for transferring juveniles for adult prosecution from age 15 to age 13 for certain serious violent federal offenses.[53]

Reasons for Transferring Juveniles

There are three primary reasons for transferring juveniles to criminal court. The first involves the seriousness of the offense. Most serious juvenile offenders, particularly those who have committed violent crimes, can be prosecuted by the criminal courts where harsher punishments, including the death penalty, may be imposed.

Second, some youths, mainly those who are older and have long criminal records, are perceived by many juvenile justice officials as not amenable to treatment programs provided in the juvenile justice system. Their patterns of delinquent behavior and responses to the juvenile justice system suggest that either the programs are not effective or the youths are not responsive to the treatment efforts of rehabilitative staff.[54] It is believed that the more punitive environment of adult prisons may have a positive impact on these youths by giving them a taste of adult punishment.

A third reason stems from society's frustration with serious juvenile offenders. Many citizens and penal experts are uncertain about the need for harsher punishments or the ability of adult corrections to rehabilitate these youths effectively, but they argue that long-term incarceration will at least remove these offenders from the streets for a longer period of time.

Legal Criteria for Transfer

In the *Kent* case, the Supreme Court stated that there is no constitutional requirement for a separate juvenile court system; it would therefore be constitutional if states wished to prosecute juveniles and adults within a single system. However, the Court held that when such a juvenile court system is authorized by statute, a juvenile may not be deprived of his or her constitutional rights (for example, transfer to criminal court) without ceremony. Specifically, the Court stated that there is no place in our legal system for reaching a verdict of such tremendous consequences without a waiver hearing, without effective assistance of counsel, and without a statement of the reasons for transfer of a youth.

The juvenile courts in most states have original jurisdiction over all youths who are under age 18 at the time of arrest. In 37 states, the District of Columbia, and the federal districts, 17 is the upper age limit for jurisdiction; 10 states set the limit at age 16; and three states (Connecticut, New York, and North Carolina) set the upper age limit at 15. Most states also set minimum ages at which a juvenile may be transferred to adult court.[55] Table 14–2 lists the youngest ages for transfer in each state.

The Transfer Process

Three procedures are used for transferring youths to criminal court: judicial waiver, legislative exclusion, and prosecutorial waiver or direct file. These transfer methods are also known as certification or remands to criminal court.

Judicial Waiver   Historically, **judicial waiver**, in which the juvenile court judge is the primary decision maker, has been the most common method for transferring youths to criminal courts. It is seen as the method most consistent with traditional juvenile justice philosophy. In all states except Nebraska, New Mexico, and New York, juvenile court judges may waive

Table 14–2   Minimum Age at Which a Child Can Be Tried as an Adult

MINIMUM AGE*	STATE
No age minimum	Alaska, Arizona, Delaware, District of Columbia, Florida, Georgia, Hawaii, Idaho, Indiana, Maine, Maryland, Nebraska, Nevada, Oklahoma, Oregon, Pennsylvania, Rhode Island, South Carolina, South Dakota, Tennessee, Washington, West Virginia, Wisconsin
10	Kansas, Vermont
12	Colorado, Missouri, Montana
13	Illinois, Mississippi, New Hampshire, New York, North Carolina, Wyoming
14	Alabama, Arkansas, California, Connecticut, Iowa, Kentucky, Louisiana, Massachusetts, Michigan, Minnesota, New Jersey, North Dakota, Ohio, Texas, Utah, Virginia
15	New Mexico

*Most state judicial statutes identify specific offenses which, when committed by juveniles, are waivable. This table shows only the youngest age at which a juvenile may be waived without regard to the specific offense.

Source: Howard Snyder and Melissa Sickmund, *Juvenile Offenders and Victims: 1999 National Report* (Washington, DC: National Center for Juvenile Justice, 1999), p. 106.

jurisdiction over certain cases and transfer them to criminal court.[56] According to Donna Bishop and her associates,

> When a state seeks to transfer a youth to criminal court via judicial waiver, it bears the substantial burden of marshalling evidence sufficient to convince a presumably treatment-oriented juvenile court judge that a youth poses a serious danger to the community and is not amenable to treatment within the juvenile justice system.[57]

The judge, acting according to the *parens patriae* philosophy of the juvenile court, is believed to be in the best position to consider all relevant issues of the case. The judicial waiver method requires that the state file a motion for waiver of jurisdiction to have the juvenile tried as an adult. The court then holds a waiver or transfer hearing to determine whether a transfer is in the best interests of the child and the community.

Legislative Exclusion   Many states have established the use of the **legislative exclusion**, whereby the most serious or persistent offenders or those over a certain age are excluded from juvenile court jurisdiction and automatically prosecuted as adults. This procedure is based on the idea that "the 'right' of a juvenile to be in juvenile court is entirely a statutory right. It is something that is granted by legislative largess and can be summarily eliminated."[58] In other words, some states have chosen to take away some youths' "right" to have their cases heard in juvenile court. In addition, some observers believe that certain types of youthful offenders are not fit for juvenile court.

Should there be a defense attorney waiver in which the defender of the accused acknowledges that certain individuals are beyond rehabilitation? If such a waiver did exist, would it ever be used?

In 1978 New York State representatives passed get-tough legislation against violent juvenile crime. These policy makers were reacting, in part, to the increased use of 13-, 14-, and 15-year-olds by adults for the commission of serious crimes, including contract murder. If the youths were caught, the old law required that they be subject to the rehabilitative orientation of the family court, and there was no judicial procedure for transferring youths to criminal court. The new legislation lowered the age of criminal responsibility to 13 for murder and to 14 for a number of other violent and potentially violent acts (such as arson, rape, and robbery), and the criminal courts were given original jurisdiction over these offenders.[59] All 16-year-olds in New York State automatically come under the jurisdiction of the criminal courts.

Prosecutorial Waiver   The **prosecutorial waiver**, or *direct file*, gives the prosecutor the authority to decide whether to file a charge against a juvenile in criminal court. Prosecutorial waivers are currently used in at least 15 states. In these states, the prosecutor possesses concurrent jurisdiction over most cases involving violations of criminal law and has the discretion to file charges in either juvenile or criminal court. For example, the prosecutor may choose to file a serious charge in criminal court against a juvenile meeting the minimum-age criterion (cases involving capital crimes, however, must be submitted to a grand jury for indictment) or to file the charge in the juvenile court.

At least 23 states provide some mechanism, typically known as a **reverse waiver**, whereby a juvenile who is being prosecuted as an adult in criminal court may petition to have the case transferred to juvenile court for adjudication or disposition. Generally, if the juvenile was transferred to criminal court by direct file or statutory exclusion, the court would evaluate the petition for reverse waiver on the same grounds and using the same standards that the juvenile court would use in deciding whether to waive the youth to criminal court. In some states, such as Kentucky, Mississippi, and Tennessee, reverse waivers are usually authorized only if the juvenile court's decision to initially waive the juvenile was groundless or if other "exceptional circumstances" could be shown.

Interestingly, some states provide for a **demand waiver**, whereby a juvenile may request to have his or her case transferred *from* juvenile court *to* criminal court. Such requests are uncommon and are typically used when a youth desires to have a jury trial, believing that he or she will more likely be acquitted by a jury, or when the sentence in criminal court would be substantially shorter than one likely to be imposed by the juvenile court.

Who Is Transferred?

Just under 1 percent (about 8,400) of all petitioned delinquency cases in 1997 were judicially waived to criminal court. In addition, over 3,000 additional youths were handled in the criminal courts as a result of legislative exclusion and prosecutorial waivers.[60] In most states, except in those that use legislative exclusion based on a youth's age or offense, most juveniles who meet the statutory requirements for transfer *are not transferred* or even formally considered for waiver hearings.[61] Given the discretion of prosecutors, what characteristics are most important in determining who gets transferred?

Prior to 1992, property cases outnumbered person offenses among juveniles waived to criminal court. However, this trend was reversed in 1993 as offenses against persons accounted for a greater proportion of waived cases. By 1997 juveniles waived for crimes against the person only slightly outnumbered those charged with property crimes (40 percent versus 38 percent).[62]

There may be no greater disparity in juvenile justice processing than that found in sex differences in waiver (with the exception of death penalty cases). Males are significantly more likely than females to be waived to criminal court, comprising 95 percent of all waived cases. Over 85 percent of waived cases involve juveniles who were age 16 or older at the time of court referral. Significant disparities are also found in race of waived juveniles. In 1997 white youths accounted for 50 percent of waived cases, black youths comprised 46 percent of the cases, and youths of other races accounted for 4 percent. White youths are more likely to be waived for property offenses, while

15-year-old Charles "Andy" Williams killed 2 fellow students and wounded 15 in a rampage at Santana High School on March 5, 2001. Should Williams be prosecuted as a juvenile or adult? Why?

Table 14-3   Percent of Youth Waived to Criminal Court, by Race and Offense

MOST SERIOUS OFFENSE	WHITE	BLACK
Person	36	43
Property	47	27
Drugs	11	21
Public Order	6	9

Source: Charles Puzzanchera, Anne Stahl, Terrence Finnegan, Howard Snyder, Rowen Poole, and Nancy Tierney, *Juvenile Court Statistics, 1997* (Washington, DC: U.S. Department of Justice, 2000), p. 31.

black youths are much more likely to be waived for crimes against the person (see Table 14-3).

Juvenile offenders are also likely to have extensive prior arrests, adjudications, and commitments. For example, in South Carolina, 32 percent of transferred youths had five or more prior court referrals, 26 percent had three or more prior adjudications, and 15 percent had two or more prior court-ordered residential placements. In Utah, 80 percent of youths approved for waiver had five or more prior referrals, 81 percent had five or more prior adjudications, and 78 percent had three or more prior court-ordered residential placements.[63]

The Impact of Race and Ethnicity in Transferred Cases

The previous discussion of characteristics of juveniles transferred to criminal court was largely based on national statistics. However, significant racial and ethnic disparities in transfers may be masked by national data. Therefore, it may be more useful to examine the transfer process in local jurisdictions. Jeffrey Fagan and his associates analyzed transfer cases in Boston, Detroit, Newark, and Phoenix and found that black youths were 75 percent more likely to be waived to criminal court than were white youths, although race had no independent influence on the waiver decision when seriousness of offense and prior record were controlled.[64] Similarly, Marcy Podkopacz and Barry Feld report no racial disparities in waived cases in Minneapolis when controlling for offender, offense, and court process variables.[65]

A more recent study of juvenile transfers in 18 jurisdictions suggests that race and ethnicity play a significant, but complex, role. Jolanta Juszkiewicz analyzed all juvenile cases filed in 18 criminal courts during the first six months of 1998.[66] The jurisdictions included cities such as Birmingham, Phoenix, Los Angeles, Miami, Orlando, Indianapolis, St. Louis, Brooklyn, Queens, Philadelphia, Houston, and Milwaukee. Disparities affecting black and Latino youths were found throughout the process. For example:

Would you describe the juvenile court as a gutsy or gutless social institution? Use evidence from the chapter to support your opinion.

- Black youths were disproportionately transferred to criminal court based on their proportion of felony arrests.
- Black youths comprised two-thirds of all juveniles arrested for felony drug offenses, but accounted for three-fourths of juvenile drug cases in criminal court.
- Disparities in some jurisdictions were extreme. For example, black youths accounted for 30 percent of felony arrests in Jefferson County (Birmingham), Alabama, but were 80 percent of transferred cases to criminal court.
- White juveniles were more likely than minority youths to have violent offenses filed in criminal court in half of the jurisdictions.
- Conviction rates were significantly higher for white and Latino youths (76 percent and 72 percent, respectively) than for black youths (57 percent).
- Black youths were nearly three times more likely than white youths to have their cases transferred back to juvenile court (13 percent versus 5 percent).
- Black (43 percent) and Latino (37 percent) youths were more likely than white (26 percent) youths to receive prison sentences.
- Black youths sentenced to prison had longer sentences than white or Latino youths for nearly all offense categories.

But, as noted earlier, most youths who meet the offense and statutory-age criteria for waiver are not transferred to criminal court. Most are handled in the juvenile courts, and if their cases result in adjudications of delinquency, the youths then face disposition. The next chapter will examine the range of disposition alternatives available to the juvenile court including probation, restitution, and confinement in correctional institutions.

Conclusions

This chapter has explored the nature of the juvenile courts and the specific stages and procedures of the court process, from arrest and court intake to detention and adjudication and disposition hearings. In its decisions on a number of landmark due process cases, the U.S. Supreme Court established guidelines as well as legal constraints under which the juvenile courts must operate. Other court decisions, and statutes established by state legislatures, have placed constraints on the public nature of juvenile court hearings, although public access to court proceedings and information has increased in recent years.

A very important issue today involves the transfer of serious juvenile offenders to criminal court for prosecution as adults. In most states, juveniles who are charged with certain serious crimes (for example, murder or armed robbery) and who meet the minimum-age standard for waiver, may be transferred. Once transferred, they face the same prosecution process that adult defendants face. Some states rely exclusively on judicial waivers, while an increasing number of states permit the prosecutorial transfer of youths. Most youths tried in criminal court, however, are there as a result of legislatively mandated transfers. Given the growing get-tough sentiment of the public and of politicians, it is reasonable to expect that an increasing number of youths will be tried in criminal courts for their crimes in the next few years.

Key Terms

adjudication hearing: *A hearing held to determine whether the child committed the offense of which he or she is accused.*

Breed v. Jones: *Criminal prosecution of a child following a juvenile court hearing is unconstitutional because it constitutes double jeopardy.*

demand waiver: *A juvenile may request to have his or her case transferred from juvenile court to criminal court.*

detention: *The temporary confinement of children pending adjudication, disposition, or implementation of disposition.*

disposition hearing: *A juvenile court hearing in which the court determines what action will be in the youth's and community's best interests; the equivalent of the sentencing stage in the criminal court process.*

double jeopardy: *The prosecution of an individual a second time for the same offense. It is prohibited by the Fifth Amendment.*

In re Gault: *Juveniles may not be denied basic due process rights in juvenile adjudicatory hearings.*

In re Winship: *Juveniles, in delinquency cases, have the right to be convicted only if there is proof beyond a reasonable doubt.*

informal adjustment: *Cases that are handled through discretionary nonjudicial dispositions.*

informal probation: *A case adjustment practice in which the child and family comply with requirements of probation personnel without a formal court order.*

intake: *The initial case-screening process in the juvenile court system. It is designed to screen out cases that do not warrant a formal court hearing.*

judicial waiver: *A method used for transferring youths to criminal court in which the juvenile court judge is the primary decision maker in determining whether the youth should be transferred.*

Kent v. United States: *A formal waiver hearing must take place before transfer of a juvenile to criminal court.*

legislative exclusion: *A method used for transferring youths to criminal court, whereby the most serious or persistent offenders or those over a certain age are excluded from juvenile court jurisdiction and automatically prosecuted as adults.*

McKeiver v. Pennsylvania: *Juveniles do not have a constitutional right to a jury trial in juvenile court.*

petition: *A document setting forth the specific charge against a juvenile.*

prosecutorial waiver: *A method used for transferring youths to criminal court in which the prosecutor is the primary decision maker in determining whether a youth should be transferred. The prosecutor typically has concurrent jurisdiction to file charges in either juvenile or criminal court.*

reverse waiver: *A juvenile who is being prosecuted as an adult in criminal court may petition to have the case transferred to juvenile court for adjudication or disposition.*

Schall v. Martin: *Juveniles may be held in preventive detention while awaiting adjudication if they are determined to be "serious risks" to the community.*

Getting Connected

There are a number of web sites that provide legal, statistical, and policy-oriented reports and publications. The Office of Juvenile Justice and Delinquency Prevention's (OJJDP) website is one of the most comprehensive locations for government documents dealing with juvenile delinquency and the juvenile justice system. It is located at:

http://www.ojjdp.ncjrs.org/

1. The OJJDP maintains extensive files of abstracts of public opinion polls on American youths. What are Americans' attitudes toward juvenile justice?
2. The OJJDP maintains extensive files of abstracts of public opinion polls on American youths. What are Americans' attitudes toward the drug problem?
3. The OJJDP maintains extensive files of abstracts of public opinion polls on American youths. What are Americans' attitudes toward "kids these days"?

The OJJDP page focusing documents and reports relating to the juvenile courts can be found at:

http://www.virlib.ncjrs.org/Courts.asp

1. What are "teen courts"? For what kinds of cases are they an alternative to the juvenile court?
2. What is juvenile court waiver? What lessons were learned in the study "Juvenile Transfers to Criminal Court in the 1990's: Lessons Learned"?
3. Find the study "Juveniles Facing Criminal Sanctions: Three States That Changed the Rules." What did these three states do differently?

The American Bar Association (ABA) Center on Children and the Law maintains a website at:

http://www.abanet.org/child/

1. Find the issues section, then the court improvement fact sheet. Why was this initiative developed?
2. Find the "center materials" section, then the page on the *Children's Legal Rights Journal.* What recently published articles are particularly related to juvenile delinquency?
3. What are the main activities of this division of the American Bar Association?

The United Nations Standard Minimum Rules for the Administration of Juvenile Justice (The Beijing Rules) can be found at

http://www1.umn.edu/humanrts/instree/j3unsmr.htm

1. How influential are United Nations documents in developing American policy toward juveniles and juvenile delinquency?
2. How does this document define a nation's responsibility toward juveniles?
3. Read article 17.2 in light of American death penalty policy.

The National Council of Juvenile and Family Court Judges, located in Reno, Nevada, provides education, training, and informational reports and publications at their website. You can visit it at:

http://www.ncjfcj.unr.edu

1. Link to "Brevity on the Internet." What kinds of issues have been raised most recently?
2. What are the main activities of the Alcohol and Other Drugs Division of the NCJFCJ?
3. What is the National Center for Juvenile Justice?

Endnotes

1. Robert Mennel, *Thorns and Thistles: Juvenile Delinquents in the United States* (Hanover, NH: University Press of New England, 1973), p. 132.
2. Evelina Belden, *Courts in the United States Hearing Children's Cases: Results of a Questionnaire Study Covering the Year 1918* (Washington, DC: U.S. Government Printing Office, 1920), p. 13.
3. Mark Haller, "Urban Crime and Criminal Justice: The Chicago Case," *Journal of American History* 57:619–635 (1970).
4. Sanford Fox, "Juvenile Justice Reform: A Historical Perspective," *Stanford Law Review* 22:11871239 (1970).
5. Frank Miller, Robert Dawson, George Dix, and Raymond Parnas, *The Juvenile Justice Process*, 4th edition (New York: Foundation Press, 2000), pp. 215–216.
6. Charles Puzzanchera, Anne Stahl, Terrence Finnegan, Howard Snyder, Rowen Poole, and Nancy Tierney, *Juvenile Court Statistics, 1997* (Washington, DC: U.S. Department of Justice, 2000), pp. 5–6.
7. Miller et al., note 5, p. 291.
8. Martin Gardner, *Understanding Juvenile Law* (New York: Matthew-Bender, 1997), p. 247.
9. Puzzanchera et al., note 6, p. 8.
10. Barry Feld, *Cases and Materials on Juvenile Justice Administration* (St. Paul, MN: West, 2000), p. 313.
11. Gardner, note 8, p. 248.
12. Ala. Code § 12–15–59(a) (1975).
13. Joan McCord, Cathy Widom, and Nancy Crowell, eds. *Juvenile Crime, Juvenile Justice* (Washington, DC: National Academy Press, 2001), p. 177.
14. *Schall v. Martin*, 467 U.S. 253 (1984).
15. Puzzanchera et al., note 6, p. 8.

16. Puzzanchera et al., note 6, p. 18.
17. Charles Frazier and Donna Bishop, "Reflections on Race Effects in Juvenile Justice," in *Minorities in Juvenile Justice*, edited by Kimberly Leonard, Carl Pope, and William Feyerherm (Thousand Oaks, CA: Sage Publications, 1995), pp. 16–46.
18. Gillian Porter, *Detention in Delinquency Cases, 1988–1997* (Washington, DC: Office of Juvenile Justice and Delinquency Prevention, 2000), p. 1.
19. Melissa Sickmund, *Offenders in Juvenile Court, 1997* (Washington, DC: Office of Juvenile Justice and Delinquency Prevention, 2000), p. 7.
20. Shay Bilchik, *Minorities in the Juvenile Justice System* (Washington, DC: Office of Juvenile Justice and Delinquency Prevention, 1999), p. 9.
21. Porter, note 18, p. 1.
22. American Bar Association and National Bar Association, *Justice by Gender: The Lack of Appropriate Prevention, Diversion and Treatment Alternatives for Girls in the Justice System* (Washington, DC: American Bar Association and National Bar Association, 2001), p. 17.
23. American Bar Association, note 22, pp., 18–19.
24. Barry Feld, *Bad Kids: Race and the Transformation of the Juvenile Court* (New York: Oxford University Press, 1999), p. 162.
25. Puzzanchera et al., note 6, p. 9.
26. See, for example, Donna Bishop and Charles Frazier, "Gender Bias in Juvenile Justice Processing: The Implications of the JJDP Act," *Journal of Criminal Law and Criminology* 82:1162–1186 (1992); Kimberly Leonard, Carl Pope, and William Feyerherm, (eds.), *Minorities in Juvenile Justice* (Thousand Oaks, CA: Sage Publications, 1995); and Edmund McGarrell, "Trends in Racial Disproportionality in Juvenile Court Processing: 1985–1989," *Crime and Delinquency* 39:29–48 (1993); John MacDonald and Meda Chesney-Lind, "Gender Bias and Juvenile Justice Revisited: A Multiyear Analysis," *Crime and Delinquency* 47:173–195 (2001).
27. Puzzanchera et al., note 6.
28. *Kent v. United States*, 383 U.S. 541 (1966).
29. *In re Gault*, 387 U.S. 1 (1967).
30. *In re Gault*, note 29.
31. *In re Gault*, note 29.
32. Feld, note 24, p. 125.
33. Jane Knitzer and Merril Sobie, *Law Guardians in New York State: A Study of the Legal Represention of Children* (New York: New York State Bar Association, 1984).
34. Janet Ainsworth, "Re-imagining Childhood and Re-constructing the Legal Order: The Case for Abolishing the Juvenile Court," *North Carolina Law Review* 69:1083–1133 (1991).
35. Feld, note 24, p. 132.
36. *In re Winship*, 397 U.S. 358 (1970).
37. *In re Winship*, note 36.
38. *In re Manuel L.*, 7 Cal.4th 229 (1994).
39. *McKeiver v. Pennsylvania*, 403 U.S. 528 (1971).
40. *McKeiver v. Pennsylvania*, note 39.
41. Joseph Sanborn, "The Right to a Public Jury Trial: A Need for Today's Juvenile Court," *Judicature* 76:233 (1993).
42. *In the Interest of G.O.*, 304 Ill.App.3d 719 (1999).
43. *Breed v. Jones*, 421 U.S. 519 (1975).
44. Miller, note 5, pp. 338–339.
45. *Schall v. Martin*, note 18.
46. *Schall v. Martin*, note 18.
47. *Breed v. Jones*, note 43.
48. Howard Snyder and Melissa Sickmund, *Juvenile Offenders and Victims: 1999 National Report* (Washington, DC: Office of Juvenile Justice and Delinquency Prevention, 1999).
49. *Davis v. Alaska*, 415 U.S. 308 (1974).
50. *Oklahoma Publishing Company v. District Court*, 430 U.S. 308 (1976).
51. *Smith v. Daily Mail Publishing Company*, 443 U.S. 97 (1979).
52. Robert Shepherd, "The Rush to Waive Children to Adult Court," *Criminal Justice* 10:39–42 (1995); Patricia Torbet, Richard Gable, Hunter Hurst, Imogene Montgomery, Linda Szymanski, and Douglas Thomas, *State Responses to Serious and Violent Juvenile Crime* (Washington, DC: National Center for Juvenile Justice, 1996); Patricia Torbet, Patrick Griffin, Hunter Hurst, and Lynn MacKenzie, *Juveniles Facing Criminal Sanctions: Three States That Changed the Rules* (Washington, DC: Office of Juvenile Justice and Delinquency Prevention, 2000).

53. 103D Congress, *Violent Crime Control and Law Enforcement Act of 1994*, Title XIV, Sec. 14000.1 (Washington, DC: U.S. Government Printing Office, 1994).

54. Feld, note 24.

55. Snyder and Sickmund, note 48.

56. Snyder and Sickmund, note 48, p. 103.

57. Donna Bishop, Charles Frazier, and John Henretta, "Prosecutorial Waiver: Case Study of a Questionable Reform," *Crime and Delinquency* 35:180 (1989).

58. Francis McCarthy, "The Serious Offender and Juvenile Court Reform: The Case for Prosecutorial Waiver of Juvenile Court Jurisdiction," *Saint Louis University Law Journal* 38:654 (1994).

59. Simon Singer, *Recriminalizing Delinquency: Violent Juvenile Crime and Juvenile Justice Reform* (New York: Cambridge University Press, 1996).

60. Puzzanchera et al., note 6, p. 13.

61. Lee Osbun and Peter Rode, "Prosecuting Juveniles as Adults," *Criminology* 22:195 (1984).

62. Charles Puzzanchera, "Delinquency Cases Waived to Criminal Court, 1988–1997," *OJJDP Fact Sheet* (Washington, DC: Office of Juvenile Justice and Delinquency Prevention, 2000), p. 2.

63. Howard Snyder, Melissa Sickmund, Eileen Poe-Yamagata, and National Center for Juvenile Justice, *Juvenile Transfers to Criminal Court in the 1990's: Lessons Learned from Four Studies* (Washington, DC: Office of Juvenile Justice and Delinquency Prevention, 2000), pp. 14, 22.

64. Jeffrey Fagan, Ellen Slaughter, and Eliot Hartstone, "Blind Justice? The Impact of Race on the Juvenile Justice Process," *Crime and Delinquency* 33:224-258 (1987).

65. Marcy Podkopacz and Barry Feld, "The End of the Line: An Empirical Study of Judicial Waiver," *Journal of Criminal Law and Criminology* 86:449–492 (1996).

66. Jolanta Juszkiewicz, *Youth Crime/Adult Time: Is Justice Served?* (Washington, DC: Building Blocks for Youth, 2001).

Chapter 15
Juvenile Corrections

I know not whether laws be right, Or whether laws be wrong;
All that we know who lie in gaol Is that the wall is strong;
And that each day is like a year, A year whose days are long.
—*Oscar Wilde,* The Ballad of Reading Gaol

To many observers, the field of juvenile corrections appears to be only an afterthought within the history of the juvenile justice system: It has consistently been low on the list of budgeting priorities and largely ignored by national debate. To other observers, juvenile corrections has been viewed as accomplishing little more than either warehousing or coddling youthful offenders while they are in state custody—money is expended but little reform is achieved.

It is interesting, however, that special attention to the correctional reform of juvenile offenders predates the creation of the juvenile court by more than half a century. As noted in Chapter 1, the first house of refuge opened in 1825 in New York for the care of wayward, neglected, homeless, and misbehaving youths. Two decades later, in 1846, Massachusetts opened the first state-run juvenile reform school, the Lyman School for Boys. In 1876 more than 50 reform schools or houses of refuge were operating around the country. By 1890 state reform schools had been established in nearly every state outside the South, and a number of states had created special reform schools for girls.[1]

Not all delinquent children were sent to reform schools. Charles Loring Brace and other child savers, during the latter half of the 19th century, established a program for placing urban problem youths in apprenticeships with farm families in the Midwest and West. Brace considered such placements to be "God's reformatories" for problem children.[2]

Correctional philosophy took another turn at the end of the 19th century with the creation of the first juvenile court in Cook County, Illinois, in 1899. Probation, or community supervision, was still in its infancy as a tool for reforming adult offenders, having been implemented at the state level in Massachusetts less than 20 years earlier. Probation was quickly adopted by the Illinois court, and it was subsequently implemented by juvenile courts across the nation. By the middle of the 20th century, probation and a variety of more recent alternatives to institutional placement for delinquent youths became the standard court disposition.

Deciding the Disposition

The juvenile court, prior to *Gault*, permitted judges a great deal of discretion in deciding a disposition. The judge could dismiss the case, place the youth on probation, remove the youth from his or her home to be placed in foster care, or send the youth to a correctional institution. Dispositions, from the early establishment of the juvenile court, were based on notions of rehabilitation and the desire to do what was in the "best interests of the child." This focus on treatment seemed to work fairly well through the first half of the twentieth century, as most children brought to the juvenile court were minor offenders.[3]

But as noted in Chapter 1, from the mid-1960s to the end of the 20th century, juvenile delinquency not only increased dramatically, it increasingly involved serious, violent criminality. The effectiveness of rehabilitation as the sole consideration for disposition was called into question, and states began to adopt more punitive and restrictive disposition alternatives based on notions of deterrence.[4] Today, about half the states use structured guidelines, mandatory offense-based minimum sentences, or determinate sentencing laws to regulate dispositions. For example, the state of Washington revised its juvenile code in 1977 to emphasize just deserts and implemented a determinate sentencing law aimed at protecting "the citizenry from criminal behavior" and to "make the juvenile offender accountable for . . . criminal behavior," and to "provide for punishment commensurate with the age, crime, and criminal history of the juvenile offender."[5]

Recent studies of judges' disposition decisions appear to support the notion that emphasis has shifted from a child welfare approach toward a crime control orientation. Research by Brandon Applegate and his colleagues found judges focusing primarily on offense characteristics and only marginally on the offender's social characteristics. However, they note that "judges may believe that secure confinement presents the best opportunities for rehabilitating youthful felons while protecting the public" and that the use of incarceration was reduced somewhat when judges believed appropriate programs were available in the community.[6] In addition, a study by Jamie Fader and his associates of juvenile commitment decisions by juvenile court judges in Philadelphia reports that dispositions are made differently for first-time and repeat offenders.[7] In cases involving first-time offenders, offense-specific variables, such as seriousness of offense and injury to victim, are viewed as key factors by judges, although significant weight is also given to child and family functioning factors. Furthermore, youths whose mothers had substance abuse problems or were known to be abusive or neglectful were more likely to be placed in institutions.[8] However, dispositions involving youths with prior offense histories were more likely to be made based on offense severity and situational factors, such as behavior since arrest, including running away from a detention facility or being arrested again. (See Box 15–1 for a discussion of the concept of restorative justice as an alternative emphasizing the needs of the juvenile, victim, and the community.)

Alternatives to Institutionalization

Most youths adjudicated delinquent for the first time are placed on probation. But probation is not the only alternative available to the court. Today, courts have a variety of dispositions to select from, including such options as home confinement and electronic monitoring, the payment of fines or restitution, and short-term placement in a boot camp.

BOX 15–1   DELINQUENCY PREVENTION
Restorative Justice as an Alternative Paradigm in Juvenile Corrections

Restorative justice is a recent, and increasingly popular, alternative to the traditional correctional paradigm in juvenile justice. Its focus is on restoring or repairing relationships disrupted by crime, holding offenders accountable by requiring restitution to victims or the community harmed by the crime, promoting offender competency and responsibility, and balancing the needs of community, victim, and offender through involvement in the restorative process. Recent implementations of restorative justice include victim–offender mediation or dialogue, family group conferencing (for example, New Zealand now requires that disposition of all delinquency cases, except rape and murder, be resolved by family group conferencing), community service, circle sentencing (practiced among aboriginal communities in British Columbia, Canada), and victim restitution.

The restorative justice movement has been heavily influenced by a variety of political interests, including feminist critiques of patriarchial justice and hierarchical decision making, liberals' emphasis on the humanistic potentials of victim empowerment and offender reintegration into the community, and conservatives' desire to secure greater justice for victims. Much of the attraction of restorative justice is its claim that punitive correctional approaches do significantly more harm than good.

However, Sharon Levrant and her colleagues question whether restorative justice can ever really be achieved and whether it is really such a desirable alternative to current get-tough approaches to the problem of serious youth crime. They note that restorative justice advocates have failed to offer a realistic blueprint for crime control and the reduction of

Probation

Probation is the conditional freedom granted by the court to an alleged or adjudicated offender as long as he or she avoids further misbehavior and meets certain conditions. Probation is usually available for every juvenile offender, regardless of the offense, and most states provide probation as a disposition alternative. Approximately 58 percent of all adjudicated delinquents receive probation.[9]

First-time offenders and tenth-time offenders are often perceived differently by juvenile justice officials. Are first-time offenders entitled to a benefit of the doubt? Do recidivists deserve any compassion?

Probation is based on the belief that misbehavior may be better corrected by trying to rehabilitate the juvenile in the community rather than in an institution. The major goals of probation are rehabilitation and reintegration, and the principal figure in accomplishing these objectives is the probation officer. Many juvenile courts have no probation services at all. Those that do usually have overwhelmingly large caseloads, forcing counseling and supervision to take the form of occasional phone calls and perfunctory visits instead of careful, individualized services. A recent survey conducted by the recidivism by serious, persistent offenders. Their criticisms include the following:

- Restorative justice systems fail to provide due process protections and procedural safeguards.
- Offenders may be coerced into participation, believing that refusal to participate in mediation will produce harsher punishments.
- Restorative justice programs may simply widen the net of the juvenile justice system to include minor offenders who would have been diverted otherwise.
- Restorative justice policies may add punishments for offenders by subjecting youths to both reparative conditions and traditional probation supervision.
- The focus on community reintegration of offenders and expanding the role of probation officers is not realistic given the current organization and limited resources of probation departments.
- There may be unintended race and class bias whereby more affluent offenders may be better able to mediate or negotiate more favorable sanctions.
- Most restorative justice programs have targeted low-risk, nonviolent offenders who are unlikely to recidivate, and there is little evidence that these programs will work with more serious offenders.

- It is unlikely that restorative justice programs will have any long-term impact on altering an offender's criminogenic needs.

Levrant and her colleagues conclude by stating "Restorative justice remains an unproved movement that risks failure and perhaps does more harm than good. Its attractiveness lies more in its humanistic sentiments than in any empirical evidence of its effectiveness."

Sources: Gordon Bazemore and Mark Umbreit, *Balanced and Restorative Justice: Program Summary* (Washington, DC: Office of Juvenile Justice and Delinquency Prevention, 1994); Shay Bilchik, *Guide for Implementing the Balanced and Restorative Justice Model* (Washington, DC: Office of Juvenile Justice and Delinquency Prevention, 1998); Sharon Levrant, Francis Cullen, Betsy Fulton, and John Wozniak, "Reconsidering Restorative Justice: The Corruption of Benevolence Revisited?" *Crime and Delinquency* 45:3–27 (1999); Gordon Bazemore and Mara Schiff, eds., *Restorative Community Justice: Repairing Harm and Transforming Communities* (Cincinnati: Anderson, 2001).

National Center for Juvenile Justice indicated that the range of probation caseload size is great, ranging between 2 and 200. The average caseload is about 41, with 30 considered optimal.[10]

Probation may be used at the "front end" of the juvenile justice system for first-time, low-risk offenders or at the "back end" as an alternative to institutional confinement for more serious offenders. The official duties of probation officers can differ between states and even between jurisdictions within a single state. In any case, the basic set of juvenile probation functions includes intake screening of cases referred to juvenile and family courts, predispositions or presentence investigation of juveniles, and court-ordered supervision of juvenile offenders. Probation orders imposed by the court for supervision of juveniles usually require that the youths obey all laws, attend school regularly, periodically visit the probation officer, remain within the community, and be at home at night by a set hour. The judge has the statutory authority to frame these conditions. Some probation departments also provide aftercare for youths released from institutions; others may administer detention or manage local residential facilities or special programs.

Since probation has historically been viewed as a "favor" to a person convicted of a crime, conditions of probation were, until recently, rarely subject to judicial review. Now, however, it is generally agreed that probationary conditions for juveniles are subject to certain limitations. For example, in juvenile courts, a major goal of probation is to rehabilitate the child by treatment and guidance while he or she participates in the community. If probation conditions do not promote this end, they should not be used or permitted.

Home Confinement and Electronic Monitoring

The search for dispositions offering alternatives to placement in jails, detention centers, and institutions has led to the development of various community-based programs. Drawing in part from the labeling perspective (Chapter 8), which holds that unnecessarily punitive confinement may have adverse consequences, juvenile courts have increasingly sought the least restrictive alternatives available.

Home confinement, sometimes called *house arrest* or *home detention*, is the intensive supervision and monitoring of a person in his or her home environment. Home confinement programs are usually administered by juvenile court probation departments. Surveillance consists of personal daily contacts with the youth and daily contacts with parents, teachers, and employers.[11] Juveniles are typically confined to their homes unless attending school, work, or other previously agreed-upon activities. Any other time the youth is not at home, he or she is closely monitored by both parents and probation department supervisors. Advocates of home confinement programs point out that the programs' costs are less than one-fourth the cost of confining youths in jail or detention centers.

A variation on home confinement is **electronic monitoring**.[12] Electronic monitoring, or tracking systems, are generally of two types: active and passive. *Active* systems are used when constant surveillance of the juvenile is desired. The youth must wear a transmitter on the ankle, neck, or wrist. The transmitter sends a constant signal (allowing for movement to a distance of 100 to 150 feet) to a receiver connected to the home telephone. The signal is then sent to a central computer that matches the signal to patterns preprogrammed for arranged absences such as school and work. In *passive* systems, the youth sends electronic signals via phone in response to computer-activated calls. The juvenile may respond either by inserting a special plug worn on the wrist into the transmitter or by speaking on the phone (his or her voice is matched to a voiceprint programmed into the computer). Both approaches allow the computer to verify that the juvenile is, in fact, at home when he or she is supposed to be.[13]

Critics of home confinement and electronic monitoring raise four concerns about the programs:

How are sanctions, such as home confinement, problematic for offenses such as alchol or drug abuse? How can such a punishment guard against in-home offending?

Electronic monitoring allows for offenders to remain integrated in the community while serving a cost-effective sentence. However, is the reliance on technology for surveillance always positive? What "Orwellian" concerns are raised by the electronic monitoring of delinquents?

1. To what extent will juveniles, who would not otherwise be placed on supervision, be brought into the net of the juvenile justice system simply because of the convenience of these new less-restrictive programs?
2. Our society has a long-held belief that "a person's home is his castle" and should not be violated by the state. To turn a juvenile's home into a prison runs contrary to Anglo-Saxon tradition.[14]
3. If the juvenile's home is turned into a prison, what is the effect on the traditional parental role? The criminal codes of most states recognize the special relationship between parent and child. Parents are often exempt from testifying against their child or even from being prosecuted for assisting their child if he or she has escaped from a correctional facility. Will home confinement turn parents into wardens or "keepers" of their own children? Will parents be subject to charges of contempt of court or contributing to the delinquency of a minor if they do not report violations of home detention?
4. Will electronic monitoring intrude on our nation's deeply held value of privacy and create a Big Brother atmosphere? Could a "least restrictive" program, in the long run, lead us toward acceptance of pervasive restrictions over all aspects of our lives?

"Widening the net" refers to the expansion of non-incarceration sanctions. A positive of this trend is cost savings; a negative is the expansion of the total correctional population. Is increased surveillance beneficial or problematic?

Fines and Restitution

Increasingly, states are authorizing that restitution and payment of fines may be used as disposition alternatives and may be included as a condition of probation. **Restitution** is a court-ordered action in which an offender pays money or provides services to victims of the offense or to the community.[15]

According to Anne Schneider, restitution programs are based on the principle that youths should be held accountable for their delinquent actions.[16] When juveniles cause damage or loss, they should repay their victims. Courts generally rely on any one of three methods to determine restitution:

1. A judge decides the amount of restitution on the basis of arguments presented by both the offender and the victim during the sentencing hearing.
2. An insurance claim is used to determine the amount to be paid by the offender.
3. The victim and offender are brought together and work out a restitution agreement that is satisfactory to both parties.[17]

A **fine** is a cash payment determined by the court and paid by the youth (or his or her parents). Fines are seldom used as the sole disposition. Rather, they are more likely to be imposed in addition to a disposition involving probation. Part of the fine may include court costs, fees for drug or alcohol treatment, or victim compensation.

Boot Camps

Boot camps for juveniles are an increasingly popular disposition alternative for adjudicated delinquents. By 1996, 48 juvenile boot camps were operating in 27 states.[18] Boot camps are modeled after military basic training with youths required to wear military-style uniforms, march to and from activities, and respond immediately to the commands of their "drill instructors." Daily schedules typically include drill and ceremony practice, strenuous physical fitness activities, and challenge programs. Juvenile inmates who violate rules are generally required to perform pushups as punishment.

These programs, like most of the boot camps for adult offenders, are designed for "midrange" delinquents—those who have failed with less severe sanctions, such as probation, but are not yet defined as "hard core" or chronic delinquents (see Chapter 2). Certain offenders are typically excluded, such as sex offenders, armed robbers, and youths with records of serious violence. Most programs are available for youths in their mid- to late teens, although the Mississippi boot camp program admits youths as young as 10, and two boot camps in Alabama take 12- and 13-year-olds.[19]

Juvenile boot camps are generally much less costly than traditional state-run correctional institutions. According to a study of juvenile boot camps conducted by Michael Peters and his colleagues, the estimated cost per offender in boot camp ($6,241) was about half the cost per offender confined in state institutions ($11,616). However, boot camps are still significantly more expensive than the costs per offender associated with traditional probation supervision ($516).[20]

Juveniles sent to boot camps typically face programs of 90- to 120-day duration, although Alabama's program is much shorter, at 30 days. During these few months, youths are generally exposed to a militaristic environment, with "in-your-face" drill instructors, an emphasis on physical conditioning, and

Three commodities are used in meting out punishment: time, status, and money. Most offenders have only time. Should delinquents from wealthy families be exploited for their wealth? Should wealthy miscreants be used to help subsidize the juvenile justice system or to create a large fund for crime victims?

As juvenile violence proliferated in the 1980s and early 1990s, so too did boot camps. Boot camps employ grueling mental and physical regimens in an effort to instill discipline and self-worth in young offenders. What are the potential costs and benefits of such a "tough-love" approach?

three to six hours of work detail each day. All the programs include an educational component, and most programs also include some vocational education, work skills training or job preparation, and drug and alcohol counseling.

Even with their popularity among lawmakers and the public, juvenile boot camps are controversial. Advocates of the camps argue that the structure of the programs promotes positive growth and change and creates a safer environment for youths than traditional correctional facilities. In addition, proponents believe that the military model builds camaraderie among youths and fosters respect for staff. Critics say the camps' confrontational environment conflicts with the creation of positive interpersonal relationships and is antithetical to quality therapeutic programming. Confrontational interactions, they argue, may cause juveniles to fear correctional staff and undermine any potential for effective therapy and educational achievement. Furthermore, critics say the emphasis on group activities ignores individual youths' problems. Lastly, critics believe the group orientation of boot camp programs, in which an entire platoon may be punished when only one member of the group misbehaved, may cause youths to view the system as unjust.[21]

A sizable research literature asserts that boot camps don't work in terms of rehabilitating delinquents. If this is true, what other sorts of benefits do boot camps provide? Is reduced crime the only purpose of sanctions like boot camps?

Most boot camp programs provide for some form of aftercare or supervision for youths who have finished the program. In some states, youths released from boot camp are assigned to intensive community supervision. In Denver, boot-camp graduates attend a special school operated by New Pride, a community-based agency, for six months. In Cleveland they are required to report for six months to a day center where case management and supervision, counseling, recreation, and other services are provided. Finally, boot camp graduates in Mobile, Alabama, report to one of seven Metropolitan Boys and Girls Clubs after school.[22]

Are juvenile boot camps more effective than traditional correctional treatment? Recent studies find no significant difference in recidivism rates for youths placed in boot camps versus youths receiving more traditional correctional treatment options.[23] On the other hand, boot camps may provide some advantages not directly related to recidivism. Doris MacKenzie and her colleagues surveyed over 4,000 youths in 27 boot camps and 22 traditional institutions in 1998. They report that youths in boot camps, compared to youths assigned to traditional facilities, perceive their facilities to be more caring and just, that programs are more therapeutic and helpful in preparing them for jobs, and that they receive more individual attention. In addition, while youths in boot camps more frequently reported feelings of being in danger from staff, youths in traditional facilities more frequently reported feelings of danger from other residents.[24]

Parole

Parole is the release of an individual from an institution before the scheduled period of commitment has ended. Juvenile parole has its origins in the early house-of-refuge practice of requiring child inmates to work several years in private homes after their term of incarceration. It was the responsibility of the receiving family to feed and clothe the child, as well as to decide when he or she had earned complete freedom.[25]

Today, the decision to grant parole and the determination of conditions of parole are generally made at the discretion of state officials, often by a parole board or the staff of the institution where the juvenile is confined. However, entrusting the important decision of whether to grant parole to the discretion of institutional staff raises some serious concerns. When coupled with the traditional provision for indeterminate sentencing, allowing such discretion gives institutional officials great power over a juvenile's life for a long period of time. Juvenile codes that do not deal with parole generally require judicial review of any modifications of disposition. This approach seems better designed to protect juveniles' rights because the review gives them the opportunity to be heard in matters of vital concern to them.

Parole, or *aftercare,* is similar to probation in that it is conditional and requires a youth to submit to supervision by a parole officer. Conditions of supervision are very similar to probation conditions—parolees are required to, among other things, obey all laws, observe curfews, attend school or maintain employment, report to their probation officers regularly, and often submit to random drug or alcohol tests. **Parole revocation** may result when a youth violates the law or one of the discretionary conditions of parole. If revoked, the youth is returned to a correctional facility deemed appropriate.

The next few sections of this chapter will briefly examine the historical context of correctional institutions, patterns of institutionalization, and the nature of delinquents' confinement prior to their being released on parole.

How might criminologists, criminal justice practitioners, and the general public differ in their assessments of parole or aftercare? Would inmates have a better chance of release with a parole board constituted by one group over another? What commonalities might exist among these groups' assessments of parole?

Confinement of Juvenile Offenders

The reality of confinement as a form of punishment or rehabilitation is harsh. Imprisonment is, indeed, one of the most frequently criticized mechanisms for dealing with crime and delinquency. However, the range of complaints reflects inconsistent public expectations of correctional institutions:

- They should reform offenders, but they fail to do so;
- They should punish lawbreakers, but they coddle them;
- They should be secure and orderly, but there are many escapes and disturbances; and
- They should operate with minimal cost to the taxpayer, but they are expensive.

Our corrections system contains a fundamental flaw: It was developed under sociocultural circumstances of an earlier era to be relevant to the goals of that particular time. But although circumstances and goals have changed drastically, the system has not. Today, it may even be seen as an obstacle to significant rehabilitative efforts.

The Institutionalization of Juveniles

In 1880, nearly 20 years before the creation of the nation's first juvenile code and court, 11,468 juveniles were held in some sort of correctional facility. Of these youths, 81 percent were male, and only 11 percent were nonwhite; their average age was 13 years. By 1997 the number of juveniles incarcerated in the United States on any given day had risen to over 107,000. Nearly 93,000 of these youths were incarcerated in juvenile facilities. In addition to those facilities specifically designated for juveniles, about 15,000 youths were held in state and federal adult correctional facilities (see the discussion later in this chapter).[26]

Not surprisingly, states with the largest populations also have the largest number of juveniles in custody. California alone has nearly 20,000 juveniles in custody on any given day, while juvenile correctional facilities in Texas have nearly 7,000 youths and Florida just under 6,000.[27] Custody rates also vary a great deal by state. Some states, such as California and Nevada have custody rates for delinquent offenders at well over 400 per 100,000, while other states have dramatically lower custody rates. For example, Massachusetts has a rate of 69, while Virginia's rate is only 34 (see Table 15–1).

Approximately 70 percent of youths incarcerated in juvenile facilities were held in public institutions while 30 percent were held in private facilities.[28] In 1997, the average time juveniles spent in public facilities was 192 days, while the average time spent in private facilities was 174 days. Most youths in custody in public facilities are placed there for serious property offenses, violent crimes, other crimes against the person, and drug-related offenses. Most youths in private facilities, on the other hand, were there for status offenses or other nondelinquency reasons.

Table 15-1   State Custody Rates of Delinquent Offenders Held in Public Institutions (per 100,000)

HIGHEST CUSTODY RATES

California	498
Nevada	446
South Dakota	416
District of Columbia	412
Georgia	397
South Carolina	368
Louisiana	368
Connecticut	361
Virginia	358
New Mexico	325

LOWEST CUSTODY RATES

Arkansas	115
North Dakota	115
Iowa	112
West Virginia	107
Pennsylvania	107
Idaho	101
New Hampshire	97
Hawaii	83
Massachusetts	69
Virginia	34

Source: Melissa Sickmund, *State Custody Rates, 1997* (Washington, DC: Office of Juvenile Justice and Delinquency Prevention, 2000), p. 3.

Race and Ethnic Disparities in Confinement   As noted in previous chapters, blacks comprise a disproportionate number of youths arrested, especially for violent crimes, a disproportionate number of delinquency cases brought before the juvenile court, and a disproportionate number of youths placed in secure correctional facilities. Of the estimated 163,200 delinquency cases resulting in out-of-home placement in 1997, 60 percent involved white youths, 36 percent involved black youths, and 4 percent involved youths of other races. Nearly a third of adjudicated delinquency cases involving black youths resulted in custodial placement, compared to 26 percent of cases involving white youths.[29]

What does evidence of disparities in confinement mean? When data indicate there is an *overrepresentation* of a particular group in custody, it simply means there is a larger proportion of that group than would be expected based on their proportion in the general population. Evidence of *disparity* in custody rates means that the probability of receiving a particular outcome differs for different groups. Disparity may in turn lead to overrepresentation. *Discrimination* means that one group of juveniles is treated differently from another group of juveniles based wholly, or in part, on their race, ethnicity, or gender. However, neither overrepresentation nor disparity necessarily implies discrimination.[30]

Disparity and overrepresentation can result from factors other than discrimination. For example, a number of studies suggest that minorities' higher rates of confinement are due to their disproportionate involvement in serious and violent crimes.[31] If minority youths commit proportionately more crime than white youths, are involved in more serious incidents, and have more extensive criminal histories, they will be overrepresented in secure facilities, even if no discrimination by decision makers occurred. However, a number of other studies suggest that disparities are the result of racial and ethnic discrimination. This line of reasoning suggests that because of discrimination on the part of justice system decision makers, minority youths face higher probabilities of being arrested by the police, referred to court intake, held in short-term detention, petitioned for formal processing, adjudicated delinquent, and confined in a secure juvenile facility.[32] In addition, a few studies claim that repressive drug laws result in disproportionate numbers of black youths being incarcerated.[33] The findings of still other studies indicate that the disparities may be the consequence of community structural factors—such as violent crime rates, minority concentration, and economic inequality—and not directly related to the characteristics of the individual offender.[34] Finally, some experts believe that differential placement of juvenile offenders in mental hospitals may contribute to minority overrepresentation in correctional facilities. For example, black youths who exhibit very aggressive behaviors are more likely to be directed to correctional facilities while equally aggressive white youths are placed in psychiatric hospitals for "treatment."[35]

Regardless of the causes of disparities, the Office of Juvenile Justice and Delinquency Prevention established the Disproportionate Minority Confinement (DMC) Initiative in 1991 to assist states in aggressively assessing the extent of DMC in their jurisdictions. For example, Pennsylvania's DMC efforts soon discovered that, although minority juveniles represented just 12 percent of the state's juvenile population, they accounted for over 70 percent of juveniles placed in secure confinement. These findings led to the development of special programs in four targeted communities (Harrisburg, Philadelphia, Pittsburgh, and Lehigh and Northampton Counties) designed to reduce the number of minorities confined in the state's correctional facilities. Prevention and intervention programs aimed at minority youths included educational, social, vocation, and recreational outreach, tutoring, development of life skills and job training, truancy and dropout prevention, and conflict resolution and impulse control training. By 1995, minority juveniles confined in secure correctional facilities had declined from 73 percent to 66 percent.[36]

Decarceration of Status Offenders   In the early 1970s, the federal government pushed for elimination of all status offenders from "secure" institutions designed to house delinquent offenders. As a result of this **decarceration** policy, large numbers of juveniles were shifted from institutions to community-based programs such as shelter-care facilities run by local Youth Service Bureaus. By 1995 only 2.6 percent of juveniles in public facilities were held for status offenses (95.6 percent were held for delinquent offenses). However, nearly 15 percent of the juveniles in private facilities were committed for status offenses, 41 percent for "nonoffender-other" reasons, and only 45 percent for delinquent offenses.[37]

Living in Custody

What about the juveniles who are placed in correctional facilities? How do they adjust to being incarcerated? What determines the nature of their adaptations? To answer these questions, we must look at juvenile institutions from the juvenile's perspective.

Institutions can be differentiated on the basis of their goals and orientations as well as how such differences are related to differences in the behavior of incarcerated juveniles. But few institutions operate according to a singular model; many mix treatment and custody orientations.[38]

Treatment-oriented institutions may officially promote rehabilitation of its clients, but this goal can be complicated by control or security considerations. Similarly, custodial institutions generally offer some minimal training or rehabilitation programs, even though their primary concern is custody. And since the mixed-goal institution attempts to combine elements of both polar types more or less equally, the result is, in terms of organizational effectiveness, often as mixed as the goals. However, comparative studies have demonstrated that the formal structure of an institution not only affects inmate responses to the institution as a whole and to the staff and programs but also affects assimilation into an inmate subculture. Related research has shown that as organizational orientation shifts from custody to treatment, the negative influences of confinement are either reduced or become positive.

Bernard Berk examined both juvenile detention centers and minimum security prisons.[39] He found that inmate attitudes toward the institution were more positive in treatment-oriented than in custody-oriented institutions. He also discovered that inmate attitudes were shaped by the prison experience. Inmates who had spent long periods of time in custody-oriented institutions were more likely to hold negative attitudes than those who had been incarcerated only a few months, whereas the reverse was true at treatment-oriented prisons.

While many criminologists have examined the problems of confinement in juvenile institutions, two studies stand out in terms of their extensive and intensive analyses of the nature of inmate adaptations.[40] In a comparative study of 10 facilities in Massachusetts, Barry Feld identified four types of institutional treatment settings in terms of correctional goals, programs, and

Education is free in the United States. Why do so many delinquents and criminals wait until they are incarcerated to embrace education? Is the "denial of educational opportunities" real or perceived? Why?

social control techniques.[41] Differences in organizational structure had a major impact on inmates' informal social systems. In the oppressive custody-oriented settings, staff roles were authoritarian and hierarchical. Staff members were strictly custodial, minimizing their contacts with inmates and attempting to maintain a high level of surveillance and control. Such practices, coupled with a high degree of institutional deprivation, gave inmates many incentives to engage in covert deviance. In this setting, there emerged a group of tough inmates who exploited weaker inmates and used violence to reinforce their own status. The use of violence by inmates, paralleling staff practices of social control, resulted in a rigidly structured authoritarian subculture in which the social distance between high- and low-status inmates was comparable to the distance between inmates and staff.

On the other hand, in treatment-oriented facilities that used a cottage system, substantially less hostility and aggression among inmates were observed. The greater harmony was largely due to the introduction of formal collaboration between staff and inmates, which increased the social solidarity of the entire institution and diminished incentives for violent solutions (see Box 15–2 for a look at a juvenile reform school in China.)

Correctional facilities present a critical mass of individuals who have committed the most serious types of crime. Why do some criminologists blame the facilities themselves for the dangerousness of such institutions. Shouldn't a correctional facility be dangerous by definition?

One of the most detailed accounts of the brutalizing conditions in the more custody-oriented institutions is provided by Clemens Bartollas, whose account is based on his study of an Ohio facility for boys.[42] Upon arrival at the institution, boys are subjected to a testing process by inmate leaders to determine whether the new boys will defend themselves when attacked and whether they have a history of sexual exploitation. The staff and other inmates offer little help to the new boys. The less able the youths are to defend themselves, the further down the exploitation scale they are pushed. Exploitative acts on this scale, in terms of increasing severity, are:

1. Taking a victim's dessert and favorite foods at meals;
2. Taking his canteen purchases and pop and candy given to him by his parents;
3. Taking his institutional clothing, toilet articles, cigarettes, personal clothing, or radio; and
4. Physically beating him or forcing him to masturbate others, play the passive role in anal sodomy, or be the receptor in fellatio.

To an inmate, being the "girl" in fellatio is the most degrading of all victimization experiences. A boy's commission of this act is publicized via an informal grapevine throughout the institution, where the act and subsequent publicizing represent a status-degradation ceremony. He is then viewed as a social outcast and avoided by self-respecting inmates, except when they victimize him. Some of the victims gradually accept their low social standing and internalize the negative perceptions others have of them. They display little outward emotion, keeping their guilt, shame, and indignation to themselves. Their personal habits deteriorate. Some boys in this situation may mutilate themselves in their despair.

BOX 15–2   A CROSS-CULTURAL PERSPECTIVE ON JUVENILE JUSTICE
A Chinese Juvenile Reform School

While juvenile delinquency in the People's Republic of China is proportionately only a very small problem when compared with delinquency in the United States, it exists and is increasingly of concern to officials and the public alike. Juvenile reform schools in China are coeducational and operate under the provincial ministry of education. According to Chinese law, juveniles under the age of 14 are not to be sent to correctional institutions but, instead, are to be reformed at home.

The Junshan Juvenile Delinquency Reform and Vocational School houses approximately 1,200 juveniles (about 1,000 boys and 200 girls) between the ages of 14 and 18. The staff considers its primary responsibility to be the reform of delinquents through reeducation. The teachers take great pains to help the youngsters develop good habits and find a better path in life. The staff members speak of themselves as "gardeners" who nurture and cultivate "young plants"—young people who will grow up to be fine citizens, respected by their parents and the community.

Because Junshan is the only reform school in the province, it houses two kinds of delinquents. About one-fifth of the school's juveniles have been convicted and sentenced for serious crimes. The remaining four-fifths have committed only minor offenses and are at the school for reform through labor. Both groups are to be educated as well as to take part in some useful work according to their ages.

For juveniles who have already completed their junior middle school education, there is a secondary vocational program that provides training for specific jobs. Among its many different classes are art and painting (for work in handicraft factories), electronics repair, gardening, raising chickens, sewing, and the making of mirrors. Classroom instruction in the morning is combined with on-the-job training in the afternoon so that juveniles can practice what they have learned.

Nearly 85 percent of the juveniles released from the school stay out of trouble after being released. The school's high rate of success is accomplished in spite of the problem that many citizens do not readily accept reformed delinquents back into the community. According to members of the school staff, for reform to be truly effective, people must be willing to help integrate offenders back into normal life. They strongly believe that young delinquents can be educated and acquire appropriate job skills, although they feel that if local people treat the youths as outcasts once they are released and refuse to give them jobs, the youngsters are likely to get into trouble again.

Source: Adapted from John Hewitt, "Gardeners Shape a New Future for Delinquents," *China Reconstructs,* August:29–31 (1987).

Unfortunately, such patterns of exploitation and victimization in juvenile institutions are scarcely unique to the facilities studied by Feld and Bartollas; they have been well documented in many settings across the country over the past 25 years.[43] For example, extensive abuses were found in Louisiana juvenile training schools in the mid-1990s including the placement of youths

Should private companies, such as the private reform school for girls pictured here, be afforded the opportunity to practice criminal justice? Are any ethical issues involved in privatized corrections? If so, what are they?

The Lancaster school provided a "homelike" milieu, emphasizing Christian family life in which reform efforts prepared the girls for domestic work—either as wives and mothers or as paid domestic workers.[50]

This emphasis on domesticity in the correctional treatment of female juvenile offenders has continued to play a prominent role in institutions even today. In girls' reform schools throughout the country, academic and vocational programs still emphasize the traditional female roles of wife, mother, and homemaker.[51] According to an American Bar Association (ABA) survey of juvenile facilities, the most frequent programs in girls' schools were cosmetology, business education, nursing, and food service. In contrast, the ABA found that institutions for boys were typically providing courses in auto shop, welding, and small-engine repair. Such differences in programs clearly determine differential career opportunities in the future—in terms of both job skills and wages.[52]

While females are half of the juvenile population, account for about a fourth of all juvenile arrests, and just under a fourth of delinquency cases referred to the juvenile court, they comprise only about 14 percent of juveniles (or just over 14,300) in residential placement. Females represent a somewhat greater proportion of juveniles placed in private correctional facilities (17 percent) than in public facilities (9 percent).[53]

Females are significantly less likely than males to be held in either public or private facilities for delinquencies, but more likely to be in custody for status offenses or other nondelinquency reasons. As Table 15–2 shows, 99 percent of males and 91 percent of females in public facilities were held for delinquencies; only 89 percent of males and only 55 percent of females held in private facilities were in custody for delinquency offenses.

Table 15-2   Reason for Placement in Juvenile Correctional Facilities, by Sex

	PERCENT OF PUBLIC		PERCENT OF PRIVATE	
	MALE	FEMALE	MALE	FEMALE
Delinquent offenses	99	91	89	55
Violent Index	30	16	19	7
Other person	7	13	10	12
Property Index	27	21	28	16
Other property	4	4	5	3
Drug trafficking	3	1	3	1
Other drug	6	4	7	5
Public order	9	9	10	4
Probation-parole violations	12	23	7	7
Status offenses	2	13	12	22

Source: Howard Snyder and Melissa Sickmund, *Juvenile Offenders and Victims: 1999 National Report* (Washington, DC: Office of Juvenile Justice and Delinquency Prevention, 1999), p. 199.

Numerous studies have suggested girls are more likely than boys to receive more-serious dispositions for less-serious offenses. That is, girls may well end up in secure confinement for offenses for which boys would be placed on probation. For example, a recent study by John MacDonald and Meda Chesney-Lind examined the processing of nearly 26,000 juvenile cases in Hawaii over a 12-year period. They found that girls were nearly four times more likely than boys to be referred to the court for running away, while boys were ten times more likely than girls to be referred to the court for violent offenses. However, "once girls were found delinquent, they were more likely than boys to be given a restrictive sanction for less serious offenses."[54] For example, less than one percent of boys given formal dispositions had been referred for running away, compared to six percent of the girls. However, boys were three times more likely than girls to receive formal dispositions for violent offenses.[55]

Social Organization

All correctional institutions contain some form of inmate culture as a response to the unique circumstances experienced by inmates. While boys engage in aggressive, coercive behaviors to establish hierarchies and define social roles, girls are more likely to respond by developing family structures parallel to those outside the institution. According to Barbara Carter

> Inmate culture in a girls' school is best understood as a complex of meanings through which the girls maintain continuity between their lives inside and outside of the institution; and as social forms established to mitigate and manage the pains of confinement and problems of intimate group living.[56]

Inmate Roles

Pseudo families are intimate relationships that substitute for those found outside the institutions. These families sometimes emerge out of continuing courtships and other times occur spontaneously. Courtship reflects traditional boy-girl relationships: recognition seeking, emotional involvement, and companionship. Consequently, such relationships can be characterized as symbolically heterosexual rather than homosexual. According to both Carter[57] and Rose Giallombardo,[58] this family structure involves only minor physical contact (hand-holding, touching, and kissing). Coercive homosexual relationships often found in male institutions are rare in female facilities. Sexual roles, ranging from "mother" and "father" and "husband" and "wife" to "sister" and "cousin," also reflect traditional male-female sex roles.

Whether inmates establish a "family" or are simply courting, sex roles revolve around *butches* and *femmes*. The butch is the masculine role in the relationship; dress, hairstyle, and demeanor are subtle indicators of the role. A girl who takes on the butch role is expected to act like the boy in the relationship but may still maintain traditional female interests such as knitting and sewing. On the other hand, a "stone butch" is a girl who has accepted the butch role as her identity. Other variations on the butch role include "half-ass butches"—girls who call themselves butches but are unable to play the part successfully—and "jive butches"—promiscuous girls who court many girls at the same time. Femmes play the traditional feminine role in an exaggerated manner and are expected to be submissive to their butches. Through courting and kinship groups, institutionalized girls maintain relatively normal interpersonal relationships.

According to Coramae Mann, pseudo families seem to fulfill at least three functions.[59] They "provide a measure of affection and belonging to girls who are lonely, isolated from their natural families, and deprived of their freedom." They offer a "form of protection from verbal and physical attacks by other inmates." And they aid the institution in maintaining social control. Institutional control is enhanced inasmuch as families (both in and out of institutions) are the primary socializing agents for the individual, teaching the rules and regulations of the institution.

Institutionalized girls take on other roles besides those found in courtship and pseudo families (see Table 15–3). Giallombardo identified four social roles among female inmates that have also been observed in male institutions:

1. *Finks, rats,* or *snitchers* are girls who provide information to staff members about illegal activities of other inmates. Because they help the staff, finks or snitchers are shunned by other inmates and may even face physical retribution.
2. A girl who plays the *junior staff* or *cop* role assumes staff functions. She "gets on the good side of the staff and does the things a staff member does."[60] Because such girls identify with the staff, they are typically despised by other inmates.

Table 15–3   Social Roles of Institutionalized Girls

ROLE	SOCIAL CHARACTERISTICS
Family or courting roles:	
Butches	Plays traditional masculine role
Half-ass butch	Displays a weak commitment to masculine role
Jive butch	Is promiscuous
Femmes	Plays traditional feminine role
Institutional Roles:	
Finks/snitchers	Provides information to staff
Junior staff/cops	Tries to assume staff functions
Independent roles:	
Squares/straights	Identifies with noncriminal values
Sissies	Has very close, stable relationship with another girl

3. *Squares* and *straights* are girls who identify with noncriminal values and may be good friends with staff members. These girls tend to avoid homosexual relationships and pseudo family involvement. They are often viewed as being too accommodating with the staff.
4. *Sissies* are girls who establish very close, stable relationships with other girls that go beyond those of pseudo families. "Sissies are best friends . . . When they call each other sissies—and everyone who is tight with someone has a sissie—it's to let everybody know that they're as close as they can ever get—like blood relationship."[61]

Are sex differences in the adaptation to prison a demonstration of nature, nurture, or a combination of both?

Neal Shover and Werner Einstadter suggest that juvenile female inmates are less violent, less committed to an inmate code, and more likely to create pseudo families than juvenile male inmates.[62] They believe that these differences may be accounted for by "differences in the preconfinement experiences of boys and girls, and traditional sex-role differences." In addition, they point out that institutionalized girls may be much more affected than boys by the loss of supportive relationships. Courtship, pseudo families, and "sissie" relationships become rational adaptations to the abnormal realities of institutional life.

Juveniles in Adult Prisons

Approximately 100,500 persons under age 18 were in custody in juvenile or adult correctional facilities at year-end 1997. The vast majority of these youths were held in juvenile facilities, although 5 percent were confined in state prisons. Juveniles comprised just under 1 percent, or 5,400, of all inmates in state prisons. Over 7,400 youths under age 18 had been committed to adult prisons at some point during that year, which was more than twice the number in 1985.

Juveniles who commit serious Index crimes often face adult sanctions. Is this an appropriate response to youth crime? Does the criminal justice system effectively "wash its hands" of juvenile delinquents who engage in dire criminal offending? If so, should they?

Most juveniles in state prisons were males (92 percent), and over 90 percent had not graduated from high school at the time of admission to state prison. Approximately 60 percent of inmates under age 18 were black, 19 percent were white, 13 percent Latino, and 8 percent Asian or American Indian. About 70 percent of state prison inmates under age 18 were incarcerated for a violent offense (13 percent for murder), 15 percent for property crimes, and 11 percent for drug offenses. Black offenders were more likely than offenders of other racial groups to be admitted to prison for violent offenses (60 percent of violent offenders in state prison were black, 20 percent white, and 20 percent Latino).[63]

One of the most serious dilemmas of incarcerating juvenile offenders in adult prisons is the problem of separating or integrating juvenile and adult inmates. Because juveniles are more vulnerable than older inmates and likely to be victimized, should they be housed in separate facilities, segregated in special units within institutions, or be placed in the general adult inmate population? States have responded very differently to this question. Most states allow underage inmates to be housed in state correctional facilities with other adult offenders as part of the general population. Six states (Arizona, Hawaii, Kentucky, Montana, Tennessee, and West Virginia) require that all inmates under age 18 be housed separately from adults. In North Dakota and California, no person under age 16 can be held in an adult prison. *Graduated incarceration* is employed in 12 states. In this system, inmates under age 18 begin their sentences in a juvenile facility until they reach a certain age (typically 18). The offender can then be transferred to an adult facility to serve the remainder of the sentence, or, if the state chooses, can be released. Eight states use *segregated incarceration* in assigning certain underage offenders to specific facilities based on age and programming needs. For example, in Florida, persons under 18 convicted in criminal court can be sentenced to the youthful offender program that separates ages 14 to 18 from ages 19 to 24.[64]

When juveniles are incarcerated in the general prison population, they are more vulnerable to victimization by older inmates. Because they are younger, and often smaller, they are more likely to be victimized. Martin Forst and his colleagues found that, whereas about half of the juvenile offenders assigned to a juvenile institution or adult prison reported being victims of property crime, juveniles in prison were more likely to be victims of violent crime than those in a juvenile institution: Only 37 percent of those assigned to juvenile facilities were victims of violence compared to 46 percent of the juveniles in prison. In addition, they found that sexual assault of youths was five times more common in prison than in juvenile facilities and that youths were 50 percent more likely to be victims of attacks by other inmates involving weapons than were their counterparts in juvenile facilities.[65]

The Death Penalty and Juveniles

In 1989 the Supreme Court was asked to decide if it was constitutional to execute a person who was under the age of 18 at the time he or she committed murder. Kevin Stanford was only 17 years old when, in 1981, he and a friend raped, sodomized, and eventually shot to death Baerbel Poore, age 20, in Jefferson County, Kentucky. Stanford murdered Poore during a robbery of a gas station where she worked as an attendant. After his arrest, Stanford told police he had to shoot her because she lived next door to him and would recognize him. Stanford was found guilty of first-degree murder and sentenced to death. The Supreme Court, in *Stanford v. Kentucky*, upheld that decision, stating that capital punishment did not constitute cruel and unusual punishment for a person who was age 16 or 17 at the time he or she committed the crime.[66] As of October 1, 2001, Kevin Stanford was still on death row.

Although juveniles have rarely been executed in the United States, at least 361 have been officially executed by the state since 1642. The first recorded execution of a juvenile took place in Plymouth Colony: Thomas Graunger, age 16, was executed for the crime of bestiality. James Arcene, only 10 years old when he committed his crime, was the youngest juvenile to be executed. Arcene, a Cherokee, was 22 when he was finally hanged at Fort Smith, Arkansas, for his participation in a murder.

Since the 1890s, juveniles have accounted for approximately 2 percent of all people executed. From the 1890s to 1930, fewer than 30 juveniles were executed in any given decade. However, in the decades of the 1930s and 1940s, there was an unusual increase in juvenile executions, with 40 and 50 such executions in the respective decades. Between 1965 and 1984, no juveniles were executed. With the execution of Charles Rumbaugh in Texas on September 11, 1985, juveniles once again faced the imposition of the death penalty.

Between 1985 and 2000, 17 persons were executed who had been juveniles at the time they committed their crimes. Of these 17, 15 were executed in southern states, 9 (53 percent) alone in the state of Texas. All 17 were males, 9 were white, 7 black, and one Latino. And all but one were age 17 at the time of their crimes. On February 4, 1999, Sean Sellers was executed in Oklahoma for three murders he had committed when he was 16 years old. In 1985, Sellers killed Oklahoma City convenience store clerk Robert Bower, and then six months later, in 1986, he shot his mother and stepfather, Vonda and Paul Bellofatto. Prior to Seller's execution, the last person to be executed for a crime committed at age 16 was Leonard Shockley, who was put to death in Maryland in 1959.[67]

Characteristics of Juveniles on Death Row

At the beginning of 2001 there were 73 people on death row who had committed their offenses while under age 18. Approximately half of all juvenile death sentences have been imposed in three states—Texas, Florida, and Alabama—with 36 percent of them in Texas alone. Blacks constitute 47 percent of the juveniles on death row, while whites comprise 34 percent and Latinos 18 percent (see Table 15–4). All 73 of these juveniles are male, and 75 percent were 17 years old at the time of their crimes while 25 percent were age 16. Nearly two-thirds of their victims were white, 13 percent black, and 13 percent Latino. Over half (52 percent) the victims were females and a fifth (20 percent) were age 50 or older.[68]

Should Juvenile Offenders Be Executed?

That the United States continues to sentence juveniles to death appears to be an anomaly within the context of the nation's traditional juvenile justice philosophy. In 1982 the Supreme Court heard the case of *Eddings v. Oklahoma.*[69] Monty Lee Eddings, a 16-year-old male, killed a highway patrol officer and was sentenced to death. Upon appeal, the Court overturned the lower court's sentence. However, the Court avoided dealing directly with the issue of whether it was constitutional to execute juveniles. Instead, it argued that the lower court had not taken into consideration all requiring mitigating circumstances. In the *Eddings* case, the sentencing judge had refused to review evidence of the boy's background, including beatings administered by his father, and his severe emotional disturbance. In a 5-to-4 decision, the Court remanded the case, indicating that the Eighth Amendment requires consideration of a defendant's background and record in addition to the immediate circumstances of the offense. And while the Court noted that youthfulness of the offender was one of the mitigating circumstances that must be considered in a capital case, it refused to rule that application of the death penalty for juveniles violates the Eighth Amendment.

In 1988, the Supreme Court held in **Thompson v. Oklahoma** that the execution of a person who was under age 16 at the time of the commission of his or her crime was unconstitutional.[70] William Wayne Thompson was 15 years old when he premeditatedly murdered his former brother-in-law by

Adam Smith once wrote that mercy to the guilty is cruelty to the innocent. What does this mean? Can this logic be used to assess the need or usefulness of executing delinquents?

On February 4, 1999, Sean Sellers was executed for a triple-homicide he committed at the age of 16. Does the age of an offender become irrelevant once the criminal conduct reaches the magnitude of murder? Why or why not?

Table 15–4   Juveniles on Death Row, December 31, 2000

STATE	NUMBER OF OFFENDERS	WHITE	BLACK	OTHER
Alabama	14	7	7	0
Arizona	4	3	0	1
Florida	3	3	0	0
Georgia	3	0	3	0
Kentucky	2	1	1	0
Louisiana	3	1	2	0
Mississippi	5	3	2	0
Missouri	2	1	1	0
Nevada	2	0	0	2
North Carolina	1	0	1	0
Oklahoma	1	1	0	0
Pennsylvania	3	0	3	0
South Carolina	3	2	1	0
Texas	26	5	11	10
Virginia	1	0	1	0
TOTAL	73	27	33	13

Source: Victor Streib, "The Juvenile Death Penalty Today: Death Sentences and Executions for Juvenile Crimes, January 1973–December 31, 2000." Online. Internet. 8 August 20, 2001. Available at http: law.onu.edu/faculty/streib/juvdeath.htm.

beating him, shooting him twice, cutting his throat, and stabbing him in the chest and abdomen. Although only 15, Thompson was transferred to adult court for prosecution, where he was convicted and sentenced to death:

> In the *Thompson* decision, the Court held what is a fundamental principle of our society that no one who is as little as one day short of his 16th birthday can have sufficient maturity and moral responsibility to be subjected to capital punishment for any crime.[71]

Part of the reasoning by the Court in setting age 16 as the minimum was that 16 years of age is generally recognized as the age separating childhood from adulthood. In most states, this is the age at which minors are legally allowed to take on some adult responsibilities, like driving a car.[72]

The Supreme Court rejected appeals in two later cases in 1989 (***Stanford v. Kentucky*** and *Wilkins v. Missouri*)[73] that could have prohibited execution of anyone younger than 18 at the time of commission of the crime. Justice Antonin Scalia, writing the majority opinion in the combined cases, noted that while Congress established 18 as the minimum age for the death penalty in drug-related murders, "this does not establish the degree of national consensus that this Court has previously thought sufficient to label a particular punishment cruel and unusual."[74]

Today, 38 states and the federal government have death penalty statutes. Twenty-four of these jurisdictions permit the execution of a person who committed his or her crime while under the age of 18. Of these 24 jurisdictions that allow for such executions, five have set the minimum at 17, while 19 states use age 16 at the time of crime as the minimum age for execution.[75]

It is interesting to note that as we move into the 21st century, the United States is one of only two member countries of the United Nations (the other is Somalia) that have not adopted Article 37(a) of the U.N. Convention on the Rights of the Child, which states that "neither capital punishment nor life imprisonment without possibility of release shall be imposed for offenses committed by persons below eighteen years of age."[76]

In *Eddings v. Oklahoma* (1982), the U.S. Supreme Court used the abusive background experienced by a criminal to mitigate his murdering a police officer. What form of justice is achieved when adversity or a "bad childhood" carries greater legal weight than the slaying of a police officer?

Conclusions

The need to preserve an orderly society has been a pervasive concern throughout our nation's history. From the beginning, correctional institutions for juveniles were quickly filled to overcrowding; staffs were largely untrained, poorly paid, and not up to the task of caring for sizable numbers of children. The institutions themselves were often inadequately built and financed. The incontrovertible evidence of institutional shortcomings and neglect and actual physical abuse of institutionalized children stands in stark contrast to the goodwill, enthusiasm, and energy of the reformers who conceived the new programs.

From both historical and contemporary perspectives, we have not obtained the knowledge we need to design, or even agree on, effective methods of reforming individuals. In addition, there has been an abysmal lack of experience and information regarding construction of institutions that would adequately house large populations. One prime factor in the perpetuation of existing programs has been the fear of alternatives. If difficult children were not institutionalized or placed under the wing of the juvenile court, where would they go? Many fear that such youths would be free to disrupt and damage the lives and homes of law-abiding citizens. In addition to developing a commitment to the ideals and dynamics of reform, we must rigorously strive to understand the realities and complexities of the challenges that face us.

Key Terms

boot camps: *Short-term confinement facilities where youths are exposed to a militaristic environment in which the emphasis is on physical conditioning, work, and education.*

decarceration: *The policy, since the early 1970s, of removing status offenders from "secure" institutions.*

electronic monitoring: *An active or passive computer-based tracking system in which electronic signals are used to verify that the youth is where he or she is supposed to be.*

fine: *A cash payment determined by the court and paid by the youth.*

home confinement: *The intensive supervision and monitoring of an offending youth within his or her home environment.*

parole: *The release of an offender from a correctional institution before the scheduled period of confinement has ended. It typically involves supervision by a parole officer.*

parole revocation: *If a youth violates the law or one of the discretionary conditions of parole, parole may be revoked and the youth is returned to a correctional facility.*

probation: *The conditional freedom granted by the court to an alleged or adjudicated offender, who must adhere to certain conditions and is generally supervised by a probation officer.*

pseudo families: *Relationships established in correctional institutions for girls and intended to substitute for those found on the outside.*

restitution: *A court-ordered action in which an offender pays money or provides services to victims of the offense or to the community.*

restorative justice: *A rehabilitative strategy aimed at restoring or repairing relationships disrupted by crime, holding offenders accountable by requiring restitution to victims or the community harmed by the crime, promoting offender competency and responsibility, and balancing the needs of community, victim, and offender through involvement in the restorative process.*

Stanford v. Kentucky: *The 1989 case in which the Supreme Court held that the execution of a person who was age 16 or 17 at the time of his or her offense was not unconstitutional.*

Thompson v. Oklahoma: *Supreme Court ruled that the execution of a person under age 16 at the time of his or her crime was unconstitutional.*

Getting Connected

The Office of Juvenile Justice and Delinquency Prevention maintains a comprehensive website that includes a page with its publications and reports about juvenile corrections available in both Adobe Acrobat and ASCII form.

http://www.ncjrs.org/jjcorr.htm

1. Investigate the publication "HIV/AIDS and STDs in Juvenile Facilities." Are recommendations made which would help juvenile facilities improve their health services?
2. Investigate the publication "Juvenile Correctional Education: A Time for Change." What are the major issues?
3. Investigate the publication Disproportionate Minority Confinement: Lessons Learned From Five States. How should the issue of disproportionate minority confinement be addressed? What lessons were learned?

The Texas Juvenile Probation Commission maintains a website providing extensive information on its organization and services and links to related sites.

http://www.tjpc.state.tx.us/

1. What are the Commission's Intensive Supervision Programs?
2. Link to Texas Kids Count. What kind of program is this?
3. Link to the Texas Youth Commission. What is this Commission's major responsibility?

The California Youth Authority home page provides information on correctional facilities and programs for youthful offenders in California.

http://www.cya.ca.gov/

1. What are the mission and values of the California Youth Authority?
2. What is the Free Venture Program?
3. What are "Six Important Areas Affecting Youth Corrections"?

The Juvenile Boot Camp Directory contains descriptions of more than 40 juvenile boot camps and youth correctional camps in the United States.

http://www.kci.org/publication/bootcamp/2000edition.htm

1. How does this site address the controversies over the treatment of adolescents in boot camps?
2. Link to one of the resources for parents. Link to one of the resources for adolescents. Discuss your findings.
3. What is the Koch Crime Institute?

Historical and current information about juveniles and the death penalty is provided at a website maintained by Professor Victor Streib at Ohio Northern University's School of Law.

http://www.onu.edu/faculty/streib/juvdeath.htm

1. How long has Prof. Streib been studying the death penalty and juveniles? Has the issue always been controversial?
2. Juveniles represent about what percent of death sentences imposed in the United States since 1973?
3. What is the status of the juvenile death penalty in other countries?

Endnotes

1. Barry Krisberg, "The Legacy of Juvenile Corrections," *Corrections Today,* August:122 (1995).
2. Krisberg, note 1, p. 124.
3. John D. Hewitt and Bob Regoli, "Holding Serious Juvenile Offenders Responsible: Applying Differential Oppression Theory," *Free Inquiry in Creative Sociology,* in press, 2002.
4. Martin Gardner, *Understanding Juvenile Law* (New York: Matthew Bender, 1997), p. 293.
5. Wash. Rev. Code Ann. ß 13.40.010(2) [West Supp. 1996].
6. Brandon Applegate, Michael Turner, Joseph Sanborn, Edward Latessa, and Melissa Moon, "Individualization, Criminalization, or Problem Resolution: A Factorial Survey of Juvenile Court Judges' Decisions to Incarcerate Youthful Felony Offenders," *Justice Quarterly* 17:328 (2000).
7. Jamie Fader, Philip Harris, Peter Jones, and Mary Poulin, "Factors Involved in Decisions on Commitment to Delinquency Programs for First-Time Juvenile Offenders," *Justice Quarterly* 18:323–341 (2001).
8. Fader et al., note 7, pp. 336–337.
9. Anne Stahl, *Delinquency Cases in Juvenile Courts, 1998* (Washington, DC: Office of Juvenile Justice and Delinquency Prevention, 2001).
10. Patricia Torbet, *Juvenile Probation: The Workhorse of the Juvenile Justice System* (Washington, DC: Office of Juvenile Justice and Delinquency Prevention, 1996).
11. Ronald Ball, Ronald Huff, and Robert Lilly, *House Arrest and Correctional Policy: Doing Time at Home* (Newbury Park, CA: Sage Publications, 1988), pp. 46–47.
12. Bonnie Berry, "Electronic Jails," *Justice Quarterly* 2:1-22 (1985); Ronald Ball and Robert Lilly, "The Phenomenology of Privacy and the Power of Electronic Monitoring," in *Controversial Issues in Crime and Justice,* edited by Joseph Scott and Travis Hirschi (Newbury Park, CA: Sage Publications, 1988).
13. Ball et al., note 11, p. 78.
14. Gilbert Geis, "Forward," House Arrest and Correctional Policy: Doing Time at Home, Ball et al., note 11, pp. 10–13.
15. William Staples, "Restitution as a Sanction in Juvenile Court," *Crime and Delinquency* 32:177–185 (1986).
16. Anne Schneider, *Guide to Juvenile Restitution* (Washington, DC: U.S. Government Printing Office, 1985).
17. Andrew Klein, *Alternative Sentencing* (Cincinnati: Anderson Publishing Co., 1988), pp. 156–157.
18. Doris MacKenzie, Angela Gover, Gaylene Armstrong, and Ojmarrh Mitchell, *A National Study Comparing the Environments of Boot Camps with Traditional Facilities for Juvenile Offenders* (Washington, DC: National Institute of Justice, 2001).
19. Roberta Cronin, *Boot Camps for Adult and Juvenile Offenders: Overview and Update* (Washington, DC: National Institute of Justice, 1994), p. 36.
20. Michael Peters, David Thomas, Christopher Zamberlan, and Caliber Associates, *Boot Camps for Juvenile Offenders: Program Summary* (Washington, DC: Office of Juvenile Justice and Delinquency Prevention, 1997), p. 25.
21. MacKenzie et al., note 18.
22. Cronin, note 19, pp. 38–39.
23. Doris MacKenzie, "Criminal Justice and Crime Prevention," in *Preventing Crime: What Works, What Doesn't, What's Promising,* edited by Larry Sherman, Denise Gottfredson, Doris MacKenzie, John Eck, Peter Reuter, and Shawn Bushway (Washington, DC: National Institute of Justice, 1997).
24. MacKenzie et al., note 18.
25. Frederick Hussey, "Perspectives on Parole Decision-Making with Juveniles," *Criminology* 13:449–469 (1976).
26. James Austin, Kelly Johnson, and Maria Gregoriou, *Juveniles in Adult Prisons and Jails: A National Asessment* (Washington, DC: Institute on Crime, Justice and Corrections and National Council on Crime and Delinquency, 2000).
27. Melissa Sickmund, *State Custody Rates, 1997* (Washington, DC: Office of Juvenile Justice and Delinquency Prevention, 2000).
28. Sickmund, note 27.
29. Charles Puzzanchera, *Juvenile Court Placement of Adjudicated Youth, 1998–1997* (Washington, DC: Office of Juvenile Justice and Delinquency Prevention, 2000).
30. Shay Bilchik, *Minorities in the Juvenile Justice System* (Washington, DC: Office of Juvenile Justice and Delinquency Prevention, 1999).
31. See, for example, Alfred Blumstein, "On the Racial Disproportionality of United States' Prison Populations," *Journal of Criminal Law and Criminology* 73:1259–1268 (1982); Patrick Langan, "Racism on Trial: New Evidence to Explain the Racial Composition of Prisons in the United States," *Journal of Criminal Law and Criminology* 76:666–683 (1985); and Merry Morash, "Establishment of a Juvenile Record," *Criminology* 22:97–111 (1984).

32. See, for example, James Austin, "The Overrepresentation of Minority Youths in the California Juvenile Justice System," in *Minorities in Juvenile Justice,* edited by Kimberly Leonard, Carl Pope, and William Feyerherm (Thousand Oaks, CA: Sage Publications, 1995), pp. 153–178; Barry Feld, *Bad Kids: Race and the Transformation of the Juvenile Court* (New York: Oxford, 1999).

33. David Hawkins, "The Nations Within: Race, Class, Region, and American Lethal Violence," *Colorado Law Review* 69:905–926 (1998).

34. George Bridges, Darlene Conley, Rodney Engen, and Townsand Price-Spratlen, "Racial Disparities in the Confinement of Juveniles: Effects of Crime and Community Social Structure on Punishment," in Leonard et al., note 32, pp. 128–152.

35. Joan McCord, Cathy Widom, and Nancy Crowell, eds., *Juvenile Crime Juvenile Justice: Panel on Juvenile Crime: Prevention, Treatment, and Control* (Washington, DC: National Academy Press, 2001), p. 257.

36. Heidi Hsia and Donna Hamparian, *Disproportionate Minority Confinement: 1997 Update* (Washington, DC: Office of Juvenile Justice and Delinquency Prevention, 1998).

37. Joseph Moone, *Juveniles in Private Facilities, 1991–1995* (Washington, DC: Office of Juvenile Justice and Delinquency Prevention, 1997).

38. Donald Cressey, "Limitations on Organization of Treatment in the Modern Prison," in *Theoretical Studies in Social Organization of the Prison,* edited by George Grosser (New York: Social Science Research Council, 1960); Bernard Berk, "Organizational Goals and Inmate Organization," *American Journal of Sociology* 71:522–534 (1966); Rosemary Sarri and Robert Vinter, "Group Treatment Strategies in Juvenile Correctional Institutions," *Crime and Delinquency* 11:326–340 (1965); Mayer Zald, "Organizational Control Structures in Five Correctional Communities," *American Journal of Sociology* 68:335–345 (1962).

39. Berk, note 38.

40. Barry Feld, *Neutralizing Inmate Violence* (Cambridge, MA: Ballinger, 1977).

41. Feld, note 40.

42. Clemens Bartollas, *Juvenile Victimization* (New York: Halsted Press, 1976).

43. Eric Poole and Robert Regoli, "Violence in Juvenile Institutions," *Criminology* 21:213–232 (1983).

44. Human Rights Watch, *Children in Confinement in Louisiana* (New York: Human Rights Watch, 1995).

45. *State v. Werner,* 242 S.E.2d 907 (W.Va. 1978).

46. *Gary H. v. Hegstrom,* 831 F.2d 1430 (U.S. Court of Appeals, Ninth Circuit, 1987).

47. Dale Parent, Valerie Leiter, Stephen Kennedy, Lisa Livens, Danile Wentworth, and Sarah Wilcox, *Conditions of Confinement: Juvenile Detention and Corrections Facilities, Research Summary* (Washington, DC: U.S. Department of Justice, 1994).

48. Lindsay Hayes, "Suicide Prevention in Juvenile Facilities," *Juvenile Justice* 7:24–32 (2000).

49. Rebecca Widom and Theodore Hammett, *HIV/AIDS and STDs in Juvenile Facilities* (Washington, DC: National Institute of Justice, 1996).

50. Barbara Brenzel, *Daughters of the State* (Cambridge, MA: MIT Press, 1983).

51. Coramae Richey Mann, *Female Crime and Delinquency* (University, AL: University of Alabama, Press, 1984).

52. Catherine Milton, *Female Offenders* (Washington, DC: U.S. Government Printing Office, 1976).

53. Howard Snyder and Melissa Sickmund, *Juvenile Offenders and Victims: 1999 National Report* (Washington, DC: Office of Juvenile Justice and Delinquency Prevention, 1999), pp. 198–199.

54. John MacDonald and Meda Chesney-Lind, "Gender Bias and Juvenile Justice Revisited: A Multiyear Analysis," *Crime and Delinquency* 47:187 (2001).

55. MacDonald and Chesney-Lind, note 54, p. 188.

56. Barbara Carter, "Reform School Families," in *Women and Crime in America,* edited by Lee Bowker (New York: Macmillan Publishing Co., 1973), p. 419.

57. Carter, note 56.

58. Rose Giallombardo, *The Social World of Imprisoned Girls* (New York: John Wiley & Sons, 1974).

59. Mann, note 51, pp. 188–189.

60. Giallombardo, note 58, pp. 214–215.

61. Giallombardo, note 58, p. 216.

62. Neal Shover and Werner Einstadter, *Analyzing American Corrections* (Belmont, CA: Wadsworth Publishing Co., 1988).

63. Kevin Strom, *Profile of State Prisoners Under Age 18, 1985–97* (Washington, DC: U.S. Department of Justice, 2000).

64. Strom, note 63, p. 10.

65. Martin Forst, Jeffrey Fagan, and T. Scott Vivona, "Youth in Prisons and Training Schools: Perceptions and Consequences of the Treatment-Custody Dichotomy," *Juvenile and Family Court Journal* 40:1–14 (1989).

66. *Stanford v. Kentucky,* 429 U.S. 361 (1989).

67. Victor Streib, "The Juvenile Death Penalty Today: Death Sentences and Executions for Juvenile Crimes, January 1973–December 31, 2000." Online. Internet. 20 August 2001. Available at http:law.onu.edu/faculty/streib/juvdeath.htm.

68. Streib, note 67.
69. *Eddings v. Oklahoma*, 455 U.S. 104 (1982).
70. *Thompson v. Oklahoma*, 487 U.S. 815 (1988).
71. Streib, note 67.
72. Kenneth Gewerth and Clifford Dorne, "Imposing the Death Penalty on Juvenile Murderers," *Judicature* 75:11 (1991).
73. *Stanford v. Kentucky*, note 66; *Wilkins v. Missouri,* 492 U.S. 361 (1989).
74. Linda Greenhouse, "Death Sentences Against Retarded and Young Upheld," *The New York Times*, June 17:1, 10 (1989).
75. Tracy Snell, *Capital Punishment 1999* (Washington, DC: U.S. Department of Justice, 2000); Streib, note 67.
76. Lynn Cothern, *Juveniles and the Death Penalty* (Washington, DC: Coordinating Council on Juvenile Justice and Delinquency Prevention, 2000), pp. 8–9.

Selected Amendments to the United States Constitution

FIRST AMENDMENT

Congress shall make no law respecting an establishment of religion, or prohibiting the free exercise thereof; or abridging the freedom of speech, or of the press; or the right of the people peaceably to assemble, and to petition the Government for a redress of grievances.

SECOND AMENDMENT

A well-regulated militia, being necessary to the security of a free State, the right of the people to keep and bear arms, shall not be infringed.

THIRD AMENDMENT

No soldier shall, in time of peace, be quartered in any house, without the consent of the owner, nor in time of war, but in a manner to be prescribed by law.

FOURTH AMENDMENT

The right of the people to be secure in their persons, houses, papers, and effects, against unreasonable searches and seizures, shall not be violated, and no warrants shall issue, but upon probable cause, supported by oath or affirmation, and particularly describing the place to be searched, and the person or things to be seized.

FIFTH AMENDMENT

No person shall be held to answer for a capital, or otherwise infamous crime, unless on a presentment or indictment of a Grand Jury, except in cases arising in the land or naval forces, or in the militia, when in actual service in time of war or public danger; nor shall any person be subject for the same offense to be twice put in jeopardy of life or limb; nor shall be compelled in any criminal case to be a witness against himself, nor be deprived of life, liberty, or property, without due process of law; nor shall private property be taken for public use, without just compensation.

SIXTH AMENDMENT

In all criminal prosecutions, the accused shall enjoy the right to a speedy and public trial, by an impartial jury of the State and district wherein the crime shall have been committed, which district shall have been previously ascertained by law, and to be informed of the nature and cause of the accusation; to be confronted with the witnesses against him; to have compulsory process for obtaining witnesses in his favor, and to have the assistance of counsel for his defense.

SEVENTH AMENDMENT

In suits at common law, where the value in controversy shall exceed twenty dollars, the right of trial by jury shall be preserved, and no fact tried by a jury shall be otherwise reexamined in any court of the United States, than according to the rules of the common law.

EIGHTH AMENDMENT

Excessive bail shall not be required, nor excessive fines imposed, nor cruel and unusual punishments inflicted.

NINTH AMENDMENT

The enumeration in the Constitution, of certain rights, shall not be construed to deny or disparage others retained by the people.

TENTH AMENDMENT

The powers not delegated to the United States by the Constitution, nor prohibited by it to the States, are reserved to the States respectively, or to the people.

FOURTEENTH AMENDMENT

Section 1. All persons born or naturalized in the United States, and subject to the jurisdiction thereof, are citizens of the United States and of the State wherein they reside. No State shall make or enforce any law which shall abridge the privileges or immunities of citizens of the United States; nor shall any State deprive any person of life, liberty, or property, without due process of law; nor deny to any person within its jurisdiction the equal protection of the laws.

Glossary

achieved status   A status that is earned. (1)

adjudication hearing   A hearing held to determine whether the child committed the offense of which he or she is accused. (14)

adolescent-limited offenders   Juveniles whose law-breaking behavior is restricted to their teenage years. (2)

age-adjusted homicide rates   Homicide rates calculated specifically for particular age groups. (12)

aging-out phenomenon   The gradual decline of participation in crime after the teenage years. (2, 7)

annual prevalence   In self-report surveys, the use of a drug at least once during the prior year. (4)

ascribed status   A status that is received at birth. (1)

atavistic   Criminals are a throwback to a more primitive stage of human development. (6)

Attention Deficit/Hyperactivity Disorder   The most common neurobehavioral childhood disorder. (6)

authoritarian parents   Parents who place a high value on obedience and conformity, tending to favor more punitive, absolute, and forceful disciplinary measures. (10)

authoritative parents   Parents who are warm but firm; they set standards of behavior for their child and highly value the development of autonomy and self-direction. (10)

Baker v. Owen   Teachers can administer reasonable corporal punishment for disciplinary purposes. (11)

behavior modification   A therapeutic technique to change behavior through operant conditioning. (6)

Bethel School District No. 403 v. Fraser   Schools may prohibit vulgar and offensive language. (11)

bond   The glue that connects a child to society. (7)

booking   The official recording of a person into detention after arrest. (13)

boot camps   Short-term confinement facilities where youths are exposed to a militaristic environment in which the emphasis is on physical conditioning, work, and education. (15)

Brady Bill   Federal legislation mandating a five-day waiting period for the purchase of handguns. (3)

Breed v. Jones   Criminal prosecution of a child following a juvenile court hearing is unconstitutional because it constitutes double jeopardy. (14)

bullying   Negative acts by students carried out against other students repeatedly over time. (11)

Child Savers   19th-century reformers who believed that children were basically good and blamed delinquency on a bad environment. (1)

children   People under age 18. (2)

Chimel v. California   Established the one-arm's-length rule: Once a suspect is arrested, police may search the suspect and the immediate area he or she occupies. (13)

chivalry hypothesis   The belief that lower rates of crime and delinquency among females reflect men's deference and protective attitude toward women whereby female offenses are generally overlooked or excused by males. (9)

chronic offenders   Juveniles who continue to engage in law-breaking behavior as adults. (2)

Classical School   Perspective that assumes people are rational, intelligent beings who exercise free will and choose to commit criminal behavior. (5)

conduct norms   Rules that reflect the values, expectations, and actual behaviors of groups in everyday life. They are not necessarily the norms found in the criminal law. (8)

conflict theory   A perspective which argues that society is held together by force, coercion, and intimidation, and that the law represents the interests of those in power. (8)

corporal punishment   The infliction of pain as a penalty for violating a school rule. (11)

Crime Index   A statistical indicator consisting of eight offenses used to gauge the amount of crime reported to the police. (2)

crime norms   Rules that prohibit specific conduct and provide punishments for violations. (8)

crimes of interest   The crimes that are the focus of the National Crime Victimization Survey. (2)

cultural transmission   The process by which criminal values are transmitted from one generation to the next. (7)

decarceration   The policy, since the early 1970s, of removing status offenders from "secure" institutions. (15)

decriminalization   The relaxing of the enforcement of certain laws, for example, drug laws. (4)

demand waiver   A juvenile may request to have his or her case transferred from juvenile court to criminal court. (14)

detention   The temporary confinement of children pending adjudication, disposition, or implementation of disposition. (14)

differential oppression theory   A theory that argues delinquency is the culmination of a process that begins at conception and evolves through adolescence; the more a child is oppressed, the greater the likelihood he or she will become delinquent. (8)

differential social organization   Neighborhoods are differentially organized. (7)

disintegrative shaming   A form of negative labeling by the juvenile justice system that stigmatizes and excludes targeted youths, tossing them into a class of outcasts. (8)

disposition hearing   A juvenile court hearing in which the court determines what action will be in the youth's and community's best interests; the equivalent of the sentencing stage in the criminal court process. (14)

dizygotic twins (DZ)   Fraternal twins; develop from two eggs fertilized at the same time. (6)

double jeopardy   The prosecution of an individual a second time for the same offense. It is prohibited by the Fifth Amendment. (14)

doubly oppressed   The notion that adolescent girls are oppressed both as children *and* as females. (9)

Drug Abuse Resistance Education (D.A.R.E.)   A program aimed at children in kindergarten through 12th grade, designed to equip students with appropriate skills to resist substance abuse and gangs. (4)

dualistic fallacy   The idea that delinquents and nondelinquents are two fundamentally different types of people. (8)

ectomorphs   Introverted, overly sensitive people with lean and fragile physiques. (6)

ego   Problem-solving dimension of the personality. (6)

electronic monitoring   An active or passive computer-based tracking system in which electronic signals are used to verify that the youth is where he or she is supposed to be. (15)

endomorphs   Relaxed, extroverted people, with round and soft physiques. (6)

exclusionary rule   Evidence police produce illegally is not admissible in court (see *Mapp v. Ohio*). (13)

falsely accused   Juveniles who are thought to have committed a crime when they have not. (2, 8)

fine   A cash payment determined by the court and paid by the youth. (15)

focal concerns   The values that monopolize lower-class consciousness. (7)

free will   People choose one course of action over another. (5)

gender-role identities   Individual identities based on sexual stereotypes. (9)

Goss v. Lopez   Students who may be suspended for 10 or more days from school must receive a hearing. (11)

Hazelwood School District v. Kuhlmeier   School administrators can regulate the content of student publications in public schools for educational purposes. (11)

hidden delinquency   Criminal activity that is not known to criminal justice authorities. (2)

hierarchy rule   In the *Uniform Crime Reports,* the police record only the most serious crime incident. (2)

home confinement   The intensive supervision and monitoring of an offending youth within his or her home environment. (15)

hue and cry   A loud call for help shouted by colonial police when they were in need of assistance. (13)

id   Represents the basic drives of the personality. (6)

In re Gault   Juveniles may not be denied basic due process rights in juvenile adjudicatory hearings. (13,14)

In re Winship   Juveniles, in delinquency cases, have the right to be convicted only if there is proof beyond a reasonable doubt. (14)

incidence   The number of delinquent acts committed. (2)

indeterminate sentence   A sentence with a minimum and maximum number of years. (5)

indifferent parents   Parents who are rather unresponsive to their child, and may, in extreme cases, be neglectful. (10)

individual justice   The criminal law must reflect differences among people and their circumstances. (5)

indulgent parents   Parents who are more responsive, accepting, benign, and passive in matters of discipline and place few demands on their child. (10)

infanticide   Homicides in which recently born children are killed by relatives who do not want the child. (3)

informal adjustment   Cases that are handled through discretionary nonjudicial dispositions. (14)

informal probation   A case adjustment practice in which the child and family comply with requirements of probation personnel without a formal court order. (14)

Ingraham v. Wright   Corporal punishment does not violate the cruel and unusual punishment clause of the Eighth Amendment. (11)

intake   The initial case-screening process in the juvenile court system. It is designed to screen out cases that do not warrant a formal court hearing. (14)

intelligence   The ability to learn, exercise judgment, and be imaginative. (6)

judicial waiver   A method used for transferring youths to criminal court in which the juvenile court judge is the primary decision maker in determining whether the youth should be transferred. (14)

justice model   A corrections philosophy that promotes flat or fixed-time sentences, abolishing parole, and using prison to punish offenders. (5)

juvenile delinquency   Behavior committed by a minor child that violates a state's penal code. (1)

juvenile delinquent   A child with a long and problematic history of involvement in crime. (1)

juveniles   People under age 18. (1)

Kansas City Gun Experiment   A 1992 program in which the use of additional police to patrol in target areas for the exclusive purpose of gun detection significantly increased gun seizures and decreased gun crimes. (3)

Keating-Owen Act   An act passed by Congress in 1916 that raised the legal work age to 14 and allowed children between 14 and 16 to work only eight hours per day. (1)

Kent v. United States   A formal waiver hearing must take place before transfer of a juvenile to criminal court. (14)

klikas   Age cohorts within Latino gangs. (12)

labeling theory   A perspective that assumes that social control leads to deviance; how behavior is reacted to determines whether it is defined as deviant. (8)

latchkey children   Children who regularly care for themselves without adult supervision after school or on weekends. (10)

legalization   The elimination of many laws currently prohibiting the distribution and possession of drugs, but not necessarily eliminating all regulation. (4)

legislative exclusion   A method used for transferring youths to criminal court, whereby the most serious or persistent offenders or those over a certain age are excluded from juvenile court jurisdiction and automatically prosecuted as adults. (14)

liberation hypothesis   The belief that changes brought about by the women's movement triggered a wave of female crime. (9)

lifetime prevalence   In self-report surveys, the use of a drug at least once during the respondent's lifetime. (4)

maltreatment   Severe mistreatment of children, including physical and sexual abuse, physical neglect, lack of supervision, emotional maltreatment, educational maltreatment, and moral-legal maltreatment. (10)

Mapp v. Ohio   Applied the exclusionary rule to state courts. (13)

master status   The status of a person that people initially react to when they interact with him or her for the first time. (1, 8)

maturational reform   The idea that many youths who participate in delinquency reduce or stop such activity as they become older. (5)

McKeiver v. Pennsylvania   Juveniles do not have a constitutional right to a jury trial in juvenile court. (14)

member-based definition   Defining a crime as gangrelated when a gang member or members are either the perpetrators of the victims, regardless of the motive. (12)

mesomorphs   Active, assertive people with muscular physiques. (6)

middle-class measuring rod   The standard teachers use when they assign status to students. (7)

Miranda v. Arizona   Established the right to protection from self-incrimination under the Fifth Amendment and the right to legal counsel under the Sixth Amendment. (13)

mitigating circumstances   Factors that might be responsible for the individual's behavior, such as age, insanity, and incompetence. (5)

monozygotic (MZ) twins   Identical twins; develop from one fertilized egg. (6)

motive-based definition   Defining a crime as gang-related when committed by a gang member or members in which the underlying reason is to further the interests and activities of the gang. (12)

National Crime Victimization Survey   Annual survey of criminal victimization conducted by the U.S. Bureau of Justice Statistics. (2)

National Youth Survey   Nationwide self-report survey of approximately 1,700 people who were between the ages of 11 and 17 in 1976. (2)

natural explanations   Theories based on data that exist in the real world. (5)

Neo-classical school   Advises us to consider mitigating circumstances when determining culpability. (5)

New Jersey v. T.L.O.   School officials can conduct warrantless searches of individuals at schools on the basis of reasonable suspicion. (11)

one-arm's-length rule   Once a suspect is arrested, police may search the suspect and the immediate area he or she occupies (see *Chimel v. California*). (13)

operant conditioning   A type of learning in which an animal associates its behavior with rewards and punishments. (6)

Operation Ceasefire   A gun prevention program in Boston involving direct law enforcement attack on illicit firearms traffickers supplying juveniles with guns. (3)

parens patriae   A doctrine that defines the state as the ultimate parent or guardian of every child. (1)

parole   The release of an offender from a correctional institution before the scheduled period of confinement has ended. It typically involves supervision by a parole officer. (15)

parole revocation   If a youth violates the law or one of the discretionary conditions of parole, parole may be revoked and the youth is returned to a correctional facility. (15)

Part I crimes   The eight offenses that form the Crime Index and are used to gauge the amount of crime reported to police; also referred to as *Index crimes*. (2)

Part II crimes   Twenty-one less-serious offenses included in the *Uniform Crime Reports*. (2)

patriarchy   A social system that enforces masculine control of the sexuality and labor power of women. (9)

petition   A document setting forth the specific charge against a juvenile. (14)

power-control theory   A theory that emphasizes the consequences of the power relations of husbands and wives in the workplace on the lives of children. (9)

prevalence   The number of juveniles committing delinquency. (2)

primary deviation   Deviant behavior that everyone engages in occasionally. (8)

probable cause   A set of facts that would lead a reasonable person to believe a crime has been committed and the person to be arrested committed it. (13)

probation   The conditional freedom granted by the court to an alleged or adjudicated offender, who must adhere to certain conditions and is generally supervised by a probation officer. (15)

prosecutorial waiver   A method used for transferring youths to criminal court in which the prosecutor is the primary decision maker in determining whether a youth should be transferred. The prosecutor typically has concurrent jurisdiction to file charges in either juvenile or criminal court. (14)

pseudo families   Relationships established in correctional institutions for girls and intended to substitute for those found on the outside. (15)

punishment   Anything that decreases the probability of a behavior reoccurring. (6)

radical nonintervention   An approach to juvenile justice whereby police and the courts would, whenever possible, "leave kids alone." (8)

rational choice theories   Delinquents are rational people who make calculated choices regarding what they are going to do *before* they act. (5)

reinforcement   Anything that increases the probability of behavior reoccurring. (6)

reintegrative shaming   The expression of community disapproval of delinquency, followed by indications of forgiveness and reacceptance into the community. (8)

restitution   A court-ordered action in which an offender pays money or provides services to victims of the offense or to the community. (15)

restorative justice   A rehabilitative strategy aimed at restoring or repairing relationships disrupted by crime, holding offenders accountable by requiring restitution to victims or the community harmed by the crime, promoting offender competency and responsibility, and balancing the needs of community, victim, and offender through involvement in the restorative process. (15)

retribution   Punishment philosophy based on society's moral outrage or disapproval of a crime. (5)

reverse waiver   A juvenile who is being prosecuted as an adult in criminal court may petition to have the case transferred to juvenile court for adjudication or disposition. (14)

routine activities theories   Focus on the *crime target,* which is anything an offender wants to take control of. (5)

Schall v. Martin   Juveniles may be held in preventive detention while awaiting adjudication if they are determined to be "serious risks" to the community. (14)

secondary deviation   Deviant behavior based on the youth's taking on and accepting the deviant role as part of his or her identity. (8)

secret delinquents   Juveniles whose crimes are not known to the police. (2)

secret deviant   Offenders whose deviant behavior is hidden from others. (8)

self-report studies   Unofficial measures of crime in which juveniles are asked about their law-breaking behavior. (2)

single-parent families   Families composed of children and one parent who is divorced or widowed, or was never married. (10)

socialization   The process through which children learn the ways of a particular society or social group so that they can function within it. (10)

Stanford v. Kentucky   The Supreme Court held that the execution of a person who was age 16 or 17 at the time of his or her offense was not unconstitutional. (15)

status   A socially defined position in a group. (1)

status offense   An act that is illegal only for children, such as truancy. (1)

stigmata   The distinctive physical features of born criminals. (6)

stubborn child law   Passed in 1641, the law stated that children who disobeyed their parents shall be put to death. (1)

superego   Develops from the ego and represents the moral code of the personality. (6)

supernatural theory   Theory based on beliefs in demons, witches, evil spirits, and gods. (5)

sweep search   A search of all lockers in schools. (11)

techniques of neutralization   Rationalizations given to explain delinquent behavior. (7)

theories   Integrated sets of ideas that explain and predict phenomenon. (5)

theory of differential association   A learning theory explaining the process children go through to *become* delinquent. (7)

30-day prevalence   In self-report surveys, the use of a drug at least once during the previous month. (4)

Thompson v. Carthage School District   School officials may legally search students and their lockers without consent. (11)

Thompson v. Oklahoma   Supreme Court ruled that the execution of a person under age 16 at the time of his or her crime was unconstitutional. (15)

Tinker v. Des Moines Independent Community School District   Students have the right of free expression as long as their behavior does not interrupt school activities or intrude in the school affairs or the lives of others. (11)

token economy   A system used in juvenile reformatories for distributing and withdrawing privileges to control behavior. (6)

Uniform Crime Reports (UCR)   Annual publication from the Federal Bureau of Investigation presenting data on crimes reported to the police, number of arrests, and number of persons arrested. (2)

utilitarian punishment model   Offenders must be punished to protect society. (5)

Vernonia School District 47J v. Acton   Students participating in school athletic activities must submit upon request to an involuntary drug test (urinalysis). (11)

watch and ward   A system of policing that allowed a constable to draft any male into service to guard the town at night. (13)

West Virginia State Board of Education v. Barnette   Students do not have to salute the flag while reciting the Pledge of Allegiance. (11)

youth gang   A group of youths willing to use deadly violence to claim and protect territory, to attack rival gangs, or to engage in criminal activity. (12)

zonal hypothesis   Rates of delinquency decline the farther one moves from the center of the city. (7)

Photo Credits

Legal Case Index

HOW TO READ A CASE CITATION

Students unfamiliar with legal case citations may find them confusing. Citations, however, are quite simple to understand, once you know what to look for and where. A case citation gives in shorthand form all the information necessary to find a copy of the report.

A typical citation includes the volume number, the abbreviated name of the reporter or who compiled the record, the page number of the first page of the report, and the year the case was decided. For example, 421 U.S. 519 (1975)–the citation to the case *Breed v. Jones*– is reported in volume 421 of the United States Reports, beginning on page 519. The abbreviated forms and corresponding full names of the reporters cited in this index are given below. Thus, you should have little trouble locating the original decisions for the cases discussed in this text.

Cal. App. 3d	*California Appeals Third Series*
Cal. 2d	*California Reporter Second Series*
CrL.	*Criminal Law Reporter*
F. 2d	*Federal Reporter, 2d series*
F. Supp.	*Federal Supplement*
Idaho	*Idaho Reporter*
Ill.	*llinois Reporter*
L. Ed. 2d	*United States Reports, Lawyers Edition*
R.I.	*Rhode Island Reports*
S. Ct.	*Supreme Court Reporter*
U.S.	*United States Reports*
U.S.L.W.	*United States Law Week*
Wharton	*[Early Supreme Court Reporter]*

CASES

Baker v. Owen, 423 U.S. 907 (1975) The Supreme Court upheld the school's right to use corporal punishment.

Bethel School District No. 403 v. Fraser, 478 U.S. 675 (1986) The Supreme Court established the school's right to prohibit vulgar and offensive language.

Breed v. Jones, 421 U.S. 519 (1975) The Supreme Court ruled that a criminal prosecution of a child after he or she has had a juvenile court hearing on the same offense constitutes double jeopardy.

Chimel v. California, 395 U.S. 752 (1969) The Supreme Court established the one-arm's-length rule.

Colorado v. Connelly, 479 U.S. 157 (1986) Absent police coercion, a defendant's mental state alone would not render a confession involuntary.

Commonwealth v. Fisher, 213 Penn State Reports 54 (1905) The state court ruling that upheld the right of the state to intervene in the lives of children without ensuring that their constitutional rights are protected.

Davis v. Alaska, 415 U.S. 308 (1974) The Supreme Court held that a defendant's Sixth Amendment right to confront witnesses must prevail over the state's interest in protecting juveniles from adverse publicity.

Davis v. United States, 512 U.S. 452 (1994) Police have no obligation to stop interrogation until the accused makes an unambiguous or unequivocal request for legal counsel *and* police have no obligation to seek a clarification of an ambiguous reference to counsel.

Eddings v. Oklahoma, 455 U.S. 104 (1982) The Supreme Court ruled that a lower court must consider a juvenile's age as a mitigating circumstance during a capital sentencing.

Engel v. Vitale, 370 U.S. 421 (1962) Students cannot be required to recite school prayers.

Epperson v. Arkansas, 393 U.S. 97 (1968) A state law prohibiting the teaching of evolution was found to be unconstitutional.

Escobedo v. Illinois, 378 U.S. 478 (1964) The Supreme Court established the right of a criminal suspect to have an attorney present during police questioning when the "finger of suspicion" points to the suspect.

Ex parte Crouse, 4 Wharton 9 (1838) A Pennsylvania court ruled in support of the doctrine of *parens patriae*.

Ex parte Sharpe, 15 Idaho 127 (1908) The state court ruling that upheld the right of the state to intervene in the lives of children without ensuring that their constitutional rights are protected.

Fare v. Michael C., 439 U.S. 1310 (1978) A child asking police to speak to a probation officer is not equivalent to requesting to speak to an attorney.

Florida v. Bostick, 498 U.S. 1021 (1991) The Supreme Court ruled that police may board buses, trains, and planes and ask passengers to consent to a search without a warrant or probable cause.

Gary H. v. Hegstrom, 831 F.2d 1430 (U.S. Court of Appeals, Ninth Circuit, 1987) U.S. Court of Appeals held conditions in an Oregon juvenile reform school violated constitutional prohibition against cruel and unusual punishment.

Gilbert v. California, 388 U.S. 263 (1967) The Supreme Court further clarified the right of the police to photograph and fingerprint a suspect and take samples of his or her handwriting, voice, and blood during booking.

Goss v. Lopez, 419 U.S. 565 (1976) The Supreme Court ruled that if a student is to be suspended for 10 or more days from school, he or she must receive a hearing.

Hammer v. Dagenhart, 247 U.S. 251 (1918) Overturned the 1916 Keating-Owen Act, which was the first piece of child labor legislation.

Hazelwood School District v. Kuhlmeier, 484 U.S. 260 (1988) The Supreme Court ruled that school officials can censor student newspapers for "educational purposes."

In re Ferrier, 103 Ill. 367 (1882) The state court upheld the right of the state to intervene in the lives of children without ensuring that their constitutional rights are protected.

In re Gault, 387 U.S. 1 (1967) The Supreme Court held that juveniles may not be denied basic due process rights in juvenile adjudicatory hearings.

In re Holley, 107 R.I. 615 (1970) The state court ruled that at a police lineup, juveniles have the right to counsel once they are charged with a crime.

In re Manuel L., 7 Cal.4th 229 (1994) The California court held that the state need only show "clear proof" that at the time a minor committed a crime he or she knew it was wrong in order to proceed with a delinquency petition.

In re McCloud, 109 R.I. 1304 (1971) In the state court's majority opinion, Justice Douglas stated that the issue of possible deprivation of liberty is sufficient to force the juvenile court into the status of a criminal court.

In re Winship, 397 U.S. 358 (1970) The Supreme Court ruled that the standard of evidence in delinquency cases must be proof beyond a reasonable doubt (whereas only a preponderance of the evidence is required in nondelinquency cases).

In the interest of G.O., 304 Ill.App. 3d 719 (1999) Illinois court held a juvenile charged with murder in juvenile court may not be denied a jury trial.

Ingraham v. Wright, 430 U.S. 651 (1977) The Supreme Court held that corporal punishment does not violate the "cruel and unusual punishment" clause of the Eighth Amendment.

Kent v. United States, 383 U.S. 541 (1966) The Supreme Court ruled that a formal waiver hearing is necessary before a case in juvenile court can be transferred to criminal court.

Lee v. Weisman, 505 U.S. 577 (1992) Official prayer during high school graduations is unconstitutional.

Mapp v. Ohio, 367 U.S. 643 (1961) The Supreme Court extended the exclusionary rule to state trials.

McCollum v. Board of Education, 333 U.S. 203 (1948) Religious education cannot take place in public school classrooms during the school day.

McKeiver v. Pennsylvania, 403 U.S. 528 (1971) The Supreme Court held that juveniles do not have a constitutional right to a jury trial in juvenile court.

Minersville School District v. Gobitis, 310 U.S. 586 (1940) Students can be required to salute the American flag.

Miranda v. Arizona, 384 U.S. 436 (1966) The Supreme Court ruled that police must create an environment that produces only voluntary confessions.

Moran v. Burbine, 457 U.S. 412 (1986) A valid waiver requires both "voluntariness" and a "knowing and intelligent" awareness of the right relinquished.

New Jersey v. T.L.O., 469 U.S. 325 (1985) The Supreme Court ruled that school officials can conduct warrantless searches of individuals at schools on the basis of reasonable suspicion.

Oklahoma Publishing Company v. District Court, 430 U.S. 308 (1977) The Supreme Court held that once information is publicly revealed or put in the public domain, its publication or broadcast cannot be restrained.

Olesen v. Board of Education, 676 F. Supp. 821 (N.D. Ill 1987) Schools may ban gang symbols, hand signals, or other actions furthering gang interests, such as recruitment of new members on school grounds.

Payton v. New York, 445 U.S. 573 (1980) The Supreme Court ruled that in all nonemergency situations the police must have an arrest warrant in order to make a valid entry into a home to make an arrest.

People v. Lara, 67 Cal. 2d 365 (1967) The California court held that whether a child is waived to adult court is to be determined by evaluating the totality of the circumstances of the case (the "whole picture").

People v. Turner, 55 Ill. 280 (1870) An Illinois court upheld the constitutional rights of juveniles.

Santa Fe School District v. Doe, 168 F.3d 806 (2000) Official, student-led prayers before high school football games are not allowed.

Schall v. Martin, 467 U.S. 253 (1984) The Supreme Court held that the pretrial detention of juveniles who pose a serious risk to the community is permissible.

Skinner v. Oklahoma, 316 U.S. 535 (1942) Ended the legal sterilization of offenders for certain crimes.

Smith v. Daily Mail Publishing Company, 443 U.S. 97 (1979) The Supreme Court ruled that when information regarding a juvenile case is lawfully obtained by the media, the state cannot prohibit its publication.

Stanford v. Kentucky, 492 U.S. 361 (1989) The Supreme Court held that the execution of a person who was age 16 or 17 at the time of the commission of his or her crime is not unconstitutional.

State v. Werner, 242 S.E.2d 907 (W.Va. 1978) West Virginia court found disciplinary practices at a juvenile correctional facility violated the Eighth Amendment prohibition against cruel and unusual punishment.

Stone v. Graham, 449 U.S. 39 (1980) The Ten Commandments cannot be posted in public school classrooms.

Thompson v. Carthage School District, 87 F.3d 979 (1996) School officials may legally search students and their lockers without consent.

Thompson v. Oklahoma, 487 U.S. 815 (1988) The Supreme Court held that the execution of a person who was under the age of 16 at the time of his or her crime is unconstitutional.

Tinker v. Des Moines Independent Community School District, 393 U.S. 503 (1969) The Supreme Court ruled that students have the right of free expression as long as their behavior does not interrupt school activities or intrude in school affairs or the lives of others.

United States v. Euge, 444 U.S. 707 (1980) The Supreme Court further clarified the right of the police to photograph and fingerprint a suspect and take samples of his or her handwriting, voice, and blood during booking.

United States v. Mendenhall, 466 U.S. 544 (1984) The Supreme Court held that citizens are not considered seized when the police stop them to ask a few questions.

United States v. Wade, 388 U.S. 218 (1967) The Supreme Court helped to clarify the right of the police to photograph and fingerprint a suspect and take samples of his or her handwriting, voice, and blood during booking.

Vandenberg v. Superior Court, 8 Cal. App.3d 1048 (1970) A California Superior Court held that parents may give police permission to search the rooms and possessions of their minor children.

Vernonia School District 47J v. Acton, 515 U.S. 646 (1995) The Supreme Court held that students who participate in school extracurricular activities must submit upon request to an involuntary drug test (urinalysis).

Wallace v. Jaffree, 472 U.S. 38 (1985) It is against the law to require that each school day begin with a one minute period of "silent meditation or voluntary prayer."

West v. United States, 399 F.2d 467 (5th Cir. 1968) The validity of a waiver depends on the child's age, education, intelligence, and on circumstances surrounding the police interrogation.

West Virginia State Board of Education v. Barnette, 319 U.S. 624 (1943) Students do not have to salute the flag while reciting the Pledge of Allegiance.

Wilkins v. Missouri, 492 U.S. 361 (1989) The Supreme Court ruled that the execution of a person who was age 16 or 17 at the time he or she committed a capital crime is constitutional (This case was combined with *Stanford v. Kentucky.*)

NAME INDEX

SUBJECT INDEX